MW00620291

COSMIC DUTY

COSMIC DUTY
A Swedenborgian's Interpretation of
Beelzebub's Tales to his Grandson (All and Everything)
by Edward F. Sylvia, M. T. S.

ISBN: 978-0-9702527-4-6

Staircase Press
books@staircasepress.com
www.StaircasePress.com

Publisher's Cataloging-in-Publication Data:

Names: Sylvia, Edward F., author.
Title: Cosmic duty : a Swedenborgian's interpretation of Beelzebub's tales to his
            grandson (All and everything) / Edward F. Sylvia. --
Description: Saint Louis, Missouri : Staircase Press, [2016] | Includes
            bibliographical references and index.
Identifiers: ISBN: 978-0-9702527-4-6
Subjects: LCSH: Gurdjieff, Georges Ivanovitch, 1872-1949. Beelzebub's tales to
            his grandson. | Swedenborg, Emanuel, 1688-1772. | Knowledge,
            Theory of. | Philosophy. | Spiritual life. | Spiritual formation. |
            Human beings. | Mysticism. | Fourth Way (Occultism) | Ontology. |
            Cosmology. | Transformative learning. | BISAC: PHILOSOPHY /
            Epistemology.
Classification: LCC: BP605.G9 S95 2016 | DDC: 149.3--dc23.

COSMIC DUTY

A Swedenborgian's Interpretation of
BEELZEBUB'S TALES TO HIS GRANDSON
(ALL AND EVERYTHING)

Edward F. Sylvia, M.T.S.
author of PROVING GOD

STAIRCASE PRESS
ELEVATE YOUR MIND

—◇— —◇— —◇—

This book
is dedicated to
all those
who think they are
good people.

—◇— —◇— —◇—

Table of Contents

Editor's Note

This is a transformative book.

Over a lifetime of study and several years of intense writing and rewriting, author Edward F. Sylvia has brought the all-encompassing work of George Ivanovitch Gurdjieff and Emanuel Swedenborg together in one place—allowing us to compare their thinking, side-by-side, on many of the issues that the human race has grappled with since the beginning of time.

It is his sincere hope that these startling ideas might help you make sense of world events and everyday modern life so you can be informed enough about mankind's true condition to objectively chart your own path toward eternity.

Cosmic Duty is not an easy read. It requires true effort. Like Gurdjieff's original allegory, (which carries the subtitle *An Objectively Impartial Criticism of the Life of Man*) you will need to read this book more than once to fully grasp what's going on. It's a challenging chapter-by-chapter examination of the early twentieth-century mystic, philosopher, composer and spiritual teacher's masterwork, *All and Everything: Beelzebub's Tales to his Grandson*. The author includes many of Gurdjieff's original large (and annoying) words for effect, but Gurdjieff's startling revelations are clarified here through the lens of ideas from the great eighteenth-century scientist, philosopher, theologian and mystic, Emanuel Swedenborg.

While these two men never met during their time on this planet, the author "met" them both on the same day while taking a college course. Almost immediately, he saw intriguing connections between the concepts each man presented to the world as Truth. The quest to truly understand the scope of what these visionaries shared with the world has shaped the author's own personal journey for over forty years. With this book, he makes it accessible for the rest of us.

The life's work of these remarkable men—Gurdjieff, a passionate spiritual seeker and teacher from western Asia and Swedenborg, a brilliant European scientist who lived centuries earlier—meshes quite beautifully in many ways. Especially concerning *conscience*.

The author makes connections here in a most unique study of their divergent, yet complementary philosophies, presenting us with an enlightnening and somewhat disturbing examination of who we are, *why* we are the way we are, and how we can work to be better.

Finding harmonies between two dynamic spiritual systems for the benefit of each:

George Ivanovitch Gurdjieff and Emanuel Swedenborg lived in different centuries, yet both claimed that a new paradigm shift was about to replace the current worldviews concerning science and theology. The legacy these prolific seers have left us includes a wealth of resources on personal development for serious seekers. Here are brief biographies of both men.

For more information about the life, teachings, and work of George Gurdjieff, as well as Emanuel Swedenborg's scientific and spiritual discoveries, you'll find some helpful links on page 508 to aid you in your search.

George I. Gurdjieff

George Ivanovitch Gurdjieff (1866?–1949) was born in the Caucasus of the Near East. His father was Greek and his mother, Armenian. As a young boy, he met many amazing individuals who were the surviving repositories of various ancient knowledge. Around 1915, Gurdjieff burst upon the European scene with an innovative system for tapping one's spiritual potentials by "combining the wisdom of the East with the energy of the West." His ideas included a universal science that embraced both the laws of nature and the laws of spiritual salvation. Gurdjieff's system, called the "Harmonious Development of Man," is viewed by the author as being highly complementary to the scientific and theological ideas of Emanuel Swedenborg.

Gurdjieff's primary published books comprised a trilogy titled *All and Everything*:

Beelzebub's Tales to His Grandson (First Series)

Meetings with Remarkable Men (Second Series)

Life Is Real Only Then, When "I Am" (Third Series)

Emanuel Swedenborg

Emanuel Swedenborg (1688-1772) was a scientist who turned theologian in later life. From 1710-1745 he studied all the branches of science in his time and even invented new ones. He was the first anatomical investigator to formulate a neuron theory of the brain which included deeper layers of neural scaffolding (substrates) that today's neuroscientists are now speculating.

From 1745 to his death in 1772, Swedenborg responded to a higher calling and left behind his scientific projects. Instead, he created a complete systematic theology based on direct Divine revelation and exploration of the Spiritual World.

Of interest to the author, Emanuel Swedenborg's scientific discoveries perfectly complement his later spiritual discoveries and may well hold the key to unifying all knowledge. Swedenborg's vast written work includes some 200 titles on scientific and theological topics.

His most noteworthy theological books include:

Arcana Coelestia (Heavenly Secrets – 12 volumes)

Heaven and Hell

The True Christian Religion

Divine Providence

Conjugial Love

Divine Love and Wisdom

CHAPTER I

INTRODUCTION TO A PREFACE
"The arousing of thought"

It is an odd experience to interpret a book where, as the interpretation gets deeper and better, its personal message gets more unflattering. This project brought me such an ever more unflattering experience.

In fact, as I was working on my fifth draft to this manuscript, I detected that my writing was breaking down and would need much more effort to make it work—and to grasp what was truly unfolding before me. My knowledge (and understanding) of spiritual transformation was weak and not quite sincere.

By the middle of my seventh draft, I noticed that my *sexual* energy had changed, which changed the whole focus of my writing. I was no longer pig-slop (and lost a kind of *inner* jittery-ness). I wanted this project to really touch people deeply. It became my *conscious labor* and *intentional suffering*.

I admit that I first entered this project with an over-developed ego, which amazingly, I was extremely blind toward most of the time. Ironically, the topic of these Tales deals with curtailing one's imagined self-importance and gaining a truer sense of one's actual cosmic predicament—and grasping reality, which includes God's grand plan for the human race and the providential directionality of creation. So, I have entered into this challenging project for both the benefit of others as well as myself. Believe me when I say that we are all well off the mark in solving humankind's deepest personal and relational problems!

Gurdjieff supplies us here with all the raw material to make a better world, but we must organize it and connect it all together. That kind of psychic *re-ordering* is what human understanding and rationality is supposed to do during genuine spiritual growth, by which evolution through the human species is continued into higher realms. This is our "cosmic duty." But we must endure the shock treatment of discovering our current personal flaws (which instead, always prefer praise and constantly seek affirmation from others).

(I strongly suggest that the reader obtain a copy of *Beelzebub's Tales* for reference and make primary source comparisons with the work before you. Plus, this will offer you a direct taste of an impartial and shocking view of contemporary humans and their negative trajectory toward a diminishing inner world of consciousness.)

Providentially, I have been put into a unique position where I can make helpful interpretations for studying the human dilemma. Any direct words and brief passages by Gurdjieff himself that are used in this book are for the purposes of reviewing, strengthening, interpreting and promoting his challenge to interested and concerned readers. This book, because of its cosmic and spiritual importance, is more than a commercial project. It is meant for obtaining sincere spiritual profit—for myself, and for my neighbors!

The cost of this book transcends its price. Full payment will come from one's personal efforts to grasp this information (with some bravery).

-◇- -◇- -◇-

In the summer of 1974, I attended evening classes at the School of Visual Arts in New York City. In one of those classes I was introduced to the ideas of two amazing individuals—on the very same day. Their names were Emanuel Swedenborg (1688–1772) and George Ivanovitch Gurdjieff (1866–1949).[1] I now believe that both men had gained a rare mastery of elevated (non-terrestrial and otherworldly) knowledge, vital for human civilization to solve its many problems and progress in a rationally spiritual way. They tapped into and shared special information that the average person was unlikely to come across while merely fulfilling the daily demands of physical life on Earth. Both men talked of an additional duty that we must each adopt. We have forgotten this duty, and as a result, we no longer know why we are here. This has led to a troubled world.

On the surface, their two belief-systems regarding human potential and inner transformation seem to be quite different from each other. Their authors represented different centuries and presented their ideas using different terms. But the more one gets involved with their ideas and grasps their essence, the more one can find powerful similarities. In fact, my studies of Gurdjieff have helped me to better understand Swedenborg and my studies of Swedenborg have helped me to better understand Gurdjieff.

Although the two men used different words and lived during two different eras in human history, the laws of genuine spiritual growth never change and are the same for everyone—in every country on this Earth.

This "dual" study of mine has now taken over forty years, including periods of actual membership in both Gurdjieff work groups and the Swedenborgian Church (in New York City and St. Louis, MO, including two years at the Swedenborg House of Studies in Berkeley, CA). I feel I am one of a handful of people who have acquired the "peculiar and bizarre thinking ability" to even be capable of attempting such a

---

1. Dates are according to Jeanne de Salzman, *The Reality of Being*.

writing project. With that said, I am not the first to find similarities in their two systems or to attempt to combine their ideas to help seekers find more successful ways of obtaining tangible spiritual growth. However, I may well be the first to unify the two systems by teasing fresh concepts out of *Beelzebub's Tales*. (I consider the book *Beelzebub's Tales* to be the official and best source of Gurdjieff's ideas.) Most writers have stayed away from addressing *Beelzebub's Tales* directly. It is too intimidating and confounding for the habitual human mind (with its "head-knowledge") to read through.

But it is only through this great literary effort that I can feel the true sense and weight of Gurdjieff's warning to us all about the true "terror of the situation." That is, we earth-humans are far worse off than we believe (especially when it comes to our self-delusions, duality of consciousness, mechanicality, hypnosis, and inner slavery—perceiving the Creator's cosmic laws incorrectly and having no bio-perception of what it takes for obtaining genuine spiritual growth). The true terror is that our usual approaches, programs and theories for personal transformation are pretentious and really don't work (sorry).

And time is running out for each one of us still here on Earth.

Gurdjieff challenges everything and touches all our raw nerves. We need to be shocked to our very core—for our own good—or we will remain in a state of psychic slumber!

(Swedenborg certainly underscores this shock treatment to our egoism by stating that *only* God lives and loves, and that we humans are mere bio-vessels for receiving these heavenly influences and gifts.)

So, keeping my interpretation true to the essence and spirit of Gurdjieff's storytelling, I will not sugar coat our cosmic challenge or put a positive spin on our real duty in life—but portray it as he portrays it. Some readers will undoubtedly find this treatise to be too "harsh" (a finding which originates in a warped human [*proprial*] view of fairness, justice, and self-importance). But I can assure you that both men's systems promote a real *agony* of spiritual conflict between our inner and outer realities (what we know in our heads versus how we actually behave from our hearts) to procure eternal victory.

At the present moment, most current members of these two systems of personal transformation by Swedenborg and Gurdjieff prefer to remain separate in order to preserve their doctrinal "purity." But neither system seems to have "caught fire" in the world of human ideas. That saddens me.

Both men certainly felt that their message must inevitably catch fire in order for humanity not to self-destruct. So how about putting them together now?

I believe these two systems are not only complementary, but that their future health and growth may well necessitate some kind of unification or meeting of minds between their members and followers.

3

That is why I have written this book. But I also realize that any real success will require the members of both systems to reject any feeling of self-importance or superiority—and fully embrace humility.

God's revelations never cease (for *living* churches), so remarkable individuals other than Swedenborg (like Gurdjieff), will also begin to appear on Earth to bring us these ongoing heavenly messages. (This ongoing revelation is divinely permitted since we live in a time where spiritual mysteries can now be explored by the human rational mind and its understanding. Blind faith is no longer enough.)

I feel that after forty years of intense study (of these two men's systems, relative to all my personal flaws), I can now identify and objectively address the real harmony between these two systems, and do so on a much more urgent and deeper level than others have previously attempted (like exploring the problem of having a split psyche). There is a universality to God's Truth and eternal plan in both systems of human salvation, but I must make these ideas more recognizable in order to help increase the reader's own personal spiritual success, eternal happiness, and hopefully to attract new seekers to these potent ideas (though not necessarily to the various *institutions* now promoting these ideas).

That is the goal of this book project—to target and prepare the individual for one's true cosmic duty.

Without bringing the two systems together, I believe the human race will never have the proper (scientific or theological) understanding of the terms "good" and "evil," particularly in regard to their relationship with our proper spiritual development and overcoming the "mechanicality" of the passive habitual mind and the "fantasy" that so strongly dominates our everyday consciousness.

This is the single most important (and hardest) discovery I have personally made over the past four decades—that I live in a *trance* of delusional ideas and the whole terrestrial world is vested in maintaining this trance. I made this unflattering and most difficult discovery by permitting myself to become my own human guinea pig for objective observation and experimentation with the uncommon ideas promoted by both men.

To give this project of harmonizing the ideas of these two great men a workable and productive structure, I have chosen to interpret Gurdjieff's major published work, *Beelzebub's Tales to His Grandson: An Objectively Impartial Criticism of the Life of Man (All and Everything)*, from a Swedenborgian viewpoint—that is, from the scientific and anatomical discoveries Swedenborg made between 1710 and 1745, and the divine revelations given to Swedenborg from 1745 to 1772. (Also, the words "Objectively Impartial Criticism" are key to judging the verity of both men in their *suprahuman* attempts to address *all and everything*!)

4

In the early 1920s, Gurdjieff had formed an organization called the "Institute For the Harmonious Development of Man" just outside of Paris, France. Obtaining this harmonious development was called *the Work*. According to Emanuel Swedenborg, the word "work" was used in exactly this same context of harmonious development to describe the Creator's activities.

"And on the seventh day God finished His work . . . (Genesis 2:2)

In other words, Swedenborg discovered that the biblical statement above, about God finishing His work, is to be *symbolically* (inwardly) understood as His divine labors to make the human race spiritual and celestial (our epigenesis).

Gurdjieff was headed in the same direction.

Unfortunately, after a "bizarre" automobile accident in 1924 that left Gurdjieff as "a bit of live meat in a clean bed" he found himself suddenly compelled to put all his ideas for harmonious development into a book—for the benefit of future generations.

But this book would be like no other (he even mocks contemporary authors).

One of Gurdjieff's original followers who read several drafts of the manuscript before its publication, often finding each new draft more difficult to grasp than the previous one, asked the author if he was purposely trying to "bury the bone deeper?" Gurdjieff's cryptic reply was that he was "burying the dog deeper." In other words, Gurdjieff not only felt one had to dig deeper to find the *truth* but to dig still deeper to discover the *living essence* within truth—or as physicist Stephen Hawking would say, finding the "fire in the equation."

It has been reported, by eyewitnesses and followers, that Gurdjieff tested earlier versions of his *Beelzebub* manuscript by having it read aloud to hundreds of people over many years—including strangers. If he observed that a listener showed signs of easy comprehension, Gurdjieff would revise his writing by making it even more difficult to understand.

Swedenborg himself knew that the more details you offered about a given topic the more obscure the category could become, because these details would often seem alien to the human habitual and terrestrial mind. It seems that Gurdjieff adopted a practice of adding more and more details into the conversation to make people work harder at deciphering new meaning.

On second thought, not all of Swedenborg's ideas are easy to grasp, either!

Nothing real is gained without effort and struggle. (Swedenborg claimed that the word "toil" is representative of spiritual pondering.)

So, I will make the attempt to bring both the "bone" and the "dog" up closer to the surface, where they can be better observed in broad daylight and adequately valued. But even this effort by me is fictitious help for the contemporary reader, because even with a further clarification of Gurdjieff's ideas, one's current worldview and modern intellect (memory function from a split psyche) will no doubt still be mercilessly challenged and even come under serious scrutiny. Nobody likes having the rug pulled out from under their feet (or ego).

A.R. Orage, who was one of the original editors of *Beelzebub's Tales*, states in his *Commentaries* (pg. 4) on this epic work that it is "devastating" to the reader. Gurdjieff wrote his Tales in a way that befuddles a reader's habitual mind (even the educated mind) to the point of intellectual "despair." C.S. Nott, in his book *Teachings of Gurdjieff* (p. 141), quotes Orage as saying, "One of the aims of Gurdjieff's book is to induce despair in the best trained minds concerning their 'type of reason'." This type of modern reasoning usually involves mere head knowledge.

This is interesting because according to Emanuel Swedenborg, the Lord God uses the same strategy of despair to break up false human pride and egocentrism (*Arcana Coelestia*, n. 6144). Currently, our reasoning (intellect) functions apart from our inner reality (heart) and actual being. Modern reasoning deals more with the stuff crammed into our memories than with self-knowledge (knowing thyself).

Beelzebub's Tales was not written for those who demand hugs, affirmation, praise and constant comfort or who place "hope" before and above immediate personal action. Instead, *Beelzebub's Tales* gives us a swift kick in the ass.

Knowing the difficulties he anticipated for his future readers (especially after his inevitable death) and that everything in God's world requires *three* distinct principles to manifest (*active, passive* and *reconciling principles*, or Father, Son and Holy Spirit), Gurdjieff offers advice as to how to optimally read his book—three times and three different ways! First, to read it just like you have already accustomed yourself to reading things. Second, as if you were reading *aloud* to another person. And only on one's third attempt, try to figure out the gist of his writings. (So, to be properly qualified to attempt this project, I have read *Beelzebub's Tales* all three ways.)

Such advice seems a bit naïve and overkill for inducing people to tackle this imposing Bible-length publication (over one thousand pages)! Not very many people would be inclined to read it even once—especially since it is so unflattering (non-sugary) to the human race in general and attempts to unpack our current feelings and flawed beliefs about reality and especially, about OURSELVES! But I am being kind here. In his own words, Gurdjieff's aim in writing the book is to "step on people's corns" and on the title page, "To destroy, mercilessly, without any compromises whatsoever, in the mentation and feelings of the reader, the beliefs and views, by centuries rooted in him, about everything existing in the world." (Sweden-borg, a proven genius, also admitted to wiping his own intellectual slate clean before submitting himself entirely to be properly re-taught by the Lord God. He said that admitting that one "knew nothing" is the beginning of true wisdom. He was also quite displeased with the academic world, saying that they "see everything but understand nothing.")

Because of his harsh approach to self-scrutiny, Gurdjieff begins the introduction of his book with a warning—rather than the usual "bombastic magniloquent" or "sugary" and "inflated" phrases implored by other authors of contemporary culture! Gurdjieff couldn't care less if he was hated or liked by the reader or critic. Furthermore, he warns his readers that they will fail to judge his writing properly if they insist on embracing the current grammatically correct ("bon ton") literary styles that have been instilled in people's psyche over time and learned by rote through modern education.

(Both men felt "modern education is one-dimensional.")

Gurdjieff takes great pleasure throughout his book in making up hard-to-pronounce new words to force the reader to make real—as opposed to automatic—cognitive efforts. He once told someone that we "have to move our brains once a day, apart from our bowels." This demanded new effort was meant to stretch both the reader's mind and heart!

An acquaintance of mine, who originally loaned me his personal copy of *Beelzebub's Tales* to read many, many years ago, had only warned me that the introduction to the book was fifty pages long—but charming. I was given no warning that Gurdjieff would place a mirror into the very depth of my inner being. This inner mirror was infinitely more uncomfortable, stinging, and real than my going to confession every month as a religious- automaton brought up in the Roman Catholic Church.

Beelzelbub's Tales certainly forced me to question my approach to life, my beliefs, and religion. The charm in the book comes from realizing that Gurdjieff loved us all—impartially. (He had to, in order to share everything he had learned.)

While some Swedenborgians (as well as other serious thinkers) might recoil from Gurdjieff's brutal sincerity and harsh criticism, preferring instead the shoring-up of their self-esteem, and circling the wagons around their delusional self-important images (mostly through mechanical acts of neighborly love and lots of hugging), I can assure all my readers that Gurdjieff is merely offering potent new ways to augment sincere self-examination. Swedenborg would agree that sincere self-examination is the key ingredient to obtaining the proper innocence required for receiving God's living spiritual love, lawfully and legitimately (*True Christian Religion*, n. 567 [5] and *Divine Providence*, n. 104, 278a, 338 [8]).

In fact, on the very first page, Gurdjieff offers a big clue that he understands a similar idea to that of Swedenborg's "remains" by which special sacred data for future spiritual growth is formed during one's childhood by God's grace. (This is because spiritual data can only be given to a person in a *state of innocence*. Once a child learns pretense, from growing up in the adult world, this innocence is lost—actually covered over by a more external and corporeal/ mechanical mind—and has to be regained through inner combat and spiritual temptation.) God providentially protects this sacred data by storing it deeper into the human psyche (subconscious mind or human internal natural mind)—to be used later in our lives for the spiritual purposes of transformation, regeneration, and salvation.

Swedenborg and Gurdjieff are the only two individuals I have ever come across who possessed this particular knowledge that humans have special God-given data stored deep (as a gift) within their psyches. On the other hand, Gurdjieff's unique introduction and warning also offers the reader plenty of time to bail out, because activating this sacred gift from God requires some personal pain (to one's egoism and false self-image).

Beelzebub's Tales is not for the faint of heart.

But if the reader endures the task of getting through the intro-duction, he or she will begin to notice the rare richness of Gurdjieff's writing style and even begin to appropriate for themselves, enhanced willpower, endurance, and a new sense of true individuality and direction (one's cosmic duty).

With his uncommon knowledge of the human psyche, Gurdjieff offers this unique information with a fresh kind of fullness—always from a *three-pronged* delivery system (law of triads) designed to resonate with the reader's own triune nature of *intellect, feelings*, and *corporeal/visceral sensibilities* contained within the physical body. This three-pronged descriptive writing style is used throughout the entire book to encompass all three distinct receptive functions of the reader's various nervous systems (head-brain, spinal cord, and solar plexus).

To serve as one small example of this three-pronged literary style, when Gurdjieff explains his disdain for contemporary authors he not only provides descriptive data for the reader's intellectual discernment and feelings, he also adds a third, "visceral/scientific" element. Such a visceral/scientific element might include describing the source of some harsh evaluation as having an anatomical *center of gravity*, that is, where his attitude and the trajectory of his thought finds its proper equilibrium within the multiple levels one's very bio-organism. Here, Gurdjieff is cleverly adding the universal laws of a forgotten objective science into his exposition. This objective science suggests that human mental process *parallels* physical process—in other words, the human mind works like the universe works! (Swedenborg concurred that all process "obeys the same rules," through universal *correspondences*.)

Be assured that Gurdjieff, like Swedenborg, tapped into a higher mind and consciousness, which remains dormant for most of us who only think under the tyrannical reign of our "normal" habitual/mechano mind. We can thank modern education for this awful one-dimensional predicament of terrestrial slavery.

Having mastered close to a dozen languages (Swedenborg studied eight languages), Gurdjieff amusingly informs us that he had difficulty deciding which language to use to write his book. Obviously, he is no ordinary thinker and is in the perfect position to point out how our usual way of thinking is seriously defective (again, our strange *type of one-dimensional reasoning*). In fact, both Swedenborg and Gurdjieff claimed that our ancient ancestors surpassed modern humans in intelligence, wisdom and perceiving reality. The human psyche is degenerating! Gurdjieff even suggests that a similar (corresponding) degeneration has occurred to all modern languages. This degeneration perfectly reflects the diminishing qualities of the human psyche over its history.

Gurdjieff's introduction is titled *The Arousing of Thought*. But it could also have been titled *The Arousing of Inner Conflict*, since he purposely cultivates this conflict in the reader. He knows that this psychic conflict is the only means for humans to develop true contemplative and objective thought—as opposed to the ordinary mechanical or associative thinking now operating in humans. This psychic conflict is everyone's God-given duty and represents the true sacred purpose for all religion on Earth! (Swedenborg calls it temptation.) Without it there is no genuine spiritual growth in our lives, because it takes such inner conflict for our terrestrial minds to make contact with, and develop our deeper sacred God-given data into a living bio-plane of *conscience* (turning our spiritual remains into a *higher* organic body).

Right out of the chute, Gurdjieff shares his unique opinion that contemporary culture has turned humans into *automatons* (literally, puppets). That is certainly an unflattering position and a most difficult idea for anyone to accept who embraces the idea that technological advancement means evolutionary advancement.

Even worse (for our egoism), since a stick has "two ends," Gurdjieff confesses that in writing his Tales he has taken it upon himself to grab hold of the "good end" of the stick. So the poor reader must get whacked on the head with the other—the "bad end." Gurdjieff deservingly grabs the good end of the stick in this literary effort because he personally escaped his own robotic fate of the habitual mind through his unique education growing up in the Caucuses (an area which still preserved many ancient and wise customs). His unique upbringing led him to create his original writing style for the book. Gurdjieff talks about everything in ways that are much different from those we have long become unaccustomed to. This is his strategy for breaking through (with mental shocks) and shattering the flawed self-views of our habitual minds.

Even his humor is unexpected (but deadly relevant).

Again, Gurdjieff is well aware that his mocking assessment of contemporary authorities and experts for contributing to the diminished psyche of modern people will create great doubt and suspicion for many of his readers (who would rather be "titillated") concerning the inner quality and intent of his own personal character. (Later, I will relate a funny story that Gurdjieff tells, about a man observing a frustrated dogcatcher, who gave him a great idea for developing a unique response to making himself immune to all the malice that might come from others, while performing his daily duties.)

But first, Gurdjieff admits that as far as his own official education went, "nothing stuck." This was not because he was a bad student—far from it. Nothing "stuck" because none of it addressed his inner being. (This is why current education is failing to reach many young students.)

One of the important life lessons (vivifying factors) which did stick, and which formed the *foundation* for Gurdjieff's unusual education, therefore allowing him to escape the destructive limitations of contemporary schooling and culture, came from his grandmother—at her deathbed. On her deathbed, while each person was touching the other's hand, she whispered into the young boy's ears these important words: "In life, never do as others do." Gurdjieff took this advice to heart and when his family and friends had later gathered at the cemetery for a solemn ceremony of her passing, he suddenly bolted from the crowd and began to skip around the grave, singing:

> *"Let her with the saints repose,*
> *Now that she's turned up her toes,*
> *Oi! oi! oi!*
> (Then repeating)
> *Let her with the saints repose,*
> *Now that she's turned up her toes."*

Few events offer us a better display of our automatized habits than funerals. Obviously, the young Gurdjieff resisted "drinking the Kool-Aid" and defied acting mechanically like others, even at this most solemn of ceremonies (where people are pressured into conforming).

Such an unorthodox approach to living his life forever in this unusual and non-conforming way saved the young Gurdjieff from any form of *suggestibility* taking hold in his psyche and closing it up. (Gurdjieff later called this human conformity "a magical circle from which there is no escape.")

All through Gurdjieff's boyhood, he continued to do things in ways that were completely different from what was (automatically and mechanically) expected. He describes playing catch by trying not only to catch a ball using a different hand, but with different finger combinations. Then he would add a somersault before making the catch. Other odd manifestations of his personal non-conformity campaign included sniffing or putting a pastry to his ear as if listening to it rather than eating it. Or he would swallow the first bite of the pastry quickly without savoring the taste as the other children and "biped" friends were doing.

Again, such odd actions opened up for him new freedoms that others could not enjoy. He simply became unaffected about what others thought of him or by any external pressures to blend in.

Gurdjieff describes a second event in his childhood, which allowed him to use his brain quite differently than all the others around him. He describes an incident that led to his getting a wisdom tooth knocked out by a punch from another boy. When he took the tooth out of his mouth he observed it had seven roots, each containing a small drop of blood, which were tinged with the seven different colors of the light spectrum. Why? After that event, he became intellectually curious about every suspicious "actual" observation he made in life. Most people lose this sense of curiosity by adulthood.

From this curiosity, another principle (the third) was adopted from his youth. He decided that he was to go the "whole hog, including the postage" in every serious endeavor he undertook (like satisfying his curiosity about the seven tinges of color on the roots of his wisdom tooth). So he threw himself completely into everything he did (otherwise he could not have written his book). In fact, as a result of these three orientations during his early life, he noticed that his odd behavior was creating something substantive and indestructible (which indeed stuck) within his inner reality. He was making real changes to the very bio-fibers of his spirit!

Yes, as a young boy he was already observing real substantial changes taking place in his inner world. He had found the secret to freeing himself of the laws of heredity and the influences of his outer physical circumstances (which Swedenborg claimed that the Lord God accomplished on Earth). The young Gurdjieff attributes these three strange approaches and attitudes that he adopted early in life for helping him to "honorably fulfill his duty" within God's universe.

So he further warns the reader that he has also applied this unusual three-pronged "psycho-organic principle" to the writing of *Beelzebub's Tales*. After all, to effectively communicate his unique findings, he had to put the reader through the same conditions as he himself experienced, including taking them through the "whole hog" of his discoveries. In this case, going the whole hog means writing not just about "paltry" terrestrial events, but writing about the trajectory of the whole universe—its *inner* and *outer* realms! Gurdjieff boldly asserts that his writing efforts will help to put the planet Earth in its proper place (harmonic equilibrium) within the grand cosmic scheme of the universe!

He promises to introduce true heroes into his narratives who have shed themselves of the human vices that plagued many of history's most famous personalities and that falsely made these flawed individuals seem special in the eyes of other terrestrial humans. And again, going against the flow, and against the automatically contrary impulses of contemporary society, he chooses the character Beelzebub (the god of flies) to become the chief hero of his Tales.

Swedenborg described "Beelzebub" in Holy Scripture as symbolically representing "falsities of the sensual man." Therefore, if anyone can serve as a poster boy for turning his life around, Gurdjieff's decision to use Beelzebub as the main character was an insightful and calculated one.

The major "unpopular" and anti-intuitive claim by Gurdjieff (despite modern education and technological advances) is that humankind has been suffering and continues to suffer from a weakening of the function of mentation (one's mental activity). He knows he is "poking a stick in a hornet's nest" by saying this and that he will be making few new friends. But he recalls a supposedly true story about a railway station in Tiflis (Armenia) that had a "steam whistle" and uses this as an analogy to express the reality of his own situation of annoying people's comfort by performing his personal daily duties.

The steam whistle would wake up many of the townspeople from their peaceful sleep every morning and be just as annoying in the evening. Rumor had it that the person who pulled the rope of the whistle each morning would first turn in every direction so that he could "curse all the townspeople beforehand."

(Here comes the dogcatcher story that I promised earlier.)

Gurdjieff claimed to have visited this unpopular person and over a glass of wine asked him why he always cursed the townspeople before pulling the rope to the steam whistle. Seeing that Gurdjieff was drinking his wine in a manner different from others, the man decides he can be trusted and opens up to him. The man confessed that he began *feeling ill* while he was on the job and couldn't figure out why. Two years later he met up with a friend, a dogcatcher, who described an incident whereby the untimely ringing of some church bells scared a dog away right before he was about to make his capture. The dogcatcher became so enraged he threw down his net and cursed out loud at this unacceptable situation.

Immediately, the man who pulled the rope to the steam whistle every day understood why he was always feeling so ill at his job. Everyone in town was obviously cursing him as well, and his body sensed all their *vibrations of malice*. He concluded that if he cursed everyone in town before pulling the rope he would become immune to all their malice. This strategy seemed to neutralize the man's "instinctive uneasiness." Gurdjieff takes this same attitude with all those who might curse his efforts for waking them up and making them feel uncomfortable.

End of the message/warning!

And this also marks the end of Gurdjieff's preface to *Beelzebub's Tales*. Humor aside, Gurdjieff signs off on his foreword with the seriousness of putting his name on a legal contract. The stakes are that high!

Even a casual and skeptical reader will have to admit that Gurdjieff possessed rare enormous *outer* and *inner* freedom. In fact, he writes with the special knowledge that human mentation comes in two distinct forms—*outer* and *inner* (also supported by Swedenborg). This psychic split produces an outer human mentation from mere words or memory-data, and a human mentation from the deeper, inner content of those words and ideas. (See Swedenborg's *Arcana Coelestia*, n. 4748 [3].) Unfortunately, modern education promotes only the former, more external process of human thinking.

Gurdjieff simply won't let this outer form of thinking happen with the reading of his book. He writes to communicate the *inner content of ideas* in a way that can be universally understood and experienced by all people from all geological localities—reaching all the way into the subconscious level of the human spirit, where it can reach God's sacred and protected data—if they are sincerely ready to make the effort. (Gurdjieff believes that the human subconscious ought to be our real consciousness in life. In Swedenborg's terms, the human subconscious is called the *internal natural mind* and represents our proper and essential mind. Both men believed that God's sacred knowledge is stored in that deeper mind.)

Gurdjieff's strategy is to cut through all the bull crap of our normal ways of thinking about the world (and ourselves) and reach that deeper and ignored level of human conscience that the Lord God has placed all his hope in for building a heavenly kingdom of mutual love in our lives—our deeper, *inner* lives.

Oh, I left out one amusing little story in his preface that I hope will offer my unsuspecting readers a further "heads-up" to the fact that every chapter of this unique book will challenge current worldviews by providing concepts that are formulated to increase one's *logical confrontation* and to purposely ruffle feathers.

Gurdjieff indeed made this next little story of his prologue a powerful visceral analog to his initial warning to the reader, concerning the real indigestion that will be caused by the contents of his book.

Anticipating the full and uncomfortable effect of one's purchasing and actually reading his book, Gurdjieff relates a story about a certain Transcaucasian Kurd that is very similar to Swedenborg's deeper, spiritual interpretation of Revelation 10:9–11, where John eats a book (or scroll) and later gets *indigestion*. This Kurd notices some beautiful looking red fruit displayed at a marketplace. He is so taken by the beauty of this fruit that he assumes it is delicious and buys a whole pound of it with his last few coins. The fruit turns out to be extremely hot red pepper pods! But because the Kurd has paid good money for it, he compels himself to eat it and suffer the consequences of his decision.

Spiritual growth has the same character—it first looks like a wonderfully sweet and delicious notion to the intellectual mind, but once the real process of eating and digesting (appropriation) has begun, it becomes more of a challenge and even distasteful for our well-established and equally well-defended comfort zone.

Both genuine spiritual transformation and red hot pepper pods are not to be trifled with! Both demand a resolute mind.

Anyone is capable of observing and grasping that something is terribly off-kilter with ordinary existence and the ways humans go about their lives. Everyone can see that we live in a "crazy world." Gurdjieff described his enigmatic work as his "soldiers" to help him fight against our old and flawed worldviews and to utterly destroy them. Only then can a new worldview of God, the universe, and why we are all here, be born and emerge within the hearts and minds of contemporary men and women. This psycho-spiritual battle and confrontation, implied by Gurdjieff, is similar to Swedenborg's novel theological insights into the *deeper* levels of meaning portrayed and depicted by the numerous "wars" and "conflicts" of the biblical narratives—which symbolically represent battling worldviews and belief (faith) systems. "Truth" represents God's soldiers!

Swedenborg made the bold claim that a "New" Church (the *New Jerusalem,* spoken of in *Revelation*) was now being established upon the Earth by the Lord God of Heaven—through a new divine dispensation. Similarly, Gurdjieff once told one of his pupils that a new kind of "school" was currently being established on Earth. Both claims represent a conformable cosmic sensibility that something very new was coming to humanity from a special place (from "Above"). Swedenborg would also agree that a "church" is a place of instruction and thus, is really a "school." Swedenborg also pointed out that after being born in a stable, the Lord was placed in a manger—which *spiritually symbolizes* a place of learning a place of learning—since feeding and caring for "animals" in Holy Scripture actually corresponds to the teaching of the human heart (and its emotions).

Potent new information (a new Divine dispensation) is now being made available to the human race here on Earth. And both Gurdjieff and Swedenborg want everyone to have access to it and begin to be able to decipher it, then apply its principles to their lives!

I now believe that *Beelzebub's Tales* is a part of this new information/dispensation, and the Lord God's providential plan to allow us terrestrial humans to make a rational exploration into the mysteries of faith! (Swedenborg even worded this divine strategy as "Nunc licet intrare intelligenter in arcana fidel.")

Gurdjieff made no attempt to legally protect his epic work *Beelzebub's Tales* and for good reason. It did not just contain new knowledge but a whole new *understanding*—which one cannot copyright. He believed that if someone really understood something, it then became the lawful property of that individual. But Gurdjieff could not share higher levels of understanding without challenging people into a commitment toward making the proper self-struggle and mental effort. So he wrote in a way that would boost this self-struggle in the reader. That was the sincere fulfillment of his sense of duty (and love) toward his fellow man.

Having myself, as a Swedenborgian, thoroughly chewed on and swallowed these "hot peppers," it is my hope that my exposition of *Beelzebub's Tales* can bring down the heat level just a tiny bit and make this great work more digestible (and causing less diarrhea). I, equally with Gurdjieff, wish you "bon appetit," and true spiritual success with all my being as you carefully and consciously turn the pages of this challenging book and attempt to ponder it all.

It is your cosmic duty!

SUMMARY

- Read *Beelzebub's Tales* *three* times, and *three* different ways:

    1) Like you would read a newspaper.

    2) Like you would read to another person *out loud*.

    3) Finally, to ponder its meaning and jist.

- Swedenborg and Gurdjieff have similar ideas concerning the human predicament and the true challenges of spiritual transformation. Their works deal with the *inner history* and trajectory of the human race on Earth.

- We all have *sacred* data, implanted at a young age within us, by God's grace, which now lies dormant deep within our psyches. Gurdjieff designed these Tales to "awaken" and connect the reader's habitual mind with that sacred data.

- Gurdjieff interjects the unique notion that the human subconscious mind (Swedenborg's *internal natural mind*) ought to act as the real consciousness of humans.

- Human thinking skills have diminished over history (in spite of technological advances).

- We are mere automatons. (This is by far the most difficult notion to share with—and prove to—contemporary humans.)

- Three Principles for creating true (and *indestructible*) individuality:

    1) Try to do everything differently than others around you do it.

    2) Don't ever lose your curiousity about odd things you've observed.

    3) Take every chosen project and challenge completely through to its final end (going on a spree and going the whole hog), then add some additional effort (the postage).

- You are going to have your "corns" stepped on by reading this work.

- Gurdjieff sincerely wishes you, the reader, all the best. (So do I!)

CHAPTER 2

INTRODUCTION:
"Why Beelzebub was in our solar system"

Gurdjieff calls Chapter 2 the actual "Introduction" to his book. To provide you, the reader, with the largest possible theater of experience and scale, Gurdjieff's breathtaking story opens on a great "transspace" ship, the Karnak, traveling through the vast Milky Way galaxy (this is in 1921) toward a solar system called "Pandetznokh" whose sun is identified as the "Pole Star."[2]

Beelzebub, his grandson Hassein, his faithful old servant Ahoon, and various crewmembers were all making this incredible interstellar journey on their special spaceship (special, because it could also travel between dimensions). They were all headed from Beelzebub's own birth planet "Karatas" to a different planet called *Revozvradendr*, existing in a different solar system of the great Milky Way. The reason for this journey was that Beelzebub had been invited to attend a conference on the planet Revozvradendr by some of his long time friends.

This ultra-fantastic scenario should alert the reader that *Beelzebub's Tales* is an allegory containing *deeper levels of meaning*. That is, it contains meanings beyond our literal or normal "Earth" experience (similar to Stanislav Grof's holotropic and *nonordinary states of consciousness*). In fact, John G. Bennett, who was a leading student of Gurdjieff's ideas and had personal contact with Gurdjieff, states in his own commentary on *Beelzebub's Tales* that the story actually represents a history of the "spiritual" or "inner life of humanity" (*Talks On Beelzebub's Tales*, p. 112).

The reason for using allegory or symbolic language is that common words and ordinary meanings cannot adequately provide verbal formulations capable of transmitting ideas that can only be grasped by higher states of consciousness—that is, by an elevated mind. In fact, the writing style used in *Beelzebub's Tales* was carefully designed to thwart our customary thinking, so that we could gain a more *eternal view of reality*.

(This is music to a Swedenborgian's ears. Swedenborg's theology is based on the concept that God's Holy Word, and the natural world,

---

2. Also called the North Star. (Wikipedia)

contains deeper levels of meaning. One of these levels deals with the *inner* or *spiritual history* of the human race—which is unknown to most of today's terrestrial historians and academics, and can only come through divine revelation. This symbolic language was understood and used by our ancient ancestors (*Arcana Coelestia*, n. 7729) who enjoyed using a higher level of mental functioning, and that its loss is the reason why both Swedenborg and Gurdjieff held the view that the modern psyche has atrophied—an idea that is a slap in the face to the modern notion of human history and its supposed "advancement." So, I will be seeking out and comparing more possible similarities between both men's *multi-leveled* worldviews. It is my hope that Gurdjieff's writing will help provide a deeper understanding of Swedenborg's theological works and vice versa.)

The main character of this story—*Beelzebub*—seems to allegorically represent a more original race and higher genus of human beings who had direct perception of God's kingdom (according to Swedenborg, early men and women on Earth were of a different genus than modern humans and enjoyed this special spiritual perception before their "Fall"). Gurdjieff is also cleverly using the name "Beelzebub" to arouse certain pre-conceived mental associations in the reader (automatically learned from the world) and cause him or her to question these planted associations.

As the Tale unfolds we are informed that Beelzebub, in his youth, was living harmoniously according to God's plan and aligned himself to the divine dictates and influences of the "Sun Absolute" which served as the chief dwelling place from which the Creator governed the universe. Beelzebub's birth planet, "Karatas" was located within the direct influence of the "Sun Absolute" at the *center of the universe*. (Those who have studied Swedenborg's theology can easily recognize the *Sun Absolute* in these Tales as representing the *Spiritual Sun* in Heaven from which God's infinite love and truth flows forth as *divine light* and *warmth* to sustain and vivify all created things—especially the inner human spirit.)

Unfortunately, like most teenagers whose minds have not fully matured, Beelzebub eventually rebels against this divine arrangement, preferring his own self-judgment as to how things (especially justice) ought to be run in the universe. (Swedenborg stated that self-guidance, where one is inclined to favor his "Own," leads to falsities—*Arcana Coelestia*, n. 151.) He then convinces his closest buddies on Karatas to adopt a similar viewpoint. God is then forced to banish Beelzebub and his impetuous friends to a more *remote* corner of the universe, which is identified as the solar system that contains the planet Earth. (This is how he originally came to our Solar System!) Great symbolism!

The planet Earth occupies a lowly place in the universe, symbolized by its remoteness from the center. (Similarly, Swedenborg stated that the planet Earth *psycho-spiritually* represents lowly corporeal/sensual perception in humans—as opposed to a "perception from eternity."[3] Swedenborg's theological writings represented a perception from eternity, that is, beyond our normal finite terrestrial scope because it came from the Lord God.)

Beelzebub's banishment is the exact type of symbolic scenario described in Genesis by God banishing Adam and Eve from the Garden of Eden. Swedenborg describes this "fall" as representing an inward desire by humanity to always favor their own self-judgment (as Beelzebub did in his youth), based on the fallacies of the external senses, which inevitably brings on a diminished and partial state of consciousness in which reality is no longer correctly seen by humans.

Symbolically (psycho-spiritually) speaking, humankind was not simply removed from a terrestrial garden but removed from God's wisdom (and the rays or sacred influences from the Spiritual Sun). This is essentially the same thing as Beelzebub being exiled into a more "remote" place and further from the benevolent influence of the Sun Absolute (God's enlightening influence and spiritual abode).

I find this psycho-similarity of our own ancient exile highly plausible because in Holy Scripture, Beelzebub symbolically represents a lower cognitive state by which humans become *susceptible* to falsehoods from their relying on the five outer senses alone. Gurdjieff seems to have simply engineered a new, more modern myth for representing our banishment from the Lord God's wise influence, in order to explain similar theo-concepts about the *botched* inner history of earth-humans. This modernization of mythology or symbolic language properly employs a spaceship for banishment from a planet (plane of consciousness) that was under the influence of God's Spiritual Sun, rather than on removal from a garden, which grew from the rays of such a special sun. According to Swedenborg, both a "garden" and "vehicle for travel" can be used to symbolize a doctrine, belief system or worldview, but the latter refers more to the codes we travel by.

So Beelzebub and his followers, after falling from their original "angelic" state of *innocence*, were forced to settle on various planets of the solar system that the planet Earth also occupied. Beelzebub himself first sets up camp on the planet Mars where he constructs an observatory and telescope so that he can study the other planets around him as well as more distant cosmic formations in the universe.

Because of the remoteness of this solar system (called "Ors") to the positive and direct influences of the Sun Absolute, we learn that God would systematically send "messengers" (such as prophets) to its planets in an attempt to normalize things and help their "three-brained" inhabitants* to live in harmony with God's governance and holy laws. (I will explain later why Gurdjieff describes humans of all kinds living throughout the universe as *three-brained* beings.)

---

3. A phrase used by Anthony Blake in his 2007 *Foreword of Talks on Beelzebub's Tales.*

Apparently, one of these special divine messengers, named Ashiata Shiemash, was sent by the Creator to the planet Earth during one of its earlier civilizations, and his successful mission was helped by Beelzebub. This resulted in Ashiata Shiemash putting in a good word so that the "fallen" Beelzebub could receive a pardon from God and return to his planet Karatas at the center of the universe (a realm ruled by the Sun Absolute or Spiritual Sun). After this pardon was granted, Beelzebub was permitted to return to his home planet Karatas, near the center of the universe.

After the divine pardon and his return home, Beelzebub boards the spaceship Karnak with his grandson Hassein, and was now making a special trip to the planet Revozvradendr from the center of the universe.

Because of this divine pardon and turnaround in Beelzebub's life, plus important events also occurring among his longtime friends on the planet Revozvradendr, he was invited to a conference concerning the amazing changes taking place. This is why Beelzebub was now traveling through the Milky Way system of stars.

To make the long space trip more enjoyable, Beelzebub would often share what he learned about the planets he visited during his time in exile with his beloved grandson Hassein, because he had also personally taken on the responsibility of educating the young lad.

On this particular trip, and in the middle of one of these intriguing and educational discussions with his grandson, Beelzebub was informed that the ship's captain urgently needed to speak to him about some impending trouble that lay ahead.

SUMMARY

▪ One of the chief challenges of interpreting these Tales is the task of deciphering Gurdjieff's modern use of symbolic language.

▪ The story opens on Beelzebub, his grandson Hassein, and the faithful servant Ahoon traveling across great distances in space to attend a conference on a planet in the Milky Way Star System.

▪ Again, Gurdjieff seems to be using a more modern form of symbolism (with spaceships) to convey his "mythological" story, which I believe parallels Swedenborg's discoveries concerning the *inner life* of humans on Earth.

▪ Beelzebub himself symbolizes a "fallen" angel, who in his youth, rebelled against God's government (from self-guidance) and was banished to a distant solar system, which included the planet Earth.

▪ The "Earth" symbolizes a lower (corporeal/sensual) functioning of the human intellect and further removed from God's sacred influence. Beelzebub originally came from the planet Karatas, which was a part of the cosmic system of the Spiritual Sun (Sun Absolute) and its sacred influence—meaning that Beelzebub's inner consciousness was originally open to receiving God's love and wisdom *directly*. He was "exiled" from this original mental state.

▪ Beelzebub was eventually pardoned by the Creator God for assisting in the important work of the divine messenger Ashiata Shiemash, who was sent to Earth to help the humans living and breeding there.

▪ After the pardon, and his return to his home planet, *Karatas*, Beelzebub was joined by his grandson Hassein for this particular space trip to the planet Revozvradendr. To pass the time during the long journey, Beelzebub shares with him the things he learned about the planets of that "distant" star system—including happenings on the planet Earth.

CHAPTER 3

"The cause of the delay in the falling of the ship Karnak"

One of the great ubiquitous laws of the universe identified by Gurdjieff is that opposition and obstacles only appear on the scene once you have chosen a goal (or path). In theological terms, Swedenborg would say that spiritual conflict (temptation of the heart) only appears when one consciously and sincerely chooses a spiritual path (as their "active" principle in life). These obstacles and challenges that emerge, while uncomfortable, are important "passive" *principles* to all process because they define the parameters and constraints by which we may obtain real success and reach real goals. As passive principles, these obstacles serve to provide the inner and outer environmental boundaries by which the quality of our efforts can be determined (fixed) and discerned. (Unfortunately, in our desire to change the world, it is often these very obstacles that we take aim at and wish to destroy.)

Even God's Divine Love, flowing out into the universe, must be modified by law, which puts limits on sacred action in order to give it real form and extension in spacetime and beyond it. These laws, which give form and existence to the force and the endeavor of Divine Love, are what Swedenborg calls *Divine Truth*—the spiritual laws by which God's Infinite Love finds all its true structure, trajectories and qualities.

The *theodicy issue* (or the issue of "evil" and misfortune in the world) results from our limited understanding of these universal laws. Swedenborg states that the Creator only permits negative things to happen if they can help the larger Divine Plan to succeed. We cannot expect to be born on a bed of roses and expect growth.

So it is according to this universal law concerning the necessity of obstacles that we gain a big clue for understanding the miscalculated actions of certain Higher Sacred Individuals (in Chapter 9) that would add great difficulties and obstacles to the spiritual growth of earth-humans.

Also, an obstacle can become a force bigger than any individual or group of individuals can handle, like the one now threatening the path of the space travel of this unique group of travelers—for the Captain of the spaceship Karnak informs Beelzebub that they are heading directly into the path of a dangerous comet (representing a very big opposition).

Even though the comet will cross their path an hour before they get to that same spot in space, the travelers know that it also gives off a poisonous gas (harmful after-effects), which is identified as being similar to "cyanic acid" (a colorless flammable poisonous gas). The Captain wishes to know if Beelzebub would like to stop the forward process of the ship or change course and take a detour.

Curiously, the forward thrust of the ship through space is described as "falling." (I will return to this important subject in the very next chapter.)

Beelzebub thinks about the situation for awhile, then quotes a wise saying that he learned from an Asian sage from the planet Earth named Mullah Nassr Eddin: "You cannot jump over your knees and it is absurd to try to kiss your elbow." In other words, one must not be a fool—one should learn to submit to forces and situations greater than oneself. Further discussion on the ship reveals to me that Beelzebub had adopted a principle in this situation that is very similar to one of Swedenborg's Rules of Life—*To be content under the dispensations of God's providence.* Also that one cannot fight off bad influences alone or without God's help.

(Keep in mind that this story of space travel also has another—psycho-spiritual—level of meaning. For example, Swedenborg claimed that asteroids or shooting stars and comets symbolized *false* principles within one's belief system or worldview. Such a false principle would represent a dangerous influence, even poisonous to one's soul—just as cyanic acid would be a danger to one's material body.)

Even though diverting their route around the comet's path would be quicker, coming to a complete stop would save on the wear and tear of the ship's various parts. So Beelzebub chooses to stop the ship's forward motion and wait out the danger (similar to waiting out personal temptations rather than spending the extra energy and stress to get around them).

Beelzebub then decides that he can also make positive use of this extra waiting time to talk about the new advances being made in the more contemporary spaceships now in use that are both superior and simpler to operate than the ships being used back at the time of his exile. So he asks the Captain, who is an expert on these things, to share his insights on these new improvements for space travel when he comes back.

The Captain heads off to the engine room to bring the spaceship to a complete stop. Beelzebub's promise of a discussion on the new spaceship improvements greatly delights his grandson Hassein, who totally enjoys listening to all his grandfather's highly informative and illuminating talks. (Here, rather than being depressed by this sudden change in plans, Hassein is wisely taking full advantage of the providential outcomes of the works of the Lord Creator God.)

Meanwhile, as they are still waiting for the Captain's return, Beelzebub offers to talk to his grandson about any additional topic he might be interested in. Hassein is quite curious about whether other *three-brained beings* live on the planets of the peculiar solar system in that corner of the universe that his grandfather had been exiled on. And if they do, Hassein is anxious to know whether the three-brained beings on these planets have the same possibilities of coating their higher being-bodies like others in the universe. (In Swedenborg's language, this means forming the psycho-organic membranes and organs of a *new spiritual body* within the physical or terrestrial body, in order to live fully in higher spheres after one's physical death— these higher spheres include God's heavenly kingdom.)

Beelzebub replies that individuals do indeed live on these planets and have the same potential to coat these *higher being-bodies* as all other three-brained beings in God's universe. He then informs Hassein that the external forms (physical bodies) of the inhabitants of the various planets in that solar system are formed in conformity with the physical conditions of those planets, particularly with their atmospheres. (Swedenborg would agree with this notion and the idea that the universe is teeming with intelligent life.) However, Beelzebub's physical descriptions of some of these aliens are so bizarre that they can be easily dismissed by the habitual human intellect.

For instance, Beelzebub describes beings on the Moon as having the bodies of large ants and those on Mars as having planetary bodies that include a broad trunk, large eyes, two large wings and small feet with big claws. While Swedenborg gives us a more human notion of the forms of intelligent life on other planets, I believe Gurdjieff employs his strange bodily descriptions of alien beings to force us to look deeper into what constitutes true humanness throughout God's universe— regardless of exterior bodily form. (And remember, Hassein wants to know if these aliens have similar opportunities for developing inner bodies.)

When Beelzebub finally describes the three-brained beings (humans) of the planet Earth, he informs his grandson that they are externally similar to their own kind—except that their skin is a bit slimier and they have no tails, hooves or horns. Even worse, although earth-humans also possess all the data required to coat higher being-bodies[4] within their external (physical) forms, unfortunately they lack the "strength of spirit" to do so. (This is the first reference to the fact that something is wrong with earth-humans.)

Beelzebub also throws in the peculiar comment that the planet Earth must constantly maintain its Moon's existence (as we will see in later chapters, this cosmic requirement creates a problem for human spiritual transformation as well).

Beelzebub tells Hassein that apart from the obvious imperfections of the earth-humans' exterior forms and physical bodies (compared to their own) the reasoning powers of earth-humans have also diminished over time and have become "uniquely strange" in all the universe. (This negative description is anti-intuitive to the reader who falsely believes that improved earth-technology is a sure sign of modern superiority and its advancement. Here, Gurdjieff is beginning to chip away at human fantasy and delusionalism, focusing on a deeper and more spiritual view of reality.)

At this moment, the Captain returns to their quarters.

Beelzebub, hoping to make the next conversation a bit more interesting, asks the Captain to first describe his career and then talk about the new advances in long-distance transspace ships that have been made during his long career. The Captain states that he, like his father before him, was promoted to the position of captain for his blameless service to HIS ENDLESSNESS. Therefore, both father and son received a spiritual promotion! (To a Swedenborgian, this can be easily interpreted as performing uses and duties in accordance with God's divine tenets.)

The fact that these spaceships are described in this story as being used for *intersystem* and *interplanetary communication* suggests something is being addressed here that is beyond mere rocket ship technology or mere physical travel. Symbolically, I believe this discussion actually concerns improvements made on *inner* or *psycho-spiritual* travel due to simpler doctrines. It is easy for the habitual human mind to run off the rails when faced with an allegorical tale that contains higher (yet hidden) meanings. But we must make the intellectual effort to elevate our thoughts or little of this will make any sense. In other words, these special spaceships symbolically represent something higher and psycho-spiritual—like the *belief systems* that carry us to our chosen goals and destinies. Such destinations can include spiritual *salvation*.

In Swedenborg's terms, the word "communication" symbolizes conjunction and reception of God's universal truth. This is why I believe that the advances being made in these transspace ships represent doctrinal improvements and a simplifying in the receiving of God's heavenly influences.

The Captain explains that the original ships used "elekilpomagtistzen," a substance made from two separate elements of the omnipresent Okidanokh (I believe this is electrical energy) to power them. This system of propulsion by *opposing forces* (symbolizing the dualistic notion of "good and evil") proved bulky and was later improved upon by the ships (doctrines) designed by Saint Venoma. (Again, in Swedenborg's terms, this means that more efficient and

---

4. Although Swedenborg talks about spiritual bodies, those who follow his ideas emphasize "good works." But when good works become a fixed trait, this is evidenced by the organic evolution of higher bodies and structures within us.

streamlined methods were developed by heavenly intelligences to help all humans more easily obtain spiritual ends that were much less artificial and cumbersome than our memorizing, by rote, what was to be deemed "good" and what "evil.")

Saint Venoma represents a higher, God-inspired intelligence for improving our receptivity toward the spiritual doctrine of truth. More details of this Saint's new and improved system for travel (doctrines that allow us to advance more easily toward our heavenly goal) will be offered in the next chapter.

SUMMARY

■ Beelzebub's spaceship journey runs into a deadly obstacle—
a comet, which contains a psycho-spiritual lesson concerning the
necessity of negative principles and obstacles. From this, we must
learn not submit to forces and situations greater than ourselves
while learning to take advantage of opportunities within God's
providence—including strings of bad luck!

■ (This predicament of a comet offers the reader a clue for
understanding an important principle that will come up in
Chapter 9, concerning the genesis of the Earth's Moon.)

■ The theodicy issue, or issue of "evil" in the world, comes from
humans not understanding our true situation, or what is necessary
to procure a permanent spiritual life within oneself.

■ Beelzebub asks the Captain to explain the enormous advances
made in new spaceship technology during his lifetime. Since, this
new technology was invented by a "Saint," we can assume it means
that this noble individual made some modification to our acquiring
more spiritual aims and heavenly happiness.

■ Hassein wants to know if there are any other intelligent beings on
the planets his grandfather was exiled on, and if they had the same
opportunities for spiritual growth as their own tribe enjoys. They do.

■ While Swedenborgians emphasize "good works," when such
spiritual characteristics become "fixed" within one's life choices,
it leads to the further development of higher organic structures
and inner bodies.

■ Beelzebub informs Hassein that the humans from the planet Earth
have spiritually degenerated over time and now act quite peculiarly
for three brained-beings (those who have a *head-brain*, a *spinal column*
and a *nerve plexus* in the breast).

CHAPTER 4

"The law of falling"

When Sir Isaac Newton observed an apple falling next to him it inspired him to investigate and discover what would become known as the *law of gravity*. He found that if for instance, you shot a cannon ball, it would take a mathematically precise trajectory and "fall" at some mathematically precise place. The more gunpowder, the farther (and faster) would be the trajectory of the projectile and its descent. From this notion came the idea that if one used enough gunpowder, in a sufficiently large cannon, the projectile would hit a trajectory and speed in which it would not "fall" to the ground but fall into an orbit around the earth! This orbit would represent where the projectile found its proper (and corresponding) stability.

(It is a universal law, known even to all earthly physicists, that everything put into motion seeks its equilibrium or point of stability.)

According to the captain of the ship Karnak, it was not Newton but Saint Venoma who first discovered this ubiquitous law. He called it the "Law of Falling." This saintly being made certain that in a universe where *everything is process* and constantly moving, all things seek (tend toward) some appropriate "bottom." The bottom is different for different phenomena in the universe. In each case, or on any scale, the bottom represents the nearest "point of stability" (equilibrium) where all lines of force are converging.

In his anatomical book *The Fiber* (Volume lll of the *Economy of the Animal Kingdom*, n. 65), Swedenborg concurs that all things are in an endeavor toward equilibrium, which is toward the center of their sphere. He also called this point of stability the *"punctum immobile."*

The *center* of every star or planet in the universe represents points of stability (or centers of gravity). Each astronomical formation represents the lowest point of some distinct quality of forces and where they lawfully concentrate within the arena of universal processes. The Law of Falling discovered by Saint Venoma was not simply an anticipation of Newton's later physical discovery—it included the concept of *gravitational order* within the scheme of a *multilayered* universe. This covers more than why a helium balloon finds its stability in a different place and "falls" in a different direction than a brick does. It involves how nature incessantly strives toward organization (whereby many successive operations find a *common equilibrium*).

Everything finds its rightful place in this great universe of dynamical and organizational process—*including our wishes and intentions!* Our desires and intentions come under the same law of falling and arrange psychical order (common equilibriums) to the values held in the human mind. This psychical order embraces real bio-structure (mental substrates) and determines the ultimate form of our spiritual body.

I cannot stress enough how important this topic is. It offers a scientific and rational view of the universe that includes the structured (ordered) arrangement of biological and psycho-spiritual phenomena. Swedenborg discovered that in the biological processes of the human body, these processes advance from one center to another through a series of unified organs. Later, in his theological writings, Swedenborg indicated that in the afterlife, our spirits similarly find their equilibrium by heading in the direction of our hearts (and intentions).

A system of using gravity for moving about constitutes a universal and spiritual form of propulsion. According to Beelzebub, Saint Venoma sought to incorporate this ubiquitous law into the design of a whole new order of spaceships (doctrines).

Saint Venoma made his famous discovery after he was providentially moved from his home planet "Soort" to the holy planet "Purgatory" in order to perform greater uses for the Creator. He must have noticed that any change of his heart created a change in his "placement" (equilibrium) in the spiritual realm. Swedenborg would completely agree with this spiritual or non-physical dynamic of motion and directionality.

Since it was Gurdjieff's strategy to always "bury the dog deeper," the Captain's story on spaceship technology forces the reader to withdraw his or her habitual mind from normal sensuous functioning (of mere terrestrial ideas and memory-data), which can suffocate the higher mind from operating. Both Gurdjieff and Swedenborg were in agreement that the lower habitual mind in humans is kept closed and immersed—even imprisoned—in worldly terms and terrestrial ideas.

Gurdjieff masterfully cuts through this *word-crap* by creating odd scenarios and terms that render our normal cognition useless, forcing us to think in new and uncomfortable ways (even to the point of *despair*). As a student of Swedenborg's theology, this is the same strategy employed by the fantastic nature and style of many of the Bible's fantastic stories—which attempt to challenge a mere linear or purely historical/literal interpretation of events (*Arcana Coelestia*, n. 5089).

We are being challenged to raise our thoughts (and spirits) to a higher "bottom" or point of stability.

The Captain continues his odd talk about an angelic being on a higher plane of existence, who upon discovering this law of falling, begins to wonder if this same principle could be incorporated into the technology of a spacecraft. This saintly individual finds that such an idea of using gravity for propulsion indeed works well in free space (a vacuum) but runs into trouble because solar and planetary atmospheres would hinder the forward progress of any spacecraft (due to the same law).

Here again, Gurdjieff interjects the idea that any path taken will eventually come under some resistance. These solar and planetary atmospheres are metaphors for the human condition and represent resistances coming from the different influences of individuals and organizations, which can slow our personal progress and intentions, but which are all necessary!

Saint Venoma concentrated on solving this issue of atmospheric resistance with a solution that involved vaporizing the atmosphere ahead of the ship with a *ray of energy,* so that the space it was entering was always empty. The Captain admits to being present at the trials of this new type of spaceship technology. It was, soon after, approved by a special Commission of Inspection headed by another archangel. (Saints, angels and archangels involved in improving space travel? Again, this story cannot be a taken literally. The *ray of energy* most likely represents the light or force of God's Divine Truth removing imagined obstacles in the human spirit.)

As a Swedenborgian, I understand that angelic beings find their greatest joy in serving others and creating the kinds of things that provide real and eternal benefit to others. In other words, angels will only undertake projects that benefit a person's path toward spiritual salvation and well-being. Therefore they would only devise a means of propulsion that would help God put the human race on a truly faster spiritual trajectory and journey. (Having been associated with other members within various Gurdjieff work groups, I have heard this story of improved spaceship technology interpreted as the simplifying of a higher teaching or doctrine by which one can more effectively obtain inner [heavenly] freedom—and happiness.)

This interpretation fits well with Swedenborg's use of symbolic language pertaining to vehicles of all types that inwardly represent various doctrines and belief systems, all designed to "carry" us through life and transport us to where our hearts and minds seek their ultimate stability. I strongly believe that this is the kind of transcendental "craft" Saint Venoma was working on.

So the valuable nugget hidden or buried deeper in this chapter is that according to both Gurdjieff and Swedenborg, the center of gravity in the "law of falling" can also represent a person's quality of love or intentions and represents a psychical, rather than just a physical, state of stability and equilibrium. Swedenborg addresses the concept of a spiritual center of gravity in his work *Apocalypse Explained*, n. 159 [3]. When Jesus told Pontius Pilate that His kingdom was "within," He was talking about a spiritual center of gravity that the human heart and mind must gravitate toward.

The Captain continues his story by saying that the spaceship designed by Saint Venoma, although it was an improvement over previous ships, still had severe "steering" problems and had to be slowed down immensely when passing near suns and planets, especially those with lots of comets.

So, the Captain next talks about an even better spaceship design for intersystem and interplanetary *communication* that was invented by the Archangel Hariton. As said before, the term "communication" tells me again that these "space vehicles" are designed to improve an individual's efforts (spiritual travel) to come closer to God and reciprocate—like acquiring an improved theological doctrine.

So what does this new multidimensional spaceship technology consist of, and what would it symbolize to the human spirit—that is, the human heart and mind? We'll find out.

SUMMARY

■ Earth-humans have the same spiritual potential as other humans living throughout the universe. But unfortunately, they have weaker spirits.

■ The Captain of the spaceship *Karnak* gives a history of the changing technology used for multi-dimensional travel.

■ Saint Venoma was transferred to a higher post (new planet/plane) because that's where his cosmic usefulness (and center of gravity) was tending.

■ There, he began work on incorporating the "Law of Falling" into the locomotion of spaceship technology (which symbolizes a more efficient spiritual doctrine and world view to get to where we're going).

■ The "Law of Falling" includes the thermodynamics and psycho-spiritual dynamics of gravitational organization, whereby one's spirit travels and finds stability in the directionality of one's *love* (inner goal and its inner environment). In other words, love is *spiritual* gravity!

■ Archangel Hariton adds a unique improvement to Saint Venoma's technology and system for traveling through different levels of "space" while encountering various obstacles and different spheres.

■ Heaven (and its eternal happiness) is the ultimate destination of all life's human travelers.

CHAPTER 5

"The system of Archangel Hariton"

As the Captain of the *Karnak* continues discussing his personal history with Beelzebub, Hassein and Ahoon, the reader now hears about how a different archangel was brought into the challenge of designing a newer and better transspaceship technology—especially on the issue of steering in the atmosphere's cosmic units. In Swedenborg's terms, an archangel corresponds to a *celestial* angel—the highest angel in God's heavenly kingdom. But as I hinted earlier, saints and angels would only be concerned with transspaceship technology if it brought us closer to the Creator! (Which means an improvement over spiritual doctrine.)

That is why I so strongly believe that this allegorical story concerns the *inner travel* of the human spirit—not just physical travel. (It is this rarefied information that all allegory contains that the habitual human mind finds so difficult to grasp.)

A noble being such as a saint or archangel would have deeper insights and greater *doctrinal* solutions for simplifying travel for the human *spirit*. The improvement made by this next archangel was with the various atmospheric resistances a transspaceship would encounter traveling through the spheres of stars and planets along the way. (This is similar to our dealings with other human beings as we travel though life.)

So again, this story presents a problem for the reader who only gets caught up in external, worldly ideas and definitions, and can only visualize physical travel. God's Heaven and its angels do not exist in a material or physical realm. Nor are angels concerned with physical travel between actual physical stars and planets. It is worth repeating—they are only concerned with constantly finding ways to help the Lord God improve the means by which terrestrial humans can become *more spiritual* (through improved doctrines) so that their inner lives can return to the source of creation—the Holy Sun Absolute (Spiritual Sun). This notion of inner travel is supported by the fact that Beelzebub's current spaceship can travel or "fall" to the spiritual center of the universe, which is beyond the spacetime arena.

Emanuel Swedenborg describes nature as a being a "complex of means" (*Arcana Coelestia*, n. 5094) by which all things are divinely inspired to be disposed toward God's ultimate *end*. Gurdjieff and Swedenborg both are in agreement that the ultimate end of creation is to create spiritual and heavenly beings (with higher being-bodies) from the physical human race (which exists throughout the starry universe). But this requires that the human psyche learn to distinguish between exterior (worldly) and interior (spiritual) communications.

By the ship's captain next describing the materials and blueprint of Archangel Hariton's new design, Gurdjieff slyly uses seemingly familiar terms to show how easily the reader can be led away from the deeper message that is intended. These mentioned materials must be grasped psycho-symbolically. (For instance, Swedenborg states that all the materials and construction of the sacred temple that Aaron alone would enter (as described in Exodus), actually represents qualities of God's intelligent and purposeful design for how the human spirit (mind and heart) can approach closer to divine truth and goodness. Concentrating merely on the physical materials described in the construction of this temple and their literal meanings only leads one astray from the deeper sacred communication and symbolic meaning contained within—all to help us travel spiritually. The same communication is incorporated into the new design of Archangel Hariton's mechanism for propulsion.)

The human brain has no problem understanding and traveling to these deeper ideas when it is elevated into more rarefied or higher planes. But on lower planes of human mentation, symbolized by terrestrial planets and their different atmospheres (lower points of stability or centers of gravity), which offer resistance to our traveling to more interior realities, a simpler means must be devised for communicating and applying rarefied ideas so that one can travel to these deeper realities—unhindered.

The new system of propulsion devised by the Archangel Hariton (and now employed in the spaceship *Karnak*) consists of materials put in a *special order* from *inside* a special chamber and separated by "amber." So let's take a look at the possible symbolism being used here. The phrase *special order* is code for expressing God's *sacred* order (the Divine order of Truth as it advances.) According to Swedenborg, amber also has a very special spiritual significance. Amber represents a mediating substance by which lower or natural things can be *connected* to the influences (influx) of higher spiritual things, which result in God's Truth reaching the ultimate, worldly plane (this is the symbolic meaning of amber given by Swedenborg's Bible interpretation as well).

When Archangel Hariton's ship comes in contact with a planet's atmosphere (worldly notions) and the elements of this atmosphere enter the special chamber, where they are submitted to this new arrangement (and order), they next expand and exit the chamber, providing thrust. (New effort in the human will.)

This expansion (and thrust) can happen to our normal ideas and concepts, which, when put in the proper cosmic or divine order will be expanded in our minds and push us, with greater power and velocity, toward our God-given goals.

Spiritually speaking, Archangel Hariton was designing a means by which humans could take in worldly or ordinary knowledge from the outer senses and expand it in a way that provides new thrust for our spiritual growth and obtaining a heavenly direction in life. What makes this new form of "travel" simpler than past means is that instead of removing and destroying all resistance, it makes use of all kinds of resistance as the fuel to provide the actual propulsion for moving forward (and upward).

There is an important message here concerning our spiritual travels (goals). As an analog to streamlining spiritual progress (inner motion), we can use all our resistances (from egoism) to God's heavenly plan as the perfect material to create a heavenly thrust! One of Swedenborg's most powerful messages is that we must identify our character flaws (resistances) in a way that they then become the fuel for our regeneration and change (positive spiritual motion). What could be simpler and more readily available for fueling our inner progress than our own flaws?

The purpose of Gurdjieff's book is clearly to provide a means of reaching spiritual goals through a new kind of (mental) propulsion, which makes wise use of our readily available personal imperfections. If you are skeptical of his writing style as containing a deeper psycho-spiritual level of meaning, then you will be left with merely ultra-fantastic and inexplicable stories that defy ordinary comprehension and provide no practical help.

(This kind of knowledge is not made available through modern education. It originates from higher sources of wisdom and involves educating and elevating the heart and not just the intellect (with its memory-data). The new means of spiritual propulsion [through sincere self-examination and comparing it to Divine order] mentioned above will someday be in wide use by all those who come to inhabit the Holy City, The New Jerusalem.)

Since Gurdjieff's first attempt at writing *Beelzebub's Tales* took him seven years, after which he started the whole process all over again to make modifications and improvements, it seems highly doubtful that he would focus all this labor-intensive energy and time on expressing mere nonsense and silliness.

SUMMARY

▪ Spaceship technology symbolizes the doctrines and belief systems that carry us to our life's destinations.

▪ Angels and Archangels are only concerned with improving *spiritual* travel—not physical travel.

▪ Archangel Hariton makes a further (and simpler) improvement to Saint Venoma's transspaceship propulsion system. This wise improvement in propulsion uses the various resistances to forward progress (found everywhere) as a completely new form of fuel!

▪ According to Emanuel Swedenborg's theology, a person's inner evils (resistances to God's plan) can also become the means for reformation and repentance, which fuels regeneration (spiritual progress).

▪ This deeper knowledge is not given in modern education or religion. It can only be gained by an elevation of the mind (and heart) through God's heavenly help, by which worldly ideas are given higher, corresponding meanings to represent spiritual (non-material) qualities and realities.

▪ Angelic beings not only have heavenly hearts, their intellect constantly strives to learn new things.

CHAPTER 6

"Perpetual motion"

One of the seemingly oddest ideas in *Beelzebub's Tales* is that angels and archangels are portrayed as being in a continuous pursuit of knowledge, especially concerning the laws of *world creation and maintenance* (God's universal laws). This perpetual activity sounds more scientific than angelic. Whether we believe in angels or not, our culture has taught us that angels are spiritual beings with large and caring hearts—not rocket scientists with curious minds.

However, Emanuel Swedenborg, through his visionary insights and direct observation of phenomena in the Spiritual world, learned that angels (who are finite human beings from various planets throughout the universe) continue to learn new things throughout eternity. They seek to increase their wisdom and intelligence concerning God's laws of divine order (divine truth) so that their love and hearts can be rationally directed toward activities and usefulness that are increasingly beneficial to others. In this way they perpetually help the Creator to increase the mutual love in Heaven and the harmonious design of the universe.

Swedenborg claimed in both his scientific and theological works that "existence is perpetual subsistence." Said another way, subsistence is a "perpetual coming into existence." This *dynamic of everlasting existence through sharing* represents the universal laws of world creation and maintenance (Gurdjieff's *Trogoautoegocratic* principle) and embraces every topic of inquiry from creation to evolution to spiritual salvation. Swedenborg also stated that conscious action was perpetual will, because the will is eternally seeking to find itself in real action, form, and structure. Similarly, all physical motion in the universe is the result of a perpetual endeavor (called conatus), because endeavor is an internal state of perpetual effort tending (as a creating force) to move itself out from itself through a spinning progressive motion (displacing itself). This perpetual spiral flux into circular motion creates geometrical limits (passive constraints and form) through delineating points, lines, surfaces, and volumes.

So *something perpetual and infinite is running the universe!* (Something perpetual and infinite created finite geometry and nature—all at the same time!)

Swedenborg discovered that the laws of world creation and maintenance represent the *dynamics* and *laws of Love* (God's character expressing itself formally), which ultimately addresses both fundamental *being* (Esse), and its *coming forth* (Existere). These ideas represent the "bone and dog" that Gurdjieff keeps burying deeper, and challenges the reader to work ever harder at digging out.

That I have put this ubiquitous notion of perpetual dynamics right in your lap doesn't make things any easier, either, because the idea that Love is fundamental reality and primal substance (which makes it a topic worthy of scientific investigation) is not easily grasped by normal human cognition. Love, in Swedenborg's and Gurdjieff's terms is more than a principle of romance, or something we acknowledge on St. Valentine's Day. Love powers the manifest universe from a perpetual principle! So there still remains a lot of mental digging (contemplation) before us.

At this point in the story (Chapter 6) Beelzebub interrupts the Captain by saying that his account of God's high-ranking angels improving on the design of their ships reminds him of the time on Earth when he observed earth-humans going crazy trying to invent *perpetual motion* machines (in which God is taken out of the picture). Beelzebub expresses disdain for those who from vanity, self-love and who seek worldly honors, attempt such a project without the proper *internal data* (which genuine angels possess). Earth-humans love to make stuff up and concoct things from their own misguided sagacity and egoism (without God's input). Instead of wisdom, these misguided earth-humans pursued this most difficult challenge of perpetual motion through their cunning and cleverness—in order to seek worldly honors and status. Beelzebub adds the word "psychopathy" to this misguided effort by earth-humans.

In his scientific work, *The Economy Of The Animal Kingdom* (Vol. II, ch. 3, n. 209) Swedenborg makes a similar point about the human psyche and its odd proclivities. He states that there is nothing more common to the human race than to quickly move from the lowest sphere to the highest sphere merely from the love of self and love of worldly ambition—which is counter to God's scheme (proper internal data). He states:

"Thus every sciolist and tyro aspires from the rudiments of his science forthwith to its loftiest summit; as from the rudiments of geometry to the quadrature of the circle; from the rudiments of mechanism to perpetual motion; from the rudiments of chemistry to gold and alkahest; from the rudiments of philosophy to the substantia prima, or first substance of the world; and from every science to the human soul."

Swedenborg concludes with this theological warning:

"Thus the ambition of Adam remains deeply rooted in the nature of his posterity, and every one as a son of earth still desires to touch the heavens with his finger."

Only the Lord God provides the proper *internal data* for understanding perpetual motion within the cycle (orb) of change and process through His Divine Providence. (Swedenborg calls such a sacred series of coherent and connected events "the power of truth advancing.")

This chapter concerns how misguided humans prefer their own self-judgment in obtaining the highest possible knowledge, and bypassing the divine and lawful means for obtaining such rarefied knowledge about reality. However, these rarefied concepts cannot be expressed by common ideas or by the partial information provided through an individual's five sensory organs. This is why Gurdjieff floods the reader's senses with many uncommon ideas—like angels building *transspace* ships. (Angels represent higher and holy intelligences, always oriented toward God, thus manifesting purely noble motives.)

But even without moving the human mind toward new realms of mental abstraction—toward unified process (like the angels possess)—I believe the reader can still get a good "feel," or more interior perception (revelation) for what is lacking in the finite and modern human psyche, and by the frivolous efforts of a self-centered ego.

Perpetual motion comes only from the infinite Lord God! But the idea of an infinite and perpetual divine effort is utterly incomprehensible to the finite human mind—that is why only a condition of psychopathy would cause men to believe that such a challenge is a "simple matter," needing only ingenuity and cleverness.

The common human intellect (worldly habitual mind), by itself, is almost useless for interpreting *Beelzebub's Tales*. The higher human spiritual heart must come in to aid the ordinary reader, for wisdom cannot be obtained from God without a good or innocent heart. (And I cannot leave out the fact that Gurdjieff also wants us to read this challenging book *out loud,* so that we can also bring our motor nerves and our physical bodies into the experience of these unique Tales— all to help us get a more visceral grasp of his sacred message.)

In fact, in this short chapter, Gurdjieff has created a modernized version of the biblical story of the Tower of Babel. Symbolically speaking, each human invention for producing a perpetual motion machine represents a (hand-hewn) brick for the raising of this artificial and fabricated tower. The human race does not understand its true duty in God's universe or how to reach a true "heaven" (and not one of our deluded mind's own making).

The topic of perpetual motion simply serves to illustrate this flaw in human mentation by showing that those who attribute all things to nature and nothing to God fail to consider that all process is annihilated when disconnected from first principles—the Divine Infinite activity.

Perpetual motion comes from being connected to, and in constant reciprocal partnership with, God's eternal activity.

SUMMARY

■ Since Archangel Hariton's new design will work for as long as the world exists, it reminds Beelzebub of a time on Earth when he personally witnessed foolish men engaged in constructing inventions for perpetual motion (without any proper "inner" data or input from God's laws).

■ This chapter concerns earth-humans' egoism.

■ Men's cunning and cleverness is no substitute for spiritual wisdom.

■ Because of these silly (egoistic) inventions, the earthmen-inventors were kept from fulfilling their real obligations and cosmic duties arranged by God.

■ Archangel Hariton's design (a special cylinder-barrel that expands atmospheric substances for engine thrust) was exactly what the Earth's inventors were looking for—but its construction was based not on cleverness, but on universal and holy laws.

■ Archangel Hariton's improvement was directed toward *spiritual* locomotion, by which worldly ideas were put into a new sacred order where they would be expanded. This expansion of ideas provides additional thrust for one's psycho-spiritual travel to inaccessible places.

CHAPTER 7

"Becoming aware of genuine being-duty"

This chapter inspired me in finding the title of the book you now have in your hands—*Cosmic Duty*. It points to what God expects of us and in exactly what God placed His hope for creating the human race.

Beelzebub's Tales has become much more theological to me since I first read it back in 1974. I also have to admit that studying Swedenborg's theology through the years has made my mind much more attuned to the religious/spiritual elements incorporated into its topics. Gurdjieff uses so many odd words and seemingly non-religious scenarios that one can fail to notice that God is mentioned practically everywhere among its pages (and often described as HIS ENDLESSNESS or COMMON ENDLESS CREATOR). Gurdjieff seeks to elevate human consciousness through universal *spiritual* laws. Without such an elevation of heart and mind we cannot possibly see reality or our true purpose.

If Chapter 1 is the arousal of thought, then Chapter 7 is the arousal of new feelings. In this chapter, Beelzebub's grandson, Hassein, is struck with sadness after hearing the Captain's story about all the advances made in transspace ship technology. Concerned, Beelzebub inquires about the source of this melancholy.

Hassein replies that in the universe of our ENDLESSNESS (God's creation) it has now become clear to him that all the wonderful things and inventions he has become accustomed to—that make his life more comfortable and convenient—did not always exist. These things were created by the real efforts of other people who lived before him.

Hassein is sad because up to that point in his existence he accepted these things naturally and took them all for granted. He was born into them. But now, Hassein is humbled by his newly increased awareness of the labors of those who came before him. Certainly, one must be thankful to those whose efforts have improved the welfare of his society. (That we mindlessly accept all of life's improvements over the years is a sure sign that we live in some kind of a trance.)

Hassein asks his grandfather what obligations he is under for all the efforts and fruits of labor by those individuals who preceded him. Because of Hassein's new and widened state of consciousness, he now admits to his grandfather that he is experiencing real *remorse of conscience* for not having given any consideration to the efforts of those who lived earlier.

Beelzebub tells him he is still too young to be concerned about such an important *essence-question*. However, he advises Hassein that every morning at sunrise, while observing its splendor, he should attempt to connect his conscious mind with various parts of his unconscious functioning and treating them also as if conscious, imploring them not to *hinder* future efforts to become a good servant of our COMMON ENDLESS CREATOR nor to interfere with the important obligation of *"paying for your existence."* (Apparently, there are many forces working against us that we need to consciously discover from within and use as the thrust for our individual strategies of self-transformation.)

This deep connection and its resulting inner conflict (temptation), within an individual, produces increased conscience—as an *equilibriating* force.) Swedenborg insisted that all spiritual transformation emerged from the enlargement of this special interior plane of conscience because it represents a plane in which God's influx of love and wisdom can become fixed (coated) in the individual. (This is what led me to believe that *spiritual conscience* and the *remains*, implanted by God, represent the same sacred mental substrate of the human natural mind!)

Beelzebub must certainly be happy with his grandson's question, since Hassein is starting to develop real *conscience*, without which one cannot ever hope to be called a "genuine son of our COMMON FATHER OF ALL THAT EXISTS." (p. 368)

It is here, in Chapter 7, that Gurdjieff introduces the concept of one's personal duty to God, to the universe, and to the neighbor. Later in the book, Gurdjieff calls this most sacred obligation one's "being-Partkdolg-duty" (being-duty for short).

The topic of cosmic duty—of properly re-paying for one's existence through spiritual labors and toil—is a great lead-in for Hassein to now ask his grandfather to tell him more about the strange *three-brained* beings who inhabit the planet Earth.

Why strange?

Is there something wrong with earth-humans in the cosmic scheme of things and their sense of duty?

In Swedenborg's terms, there most certainly is—the human race is reluctant to take up the Lord's "Cross" (which is the essence of our being-duty and paying for our existence). Unfortunately, most earth-humans are oblivious to this higher cosmic duty and go through life only addressing their immediate physical needs.

Thus, we end the first "octave" of *Beelzebub's Tales.*

SUMMARY

▪ Hassein gets a humbling new insight, which brings about remorse (and prepares him for understanding future cosmic obligations as an adult).

▪ We shouldn't take anything for granted. Not everything we enjoy always existed as it now does—it came from the efforts of those who preceded us.

▪ Individuals who lived previously, suffered and labored long and hard to bring us all the amenities and comforts we now enjoy (even though they had no awareness of us).

▪ We all have to pay the universe (and God) back for our existence. But this takes an increase in our consciousness and our serious pondering about real essence-questions.

▪ We must convince our unconscious nature (our subconscious mind, with its often opposing appetites and desires) not to screw up our proper functioning in the external world. Otherwise we will never succeed in paying the universe back for the gift of our existence.

▪ Although this payback is our proper duty, it is not demanded by life—that is, until we reach the age of responsibility and maturity (proper reasoning).

▪ Everything has its time.

CHAPTER 8

"The imprudent brat Hassein, Beelzebub's grandson, dares to call men 'slugs' "

Beelzebub opens the next octave of his Tales (my conjecture) by offering a new *evaluation* (the "Do" in a psychic octave) of earth-humans and their status in the universe—meaning, us! This new evaluation is not very flattering. (Swedenborg, in his work, *Worship And Love Of God*, n. 122 [b], describes this new evaluation of a mental series as the mind immediately seizing things that will be instrumental in gaining a new and helpful knowledge of things. Also, in Swedenborg's spiritual symbolism, the number "8" (as in octaves) corresponds to a new beginning or start of a new series of events. This next unfolding mental octave from this series of functioning will provide additional evidence for entertaining Gurdjieff's negative evaluation of earth-humans for furthering our enlightenment.)

Vaguely remembering that Beelzebub had described the three-brained beings living on planet Earth earlier in the Tales as having skin a bit *slimier* than their own, the grandson Hassein, acting like a typical young brat, states that he wishes to learn more details about these "slugs" (which also have slimy skins).

Beelzebub is at first taken aback by this crude assessment because he does not at first understand exactly whom Hassein is referring to. Then he laughs that his lovable grandson was merely calling the three-brained beings of the planet Earth "slugs" from hearing his own earlier description of them as having slimier skins. (This is another conscious attempt by Gurdjieff to bring the reader's egoism down yet another notch.)

But Beelzebub warns his beloved grandson that using the comical term "slugs," even innocently, is no joke when it comes to having any deep or serious discussion concerning these particular three-brained beings that Hassein has suddenly become curious toward. Hassein's grandfather explains that earth-humans will often seek revenge on hearing such insults. (Earth-humans not only have slimier skins, but also thinner skins.)

In spite of Hassein's childish insult, Beelzebub, having observed the planet Earth with his powerful telescope (from Mars) and even living among these inhabitants or "men-beings" of the planet Earth for several long periods of time, admits to his grandson that much valuable material can be obtained from a discussion of their peculiar lives (which is the real reason they should be called "slugs" in the universe).

He tells his beloved grandson that the men-beings of Earth manifest traits not found on any other planet of the universe. (Swedenborg certainly agrees that spiritually, humans on Earth have fared worse than the inhabitants of other planets and solar systems.)

So this is not a good sign. The message here is designed to destroy any notions that earth-humans enjoy some level of superiority over all things in the manifest universe.

Beelzebub is so old that he tells his grandson that he not only observed, from the planet Mars, the arising of humans on Earth but he witnessed the full formation of the planet Earth itself from a time when it had not yet cooled off. (So Mars is older than Earth.)

Beelzebub informs Hassein that from the very beginning, the planet Earth was a big problem for God (another cosmic bummer for the reader). In fact, Beelzebub has nothing remotely flattering to say about the human race or the planet they inhabit and breed on. (This is actually positive spiritual input because Swedenborg assures us that any weakening of the human ego and its self-centered nature brings strength to the inner human soul—which is what the Lord God actually wants.)

Hassein is now completely interested in listening to his grandfather tell him about the general cosmic character of this particular astronomical concentration called "Earth" and how this planet came to be the cause of so many serious troubles for our ENDLESSNESS (God).

Again, Gurdjieff obviously wants to thoroughly demolish any thoughts his readers might entertain that the inhabitants of Earth are to be viewed as somehow special. The planet Earth is an eyesore in God's great universe. And Gurdjieff uses Beelzebub (who was once a fallen soul, but now pardoned) to explain how this situation came to be.

Swedenborg underscores this unflattering notion by reminding us that Jesus came to the planet Earth—and only the planet Earth—to spare its human race from extinction and preserve salvation.

SUMMARY

■ Earth-humans have slimier skin than that of Beelzebub's race (and no horns, tails or hooves). That is why young Hassein calls them "slugs."

■ Never call earth-humans anything negative (like slugs). They will retaliate in nasty ways.

■ Beelzebub is so old that he witnessed the formation of the planet Earth and the rise of men-beings on it.

■ From the very beginning, the planet Earth became a big cause of trouble for God.

■ Mars is much older than the Earth.

■ Earth-beings are the most peculiar kind of humans—in all of the universe.

■ Hassein becomes ever more curious about the planet Earth and wants his grandfather to share his observations, made over a long period of time, about these odd earth-humans.

CHAPTER 9

"The cause of the genesis of the Moon"

My poor noggin is still very much challenged by this odd chapter because I believe that Gurdjieff may be straddling both true (outer) physical astro-history and human (inner) psycho-spiritual history. Both histories offer us interesting views on how the planet Earth and we humans must automatically serve nature's built-in demands (for cosmic equilibrium), whether we know it or not—or whether we like it or not.

More amazingly, both outer planetary and inner human histories correspond to (mimic) each other, here. (Modern science cannot handle such fine-tuning and inner consistencies of law.)

In Chapter 9, Beelzebub tells his grandson why the planet Earth became such a challenge for the Lord God (and God's divine plan for earth-humans to engage in their proper cosmic duty).

Angels and archangels help the Creator to oversee and carry out the duties of maintaining order and balance in the universe. They have the proper intelligence and bent to assist God in His governance (Divine Providence) of the world and all things existing in it. But angels and archangels are still imperfect finite beings. They have imperfect knowledge and can make miscalculations (but we will see how God can still providentially use even these angelic miscalculations—which caused the genesis of the Moon—to provide a potential advantage for earth-humans).

According to Beelzebub, one of these highly intelligent helpers of HIS ENDLESSNESS (God) indeed made a slight miscalculation concerning the path of a particular comet "Kondoor" and it collided with the Earth at a time when the planet was still cooling and was most vulnerable, before it had time to develop an atmosphere that could help deflect the comet. (There is an actual scientific theory out there that the Moon was created by a great collision. But please, also keep in mind that this account of an astronomical collision is also being used as an ingenious allegory concerning the inner history of the earth-human psyche. Something "far-out" collided with human perception.)

Beelzebub recalls for his grandson that on one day when all of his tribe was very busy settling into their new surroundings, the entire planet Mars was suddenly shaken. A little later, a choking "stench" affected the whole planet. Beelzebub tells Hassein that he felt something "indescribable" had gotten mixed into the normal functioning of the universe. (The foul odor is strongly suggestive that this unfortunate cosmic event also mimics something "stinky" that was happening within the normal harmony of the earth-human psyche.)

The cause of this terrible shaking and powerful stench (which must have forced everyone in that solar system to hold their noses) was the aftershock of the collision between the Comet Kondoor with the planet Earth. Only later, when competent Sacred Individuals visited the scene (Beelzebub can converse with angelic beings!), and explained to him that a miscalculation was made by one of them, which unfortunately caused the comet to collide with the planet Earth on its very first orbit, did he grasp the seriousness of this cosmic calamity. The collision caused two large fragments to break away from the planet Earth and fly out into space. The larger of these two fragments is today called the "Moon."

God was also immediately informed of this cosmic misfortune and as a result a Most High Commission of Angels and Archangels, specialists in the important work of World-creation and World-maintenance, was sent from the Spiritual Sun to fully investigate the matter and make sure no further damage would occur to upset and threaten the equilibrium (divine order) of the universe.

Further observations by this Sacred Commission, as told to Beelzebub, were that they discovered that these two fragments, having lost their original momentum, began falling back toward their fundamental planet—the Earth. Because the Earth is also moving, this falling back also began to come under the influence of the "Law-of-Catching-Up." The result of following both the "Law of Falling" and "Law-of-Catching-Up" caused these two fragments to safely assume regular elliptical orbits around the Earth. Peaceful existence and equilibrium was again re-established in that solar system. Danger gone? Maybe.

Just to be on the safe side, this Most High Commission sent from the spiritual center of the universe, made some additional calculations to see what might happen from this event further into the future. They concluded that because of certain displacements (that they had conjectured), the two fragments might someday still leave their orbits and again threaten to bring "irreparable calamities" to this solar system, and even to other solar systems.

On further reflection, these Sacred Individuals then devised a strategy to neutralize any possible future problem. They believed that the best measure that could be taken was to make conditions possible on the Earth's surface to send the sacred vibrations "askokin" (living force) to maintain the two fragments. According to Beelzebub, this sacred substance can be formed on planets when the two fundamental laws of the universe function together in an independent way and on smaller scales (as in organic lifeforms). These two laws are the *Law of Three-foldness* and the *Law of Seven-foldness*. When these two laws function together as a new independent entity (living unit) it is called "Ilnosoparno."

The High Commission then returns to HIS ENDLESSNESS to gain approval of their plan and obtain the proper divine sanctions so that the Ilnosoparnian process can begin taking place on the surface of the planet Earth. (That they gained God's approval means that it was permitted by Divine Providence.)

From then on there began to arise something "CORRESPONDING" to the great laws of the universe on the planet Earth—but on smaller scales. These corresponding independent formations or "Similitudes-of-the-Whole" were the results of the evolution of organic life on the planet Earth. The death of these organic species on Earth then became the means of releasing "askokin" (their life force) from the Earth to maintain the proper functioning and stability of the two broken off fragments.

Whew! From that time on, the planet Earth (with all its various lifeforms arising and dying on its surface) became cosmically responsible for maintaining its satellites' proper existence and orbits.

You, my friendly reader, have before you once more, a wonderful example of how Gurdjieff buries the dog deeper. In spite of the strange physical events described by Gurdjieff (through the character Beelzebub), his spectacular cosmic scenario and story represents a profound metaphor that also portrays the *inner spiritual history* of the human race. If it were not for Swedenborg's *Doctrine of Correspondences* (sacred and spiritual symbolic language) my poor brain would have short-circuited from reading this most challenging part of *Beelzebub's Tales*.

As I hinted earlier, the collision of the comet at an early stage of the Earth's development also symbolizes a corresponding event that took place deeper within the psyche of our ancestors from a much earlier time. In his theological writings, Swedenborg describes the "Earth" as the symbolizing the quality of human worship, and moving objects in the "Sky" (like comets and meteors) as representing *principles of falsities* or falsehoods that could collide with—and affect—that pristine quality of worship.

So, Gurdjieff's story, taking place on the great astronomical scale of a comet hitting a planet, symbolizes that an *immense* principle of falsehood collided within the early human psyche (before it could protect itself) and changed things forever in human perception. The collision with this huge "false principle" also caused the human psyche to fragment and divide into more external and *distinct* forms of cognition. The Moon represents a more *external* intellect based on memory data collected from the outside world by the five senses and its imagination. (I am not sure about this, but the second smaller fragment probably represents something more obscure, hidden and seemingly less important to daily human functioning because it cannot be easily detected—like our hidden agendas and ignoble passions).

According to Gurdjieff, this smaller "satellite" was known by those earlier beings living on the former continent called "Atlantis" (more ancient symbolism). That is, they understood what this smaller fragment represented, until another unfortunate cosmic event took place on the planet Earth. This second unfortunate event was again a part of the unintended consequences of *angelic engineering*. It led to the separation (and burying) of conscience from a human intellect that was oriented to external stimuli, and represented by the "Moon."

My knowledge of Swedenborg's symbolism (correspondences) leads me to believe that Gurdjieff's tale of a major collision in the early solar system is simply a newer form of mythology, substituting for the biblical story of humankind's fall from grace and their removal from the Garden of Eden. (By creating a new myth, Gurdjieff can escape the strong resistance of many people to traditional religious subjects and the authority and inerrancy of the Bible.)

The reason for my believing in this similarity of symbolic communication is that both Gurdjieff's story and Swedenborg's deeper exposition of the Genesis story in the Garden of Eden involves our ancestors accepting a false principle as truth, inverting their values, and thus seeing reality only in an inverted way. Swedenborg claims that this early genus of human beings on Earth did not have psycho-spiritual protection from the passions of an evil heart and will and as a result, they became slaves to their own fantasies. (They maintained these fantasies with the same life-energies that went into maintaining the Moon's equilibrium.)

The angelic miscalculation in all this symbolizes the unintended consequences of preserving earth-humans' *free will* because this freedom can be abused and lead them to preferring their own prudence and judgment rather than God's Wisdom. Again, God permitted this unfortunate outcome in humans to take place, because a passive or counter (opposing) principle was providentially needed to lawfully fix spiritual knowledge into their very bio-fabric through inner combat. Only in this way could the process of salvation be preserved to allow genuine inner growth (of spiritual bodies) to proceed in the life of earth-humans!

I will explore this seemingly "unfair" hypothesis about heavenly forces taking part in humankind's inner history and their "fall" further in the next chapter.

SUMMARY

■ A comet hit the young Earth (through a miscalculation by higher angelic beings) causing two fragments, one large and one smaller, to fly off into space.

■ These two "satellites" eventually settled into orbits around the Earth. The larger of these two fragments is called the Moon."

■ This scenario, which may be historically and astronomically true, is also an allegory and metaphor of the same deeper processes taking place in the splitting up of the human heart (will) and mind (intellect). So, just as the Moon became a more external point for God's forces to terminate, the human mind also had its intellect (and imagination) moved further from the center of reality.

■ So the "angelic miscalculation" of the comet and Earth's orbit also represents an unforeseen result of what would happen when human *free will* (and its original God-design), collides with a false and misguided principle. This "counter principle" was allowed under God's providence because it was now lawfully needed to qualify and "fix" spiritual progress into the human spirit and psyche.

■ This scenario closely follows the *inner meaning* of the "Fall" in the Bible's story in Genesis, in which earth-humans felt lonely (wishing they could love and be full of themselves) and began to embrace a false principle of self-centeredness that favored their own sagacity and imagined self-importance.

CHAPTER 10

"Why 'men' are not men"

As the second step in a new octave of these Tales and new evaluation of the earth-humans' falling status, Chapter 10 represents a stretching out ("RE") of the topic for our continued pondering.

Here, we start learning some of the details of why earth-humans have become such a problem for the Lord God and His administration of the cosmos. Gurdjieff continues to be merciless in his efforts to rain on our egoistic parades. The human race is in a "fallen" state and now has to be rudely awakened out of this inverted situation.

Beelzebub continues his tale to his grandson by noting that after the collision with the comet "Kondoor," the orderly processes of *involution* and *evolution* eventually returned to normal on the planet Earth—after the "Ilnosoparnian" process (top-down and bottom-up flow from the unified laws of three-foldness and seven-foldness within bio-units or lifeforms) was incorporated. Because of this return to cosmic normality, the three-brained beings of Earth enjoyed the same opportunity to "crystallize" (fix) the proper data for acquiring objective (spiritual) reasoning as those individuals on other planets in the universe.

Unfortunately, recounts Beelzebub, if it were not for a second visit to the planet Earth by a Most High Commission, perhaps later screw-ups in the behavior of the biped human beings living on that ill-fated planet might not have ever occurred. This second commission was still not convinced of the impossibility of some undesirable surprise happening in the future to this solar system. The Commission became particularly concerned that if the mechanical instinct of the three-brained beings of planet Earth were to develop to a higher level of Objective Reason they would quickly find out why they now came to be—namely that through their existence and death, the two fragments (satellites) could be continuously and automatically maintained. Earth-humans, if they discovered this before the time was right, might resist such cosmic servitude and slavery to God's universal laws of cooperation.

Swedenborg referred to this cosmic servitude to universal laws by the heavenly angels as spiritual "uses," and it involved perfecting mutual love and the conscious choice of cooperation as one's ultimate freedom.

(There is a scientific theory of interrelationships in which if something moves, it affects the movements of everything else. In a multi-dimensional universe this relationship even includes the moral decisions of the human heart and mind. Swedenborg claimed that the universe is a world of mutual *utility*. God's providence (governance) ensures that everything we do (good or bad) plays some role in preserving the harmony and balance of everything—everywhere. Existence is relationship! Because humans represent a "universe in miniature" their activities affect all levels of existence—other planets, other humans and even subatomic phenomena. This means that all individuals have a responsibility to maintain the healthy order of the whole—rather than seeking to fulfill only their limited personal pleasures. Self-centeredness is abhorred in God's universe! I will say more about this a little later.

To thwart the slightest possibility of a rebellion by earth-humans against this cosmic setup of *mandatory* cooperation, that would cause big trouble for the stability of the world's processes (common-cosmic Harmonious Movement), the Sacred Commission decided to implant a special organ at the base of their spinal columns.

This organ was called the *Kundabuffer*. Its functioning would cause earth-humans to see reality topsy-turvy and stimulate all the right factors for evoking physical "pleasure" and "enjoyment," rather than spiritual self-sacrifice. This deluded state in men-beings of the planet Earth would ensure that their sacred substance or lifeforce "askokin" would be released at the time of their death to help maintain the harmonious movements of the Moon and Anulios and keep cosmic order.

Although a visit from a third Most High Commission later removed this maleficent organ from the base of people's spinal columns, it still had left its mark on their psyche and habitual behavior of the earth's three-brained inhabitants (from habit, its influences became crystallized and second nature). Because of this, earth-humans could no longer perceive truth (and couldn't care less). Owing to this sad condition, they could then be led to slaughter (their physical deaths) in order to release the substance "askokin" and be safely oblivious to—and never suspect—their mandated support of the Moon and Anulios.

Time ticked by.

Beelzebub tells Hassein that all during this time he had been using his telescope to make detailed observations from Mars of both the remote concentrations in the far reaches of the universe and the planets of that particular solar system that they had been exiled to. This included observing the planet Earth from time to time (viewing earth-humans from a higher vantage point—from a superior or elevated intellect).

Eventually, Beelzebub noticed weird phenomena occurring on the surface of the planet Earth. He tells his grandson that he observed periods of time when the population of the earth-humans exploded and other times when the population became greatly diminished. Both the rapid increase and rapid decrease of men-beings on Earth was a result of situations he had never seen on other planets.

At this point in the story, Beelzebub only addresses the reason why the decrease in the population of earth-humans is troublesome—they are killing each other off (as in wars) which is in opposition to God's Commandments.

If Beelzebub and his tribe had not made this observation concerning the fluctuating human populations on Earth, they would never have noticed anything weird or unusual taking place on that planet. Beelzebub and his clan are forced to assume that the large population of humans either being born or being killed on the Earth's surface was quite necessary for the needs of maintaining the common-cosmic Harmonious Movement.

At the end of this chapter, Gurdjieff takes another poke at the men-beings on Earth by having Beelzebub admit to his grandson that he personally liked the three-brained beings of the planet Saturn best. These beings of Saturn acted according to the golden principle: "Do unto another's as you would do unto your own." They lived noble lives in spite of having an exterior form (coating) of the being-bird called "raven." (A raven? Again this is Gurdjieff's attempt to disturb the reader into mental despair and to focus on deeper levels of the intellect, which can be quite different from judging mere outer forms and external characteristics. In fact, according to Swedenborg, a "raven" has a similar symbolic meaning of creating a disturbance to the human belief system. Beelzebub, of course, loves the sound that these Saturnian-bird-beings made—after all, he loves creating disturbances himself.)

Now I will have to put on my Swedenborgian cap again to further address the issue of personal responsibility in the universe (as I promised earlier). Emanuel Swedenborg discovered "from things seen and heard in the Spiritual World" that everything was created for some *utility* and *use*. Every created thing in God's universe pays for its existence by supporting and promoting the proper functioning and greater good of the *Whole*. (In Scripture, and in theological terms, this universal usefulness is called "charity" and "good works.") Nothing created can escape this holistic law, otherwise, all these unifying activities of cooperation would cease to harmoniously exist and the physical universe would turn to a froth. This is why the universe has been purposely designed under an *organic* scheme of mutual cooperation and support—by a *living* God of Infinite *Love*. Plants and animals (static lifeforms plus animate creatures with one- and two-brained systems) automatically and instinctively live according to this divine order by filling various niches in the ecosystem.

However, the human race, because it has been given *free will*, can choose to avoid this noble responsibility, and instead, merely seek to satisfy their personal selfish needs and pleasures. It is *free will* that allows humankind to either rebel and reject their cosmic duty or choose wisely. Since human free will is a sacred and protected gift from the Lord God, it is said that because of this divine protection, the problem of human rebellion originated from on high. But earth-humans have also been given the intellectual potential and capacity to rise above their natural and worldly loves—if they connect with their God-given consciences and spiritual remains.

According to Gurdjieff the sacred and proper division of labor, through reciprocal utility, creates the sacred vibrations called "askokin" which helps maintain all things in their proper equilibrium and serves God's higher and ultimate purpose. All life forms are required to contribute to this grand scheme and serve this higher purpose either with their life-design or with their death, or both. Nothing in nature is wasted, not even human evil (which Swedenborg claims that God providentially uses to maintain balance in the higher spiritual realms—and which flows down into lower worldly realms).

Everything lives for everything else. This interrelated, interconnected and interdependent scheme is the physical analog of heavenly mutual love! Swedenborg would say that in the case of men and women on Earth, this "sharing" can be elevated to the level of genuine spiritual love—to God and the neighbor. This is religion's true purpose—to give nature's interrelations, interconnections and interdependence an elevated, non-physical or spiritual expression. This is God's hope for the human race.

If humans consciously choose (from free will) to grow spiritually through loving helpfulness, they contribute a sacred energy and higher living force (more spiritual forms of "askokin"), which God can then use for the maintenance of a heavenly kingdom and eternal happiness. Those who don't comply will contribute just as well—but through their eternal suffering of frustrated desires and wants.

Swedenborg provides one more unexpected angle to this important topic. He states that God's influence (influx) descends into the various levels, structures and life forms in the world. In animals, this sacred energy passes through their organic forms, is dissipated, and leaks out into the world, where it vanishes and never returns (*Arcana Coelestia*, n. 5114). In other words, God's sacred energy and influx moves on to more external *centers of gravity* and "lower" structures, where it ultimately terminates—unless it finds a higher plane (developed gravity center) in the hearts and minds of three-brained human beings.

Gurdjieff implies in *Beelzebub's Tales* that the two fragments (one being the Moon) become the benefactors of this energy leak because they exist at the lowest point where God's energy can terminate. On a deeper psychological level, which Gurdjieff's unique mythology is designed to also communicate, this could be understood symbolically as humans having to maintain a "fragmented" and more external mind (divided consciousness) after having absorbed the impact of a false principle in their belief system (symbolized by a comet's collision).

However, instead of serving as a cosmic sieve to Divine energy as most other life-forms automatically do, humans have the God-given potential to create *new planes of understanding and love*—which not only holds the heavenly influx from going further outward and downward, it can return that love back to God through spiritual *evolution*. It is by such a reciprocal relationship and partnership with God that humankind can create a fixed spiritual plane or biosphere (called Heaven) to serve a higher purpose and obtain the means to eternal life and happiness.

As I alluded to earlier, Gurdjieff's story of the organ Kundabuffer and angelic surgery has a similar meaning to Swedenborg's deeper, symbolic interpretation of God's divine surgery, forming Eve out of Adam's *rib bone* in Genesis (*Arcana Coelestia*, n. 147–162). The passage in Holy Scripture where Adam feels "alone" represents humankind's desire to fill this empty feeling by being able to discern reality for oneself and to do "what's pleasing for oneself." This desire for self-guidance represents the false principle and comet that hit the Earth! God had to allow this to happen (just as the Most High Commission in Gurdjieff's story always sought God's sanction for their actions) in order to preserve human free will (and prevent a disastrous rebellion that would undermine cosmic stability).

Swedenborg made it clear, over and over again, that without protecting human *free will*, God cannot save anyone. (The human intellect must be free to have preferences and to make choices.) So God put mankind to "sleep" as a trade-off and divine compromise. God preserved human free will by allowing humankind's psyche to become fragmented in order for them to falsely see their illusions as reality and want to continue living. This illusion (cosmic pacifier) helped the human race to at least become re-energized from the more limited principle of self-love and self-centeredness. The illusion was granted by God Himself, through His putting Adam into a state of deep sleep (trance).

This false principle of self-love is further symbolized in Holy Scripture, not by a dead comet, but by God's forming an intimate partner, "Eve," from Adam's "rib bone" while he was in this state of trance or deep sleep. In symbolic terms, a rib bone, which is positioned near (actually outside) the more vital organs of the chest, such as the heart and lungs, but is relatively less alive, represents a human attraction to something more external and dead (less vital to one's spiritual life). That a comet collides with the Earth in Beelzebub's story symbolizes the human psyche tending in this same direction as favoring a false principle (there is no other reason why such a collision would cause such a big "stink" all around).

Similarly, Eve represents humankind's new psychic *center of stability* (where human inclinations were now tending) further removed from God's fundamental or spiritual qualities. Whether we talk about Gurdjieff's organ Kundabuffer planted at the base of the human spine or Swedenborg's rib bone, a psychological disposition and proclivity to seeing reality upside down is meant. Adam and Eve were not removed from an earthly or physical garden—they were removed from God's wisdom and teachings.

It is now one's personal duty and obligation in life to regain this wisdom in order to be of true service to God's great plan of creation.

But as things now stand, God's influx—meant for higher aims—must flow down to a lower and more disconnected and corporeal/external fragment of human cognition where it will vanish in the memory/imagination function and never be used for genuine spiritual rebirth.

But again, nothing is completely wasted, not even from this terrible situation, because for the purpose of maintaining cosmic stability, this "trance state" in humans will allow them to calmly and unknowingly sustain the Moon, both outside of us and inside of us—automatically and with few complaints. Whether we want to or not, God's providence will make use of our quality of life energy to sustain creation wherever needed. Nothing is allowed to exist without having some usefulness in this grand unified plan.

Gurdjieff returns to the subject of the Sacred Askokin later in his Tales. But in a nutshell, all organic and inorganic structures in the created universe serve as an apparatus to transform energy either *upward* or *downward*—upward toward God (evolution) or downward (involution) toward the physical world. (Swedenborg calls both these operations "uses.")

Those people on Earth who neglect their sacred duty to God, to the universe and to the neighbor, act to facilitate the further downward and outward trajectory of universal forces and influx (which maintains the Moon and its representative memory/imaginary function in humans). The human race is special compared to all other living creatures, in that they can decide, up or down, where their vital energies find their ultimate stability (center of gravity in the Law of Falling).

Again, Gurdjieff's unique writing style is aimed at helping us transubstantiate important and rare knowledge in a unique three-dimensional way—through our *hearts, intellects* and *corporeal/sensual bodies.*

Swedenborg concurs with Gurdjieff that the human race on Earth now sees reality in an upside-down manner. In fact, Swedenborg claimed that the knowledge of earth-humans is always finite and what they do not know is always infinite. Therefore, there is no basis for human egoism. We are each dependent upon God to see reality and gain a measure of wisdom. If we do not engage in this cosmic duty, we cannot be called real men.

SUMMARY

■ Loving God and the neighbor cannot be looked at apart from one's living structure. "Coating" a higher-being body (spiritual body) represents making noble characteristics a fixed part of one's organic fabric.

■ During Beelzebub's exile he discovers that there are many problems with the men-beings on Earth because he notices that there are strange periods of population increases and decreases.

■ A third visit by a High Angelic Commission from the center of the universe creates another miscalculation and they become responsible for humans perceiving things in an upside-down (topsy-turvy) manner.

■ This miscalculation ensures that humans will unconsciously create the proper (involutionary) energy to sustain the Earth's satellites.

■ Because everything is connected, no one is free from the law of usefulness.

■ Even though the organ Kundabuffer is eventually removed, its negative influences become fixed within the human psyche and even increase.

■ The organ Kundabuffer is similar to the *rib bone* in the Genesis story of God creating "Eve." It represents the human passion for clinging to a false dream and comparatively dead worldview.

■ Beelzebub likes the beings of Saturn best. He describes them as having physical bodies like "ravens." I believe this is done in order to disturb the reader and force one to look at humanness beyond mere outer forms.

CHAPTER 11

"A piquant trait of the peculiar psyche of contemporary man"

I have no doubt in my mind that many of my readers will find it a rather odd notion that God and a group of His highest ranking angels could ever be involved in a miscalculation that put human-kind on Earth in such a precarious position. Some might even find this idea detestable and a terrible *injustice* by heavenly forces.

But in this regard, Swedenborg would most certainly come to Gurdjieff's defense. In Swedenborg's deeper (and spiritual) exposition of Genesis described in his *Arcana Coelestia* (Heavenly Secrets) he reveals that the human race on Earth indeed found itself in need of divine surgery. God's original human brain-design was ultimately flawed in that it offered no intellectual defense against false principles that might affect the human heart and will (just as the young planet Earth had no defense against a comet's collision).

Swedenborg explained that earlier races of earth-humans were of an entirely different genus and could not separate their thoughts from their wills. Therefore, they could not raise their thinking function above their passions (which were headed for the garbage can). This problem is what is symbolized by Gurdjieff's claim that "higher" intelligences made a miscalculation when it came to the human race colliding with destructive ideas and false beliefs.

But this tragedy was inevitable to make our choices stick.

God originally designed humans to be cerebellum-focused (which according to Swedenborg, was directly connected to heavenly inputs and represented the seat of the human heart). This is evidenced by the fact that early humans had pronounced *occipital morphology* in the back of their skulls. Fossil evidence shows that evolution suddenly began to favor cerebrum-focused humans, as seen from Neanderthals being replaced by the Cro-Magnon race (who had a more vaulted forehead).

This original design held up as long as humans were properly focused (upward) on God and living according to His spiritual tenets. But this brain system broke down when egoism and self-love entered into the picture (represented by a comet). God then wisely saw the necessity of enlarging the prefrontal lobes of the cerebrum so that humans had a degree of autonomy and they could gain the freedom to raise their understanding and intellect above their now flawed hearts and wills.

Unfortunately, this wise solution (from Above) also had a downside. Now humankind had to investigate "truth" from the physical world—by a more external means, rather than from interior perception and direct revelation from God. Instead of inner perception, God implanted conscience between their separated mental functioning and their involuntary/instinctive mind.

This gamble, while preserving *free will*, led the human race on Earth to continue heading in the wrong direction because they greatly favored their own misguided psyches. Humans simply learned to ignore God with their new functioning intellects and felt that they could now interpret reality quite well on their own.

Gurdjieff's description of an "angelic intercession" by heavenly forces to implant a new organ *at the base of the spinal column* in humans is a clever way to describe the re-tooling of their psyche to become more outwardly focused and oriented to the physical world and its external data, thus see things upside-down. In his anatomical works, Swedenborg describes the cortical cells (neurons) of the head-brain and the spinal column as being oriented in opposite directions. Therefore, the neurons in the spinal column act as a *reagent* or *passive principle* relative to the *active* operation of neurons working in the head-brain.

Putting a new organ (the Kundabuffer) at the base of the spinal column is a wonderful organic metaphor for depicting a situation which required putting more weight on the passive, external/sensory or worldly side of the human psyche. This produces an "inverted" state in human cognition with the terrestrial world gaining utmost importance and God's Heaven taking a lower position. Swedenborg claimed that the biblical symbolism of the serpent in the garden was that a snake is almost all backbone and lured the psyche of early humans to become engrossed (from head to tail) in the material world. The serpent being forced to crawl on the ground represented this psychical shift in earth-humans toward lower and earthly values.

This psychical shift, although flawed, allowed earth-humans to at least feel more comfortable about themselves and the choices they made with their free will intact. Unfortunately, this also "put to rest" any real possibility of them escaping from their faulty predicament on their own.

So Gurdjieff and Swedenborg are in complete agreement that God took drastic steps to make organic changes to the human race on the planet Earth that could preserve and potentially restore their proper cognitive *polarity* toward Heaven. According to Swedenborg, without this Divine intervention and Divine strategy, the human race would have perished. But this Divine solution, while potentially allowing for a better possibility, still left problems for God, because humankind on Earth began mistaking *license* for *free will*. And, their new cerebrum-focused brains (relying on information of the physical senses reaching them from the spinal column) could adopt any fraudulent belief system that favored their passions (instead of relying on their more inner, sacred, God-given conscience, which could challenge their assumptions).

More will be said about the organ Kundabuffer later.

Returning to the Tale, Beelzebub tells Hassein that he is grateful that they are both out of the reach of earth-humans after making such an insulting comment "to their dignity" as to call them "slugs." (Swedenborg states that anger, outrage and indignation comes mostly from the principle of *self-love*.) Beelzebub is truly horrified by the thought of what these men-beings from Earth would have done to his poor grandson if they had heard this unflattering assessment and had gotten their hands on him.

Here, the reader is confronted with the uncomfortable truth of *man's inhumanity to man*—especially if you step on their toes.

Having studied the psyche of the three-brained beings inhabiting the planet Earth over long periods of time, Beelzebub feels he now has the knowledge (and the perfect moment) to teach his naïve grandson why humans would behave in such a harsh way if they had learned about Hassein's giving all of them such an unflattering "nickname."

Beelzebub describes the current quality of mental discrimination in modern humankind (including its best scientists) as a "pouring of the empty into the void." (So they might as well be called "slugs.") Again, since readers of *Beelzebub's Tales* are obviously earth-beings, with the potential of sensing an unjustified personal attack by being called a "slug," Gurdjieff cleverly has his audience stand back a little by placing this discussion on a spaceship traveling through the greater arena of outer space. This vast arena gives the reader the cover of believing that these Tales are far-fetched and can be considered "way out there."

But humans would still be offended by Hassein's uncouth "slug" remark.

Beelzebub then explains to his grandson the full horror of his insult and how these peculiar men-beings of the planet Earth would even go through official circles to "anathematize" and curse him. They would bring in specialists and experts from every institution, whose credentials cannot be denied. Then, these special officials and important individuals, on designated special occasions and well-established ceremonies, would wish evil upon the youngster, who luckily remains out of their legal and physical reach.

But even when such an "enemy" is found to be out of their reach for delivering punishment, the real, more *interior* problem presents itself because they will not give up their burning hatred for the lad—ever!

In spite of the dire warnings about the danger Hassein has put himself in, Beelzebub ends this chapter with a smile toward his lovable and inquisitive grandson. (Swedenborg teaches us that youngsters are in *innocence* and even their transgressions cause adults to find cuteness in all their manifestations.) Unfortunately, Hassein is probably a bit older (a tween or a teenager), and therefore would probably not be afforded such clemency among earth-humans.

But the genius of Gurdjieff, through the character of Beelzebub, has succeeded in making *this writer* more aware of a negative "piquant" trait lurking within myself. I wouldn't want to be called a "slug" by some snotty-nosed little brat. But this self-discovery is even more irksome when I can see it in myself! So Gurdjieff's indirect method of shining new light upon an uncomfortable subject allows me the perfect chance to make such an unflattering self-discovery—if I allow it.

The "piquant" trait revealed here is a real biggie and it gets to the heart of self-love (which is always counter to heavenly love) and spawns human hatred.

SUMMARY

▪ The apparent miscalculation of "higher" beings toward earth-humans is that their original brain organization had no defense against self-love, but without self-love and the delusion of self-importance, they would reject all responsibilities and end their lives. This would challenge the equilibrium of the universe and God's ultimate plan of a heavenly kingdom.

▪ More explanation is given here as to why higher intelligences (including God) played a part in allowing men's and women's psyches to become so degraded.

▪ The so-called "piquant" trait of earth-humans is self-love, which is the source for hatred when their "dignity" is challenged or shown up.

▪ Self-love (and hatred) will rule within the human heart even if one's perceived enemy remains well out of physical reach—it is internal, not external.

▪ Self-love will even hide behind "official" ceremonies (which are just puppet shows) and gather more similarly misguided allies in order to gain a false sense of respectability.

CHAPTER 12

"The first 'growl'"

Gurdjieff would not use the word "growl" in this chapter heading unless he had some sense of its *psycho-spiritual* or symbolic meaning. The word offers us some insight into the strange psyche of the human species that now inhabits the planet Earth.

Symbolically speaking, the term "growl" used in the context of the general psycho-spiritual quality of the human race is obviously not a good thing. Gurdjieff uses this *beastly* term to add a more colorful description for the outward trajectory (and mental deterioration) of the human race toward manifesting the negative consequences of the aspects of blind self-love and love of the physical world. This condition is an *inverted* state from that of loving God and the neighbor and a perversion in the human consciousness of separating (and giving importance to) external ideas and data in the world from their deeper spiritual significance.

A "growl" represents three-brained beings acting like two-brained beings (mammals), which lack true reasoning. (Swedenborg even records hearing various growls from spirits in the spiritual world who continue, from free will, to embrace and manifest this lower corporeal behavior.)

Beelzebub continues discussing his observations concerning these unfortunate earth-humans in order to educate and offer extremely valuable lessons to Hassein (and the reader) about their peculiar and flawed psyche. Besides observing these men-beings through his telescope from Mars, Beelzebub states that he made *six* personal visits to the planet Earth (over long periods of time). He made many interesting and valuable observations during each visit to this strange planet. He then tells his grandson about a negative situation that occurred on his very last (sixth) visit.

He describes a certain fairly recent author on the planet Earth, who (from self-love) felt compelled to write an "important" book. Looking over the titles on the bookshelves of his personal library, this writer spots a copy of the four Gospels of the New Testament and suddenly feels that he can write something every bit as profound, which could be received by the public as the "Gospel Truth" as well, and assure him of future financial success. This writer certainly believed he was more educated, cultured and sophisticated than

"Matthew, Mark, Luke or Johnnie." (Swedenborg also observed that worldly humans often feel that the narratives in the Bible are inferior forms of writing, when compared to the writings of more properly educated and talented humans throughout history.)

This scenario is obviously presented by Gurdjieff to underscore humanity's proclivity to invent (fabricate) great truths all by themselves—while ignoring God's perennial wisdom (which the apostles praised and taught). The theme of *Beelzebub's Tales* highlights the continuous organic need for men-beings on Earth to constantly find self-importance at the expense of God's objective and spiritual truth.

According to Beelzebub, nothing out of the ordinary would have happened to this new and concocted "Gospel" if it were not for the fact that many of the politicians of that time were having bad luck at gambling with other people's money and the resulting new demands for more tax dollars caused the ordinary citizenry there to snap out of their usual torpor and they "began-to-sit-up." This also alarmed the "power-possessing" beings (rulers) who then felt it necessary to keep the citizenry in a perpetual state of hibernation and calm. It was at this precise time that the said author's "Gospel" was published. The power-possessing beings sensed that this new book might arouse the public further and conspired together as to how to get rid of this possible threat.

At first they denounced the author and his new book. Then, they did an unexpected about-face.

The reason for this about-face is that the more these leaders and politicians made a fuss about this author and his new book, the more the public became interested. In fact, the more often the information about this author and book were repeated, the more the public came to regard this author (through constant suggestion) as having an extraordinary mind concerning the psyche of his fellow earth-humans and that anything he wrote must be regarded as full of indisputable truth. So various politicians hopped on board and used this form of *suggestibility* to get the unwanted attention of the voters away from themselves and began praising this new author's work.

As a result of human suggestibility, upon merely hearing this author's name, even those men-beings who had not read any of this author's books would *associate* this person with being an extraordinary individual. (I suspect Gurdjieff is referring to Sigmund Freud here, but this is mere conjecture on my part.)

Gurdjieff is commenting here on the deplorable human traits of suggestibility, mechanicalness and blind self-love, which lead to mental laziness (spiritual sleep) and resisting our true God-given duty in life. We have become *spiritual couch potatoes.*

Swedenborg tells us that "growling" in the psycho-spiritual sense represents *devilish* loves being expressed from the principle of self-centeredness—which is pure fantasy (again, spiritual sleep) and not proper for human or rational behavior. This flawed trait of suggestibility can become hard-wired (mechanical) in the human brain, due to the habitual repetition of our always seeking "titillation" through various forms of affirmation and praise from others around us.

I think this "devilish love" engrained in human behavior is what Gurdjieff had in mind when he came up with the "inhuman" and "beastly" title for this chapter.

If you think this is an overly harsh criticism of humans living on Earth, you are about to be astonished. More evidence awaits us.

SUMMARY

■ The psycho-spiritual meaning of the word "growl" says a lot about the mental state and current predicament of earth-humans.

■ Swedenborg gives us the psycho-spiritual meaning behind the term "growl" and this offers us further evidence that Gurdjieff also can tap into these rarefied and symbolic meanings.

■ The "growl" is further explained in *Beelzebub's Tales* by an *everyday* author, who thought that he could create (concoct) a work that was every bit as profound and important as the writers of the Gospels in the Bible.

■ Contemporary humans, from a misguided principle of self-importance, are deluded into thinking that truth can emerge from their very own minds.

■ The flawed books from these types of authors further speed up the degeneration of the human mind and fill it up with complete nonsense.

■ The modern human mind is greatly influenced by suggestibility and things repeated over and over again.

CHAPTER 13

"Why in man's reason
fantasy may be perceived as reality"

At this point in the story Hassein becomes even more curious about the peculiar psyche of men-beings living on the surface of the planet Earth. He now wants his grandfather to explain to him how it is that these three-brained beings so easily accept fantasy as reality.

As a student of Swedenborg's theology, I am very familiar with the idea that those who seek ultimate truth from the physical world alone (without God's guidance or from spiritual conscience), and favor their own sagacity and judgment, are prone to *fantasy* and *delusion*.

This is particularly so when the human psyche (from a lower worldly or purely natural affection) favors reward, self-glory, honors, status and temporary earthly riches over the *internal obligation* (duty) to appropriate eternal life and happiness for oneself and for others. Swedenborg says that such individuals are not motivated by a sincere internal obligation unless they have developed a "conscience of spiritual truth" (*Arcana Coelestia*, n. 4988 [4]). Swedenborg also equates such worldly people as having a *faith of knowledges* rather than a faith of life (*Apocalypse Explained*, n. 242b).

However, this *inner mirror of conscience has now become hidden* from earth-humans and prevents them from grasping reality—and how to obtain legitimate and everlasting spiritual success. This predicament is communicated in the Holy Word by the passage "Behold, my master knoweth not what is with me in my house" (Genesis, 39:8). Translated spiritually, a person's "lord" or master most often represents being ruled by worldly values, which can teach nothing real. Nor is this "imposter–master" interested in developing the inner qualities of the human spirit (which represent what is really going on inside one's inner "house").

Swedenborg further adds that this principle of self-delusion is behind the cryptic warning given in the biblical passage that "a man's foes shall be those of his own household" (*Matthew* 10:36). Without developing spiritual conscience we don't see ourselves (or our habitual loves and pleasures) as the enemy, but as our closest friend and comforter. Swedenborg even suggests that this kind of Godless worldview is nothing but pure insanity.

Beelzebub now offers Hassein more detail as to how men-beings became increasingly fixed, not on reality, but on merely earthly, bodily and worldly things, denying and loathing heavenly subjects concerning their *cosmic duty* or obtaining true and lasting happiness. This negative trajectory is first contracted in one's childhood and then augmented by our worldly education, which helps divide the human mind.

A divided mind created in childhood?

Yep!

In a nutshell, Swedenborg agrees with Gurdjieff's assessment that children learn early to divide their minds for the sake of *pretense* (*Arcana Coelestia*, n. 8247) and that the natural or corporeal/ sensual mind in humans, when separated from higher reasoning functions and vigilance, can be easily persuaded by false principles—especially if those principles promote and confirm the things we personally favor, desire and which offer us earthly reward and pleasures (*Arcana Coelestia*, n. 5033).

Beelzebub explains that men-beings (three-brained beings) of Earth gradually allowed the predominant part of their psyche (the active and spiritualized part called one's *Ruling Love* or "main" feature) to drop its responsibility for overlooking the perceiving of reality by the other psychic functions (being-centers). This lack of inner responsibility causes the human psyche to become loosened, fragmented and unconnected, whereby its distinct functions can no longer assist each other (one's personal *djartklom* or separation of being-forces) in the more important operation of spiritual unity and transformation. (What else would unify all of a person's psychic functions toward a spiritual goal than performing his or her cosmic duties in a more complete way—through the *heart, mind,* and *body*?)

But because of this psychic laziness, disconnection and disharmonious mental arrangement in earth-humans, any external information (data) coming in through the five senses from the external world can now only be crystallized (become fixed) and validated by the mere repetition of this external data (but learning by rote has nothing to do with perceiving reality correctly). So any darn thing can be believed in if it is repeated often enough in the divided human psyche. This repetition is why an "unnamed" writer in this Tale (again, probably Freud), is now considered a great psychologist by many of those in the community who have abandoned their God-given cosmic duty, thus basing their conviction of his greatness on hearing this praise often enough, and without any real active and sane deliberations (rational pondering) on their part.

Beelzebub insists that this regrettable outcome was not to be blamed on either the comet Kondoor hitting the Earth or by the implantation of the organ Kundabuffer by Saintly Individuals. It resulted from the continual abnormal condition of *external* habitual being-existence that gradually established itself in the earth-human psyche as a principle for their own "Self-Calming." (For instance, when people seek affirmation from others, this kind of activity is a form of *self-calming*, since it puts the kabosh on sincere self-examination and the possibility of waking up one's spiritual conscience toward one's personal flaws.) Beelzebub also describes this practice of self-calming as a result of people's inner "Evil-God"—the false ruling master of their existence. Today, it is called political correctness.

In John 5:44 we are warned against seeking glory from other men. (This is how we appease our "Evil-God.")

Swedenborg confirms that externally oriented individuals experience God's vital influence to initiate spiritual combat within one's conscience only obscurely— and they feel it as a simple anxiety (*Arcana Coelestia*, n. 5036 [2]). The point here is that people will go to great lengths to calm these anxieties percolating up from their inner spirit so as not to disturb the predominant part from its slumber (Ruling Love of egoism and the *proprium*) and keep it from enjoying its present dreamlike situation.

Swedenborg and Gurdjieff both insist that humans have brought this sorrowful state of obscurity and fantasy upon themselves, and always have the freedom to escape this abnormal predicament—if they would only make the proper decisions and effort.

"If?"

At this point in the story, Beelzebub is interrupted by one of the ship's servants with an "etherogram." After he finishes listening to the recorded message, Hassein begs his grandfather to continue talking about these strange and interesting inhabitants of the planet Earth. Beelzebub smiles to his grandson in a "special way" that includes a very strange head gesture. He then continues on with his story of earth-humans.

(If you feel that Gurdjieff is providing too many anti-intuitive ideas, too quickly for your brain to absorb, I promise that all these topics will be given expanded explanations in the later chapters. Gurdjieff is simply "softening the beaches" in the early chapters of these Tales to prepare his readers for the totally unflattering notion that most earth-humans actually go through life in a *hypnotized* state, resulting from their spiritual snoozing and self-calming preferences).

SUMMARY

- Hassein wants Beelzebub to tell him why earth-humans prefer fantasy over reality.

- The big reason why earth-humans only see non-reality is that their predominant part (Ruling Love) became passive (fell asleep) and no longer participated in their cosmic God-given duty, gradually allowing other independent (distinct) psychic functions to also perceive all new incoming impressions without this same duty and vigilance. This allowed men and women on Earth to receive information about the world without a proper and unifying conscience.

- One cannot properly perceive reality in the absence of cosmic duty (performing heavenly uses).

- Without acknowledging one's cosmic and God-given duty, all that is needed to create personal conviction in any matter whatsoever is mere *repetition of the idea* (which leads to suggestibility).

- The organ Kundabuffer and the Saintly Individuals who placed it in earth-humans are not to be blamed for this awful predicament, but men and women themselves, who instead of developing their spiritual *conscience*, now only want to calm their inner world from any anxiety to their self-esteem.

- This "Self-Calming" (of their inner "Evil-God") in human individuals demands constant affirmation from the world of men—whether something is true about themselves or not. (This is why the phrase "Flattery will get you everything" has made it into our lexicon. Also, Scripture warns us against seeking praise and glory from fellow men, instead of God – John 5:44.)

CHAPTER 14

"The beginnings of perspectives promising nothing very cheerful"

(I understand this chapter to represent a new beginning [the "DO" of a new evaluation] and thus another new octave in the unfolding of this Tale.)

Beelzebub assures Hassein that the men-beings of the planet Earth who have caught his curiosity were originally just like all the other "Keschapmartnian" three-brained beings (dual gender) in the universe and enjoyed a similar duration of planetary existence. (Swedenborg observed that men-beings from other planets in the solar system and beyond were more spiritually noble than the inhabitants of the planet Earth, except for those original celestial earth-humans who lived in more ancient times.)

Here, Beelzebub introduces a real physical downside to seeing realty incorrectly and selfishly, as he starts to hint that the human "lifespan" on Earth is diminishing—not in the sense that humans are living fewer astronomical years but that their sensing of the flow of time began speeding up in their psyche. Earth-humans started "missing" (not noticing) the more important details of life—which shortens our sensing of all things!

Another big "outer" element in diminishing of the lifespans of earth-humans' was the growing phenomenon of "war."

He tells his grandson that most of the ill effects taking place in the presences of these men-beings occurred after the continent "Atlantis" became submerged within their planet. This was the second big misfortune to occur on the planet Earth (the first was the collision with the comet Kondoor).

The story of Atlantis, like all genuine ancient legends, contains a deeper psycho-spiritual meaning and truth about humankind's *inner* or *spiritual* history. So for now, my valuable reader, simply entertain in your mind that this second great cataclysmic event— the sinking of Atlantis—symbolically refers to something negative that happened *within* people's noggins—something essentially important (like conscience and innocence) sank deeper and was lost to human consciousness.

According to Beelzebub, the submerging of Atlantis also was a reason why earth-humans began noticing less, therefore experiencing time-flow moving more quickly, because it represented a further (diminishing) change in the qualities of their psyches' abilities to receive sensory inputs objectively and completely.

I will address this topic later, but to offer my Swedenborgian readers a juicy "carrot" here—this *sinking of Atlantis* has a lot to do with understanding the doctrine of "remains," which when buried (sinks), causes the earth-human psyche to become fragmented and divided into *inner* and *outer* functioning. This fragmentation also speeds up our experiencing and sensing of the passage of time (which again, is a shortening of life) because it limits our perception of universal process, reality, and all its sequences.

In this chapter, Gurdjieff is providing us with a unique and humbling new view of the consequences of people ignoring their personal duty-bound responsibility—as nothing less than an event *on the cosmic scale of a major continent on the Earth sinking!*

Remember, God's universe will always get what it needs—whether humans consciously care or not—by either gathering needed radiations through the way people choose to live their lives or through their physical death.

If humans fail to reach their spiritual potential and continually lower the quality of their radiations (organic sphere of the influences of their "works" and "utility"), which are necessary to stabilize universal processes (including to help maintain Heaven, as well as the former parts of their planet—like the Moon), nature will respond by making appropriate adaptations to restore universal equilibrium. If Nature cannot get the quality of radiations she wants, she will be forced to rely on quantity alone (thus increasing human births and death rates).

You guessed it. Because of the low-quality radiations now given off by earth-humans, due to the abnormal conditions of external being-existence established by their own choices, God's Great Universe has been compelled to furnish its cosmic needs through various "population explosions" and increased periodic wars—all to make the necessary *askokin* (life-force) available for cosmic equilibrium through the killings and deaths of many humans.

Beelzebub tells Hassein that nowhere else in the entire universe does such a "process of the destruction of each other's existence" (through wars) take place among three-brained beings—except on the planet Earth.

So, war is an abnormal Earth-phenomenon only! (Swedenborg would concur with this unflattering assessment.)

Other ignoble traits crystalized (becoming organically fixed) within the Earth-human psyche (further increasing nature's need for obtaining a quantity of radiations) were *egoism, self-love, vanity, pride, self-conceit, credulity,* and *suggestibility*. Beelzebub further informs his grandson that *suggestibility* is the most terrible of all the abnormal psychic peculiarities plaguing these unfortunate beings of God's great universe and most responsible for diminishing their existence (experiencing the flow of time faster and faster).

After some contemplation, Beelzebub decides that the best way he can more specifically inform Hassein about the strangeness of the psyche of the three-brained beings living on the surface of the planet Earth is to describe in detail his six personal visits to this odd planet and the circumstances involved with each. (These six visits are a cleverly hidden exposition of Swedenborg's *coordination and subordination of all things through successive and simultaneous order*—God's Divine Order, which is *the power of truth advancing*.)

Everything in the universe advances by the same rules, whether physical, mental or spiritual. Today's scientists, because their proper duty (and remains) has also become buried and put to sleep, cannot now accept or see such an intelligently coordinated reality in the profound fine-tuning of laws ruling the universe. Yet, they admit that the universe is somehow unified—they just don't know how. (And attempting to unify relativity theory with quantum physics will not provide them with an adequate multi-dimensional theory of gravity [quantum gravity] that both Swedenborg and Gurdjieff easily embraced).

SUMMARY

▪ This chapter may represent another new octave (new evaluation) in the story, even perhaps now including octaves within octaves!

▪ Originally, earth-humans had the same spiritual potentials as other "Keschapmartnian" three-brained beings arising throughout the universe and enjoyed the same duration of lifespan—that is, their sensing of time and process was originally normal.

▪ A second misfortune happened to the planet Earth, which had an even worse consequence for earth-humans than the comet collision. This second misfortune was the sinking of the Earth's chief continent, called "Atlantis."

▪ Atlantis (as a "chief" continent) inwardly refers to an important function in humans that was submerged and lost. (Atlantis is the

SUMMARY

mythological equivalent to Swedenborg's doctrine of remains and conscience, which is buried deep in the human psyche. This event brought negative conditions to all future religions and the state of worship on Earth.)

■ Because of this "sinking," the universe was compelled to modify earth-human perception so that the proper quantity (no longer quality) of radiations could be obtained from these beings in order to preserve and maintain the harmonious development of the Earth's fragments (Moon and Anulios).

■ This new need for quantity of vibrations required increasing the populations of earth-humans, then speeding up their deaths—over the entire surface of the planet. From that moment on (after the sinking of Atlantis) humans also began sensing the flow of time as moving ever faster and faster.

■ Beelzebub believes that the best way to give his grandson a clear understanding of the peculiar psyche of the three-brained beings living on the planet Earth is to share his observations and experiences gained from his six visits there throughout the planet's history.

CHAPTER 15

"The first descent of Beelzebub upon the planet Earth"

Having studied Gurdjieff's ideas for about 40 years, I have come to assume that he sneaked as much important information into every nook and cranny of his story as possible. Instead of expressing information by way of major octaves, it is my suspicsion that he is now expanding his Tales to include *octaves within octaves* (inner orbs)! Each reading has given me new insights into the human predicament (especially my own) and the laws ruling the universe (to my amazement, these discoveries were enhanced by my reading Gurdjieff's book [*Beelzebub's Tales*] *out loud*). Much valuable information was overlooked before I read the entire book in this way.

For instance, in earlier readings, I overlooked that Beelzebub had described his particular race of three-brained countrymen as his "tribe." The word "tribe" is used several times in this chapter. It is an odd way to describe one's kinsmen, especially in modern times. I believe Gurdjieff used the word quite consciously. So the word "tribe" itself became suspicious to me after several readings and I eventually wondered what deeper meaning, if any, this word might contain.

Bingo!

According to Swedenborg, the word "tribe" has a definite spiritual meaning that is kindred to the first words of the title "All and Everything" in *Beelzebub's Tales*. Psycho-spiritually, the word "tribe" means "all things of truths in one complex" (*Arcana Coelestia*, n. 5054 [4]). In other words, Beelzebub's "tribe" represents knowledge concerning the fullness and unity of universal laws, processes and order, issuing from God's foresight and providence—in the form of *comprehensive wholes*. The term "tribe" describes an inner organization and holy relationship between kindred and relational ideas within a genuine spiritual belief system or doctrine. Beelzebub's tribe embraced this knowledge.

Like many of the seemingly "fantastical" narratives in God's Word, the account Beelzebub gives to Hassein concerning his various travels to Earth would be farfetched, at best, if they did not contain deeper and relevant symbolic (psycho-spiritual) meanings (inner octaves).

The story of Beelzebub's first "descent" to Earth starts with a visit from a number of individuals from his tribe (representing a belief system). They reported that an unhappy situation had occurred with one of their "young" (inexperienced) kinsmen who, because of his innocence, got himself into a big mess down on the planet Earth. This mess now had negative consequences for their whole tribe. These tribesmen sought out Beelzebub's wisdom and convinced him to travel to Earth and correct this unfortunate situation. (Earlier in this Tale, it was mentioned that some of Beelzebub's clan and friends, after being exiled from the "Center," had decided to settle on various other planets of this far-off solar system, including the planet Earth. This particular young kinsman who got himself in trouble had chosen to live on the planet Earth many years earlier.)

Beelzebub immediately decides he must travel to Earth and soon lands on the chief continent there, called "Atlantis." He travels to Earth on a spaceship named Occasion which had been given him from "Above" and which his clan had originally used to travel to this lonely solar system in the Milky Way.

Gurdjieff adds this detail to the story to communicate the idea that Beelzebub descended to Earth under a more original and different type of psyche or brain design than that of the earth-humans living there.

He finds out that the young and inexperienced kinsman of their tribe, who was at the center of the problem, had made friends with "King Appolis," ruler of the city "Samlios," the largest and most prosperous community on the continent of Atlantis. The two would often have diner together and discuss various topics. (According to Swedenborg, a "chief continent" symbolizes the quality of the main church or form of worship on Earth. A king spiritually represents one who rules from the love of God's truth. Thus, the "largest city" of a community represents a state where a church's spiritual doctrine is most elucidated and lived—or followed.)

In one such discussion, this young and innocent member of Beelzebub's tribe voiced his opinion that he did not approve of the king's harsh methods for getting his subjects to roll up their sleeves and maintain the wealth and grandeur of the City Samlios. These methods would often include physical threats and punishments and seemed quite *unjust* to the judgment of this younger member of Beelzebub's tribe.

At the time of Beelzebub's first visit to Earth, it is pointed out that the organ Kundabuffer had already been removed from earth-humans. However, this organ began leaving behind its negative influences (through habit), which caused some of these beings not to take *conscious responsibility* for any duties given them. Laziness began to creep into the human habitual mind. The king's threats and punishments were used to instill fear in such increasingly lazy individuals of his great city.

Having a completely different psychical orientation and innocence than the earth-humans around him, and not grasping the organic reason for their psychic leanings toward laziness, this young "simpleton," a kinsman of Beelzebub's tribe, told the king (who spared neither his own wealth nor labor to sustain his city's greatness that had been entrusted to him, and expected the same efforts from his subjects) that things would go much better *if he could just trust his populous to do the right thing.*

Sounds noble and just.

The King did not think such an approach would work, so the young kinsman from Beelzebub's tribe made him a "wager." He said that if trusting people's better nature failed, he would take full responsibility for maintaining the greatness of the city—including keeping the tills of the treasury properly filled. The King then agreed to soften his approach and allow for such an experiment. The two of them even wrote down and signed this agreement with their own *blood.*

This incident reminds me of the phrase "you can attract more flies with sugar than with vinegar." The problem with this idealistic notion is that once you use sugar (kindness) you are left with a whole lot of disgusting flies and there is no guarantee that all these flies will make the proper individual efforts to become beautiful butterflies. This same ideal is symbolically communicated in the New Testament story of Jesus telling his disciples to cast their nets on the right side of their boats (representing right-brained kindness and love) to catch more fish.

In human terms, we are the "fish" (as depicted in early Christian symbols) but after being captivated (captured) by this show of kindness we must next allow ourselves to be completely changed, that is, be "eaten" and absorbed into the belly of a higher system of life (a spiritual system) where we can be reconstituted into its bio-societies. This cosmic process of "digestion" allows us to die as to our old nature (of self-centeredness) and become something new (more vital and essential) and enter into a more special plane and spiritual bio-fabric of reality (called Heaven). This is how we feed and support God's growing spiritual kingdom.

Swedenborg observed that the spiritual world, taken as a whole, represents a Grand Human, and that when we die, we enter its digestive system where we are prepared for some appropriate society of this great organic design of angelic utility and mutual love. Angelic teachings act as the spiritual enzymes. If we resist these angelic teachings and take a hardened stance, we are deemed unusable (undigestible) to this great organic scheme of mutual support (*trogoautoegocratic* system) and are jettisoned from this eternal arrangement of profound unity as waste material—right out of the great spiritual "butthole."

Swedenborg insisted that the only way for humans to elevate their thoughts above themselves (and their usual natural thoughts) and properly examine their actions was through *spiritual affection* (*Apocalypse Explained*, n. 242).

We, like Beelzebub's naïve kinsman, often don't take into account that human nature is greatly flawed from its core and therefore cannot be merely left to its own self-judgment. (That is what got us into trouble in the first place!) While the king's punishments toward lazy individuals may seem harsh and insensitive to human dignity, Swedenborg concurs that such laws are absolutely necessary for maintaining order in a "fallen" society. In his *Arcana Coelestia* (Vol. 12, n. 10791), Swedenborg states that all humans are born into a state of flawed intentions (inherited evil) and must therefore be kept in bonds by laws that carry real punishments—just like those the king was handing out.

Beelzebub tells his grandson that this young kinsman of their tribe had no experience in dealing with the three-brained beings of Earth—who were the descendants of those who had come under the influence of the organ Kundabuffer planted at the base of their spine (thus living in self-delusion and enjoying it). And, as said before—although this organ was later removed, also by God's angelic bio-engineers—its negative consequences started to become organically fixed (hard-wired and second nature through repeated actions) within the psyche of these unfortunate earth-humans.

The worst of these negative consequences involved the natural disappearance of any "remorse-of-consciousness" in these three-brained beings while being lazy and not fulfilling their cosmic duty within God's universe of shared utility. So, earth-humans all needed a "swift kick in the pants" by the king to be persuaded to do anything of real value for society. Again, this young individual of Beelzebub's tribe did not grasp the bio- and psychical-reason behind earth-humans needing a boot in the ass to get things done (because no one in their tribe ever needed these peppery motivations to do the right thing).

But through his persistence, this young lad persuaded the king to relinquish his forceful ways, anyhow. Did it work? Nope!

So, when this suggested new system of governance (through kindness and trust) was put into place, the king's subjects not only stopped making efforts to maintain the wealth and grandeur of their city, but they began to actually drain the system of its "money" (sound familiar to modern realities?).

As agreed (and written in blood), the young kinsman from Beelzebub's tribe now became responsible for balancing the city's budget. Not having the personal wealth himself to continue payment, he began calling on others of his tribe to chip in. It was foreseen that everyone in Beelzebub's tribe would soon be picking up the tab for the young kinsman's error in judgment. (This experiment's negative outcome unfortunately backs up Swedenborg's claim that the human heart and will has become totally degenerated, insane and infernal.)

We all have to pay for the mistake of putting our trust in mere human edifices and constructs (which lead, symbolically, to the building and crumbling of a "Tower of Babel," which is built from false, hand-hewn principles.)

Soon after, high-ranking members of Beelzebub's tribe assembled and realized that they had to return the Atlantean city of Samlios to its former mode of operation and greatness, but how? They would be damned if they did and damned if they didn't. You see, they also ascertained that if they restored the old forceful code of governing to the city, the bad effects from the consequences of the organ Kundabuffer would cause many of the king's subjects to immediately *revolt* and seek to both destroy property (vandalism) and demand someone's head—out of an imagined sense of social justice.

(So again, we are dealing with the concept of revolt and disorder within an otherwise working scheme, which Beelzebub himself had been caught up in during his more fiery and youthful days—and which was the reason for his exile. I also sense that by this repetitive approach in storytelling (his use of individuals making miscalculations—this time by a member of Beelzebub's tribe), that Gurdjieff's Tales are designed in a format that contains *repeating cycles*. These steps show order in the universe even when things are headed off course—and the order by which things can return to normal. More on this later.)

Because this great calamity was not the king's fault, the assembly of wise elders from Beelzebub's tribe, including Beelzebub himself, decided that the calculated wrath of the revolting citizenry should be directed at those who made up the king's *administration*. But this action would not be true justice, either—especially since it was one of their own tribe members who caused this problem to occur. So the wise elders decided further that various members of their own tribe would replace the officials (and all those holding responsible posts in the city's administration) and personally take the heat off of the good king.

Because of the inevitable and unfortunate outcomes of revolution by the city's citizenry, Beelzebub tells Hassein that under such periods of revolutionary "psychosis" it can be expected that not only will some of the city's property end up being destroyed by these mindless hordes, but even worse, the valuable knowledge accumulated over centuries to inform people how to lawfully engage in the process of spiritual evolution—which is the proper cosmic duty of all three-brained beings in the universe—is also destroyed.

Things in the city of Samlios eventually returned to "normal" as its citizenry began to feel pity toward their poor king. But they continued to reject being governed by an *inner dictum* (like conscience), only understanding the wisdom and the convincing effectiveness of a leader who constantly applied the threat and power of physical force to get things done (might is right).

For reasons I can only discuss later, (and at the risk of becoming more obscure) this period covering the inner history of the human race (Atlantean) seems to correspond well to Swedenborg's account of the vastation of the Ancient Church (called Noah) on Earth, which had its own special divine knowledge and revelation—a Bible before the Bible—which is now lost to the world. This very ancient and sacred document (Noachian *Book of Enoch* and *Book of the Wars of Jehovah*) contained the *growth of conscience* and one's God-given *"remains,"* but was expressed in an even more remote symbolic language than that used within the current Bible narratives.

This higher sacred knowledge was designed to create an inner dictate within earth-humans' hearts and minds before it became lost to the world, causing the human *conscience* to "sink," whereupon men-beings of Earth began building the *Tower of Babel* (artificial worldviews) from their own personal sagacity.

Swedenborg brought the key to unlocking this ancient symbolic language, called *correspondences*, back to the human race—so that *"dry ground"* could resurface again within the human psyche (the reverse of the sinking of Atlantis as represented in the "third day" mentioned in Genesis 1:9).

For instance, Swedenborg claimed that the biblical phrase "the uprising of the sea" (Psalm 89:9) symbolizes man's exalting his own natural or terrestrial knowledge over and against the Divine (*Apocalypse Explained*, end of n. 275a).

The next time we hear of Atlantis in *Beelzebub's Tales* it has sunk down into the ocean of the planet Earth.

SUMMARY

▦ A "naïve" young member of Beelzebub's tribe convinces the king of the largest, most splendid city in Atlantis not to use threats of punishment, but instead, to trust his subjects to be properly self-responsible. He further promises to personally make up any financial debt in the city's treasury should this new and more kindly direction fail to produce results.

▦ At this time (during Beelzebub's first visit to the planet Earth), the accursed organ Kundabuffer had been organically removed from earth-humans, but through habit, its negative influences had not only taken hold, but even began to increase. (This caused certain humans to begin to no longer feel any kind of remorse from their being lazy.)

▦ The "kindness" strategy failed—because of the deteriorating earth-human psyche, in which egoism and laziness had become too overpowering. Having no understanding of the true nature and depth of human egoism, the young kinsman from Beelzebub's tribe was now on the hook to pay the funds necessary for maintaining the Atlantean city's treasury and greatness.

▦ Of course, unable to meet such a debt, the young kinsman asked other members of his tribe for help to bail him out. These other members (wise elders) eventually approached Beelzebub to help them solve this irksome problem.

▦ The difficulty is that once you allow your citizenry to abandon their essence-responsibilities and then later attempt to bring back original and harsh laws, the people will revolt and even ask for heads. This "psychosis" of the citizenry also results in their destroying any previous knowledge gained by others for freeing oneself of the negative influences (crystalizations) of the organ Kundabuffer (false outer convictions).

▦ Beelzebub and certain of his tribal elders decided to reinstate the "Old Codes" of negative (forceful) prompting to this earth-community but then also cleverly shift the blame (and anger) away from the innocent king to the members of his administration. To do this, the members of Beelzebub's tribe voluntarily took up various posts in the king's administration to take the heat. They gradually returned these positions to most of the original staff as the anger of the citizenry faded.

▦ But this was the beginning of the end of *sincerity* in the earth-human psyche (and the continent "Atlantis," which symbolizes the functioning of genuine and sincere conscience becoming buried and submerged).

CHAPTER 16

"The relative understanding of Time"

Since Beelzebub claimed that the sensing of Time became different in later generations of earth-humans (perceived as moving faster), Gurdjieff takes the opportunity here to explain what Time really is.

We all know that as children we experienced Time more slowly and it "speeded-up" as we got older. This is evidence that something very basic (and detrimental) has happened to all of us!

In his book *The Emperor's New Mind*, world-renowned theoretical mathematician Roger Penrose states, "It is my opinion that our present picture of time is due for a grand shake-up . . . " (p. 480). "Human consciousness seems to be intimately tied to the sensation we have of the flow of time. Time is how we experience change within the dynamical universe." However, Penrose sees a problem between the way modern physics treats Time—versus one's own personal observation—in that he feels there is "something very odd about the way that time actually enters into our conscious perceptions . . . " [5]

Einstein's theory that spacetime is continuous is flawed.

In this part of the story Beelzebub now apparently takes a detour to explain to his grandson how Time should be properly understood. However, this discussion is intimately connected to the theme of the gradually diminishing cognitive powers of the earth-humans throughout history. Because of this, earth-humans currently sense Time differently than those living in former epochs or even on other planets. (Penrose would easily grasp the notion that humans have experienced *change* differently over different epochs.)

Beelzebub first explains to Hassein how earth-humans formed units of Time calculation according to the Earth's revolutions around its sun ("Falling and "Catching-up") and the rotations of the Earth on its axis. While this seems obvious, it underscores an idea that Swedenborg also embraced—that Time is meaningless without *periodicity*. This allows Time to be *packaged in a series of repeated changes*—on different scales! (Hold that thought.) Sweden-

---

5. *The Emperor's New Mind*, Roger Penrose

borg communicates this observation of orderly cycles in nature early in his unique book, *Worship And Love Of God*.

But here comes the kicker.

According to Beelzebub, Time itself has no objective or onto-logical reality. Time simply does not exist. Again, this is different than what Einstein believed. Time is a derivative of process. It emerges or is a byproduct of all the phenomena occurring in a given place. So it can produce a similar order on different scales. (Swedenborg describes these phenomena as a coming forth from the Lord God's Divine Proceeding and since all created things are receptacles of this divine flow, they all experience this process subjectively—but in a similar sequence.

Beelzebub further informs Hassein that all the phenomena in the Great Universe represent lawful "Fractions" of some greater *comprehensive* whole issuing out of the "Most Holy Sun Absolute" (Swedenborg's Divine Proceeding from the Spiritual Sun).

These law-conformable "Fractions," whether taking part in a series of changes moving away from God (creation and invo-lution) or back toward God (spiritual evolution) proceed in a *seven-fold* series (seven mathematically precise steps of stability, or gravity centers, that form a common equilibrium, whereby the first step corresponds—even mathematically—to the last step).

Symbolically, most people already sense that "seven" is a Holy number. The reason for its holiness is that it signifies a *complete* series of subordinated and coordinated events, proceeding in all completed (whole) processes, according to divinely established patterning principles (sacred divine order and providence). This holistic pattern will be more fully explained in later chapters.

Swedenborg and Gurdjieff are in full agreement that all things in the universe have their origins in the activity and emanations of the Lord God's Spiritual Sun or Sun Absolute (which represents God's Word and Divine Truth advancing). Time is merely an outcome and derivative of this orderly activity.

Swedenborg also claims that heaven's angels perceive all phenomena as ordered into *comprehensive wholes* (the bigger picture). Gurdjieff calls this holistic angelic cognition "Egokool-natsnarnian-sensation." In spite of using strange new words, this suggests to serious students of Swedenborg's theological writings that Beelzebub is sharing angelic knowledge (objective or holis-tic knowledge) with his grandson. (As I hinted earlier, the term "tribe" in Holy Scripture symbolically represents "all truths of faith in one coherent system.")

Beelzebub next tells Hassein that of all the objective cosmic phenomena occurring in the universe, Time alone has the distinc-tion of being the "Ideally-Unique-Subjective-Phenomenon" in the whole world. In other words, Time is packaged in the same sequence and order *on all scales* of reality, but sensed with different speeds on these scales. A microbe for instance, which is also a recipient bio-form of God's influx, goes through the same process of birth, youth, old age and death as humans do. (As I mentioned above, Swedenborg observes this same universal order of process in the opening of his unique book *Worship And Love Of God*—as the change of seasons.)

So, even the greater stars and planets go through this orderly process—only the relative scales and durations differ. Therefore, Time is sensed according to the vivifyingness of the vibrations present in a given space, structure or living organism. In human perception, this includes sensing Time not just physically but from a deeper psycho-spiritual state of mind (this is why humans lose all sense of Time when they are having fun—and living in their element of what they "love.")

Beelzebub informs his grandson that their kinsmen perceive Time on a different scale than earth-humans do. The reason for this is that their psyche contains more *activated* levels of awareness. They sense things more fully than do earth-humans. Each new activated level in the human psyche is like adding a new string to a guitar—one that is also capable of vibrating much faster than the other strings. Therefore, an extra dimension of consciousness (like an extra vibrating guitar string) causes a three-brained being to sense Time more fully and richly, thus lengthening the experiencing of one's lifespan.

When I was personally attending a Gurdjieff work group, one particular discussion involved the phrase "Time is of the essence." Gurdjieff had made a distinction similar to Swedenborg's model of human cognition as having both an *internal* reality and an *external* reality. Gurdjieff described the internal part of human intelligence as essence (Swedenborg called it *the internal natural mind*) and the external part as *personality* (mask). Both Gurdjieff and Swedenborg claimed that the human race had become disconnected from this deeper, inner essence of consciousness due to their more sensual orientation and focus upon merely earthly, bodily and worldly (lower) things.

As this external focus strengthens, the sensing of time speeds up.

This outer, more external form of consciousness traps knowledge in the human memory and imagination, keeping it from going deeper into the psyche where the human spirit or *essence* of a person resides—and thus is left starving and underdeveloped. This mental barrier (or split psyche) makes humans vulnerable to fantasy, illusion and negative compulsions, because it keeps our better head-knowledge at bay, preventing us from using it as a comparison to what is really going on inside us.

So we are kept from sincerely self-examining our inner motives.

This split situation also causes the experiencing of time to lessen in humans by speeding life up. Again, we all remember that as children, time seemed to last much longer, but as we grew up, time seemed to flash by more and more quickly. The instructor of the Gurdjieff work group I attended stated that in our childhood we still live in our essence (Swedenborg's internal natural mind) or spirit (and in a state of innocence). As we grow up and learn the ways of the world, this instinctive functioning is thwarted from expressing itself and is eventually replaced by a more artificial, fabricated and external functioning called the "personality and its mask," which expertly expresses how we wish to be seen in the world and hides who we really are.

So, if *Time is of the essence,* its experiencing would depend on the quality of our essence, internal natural mind or inner spirit. As children in innocence, this essence lives at the surface.

But, because of the abnormal external conditions gradually set up by humans throughout history, this interior or essential part of the human psyche was driven deeper within us—it was submerged (like the sinking of the continent "Atlantis"). Unfortunately, this deeper level needs to be reached in order for God to build a new foundation in our lives for our spiritual evolution, because this is the plane from which God implanted the sacred concepts held in our *remains* and *spiritual conscience,* which alone can re-emerge as "dry land" (as illustrated on Day Three of the Genesis *Creation Story).*

Both Gurdjieff and Swedenborg claimed that under such abnormal conditions, humans experience life (and inwardly "growl") much as irrational animals do (see *Arcana Coelestia,* n. 5125). Furthermore, Gurdjieff states that earth-humans, under this "incomplete" psychic condition, live and sense the "tempo of time" under the same principle as all the one- and two-brained creatures do (lower animals). He calls this limiting perception of tempo and flow the principle of "Itoklanos" (*Beelzebub's Tales,* pgs. 130-131). As an illustrative example of this diminution in our sensing of Time, Beelzebub claims that his 12-year-old grandson (Hassein), has lived for *four thousand six hundred and sixty-eight years* according to our earth-human time calculation.

Again, the reason for this diminuation has its roots in our spiritual laziness.

Nature is forced to correspondingly adapt the human psyche to this situation and limit perception when earth-humans cease to sense and perform their God-given duties. But when humans re-connect with their true inner selves and sense of cosmic responsibility and make the effort to bring it back into proper divine order, their experience and delight is increased a *thousand-fold* (see *Arcana Coelestia,* n. 5125 [2]). This increased delight increases the perception of reality and the duration of the experience. Gurdjieff calls this more noble principle of time perception "Fulasnitamnian," which is proper to all three-brained beings of God's Great Universe who are capable of becoming spiritual and angelic.

This sensing is different than time slowing down from mere boredom and lack of interest. In this present discussion, time slows down because its sensation (passage and duration) in earth-humans becomes fuller. This fullness of perception occurs as a man's interior reality also begins functioning and adds a deeper level of consciousness to the human experience of "flow." Again, Time is of the *essence* because humans experience time according to the development of one's essence (or the lack thereof). Human essence and spirit is according to the quality and richness of one's *Ruling Love*, which alone, through spiritual transformation, can build the strength to genuinely embrace reality to its fullest.

Gurdjieff adds that earth-humans who do not participate in God's plan for spiritual evolution do not create the sacred substances required for developing their essential spiritual bodies in the proper (heavenly) way, but create only those gross substances and living forces that benefit the harmony of the physical solar system, their planet Earth and the Moon—upon our deaths.

It is our duty to create both sacred as well as physical substances during our lives, or time will whiz right by us and nothing will ever be accomplished that has any real importance.

SUMMARY

■ Beelzebub calls Time (also the "Heropass") the "Ideally-Unique-Subjective-Phenomena" in the universe. It flows according to our perception.

■ Time flows in the same sequence on all distinct scales of the universe. That is, on every scale, birth, maturity, illness, the urge for self-perfection, old age and finally death is experienced in the *same sequence*—whether a "being" is large or tiny (like a microbe).

■ Swedenborg makes a similar observation about the lawful sequences of Time and its seasons in the opening chapter of his unique book, *The Worship And Love Of God*.

■ Hassein, although 12 years old, has lived *four thousand six hundred and sixty-eight years* compared to earth-human time calculation.

■ Earth-humans, rejecting their essence-duty, no longer sense time properly (Egokoolnatsnarnian sensation) that is, completely or fully.

SUMMARY

▪ Earth-humans sense time more quickly than those citizen of Beelzebub's planet because nature was forced to correspondingly adapt their experience (and their psyche) gradually from their living so abnormally, and thus, to sense the sequence and duration of time ever more quickly. This diminishing sense of time is not proper to their normal (God-intended) existence, and relatively speaking, this duration now comes to almost "nothing." Life is short.

▪ Nature caused earth-humans to sense time by the "Itoklanos" principle (which all lower forms of life exist by) instead of the original "Fulasnitamnian" principle—because earth-humans no longer assisted the common-cosmic-Trogoautegocratic-process of transmuting the proper substances needed for maintaining God's universe and heavenly plan.

▪ Lower life forms and animals only generate the substances required by their own planets or for their sun. But humans were created to produce higher substances to maintain another distinct realm. These valuable substances also coat their spiritual bodies or bodies of the soul.

▪ Without this sacred utility performed on Earth by earth-humans, nature was forced to get the required substances for maintaining the Moon and Anulios through the "quantity" of human deaths (and ritual animal sacrifices). Also, earth-humans were no longer capable of correctly sensing and grasping cosmic phenomena, that is, having the "instinctive sensing of reality" that other human species enjoy throughout the universe.

CHAPTER 17

"The Arch-Absurd: According to the assertion of Beelzebub, our Sun neither lights nor heats"

This was at first, a most difficult chapter for me to interpret—especially in a way that could be explained by Swedenborg's theology and cosmology. It challenges my everyday beliefs. But I did finally happen to locate similar concepts mentioned by both these amazing men.

In this extremely challenging chapter, Beelzebub gives his grandson Hassein, examples of how far earth-humans have degenerated in their "instinctive sensing of reality." Their diminished function (mental-fantasy and foolishness) in perceiving reality began to speed up after the *second Transapalnian perturbation* took place on the planet Earth—the sinking of the continent "Atlantis." Now things have become so bad that when people are told the truth they see it as an "absurdity." (Swedenborg speaks of a spiritual condition in which humans see truth as falsity and love as evil.)

In fact, many people find Swedenborg's assertion that he was given a special Divine commission to observe phenomena in the spiritual world and write about it for almost three decades as pure malarkey.

Gurdjieff remains unrelenting in destroying our fabricated worldviews, whether they are scientifically supported or not—especially concerning our deluded self-images and flawed perception of reality (God's creation). So let me take the hit first and be the guinea pig for showing how I was being led—and therefore, am not who I think I am.

Nothing exists alone, not even human thought and feeling. Everything (including the human brain) is a form and organ receptive to the living influences from the Lord God (or other *a priori* spiritual sources). We humans are not even alive from ourselves. (Nor does the sun give off heat and light from itself!)

All comes from God.

First, in order to convince you, my reader, that I have no intelligence or thought from myself (which is an important conviction for properly perceiving reality and freeing oneself of the negative consequences of the organ Kundabuffer and its promotion of egoism), but that my thought processes and life is actually "borrowed" from another more sacred and Holy source, I must now confess to you that I have enjoyed many extraordinary and meaningful coincidences (what C. J. Jung called *synchronicity*) while working on this most challenging project.

I often prayed to the Lord God (a holy source) to enlighten me before beginning the reading of each new chapter of *Beelzebub's Tales*. Then, the extraneous help I needed came to me in a "meaningful coincidence." It just so happened that I was also providentially reading Swedenborg's *Arcana Coelestia* (Secrets of Heaven) and his *Divine Love and Wisdom* at the exact same time that I was working on this chapter. I would have found this chapter of *Beelzebub's Tales* way over my head—and truly absurd—if I had not found a similar topic being discussed by Swedenborg on the very pages I "luckily" happened to be reading from his writings on that very same day! I was being providentially guided by outside help.

Thank you, God!

In previous chapters Beelzebub takes shots at contemporary authors and their "bon ton" literary style. Now he goes after the scientists, who live and think under the same abnormal conditions as everyone else in contemporary human society (because they also suffer from the residual effects of the organ Kundabuffer). Attacking the modern scientific view of reality is, therefore, a necessity.

Since the writing of *Beelzebub's Tales* began around 1925, Gurdjieff would have been sufficiently familiar with the two pillars of modern physics—Einstein's general relativity theory and quantum physics. In the previous chapter, Gurdjieff deals with the relative understanding of time (unlike Einstein, he also does not see space-time as a continuum, but as consisting of *discrete* packets and scales in a multi-dimensional or "sandwiched" scheme). Now he moves to explain that all physical substances are actually dead (Swedenborg also claimed that nature was dead) and must get their dynamical and vivifying qualities from another, more dynamic and theological source.

In quantum physics it is believed that units of light or photons carry electromagnetic energy throughout the universe (as a radiation). The human eye "sees" things because photons are constantly entering ("bombarding") into it. Yet, I have never heard it explained how these tiny units of radiation carry data via *constantly changing* images of the world to the human eye. Photons must be quite malleable and adaptive to carry different kinds of information in such an instantaneous way—merely by bouncing off or hitting objects.

In this challenging chapter Beelzebub tells Hassein that scientists of the planet Earth are completely wrong to think that light and heat arrives to their planet "ready-made, 'd-i-r-e-c-t-l-y' from their own astronomical Sun." This bogus idea had not entered into the noggins of earth-humans until after the sinking of the continent Atlantis, which engendered in the human psyche the mental property of "fantasy."

Beelzebub tells his grandson that sacred information had been properly "implanted" in his mind from an education based on living life according to God's commandments (this sacred implantation of information is also Swedenborg's concept of "remains" and "conscience").

Because this sacred information and proper inner education has been kept alive among his tribesmen, Beelzebub informs Hassein that if he should ever find himself living among these odd earth-humans, he would break out in uncontrollable laughter if he were able to observe their facial expressions at the moment they found out the truth that their Sun is not the source of either heat or light for their planet. (I seem to recall reading somewhere that the Sun is even closer to the Earth during winter than summer. Hmmm...)

Beelzebub then says something quite astonishing. He describes the Sun, like all other *physical* Suns of the universe, as being more icy and frigid than the "North Pole." Therefore, any astronomical sun must borrow this energy from another source. This statement by Beelzebub, of course, seems absurd to the ordinary reader (and especially the scientist). I too, originally thought this was a nutty notion. An "icy" Sun? That certainly is an anti-intuitive idea—if not totally absurd!

Enter Swedenborg. (Providentially, I was also reading his theological work, *Divine Love and Wisdom* while going through this seemingly anti-intuitive and challenging chapter.)

Swedenborg claims in his book (*Divine Love and Wisdom*, n. 157-159) that the physical sun is dead and indeed receives its life-giving properties of heat and light from another source—the Spiritual Sun (what Gurdjieff calls the Most Holy Sun Absolute). The natural sun of the physical universe has no vital power of its own!!!

While I was going through this particular chapter of *Beelzebub's Tales* I also came upon the statement by Swedenborg in his *Arcana Coelestia* that those individuals who get all their information from the light of the physical Sun put their reasoning powers in a light much like that of "winter," which is devoid of life. This "light" is seen by higher angelic minds as a "snowy wintry light" and as soon as the light from the Spiritual Sun (original source), enters into the picture, this fatuous (and "icy") light is darkened like the dark of nighttime. The message here is that most contemporary humans (including scientists) live in this mental, icy darkness.

So Swedenborg, as well as Gurdjieff, gives full credit to the Spiritual Sun (God's dwelling place) as the sacred source for the creation and maintenance of the manifest universe as well as the inmost sacred source of heat and light.

All the laws of the universe were purposely designed and actualized by God (through the emanations of His Spiritual Sun), so that all created (limited) things would participate in a *reciprocal exchange* of uses, substances and energies. This universal reciprocation and cooperation is a physical analog for spiritual Love (and God's essential character), which perpetually seeks to unite all created things by a process of sharing. (This is why nature is in a constant endeavor toward self-organization and arranging things into orderly systems.) Physical thermodynamics cannot create organization (simultaneous order), but can borrow this ability from God's pulsating heat (Divine Love) and sacred unifying intentions and ends.

Gurdjieff uses the term "Etherokrilno" as the prime-source substance of the world from which all created things arise. Swedenborg identifies this primal unifying substance as Love (Divine Will), becoming pure endeavor (conatus) as a *motion in the Infinite* (which may seem Arch-Absurd to a great many of us). Gurdjieff also describes the resulting Divine reciprocal system of world creation and maintenance from this prime-source unifying substance as the "Most Great Common-Cosmic Trogoautoegocratic-process."

This sacred cosmic process of universal reciprocation proceeds under two sacred laws that were mentioned earlier in this story—the *Law of Threefoldness* and the *Law of Sevenfoldness*. Together, these two laws constitute the WORD OF GOD (Theomertmalogos) and determine how Etherokrilno (pregnant void of potentials or universal soul) creates all the forms, scales and structures (organic and non-organic) in the world.

Beelzebub then relates to Hassein that scientists of the planet Earth confuse the concepts of "radiation" and "emanation." (God emanates, not radiates.) In Swedenborg's terms, this means that contemporary earth-scientists misunderstand the concept of flow (influx) in a top-down casual pattern of process that is (discrete) and requires a *correspondence* for connection between higher spiritual (non-physical) realities and lower (physical or spacetime) realities. Correspondence is not radiation, but an analogous and lawful mimetic response to God's emanations and flow.

During the process of creation, God's prime emanation (Theomertmalogos or God's Word) from the Most Holy Sun Absolute, together with a new blending of its three holy influences (end, cause and effect) upon Etherokrilno (non-manifesting endeavor in pre-space or potentiality space) creates a special new entity called *Okidanokh*. This new production represents the first created active element "outside" the Spiritual Sun.

This new active element, while the first unit of physical creation, has the same (or corresponding) aspects as the spiritual elements and laws preceding it from pre-space (becoming an analog of God's *living* Will and Wisdom) so that the original creative action and divine thrust is repeated on a lower and more limited (finite) level of existence. Here, the true science of creation and theology (Trinitarian doctrine) are unified.

(Some people believe that a rational unification between science and theology is absurd, but this belief will change in the future.)

Etherokrilno and Okidanokh are highly abstract substances and difficult to grasp—let alone explain. But I will try from my Swedenborgian point of view! The first substance (Etherokrilno) exists before the actual (formal) creation of the physical universe (and its spacetime arena) because it represents *pure potentials* (like a sphere of virtual entities).

Swedenborg addresses the first primal substance theologically as God's Love (which fills all potential space) in his book *Divine Love & Wisdom*. And the second major substance, from God's Love in his book *Principia*. He defines this second substance as a "first *ens*" and a non-dimensional "point" of pure activity (a motion in the Infinite) by which nature and geometry both have their beginnings. (It is a primal form that contains all form.) I understand Okidanokh to represent the first elemental, which contains all God's three forces.

John G. Bennett, a principle promoter and disciple of Gurdjieff's ideas, stated in his own translation of *Beelzebub's Tales*[6] that Etherokrilno represents primal space and Okidanokh is the substance of will. These are good descriptions but I prefer to call the first cosmic substance *potential* or *possibility space*, or what Buddhism calls *sunyata*—the "pregnant void." As to Okidanokh, Beelzebub also describes this omnipresent substance as an "element" created *outside* God's Sun. (That is a helpful clue, because in Swedenborg's terms, an "elemental" contains all three forces—active, passive, and neutralizing.) So the elemental substance immediately produced from this pregnant void is a corresponding striving of conscious aim, with a formal existence, and containing all three aspects of God's directed holy forces.

At each downward step (involution—away from God and His Spiritual Sun) in the process of physical creation, new cosmic units lose the vivifyingness of their vibrations, because they are moving further away from the origins of the vital and living forces of the first heavenly cosmos, or Protocosmos. Each step lawfully and orderly advances to a new "bottom" or *center of gravity*.

The full topic of Creation (from God) will be addressed in greater detail in Chapter 39, but for now, simply think of this primal active element (Okidanokh) as containing a similar endeavor (or striving) as God's Universal Will—which is to keep on creating new substances through these same three (Trinitarian) forces and principles and taking their orderly placement within the layered structure and providential scheme of creation.

This allows each newly created finite formation to act as its own creator (or first principle) for further development. Each step imploring these same three forces to unify on yet another distinct scale. In

---

6. *Beelzebub's Tales to his Grandson*, translation by John G. Bennett © 1950, etc.

his book *Divine Love and Wisdom* (n. 169), Swedenborg concurs that three distinct forces must enter into all created things.

(The Law of Sevenfoldness also takes part in this sacred process of creation but because it demands much additional explanation, it will be addressed later in its own chapter).

Beelzebub also informs his grandson about another kind of "substance" that acts as a superior and purifying substance. It is also created from Etherokrilno and the three holy forces of the sacred Theomertmalogos (emanations from the Lord God through His Spiritual Sun). This substance doesn't simply blend with the continued creation of new structures (crystallizations). Instead, when coming into contact with any newly arising unit (and this is key—and acting as a higher *purifying* principle, relative to that unit) it serves to actually disperse and separate the three fundamental forces that went into that unit's arising to correct them (similar to how gold is completely melted down into its constituent parts and *purified* by the activity of extreme heat and fire).

This process of separation of the three different forces contained within any newly created whole unit is called by Beelzebub, "Djartklom." This Djartklom, or separation of the triunal forces making up any created entity is also referred to as the *remorse of matter,* which is analogous in humans when they are experiencing remorse-of-conscience and a need for self-improvement. Without this separation and "remorse" by the three forces, which allows each of them to able to "criticize" one another, there would be no process of purification in nature (or in human minds).

Not that any of the information of this chapter is easy to mentally digest, but Beelzebub's explanation of "Djartklom" to his grandson really stretches one's neurons. He tells his grandson that when any cosmic arising comes into increased contact or influence with either the Spiritual Sun or any astronomical Sun (as an active and purifying principle), the process "Sacred Aieioiuoa," or *Djartklom* occurs, creating an agitation or friction among the three forces occupying the given cosmic unit. (Djartklom from God's *Spiritual Sun* causes psychic friction in people, while astronomical Suns can only cleanse and purify physical substances.)

This friction during "Aieioiuoa" (Djartklom) is again a result of the separation and criticism of a unit's three distinct fundamental forces—so that they can then judge each other's actions. This is a clever way of saying that lower realities should serve and align themselves with higher (more active) realities in accordance with the divine law of subordination and coordination to maintain Divine Order. So, under the influence of a higher (active) reality, lower realities "suffer the chastening effect" of superior influences.

In Great Nature it is self-evident that the biosphere is under a constant operation of purification and orderly distribution. This cleansing influence always comes from "Above" (higher principles). Swedenborg observed that when the Lord God approaches individuals more closely *from within,* their negative traits become more disturbed, which prompts one to suffer spiritual temptations (inner combat) and increased personal criticism. Gurdjieff called this process *Djartklom.*

To put this all into layman's terms, when we hear a good sermon or receive expert advice, the human mind ponders what it hears by separating its distinct functions (*Aieioiuoa* or *Djartklom*) and self-examines its thoughts, feelings and physical actions, to see what function needs to be improved upon.

Spiritual conscience and personal unity is lawfully expanded under this purifying or self-criticizing action.

Similarly, when the Earth's atmosphere comes under the influence of the Sun, (which serves as a medium to deliver the vital forces from the emanations of God's Spiritual Sun), the circumfluent molecules of air and units of ether also become agitated by a kind of higher "scrutiny." As a result, physical heat and light is generated at the spot—by reciprocal reaction and correspondence, not by anything physically traveling through physical space—which would be a *radiation* rather than an *emanation.* (Winter and summer are according to the angle of the Earth, not its physical closeness to the Sun.)

So, the same process of remorse (Aieioiuoa) in nature takes place when humans allow themselves to self-criticize and experience the higher influence of God's teachings. Spiritual chastening occurs in the human psyche when it splits into different functions and allows friction to occur from a critical exploration between one's three forces—the *will, thoughts,* and *motor actions*—in relation to God's Holy teachings and commandments.

Swedenborg calls this process of scrutiny *temptation,* whereby one who sincerely embraces the influences from The Lord God's Spiritual Sun (or Word) gains an "active" heavenly principle to challenge and combat one's personal disharmonies (falsities and evils). See *Apocalypse Explained,* n. 246-247.

The resulting psychical agitation, friction and self-chastening creates *spiritual heat* and *light* (enlightenment), which forges a higher-being body. Because after separation and purification, one can then re-blend his three forces (heart, thoughts and actions) into becoming a newer harmonious structure and creation—a more advanced and spiritual being. This is what is meant when Beelzebub states that in the separation of forces that occurs during *remorse of conscience,* Etherokrilno (substance of possibilities that have the power to unite and form new unities) is temporarily set free so that it can return to re-connect everything. This time, these separated and purified forces can re-blend and be re-organized into a more noble enlightened principle and organic structure of mutual love.

In terms of universal cosmic process, this becomes *the power of God's truth advancing* within our lives. Theologically, God's perpetual presence in our lives is the divine hope for us to let Him walk through our psycho-spiritual door of consciousness when He "knocks."

But bad things can also happen. And they do.

This separation of forces can have negative consequences according to various qualities or being-impulses of delusional self-love and worldly love that we often warm up to (choose to embrace). This results in a disconnected mind.

Unfortunately, when we are *asleep at the wheel,* the separated forces in a disconnected psyche provide no self-correcting feedback to each other or the necessary inner critiquing (self-examination) for our proper spiritual transformation.

And, this negative circumstance certainly has eternal consequences for us and for our inner (spiritual) organization. That is why Holy Scripture is constantly warning us to "awaken" and "sleep not." We always have to be vigilant and on guard for negative or false influences, which can exploit and take hold of a disconnected and divided human psyche.

Beelzebub tells Hassein that the *great terror of this situation* is that when it comes to most contemporary earth-humans and their conscious using of this cosmic process of separation (personal Djartklom) for positive inner growth—and for one's own self-perfecting—such noble and God-given possibilities now simply "beat their wings in vain."

To underscore this terror he next offers an explanation as to what is meant by a "three-brained being."

Humans literally possess three distinct neural organizations or systems (even though we identify ourselves as being a single person). The neural cells of the head-brain (gray matter) is where the Holy-Affirming or active force of the sacred Law of Threefoldness is localized and functions in humans. The spinal column is where the Holy-Denying or passive force functions in earth-humans. (Swedenborg had keenly observed in his anatomical researches that the nerve cells in the spinal column had an *opposite* orientation to those in the cerebrum.) And finally, the nerve nodes and ganglia of the various plexuses in the chest area act as the Holy-Reconciling (harmonizing) force.

In theological terms, these three distinct operations are formulated as "Father," "Son" and "Holy Spirit." Swedenborg also interpreted these three forces as *Divine Love, Divine Wisdom,* and the *Divine Proceeding* (all going forth together). This sacred patterning principle is why three-brained beings (like earth- humans), are said to be created in the image and likeness of God.

But here is where things go horribly wrong.

When an individual is not on a genuine spiritual trajectory (from embracing the Lord God's teachings) these individual forces do not strive to blend back together harmoniously, rather, they go their own happy ways, maintaining their separated and limited status quo. Beelzebub explains that such a disconnected operation and outcome in beings with three-brained systems (resulting from their inner laziness and neglecting their cosmic responsibilities), instead results only in the development of their physical (planetary) body alone. This condition only leads to the promotion of the (passive) functioning of the Holy-Denying principle within their Cosmic Omnipresent-Element-Okidanokh (a downward expression of forces operating within the limited preferences of seeking pleasure).

Proper reasoning and spirituality are not developed or "crystallized" in such disjointed earth-humans, and therefore, both the "Active" and "Neutralizing" being-functions of their brains, having no fixedness or matrix in these men and women. So their life energies are siphoned off for the needs of the universe—like the Moon. (Remember that the life-energy, *askokin*, is needed from all life-forms to maintain the proper equilibrium of the physical universe.)

This *unconscious* and mandated responsibility to fulfill the needs of the expanding universe amounts to *human inner slavery* and bypasses the orderly arrangement of one's spiritual integrity. However this orderly arrangement is critical for producing the substances needed in coating spiritual bodies and obtaining eternal happiness in the afterlife. All living beings must provide for the universe's needs, including the spiritual realm.

I feel the need to return to the topic of Etherokrilno and Okidanokh. They are related but distinct substances. Etherokrilno exists before spacetime and is non-material. Okidanokh is the first spacetime *elemental* substance and is formed out of Etherokrilno (ground of possibilities) from the direct influences (emanations) of the Spiritual Sun (God's Word).

As I mentioned earlier, Swedenborg describes something very similar to the substance of Etherokrilno as a "motion in the Infinite" or pure endeavor or conatus that contains all possible forms and exists before time and space. Beelzebub seems to support this model. He states that Okandanokh is the first elemental substance created from this primal non-material situation but that it operates *outside* the Spiritual Sun. Swedenborg further adds that this elemental unit enters spacetime when its striving turns into an actualized or formal displacement through a multiplication of itself, creating and defining real motion and thus occupying true physical space (through God's activity or Divine Providence).

(You may again wonder if this topic of Creation could be explained in a simpler and more accessible manner. I do not know.

But Gurdjieff wanted to make sure that this uncommon information would penetrate deeper than any mere memory-data [which is like food in the stomach before it gets into one's blood] and be transubstantiated by one's deeper reasoning and spiritual cognitive functions. He does not want this information to merely collect in a person's passive being-function or memory where it can putrefy— but rather, to become material appropriated inwardly to help create a new foundation by which the Lord God can fashion one's proper spiritual design—or bodies—for the soul.)

This inner development and unity is not possible without real effort (and conscious suffering) from the reader (one's Kerkool-nonarnian-actualization) because it cannot be transmitted via the impoverishment of everyday word formulations that are usually embraced by the habitual human mind. Gurdjieff writes in a peculiar style (as you are no doubt experiencing) that forces readers to suffer through these Tales (hoping to create inner Djartklom) and make the extra effort.

As John Bennett states in his own interpretation of *Beelzebub's Tales,* "Explanation is often fictitious help" (*Talks On Beelzebub's Tales,* p. 31). This is because data, by itself, is only one-dimensional in humans, and possessing it as mere head-knowledge often gives one a false sense of accomplishment.

In Gurdjieff's earlier work, *Views From The Real World,* and in the first chapter called *Glimpses of the Truth,* it is explained that people cannot be given something that they are unable to receive—no matter how carefully it is verbally formulated. Swedenborg calls this fictitious help or one-dimensional data mere *memory-knowledges*—which is only a doorway into the deeper human mind.

But hold on to your hat. Beelzebub next wants to describe a scientific experiment he personally observed concerning the cosmic Omnipresent-Active-Element-Okidanokh, and conducted by an unusual friend of his from the planet Saturn!

SUMMARY

▪ Beelzebub believes that because of the diminished quality of the human psyche, universal truths would be perceived by them as absolutely "absurd."

▪ The process of "Remorse-of-Conscience" in humans is a psychical analog of the process of purification in nature when a higher source and form of "vivifyingness" approaches a lower, more static form. This is why fire purges mineral rocks of their more valuable metallic ores.

SUMMARY

▪ Everything in the universe, including Love (will and consciousness), is a substance with actual form and structure.

▪ "Okidanokh" is a primal substance arising out of Etherokrilno from the emanations of the Spiritual Sun (God's sacred Word) that contains consciousness and is constantly in an effort toward purification. When under the influence of higher emanations (producing the process of Djartklom) this substance separates into three parts where each becomes capable of scrutinizing one another for the purpose of sanitizing, re-blending and transforming into something new and special.

▪ Emanations and radiations are different (like moving waves vs. moving particles). Emanations lose nothing from their action, while radiation spits out little particles from its source. God emanates life and truth through His Word.

▪ In humans, Okidanokh works its separated actions through our three-brain systems—head-brain, spinal column and solar plexus (Beelzebub remarks that the "third" brain in contemporary humans is actually scattered among many nerve plexuses and ganglia). Okidanokh enters the human organism on different levels through physical food, air and sensory perception, and the results of the scrutinizing action between these brain centers are according to an individual's evaluation of cosmic duty (which determines how "well fed" these distinct brain centers become and develop, and how they harmoniously contribute to our spiritual growth).

▪ Okidanokh, because of its potential powers, blends (correspondingly) with various perceptions according to a person's leanings and can potentially serve as one's conscious means for self-perfection (or destruction). Unfortunately, this process favors what humans favor because Etherokrilno, through Djartklom, re-unifies the entire blending process according to a person's actual wishes. This process of bio-fusion is what creates our spiritual reality, spiritual bodies and ultimate eternal abode. That is why we must keep up self-vigilance toward the things we embrace and seek—and compare them with noble ideas.

CHAPTER 16

"The Arch-preposterous"

Gurdjieff is a master at discussing seemingly unconnected topics and challenging the reader to connect everything together into a sane belief-system. Same thing happens here—in this wacky chapter. Except we now go from the Arch-absurd to the Arch-preposterous!

One of the advantages of Gurdjieff using allegory and symbolic language over that used in Swedenborg's era is that he is the more contemporary figure. While their ideas are profoundly similar (concerning universal order and the order of genuine spiritual transformation), Gurdjieff can take advantage of using more modern technologies as metaphors, such as electrical (artificial) light, to make his point. And that is exactly what he does in this neuron-stretching chapter. Here we learn some new details about "Djartkolm" and the various re-blending of Nature's forces.

Once again we are confronted with a situation more bizarre than the last (to our normal [or habitual] way of thinking), and we must fight our way back to obtain its vital message *with our whole being.* Our normal, worldly education cannot help us here—in fact, it will only frustrate us.

Beelzebub now shares with his grandson the story about how he became close friends (actually essence friends) with a scientist who lived on the planet Saturn. His name was Gornahoor (which means Mister) Harharkh and who has the exterior body of a bird—in fact, a raven! So the human habitual mind is challenged to take seriously a conversation between someone with hooves, a tail and horns with someone else, who has feathers and a beak—on the planet Saturn, no less!

This description of Gornahoor Harharkh as having the body of a bird was at first quite perplexing to my Swedenborgian sensibilities since a "raven" in the Holy Bible symbolizes false ideas making a disturbance and also representing those who are in the dark because of false notions as to what constitutes truth.

Outer appearances do not constitute truth, and according to Swedenborg, humans do not ever get beyond the appearance of truth, as opposed to perceiving truth in its naked forms. So my take is that Gurdjieff is indeed making a "disturbance" by challenging our learned prejudices about judging things from exterior forms only—thus he uses a raven in this case. He may also be expressing a profound knowledge of biblical symbolism.

As I later found out, Holy Scripture (1 Kings 17:4-6) has a curious comment about Elijah drinking from a special brook and being fed by "ravens." Hmmm… Since this biblical event was commanded by God, Swedenborg tells us that it represents an early stage in human salvation—where proper spiritual knowledge is gained (drinking from the special brook) while one is still holding on to some false beliefs (that is, being fed by ravens).

So a raven is the perfect entity to perform the mind-changing (and somewhat disturbing) experiment of this chapter, especially since its benefits—and Gornahoor Harharkh's thinking—will be challenged by his son in a later chapter.

As the Tale unfolds, we learn from Beelzebub that this brilliant Saturnian scientist had created an invention which could not only collect the *separated* parts of Okidanokh through various *vacuum pumps, dynamos, generators,* and *accumulators,* but through additional various levers could allow one, two or all three of these sacred "force-strivings" to be amplified (mixed together) in his unique experimentation room.

Beelzebub and Gornahoor Harharkh had to put on special protective suits for this experiment because they would be making their observations in a vacuum. They were also able to continue communicating with each other while wearing these protective suits. Again, my suspicions as to why Gornahoor Harharkh is described as having the planetary body of a raven is because he is in relative darkness (spiritual falsity) himself, concerning how the outcome of his experiments would prove to have a negative effect on the solar system in the long run.

While the experiment and its complicated details are difficult to follow, simple results can be recognized.

In the main chamber, when Harharkh mixes only the Active part (Anodnatious) of Okidanokh with its Passive part (Cathodnatious), the opposing and conflicting two forces, from their clashing together, create electrical or "artificial light" in the room. Furthermore, when only the passive force is increased in the room, by manipulating the levers of the apparatus in another way, Harharkh artificially aids a substance (in this case, "copper") to go through a further process of *involution* (passivity) and transform itself into another distinct substance with increased (denser) mass and less vivification of vibrations.

(Because our own passivity makes us "heavier" as well, we are cleverly being informed here that psychic principles of process are the same as those operating in the physical world.)

Beelzebub remarks that through his special telescope (which Harharkh helped him build) he had witnessed from the planet Mars, this very same process of *involution* taking place on Earth, after some war or another changed many living earth-humans into *corpses* by which their bodies began manifesting less vivification and taking on another trajectory (like rotting).

One can further surmise that by increasing the first or "active" force, a more evolutionary trajectory with increased vibrational rates would be obtained.

Gornahoor Harharkh's invention and experimental room (laboratory) is actually a representation of the human psycho-spiritual design, which can change the parts of Okidanokh operating in a person's life. (In an earlier work, Gurdjieff described the removal of the reconciling or third force of Okidanokh in our human perception as being "third force blind.") Swedenborg, in his anatomical works, even described the human body and its distinct functions as a "laboratory."

As I touched on in the previous chapter, we have all been constructed to separate the three sacred forces of fundamental reality (in our personal Okidanokh) when coming into contact with a higher influence (like religion). This happens through the three distinct bio-apparatuses of the head-brain, spinal brain, and ganglia of the various nerve plexuses in the body. And, we are free to re-mix these sacred strivings according to our proclivities and free will. The result is that we can perform this cosmic operation in such a way that we can either evolve *upward* spiritually, or toward a more *downward* trajectory that leads to spiritual decline. This latter direction creates a fatuous and *artificial enlightenment* (from the clashing of two of the three forces) that allows us to keep seeing and doing things, but without any true understanding (spiritual darkness).

When we close our eyes, we can still think and see objects in our mind. This mental light, according to Swedenborg, comes from the triune forces emanating from God's Spiritual Sun. However, when we separate what we know (data) from our real life choices, where they are no longer harmoniously unified, we create only artificial Djartklom from mere opposites—that is, artificial or fatuous light in the mind's eye. This occurs when we reject our spiritual duty within God's Universe and fail to both grasp God's full plan (why we are here) and put this plan into tangible practice (which causes the reconciling [third force] or equalizing action of unifying spiritual love and knowledge into harmony).

Similarly, when a church creates a clash between charity and its good works (Anodnatious) from faith and doctrinal data (Cathodnatious), a fatuous or artificial light is produced in one's inner spirit and mind, which only sees everything in terms of literal opposites—like black and white, or I am right and you are wrong.

This limited condition of clashing opposites is the "disturbance" (symbolized by a raven's irritating squawking sounds) that results from incomplete and false belief systems that grate and wrongly "turbinate" the sensing mechanisms of our neurons. This incomplete sensing causes us to perceive only fantasy and all things in the world under an artificial (spurious) light, rather than seeing or understanding the whole picture as it really is.

This is why the Bible says men can live in darkness—even with their eyes wide open, or merely follow the blind. This species of spiritual darkness is called "sleep" in Holy Scripture and cannot be dispelled without the Lord God's wise help (true Djartklom).

The purpose of true religion is to teach the human race how to bring the third striving (Holy Spirit) into our lives and restore our *wholeness*. The only way to do this is through adopting the spiritual *duty* (and proper utility) given us by God's heavenly commandments, so that everything we do in life is focused on being useful to other people's eternal welfare rather than on their temporal needs.

As I mentioned earlier, we earth-humans (in our fallen spiritual state) create false thinking in our minds by a process analogous to making artificial (electrical) light from a clashing of positive and negative influences. (Again, Swedenborg did not have access to such modern technology as electricity for making his analogies and metaphors about the unregenerate human mind.) Electricity helps us see at night just as falsity helps us see during mental darkness.

Curiously, during Harharkh's experiment with the element Okidanokh, and his producing a vacuum in the experiment room so rapidly, Beelzebub begins to experience a kind of "death" happening to parts of his body and the other two of his three-centered brain functionings. (Thus, he questions whether he has a deeper *inner* life.) He then begins sensing things from his higher spiritual essence *alone* (his usual associative thinking was no longer available to him under these rapidly changing conditions). Apparently, these dying functions were dependent on the normality of atmospheric conditions, and so were now being forced to pass their abilities and powers on to Beelzebub's *thinking center*. I believe this represents a new kind of reasoning (a change of the center of gravity in his "initiative-of-constatation" without the physical body and from the deeper inner spirit) from which all new incoming impressions were then evaluated and fixed by a more intensified and unusual perception. (Swedenborg states that our spiritual essence can perceive things many times faster than our terrestrial functions.) This was also the only time Beelzebub allowed the fear of death to creep into his consciousness. His normal being-experiencing returned from this rapid change when he saw his friend Harharkh floating around weightlessly in the room.

Later in *Beelzebub's Tales*, we learn that Gornahoor Harharkh's own son would reject his father's accomplishments because there were unexpected destructive results obtained by generating this artificial light (and electricity) from the clashing of only two of the sacred strivings in the Okidanokh. This clashing can never bring about a healthy outcome for three-brained beings.

The reliance on artificial light and electricity today has led humankind to evolve technologically and *outwardly*, but not spiritually or *inwardly*. Our knowledge (even our scientific knowledge) is just as artificial as our technology. The encrusting of this artificial knowledge upon the human psyche over the centuries has "covered over" our internal reality, which holds our spiritual conscience and the instinctive need for spiritual responsibility.

God even provides a special strategy, unknown to most religions at this day, to potentially offset this terrifying predicament that the human race has put itself into. God's great plan is to offer us new knowledge through additional revelations. I believe that Swedenborg and Gurdjieff both play key roles in dispensing this new knowledge from "Above."

SUMMARY

■ Beelzebub observes experiments with the substance "Omnipresent Okidanokh" done by his close friend, Gorahoor Harharkh on Saturn (Harharkh also helped Beelzebub construct a powerful telescope which allowed him to observe the goings-on of the processes on the surfaces of the other planets in that solar system.)

■ Gornahoor Harharkh is a prominent scientist, but has the body of a "raven."

■ His experiment involves appliances like vacuum pumps, electric lamps, dynamos, generators, and accumulators which can extract the Omnipresent-World-Substance-Okidanokh from all kinds of physical processes, then separate and study each of its three independent properties and forces, re-blending them in certain proportions, or even leaving out one of the fundamental forces altogether.

■ When the neutralizing force (third property) is removed from the normal process of "striving to re-blend" with the other two, electricity and artificial light is created. In Swedenborg's terms, this clashing of positive and negative forces causes the atmospheric ether to turbinate and create light waves—but in an artificial manner. This process does not correspond to the living light (wisdom) emanating from the Spiritual Sun.

■ Harharkh's invention is symbolic of human psychical processes, which can change the proportions of those same three properties within one's own Okidanokh (soul element) according to individual

SUMMARY

propensities (Ruling Loves). Apparently, modern human thinking usually goes on without a proper third property and creates artificial mentation and thought. Psycho-spiritually (symbolically) the third property is the alchemic secret behind humans being able to change base metals into "gold" (change natural desires into spiritual loves).

■ During the witnessing of these experiments with Okidanokh (and first element), Beelzebub begins experiencing from his deeper spiritual essence, a strange process similar to "death" taking place in some parts of his body (its feeling and moving centers). It seems that these "dying" brain systems were passing their individual functioning to Beelzebub's deeper thinking center, increasing the intensity of its activity.

■ By changing the proportions of the three forces in the Okidanokh, you can obtain the process of either *involution* or *evolution* of substances into other substances through "Symmetrical-blending" (resonance through correspondence). These new substances take on similar properties to Okidanokh in that they can also become carriers of either *active, passive,* or *neutralizing* forces for the reciprocal-feeding-of-everything existing (universal cooperation). The resulting reciprocally acting *contact* is what causes the planets to gradually change their densities while ensuring stability.

■ Again, this same process creates psycho-spiritual substances in humankind's inner reality that will coat their inner bodies and change their densities and vibrational qualities to newer levels.

CHAPTER 19

"Beelzebub's tales about his second descent onto the planet Earth"

Here, Gurdjieff is most definitely using a new chapter to represent a change in the form of a new mental gravity center for his Tales and describing the inner history of earth-humans, according to the Law of Falling and moving toward a common equilibrium (goal). The sinking of Atlantis, when understood as allegory, represents an unfortunate change of gravity centers within the human psyche.

The purpose of legends and mythology is exactly that—to communicate the *inner history* of the human race, that is, our deeper spiritual trajectory of blundering and then being reformed and saved by higher influences (like God). *Beelzebub's Tales* represents such an inner story and strategy. The fantastic scenarios, described by all the imaginative narratives of mythology (including *Beelzebub's Tales*) were never intended to be understood simply in a linear or literal fashion. These stories embrace a symbolic language that has ontological relevance on higher (deeper), non-physical planes of reality. Nevertheless, the trajectory of these stories follows the same rules (and distinct gravity centers) as found in all completed processes of the universe. As above, so below—all process in the universe perfectly corresponds to and follows the same rules of order.

The deeper your mind can go, the more enlightenment you will receive from this ancient form of communication, which again, follows the universal laws of order (according to Swedenborg, this unexpected relationship protects higher knowledge from being profaned by unprepared or egoistic human efforts).

These days however, when some story from the past is seen as untrue, it is called a "myth." This is laughable and it points to the decomposing nature of the human intellect—in spite of modern inventiveness and all its technologies. Both Gurdjieff and Swedenborg are in agreement that our more ancient relatives had the *elevated* minds to cultivate this rarefied knowledge into their myths, legends, allegories and storytelling.

And there is a profound spiritual angle to this lost knowledge because it always deals with the more invisible inner world of humans and improving their psycho-spiritual quality.

In his great 12-volume work *Arcana Coelestia* (Secrets of Heaven), Emanuel Swedenborg provided tons of evidence that God's Holy Word (Bible) was also written in the same kind of symbolic language that I have been alluding to, called *correspondences*. Correspondences are based on a top-down symmetry whereby everything we see in the physical spacetime arena mirrors some higher psycho-spiritual event or process. This type of *multi-leveled* language is based on mirroring the purposely designed multi-level (sandwiched) architecture of reality, and can only be deciphered when one understands this principle and knows how to distill deeper, psycho-spiritual meaning from ordinary words and their physical connotations. Again, that these higher meanings have been mostly lost to the modern world (and contemporary education) suggests that the human race has undergone a diminished functioning of their original cognitive powers. (I know that no one today wants to hear this, but it is true.)

Swedenborg describes the Genesis story of the "fall of man" as having started with the spiritual quality of an ancient race of humans who lived in *innocence* but later began to prefer to be under the "Master" of their own self-guidance (Arcana Coelestia, n. 151). They focused only on the material world for getting input on judging reality. This *inversion* of the human psyche for preferring to investigate worldly material things without spiritual guidance is represented in *Beelzebub's Tales* as the implanting by angelic beings of the organ Kundabuffer in the lower spine of earth-humans. (Swedenborgians can simply replace the words "falsity" for "comet," and "rib bone" for the organ "Kundabuffer.")

This false preference brought about even more disasters down the road for the original human race. The human race, which originally enjoyed open communication with angels and a heavenly perception of reality, then became extinct (because their breathing was tied to their heavenly perception, which they were losing) but who were providentially replaced with a more pre-frontal developed genus and species of humans. These new humans were given a new kind of dictate called *conscience* instead of direct heavenly perception (*Arcana Coelestia*, n. 607). Conscience would serve as a medium between the human rational mind and the now insane (hellish) human will—until this dictate later became submerged by human pretense.

According to Swedenborg, this new pre-frontally focused race of humans—who could no longer communicate directly with angels—were, from divine mercy, given similar heavenly (elevated) knowledge (called the "science of correspondences"), except now through codices and extant writings for the benefit of their cerebrums. These original sacred (and symbolic) writings represented a *Bible before the Bible*, that is, an even more ancient Word than the Hebrew version, which also represented a revelation from God (to Moses).

This more indirect or synthetic means of enlightenment could be considered as providing a higher influence for producing a better type of *Djartklom* in order to bring about *remorse of conscience* and a striving for genuine spiritual growth. This strategy included creating imaginative symbolic stories designed to teach an individual of the eternal importance of forcing one's learned (head) knowledge to make contact with one's innermost motives and life-choices (in the heart). The hoped-for result from the clashing of any contradictions is that a new heavenly life and heart could then be implanted and begin to emerge from within people's expanding rational minds.

But earth-humans even screwed up this sacred design. This new divinely inspired strategy (from God's mercy) of giving the earth-humans *conscience* had flaws. Conscience can be ignored—buried and covered over by laziness, artificial knowledge and especially pretense.

-◆- -◆- -◆-

In this chapter, Beelzebub tells Hassein that on his second visit to the planet Earth a *second catastrophe* had already occurred. The continent of Atlantis had "sunk" into the Earth. Symbolically, Swedenborg tells us that a land mass or continent represents the quality of a "church"—the quality of the relationship between humans and God. The legend of Atlantis represents the sinking of *conscience* deeper into the human psyche (forming the subconscious) as well as the disappearance of instinctive knowledge concerning one's cosmic duty.

Speaking of great knowledge, nowhere else is this doctrine of conscience and its sinking deeper into the human psyche obtained, other than from Divine revelation. Only Swedenborg and Gurdjieff show a similar understanding of this special knowledge implanted by God's mercy. Both men agree that this submerged part of the human psyche (the *subconscious* or *internal natural human mind*) is where God secretly stores sacred data from which a plane for conscience and innocence can be preserved, and later re-emerge in mature humans as a striving for inner development.

Whereas, Swedenborg had learned of this heavenly detail by means of a new dispensation from the Lord (and originally called it the "remains"), Gurdjieff seems to have discovered it from fragments of the pre-Hebrew (Ancient) Word (as well as submitting different people to hypnosis and gaining access to their "sunken" and subconscious minds).

The sinking of Atlantis therefore seems to represent a transition (change of gravity centers) from earth-humans having an *internal* form of worship to a more *external* form. Swedenborg calls this transition the "second" ancient church (called "Eber"), which followed after Noah—and which included animal sacrifices.

The reason for Beelzebub's second trip to Earth is that another committee of angels "from the center" had paid him a visit on Mars to seek his help. This important angelic commission was even escorted by one of God's Seraphim (which represents a divine guard or heavenly protection)! The fact that Beelzebub can communicate with angels means that he has more in common with the original race of earth-humans (whom Swedenborg described and who lived on this planet before the "Fall") than with modern-type humans.

This High Commission, sent from the Spiritual World, had ascertained that the second catastrophe on the planet Earth, which swallowed up the continent of Atlantis, was due to the Earth and Moon finally finding their true "centers-of-gravity" after that collision with the comet. In other words, changing functions of the human psyche found their new place of stability in a more outward (external) scheme of things. This change in the center of gravity of earth-human mentation means that their focus became fully adapted to external/corporeal thinking—at the expense of an internal functioning.

The Earth's Moon is represented in each of us as the influence of the organ Kundabuffer (*Glimpses of the Real World*, pg. 102), which keeps us hypnotized.

The Moon, which finds its stability on the lowest rung in the top-down hierarchy of cosmic structures and cosmic order, begins to make demands to fill its own needs. These new needs caused Atlantis to sink, that is, caused true religious principles (on a psychical level) to go under and be replaced with new continents (fictitious worldviews and concocted belief-systems). Psycho-spiritually (symbolically), the Moon represents the human mind functioning in a more external (lowest rung) way, adding an additional (and less vital) layer of cognitive functioning, which Swedenborg described as being more like the shell of an egg or bark of a tree. This development (sinking of conscience) splits human consciousness into what Swedenborg calls the *external natural mind*—one's worldly personality—and the *internal natural mind*—one's deeper essence. (See *True Christian Religion*, n. 593.)

So the splitting off of the Earth-fragment called "Moon" in this story represents a trajectory and center-of-gravity further removed from God's heavenly influence and influx. The Moon's new needs symbolize a requirement in the human psyche to find stability in accumulating *external-data* for "feeding and maintaining" the memory function (and its imagination) only. This produces only "head-knowledge" that has been separated from genuine spiritual duty and goodness (this creates fantasy and directs the human life force toward supporting the Moon's development—which also corresponds to the support of a more external mental functioning).

This predicament is the origin behind the term "lunatic," because memory-data acts like a mere satellite for the real human mind, yet can suck up all its focus.

The Moon represents a state in humans where the function of memory and imagination has gained greater support and importance to people rather than the development of one's inner spiritual *conscience*. So we fail to form an adequate plane or matrix in our intellect that is capable of holding (receiving) God's Love and Wisdom, thus evolving human consciousness upward toward Heaven.

Divine Love, with no appropriate place to settle (terminate and become a fixed quality) within the human psyche, escapes further outward (like water in a sieve)—moving on into lower and more external levels where it eventually becomes twisted and turned into opposites—that is, into insanities (Arcana Coelestia, n. 5145 [1-6]). The coating of higher spiritual bodies fixes God's noble principles into our lives and expands conscience.

The Moon in this highly symbolic story represents this most exterior degree of cognitive functioning in earth-humans, especially since it has become further separated from the life of its planet and higher influences from God. This situation causes us to become delusional and susceptible to bouts of "lunacy."

God had wisely counteracted this downward situation of the human race by secretly allowing the implanting and deeper storing of more essential spiritual data to be protected within the *internal natural mind* during our infancy and innocent years of our youth. But now this sacred data has been covered over by our later learned behavior of pretense, which functions as the more worldly and artificial (external) intellect in our adulthood. Still, God's hidden plane of innocence (spiritual affection and conscience) in earth-humans is protected in our subconscious minds, and can be re-activated through our genuine spiritual growth and rebirth.

So *conscience*, which is implanted by God's mercy, indeed sinks like Atlantis as we grow older and learn from the world, but is providentially preserved and not destroyed. According to Swedenborg, God allows this important functioning to become submerged to protect its sacred information from the ignoble influences coming from the various vanities and allurements of the external world. As I have previously stated, Swedenborg calls this original divine storehouse the "remains." Later, it became conscience. Without this special sacred matrix or conscience, God's spiritual energy would have no place to focus and take part in human life—and as a species, we would quickly become monsters, then we would cease to think or exist. Swedenborg even states that the Lord God works only from this secret plane (of *conscience* and the remains) in humans. This sacred plane is His representation and Divinity within us!

Life and salvation are from the Lord alone and only come from Above!

Should an individual decide to take up the challenge and responsibility of spiritual evolution and its duties, this noble plane acts as the matrix (land mass) for spiritual conscience to re-emerge from its depths and develop (evolve) into new spiritual bio-structures (spiritual bodies). This evolutionary trajectory also keeps God's sacred influences from leaking out and becoming scattered, adulterated and moving further outward.

As I alluded to earlier, the symbolic meaning behind the Seven-Day Creation story in Genesis is the awakening and spiritual development of this secret plane (and spiritual conscience) within our lives. This awakening is illustrated by the emergence of "Dry Land" on the third day (the reverse situation of the sinking of Atlantis into the watery sea)!

Also, the legend of the sinking of Atlantis has a similar spiritual meaning to the Bible story that leads to the Tower of Babel, whereby an inner state is formed in humans who foolishly believe they can reach Heaven (true happiness) from the activities and fabrications of a *divided* mind and *external* worship instead of conscience. In this way, humans became totally confused and *divided* after this botched project to reach "Heaven" from relying on their own sagacity and prudence (human edifices and towers). The human race became "scatter-brained" with the loss of spiritual conscience.

Beelzebub tells his grandson that after its sinking, Atlantis is replaced by all new land masses (new worldviews and invented religious doctrines). On one of these new major continents, called Ashhark (Asia), three new religions suddenly popped up. These three different emerging forms of worship were an analog of the divided human psyche caused by the submergence of a unifying conscience and a diminished sense of objective spiritual knowledge and connection with the Creator.

Earth-humans turned their *three-centered brains* and logical mentation toward acquiring personal cunning instead of wisdom.

The first area of this new land mass described by Beelzebub (and replacing Atlantis) was called *Tikliamish* (Caucasus and Fertile Crescent, which included the land of Canaan), the second, was called *Maralpleicie* (now the Gobi Desert) and *Pearl-land* (India) was the third.

Increased divisiveness of the human psyche was further personally observed by Beelzebub himself on this second visit, when he noticed whole populations of earth-humans trading in their "needful-striving-for-self-perfection" for a new kind of psychic need. This new psychic need involved convincing people from other parts of the planet to accept their particular country as the "Center-of-Culture" for the entire planet. (This new organic need symbolizes a *change of gravity* in one's heart to convince everyone—from a principle of false self-importance—that one's particular religion and worldview is better than all others.)

The angels themselves became increasingly concerned about these developments because the practice of sacrificing animals had now taken hold in these newly "popped-up" religions, which promoted false gods. (As we will see in a later chapter, this killing of animals further upset the harmony between the Earth and Moon's movements). The angels knew that these sacrificial offerings were done to merely honor earth-humans' false gods and idols (hoping this would validate their self-importance and reward all their wishes for personal pleasures).

They also saw that this senseless custom not only had nothing to do with true spiritual evolution but it had become so widespread on the planet Earth that the "Sacred Askokin" (life force from all living creatures) which is released for the needs of sustaining the two broken-off fragments from the Earth (Moon and Anulios) through the natural process of physical death, was now in such great abundance that it threatened to again put things out of whack.

The action of men deluding themselves by this deadly *external* ritual was creating potential cosmic harm. (Remember, everything is interconnected, interrelated and interdependent.) Specifically, this surplus of life-energy ("Sacred Askokin") being released from the misguided actions of earth-humans sacrificing many animals was hindering the proper exchange of substances between the Moon and its developing atmosphere, which if it developed incorrectly, had the further potential of threatening the harmony of the larger solar system—and even beyond.

The symbolism here refers to what happens when we humans overload the memory with false principles and skirt our true God-given responsibilities—it leads to horrific and negative outcomes (imbalances) within the spiritual ecosystem of the soul, and this eventually affects the outer ecosystem of our solar system. The terrible practice of animal sacrifice creates a toxic atmosphere within the human mind that has the potential to consume and destroy all goodness there and beyond, because it can also spread to others who are equally gullible.

Swedenborg observed in the spiritual world that evil spirits projected poisonous atmospheres around them. If this harmful influence was not curtailed by God's divine strategies, bad things would happen. So God stored sacred knowledge within the submerged part of the human psyche (internal man) and was born into the physical world with a human body. Having a human body allowed him to be personally attacked by Hell's full fury and gain final victory through inner combat.

Without this divine effort, Heaven and all its angels would have succumbed and fallen victim to these poisonous spheres (which would then have destroyed the human race). This is the great danger that the angels were anxious of while communicating to Beelzebub—that the evil practices of animal sacrifices carried out on Earth could have the potential to spread and harm the harmony of the whole world and all humanity, including the higher reaches of Heaven itself!

Beelzebub tells Hassein that he fully concurred with this new angelic commission and agreed to visit the planet Earth for a second time and attempt to come up with some plan to persuade earth-humans to stop the senseless slaughter of helpless animals—especially just to please their false (and concocted) gods. (He also hopes that this important task of eliminating animal sacrifice on Earth will help him to become a "particle of everything existing in the Great Universe," or as Swedenborg would say, to become the smallest "unit of Heaven.")

His spaceship lands at the Caspian Sea in the country of Tikliamish in Asia. There, Beelzebub finds himself in the city of Koorkalai and visits various places where its citizens congregate. At one of these establishments he meets a "priest" named "Abdil."

They eventually become essence-buddies.

Beelzebub had noticed that the being-impulse of "compassion" and "sensitivity" toward other beings (a function of a healthy conscience) had not yet completely atrophied in this particular Asian priest. Surely, here was an individual that could respond to Beelzebub's plan.

A long discussion takes place where Beelzebub convinces the priest Abdil that all the creatures in the world serve some important purpose within the Creator's grand scheme (cosmic ecosystem). Thus, the practice of destroying the existence of other creatures to somehow obtain "sainthood" puts the kibosh on any true striving for genuine human self-perfection and on the hopes of the COMMON FATHER CREATOR to augment His conscious scheme (which is, creating a heavenly kingdom of mutual love).

Instead of acting "in-the-likeness-of-God," earth-humans, because of these unfortunate rituals of animal sacrifice, were turning themselves into "being-monsters." (Swedenborg was adamant that if the Lord God had not made Himself present on Earth to combat Hell's influences on the organic human mind (which the Lord equally possessed while in the physical world) the entire human race would have morphed into actual *monsters* before going extinct.

As the conversation continues, Beelzebub throws in another very "Swedenborgian" concept—that *GOD forgives everything*. But he stresses that humans must be careful not to abuse this All-Gracious and Everywhere-Penetrating Goodness, but dutifully help the Creator to care for and maintain all things of His creation. In other words, God's forgiveness does not stop humans from continuing their ruling focus—good or bad. So we can be forgiven by God yet have our preferred Ruling Love still drive us toward a bad eternal trajectory. True worship (and conscience) addresses and purifies both *inner* and *outer* ecologies in humans and their dual cosmic environments.

Beelzebub's eco-friendly conversation makes such a powerful impression on Abdil that the priest begins to preach against the practice of sacrificial offerings to everyone in his congregation. This news spreads fast and gains momentum in other communities far and wide.

Unfortunately, those who oversaw and profited from the rituals of animal sacrifice began to feel it in their pockets. (This situation reminds me of Jesus in Jerusalem, overturning the tables of the moneychangers and those selling doves for sacrifice.) These profiteers not only banded together to destroy this priest's reputation, they even ended up hacking him to death (a real monstrous act indeed).

Beelzebub is forced to take Abdil's mangled physical body back to Mars for a proper burial and to protect it from further atrocities by those beings on planet Earth who have developed the strangest psyche of all three-brained beings existing in the entire universe. (If you get in the way of a person's means for making money, even if it is a crime, they will certainly kill you!)

On the bright side, Beelzebub informs Hassein that Abdil's preaching continued to have a strong lasting affect on many earth-humans. Gradually the number of animal slaughterings for religious and sacrificial purposes began to diminish in Asia.

Again, in my humble opinion, this period of Beelzebub's second visit to the planet Earth corresponds externally and internally to the period described in the Holy Bible just after the "Great Flood" and "Tower of Babel" events, with the emergence of Eber (the Hebrew) upon the scene (Genesis 11:14), who according to Swedenborg, represents a state of humanity, where from the principle of self-love and avarice, there was no longer any *internal worship* but only *outward* worship— which made it easy for the ritual of animal sacrifice and idolatry to become incorporated into people's worship (*Arcana Coelestia*, n. 1343).

True *conscience* has less and less influence on such external and deluded forms of worship. These external rituals and beliefs only bury conscience (and God's characteristics) more deeply into the human psyche. Swedenborg also suggests that from the ancient country of Syria, from where both Eber and Abram originally came, the name "Jehovah" was preserved and later brought forth the Hebrew and Israelite religions. These later religions (called the "third" ancient church) continued the practice of animal sacrifices, because under strict rules, God had permitted it, by instilling a heavenly way to make these practices represent and symbolize (through correspondences) deeper and more sacred Holy processes. These symbolic rituals included offerings other than animal lives (like the burning of incense).

Unfortunately, these symbols and representations were not understood and therefore, had no deep effect on those who clung merely to the more *external* forms of worship, rituals and actions.So another (third catastrophe) hits the surface of the planet Earth, producing wind storms and deserts. (Symbolizing the diminished quality of the human psyche.)

How am I so sure that Gurdjieff actually understood the sacred language of correspondences as Swedenborg did? Well, in this chapter, he (Beelzebub) states point blank, that there is a cosmic law in the universe where "everything-gives-birth-to-its-corresponding-result."

And humans were getting worse.

SUMMARY

■ On this second visit to the planet Earth, the continent "Atlantis" has already sunk below the surface.

■ New (egoistic) values are adopted by earth-humans, including animal sacrifice. (According to Swedenborg these new rituals were performed during the time of *Eber*—representing the "second" ancient church—who was the first actual historical individual identified in the Holy Narratives of the Genesis story).

■ All created things in God's universe have a purpose. Earth-humans were created, to be a "field-of-hope" for bringing God's sacred organization and order into their very lives—through the coating of spiritual bodies, in order to be more useful in this grand holy scheme.

■ Animals (with two-brained systems) do not have the ability for *logical mentation* or *reasoning* that beings with three-brained systems have. But earth-humans have turned logical mentation into *cunning* instead of searching for wisdom.

■ Sacrificing animals causes great disharmony to God's scheme of cosmic mutual support.

■ On this second visit to Earth, Beelzeub succeeds in at least minimalizing the number of animal sacrifices taking place.

■ In this chapter we also learn that a third catastrophe hits the Earth (after the sinking of Atlantis). This catastrophe causes an accumulation of sand, whereby deserts appear on the Earth's surface. Symbolically, a "desert" represents a state in the human heart and mind that is lacking (desolate) of objective (heavenly) truth. "Sands" symbolize data and knowledge accumulated and locked up in the outer corporeal memory, where it lacks order and is unavailable for our deeper spiritual process to grow one's conscience.

■ This third catastrophe corresponds to the further diminishing of the human psyche, symbolized by great windstorms (inner disturbances).

CHAPTER 20

"The third flight of Beelzebub to the planet Earth"

After receiving his divine pardon and arriving back to his home planet Karatas to spend some time with various relatives, Beelzebub quickly returns to Earth for a third visit. He tells his grandson Hassein that he needs to finish his job of uprooting that terrifying custom of animal sacrifice by earth-humans (which had been done all in the name of their doing "Divine work").

(Who doesn't see the insanity of such destructive forms of worship and that these rituals were all fabricated by the flawed—and split—minds of earth-humans?)

This time Beelzebub lands among the second of the three major groupings of earth-humans on the Asian continent (after the sinking of Atlantis) who had built their civilization where the Gobi Desert now exists.

To set up his story for the benefit of his grandson's understanding, Beelzebub then goes even further back in time when Atlantis was still existing (above water), and some silly individual there concocted the strange idea that the horns of a particular deer (called "Pirmarals") could be turned into a medicinal powder with wide-ranging curative effects. This concocted practice spread and was another reason why human worship turned *from internal to external* and that Atlantis (*spiritual conscience*) would eventually have to become submerged in order to allow for such foolish thinking to occur and go mostly unchallenged. (Today we have many similar beliefs and customs, like acquiring rhinoceros horns, tiger parts and bears' gall bladders for some curative and self-centered purpose.)

"Hunters" in this pre-sunken Atlantian timeframe hunted these ancient deer to the point of extinction. Symbolically speaking, these hunters represented the intellectual inquiry and favoring a belief system from their sensual inclinations that could persuade (captivate) others. In other words, they wiped out the ability of true natural freedom in reasoning from their mind's diminishing conscience. Now they were forced to go hunting for these rare horned creatures on other continents (meaning spiritually, to abandon the function of spiritual conscience and head for a new belief system or "psychical turf" that permitted such false beliefs to take hold). Since hunting these deer was a complex job, they had to take their families along with them (taking with them all the *related* ideas of their psychical household).

After the sinking of Atlantis these families settled down on the continent now called "Asia." These hunters of Pirmarals, and their families, so liked this new area that they had no desire to return to Atlantis, and they did not miss it (return to their original form of internal worship through the proper functioning of spiritual conscience).

Again—and putting all this in Swedenborg's theological terms—I believe that the period of the sinking of Atlantis (conscience and remains) and that of the practice of sacrificing animals and a more external worship, corresponds to the biblical period between "Noah's Ark" and "Eber" in Genesis. There were no animal sacrifices during the time of Noah (the Noachian Church, which enjoyed conscience, but there was indeed ritual animal sacrifice by the time Eber came along).

All this points to the fact that the human psyche and its consciousness were changing for the worse.

Both Beelzebub's story and the biblical narratives, when understood symbolically, depict this negative change in the quality of human spirituality. "Hunting," according to Swedenborg, actually represents teaching (persuasion) from external (outer) and sensual things about deeper doctrinal matters, in a way that can captivate (capture) men's minds. Similarly, animal horns ground up to be used as medicine represent attributing all the power of truth to external forms only and thus separated from their deeper internal meaning and heavenly power.

This idea of external medicinal powers, an invention of egoism, captivates many, many human minds, because it favors their inclinations. That these hunters had no desire to return to Atlantis means they were embracing a new belief system and worldview that they imagined was extremely fertile (self-beneficial), yet in reality was devoid of real spiritual conscience (internal worship) and any sense of cosmic duty. (This false thinking caused deserts to form in the inner ecosystem of their spiritual realities.)

Also in this same area of Asia there was already another earth-human from Atlantis who belonged to that highly learned society called *Akhaldans*. (I believe Swedenborg would have called these Akhaldans, *Noachian*—the representatives of the "Church of Noah," who possessed divine heavenly teachings that became their "Ark.") Beelzebub states that the Akhaldan society possessed the greatest knowledge among the Atlantians (the greatest knowledge of those who had a genuine spiritual conscience).

This special society of Atlantians also sensed that something bad was going to happen but couldn't put a finger on it. So they sent various members of their society out to the other continents and islands, including this particular individual, to make detailed observations of the various phenomena occurring there in the hope of finding out what bad outcomes lie ahead in the future for them all.

This particular member of the Akhaldan society eventually hooked up with the Pirmaral hunters in Asia who had also once been citizens of Atlantis. Shortly afterward, the continent Atlantis sank and this special individual had no place to return. However, because of his great wisdom he was later named chief among the hunters there and even married one of the hunters' daughters.

(For me, Gurdjieff makes the sequence of this story difficult to follow but it caused me to make extra personal effort, which I am grateful for.)

Much time passed until we get to the current point in this story when Beelzebub makes his third visit to the planet Earth, and where he witnessed the arising of this new center of civilization existing in the same place known as the Gobi Desert.

Now a new king is ruling there who, coincidentally, was the "grandson of the great grandson" of the king who had become the original leader for the Pirmaral hunters. This new king's name was Konuzion. The inheritance of duty for this new king included the invention of a new "religious doctrine." How this new religious doctrine came about is what Beelzebub now wants to share with his curious grandson.

Here, a new wrinkle is thrown into the trajectory of earth-humans' psychic decline that went deeper than the hunting and killing of Pirmarals.

At the time when King Konuzion was ruling over this developing new territory in Asia, he began to notice a strange behavior among his subjects. He wanted to know why this was. And he found out (and seemingly, this was the bad outcome that the Akhaldans sensed was coming to their planet).

The "grandson of the great grandson" of the King symbolically represents the remnants of great knowledge passed on down from the original Akhaldan society of Atlantis to continue as ruling principles (again, Swedenborg would identify this great knowledge as the ancient knowledge of the Noachian Church, which represented their "Ark" or divine lifeboat). This important knowledge included the proper *duties* of three-brained beings within God's grand universal scheme. This sacred scheme began to be seriously challenged by the deteriorating manifestations of many of Konuzion's subjects. King Konuzion began to notice that many beings in his community were becoming *less useful* and *lazy*. Simultaneously, crimes such as robbery and violence were on the increase.

The King eventually discovered that this negative change in the psyche of many of his subjects came from their chewing on the mind-altering seeds of the poppy plant (symbolizing dreamlike thoughts and feelings that calm our conscience with pleasurable effects, but keep us from our true—and more difficult—God-given duties and challenges).

At first, the King devised various punishments and fines, which he discovered had only a temporary effect and things eventually became much worse for the kingdom. Even those who never chewed on poppy seeds before, now began to do so from mere curiosity. This activity for obtaining "bliss" (without much effort) among his subjects was threatening the greatness of his community and especially its treasury.

Beelzebub then explains to Hassein that the King realized external punishments alone, even executions, were not the solution to the loss of spiritual conscience and cosmic duty among his subjects. He then felt the need to invent and interject a new and deeper dictate, such as a "religious doctrine" into their psyches (as a replacement for their now submerged *inner dictate* called conscience).

The King's new and ingenious religious doctrine stated that far from his subject's own continent of Asia was an even more special island that "Mister God" existed on. God had given humans physical bodies merely to help in carrying out certain cosmic duties so that when they died, their "souls" would be taken directly to this blissful land flowing with milk and honey (and well-stocked with beautiful women of all races). In this disease-free "Island Paradise" everyone's needs would be forever taken care of, including unlimited dishes made from poppy plants and hemp. The King based his inventive ideas from his realization that for his new religious doctrine to take hold, it would have to be cleverly described as a place of *eternal pleasure.*

However, this new religious doctrine (of coercion) also pointed out that on another, smaller island, God sends the souls who lived their physical lives in idleness and not according to His Commandments. This place of great pain and suffering was called "Hell." Furthermore, God gets his information about everyone from attendant "spirits" who continually spy on each one of us. While invisible to us, these spirits see absolutely everything we are doing—or not doing (kinda like Santa Claus).

This strategy by the king worked beautifully because it corresponded to the weaknesses of his subject's psyches at that time in history! (Swedenborg's direct observations of the "beyond" showed him that *duty, usefulness,* and *utility* from those individuals who have made the conscious choices to do so is continued in spiritual society and not from spies. This chosen mutual support is what makes Heaven a heaven and offers true eternal happiness—rather than just bodily pleasure—which is the only thing the King's subjects understood.)

It was long after this King's death that Beelzebub made his third visit to the planet Earth, and his first visit to this particular part of

Asia (where the second major grouping of individuals were breeding) that is now called the Gobi desert.

Once again he set out to make friends with someone in this community to get the "lay of the land." He becomes friends with the proprietor of a large drinking establishment where many citizens congregate. He next makes himself familiar with the manners and customs of this second Asian group, including some of the finer details of the special "religious doctrine" of theirs (invented by the former King) that was now in "full bloom." From his observations and research of this particular Asian group, Beelzebub decides to cleverly add an "extra modification" to this popular religion in order for him to attain his aim of completely destroying the horrible ritual of sacrificing animals.

Beelzebub feels he can convince everyone that the actual "spirits" who are spying on everyone in the community and who report back to Mister God are the very animals they are killing during their rituals. So, instead of killing these innocent lives, earth-humans ought to win over the favor of these creatures so that they can give Mister God a favorable report on them.

Beelzebub starts planting this extra idea into the head of his new friend who then immediately begins to repent and begins preaching this new doctrinal wrinkle to all the customers at his drinking establishment. (Swedenborg discovered that *tipsiness* and *drunkenness* symbolized inner states where one can only believe what can be grasped sensuously.) Soon this idea and its "indubitable truth," spreads to other establishments, including markets and holy places where other large numbers of people congregate and co-mingle.

After that, anyone treating an animal badly was attacked by mobs of people—who would rough him up a bit. Every measure was taken to see that these two-brained creatures were now well fed and watered within the city. On a more humorous note, people began listening, with reverence, to all the sounds these animals were making. When they would hear the bray of a donkey they would immediately ask for Mister God's blessings, even fall prostrate to the ground while doing so, as a sign of their sincerity.

(Humans are indeed capable of such foolishness from some strong principle of *suggestibility* and egoistic, self-centered belief.)

Ahoon, Beelzebub's longtime faithful servant, interrupts the story and jumps into the discussion. He reminds Beelzebub how comical it was that in order to not raise suspicion or unwanted attention to themselves while on the planet Earth, they too would flop to the ground along with everyone else whenever a creature made some sound or another. (Remember, Gurdjieff began to consciously escape this form of mechanical slavery, when as a young lad, he unexpectedly skipped and sang a silly verse at his grandmother's otherwise solemn funeral service.)

Beelzebub admits that there were times that he was unable to refrain from bursting into laughter when earth-humans acted out in this way but was always careful not to offend anyone, since it was against all morality to outrage anybody's religious sensitivities or belief systems (more political correctness?).

He adds that because of the abnormal conditions of ordinary external existence now on the planet Earth, no honest individual who resists acting absurdly will ever become famous or even be simply noticed. (Today, many people obtain their celebrity status from doing outrageous and questionable things.)

Beelzebub also observes that earth-humans at this time in history were becoming incessant liars.

After feeling that he had accomplished his goal of destroying the horrible religious practice of animal sacrifice among these particular Asiatic people, Beelzebub next takes aim at Pearl-land, now called India.

Again, Beelzebub himself symbolizes a primal striving to lawfully return back to the Creator and source of all reality—from a fallen state. This is the cosmic duty of all three-brained beings (including earth-humans) in the universe. So he strives to help the human race on Earth as the proper repentant means toward working out his own ultimate salvation. Swedenborg calls this conscious decision toward repentance (and inner purification) true charity toward the neighbor and love toward God.

SUMMARY

■ Beelzebub, after his divine pardon, feels he needs to return to the planet Earth for another visit in order to complete his task of eliminating animal sacrifice from religious rituals.

■ He now comes in contact with a second major group of earth-humans who settled in Asia as a result of the sinking of "Atlantis." They are moving further away from the influence of their God-given conscience.

■ Worship is becoming more external.

■ Another "evil" makes itself known, due to the further diminishing of the human psyche in this group of earth-humans—*laziness*, through the chewing of poppy seeds and seeking only physical comfort and pleasure.

■ Prior to this visit, the king of this second Asian community discovered that external punishments were not enough to replace humankind's loss of conscience and responsibility. So the king invents a new "religious doctrine" for his lazy subjects, which will provide a new kind of *inner dictate* to guide their actions. This "invented" religious doctrine worked, and even survives in various forms in many people's minds, to this day.

■ On this visit, Beelzebub decides to add an extra idea to this newly invented religion that will stop worshippers from making animal sacrifices. While the idea stops this horrible practice, earth-humans begin acting in a way toward all animals that becomes a "comical farce."

■ If we fail to notice (and laugh at) our silly actions in life, Beelzebub is more than willing to do it for us.

■ Also, earth-humans are becoming more egotistically proud and touchy, having no patience for those who criticize their manifestations. Individuals have also learned that the more ridiculous they act, the more noticed and thus, more famous they become (sound like anyone you may know?).

CHAPTER 21

"The first visit of Beelzebub to India"

There are other "comical farces" when it comes to human behavior.

This chapter does not bode well, spiritually, for people who adorn their exteriors with body tattoos or body jewelry. Being outwardly "cool" and promoting "specialness" to get noticed is a form of lying and stupidity that keeps people from making the appropriate efforts toward genuine *inner* transformation.

What efforts am I alluding to?

When Gurdjieff was running his *Institute For The Harmonious Development of Man* in France, he had the uncanny knack of finding, within any group of people, those who would experience the most friction and grief when paired up with each other. These people would often and "miraculously" find themselves in close quarters and working together on a particular project or challenge—with the very individual who most annoyed them! There was even a particular Russian individual among their work group in France who was so annoying to all the rest of the students that Gurdjieff actually paid him to stay and continue bothering people. (Apparently, he made a horrible sound with his teeth and tongue, which would force all those around him to have to make extra efforts toward maintaining their own spiritual gyroscope, composure and inner peace).

That was Gurdjieff's brilliance. He would always supply his followers with personal shocks in order to get them to make fresh (and appropriate) observations concerning the actual status and quality of their inner worlds. Since *Beelzebub's Tales* would be published after his death, Gurdjieff knew the book would have to be written in a style that would continue this unflattering strategy in order to point out people's self-pride, touchiness and resentfulness toward others. (Critics of Gurdjieff always felt that such a strategy was the opposite of love. Actually, it was the opposite of titillation.)

With that said, in Chapter 21, Gurdjieff promises to give away his biggest secret toward approaching our God-given cosmic duty, and the fastest, most productive way to apply this duty to our everyday lives. This highly concentrated technique is the "bitter pill" that we all have to swallow for obtaining sincere personal transformation. It has to do with abrasive conditions between people mentioned in the above paragraph.

Beelzebub's story continues with his desire for additional travel to end the religious ritual of animal sacrifice also occurring in Pearl-land (India), whose population represented the third major religious group in Asia. The reason why the area of this next group of Asians was called "Pearl-land" is because lots of pearls could be harvested from its surrounding waters. Asians from other neighboring communities considered these pearls vary rare and valuable.

In order to further elucidate for Hassein the peculiarities of the abnormal psyche of these Asian types, Beelzebub shares his opinion that these earth-humans turned these pearls into "precious trinkets" from an instinctive need to offset the "value-of-their-inner-insignificance." This psychic peculiarity of self-adornment (calling attention to one's outer being) was also a consequence of the properties of their organ Kundabuffer, which, as was pointed out earlier, made them see reality in an inverted or upside-down way (heaven below and the physical world above).

Swedenborg claimed to have actually seen individuals in the spiritual world who lived in an *inverted* position (because they had an inverted mental orientation).

After a month's overland travel by caravan, Beelzebub and his faithful servant Ahoon came to the City of "Kaimon" in Pearl-land. Beelzebub now finds it necessary to give his grandson a little history lesson about this third group of Asians living in India. It seems that not long after the hunters of Pirmarals from Atlantis settled on their new continent, this third group of Asiatic beings had overharvested pearls and killed off all the oysters from the waters around Atlantis for their own self-gratification and egoism.

Hmmm... So like the group of Pirmaral hunters, these "diving" professionals also moved on to other "richer" pastures, but in their case, to new water-areas where pearl-producing creatures could still be found.

Speaking symbolically, we have another group of people and another religion that appears on Earth by a "migration" moving further away from the original continent of Atlantis (which represented a genuine church with genuine knowledge). This move represents another *psychic* change, and a migration of *beliefs* away from an original (and more genuine) belief system, in which conscience (inner dictates) once ruled at the core of human activities—but now no longer.

The particular earth-humans of this third group had abused (overharvesting pearls) the knowledge of God's living influence in their memory-noggins, where what they knew no longer had any connection with true spiritual living. So pearls lost their inner value and instead, gained a new outer value.

Continuing the allegory, Beelzebub says that a "storm" (the dispersion of divine order and displacement of objective truth) brought their search rafts to this new *land* (state of mind). Both Pirmaral hunters and pearl divers of these two Asiatic groups chose to swap their now emptied-out inner worlds for a more external and fabricated one.

This change of continents reflected the changes taking place deeper within these Asians' *inner* (psycho-spiritual) ecology. So even when Beelzebub is describing outer geological features of the Earth and formation of new land masses he is only using these physical descriptions to illustrate the things going on deeper in the inner ecologies of the human heart (will) and mind (understanding). That is the only way to portray the more important *inner history* of earth-humans.

Beelzebub now decides that he can stop the senseless destruction of other creatures by this third major group of three-centered Asian humans by again adding a new twist to their religious teachings. But this group of Asians had many, many religious teachings among their large population, so he decides to focus on studying the teachings of Saint Buddha, who had the largest following there.

He tells Hassein that there are two basic kinds of religion on Earth.

One is completely man-made (fabricated) and has its origins from the organ Kundabuffer, which engendered fantasy in earth-humans. The other comes directly from the Creator/God, and the various genuine Messengers (prophets) God sent to Earth to assist its inhabitants in destroying the many negative consequences of the properties of the organ Kundabuffer that had become fixed into their psyche (like seeing reality upside down from a self-centered perspective).

Without grasping the significance of the organ Kundabuffer (and its effects on the human psyche), one will never grasp the need nor make the correct approach to achieving spiritual liberation. (Today, we still overlook our negative properties by simply engaging in acts of *outward* goodness. This approach is fabrication and spurious, rather than acts of genuine spiritual charity and love.)

So even though the physical structure of this maleficent organ had been later removed from the base of the human spinal column, its various inclinations and compulsions, were still planted (fixed) into the human heart and mind from habit— until its negative influences became *second nature*.

Saint Buddha attempted to explain all this to earth-humans in his religious teachings.

According to Beelzebub, Saint Buddha was a genuine messenger sent by God to this part of the Earth's surface to specifically help these Asiatic beings remove these negative properties (that were upsetting the normal flow of universal cooperation and order). Buddha's strategy was to lead these earth-humans into freedom through the *increased enlightenment of their Reason*.

Taking in the fact that these earth-humans had their reasoning function inverted at that time, to the point where they no longer could be reached on the deeper level of *conscience*, but only through external/literal teachings, Saint Buddha had to devise special *external* doctrines of "Truth" more suitable to influencing their cockeyed worldly (and inferior), corporeal/sensual cognitive functioning. This Prophet had to teach them with stern *warnings*.

One of the warnings that came from the new teachings of Saint Buddha was that these unfortunate Asians were all victims of an unforeseen accident in the past that required *higher beings* to introduce a new organ into their ancestors, to alleviate any bad consequences (like a full rebellion) from ever upsetting universal processes and their required harmony.

According to Beelzebub's discoveries, Saint Buddha's original teachings included this cosmic explanation of why the superfluous organ Kundabuffer was allowed, by higher-ups, to be formed within the planetary bodies of their ancestors—an organ whose "artificial" properties caused a change in their cognitive functioning to make them perceive reality incorrectly. (This perfectly parallels Swedenborg's descriptions of the later stages of those humans living in the *Golden Age*, who began to prefer gaining knowledge on their own— from the external world. This sensual inclination for self-guidance still holds today and is symbolically represented by the Serpent who was forced to crawl on the ground—on its belly, that is—to be closer to the Earth and totally immersed in physical inputs. This represents a psycho-spiritual inversion).

Buddha also taught that although this maleficent organ was later removed in their ancestors by a similar angelic intervention, its predisposition remained as a permanent fixture in their cognitive functioning (just like Adam's rib—which was turned into "Eve"—and has become a permanent fixture and partner in our unregenerated hearts and minds). These predispositions are now passed on through heredity and keep getting worse in each new human generation.

While Saint Buddha offered a genuine system by which earth-humans could successfully escape the inherited influences of the former organ Kundabuffer, his own eventual death and departure from Earth caused many three-brained beings to return to their old "Hasnamuss" (non-regenerative, self-delusional) habits. In fact, things went from bad to worse when these earth-humans began to distort Saint Buddha's original and actual teachings. This distortion is an example of a man-made religion.

For instance, one of the best means for removing the negative consequences of the organ Kundabuffer is called "intentional suffering." Swedenborg identified this process as *spiritual combat* or personally choosing to allow one's self-centeredness to suffer (and die) by sincere self-examination, repentance, doing God's will, and in loving others. This "voluntary death" produces proper humility and an increase in *innocence*. (In fact, this is the "death before the second, or physical death" mentioned in God's Word).

And, as I promised to divulge, in the second paragraph of this very chapter, Gurdjieff's secret method in applying "intentional suffering" by the fastest possible means was to for us to willingly *endure* (to suffer oneself) the displeasing manifestations of others—especially those manifestations directed toward one's self and one's self-image.

This *inner suffering* is a necessary and lawful strategy for uprooting one's misguided self-love and self-importance. (Seeking personal affirmation and a higher self-evaluation of oneself from others only thwarts this purifying activity from taking place, and leads to another comical farce.)

Pearl necklaces don't help, either.

Anyone can see how this type of *voluntary pain* and *death*, when sincerely and consciously pursued, can't fail to promote spiritual *innocence* and a greater sensitivity toward genuine neighborly love or *love of kind*. (Nor can it be accomplished in isolation—where one cannot be properly challenged.)

This practice of "enduring" another's manifestations is Gurdjieff's big secret to spiritual transformation. This practice also allows one to increase the accumulation of positive data by which the *active force* of God's three holy forces can properly counter and even overrule one's *denying* or *passive* forces (which the organ Kundabuffer exaggerated from its original location at the base of the human spine). Without such conscious (active) efforts and corresponding (passive) opposition, one could not carry out or fulfill their eternal duty in the universe or expect to evolve spiritually in any kind of lawful manner. Rather, spiritual transformation would become only an imaginary and dreamlike thing.

According to Beelzebub, a special kind of "endurance" was created in those individuals who consciously and intentionally participated in this self-conflict (spiritual combat). An individual who has sufficiently developed this special inner (spiritual) endurance lives beyond worldly identification (or as Swedenborg would say, is "of the world" but not "in it") and the desire for projecting of a false self-image to others for the sake of popularity and greater acceptance.

Swedenborg also claimed that God's Word uses the term "endurance" to have the exact same *inner* meaning of spiritual combat, which is necessary for humankind to *conjoin* internal and external parts of their dual being (*Apocalypse Explained*, n. 156). This contact, between inner and outer influences in humans, is a psychical bridal chamber, and not easily grasped or acknowledged by those who wrongly believe that their mental functions are already unified with their hearts, rather than discretely split (divorced). As a result it becomes quite difficult to get people to acknowledge the false self-image of their individuality. Swedenborg further describes this special inner contact as a *conjunction between knowledge and goodness*, each of which enters through its own distinct doorway or gate (upper and lower) in the human mind. (Also see *Apocalypse Explained,* Vol. 1, n. 208a.)

But after Saint Buddha's own death and departure, earth-beings, just two generations later, began to "concoct" their own self-deluded versions of this special kind of "endurance" into their religious doctrines. (Through the divine guidance in his great work *Apocalypse Explained* [n. 149], Swedenborg properly described this spiritual *endurance* as connecting the internal and external human minds through a form of self-suffering and combat called *temptations.*)

Connecting? Split minds? Yep!

Not only are earth-humans oblivious to their having a split dual nature (after the sinking of Atlantis), they have also decided that instead of applying this special endurance and sacred suffering while in the presence of others in their community, they would seek solitude and form monasteries where they could "save their souls" in a more private (and hidden) setting. (Swedenborg, in Chapter 55 of his popular book *Heaven & Hell,* concurred that acquiring spiritual life was to be done while living among others.)

The practice of isolation from the world removes people from experiencing the necessary *irritations* of life. (An oyster makes pearls from *irritation,* but after earth-humans removed this important inner consideration from their psyche by "over-harvesting" them for quick profit, they took irritation out of the equation. Buddha was sent to fix this condition.)

I have also heard that "wisdom" can only be used where it is gained. If wisdom is gained somewhere isolated from other people— like on a mountain top—it cannot be used around people in the city below, and therefore, would no longer be considered real wisdom or evoke perpetual spiritual compassion.

Beelzebub tells Hassein that if Saint Buddha himself could return again to that same place on Earth, he would not ever suspect that the current ideas of Indian philosophy could have come from his original teachings.

Another misunderstanding also took place concerning Saint Buddha's teachings with these abnormal three-brained beings of that part of Asia. They began believing that they could re-emerge (unify) with the wholeness of the universe by absorbing a unique substance called "Holy Prana" (literally, God particles).

Unfortunately, later generations of deluded earth-humans believed that this healthy Holy Prana is naturally activated within each of them from birth and continues to develop without their essence-responsibility of self-examination or any inner effort to change anything about themselves.

But the terrifying danger of this belief is that they never suspect that this special *holy substance (God's Love),* which they believe is so valuable and always working within them, will only blend with one's individual proclivities (and chosen affections)—which can be good or bad.

So, we must be careful and vigilant that this spiritual substance participates only in the proper growth of our spiritual reasoning and life values. (Without spiritual conscience, human free will can distort the action of this spiritual substance within us because it will flow into any passion or wish and give it life.) Swedenborg was a strong proponent that we had to discover our actual motives and compare these motives with heavenly dictates.

Beelzebub then tells Hassein that it was in the distorted teaching about this Most-Sacred-Prana that he found another opportunity to add a new detail that was designed to discourage earth-humans from destroying one- and two-brained creatures. So he began to spread his extraneous invention of Buddha's idea that this sacred unifying substance not only already existed within them, but within all the other living creatures as well. Very quickly this changed the relationships these Asiatic beings had with other life forms. Great care was made in people's lives not to accidently step on even the smallest bug!

According to Beelzebub, only one thing survived intact from Saint Buddha's authentic teachings—the first half of the word *Kundabuffer*. In more recent times this word was changed to "Kundalina" from coincidental etymology and poor translation—where it took on a new meaning as representing something "good to activate." In other works that I have read, Gurdjieff stated that activating Kundalina was not a good thing. It is our enemy. It represents the involving force in us to pervert reality and to fantasize (it is the representation of the "Moon" within us[7]). Swedenborg concurred that reflective light (which the Moon manifests) was not the real thing and often represents the intelligence or head-knowledge of worldly men—*or natural faith detached from spiritual faith*. (This is also why, the biblical Revelation chapter and sacred text of Holy Scripture depicts a pregnant woman standing "above" the moon.)

This involving force causes our life energy to pass us by (our essential being) and move toward a more external *center of gravity* in our psyche, creating a form of "lunacy" and delusion (imagined reality through false self-importance and thinking). This lunacy is the false belief that the knowledge stuffed into our memories represents who we really are—rather than our life-choices and actions do. The main properties of the organ Kundabuffer are to keep us from seeing the inconsistencies between what we know and how we actually behave, which would quickly upset our calm and our self-importance.

Beelzebub ends this chapter of his Tales by telling his grandson that much of "Indian philosophy" is now based on this word *Kundalina*, which no longer explains anything of real value.

---

7. *Views from the Real World: Early Talks of Gurdjieff,* page 102, 198

SUMMARY

■ Jewelry, such as that created from "valuable" pearls, became merely fabricated baubles to cover over people's inner nullity.

■ This inner nullity came from earth-humans and their belief systems migrating away from a state of genuine conscience (the over-hunting in Atlantis).

■ Saint Buddha was sent by the Creator-God to help the people on this part of the Earth's surface to reverse the properties fixed into their psyches by the organ Kundabuffer. This reversal is now the essential human responsibility and duty in God's created universe (and is the true purpose of all religion).

■ Buddha informs this Asiatic group of how the organ Kundabuffer was originally implanted in their ancestors to preserve harmony and then was later removed. However, its properties of fantasy must still be rooted out from the human psyche.

■ This third Asiatic group (in India) and its derivative religious practice began to misinterpret Saint Buddha's concept of "endurance," especially after his death. And they began building isolated monasteries for developing this spiritual ability of inner combat, instead of enduring the manifestations from living among other earth-citizens in their towns and cities. This isolation causes an individual to throw away much valuable material that could be available for one's genuine work of redemption.

■ One finds his or her proper wisdom (and endurance) from where one providentially finds oneself living among other human beings.

■ Later generations misunderstood Saint Buddha's explanation of Holy Prana, as well. Unfortunately, this sacred substance flows into everyone's Ruling Love, vivifying it and giving it life. So it has to be acquired only through proper spiritual transformation.

■ Beelzebub uses this misunderstanding to put a stop to animal sacrifices in India by instilling a new belief that all animals had this "Holy Prana" as well, and therefore should not be destroyed.

■ The word *Kundalina* came from a misinterpretation of the word *Kundabuffer*. Today, people wrongly believe (and imagine) that activating "Kundalina" is a positive thing according to Indian philosophy. But it leads to fantasy (and lunacy).

CHAPTER 22

"Beelzebub for the first time in Tibet"

Beelzebub decides next to take an unexpected detour through the land now called Tibet. (So his third visit to the planet Earth included visits to three destinations—Gob, India and now Tibet.)

He continues his story concerning the ill-fated planet Earth with his grandson by telling Hassein that he next organized his own caravan to make the perilous journey to Tibet. The reason for the peril was the constant threat of lions, tigers and hyenas at nighttime. While such threats in a wilderness journey seem expected, there is good reason to conjecture here that this scenario also parallels the dangers to the human psyche when it makes its various life-journeys in a state of cognitive obscurity and darkness (a mental state of night-time), which makes one prone to attacks from non-human emotions (deadly beasts). And sure enough, Beelzebub hints that his caravan helpers were only involved in *semiconscious* work (half-awake) to accomplish this dangerous mode of life travel.

Eventually Beelzebub's caravan came to an early settlement called "Sincratorza" or Tibet. These Asian people had come from India and settled in this remote part of the world in order to remove from themselves the negative consequences of the properties of the organ Kundabuffer, according to their own (flawed) interpretation of the instructions of Saint Buddha concerning self-suffering and building personal "endurance." (While conscious self-suffering is a legitimate strategy for spiritual transformation it can be approached incorrectly, as happens when one choses to do this special suffering in solitude.)

Beelzebub states in passing that no sooner does a new religion arise on Earth than it splits into various sects or schisms and the sect with the greatest "firepower" (guns and weapons) becomes the mainstream religion. This split in religion is again a natural consequence of the divided human psyche, especially after spiritual conscience becomes buried and disappears. Beelzebub calls the two main splits "Orthodoxhydooraki" and "Katoshkihydooraki." (Similar "splits" have even happened within the current Swedenborgian Church.)

The sect Beelzebub focuses on in Tibet are the Orthodoxhydooraki group of worshippers called the "Self-tamers." Their particular distortion of the original Buddhist religion involved purifying their souls through "suffering-in-solitude."

They had developed a form of *isolated* suffering that involved locking "deserving" individuals into special chambers where they were completely shut off from the outside world—except for small openings where a little bread and water was given them daily. These "deserving" individuals were to go through this purging of their thoughts and emotions and suffering process until their eventual physical deaths occurred, whereupon they would theoretically re-blend with the "All-Embracing Holy Prana" in the universe. Next, someone else would get their turn to purify themselves in solitude and immurement in these special "sentry-box" chambers. These isolated places for self-suffering were called *monasteries*.

A schism and split from this sect (creating the "Katoshki-hydooraki") occurred because the families, and particularly the wives of these individuals, rebelled against this unnatural procedure and renounced its obligations. This schism became more lax with the rules.

Here, Beelzebub also points out another peculiar psychic need by the adherents (fanatics) of various religions to become skillful in creating special arcana for their doctrine, whereby it will always remain as a "mystery" to outsiders and thus be safe from all rational criticism. (Swedenborg calls this concocted obscurity in religion the "Mysteries of Faith" but said that it was also now time for deep religious principles, and their mysteries, to be explored by the human rational and critical mind. In fact, he stated that it was the Lord God's Divine wish to reveal heavenly secrets to the comprehension of earth-humans. The resulting new spiritual understanding represents a "Second Coming.")

Now Beelzebub further addresses the foolish idea of trying to find cosmic fulfillment in solitude to his grandson. He asserts that the foolishness behind this fanatical monastic immurement is unmasked by the fact that all genuine spiritual growth is to proceed while one is among other similar beings and when fully engaged in social life. (Swedenborg stresses this point in his book *Heaven & Hell*, Chapter 55, and that spiritual growth should occur while living in the world and not isolated from it.) And as I said earlier, a person can only use his or her wisdom in the same place where they found that wisdom. Any wisdom found in solitude can only be used in solitude and would not work in the midst of a populated, bustling city. Besides, such solitude spares an individual from the true spiritual work of gaining compassion—which includes *enduring* the manifestations of others, especially when these manifestations are directed at one's self and self-image ("turning the other cheek").

But these unfortunate Asiatic beings believed they were following the exact instructions of Saint Buddha. Instead, the foolish properties of the organ Kundabuffer (Swedenborg's human *proprium*) were being drafted to solve the foolish properties of the organ Kundabuffer. (Ego does not lead one out of ego.)

As Beelzebub finally departs from the sad and melancholy monasteries of Tibet to return to the planet Mars, he remarks about the great height of the mountains there (Himalayan mountains). He tells Hassein that these mountains were even higher by the time he made his sixth and final visit to Earth.

A big clue that these growing mountains symbolized some human abnormality and vanity rising to new "heights" is Beelzebub's statement that one could climb to the top of these mountains, and with the assistance of a telescope, see clear across to the other side of the planet Earth. This absurd statement could only rationally (as a *lawful inexactitude*) refer to the great height to which human pride will rise (like the Tower of Babel) with people's self-delusional conviction of being "know-it-alls."

Beelzebub tells Hassein that he feels the abnormal height of this mountain range contributed to planetary earthquakes and could possibly lead to the planet Earth experiencing some future misfortune (just as human vanity can lead to a *shaky* life and even to one's future demise). His explanation is that the excessive elevations of these mountains could eventually push the influence of the Earth's atmosphere ("Blastegoklornian-circumference") far enough out into space that it will "hook onto" other planets and comets of the solar system—leading to planetary tremors and earthquakes from the resulting astronomical tensions.

Everything is connected!

Therefore, the haughty nature of humans can spread its sphere of influence and become contagious to other humans throughout the universe and cause real tensions in all their relationships and world-views. (Swedenborg also agreed that earth-humans could poison the spheres of all other humans, spirits and angels in existence. And indeed this was happening before the Lord God Himself came into the world to battle these contagions—inside and out. Swedenborg even observed human spirits from other planets not wanting to have anything to do with any earth-human spirits.)

Beelzebub tells Hassein that he feels sure that before these lofty mountains can become a further menace to the Earth and its solar system, appropriate measures will be taken by some future angelic committee to remedy the situation.

The servant Ahoon suddenly jumps into the discussion by telling Beelzebub and Hassein that during earlier conversations with certain angelic beings, he had heard that the problem of the abnormal growth of certain elevations on planet Earth were indeed brought to the attention of our ALL-GRACIOUS-ENDLESSNESS who immediately dispatched an archangel to look into the matter (a big hint that this issue of abnormality on Earth actually refers to spiritual and psychical matters).

Hearing this new heavenly news from Ahoon helps to alleviate some of Beelzebub's anxiety about the possible bad future and complete destruction of the planet "Earth" (symbolizing the Lord's church).

Beelzebub then goes on to tell Hassein that he returned to Mars and that a long time passed between his third and forth visits to Earth (a lengthened interval in a sevenfold process?). He is content just to observe the Earth from time to time through his special telescope that magnifies objects by 7,285,000 times. Instead, Beelzebub becomes more interested and totally consumed in the operations on Mars to build water canals.

Real water canals on Mars?!!

While both Gurdjieff and Swedenborg promoted the idea that human-type beings lived throughout the universe, including the planet Mars, I have no direct experience of this challenging matter of Martian canals to move water. However, I can attempt to look for deeper meanings within these fantastic disclosures.

Beelzebub ends the chapter by seemingly going off-topic—way off topic—with some very bizarre and incomprehensible statements concerning the planet Mars' surface—that it is *half land* and *half water*. Hmmm... Is most of this water held in the planet's soil? It is my belief that Gurdjieff is burying the dog deeper, yet again, and providing unique new symbols to express God's universal holistic process.

He describes the planet Mars as representing a "Mdnel-outian link" within the holistic economy or exchange of substances of that solar system. (Since a *"Mdnel-In"* is an aperture to allow outside forces to enter into a system and feed it, I assume a *Mdnel-outian link* acts to jettison unnecessary and non-useful material from the system.) Mars may symbolize a place in our particular planetary solar system where non-compliant and heterogenous (wrong) ideas and influences are purified or removed.

Apparently, because of this "excretion" or purging function of acting as a *Mdnel-outian link* within the greater organic scheme of a solar system (that always follows a universal hominine design) the surface of Mars becomes problematic for growing "wheat," since little water is directly available for this crop to mature (ascending or evolving "Djartklom" is hard to maintain on a planet that functions to promote descending and outgoing influences in the solar system). The building of the special canals, therefore, is to irrigate the "wheat." Symbolically speaking, bread and wheat represent *heavenly food* by which the human race can be provided with the divine nutrients that lead to an *advancing state of Love*.

Beelzebub's preoccupation with the building of these complex canals possibly symbolizes the careful and conscious effort necessary to ensure the success of this important process through constructing channels of communication—for truth to flow (spiritual water) and ensure the proper growth, watering and cultivation of spiritual life. (I have to confess that if Gurdjieff is using allegory here, it may well be above my pay grade to decipher.)

Swedenborg doesn't offer me easy help here with any satisfying interpretation, either. But he does say that all things in the created world tend to the human form and its relative functions (ultimately forming a "Grand Human" bio-organization of connected societies in the Spiritual World) and even describes Mars as representing a mediating influence in the Grand Human design (*The Earths In The Universe*, n. 88). On the smaller scale of the individual human mind, this mediating influence (just like *conscience*) is between the human intellect and human will—anatomically speaking, between the voluntary cerebrum and the involuntary cerebellum. Now symbolically speaking, a function that mediates between the human heart and intellect would be similar to a canal connecting a planet's water supply with its landmass.

I believe that those who inwardly live in such a psychical mediating "province," in which conscience connects knowledge (water) with Love (land), are incapable of dissimilation and pretense (and therefore automatically reject or excrete false ideas and principles). But these symbolic details (and my conjecture) will at best only obscure the story, so I will move on.

SUMMARY

According to Beelzebub, groups and families of Asians moved from India to Tibet in order to create the isolated onditions for "suffering-in-solitude," so that they could absorb more "Holy Prana" and become a particle or unit of everything existing.

This is a mistake and did not accurately reflect Saint Buddha's original teachings.

The fastest method for spiritual growth is enduring the manifestations of others toward yourself. In other words, we must make our best spiritual efforts while in the company of others—even those we do not like or agree with.

Beelzebub, using symbolic language, implies that not only is Tibet's abnormally high mountain range responsible for most of the Earth's planetary tensions, but these same tensions are experienced and symbolized within the abnormal and "heightened" human ego.

Also using metaphor and symbolic language, I believe that the building of "canals on Mars" represents the psycho-spiritual connecting and mediating operations of conscience, which conjoins intellectual knowledge to our heart's affections and actual behavior.

CHAPTER 23

"The fourth personal sojourn of Beelzebub on the planet Earth"

Chapter 23 is a rather long chapter relative to the others and full of additional "shocks" to open up the reader's mind from mental snoozing. This chapter will certainly give each *gender* a whack on the head! But it is also quite hilarious.

Beelzebub tells Hassein that the reason for his fourth trip to the planet Earth came out of further discussions with his essence-friend from the Planet Saturn, named Gornahoor (Mister) Harharkh. Gornahoor Harharkh had helped in the design of Beelzebub's powerful telescope and had also become highly interested in the observations made of the strange three-centered beings living on the planet Earth.

Beelzebub often made visits to Saturn to enjoy the company of his essence-friend, Harharkh, and carry on with various conversations. This again may be pure conjecture on my part, but it seems that when Beelzebub visits various planets he uses words like *ascends* and *descends*. (This tells my Swedenborgian mind that the planets represent and correspond to different planes—higher or lower—of inner experience and a quality of consciousness. In his unique work *The Earths In The Universe*, Swedenborg even specifies that the men-beings on Mars are spiritually superior to all others in the solar system. So from Earth, one would "ascend" to the plane of Mars to experience its superior spiritual quality.)

During one of their "subjective exchanges of opinion" or conversations, Gornahoor Harkarkh asked Beelzebub if he could again make a special visit to Earth and bring back creatures there called "apes" for his own scientific investigations.

At this precise point in Beelzebub's story he receives a coinciding message— an "etherogram" from Mars stating that the men-beings on Earth, especially in a place called America, had just revived the agitating and divisive topic called the "Ape question." The agitation resulted from conflicting theories as to whether humans emerged from apes or that apes emerged from humans. (The answer has spiritual significance.)

To this message, Beelzebub informs his grandson that this very same debate first began after the sinking of Atlantis and in the Asian civilization called "Tikliamish (Caucasus and the Fertile Crescent).

The earth-humans who were considered "educated," and later arose on planet Earth after the disappearance of Atlantis, were called by Beelzebub "learned beings of new formation." In other words, they had a new kind of psyche from those who had preceded them—a warped psyche from the inherited influences of the organ Kund-abuffer, which left them highly prone to wiseacring (bullshitting) and fantasy. (This warped psyche even includes the post-modern human mind and academia of the 21st century.)

According to Beelzebub, one of these newly formed "learned beings" or "freaks" (*Hasnamuss* individuals) named Menitkel, who was financially secure from an inheritance left by his rich father (who was a pawn shop proprietor), began during his excessive downtime, to concoct an elaborate theory concerning the origins of these "fellow apes" by providing many so-called "logical proofs" that these strange creatures descended from "people who became wild." In his theory, therefore, apes were given the same *spiritual status* and importance as three-brained beings.

(There are naturalist/scientists today whose research again seems to be blurring the differences between humans and apes—because some apes can use sticks as tools. This extends to the notion that dogs, and our precious pets, all go to heaven. I even had a highly intelligent and educated person once tell me that she could see the "wisdom" in a frog's eyes—despite the fact that frogs live in mud, eat bugs and the lusting males gang attack female frogs.)

Over time, the ape question disappeared, but Beelzebub informs Hassein that because of the *periodicity* inherent in the cosmic funda-mental law of Heptaparaparshinok (Sevenfoldness), this question of who is descended from whom, periodically (and lawfully) re-emerges from the abnormal Reason of these three-brained beings of *new formation*.

One new stimulus for the revival of the ape question was a great learned-being on Earth named Darwin, who from the same warped (and Hasnamuss) reasoning, came up with a completely opposite theory—that earth-humans were descended from these "Mister apes." Such a theory among these three-brained beings now represents for them the proper knowledge by which they can obtain the "highest manifestation of Reason."

Beelzebub next offers a shocking solution by which one should properly approach the genealogical problem of how apes arose. He quotes an apparently misogynistic statement from his favorite earth-teacher, Mullah Nassr Eddin, to his eagerly listening grandson that: "The cause of every misunderstanding must be sought only in women." While the feminist movement would no doubt be appalled by such a proclamation, Beelzebub next provides an explanation of this statement that is so rich in meaning that it transcends modern social sensitivities and political correctness.

Beelzebub explains to Hassein that apes neither descended from humans or humans from apes, but instead, the blame for this misunderstanding fully falls on the shoulders of "women." (Beelzebub is referring to *psychical* females—to human affection.) The clue to this symbolic language is that the various apes that Beelzebub is referring to never existed prior to the second "Transapalnian perturbation" that caused Atlantis to be swallowed up by the sea.

The two main causes leading to the arising of these "misconceived" being-apes began way back in time from the mistakes and lack of foresight by higher, angelic beings that helped to implant the organ Kundabuffer in earth-humans to mechanically ensure cosmic harmony. (As mentioned over and over again earlier, Swedenborg confirms that this apparent heavenly "disaster" is treated in Genesis, when God puts Adam to "sleep" and allowed a diminished state of cognition to take hold of the human race—all to preserve the equilibrium necessary for humankind on Earth to continue to enjoy free will).

The second cause was the abnormal conditions of being-existence that humans established themselves, from abusing their protected free will and turning it into *license*. In other words, free will is both necessary for salvation, yet contains real hazards. "Free will" gets its marching orders from one's Ruling Love, which can be good or bad.

The story now gets ultra-symbolic (continuing the theme of the *divided* nature of the human psyche with its *male* and *female* functionings).

According to Beelzebub, when the continent of Atlantis sank, those men and women who survived and reached other land masses became separated for a time. In this separated condition, men and women embraced different methods of obtaining sexual pleasure and gratification (seeking imagined happiness). "Men" were content with artificial and anti-natural strategies for the removal of their sacred substance "Exioëhary" or sperm, such as "onanism" (masturbation) and "pederasty" (anal intercourse). I find it amusing that recent surveys show that there is increased interest in anal intercourse.

"Women" preferred more natural approaches to satisfying their impulse for pleasure (imagined completeness and happiness) and sought out beings of other forms of life to be their "partners." In some cases, due to the sacred law of Triamazikamno (threefoldness), the passive Exioëhary (ovum) of three-brained females can be impregnated by the active Exioëhary (sperm) of male two-brained beings.

The results ("Terbelnian results") of this union with improper prolific principles (seed) produces "apes," that upon observation, display various female expressions on their faces and in their "automatic postures." These apes are also quite fond of "titillation."

Whatever your reaction to this story, Gurdjieff offers the reader an interesting way to portray the diminished state (and splitting) of one's modern cognitive abilities and its genealogy (mental offspring).

He even describes this story as an enigmatic question (riddle), which we are to attempt to decipher. As I have already warned, this absurd scenario can only be understood symbolically, that is, psycho-spiritually.

Let me take a crack at it.

First of all, it is a far-fetched (even hilarious) notion that men and women could be so completely split up from each other after the sinking of Atlantis that they could no longer mingle. *So another, deeper, kind of split is being described here.* The point of this part of the story is that after the sinking of Atlantis (and the function of conscience) the human psyche became divided and disconnected. (Beelzebub is unconcerned with any issues that are not directly related to this human predicament.)

Each of us has a male and female component to our mind and each has its own form of gratification. When conscience is lost, these distinct male and female functions become split off from each other. The result of this psychical split is that the human intellect or thinking part (male aspect) of the human psyche becomes gratified by focusing on artificial or anti-natural knowledge (just data), while the human heart or feeling part (female aspect) of the human psyche is left with only primitive and undeveloped animal instincts to embrace—the level left to it in which it has some affinity or correspondence. The limited *conjunction* or "intercourse" within the female aspect of the human psyche, with its undeveloped potentials serving as the active factor, gives birth to additional primitive feelings that are half human and half animal, and on par with those of various apes. Animals *symbolize* our natural (earthly) emotions, which are undeveloped relative to spiritual affections.

In Swedenborg's deeper terms, this disconnection gives rise to the split in the human psyche into distinct exterior and *interior* levels. One level—the outer level—is artificial and the other, more interior level remains underdeveloped or primitive (again, like apes, which have a human external appearance. And no real rationality. See *Divine Providence*, n. 298 [4] [c]). We will see in a later chapter that God has provided a special means to correct this disconnected state of the human heart and mind with the "remains," which allows conscience to re-connect our inner and outer realities, and rise up back to the surface (above the subconscious) as "dry land" and develop in the light of day.

This divine strategy of conjunction allows the sacred substance Exioëhary ("sperm" and the spiritual prolific principle within it) to have the proper matrix (spiritual or mental ground) to inseminate and evolve further, functioning in a way that creates a new "angelic spiritual birth" within the individual. Beelzebub even states that this sacred prolific substance is necessary to coat higher spiritual bodies for the human soul. There is no spiritual rebirth without one creating these inner bodies.

Otherwise, in our current split state, only "apes" are created. (People that only look human.)

How can I be completely sure that this symbolic message is what was actually intended by Beelzebub's storytelling, instead of him making a seemingly insensitive misogynistic comment? Well, after finishing this part of his Tales, Beelzebub gives his grandson Hassein a "special smile," indicating that the story he had just communicated had a *double* meaning. (A double meaning means symbolism, allegory, parable or correspondence.)

We find out next that the various etherograms continuously sent to Beelzebub on his spaceship, keeping him informed of the comings and goings down on Earth, are coming from that particular member of his tribe that caused him to visit Earth in the first place. This member had now properly matured and became the tribe's leader on Mars. Beelzebub gave this tribal leader the use of his special observatory while he was away, and from sincere gratitude, promised to report monthly on what he had observed taking place on the planet Earth. This new chief and leader of their tribe also received reports from three other tribe members who decided to live covertly among the inhabitants of Earth.

Beelzebub remarks in an amusing way that these three extra-terrestrials from his tribe were in a perfect position to observe the conditions of existence on Earth because of their "special" kinds of employment. One such tribal person operated an "undertaker's business" in one Earth city, a second ran a bureau for matchmaking and divorce in another city and the third individual was the founder and proprietor of many offices, in many cities, dealing with "money exchange." (You can't beat those three occupations for getting a fix on the human situation on Earth.)

Returning to the theme of going back to the planet Earth for the fourth time to collect "apes" for his close friend Gornahoor Harharkh of Saturn, Beelzebub states that he landed on the "Red Sea" and headed toward the continent Grabontzi (Africa) and the future country Egypt, where they settled in the capital city called Thebes, and met up with other members of his tribe. The continent Africa after all, was the place on Earth with the greatest number of apes. (Africa was also one of the new *land masses* that the former inhabitants of Atlantis migrated to, and brought their new belief systems to.)

While in Thebes, Beelzebub temporarily postpones his original aim to collect various species of apes because one of his tribesmen who lived in Africa informs him of special constructions there that were designed for observing other cosmic concentrations from the planet Earth. Having been involved in the construction of his own telescope on Mars for observing similar cosmic concentrations, he naturally wants to learn more about these particular African constructions and travels down a tributary of the Nile to the outskirts of what is today called "Cairo."

At the time Beelzebub arrives (in pre-sand Egypt), a Pharaoh and his grandson had completed some of these constructions. These constructions allowed not merely observation of remote cosmic concentrations (stars and planets) but the reciprocal effect they each had on the planet Earth, and even to the psyche of earth-humans. These constructions differed from Beelzebub's observatory in that they were built down into the ground instead of on the planet's surface. (Modern archeologists are indeed discovering more underground compartments and tunneling all the time in their excavations.)

The Egyptian specialists at that time who made these observatories were called "Astrologers," and only later, as human cognitive abilities continued to diminish, they eventually came to be called "Astronomers." And these astronomers were only interested in physical descriptions of the universe. (The New Testament story of the three Magi is an example of the extraordinary knowledge the ancient astrologers could obtain from watching the skies—beyond obtaining merely numerical quantities, ages and distances of cosmic concentrations.)

One of the main duties of these original Astrologers was to find the proper mates for the individuals of their community and draw up additional horoscopes for their children at the time of their birth. By the child's seventh year of existence these Astrologers would identify the proper conjugal mate, and so these sacred unions were based not on flawed personal preferences, but according to the cosmic laws flowing (at the time of one's birth) from the motions and interactions of large astronomical structures that affect the essential nature of the human psyche. This practice ensured that each partner, under the astrologer's careful guidance, would find his or her appropriate *essence-type* partner. According to Beelzebub, after centuries of practice, these Astrologers became experts at matching the sexes as to which type of male *corresponded* best to which type of female. These Astrologers also provided helpful instructions for individuals of their communities who later developed various disharmonies in their lives.

Beelzebub further states that if these kinds of original and highly knowledgeable Astrologers had continued to exist, the human race would have lived in relatively normal conditions. Unfortunately, they were replaced by beings of new formation (contemporary "titillators"), who studied these same cosmic concentrations, but came up with "ultra-fantastic" theories offering no explanation or enlightenment for pondering the true sense and meaning of creation and human life. (For instance, theories on black holes and the Higgs boson offer no insights into the human predicament.) Again, these new types of investigators (*beings of new formation*) who mostly came upon the scene after the sinking of Atlantis were called "Astronomers" and were only concerned with physical measurements—making them the actual apes.

(It is well known that modern science separates "facts" from "values." Also, modern science focuses on the "how" of creation rather than the "why." But Swedenborg is adamant that "Love" is the primal substance and great mover of the universe and has a spiritual goal of heavenly unification.)

Beelzebub informs Hassein not to get angered by this unfortunate outcome in earth-human scholarship, because although these new Astronomers (freaks) only provide worthless results for themselves and their communities, they at least cause little harm by wearing their special smocks (from England) and spectacles (from Germany). If these investigators were to become otherwise unoccupied and bored, they might busy themselves in something much worse—like leading the struggle of "five against one," that is, ganging up on others that they disagree with. Such practices lead to *harmful* radiations (bad vibes) and negative spheres that spread out into the whole community and easily affect others.

It is also made clear in this part of the story that the famous Egyptian Pyramids were among those specific constructions that were used as observatories, but again, the main design for viewing distant cosmic phenomena was dug underground. More important, one type of Egyptian construction had particular significance for Beelzebub. Among the special constructions Beelzebub observes in Egypt during this fourth visit was a spiritual remnant (an allegorical being) from the prior accomplishments of the learned society Akhaldan, which served as a special emblem on the continent Atlantis before it vanished into the ocean.

At this point in the story, Beelzebub feels it is first necessary to provide some background information concerning this once great and learned society.

Beelzebub informs Hassein that despite the continent of Atlantis going "under" and human life becoming more abnormal (external) as a result, the attainments of the learned society Akhaldan were passed on, by inheritance, to many of their remote ancestors.

Beelzebub also admits that he learned about the special history of this mental trajectory in earth-humans through "Teleoghinooras" which are ideas and thoughts fixed within the atmospheric substances surrounding the planet where three-brained beings had arisen—kind of like a sensitive cosmic membrane which stores the memory of a planet's past events. (An individual who has reached a certain level of spiritual development can tap into these thought-records imprinted on the subtle atmospheric substances existing in different spheres of a planet.) A sequence or series of these "Teleoghinooras" concerning any coherent event are called "Korkaptilnian thought tapes."

Beelzebub claimed to be able to tap into and interpret, through "Soorptakalknian contemplation," the information from those atmospheric thought-tapes. (Swedenborg claimed that human spirits remain close to the spheres of the planets of their arising and from both spiritual substances and the finest substances of nature form a certain "limbus" or cosmic *cutaneous covering*, representing a psychic border for everyone's life's memories. This would mean that human experiences and memories are preserved for all time in deeper nature as an organic realm or fixed plane of records in reality.

Beelzebub had learned from these thought-tapes that an individual on the continent Atlantis, named Belcultassi, was once contemplating on the sense and aim of his existence. To his shock, it became clear to him that something was amiss. He noticed that his manifestations (actions in life) were not in sync with his most noble ideas (data lodged only in his memory function and not applied to his heart).

Belcultassi decided to devote the whole of his existence to getting to the bottom of his proclivity toward negative human being-impulses, such as "self-love," "pride," and "vanity." This proclivity came in spite of his also possessing noble ideas and knowledge that conflicted with these very passions he was manifesting.

He eventually built up an inner "potency" to be mercilessly *sincere* with himself and resist these ignoble impulses and their accompanying heterogenous thought-associations that had become habitual (second nature) in the daily functioning of his common presence—due to automatic and abnormal reactions to various outside influences (vanities and allurements) from the world. (Swedenborg states that this inner potency comes from one's sincere desire to engage in spiritual combat and resisting ignoble principles, which is called temptations.)

Through intense self-reflection, Belcultassi even analyzed exactly what impulses affected his *body*, his *mind*, and his *feelings*, and whether he responded consciously or automatically to these distinct impressions coming to his threefold being from the outside world. (I have to admit this level of self-scrutiny goes far beyond merely lumping all bad impulses together, and is far beyond what I—as a Swedenborgian—have been taught to do in my attempt to overcome behavioral flaws). This individual, Belcultassi, became conscious of these three kinds of impulses and learned to tell whether he was acting as a representative of God or merely on automatic pilot (from one of his three disconnected psychic functions).

This unusual and exhaustive inner search convinced Belcultassi that his ordinary life was full of inconsistencies and proceeded in ways that made no sense to sane being-logic (rationality). To further his growing convictions, concerning the reality of his own abnormal psychic organization, he next sought to find out if these same conclusions could be verified by the experiences of other individuals as well. Would others make similar self-discoveries about themselves if they made similar genuine efforts?

Rather than relying on what some trained priest would tell him, he assembled a group of individuals and friends capable of a similar *self-sincerity*. These friends not only became interested in this same inner dilemma, they also began to meet regularly to find ways to remedy this unexpected, unflattering and odd condition. Together, Belcultassi and his new associates formed a group which they named the "Society of Akhaldans." The word Akhaldan means "the striving to become aware of the sense and aim of the Being of beings." In other words, why did God put us here? What are God's expectations and hopes for the human race? This group was entirely concerned with spiritual regeneration and transformation, which the ancient Church of Noah would also embrace.

Later, it was realized that no one individual in this group of seekers could acquire the immense and detailed knowledge necessary to fulfill their aim, alone. So they divided themselves up into *seven* special branches of knowledge in order to obtain their common noble goal. Beelzebub informs his grandson that this undertaking represented the birth of true objective science on Earth and it developed normally until the sinking of Atlantis. (Again, I believe that this special society of learned beings corresponded to Swedenborg's *first ancient church*, which was called "Noah," and was given special knowledge from "Above.")

The first branch of knowledge created by the Akhaldans focused on the study of the planet and its reciprocal or ecological relationships among its various parts.

The second group studied the radiations given off by all the planets in their solar system and how these radiations interacted with each other.

The third branch was concerned with mathematics.

The fourth area of investigation involved psychology, whereby they made observations of the perceptions, experiencings and manifestations of other three-brained beings.

The fifth group was engaged in chemistry and physics.

The sixth branch of study involved sensory data coming from the outside world and how this data is erroneously perceived.

The seventh and final group made a study of how outer cosmic influences, rather than memory data and viewpoints already present, influenced people's manifestations.

Eventually the learned society of Akhaldans caught wind that something serious was about to occur to their continent in the near future. Anticipating a catastrophe, they began to disperse and immigrate to other lands. After the sinking of Atlantis, many of them gradually came together again on the continent Grabontzi (Africa) where they then moved to *pre-sand* Egypt to re-establish the aim and work of their former learned society. (Swedenborg concurs that

Egypt originally possessed great knowledge—received from an even more remote past.)

Beelzebub informs Hassein that soon after the survivors of the Akhaldan society moved to Egypt, all the members of his extraterrestrial tribe migrated to the same spot. These clansmen who had a relationship on Atlantis (in the city of Samlios) again resumed their friendships and tasks in the land of Egypt.

Beelzebub laments that these surviving Akhaldans failed to fulfill their goals, but due to their great efforts, at least the "instinctive conviction" of the necessity of becoming a "completed personal being" was passed on to future generations.

And something else survived from this period up to the present time—the unique constructions Beelzebub had witnessed with his very own eyes that were being erected during his fourth visit to the planet Earth. But before he identifies any of these remaining constructions, he describes to Hassein that the organs of perception in the three-brained beings of planet Earth had seriously atrophied (this atrophy includes human reasoning or inner sight).

While these surviving Akhaldan earth-humans were still living relatively normal lives, amazingly, they could view the most far-away cosmic concentrations—day or night. Those who lawfully and consciously increased their perceptive powers could actually see phenomena issuing from the emanations of the Holy Sun Absolute (Spiritual Sun). In Swedenborg's terms, to perceive the emanations of the Spiritual Sun is to be given spiritual enlightenment and to see God's Divine Truths.) But because of the abnormal conditions of life created by the three-brained beings on planet Earth, these special powers of sight (not simply eyesight) degenerated to that of other natural animals, and they could only observe distant cosmic concentrations at night.

Despite the degeneration of the powers of perception in the three-brained beings of *new formation* (which included losing the deeper, spiritual sight of the human intellect), the observatories created under the supervision of Egypt's high priests (descendants of the Akhaldans) allowed them to still observe distant cosmic concentrations, both day and night—concentrations that were dependent on reciprocating with the harmonic laws and influences of the Spiritual Sun (*the Word of God*).

Beelzebub describes these ancient observatories as being built deep into the ground with special bored-out shafts or pipe-like hollows aimed outwardly in different directions related to the Earth's horizon. With this setup, the Egyptian astrologers could effectively observe the results of the *reciprocal* actions of distant cosmic concentrations. Beelzebub also hints that these constructions were also used to affect *climate change* (in a positive way).

Beelzebub had personally observed that all these constructions were enclosed by a special latticework made from a plant called "Zalnakatar." But what struck Beelzebub the most was a large stone statue that stood guard of the main entrance to this enclosure.

The Sphinx!

This stone statue strongly reminded Beelzebub of a statue that he had seen in Atlantis and that stood opposite of the chief cathedral there. This statue was an emblem (or logo) for the society Akhaldan and was called "Conscience." This allegorical creature contained the body of a *bull*, the legs of a *lion*, the wings of an *eagle*, and for its head were the *breasts of a virgin* that were attached to the main body by a piece of "amber."

Each of part of this allegorical being was designed to remind its citizens of their cosmic and God-given *duty* to remove their undesirable impulses. The bull represents striving for spiritual advancement and freedom with indefatigable stamina and effort, such as the physical endurance that a bull would have. The Lion represents the courage of heart needed for the undertaking. The wings of the Eagle symbolize that we must keep our mind raised (elevated) above ordinary, everyday or habitual being-existence. The "breasts of the virgin" represent *spiritual Love* and the ultimate hope that our Common Father has placed within humanity.

Beelzebub then explains to Hassein that "amber" is one of seven substances whereby all *three* parts of God's Divine influx (*active, passive,* and *neutralizing* forces) take part in equal proportion—thus defining a mediating material for impeding the independent or increased flow of one or more modes of God's triunal action. (This also means that any effort to obtain spiritual advancement other than through God's divine dictates will be impeded.)

In Swedenborgian doctrine, such an allegorical being is called a "cherubim," which stands guard over God's Providence (advancing truths) so that individuals will not insanely enter into the hidden and deep mysteries of faith from their own worldly (sensual impediments) knowledge and self-centeredness. A proper *conscience* emerges from the strategies symbolized by the different parts of this biblical allegorical being. So it was a worthy emblem for this ancient society that was focused on spiritual regeneration and growth.

Swedenborg also alludes to "amber" as being an *impeding* material for the proper equalization of divine action by symbolizing God's teaching and Word reaching down into the lowest or outermost realm in its full and harmonious influence (without any lopsided condition caused by any single element of God's threefold action becoming more dominant than the others).

Therefore, the sinking of Atlantis (with its emblem) represents conscience being driven back, deeper into the human psyche. Because of this calamity and others to the planet, including humankind's perverse "organic need" to destroy everything of spiritual value on Earth, Beelzebub can't help but conclude that conscience still must survive in humans, although somehow now protected for people's own future good. Swedenborg concurs with this surviving and protected divine influence—a gift stemming from God's mercy—and calls it the "remains," or the Lord's presence with Man.

After Beelzebub's "sorrowful reflections" about this outcome of the inner history of earth-humans, he moves on to the more southern parts of Africa to collect a number of ape-beings for his friend Gornahoor Harharkh. We are never told what was finally done with these apes. Instead, Beelzebub finds himself traveling to Saturn to attend a family ceremony for Gornahoor Harharkh's firstborn son, named Raoorkh. Beelzebub was to take on the special duty of being Raoorkh's "godfather."

Swedenborg and Gurdjieff were in complete agreement that the lower mammals (including apes) were made from a different (and distinct) formula than that of the human species. Animals can be inventive and show emotion, but they are incapable of true reasoning and discovering the Lord God. Animals cannot detect emanations from the Spiritual Sun (Sun Absolute) and therefore cannot reason about or enjoy the Lord God's heavenly kingdom.

I offer my sincere condolences to all pet owners.

SUMMARY

■ Gornahoor Harharkh and Beelzebub continually talk about the strange three-brained beings living on planet Earth. Harharkh becomes so fascinated by this human species that he wants to be kept informed concerning Beelzebub's observations of them. Gornahoor Harharkh also wants Beelzebub to go back to the planet Earth and bring him some "apes" for research.

■ "Apes" in this story depict the comical outcome of the emotional (female) part of the *divided human psyche* (after the sinking of Atlantis) to find happiness and imagined completeness through worldly pleasure alone. Apes represent those who do not act in human or rational ways.

■ Beelzebub goes to Africa because they have the most apes. (Africa was one of the main landmasses that the inhabitants of Atlantis migrated to.) But in Egypt he becomes more interested in studying its unique constructions. He believes that these unique Egyptian constructions were used to observe cosmic concentrations and were designed from an elevated knowledge.

SUMMARY

■ Beelzebub claims that early Astrologers understood reality better than modern astronomers do.

■ *The Sphinx* in Egypt reminds Beelzebub of a similar statue that he observed earlier in Atlantis, which was located opposite a place of worship. He describes this original monument's features, then gives the psycho-spiritual meaning of these features. In total, this monument/insignia represented the pursuit of spiritual *conscience*.

■ Beelzebub learns further (from "Soorptakalknian contemplation") extra details about the learned Akhaldan society in Atlantis—from his tapping into the "Korkaptilnian thought tapes" or memory "texts" of stored ideas and thoughts that surround the planet Earth's atmosphere. I believe these "thought-texts" are similar to what Swedenborg called the *Limbus*.

■ Beelzebub discovers that an individual named *Belcultassi* founded the Akhaldan society on Atlantis after making the unflattering self-discovery that his passions were often at odds with his most noble and valuable ideas. He convinced other friends to look into their own psychic realities to see if they would make the same observations. This group became the Akhaldan society.

■ This learned society divided itself into *seven* additional groups to study the various branches of knowledge needed to obtain their great aim. After the sinking of Alantis, this learned society moved to Egypt and created its unique constructions—including the Sphinx, an allegorical being which symbolized their spiritual convictions. It was not an exact replica of the Atlantian insignia.

■ Humans eventually lost the ability to perceive things from the Spiritual Sun, which is God's love and truth.

"Beelzebub's flight to the planet Earth for the fifth time"

Swedenborg and Gurdjieff both addressed the *inner experience*—the spiritual history of the human race—which takes place in the human heart and intellect (that is, our spirit). The induced sleep put on Adam and his eventual removal (with Eve) from the Garden of Eden, or Paradise, corresponds to Beelzebub's first *Transapalnian perturbation*, resulting from the Earth's collision with a comet and the later the implanting of the organ Kundabuffer at the base of the human spine. This induced sleep by higher intelligences (working through God) was to ensure that earth-humans would not find out about their life energies being automatically used to support the Moon's ongoing existence.

The comet Kondoor slamming into the Earth represented the human psyche taking a direct hit from false and extraneous principles (that it had a yearning for). This cosmic disaster and its temporary fix by higher intelligences symbolizes that the center of gravity or stability of the human psyche had moved to lower and more external or worldly things (represented by the serpent having to crawl on the ground and eat dust). What was significant to the inner trajectory of humankind was that this new state of mental equilibrium was an *inversion* from what the Creator deemed most important—spiritual Love, Truth and its life. Providentially however, this psychic degeneration and atrophy was a necessity to preserve human free will (or humans would have rebelled against the true nature and cosmic responsibility of their existence as having to support the great scheme of things). Humans were also given a new ability to separate their understanding from their hearts' desires—to challenge their intentions.

The Moon represents this first psychic split. It symbolizes human consciousness drawing off energy from one's genuine essence (like when we fill our memory with mere data and begin to *imagine* false abilities about ourselves from that data). The memory function is only an intellectual satellite to our true deeper essence. Just like the Moon is a satellite to the planet Earth.

The second big unfortunate event for the earth-humans was the "sinking of Atlantis." This symbolizes another division, but now, in the natural human mind into *outer* and *inner* operations. Swedenborg addresses this split in the human psyche in his book, *The True Christian Religion*, Vol. 2, n. 593. According to Swedenborg, the Lord God used the resulting subconscious (sunken) or interior natural level of the divided human psyche to store and protect sacred mediating data for use at a later time. Swedenborg called this divine storage the "remains."

When the Lord God reactivates these protected mediating remains ("the spirit of God moving across the faces of the waters" in Genesis 1:2), during an individual's spiritual growth, one would sense new spiritual feelings being stirred up from within—especially a desire for spiritual growth and elevated knowledge. The activation of one's divine remains allows spiritual conscience to begin to re-awaken and re-emerge within one's worldly consciousness and daily activities.

The *third* disaster to hit the planet Earth occurred due to further disharmonies with the Moon trying to find its proper balance among all the changes occurring. The result of this striving for balance, *strong winds* and *sand* storms were created on Earth, whose erosive action created the great deserts that covered over many former earth-human civilizations. This great "storm" inwardly symbolizes a disharmony that allowed great knowledge from the past to be covered over and lost to humankind.

Gurdjieff and Swedenborg both intended to return this lost and great knowledge to the human race on Earth.

When Beelzebub resumes his Tales, he informs Hassein that the great deserts that were formed from these windstorms happened between his fourth and fifth visits to the planet Earth. During that time he had observed through his telescope from Mars that the earth-humans had now populated most of the land masses on Earth, and that because of their chief psychic peculiarity, would from time to time, destroy each other's existence—such as in wars.

After the great windstorms, and on Beelzebub's fifth arrival on Earth, the two ancient Asian centers of culture in the countries of Tikliamish (Middle East) and Maralpleicie (Gobi) ceased to exist. Certain parts of Pearl-land (India) and Grabontzi were also covered by sands (African Sahara). Beelzebub again informs his grandson that the Moon was responsible for generating these powerful winds.

So, what could this mean symbolically, concerning the inner history of human experience? (According to Swedenborg, storms symbolize a dispersal of knowledge and truth from agitated human minds.) As mentioned above, the Moon was still trying to find its proper equilibrium, and in doing so, created large wind currents on the planet Earth. One cannot help but sense that the Moon represents something in the earth-human's psyche that was still trying to settle itself, but having an erosive effect while doing so (as I hinted before, this explains why the term "lunatic" comes from the word "Moon").

Biblically speaking, the separation between the Earth and Moon can be spiritually seen to represent a split between the human heart and human intellect, (and is also portrayed by the competition between brothers—like Cain and Abel, Ishmael and Isaac, or Esau and Jacob). As I mentioned above, the Moon represents the formation of a more external or corporeal intellect—which has become separated from its primal living source.

Next, the sinking of Atlantis, due to the first calamity, represents a further split, but now of the natural human mind. The splitting of this new external mind and its habitual consciousness represents the emergence of humans of "new formation" (mechanical and corporeal thought). This second split led humans to acquire a more stormy disposition, due to their having lost the ability to *unearth* deeper knowledge or use knowledge without creating a false outer impression or *pretense*.

Hypocrisy and pretense is evidence that earth-humans have a divided mind.

These violent wind storms (occurring both outside and inside of our ancestors) caused great migrations to occur across the Earth, whereby humankind was redistributed (dispersed) to China, Persia, Europe and over the whole of the Earth's surface, corresponding roughly to Genesis 11:8 where the Lord God "scattered them from there over all the Earth." These "windstorms" represented the "abrasiveness" between divisive and conflicting morals and the subjective opinions among three-brained beings on Earth (who, as beings of *new formation*, began fabricating knowledge and worldviews from their egoism). In Holy Scripture, this fabricated knowledge is symbolized by the phrase, "hand-hewn bricks." As said before, the resulting "deserts" which spread over the Earth also symbolized a mental state of desolation where genuine Truth had become scattered and was covered over by mounds (sands) of *disconnected* data.

So Beelzebub's fifth visit to Earth was after the time of this population redistribution among the groups of the communities of these earth-humans, whose inner psychic qualities were continuing to diminish.

Beelzebub admits that what piques his interest in these three-centered beings is their periodic need to destroy each other. He is determined to find out the exact causes of this horrible phenomenon that is so peculiar to the rest of the universe. (He also was able to observe that the lifespans of those humans living on Earth were uniformly getting shorter and shorter, and furthermore, that they were becoming more prone to certain "illnesses." Concerning this second problem of increased illnesses, Beelzebub also resolved to find out their causes.

On this fifth visit, Beelzebub's original spaceship *Occasion* moors on the Persian Gulf and his party moves up the river Euphrates to the majestic city of Babylon. According to Swedenborg, the river Euphrates symbolizes a psychic boundary of the most external or lowest functioning of human cognition, such as memory-data (*Arcana Colestia*, n. 118). The human memory serves as an outer or external boundary for human intelligence. Both true and false ideas can occupy this lowest plane (or boundary) of the intellect as mere sensory data.

So Beelzebub is traveling to a place (or state) of diminished thinking capacity among earth-humans—called Babylon! (And sure enough, Swedenborg had discovered that "Babylon" symbolized a split in the human psyche where one's outer (or externals of) life appear holy, but the internals are profane.)

And, on this fifth trip, Beelzebub happens to reach Babylon at the time when it was preparing something that would eventually lead to the accelerated atrophy of the human mind and its "psychic organization." As a result of this new Babylonian "push," earth-humans, with their split psyche, began to lose their connection with the instinctive functioning in their presences which give rise to the genuine being-impulses of "Faith," "Hope" and "Love." And instead, these proper being-impulses were replaced by an *artificial* and corporeal mentality in which nothing is ever verified or truly sensed. Just counterfeited.

Because of these artificial and concocted values, the *learned beings of new formation* in Babylon (those who only had their outermost or external corporeal consciousness given any value) were unable to sense and grasp universal cosmic truths in the way prior civilizations could, or as other learned humans do throughout the universe. Beelzebub stresses that from the time of the Tikliamishian civilization up to the present, earth-humans began to collect and mechanically *learn by rote* all sorts of vacuous and dead information (the piling up of mere memory-data).

Despite this mental atrophy taking place in earth-humans, the more one continued to collect information in this way (by rote), the more learned that person was considered to be by the rest of these odd Earth-people. In reality, these Earth-humans *of new formation* (with their deluded sense of importance) were only capable of *feeding the Moon* (their imagination) from the energy of their lives, regardless of education levels obtained.

We need to have our knowledge challenged and contemplated.

Swedenborg observed in the spiritual realm that when an individual received some "truth" they would immediately be given a counter thought, so that real effort would be made whereby he or she could come to a personal conclusion about that truth—all while strengthening their own powers of reasoning (*Arcana Coelestia*, n. 7298.2). Nothing was to be accepted directly or quickly without contemplation. Modern learning "by rote" thwarts this proper mental process of acquiring rationality in an orderly fashion (and creates *learned beings of new formation*).

Here, I will recount a lesson given long ago to my high school class by our science teacher concerning the meaning of educational Degrees. There was first a "B.S." degree (meaning "bull shit"). Then one could obtain an "M.S." ("more of the same"). Finally, one could earn a "Ph. D" ("piled higher and deeper"). Jokes aside, I believe such comments come from a deep instinctive feeling within us concerning the artificiality of contemporary learning.

When Beelzebub had reached the city of Babylon, he found that it was populated by a great many of these *learned beings of new formation* (that is why he crossed the Euphrates to get there, which symbolizes the collection of sensual knowledge). Many of these "learned" individuals were even gathered from all parts of the Earth by the Babylonian King at that time.

It seems that this compulsive Persian King wanted to accumulate as much gold as possible. He became acquainted with the idea that certain learned individuals could change any abundant metal on Earth into gold. However, the King, because of the strange properties of the organ Kundabuffer, understood this mysterious alchemy only literally, and not as a metaphor for obtaining a *heart of gold* from personal spiritual growth. So as this Persian King conquered other territories, he seized all their most educated individuals in the hope that perhaps one of them would know the secret to turning cheap metal into more valuable gold.

Because the quality of vibrations was being systematically lowered by the mental atrophy of the learned beings of Babylon, their "birth rate" had to increase (and their lifespans had to diminish) in order that Great Nature could meet its demands for harmonizing universal creation and maintenance.

Beelzebub hints to Hassein that the terrifying process of "war" is related to the issue of Nature's constant adaptation to re-normalize itself and procure its material needs. Death is one of Nature's means for obtaining the vibrations necessary for cosmic equilibrium (this includes maintaining the Moon). As strange as this may sound, Swedenborg stated that the Lord God uses the death of terrestrial people to maintain equilibrium and balance the needs of the spiritual realm—depending on the inner qualities that any individual will offer for God's grand providential plan.)

Beelzebub further tells his grandson that this vain Persian King also made a "military excursion" into Egypt because most of the great "scientists" of that time were concentrated in just that region of the planet. However, over time, the Persian King lost his interest in conquering and making gold cheaply. And Babylon was left with a bunch of scientists roaming the streets.

These scientists, trying to be useful, began to congregate and attempted to solve tough intellectual questions that were, according to Beelzebub, "immeasurably beyond their comprehension." The chief question that *agitated* these scientists' minds and gave them the greatest anxiety was whether or not they and others had a "soul."

Two "catchy theories" arose from their faulty deliberations (*wise-acrings*) concerning the "question-of-the-beyond." One theory, called "atheistic," embraced the idea that there was no soul. The other theory, called "idealistic" or "dualistic," embraced the idea that we all have a soul.

It was among these strange scientists of new formation, that according to Beelzebub, he first heard uttered the phrase, the "Building-of-the-Tower-of-Babel." Beelzebub then explains to his grandson that because of the diminished mental capacity of contemporary beings living on the planet Earth, such phrases from the past instill *illusory* "being-egoplastikuri" or faulty "psychic-picturings" in their noggins concerning such events. Such a faulty *picturing* is portrayed in Scripture as the ultra-ambitious construction project to allow earth-humans to reach Heaven (true happiness) by artificial means, and understanding it *literally*, as meaning, the building of an actual, physical tower to reach "Heaven."

The ideas in these two theories themselves, proposed by these so-called scientists of new formation, represented the "bricks" used to build such a tower and celebrate human achievement and great-ness. These *hand-hewn* bricks symbolize the artificial or fabricated notions formed from the diminished cognitive capacity in humans to build their personal edifices to the greatest heights. These two theories (worldviews) came to represent either *fabricated science* or *fabricated religion*—both theories were misguided attempts to reach Heaven (again, true happiness) by all of humankind's false ideas and their wacky thinking concerning the true nature of reality.

Putting my Swedenborgian cap back on, I find that Gurdjieff is employing a very sophisticated understanding of symbolism—*a knowledge of correspondences*. Swedenborg, in his various theo-logical writings, showed that the concept of correspondences was based on the fact that all things in the physical universe (like stars, comets, rivers, mountains, minerals, trees and animals) portray *psycho-spiritual* qualities and processes. This knowledge was considered the "science of all sciences" in the ancient world (and prior to the fabricated science of earth-humans of new formation). It was this great ubiquitous, multi-leveled knowledge of correspon-dences that both Swedenborg and Gurdjieff were addressing when they described what was "lost" due to the diminished functioning of human cognition over time (and from this, the *agitation of minds* or psychical wind storms had to ensue from these educated people's severe misunderstandings).

Many of the problems readers have with *Beelzebub's Tales* are the result of their not being able to penetrate this symbolic form of knowledge—thus, most earth-humans still live behind the mental border symbolized by the river Euphrates!

Let me both remind you and give you a better taste of this special elevated knowledge that was lost to humanity but cleverly incorporated into these Tales. Beelzebub's reference to the river (Euphrates), which takes them to the city of Babylon, symbolizes that they are traveling toward the lowest boundary of human intelligence (sensory knowledge and memory data) whereby external actions in their daily rituals may appear holy, but they actually profane and pervert what is holy from egoism. The fact that the Persian King was collecting various scientists from every country symbolizes the gathering of those who specialize in gathering this corporeal/sensual data (*sensuali et scientifico – Arcana Coelestia*, n. 120) in the false hope of creating gold (something spiritually precious) from common metals. This illustrates a decline in human understanding of the importance of developing spiritual values out of earthly values. A King represents our highest principle of life—false or otherwise—that rules over our lives (and holds everything together). Gold symbolizes the "Good of Divine Wisdom" or "Divine Love" which can only be created within an individual who seeks the legitimate spiritual transformation of his or her heart and mind—and not literally to be understood as the transformation of common metals into something more precious.

So, when the King gives up his pursuit (loses interest) of finding the secret to making gold from common metals, this means that humanity had lost its directive "glue," whereby all its efforts now become disjointed and scattered. It is from this abandonment that humankind is left with only its lowest cognitive functioning to fabricate some "cock 'n' bull." Wisdom now atrophies into "cunning" and the human race loses the proper being-function to "instinctively-sense-cosmic-truths."

Gurdjieff's knowledge of the symbolic language of correspondence is further confirmed when Beelzebub informs Hassein that he made friends with an "Assyrian" named *Hamolinadir* during his trip to the city of Babylon. According to Swedenborg, the term "Assyrian" symbolizes the cognitive function of *reasoning*, which is a distinct step up (elevated) from the lower operation of merely collecting data in the human memory (which is, again, the first and outermost border of human mental functioning).

Beelzebub states that this Assyrian's inner mental qualities were less atrophied than others and that he was educated in Egypt from the "School of Materializing-Thought." (This is code for being able to properly fix great knowledge into one's physical organic fabric through proper applications to life through utility, thus into the organic spacetime matrix). Beelzebub would attend various meetings with Hamolinadir to hear what the various Babylonian intellectuals had to say about the soul. It was at these meetings that these Babylonian intellectuals developed their two competing theories—*idealist* and *atheist*.

Hamolinadir eventually gives his own speech at one of these conventions. The topic of his talk was the "Instability-of-Human-Reason."

Hamolinadir speaks about how easy it is, with faulty reasoning, to confirm anything one pleases. (Swedenborg concurs that this is what humans also do when they falsely confirm what they love, or use the literal sense of biblical stories to promote their personal and subjective beliefs.)

For this reason, Hamolinadir admits he can find logic and plausibility in both idealist and atheist theories concerning the existence (or not) of the soul. He also admits that as far as questions of the beyond are concerned, he like everyone else in the room, is just an "idiot—cubed." He then informs his audience that from all their different ideas and theories they are building a tower in which to reach "Heaven." (Again, the bricks for this tower are the fabricated, "hand-hewn," theories and ideas that people have concocted to reach their highest goals.) Hamolinadir warns the assembly of intellectuals that such a tower will eventually crumble and fall on everyone's heads.

With that said, this "sympathetic" Assyrian runs out of the hall and is never seen again!

It is because of Hamolinadir's heart-felt speech, and the effect it had on the listeners, that various scraps and phrases were able to reach contemporary earth-humans. One of these phrases was "The-Building-of-the-Tower-of-Babel."

Also handed down from Babylon to contemporary beings of the planet Earth were those two conflicting theories concerning the existence of the soul that Beelzebub had mentioned a bit earlier in the story. (These two theories, idealist and *atheist*, indeed still dominate today's thinking and discussions as well.)

Beelzebub next describes some important and illuminating details concerning the idealist (or dualist) teaching to his grandson Hassein. This theory states that everyone is born with two bodies—a visible physical body and an invisible body called a soul. Unlike the physical body, the soul is immortal. Another important facet in this theory is that everyone has, perched on each shoulder, a good angelic spirit and a bad or devilish spirit. The good spirit is perched on the right shoulder and the evil spirit on the left.

It is the job of these different shoulder-perching spirits to convince a person to do their bidding. They also take notes (a person's "Book of Life") concerning all one's choices. When a person dies, these spirits bring their notes to God and place them on the appropriate pans of a scale. The heaviest notebook and pan determines which spirit gets to cart off that person's soul to either Heaven or Hell. Heaven is considered a place of "great satisfaction" and Hell is a place of "abuse." (Swedenborg insists that Heaven consists of a life of usefulness toward others and is not a retirement destination or some physical "vacation" place.)

Upon hearing this Babylonian dualist theory, Hassein asks his grandfather "which of their manifestations do they consider *good*, and which are *bad*?"

Beelzebub, with a peculiar look on his face, shakes his head before answering. He tells Hassein that there are two kinds of understandings concerning this particular issue. The first was formulated by the Akhaldan society on the continent of Atlantis, which stated that objectively, a good deed was done according to conscience, and a bad deed produced "remorse." The second understanding, an invention from King Konuzion of the Asiatic city of Gob to stop crimes, robberies and acts of violence, dealt with cultural "morality." Beelzebub further informs his curious grandson that while morality is subjective and has the properties of a "chameleon" he insists that true conscience in people was always objective (and sacred). Swedenborg confirms this same notion by stating that morality can be either *natural* and worldly, or it can be *spiritual*.

As to the atheistic theory which says that there is no soul, Beelzebub tells Hassein that it promotes the idea that all phenomena, including human life, proceeds through physical and mechanical laws only. Any talk about God and the afterlife are considered "deliriums of sick visionaries."

Beelzebub's opinion is that both theories represent the wiseacrings of Hasnamuss-individuals (learned beings of new formation) and the promotion of both ideas leads to a most terrifying outcome— the destruction of the final remnants of proper knowledge that could be used for reversing the maleficent effects from the organ Kundabuffer.

He blames this negative outcome not on what happened just in Babylon, but on an egotistical individual living several centuries earlier named "Lentrohamsanin." This Lentrohamsanin "individual," who now lives on a small planet (psychical plane) called *Retribution* (symbolizing impending eternal punishment as deserved by an individual only seeking personal advantage) was responsible for destroying the results of the holy labors of a genuine messenger who had been sent from above.

The messenger, sent from God, was named Ashiata Shiemash.

On the surface of things, a Swedenborgian might not find much fault with the Babylonian dualistic or idealistic theory of the soul. But here is exactly where Gurdjieff will offer valuable clarifying information that is mostly overlooked, even among serious students of Swedenborg's theological writings. It concerns *pretense* and *deceit* in the framework of humans having a split (interior and external) natural mind. Because of this real split (which most people fail to detect) in the human psyche, the sacred impulses of Faith, Love and Hope, which were originally noble being-impulses, now have little effect on earth-humans' lives.

I want Swedenborgians to pay close attention to what follows.

SUMMARY

■ Between Beelzebub's fourth and fifth visits to the planet Earth, the human population had spread over most places of its surface—despite their proclivity for destroying each other's physical existence (through wars).

■ Also, a third major calamity had hit the planet during this interval—great windstorms created the planet's deserts. Because of these storms, two of Asia's main cultures (Tikliamish and Maralpleicie) disappeared, plus certain parts of India became covered, as was northern Africa, by the Sahara Desert.

■ While these storms were created by ongoing disharmonies between the Earth and Moon, they also represented deeper, ongoing frictions caused by another splitting of the human psyche (deserts symbolize the desolation of divine or cosmic truths from human consciousness by mental storms and agitated minds that dispersed sacred ideas). The migrations over the surface of the planet were due to people trying to escape these "dual" storms.

■ The reason for Beelzebub's fifth visit is to look into the causes of earth-humans killing each other (as in war). At the same time he also observed the strange phenomenon of human psychic existence becoming shorter and shorter and illnesses that developed—making it impossible to live normally until death.

■ Beelzebub lands near the city of Babylon (and crosses the River Euphrates) to study the rate of the degeneration of earth-humans' "psychic organization" and the atrophy in these human beings of the instinctive functioning of "Faith," "Hope" and "Love." Such a degenerating human psyche is symbolized by Babylon and Euphrates

SUMMARY

and concerns itself only with gathering vacuous information to fill its memory, separating itself further from its *original mass* (spiritual center)—like the Moon from the Earth.

▪ The Persian (Babylonian) King, not understanding the metaphor behind making "gold," seeks to capture the greatest minds from all around, to gain the alchemical secret to this process. After the King loses his interest in making gold, the intellectuals he captured (beings of new formation who now contemplated reality without *conscious labors* and *intentional suffering*) begin to debate the existence of the "soul."

▪ An individual at these debates on the soul, an *Assyrian* named *Hamolinadir*, whose mind was not as atrophied as the others, describes all their mental efforts as "unstable" and as "building-of-a-tower-to-Heaven." (This phrase has a symbolic meaning.) As far as the Babylonian theory proving that people have souls goes, Hassein asks his grandfather about how one knows "doing good" from "doing bad." The answer given is that evil deeds make individuals feel remorse but *good* deeds are done from conscience. Morality simply feigns outer standards. The atheist theory of these Babylonians stated that everything was the result of "mechanics."

CHAPTER 25

"The Very Saintly Ashiata Shiemash, sent from Above to the Earth"

Beelzebub now introduces Hassein (and the reader) to a "Most Very Saintly" individual named Ashiata Shiemash (introduced at the end of the previous chapter). This saintly individual was sent to Earth by the Most Gracious Command of Our OMNI-LOVING COMMON FATHER ENDLESSNESS in order to reverse the direction of the negative consequences brought about through the crystallized (fixed within the human psyche) and abnormal properties from the organ Kundabuffer. And in the Kundabuffer's place, create individuals who could inwardly represent an exact *similitude* of God's Grand Universal Human and become angels (according to Swedenborg, angels are the smallest units of God's Heaven—which has a human form).

This sacred cosmic Messenger sent from "Above" was born seven hundred years prior to Beelzebub's visit to Babylon and came from the more ancient "Sumerian Race." According to Beelzebub, Ashiata Shiemash was the only Messenger sent from "Above" whose holy labors actually succeeded (at least, for a limited time) to help the three-brained beings of the planet Earth to take advantage of the same possibilities as other three-brained beings have, throughout the rest of the planetary universe.

(The Sumerian epic of *Gilgamesh* contains many similarities to notions contained in the biblical narrative of Noah's Ark—and therefore, was written by people who possessed special inner knowledge!)

Unlike other Messengers who were sent before or after him for the same sacred mission, he alone refused to teach about or preach about the ordinary methods commonly employed by other true Messengers from God!

Rather, he took the duality of human consciousness (its split functioning) into account. He also worked directly with earth-humans. As a result, none of Ashiata Shiemash's teachings were recorded and passed along through extant or written forms to later generations—with the exception of one surviving marble tablet that is now in the possession of a certain small brotherhood (called "Olbogmek") of initiated beings somewhere in the middle of the continent Asia. This brotherhood's motto (and the meaning of their name) was "There are not different religions, there is only one God."

Instead, Ashiata Sheimash's unique teachings were passed down to proceeding generations through the brotherhood's various meritorious "initiates," by what Beelzebub calls a "Legominism." The particular Legominism containing this saintly individual's special deliberations to help earth-humans was titled "The Terror-Of-The-Situation." Beelzebub tells his grandson that while he was in Babylon he chanced to come across this most interesting Legominism.

At this point in the Tale, Hassein asks Beelzebub to explain to him what a Legominism means. Beelzebub informs him that it was a means of transferring special knowledge to special initiates of later generations, and was invented by the beings from the former continent Atlantis. These legitimate initiate/students from Atlantis were those who through their personal efforts acquired objective merits that could be sensed by others and evoked their trust and respect.

Unfortunately, illegitimate initiates (those who feign importance and wisdom from self-centeredness), who plundered and stole these noble "essence-values," without earning them, also began to arise on their planet. Beelzebub states that a Legominism is the transmission of information by true meritorious (regenerated) beings concerning events, which have occurred on the planet Earth, and therefore, its true message will always go over the heads of illegitimate leaders. (As a Swedenborgian I am in a position to say that a Legominism probably uses historical and invented events on the planet to communicate the more important inner or real spiritual history of earth-humans.)

(The Word of God is a Legominism that requires specially trained and meritorious individuals to accurately interpret its deeper spiritual meanings.)

Illegitimate initiates therefore (whom Beelzelbub refers to as "gangs") and who hadn't experienced or sensed these ideas as operating and guiding their lives, will tend to misconstrue any scraps of a true Legominism that happens to reach them. The resulting "hodgepodge" constructed from these bits and scraps by earth-humans (of new formation), are so absurd that they would make it extremely difficult for Beelzebub not to "crack-up" with laughter upon hearing them.

The richness by which Beelzebub augments this laughable predicament comes with his added sarcastic comment that when cockroaches hear this human hodgepodge of fragmentary knowledge created by fraudulent initiatives, "the evil-spirit-of-Saint-Vitus" would enter these bugs' common presences and ruin the quality of their blood. Swedenborg, who addressed the illness of Saint Vitus' dance in humans (*Economy of the Animal Kingdom,* Vol 3, *The Fibre,* n. 543, 544), would say that the hodgepodge Gurdjieff is alluding to is a poisonous worldview, which can even corrupt the makeup and quality of a cockroach's blood! Imagine that—this disharmony is so bad when it enters into *anything,* that its poisoning effect could even cause a lowly, dirty cockroach's appendages to immediately go into a contorted and involuntary "dance."

At this part in the story Beelzebub informs us that God's messengers, except for Ashiata Shiemash, had failed to communicate to the human race the true terror of the human predicament—that earth-humans have two personalities.

So, living mostly in only one of those personalities, we never use this situation to learn more about ourselves and instead, seek religion to gain comfort and affirmation (peer approval from others) of our wrongly believed essential worth and self-importance. (This is an influence from the organ Kundabuffer.)

As we are about to see, because of this peculiarity of the *divided* human psyche, which allows egoistic leanings to live unabated, the sacred strategies used by other divine messengers, such as "Faith," "Hope" and even "Love" have become distorted and no longer work on earth-humans the way they were originally supposed to work.

So Ashiata Shiemash came up with a more effective way to correct this terrifying situation. This will come as a real shocker to those who still worship the Lord God in traditional ways.

While Swedenborg (and his new spiritual doctrines) indeed addresses these issues of a *divided human psyche,* most of his followers still ignore this terrifying reality, and instead of sincere self-examination, their split-off outer, corporeal natural mind, is focusing their efforts on building a loving community, improving social issues, or joining the rest of the ecclesiastical crowd. These individuals falsely believe that imploring extra acts of friendship and kindness are the correct paths to unifying the world.

It is one big "Coke® commercial."

SUMMARY

▪ Ashiata Shiemash was a true messenger sent from God to help earth-humans regenerate inwardly (and who lived in Sumeria before Babylon had reached its worldly greatness).

▪ According to Beelzebub, Ashiata Shiemash had the greatest success among God's messengers. (Evidence of their failure is that the various traditional religions of the world have failed to make the Earth a safer place, or make humans more genuinely spiritual.)

▪ Understanding the stranger aspects of the earth-human psyche (its divided nature), Ashiata Shiemash never preached to the general public, but personally delivered to specially prepared and meritorious initiates a "Legominism" containing his special instructions.

▪ There is a surviving tablet containing Ashiata Shiemash's original Legominism called the "Terror-of-the-Situation." The special group of initiates, who now preserve this ancient tablet, live somewhere in Central Asia and are called the "Brotherhood-Olbogmek," which means, "There are not different religions, there is only one God."

▪ Unlike other divine messengers who were sent before and after him, Ashiata Shiemash brought a new direction to the ordinary methods for teaching spiritual growth, because the traditional strategies of "Faith," "Hope" and "Love" no longer worked properly on the dual human psyche, which could contaminate anything it came into contact with—including truth.

CHAPTER 26

"The Legominism concerning the deliberations of the Very Saintly Ahsiata Shiemash under the title of 'The Terror of the Situation'"

As a Swedenborgian, this is the chapter that I most did not want to write. It doesn't challenge Swedenborg's theology, but it does challenge the ecclesiastical culture that has formed from those of my "New Church" brothers and sisters who say they embrace his unique doctrinal writings. My experience with the flawed ecclesiastical culture of promoting "Faith," "Hope" and "Love" among its worshippers, is based on the hypnotic notion that, in spite of our downsides, and our failure to be self-sincere, we are still all special to God and that God will comfort us (because God loves us).

These ideas represent *passive worship* and dangerously hover over our *self-centered* feelings. The more challenging theological idea (which Swedenborg actually taught) that the Lord God's real mission is to expose the inner rottenness hidden in our divided minds is not the kind of comfort that most religious worshippers are seeking these days when approaching religion.

I have often been asked by concerned Swedenborgians to provide quotes concerning our dual personalities (split psyche). But Swedenborg touched on this topic everywhere—as in the two central trees in the Garden of Eden, Cain and Abel, Jacob and Ishmael, etc.

Reading Gurdjieff has allowed me (and given me endurance) to identify and be sensitive to his less flattering comments about human life—mine included! If indeed the biblical narratives provide a deeper look into our spiritual lives, we should expect to learn within its pages a lot about ourselves that is not very pleasant—and even adversarial to God. Both Gurdjieff and Swedenborg maintained that we have developed a unique knack (bad habit) for blaming the "other person" for all our problems. This is a rejection of our spiritual duty.

Swedenborg is adamant that humans are born into evils of every kind, have insane wills/hearts, and that heavenly goodness *only* comes from the Lord God. When we become better people, it is because God is working *through* us, although (since the "fall" of humanity) we have been permitted to mistakenly sense goodness as coming from ourselves.

With that in mind, we now return to *Beelzebub's Tales* as he explains to his curious grandson the contents of Ashiata Shiemash's terrifying "Legominism," which addresses the human split psyche. It starts with a prayer to OUR COMMON CREATOR, ALMIGHTY AUTOCRAT ENDLESSNESS—that we should always strive to be just.

Ashiata Shiemash acknowledges that he was commanded by God to be coated with a planetary body of the three-brained beings from Earth and live among them in order to help free them from the negative consequences of the organ Kundabuffer, which for *important Divine reasons* mentioned earlier, were incorporated into the presences of their ancestors. As I also mentioned earlier on, Swedenborg concurs that the Lord God permitted the human race to see reality "upside down" in order to preserve their free will. Without free will, regardless of its downside and abuse, the human race can neither choose to be saved nor could God help them.

The organ Kundabuffer represents the effects of this divine gamble. Swedenborg tells us that God replaced *spiritual perception* with *conscience* to mediate and offset these effects.

Ashiata Shiemash further acknowledged that all other sacred individuals intentionally sent from Above have used the normal sacred methods, foreordained by the Creator, to offset the maleficent properties of the organ Kundabuffer—such as the being-impulses of "Faith," Hope" and "Love." Ashiata Shiemash would come to understand that such sacred being impulses were worthless to the present inner organization of earth-humans. Worthless? Yep! The reason for this is the earth-humans' dual (divided) consciousness—which allowed *conscience* to be buried, where it safely stayed out of reach. But unfortunately, this also allowed Faith, Hope, and Love to be abused by the outer, corporeal natural mind.

Swedenborg stated that all spiritual transformation takes place in one's conscience (because it represents the *reconciling principle* between one's understanding and one's heart). But with a split psyche, one can now ignore one's own inconsistencies and falsely convince oneself (and others) of his or her spirituality simply by emulating the proper outer actions.

At the age of seventeen, Ashiata Shiemash began to fulfill his divine commission by preparing his planetary existence in a special way so that when he reached the age of maturity, he would possess the conscious function of *impartiality*.

During this process of obtaining impartiality, as he observed other human individuals of all types, an "essence-doubt" began to grow in his mind as to the effectiveness of using the traditional three sacred methods of Faith, Hope, and Love to properly change people for the better. He became convinced that the negative manifestations of the organ Kundabuffer had strangely become "second nature" in the psyche of earth-beings. (Swedenborg also believed that habit created a second [automatic] nature in people.) This second nature made spiritual transformation more difficult because one's ignoble behavior now seemed so natural and self-pleasing to the protected ego.

In order to make his choice as to what sacred method Ashiata Shiemash would use to achieve his noble aim to change earth-humans, he decides to meditate on a mountain for forty days and nights. (Lots of symbolism here.)

Then, for a second period consisting of forty days and nights he also *fasted* during his meditations.

He continued this fast and meditated on the mountain for a *third* period of forty days and nights, and every half-hour plucked two hairs from his chest. "Forty" symbolizes a period of challenge and temptation. "Three" symbolizes fullness. "Plucking hairs from the chest" represents removing the outermost and smallest particulars to get at the heart of the subject matter.

After purifying his reasoning powers and freeing himself from all bodily and spiritual associations received from the outside world, it became clear to him that to save contemporary earth-humans by "Faith," "Hope" or "Love" was already TOO LATE!

The reason for this *terrifying* discovery was simple, but still greatly misunderstood by worshipping earth-humans. Ashiata Shiemash realized that the (egoistic) properties from the organ Kundabuffer would always mix with these sacred impulses in a way that perverted them. The result was that Faith, Hope, and Love no longer functioned correctly and singularly, but were always mingled with and activated by some other subjective human quality such as "vanity," "self-love," "pride," "self-conceit," "swagger," "bragging," "arrogance," etc.

(This is what each of us fails to notice creeping into all our actions, even when we occupy ourselves with noble causes, such as helping others.)

The result of this unfortunate mixing negatively affects all religious tenets—because in place of true Faith, earth-humans will also embrace many fictions and false convictions.

The second sacred being-impulse or sense of genuine Love gets replaced in the split human psyche by sexual pleasure, or a sense of pity, or desire for submission or a craze for obtaining material things and lots of wealth. So contemporary earth-humans can never manifest love with genuine, impartial and non-egoistic love. (According to Swedenborg such a noble and genuine love can only be obtained through self-examination and self-purging—with the Lord God's help.)

Because of this terrible mixing that goes on in everyone's lives, no one had any real taste of the sacred being-impulse of genuine Love—without which no data and information can form within our inner bio-fabric for the Divine purpose of self-perfection. This mixing of values is wonderfully symbolized in 1 Kings 17:4-6 where Elijah both drinks from a sacred brook and is fed by ravens! Also, by Balaam, who understands God's truth, but is bent on destroying goodness in others (*Apocalypse Explained*, n. 140).

But according to Beelzebub, the sacred being-impulse of "essence-hope" has now degenerated into the most harmful of the three. The newly formed and abnormal type of hope now being embraced by three-brained beings of the planet Earth actually causes all possibilities for spiritual growth to become paralyzed in them, simply because they always *hope* for something better to happen instead of *doing* anything about it.

"Hope" now simply strengthens human laziness.

Ashiata Shiemash next comes down from the mountain to make additional observations of those living in the city of Babylon (symbolizing those who have destroyed God's good and truth and have nothing spiritual remaining) to determine whether there might be some other way to save humanity.

He discovers that while the sacred being-impulses of Faith, Hope, and Love have become horribly tainted in the human psyche, another impulse called *Objective-Conscience* has not yet atrophied in them, but remains buried in their presences (subconscious or internal natural mind) almost in its primordial state.

In a manner corresponding to the story of the sinking of the continent Atlantis, the abnormal conditions of life established by the external orientation of being-existence on Earth, God's gift of *Objective Conscience* became embedded in people's deeper "subconscious." While this keeps it safe, unfortunately it takes no part in the functioning of people's ordinary waking conditions and routine habitual mind. In Swedenborg's terms, this implanting of sacred data deep into the human psyche (internal natural mind) is also called the "remains." In other discussions, I believe that Gurdjieff referred to this sacred storehouse of essence-information as the *magnetic center*. (*In Search of the Miraculous*, pages 200-4.)

Ashiata Shiemash surmises that if he could find a way to make this inner dictate from God's mercy function in the general state of people's so-called "waking-existence" then it would still be possible to save earth-humans from the consequences (and trance) of the organ Kundabuffer, which spoils all our noble endeavors.

So he spends the rest of his time formulating a long-term plan for creating the conditions by which the functioning of this "sacred-conscience," still surviving intact in people's subconscious, might *make contact with* (conjunction) and take part in the functioning of their ordinary consciousness. He asks for God's blessing in this serious undertaking and with that, the Legonimism ends.

(Swedenborg also states that such a union or connection must take place between *what we know to be true* with *what we really are and do* in order to awaken the inner dictate of conscience, by which our cultured morality and outer acts can become genuinely spiritual.

Otherwise "Faith," "Hope" and "Love" become merely worldly and spurious to our lives.)

So having learned about this Legonimism during his last visit to the planet Earth, Beelzebub tells his grandson that he was determined to discover the details of the methods Ashiata Shiemash took to accomplish his great aim. At this point in the story he shares with Hassein the contents of the one surviving (from war) marble tablet and principal relic of that small Brotherhood-Olbogmek of special initiated beings in Central Asia. Its inscriptions addressed the sacred being-impulses of Faith, Love and Hope as manifested by the different three-centers of human experience:

> Faith of consciousness is freedom
> Faith of feeling is weakness
> Faith of body is stupidity.

> Love of consciousness evokes the same in response
> Love of feeling evokes the opposite
> Love of body depends only on type and polarity.

> > Hope of consciousness is strength
> > Hope of feeling is slavery
> > Hope of body is disease.

Personally, I find those statements profound and eye-opening.

Before ending this part of his story, Beelzebub decides to offer Hassein some further information as to why the contemporary and now abnormal impulse of "Hope" has become so dangerous to the modern human beings on Earth. He tells his attentive grandson that the current function of hope has engendered a strange disease in humans called "tomorrow." The terrifying consequences of this disease is that even though earth-humans might have suspicions as to what they ought to really be doing with their lives, they never make the proper effort at the time it is needed. This disease has not only stifled their efforts for spiritual growth, it has also hindered many earth-humans from honestly discharging their terrestrial being-obligations (duty and uses) indispensable for maintaining the conditions of ordinary worldly society.

This disease called "tomorrow," stemming from an atrophied approach to the notion of Hope, allows earth-humans to convince (fool) themselves that if they put things off till "later," they will do something better and do more of it.

Another negative consequence of this disease called "tomorrow" is that generally, as people age and get wiser during the end stages of their planetary existence, they begin to better sense reality. This is because of the same natural processes by which the properties left behind by the organ Kundabuffer—over the course of one's lifetime—gradually diminish. These older individuals who sense their inner predicament and sense what kind of being-efforts must be made for spiritual growth, find themselves in an unfortunate condition called "feebleness" and "infirmity." In other words, Great Nature only allows a finite amount of time on Earth for people to do the work of saving their souls, and beyond that allotted time, people's desires for spiritual evolution become only ineffectual yearnings.

That is truly terrifying!

Beelzebub's researches and investigations into the further activities of the Very Saintly Ashiata Shiemash made clear to him that this unique individual again ascended up that same mountain to strategize (symbolizing elevated thinking), over a long period of time, how to save humankind by getting their submerged sacred functioning of conscience to somehow participate in their normal daily waking experience.

As a longtime student of Swedenborg's theology, I quickly recognized this spiritual condition as the split within the modern human psyche into *outer* and *inner* functions and that unless re-unified (as a marriage between knowledge and heart), leads to pretense and shallowness. Swedenborg indeed described how a more external will and thought gradually covers over our original consciousness or essence (*True Christian Religion* vol. 2, n. 593). This new outer "crust" is the worldly personality and mask we develop in life from which we can deceive others concerning our actual nullity and worldly motivations. Swedenborg states that God wisely stores this sacred data called "conscience" in the internal part of the human psyche or subconscious where it can provide a plane for a heavenly will to take hold, emerge and have a real effect on our outer life. *Only spiritual temptation brings about this unity where conscience can come back to the surface.*

The Terror-Of-The-Situation is that we go about our lives overlooking this predicament. So taking remedial action doesn't happen often. Because of the real split in the human psyche, the outer and corporeal functioning of consciousness—which exists closest to our sensory organs—*intercepts* and *steals* all the information coming in from the outer world to fulfill its purposes and to ensure its survival. This includes having an adverse reaction and disdain for all the sacred data implanted by God in the subconscious, which would rightfully seek to gain the reins in one's life.

So whether we listen to a moving Sunday sermon or read a book on spiritual evolution, even this valuable material simply piles up in the outer corporeal memory, only to be used by our self-centeredness (proprium) in the fabrication of new masks of morality and benevolence.

Having the sacred inner data of conscience rise up into our outer daily lives is not a flattering procedure. In fact, it is a process closely related to the earthquakes and combat brought about by the Lord's

Second Coming in the Apocalypse, and why Jesus told his disciples that they could not "bear" these things now.

What is it that we must come to bear? The answer is *ourselves*!

There is a tendency to try to bypass the uncomfortable process of self-examination and simply jump right ahead into becoming a good person. This is what makes people feel immediately good about themselves, and they will congregate wherever this pleasant feeling is promoted (like a church). But this is an incomplete and flawed approach to spiritual development and will not assist in the deeper and proper inner re-organization (crystallization) of a spiritual body (which houses the soul).

Here, Gurdjieff is going for the jugular vein by seemingly challenging the very foundations of kindness and love. But the real Terror-Of-The-Situation is that the two greatest heavenly Commandments to "Love God" and to "Love the neighbor" can become empty concepts—and *puppetized*. That is, our usual and earthly efforts toward being kind and friendly to others—without engaging in genuine self-examination and spiritual combat (spiritual temptations for inner cleansing)—should be seen as highly suspect.

If I had not studied Gurdjieff, I would not have fully understood Swedenborg and if I had not studied Swedenborg, I would not have fully understood Gurdjieff concerning this most important point about salvation and spiritual combat. In terms of understanding Gurdjieff especially, I would have viewed his challenging ideas as being mean-spirited and not helpful (simply because he doesn't flatter).

My impartial observations of those who belong to the current Swedenborgian Movement is that they focus too much of their attention on ideas like *"We receive God's enlightenment, truth and grace from acts of love and goodness"* or that *"enlightenment comes from goodness,"* which are technically true, but overlook preparatory ideas like "self-examination," "inner combat" and "repentance" (which Swedenborg addresses fully in his theological work, *The True Christian Religion*). These uncomfortable experiencings are necessary activities because they will ultimately *qualify* our acts of goodness, and let God know what we really want changed in our lives. Such struggle represents the only methods by which we can re-connect (conjoin) our inner and outer realities (divided minds) and bring conscience back to the forefront. This *intentional* contact and struggle can eventually make our two separated functions of thought and feelings correspond and agree with each other.

For some reason we are not taught—and don't grasp—the true spiritual challenges and obstacles of having a divided mind (a mental situation that was verified and addressed through Swedenborg's own discoveries).

Sorry folks, but most people attend church looking for support, comfort, improved self-esteem and "hope" in something or another— not to be shown their dirty laundry. But this is why Jesus said to his disciples that they could not bear his giving them more information—because this information would be very personal.

Both Gurdjieff and Swedenborg agree that True Worship is not the happy enhancement of a positive state (which often just means "titillation"). The Lord came into the world with the same strategy as Ashiata Shiemash—to help us pull the splinters out of our butts (and the logs out of our eyes)! But a big negative property of the organ Kundabuffer (proprium) is that it allowed all our character contradictions to live side by side within us and go ignored. If we do not examine all our inner contradictions (which we have become expert at keeping calm) all attempts at *Faith, Hope,* and *Love* will be impure and lack spiritual innocence.

Heaven is a state of innocence. Otherwise, even goodness and kind deeds (loving God and neighbor) will never be genuine.

To be continued!

SUMMARY

■ During extreme meditations, Asiata Shiemash discovers that the negative properties of the organ Kundabuffer have become "second nature" to the split human psyche, and therefore, the traditional methods of salvation, like "Faith," "Hope" and "Love" were now quite useless.

■ Nothing could be more *terrifying* for earth-humans, who believe otherwise!

■ Because of their dual psyche, earth-humans, can easily feign these sacred being-impulses through pretense. Faulty and unchecked motives could thereafter mix with, and corrupt, these sacred impulses and even make a person's actions look outwardly similar to that of angels. Inwardly however, these sacred impulses become mixed with ignoble properties such as "vanity," "self-love," "pride," "self-conceit," etc.

■ Individuals are open to suggestibility if any one of those ignoble traits (abnormal forms of self-love) is evoked in their degenerated Reason. This leads to false convictions concerning the being-impulses of "Faith," "Hope" and "Love" arising in the deluded self-images of earth-humans. As a result, negative persuasions become lawfully fixed into the human fabric without any hindrance from spiritual truths and challenges.

SUMMARY

■ Today's distorted view of "Hope" is the worst of our sacred impulses, since it only helps to paralyze the human potential for spiritual growth—even thwarting those who suspect they need to make genuine efforts. Thus, nothing real is ever obtained by such individuals who always "hope."

■ Ashiata Shiemash seeks some other way to help earth-humans. He discovers that Objective (Spiritual) Conscience is still preserved, intact, within earth-humans, but in a primordial state (this is Swedenborg's concept of *remains*). Through God's mercy, Spiritual Conscience (or remains) has become deeply embedded in the *subconscious* part of the split human psyche, so it does not normally take part in one's outer habitual consciousness or "waking-existence."

■ Ashiata Shiemash devises a plan to get this "sacred-conscience" to gradually function in the ordinary and outward consciousness of earth-humans.

■ Beelzebub investigates the life of Ashiata Shiemash and discovers that almost all of the stone tablets containing his unique ideas were destroyed during a time of war. Only a tablet kept by the Brotherhood "Olbogmek" survived. It addresses and describes how various forms of "Faith," "Hope" and "Love" can manifest in the split functioning of the human psyche.

■ Usually, by the time an individual naturally senses the need for spiritual self-perfection, infirmity and old age have kicked in.

CHAPTER 27

"The organization for man's existence created by the Very Saintly Ashiata Shiemash"

Beelzebub continues his Tales by telling his grandson, Hassein, that according to his own investigations, when Ashiata Shiemash descended from the mountain for the last time with a plan to accomplish his aims he did not return to the city of Babylon (an inner state of profanation) but instead traveled to a city in the middle of the continent of Asia. There, he made contact with a brotherhood called "Tchaftantouri" which means "To be or not to be at all."

Two genuine initiates who founded this brotherhood had, through brave self-examination, discovered "something-very-undesirable" in their general psychical organization (just as those Akhaldans from Atlantis did before them). And, just as important, they also discovered that within themselves they possessed special Divine data to rid themselves of this problem. They located other beings who also responded to this same aim among various monasteries in the same region and brought them together for this all-important pursuit.

Ashiata Shiemash came upon this group and was able to offer them new insights and strategies to assist them in this essence-project (spiritual duty). This brotherhood later changed its name to "Heechtvori" which means "Only-he-will-be-called-and-will-become-the-Son-of-God-who-acquires-in-himself-Conscience."

(Amazingly, Beelzebub describes "conscience" as the *representation of the Lord God's struggles within us*. I highly embrace this *spiritual* definition of conscience because I have learned from Swedenborg that it is the Lord God who fights for us. This divine inner struggle is central to Swedenborgian doctrine in that it teaches that the Lord God, when on Earth, struggled against all the "undesirable" human traits and physical leanings he inherited from His worldly mother at birth. So when we each choose to carry His "cross," we consciously choose to engage in a similar process of salvation through inner suffering and purification from our inherited flaws. But it is the Lord God who was victorious—who still fights for us on our smaller individual scale in order to make us a microcosm of Heaven.)

Ashiata Shiemash, after establishing his teaching on salvation, sent out various members of this brotherhood to teach others that in one's subconscious (what Swedenborg calls the *internal natural mind* – *True Christian Religion*, n. 593) there was always present the sacred data (sacred remains) manifested from Above for engendering in them the divine impulse of genuine conscience—and that only an individual who through certain self-efforts, acquires the "ableness" that allows this data to make contact with the *outer* habitual mind (and deluded self-image) and has the legitimate right to be called a "genuine son of OUR COMMON FATHER CREATOR of all that exists."

The initiates of this new brotherhood (called Heechtvori) who earned the distinction of being called an "All-the-rights-possessing brother" not only succeeded in connecting their outer and inner realities, but through their "ableness-of-conscious-direction-of-the-functioning-of-his-own-psyche" they each had to convince a hundred other individuals—and prove to them that the impulse of being-objective-conscience already exists in man. And how to use this gift to allow one to respond to the real (and not imaginary) sense and aim of his existence. (Swedenborg claimed that without this protected function, earth-humans could not think rationally.)

Each of these hundred individuals had to do the same, and so did others down the line.

The term "priest" was eventually given to those initiates who, through their pious efforts, succeeded in making *conscience* an inseparable part of their ordinary waking consciousness and had therefore made tangible success in their acts of goodness toward those around them, engendering the feeling in others of true "gratitude." Today, this term "priest" has also come to be used to describe professionals belonging to a group called the "clergy" (who now mainly just preach).

Although more and more people began to be enlightened to the fact that they all contained the sacred data within them necessary for the manifestation of the Divine impulse conscience, nevertheless this impulse ultimately failed to take part in their general and everyday consciousness. As a result, this important functioning gradually atrophied to where this sacred data was unavailable for evoking the objective impulse of genuine Divine-Love.

(The big problem today with communicating this inner challenge to modern humans is that one's God-given conscience (*remains*), still exists on a deeper and discrete level of a split mind, where it is out of reach of our normal daily terrestrial thoughts and activities. Also, you cannot convince someone that they need something they think they already enjoy—like being a good person and capable of participating immediately in heavenly love.)

Beelzebub then shares with Hassein the secret of Ashiata Shiemash's discovery concerning how the factors arise for the manifestation of conscience in three-brained beings. The process is purely a spiritual undertaking by which we share in God's *suffering*. (Spiritual growth does not get more Swedenborgian than this!) As mentioned earlier, this shared sacred suffering was made clear by Jesus' challenge of inviting others to "take up His Cross," that is, to participate in the same inner conflicts and temptations that He Himself endured while on Earth. (This means one has to purify oneself first in order to make *Faith, Hope,* and *Love* genuinely spiritual. When one's inner and outer realities make contact this produces the clash and suffering necessary to expand one's plane of conscience).

(Swedenborgians have definitely been exposed to this precise teaching through his writings, especially concerning the inner struggle of the Lord's Glorification, which took place beyond the observation of human eyes, and that we must each take on a similar and humbling challenge. But the greatest obstacle and the biggest challenge of connecting people's two discrete functions of consciousness (inner and outer) is their making sincere (often unflattering) self-observations about oneself and discovering that one's daily existence is focused on simply covering over the more interior and real functioning of conscience, thus preventing it from taking part in our actual spiritual growth.

People want their lives to become *more* comfortable—not less so!)

Beelzebub tells Hassein that conscience only arises from particles of the "emanations-of-the-sorrow" of our OMNI-LOVING AND LONG-SUFFERING-ENDLESS-CREATOR. This, according to Beelzebub, is why genuine conscience in humans is sometimes called the REPRESENTATIVE OF THE CREATOR in us. According to Swedenborg, "Mercy is love grieving" (*Arcana Coelestia,* n. 5480). The human race implores this divine pity when it perceives its true predicament and grieves as well.

To be more precise, humans participate in this sacred suffering and sorrow through the "clash" between the worldly desires of their planetary bodies (to seek pleasure and comfort through corporeal and worldly things) and the opposite inner strivings from the data implanted by God's mercy in their inner subconscious minds (interior rational minds) that cause sorrow and suffering to occur (shining a light on our miscues). But this clash leads to our genuine spiritual growth.

If one *consciously* assists the inner strivings of God's data in predominating over one's outer (corporeal/sensual) compulsions and desires, he or she behaves in more perfect accordance with the cosmic scheme of our COMMON FATHER CREATOR HIMSELF. The resulting inner conflict also has real organic consequences and allows for the *bio-reorganization* and "coating" of *higher spiritual bodies* for the soul within us.

But if one prefers to simply jump straight ahead into doing good deeds without taking on such inner suffering and struggle, they will *not* become a representative of the Lord God (who participated in these identical sufferings), whereby something less genuine or less innocent will result. (Swedenborg makes it clear that on the highest level of biblical interpretation, the Holy narratives are nothing other than the stories of how the Lord God battled with and suffered the onslaught of evil inclinations and false notions in His human and earthly nature.) Our cosmic duty is to take part in this great cosmic conflict as well, otherwise our good deeds and uses will always become tainted by egoism.

(Several individuals have asked me if I thought that Gurdjieff's ideas were exactly the same as Swedenborg's. For a long time I struggled with this topic since I could not tell if Gurdjieff was aware that the highest level of knowledge and spiritual revelation concerning the Lord God's own inner struggles and grieving was a blueprint for saving humankind on Earth. Beelzebub's calling conscience the "representative of the Creator" in our lives tells me that Gurdjieff was perfectly familiar with the Lord God's sacred suffering and sorrow. Swedenborg claimed that the Lord God's ultimate victory brought Heaven and Hell into a new order—called *Glorification*. (It also allowed Divine Truth to conjoin perfectly with Divine Good.)

In earth-humans (three-brained beings) this same glorification is represented on a smaller scale by each of us harmoniously conjoining our distinct *inner* and *outer* realities, or dual minds, by tapping into our remains and spiritual conscience.

According to Beelzebub, the very saintly works of Ashiata Shiemash resulted in an unprecedented period of sanity and peace on Earth. Furthermore, all "state-organizations" and "castes" or "class systems" were abolished because their rulers were no longer chosen through elections or from mere heredity. Instead, they were chosen for their merits—particularly from their personal efforts at bringing genuine conscience into their daily lives. (True leadership has a spiritual component.) The peculiar property in three-brained beings to create state-organizations and divide people into classes was one of the results of the sinking of the continent Atlantis (humans losing touch with their spiritual conscience).

This peculiar property is known as "egoism."

As mentioned before, the sinking of Atlantis symbolizes the splitting of humankind's general psyche into two distinct levels of functioning—inner (subconscious) and outer (habitual and worldly consciousness). It is only because of this split and disconnection between the two psychical functions that egoism and self-love could arise in individuals (and even be undetected by the participants).

Thankfully, this separation was used by the Lord God to providentially preserve and protect the sacred data of conscience (also called "remains") from final degeneration (by planting it deeper into the human psyche, well beyond worldly bullshit) and which would be needed for engendering true innocence and spiritual rebirth later in one's life.

So, in a sense, God punted.

If this sacred data had not been protected and was allowed to perish, the entire human race would also have perished. (In fact, Swedenborg claimed that if this deeper plane in human consciousness had been destroyed, the human race would have morphed into real monsters before ultimately going extinct. He also stated in the *Arcana Coelestia*, near the end of n. 576, that God is stealthy at placing this special data among our deepest insanities for the future creation of a new will.)

Sadly, Beelzebub points out that what was also lost to the split or dual psyche of the human beings on Earth was the impulse called "sincerity." It is self-sincerity (from self-examination) that *reconnects* an individual's inner and outer mental localizations and puts the kibosh on "cunning," "envy," "hate," "hypocrisy," "contempt," "haughtiness," servility," "slyness," "ambition," "being two-faced," etc. But through the split in human personality, our egoism becomes completely *inoculated* from God's sacred data stored deeper within the subconscious. This sacred data would otherwise be activated to provide an inner dictate and throw light on the rotten intentions we harbor in our daily lives and motives. (This inoculation occurs from our seeking only those things that give us calm and comfort—especially through some form of titillation and personal flattery.)

Beelzebub informs Hassein that a human child on Earth is not born with this split mind. The split in the human psyche is promoted by parents and modern educational practices whereby children are forced to learn artificial (outward) behavior (called culture), which causes their God-given instinct for sincerity to be "driven-back within," where it becomes their subconscious and puts it out of helpful range. Therefore, as a child reaches the age of maturity, all the other sacred being-impulses, such as *Faith, Hope,* and *Love* get caught in the crosshairs of our worldly egoism and are subject to degeneration and perversion by the delusional and disconnected dual human psyche, which allows us to believe our knowledge equals inner development.

This can be confusing to some Swedenborgians who correctly learned that these *remains*, protected within their interiors, contain elements of angelic love and truth, which are gifts of mercy from the Lord God. But these sacred influences are implanted without our knowledge during our younger years of *innocence,* and therefore escape our later egoism—where at a later time, they can serve to challenge our faulty manifestations of Love, Faith and Hope, that we have learned to copy from the outer world. (This sacred data is only implanted during states of innocence, which we lose as we learn the ways of the world. And only our return to innocence will reactivate it and make it grow.)

As a student of Swedenborg's theological writings and the doctrines of the "New Jerusalem" for forty years, I know I harbor lots of bad traits and am not above screwing things up and muddying the waters. Identifying one's screw-ups, flaws and undesirable traits, then asking for God's help in resisting these flaws of character, lawfully re-connects one's outer habitual life to one's genuine spiritual passions, so that the remains (deeper divine gifts) can develop. The painful conflict resulting from this connection allows one's inner spiritual reality to properly unfold in *innocence* and without any *pretense*. (Swedenborg makes this cleansing process particularly clear in the chapters called *Repentance* and *Reformation and Regeneration* in the second volume of his great theological work, *True Christianity*.)

In the usual condition, however, where people's ordinary waking-existence and consciousness is disconnected from the deeper sacred information that God implants in their subconscious, maleficence, evil, egoistic and selfish tendencies go unchallenged and eventually become a fixed part of the fabric of the human psyche. This unfortunate condition usurps heavenly order and makes it difficult for humans to even want to sincerely partake in the kind of "suffering" that the Lord God experienced, yet is necessary to promote real changes in earth-humans. This process of cleansing now seems quite unnatural to our passions, and even anti-intuitive to our flawed thinking.

Swedenborg calls our ordinary thinking and worldly waking-consciousness "spiritual sleep" (a form of trance) that needs to be awakened, even shook up.

Ashiata Shiemash had designed a means for delivering special "shocks" to the human psyche to snap it out of its snooze-like state so that it could be reconnected to the divine data (remains) implanted deeper within. These "shocks" are referred to by Beelzebub in his Tales as the "Remorse-of-Conscience" or as the "shock-to-organic-shame." Only through sincere self-examination and a willingness to discover undesirable elements within ourselves can we experience the proper shocks necessary to re-awaken our spiritual potential. (This operation goes deeper than mere self-denigration and requires the awareness that we are not sources of "life" but only vessels or bio-forms for receiving life—from the Lord God.)

Beelzebub informs Hassein that during times when such shocks were freeing earth-humans from their normal "rubbish" he had more difficulty observing the events on the surface of the planet Earth (with his telescope). It seems that Beelzebub is making the point here that when people are making sincere efforts to change themselves, nothing can be observed by the eyeball (ocular sight). Such a profound change is not meant for show. He also suggests that when the process of *remorse* in humans mixes itself with other, less noble behavior, the resulting vibrations given off color the earth's atmosphere in a way that makes far-off observation more difficult.

Unfortunately, the case is that that three-brained beings of planet Earth have become experts at "squashing" these shocks and the painful "prick" of experiencing any "Remorse-of-Conscience" through highly successful means. These means include "alcoholism," "cocainism," "morphinism," "nicotinism," "onanism," "monkism," "Athenianism," and other such abusive behavior ending in "ism."

(In fact, I feel my competence in taking on this challenging writing project comes from my own limited success—actually willingness—at finding many shocking realities concerning the complete rottenness and vile nature of my own inner makeup. But I have made this my life's challenge to fix, and my "ableness" and "endurance" to do so is definitely getting stronger.)

Beelzebub goes on to explain to his grandson that one of the outcomes of the absence of God's sacred data participating in the everyday consciousness of earth-humans is that they now arrange their (outer) welfare exclusively for themselves. (God's Heavenly kingdom is a spiritual and internal state of mutual Love and cooperative sharing.) Swedenborg and Gurdjieff both discovered that we are to live for others—not just for ourselves (which is self-love).

Beelzebub reminds us that since none of the planets offer enough resources to ensure everybody's "equal" *external* welfare (irrespective of one's "objective-merits"), the worldly prosperity of one individual can only be assured through the adversity of many. "Social Justice" is therefore impossible with a planet's limited outer resources. True Justice in God's universe, however, goes much deeper than a mere attempt at redistribution of material wealth, and as just mentioned, cannot be secured even by the entire resources of a birth planet. Plus, living with amenities (and entitlements) doesn't prepare us for life after death or our preparing for eternal happiness, which is a mental state that is always victorious over any kind of adversity and challenge.

The dominant drive toward material success, which focuses only on an earth-human's own personal welfare, has fixed into their common presences the ignoble being-impulses of "cunning," "contempt," "hate," "servility," "lying," "flattery," all of which cause the gradual destruction of those inner possibilities implanted by God for His grand cosmic purpose—making a heavenly society from the human race.

But for a limited period, Ashiata Shiemash indeed succeeded in convincing earth-humans about the true nature of their situation and cosmic duty (called "being-Partkdolg-duty") to have proper relationships with each other according to God's intended plan. At that time on Earth, leaders began to be chosen for their spiritual "essence-power" and objective merits—that could be easily sensed and perceptible to all other earth-humans around them. This sacred duty, introduced by Ashiata Shiemash, which led to such objective merits and self-perfecting required *personal conscious labors* and *intentional sufferings*.

Swedenborg calls these same individual efforts, "repentance," "reformation," and "regeneration." What makes this process partic-ularly challenging to adopt is that our outer, habitual mind, with its incomplete and detached consciousness has convinced us that its flawed functioning is all there is, and represents our real and only consciousness. Under such a false assumption we are tricked (hypno-tized) into believing we can simply jump straight away into doing good deeds for others by external actions—without any self-exam-ination or addressing any of our flaws. (Swedenborg calls this inner purification the "first duty" of becoming spiritually charitable and useful.)

Emanuel Swedenborg makes it clear (at least to me) that "love to the Lord and charity to the neighbor cannot exist, except in a state of innocence" for "only *innocence* acknowledges and receives the Lord" (God's Love and Truth accepted into its very being and reality. See *Arcana Coelestia*, n. 5236 on this). And, as Ashiata Shie-mash stressed (as did Swedenborg), one can only obtain this genuine innocence through spiritual *temptation* (which allows one's habitual consciousness or external focus to *connect* and clash with the sacred data implanted in one's subconscious or interior being).

I may be sounding like a broken record but the Lord God will not permit people to experience true temptation (connecting outer realities with inner realities) unless they have been actively choosing to be regenerated for spiritual rebirth. Otherwise, unprepared people would succumb to all tests of temptation. True spiritual temptation is a posi-tive (yet uncomfortable) sign that one has genuinely entered into God's divine cosmic program.

Back to the story. So, a new generation of earth-leaders, through Ashiata Shiemash's guidance and through their own essence-labors, had succeeded in the development of their genuine conscience through five "being-obligolnian-strivings." These strivings are identified as:

The first striving required having respect for one's physical body and supplying it with that which was *really* necessary.

The second striving consisted of having a constant and unflag-ging instinctive need for self-perfection.

The third striving was the challenge to continually perfect one's knowledge of universal laws (which are the same for both science and religion).

The fourth striving was to pay back God for the gift of life and become free to help lighten God's load and Divine suffering/ sorrow.

Finally, the fifth striving—to assist in the self-perfection of others.

From these five strivings, not only was peace and normality restored during this period of Ashiata Shiemash's saintly influence on Earth but Beelzebub had even observed that the "death and birth rate" of humans on Earth began to diminish—by a fifth! As earth-humans increased the quality of their life-vibrations, through proper *inner* work, Nature's need for quantity is lowered for maintaining balance and the proper equilibrium of the universe. (I know this sounds like an odd notion, but Swedenborg himself wrote that God allows people to die in order to maintain the required qualities needed for proper equilibrium in the Spiritual World—which also rules Nature and the free will of the human intellect.)

Unfortunately, after Ashiata Shiemash's own departure from the surface of the planet Earth, humans began again to move in a downward spiral direction.

SUMMARY

▪ When Ashiata Shiemash comes down from the mountain for the last time, he travels not to Babylon, but to another community in the Middle East where he meets initiates of a Brotherhood (called Tchaftantouri) who were making similar unflattering discoveries about themselves.

▪ Ashiata Shiemash is able to enlighten and prepare these special individuals by teaching that God had implanted within them (their subconscious mind) sacred data (*remains*) that could help engender genuine conscience.

▪ This sacred data must make intentional "contact" with both one's outer worldly mind and inner desires and start a mental *friction* between conflicting values, which Swedenborg calls *temptation* and *spiritual combat*. Only those who acquire the "ableness" to create such inner contact within themselves, have the right to be called a genuine Son of our COMMON FATHER CREATOR.

▪ After some success, Ashiata Shiemash sent his brethren out to spread the word. New members who successfully applied these "truths" to their lives became a part of yetanother Brotherhood (called Heechtvori, meaning, "Only-he-will-be-called-and-become-the-Son-of-God-who-acquires-in-himself-Conscience").

▪ Conscience is the REPRESENTATIVE OF GOD in us. That is a very Swedenborgian concept!

SUMMARY

▪ Because of humankind's split psyche (outer and inner), egoism is inoculated from the opposing influences of conscience, in which our spiritual potentials have fallen asleep and become passive.

▪ For awhile, and because people were interested in developing conscience, the Asian continent experienced unprecedented peace along with the disappearance of various "state-organizations" and "class distinctions" among its citizens, both of which had caused them to live abnormally and promoted *egoism*. Birth and death rates diminished, due to these changes.

▪ Modern education (learning "head knowledge" by rote) and our abnormal upbringing (to outwardly fit in), helps drive *conscience* down deeper into the human psyche until it actually becomes totally split off. Swedenborg says that this split occurs when a young child learns *pretense* from the adult world. The outer manifestation of this split is a fabricated worldly personality (or mask).

▪ *Sincerity* reconnects the human dual psyche and allows conscience to expand and return to the forefront of our existence.

▪ A birth planet's limited resources makes it impossible for a fair distribution of material wealth to all. True justice goes deeper than social justice.

CHAPTER 28

"The chief culprit in the destruction of all the Very Saintly Labors of Ashiata Shiemash"

Beelzebub now tells his grandson how an individual named *Lentrohamsanin* helped to obliterate Ashiata Shiemash's great works. This most grievous event happened several centuries before Beelzebub's fifth visit to the planet Earth when he took personal residence in the ancient city of Babylon.

Lentrohamsanin, unfortunately, because of his "double-gravity-centered" existence (split psyche) allowed egoism to mingle with the development of his highest reasoning powers (learning) and now, after his terrestrial death, lives on a small planet named "Eternal-Retribution," that is, on a plane of existence consisting of *internal* suffering. (Sounds like Swedenborg's karmic description of Hell to me—that is, a negative inner state of mind returning to its misguided first principles, rather than an actual place of physical suffering and torture. By the way, Swedenborg, who was a genuine intellectual genius, also observed within himself that when his ego was removed from any of his scientific projects he would lose all interest in them. So ego can be the driving force operating in even the smartest, most educated of individuals—like this Lentrohamsanin fellow!)

In our flawed worldview, we tend to mix up intelligence and mental genius with the inner quality of one's heart. Wrong!

Beelzebub gives Hassein some background information concerning the history and arising of this "Hasnamuss" (bull-shitting) person of new formation (having a post-Atlantian or post-Noachian psyche), who was considered an expert and easily gained authority over others. Lentrohamsanin's father was a very rich *hedonist*, owning many camel caravans and his mother, a huckster, made her living convincing childless women that they could enhance their fertility by visiting a special "Holy" mountain (that she had personally chosen).

Because these two earth-partners had concentrated all their focus on gaining riches and living a life of pleasure, they resorted to having abortions so that their life's pursuits would be unhindered. However, upon having reached an older age they felt that they needed a child in order to be fulfilled. Beelzebub states that their sexual intercourse consisted in the blending of two *heterogeneous* "Exioëharies" (their sperm and ovum were not a harmonious match, probably meaning that they were not *spiritually* or genuinely in love with each other).

This married couple spared no expense or medical means to achieve pregnancy and also visited every "Holy-place" (except, of course, their own "Holy-mountain"). When their first son, Lentrohamsanin was born, they put all their efforts in gratifying his every pleasure and giving him the best education money could buy. They were certainly what we would call today, "helicopter parents."

According to Beelzebub, Lentrohamsanin, during his special upbringing, had his brain filled with every kind of fantastic and dubious information possible concerning reality. Since all this data/information in his split psyche had no connection to the quality of his true inner being, then because of the leftover consequences of the organ Kundabuffer, which generated impulses like "vanity," self-love," and "swagger," an ambition arose in him to become a famous person.

Lentrohamsanin meditated on how to accomplish such a thing and decided he would invent a unique theory that no one else had ever thought of before. He would also put this new intellectual invention into writing (a Kashireitleer). It was to be a new *doctrine of happiness*.

His new doctrine of happiness challenged the current existing order of collective existence among humans. He put forth the new idea that true happiness could only be obtained when an individual became fully independent and free from the influence of any other person, regardless of title. Beelzebub, in describing this scenario to Hassein, also alludes to the fact that the three-brained beings on Earth at that time had no true understanding of what freedom really was when they were introduced to this new doctrine concerning happiness.

Lentrohamsanin also challenges the "spiritual" merits by which people became chiefs and leaders of their society.

His reasoning was that if these leaders truly lived lives that were proper for their souls to secure a heavenly existence in the other world, then surely God had bestowed upon them special talents not given to the *rank and file*. Therefore, if the ideas these leaders were feeding the general public were true, then they should be able to prove it by at least changing a pinch of sand into bread. Since they could not do so, Lentrohamsanin insisted in his writings that we all must rely on ourselves to secure happiness and our real freedom.

In other words, we must bring down the old (and unfair) system, become masters of our own circumstances, and elect leaders who come from among our own ranks and who understand our own plights. These leaders will be chosen on the basis of equal rights, without distinction of sex, race or age. This sounds very much like what we are hearing in society today!

(Some students of Gurdjieff's teachings have speculated that the name "Lentrohamsanin" was created from the names "Lenin" and "Trotsky," who used the rank and file in their revolutionary movements to bring down the old system, as their "useful idiots.)

Lentrohamsanin next puts together a costly banquet and invites learned beings (intellectuals) from all over the area. After this free feast they were all introduced to the "new ideas of freedom" invented by this Hasnamuss (bull-shitting) individual. One by one, the guests began to praise these astounding new (and titillating) ideas and began patting each other on the back for recognizing the importance of these newly revealed "truths." Through this "mutual inflation," they too wanted to hop on the bandwagon and be bestowed with a similar level of importance and status.

Word spread. Egos puffed up.

Unfortunately, not everyone was convinced. So (as always) two opposing "parties" resulted—one favoring the old way and the other favoring the new way. *Hatred* grew between them. As these two differing parties swelled in membership, civil wars began to break out.

Many years later, and eager to change the "state-organization" of his own city with these new ideas for personal *happiness* and *freedom*, was the great-grandson of Lentrohamsanin. He lived in Babylon at the height of their frenzied debates about the reality of the soul. Thanks to this "grandson," who wanted a new state-organization, soon the question "of-the-soul" was turned into the question of "politics."

After more heated debates about obtaining happiness, the group of learned beings in Babylon also split into two political parties. This split, too, would have led to a civil war except the Persian King, who had originally brought them all together from his military expeditions, began a major crackdown. Some of these learned beings were executed, others were imprisoned and still others were sent back to their native countries as "mad." (Those who did not participate in this political frenzy were sent back home with all kinds of honors.)

Beelzebub adds that those learned individuals who escaped with their lives from Babylon and were now spread over the whole continent of Asia continued to fan the flames of those two famous questions concerning the reality of the "soul" and the new political question of what constitutes the proper "inner-communal-organization" for humans.

Still, small pockets of true initiates survived in Asia, where the ideas of Ashiata Shiemash were faithfully continued. But these pockets were also finally destroyed by a "clean sweep," thanks to an arch-vainglorious Greek named "Alexander-of-Macedonia."

With that said, Beelzebub decides the time is now right to tell Hassein the meaning of the phrase "Hasnamuss-individual" and its eternal consequences. Simply put, it is someone who allows *egoism* to participate in the maturing or completed formation of a person's being-individuality—regardless of the intellectual level obtained. This participation by the ego causes an individual to become a "bull-shitter." (This is also the reason why Faith, Hope, and Love no longer have any real effect.)

The greater problem is that egoism, according to ubiquitous and universal rules, can blend itself into the full spectrum (Law of Seven-foldness) of cosmic processes that start in the human mind as an original *perception*, and end in some resulting (corresponding) *behavior*. This spectrum of the human intellect, which the ego can easily partner with, always consists of seven "Naloo-osnian-impulses" (each having its own gravity-center, which contributes to a common equilibrium bent on destroying the rationality of the human psyche). These seven gravity-centers, in which the human ego (proprium) takes part, have the following distinct qualities:

1) Every kind of depravity, conscious or not

2) The feeling of self-satisfaction from leading others astray

3) The irresistible inclination to destroy other breathing creatures

4) The urge to become free from the necessity of fulfilling God's plan

5) The attempt to hide from others, by all artificial means, one's self-estimation of their physical imperfections

6) The nonchalant usage of things not personally deserved

7) Always pretending to be what one is not

(Do you recognize any of these qualities in other humans? Or even in yourself? I certainly do!)

These seven "Naloo-osnian-impulses" of egoism not only have serious eternal consequences for an individual, they can also spread to—and engender—similar hurtful responses in others. Beelzebub informs Hassein that these consequences manifest in four basic categories of Hasnamuss people, or those who mix egos with their level of intelligence. (Here, Gurdjieff attempts to connect the various egoistic outcomes with corresponding gradations of human bio-organizations. Everything we do has an organic consequence.)

The first is a Hasnamuss-individual who lives only in the physical body and memory function, and upon physical death is destroyed forever, such as he or she is. Such a Hasnamuss-individual, while living in the world, is only concerned with protecting his or her hide. Also, this type of individual starts dying (losing functions) while still engaged in his or her planetary existence.

Some Swedenborgians might argue with this cruel outcome because they are taught that all individuals live after the death of the physical body. However, only God gives life and vivifies the human experience, and those without an adequate spiritual life, who love only themselves and the world, have no real experience of genuine living, or of themselves, and are reduced to mere "sticks of wood" or "charred skeletons." Existence is not life.

The second kind of Hasnamuss-individual, who blends their egoism to the perfecting of their imagination (Astral body), after death, survives within the sphere of the planet of their arising, but in this survival they must participate in the lives of many changing lower forms, until this abnormal property of egoism has been eliminated. (This is where the idea of reincarnation comes from and does not usually end in success.)

A third type of Hasnamuss-individual has mingled his or her egoism with the development of their higher-reasoning function (coating of the more subtle, mental body for the soul). Such an individual suffers more greatly than others but still has the potential to spiritually cleanse him or herself after physical death—if they choose to suffer intentionally by removing their precious self-love.

The fourth type is similar to the third except that such a Hasnamuss-individual has lost forever the opportunity to cleanse themself after death (because of their ego and self-love confirming false principles and making these principles "one's own" during life, therefore becoming an *Eternal-Hasnamuss-individual*).

Swedenborg describes the mingling of egoism (proprium) and rationality within the biblical narratives as represented by "Ishmael" mocking Isaac (Genesis 21:9). This type of person has a fully developed civic rationality, but claims that all sagacity originates from themself (instead of God). Beelzebub is underscoring this notion by saying that such individuals must live after death on an equally "disharmonized" planet (spiritual plane) called "Eternal-Retribution," in which there are "serious-retributive-suffering-consequences." (This is the eternal spiritual state that Lentrohamsanin now lives in.)

The term "disharmonized" is a much better way to describe the conditions of Hell.

Beelzebub claims that other Hasnamuss-individuals, who have not yet lost the potential to purify themselves, can find their temporary existence on other *disharmonized* planets variously called "Remorse-of-Conscience," "Repentance," and "Self-Reproach." These three disharmonized states (or planes) of the human spirit correspond to Swedenborg's theological concepts of "Repentance," "Reformation," and "Regeneration." Each term refers to a different, but still disharmonized plane (of the spiritual world), where correction is still needed and that represent the place and inner state in the process of spiritual growth that an individual finds oneself in. These three planes all represent an orderly and organic trajectory that can take one inwardly out of egoism and hell (retributive-suffering-consequences).

Gurdjieff does not directly address the issue of children after death. However, in another book, he states that children "are closer to God," and in this current Tale, he describes those who participate in abortions (like Lentrohamsanin's parents) as "makers of angels." It is apparent, at least to me, that Gurdjieff is referring here only to the fate of individuals who have died after reaching maturity and their "age of responsibility." Swedenborg states the same thing, in that we are responsible for our life-choices only after reaching maturity—and only those choices which become the ruling principles (love) behind all our reasoning and actions.

Obtaining true freedom and happiness is a spiritual process and responsibility (duty), consisting of *conscious works* and *intentional suffering*. Lentrohamsanin tried to remove this responsibility from people's lives and titillate human self-centeredness and self-importance. Lentrohamsanin's ideas are still very seductive to the modern human mind.

He will forever suffer the consequences of wrongly guiding others.

SUMMARY

▪ An individual named Lentohamsanin destroys all Ashiata Shiemash's saintly works by inventing a misleading *new doctrine of happiness*. His motive was to become famous.

▪ This doctrine promises personal happiness by freeing people from others—even though most people did not grasp what true freedom really was. People liked that this new doctrine offered them the freedom not to have to answer to anyone or ever need to sweat over fulfilling God's plan. (However, this creates an inner slavery to one's ego.)

▪ Lentrohamsanin mocks the method of choosing chiefs and leaders based on their *spiritual* merits. And instead, insisted that leaders should be chosen from among their own ranks, who could understand their personal plights. And, these new leaders should be chosen based on "equal rights," and without any discrimination.

▪ One's egoism must also follow the universal rules of order and fully partake in the whole sequence and completing process of the unfolding of the Law of Sevenfoldness—so that it finds its common equilibrium in all its steps of destroying God's plan for proper human development.

▪ Beelzebub describes the four kinds of Hasnamuss-individuals who allow ego to enter into the cockpit of their various levels of intelligence, and what their futures hold after death.

▪ Those who still need (and want) to cleanse themselves of their egoism will find themselves, after death, on one of four *disharmonized* "planets" where there is retributive suffering, corresponding to their personal situation.

▪ Politics emerged from the debate on the existence of the human soul and how one should therefore live to obtain true happiness and freedom—a discussion that transitioned from God's government (and providence) to human government.

▪ The popularity of Lentrohamsanin's invented ideas for creating *happiness* and *freedom* was based on destroying one's cosmic responsibility—through titillating human self-centeredness and self-importance. These ideas also led to political disagreements and civil wars over what was the preferred inner organization to rule people's lives.

PART TWO

CHAPTER 29

"The fruits of former civilizations and the blossoms of the contemporary"

Beelzebub continues his lesson concerning the weird and unusual history of earth-humans for his devoted grandson. Again, this lesson includes the "inner" history (degenerating trajectory) of the psyche of the men-beings living on the ill-fated planet Earth. He now moves on to tell Hassein about the beginnings of western civilization.

Here, Gurdjieff intensifies his assault on our mostly unchallenged and most strongly held worldviews—especially concerning ourselves and our notions of the past.

The story now focuses on the *Greek* and *Roman* civilizations who, through their military might, made a "clean sweep" of all the remaining wisdom brought forth by the saintly labors of Ashiata Shiemash in Asia. Worse, these newly arising powerful countries gave birth to more types of human "nonsense" which allowed for *mechanicality* to rule and the complete atrophy of the fundamental being-impulse of "organic shame" (spiritual innocence).

Beelzebub admits to Hassein that because of his intense investigations into the life of Ashiata Shiemash, he had to commission one of his fellow tribesmen, living on Earth at the time as an "undertaker," to gather historic information concerning these early Greeks and Romans.

In the beginning, the Romans were called "Latinaki," which means "shepherds" (symbolizing guides for the heart). The other European power—the Greeks—were originally called "Hellenaki," which meant "fishermen" (symbolically, those who intellectually hunt for and teach truths on the lowest, natural level—memory stuff). So the Greeks were the main culprits who were responsible for human reasoning producing new types of intellectual "nonsense" while the Romans were responsible for destroying any last traces of "instinctive shame." Here, Beelzebub is about to describe the degeneration of both the human intellect (by Greeks) and emotions (by Romans) during the birth and arising of western culture.

Again, this part of the Tales is highly symbolic and allegorical.

According to Beelzebub, these groups of *fisherman* and *shepherds* both had to take shelter during times of "stormy" weather. While holed-up in these shelters and caves, and out of boredom, the Greeks invented their various "fiddle-faddle" sciences (a "pouring-from-the-empty-into-the-void"). The Romans, experiencing this same type of boring downtime in their own shelters, created various sex games for distraction. As these two groups came into contact, they exchanged these new inventions of theirs with each other. From the Romans, the Greeks learned how to organize their "Athenian nights," and from the Greek sciences, the Romans were inspired to produce their famous laws.

Putting on my Swedenborgian cap of symbolism again, "storms" represent an inner state of human stress from a *dispersal of truth* or the disconnection of *heterogenous things,* and "caves" represent a mental state of *obscurity.* Symbolically understood, Gurdjieff is implying that the fruits of western civilization were born from minds that had rejected objective (higher spiritual) truths, and as a result, lived in a stormy mental state of relative obscurity and darkness (otherwise, as stated before, these scenarios of human history, given by Beelzebub, would be a bit far-fetched and simplistic).

So Beelzebub blames the Greco-Roman civilization for utterly destroying the chances in earth-humans of the possibility of fixing data into their lives that would engender "sane-logical- mentation" and "being-self-shame." (Such data only comes from divine revelation and adopting God's tenets.) Instead, their "accomplishments" have left humankind with the maleficent impulses which produce a "passion-for-inventing-fantastic- sciences," and the "passion-for-depravity."

Thanks to these two "inventions" of the Greco-Roman civilization, today's "worldview," "value-system" and "priorities" consist mostly of mental fantasizing ("egoplastikoori" or mind-picturings according to one's Chief Egoistic Love) and of striving-for-sexual-gratification. (This is certainly not what we learned in our history classes at school concerning the roots of western civilization! This story causes us to contemplate and take a much deeper look into the so-called "fruits" of western civilization.)

I would like to add here that sexual depravity might also be degrading the quality of human sperm (hold onto that thought, as I will address this unique issue at the end of Chapter 39).

The historical trajectory of these two maleficent inventions of the Greeks and Romans (sexual depravity and delusional science) upon earth-humans is such that these values were eventually passed down to those of modern *Germany* and *England.* Beelzebub then describes the maleficent effect of the Greeks' concocted "sciences" on the Germans when the mental activity of acquiring knowledge had become divorced and separated (through mental storms and agitations) from one's actual cosmic duty. (Beelzebub is implying here that knowledge must always be connected to our challenges of self-improvement.

Beelzebub zeros in on five so-called "fruits" of modern (Hasnamuss) German science, which contribute only a "decomposing" as opposed to a "creative" result for humanity. These "fruits" or discoveries are (1) satkaine, (2) aniline, (3) cocaine, (4) atropine and (5) alisarine.

The first chemical invention on this list of the five German accomplishments was used as a poisonous gas for warfare. The second was used as a chemical coloring substance, which would actually lessen the life span of a product it was applied to. (Because of this property, using aniline dyes to re-color things also hastened the destruction of many valuable ancient artifacts.) The third destructive chemical substance, "cocaine," is obvious to all. (Beelzebub further remarks to Hassein that cocaine has a similar effect on the psyche of earth-humans that the organ Kundabuffer had.) The fourth chemical compound was supposedly used to dilate the eyes and enhance one's facial pleasantness. This chemical would eventually cause its users to go blind. And the last chemical, alisarine, was used as a sugar substitute. All five chemical inventions only provide help for God's great Nature by enhancing the process of *involution*, that is, *decomposition*.

This talent for hurtful "scientific" invention was also passed down from the Greeks to modern England. Instead of new chemicals, these Englanders became experts at "metalwares." These metal products included locks, razors, mousetraps, revolvers, scythes, machine guns, saucepans, hinges, guns, penknives, cartridges, pens, mines, needles, etc. Beelzebub points out to Hassein that before many of these inventions were created, it was much more difficult to kill people. Now, this misguided being-duty of Hasnamuss earth-humans, to kill others, was made much more simple and effective.

Another destructive invention that reached England from the Greek civilization was "sports," like wrestling. Because of the flawed psyche of contemporary humans, they imagined in their minds that something positive could be obtained from such strenuous physical activity. (In spite of what we are led to believe from "authorities" or TV commercials, our Olympic heroes do not represent wonderful examples of God's ultimate plan for the human race. And, in reality, athletes don't seem to age well, either.)

However, watching athletes perform does keep our minds temporarily off of our own negative situation.

At this point in the story, Beelzebub interjects that because the earth-humans have consistently resisted their true cosmic being-duty, that the invention of "sport," like other activities also hastens to diminish their lifespans.

He tells his grandson that there are two principles for being-existence—the "Fulasnitamnian" principle and the "Itoklanoz" principle. The latter principle ("Itoklanoz") naturally reins in one- and two-brained beings (reptiles and mammals) but also operates in men-beings who cease to actualize God's Partkdolg-duty in their lives for the purpose of coating their inner, spiritual bodies. (In my experience, rarely do the followers of Swedenborg's *Doctrine of Charity* view spiritual usefulness in its appropriate visceral, organic framework. Regeneration is our procuring the proper and corresponding bio-structures, for our spiritual bodies, during one's inner transformation. This situation represents real "bio-ignorance" concerning the true process of spiritual growth through real living forms. Even the spiritual world has a deeper organic human form.)

Because of the failure in human responsibility toward spiritual duty, Great Nature could not obtain all the necessary radiations for her maintenance and further progress. In order to restore "equilibrium," the expanding universe was compelled to adapt the *tempo* of human life-experiences to the less noble *Itoklanoz principle* (which lower life-forms and animals enjoy). The Itoklanoz principle in earth-humans (as we will see in Chapter 32) is an actual manifestation of blood-flow now being directed differently from the unfortunate result of "conscience" being driven down into a subconscious level of experiencing—creating the split human psyche.

Swedenborg does address the topic of our dual bloodflow in his *Divine Love and Wisdom* (n. 405)! But its importance hasn't registered in church worship.

Under the less noble Itoklanoz principle, the entire contents of a person's individuality and duration of one's lifespan comes from these seven *external* situations:

1) Heredity

2) External conditions and the environment at the moment of conception

3) The various combinations of radiations issuing from all the planets of the solar system while one is developing in the womb

4) The degree of spirituality obtained (or not obtained) by the parents during the period in which the child reaches maturity

5) The spiritual quality of those around them in their society

6) The quality and level of sincerity in the good wishes of vibrational thought waves moving through the atmosphere, coming from the people surrounding the developing child

7) And finally, the quality of a person's belief system (Egoplastikoori or mind-picturings) and the efforts one makes to identify important data and transform it into proper objective reasoning and wisdom

From these *seven* aspects and conditions of living under the Itoklanoz principle, a person growing up to the age of responsibility (maturity) forms the limits of, and quantity of impressions and associations one can experience in each of his or her three independent brain systems (*thoughts, feelings, and physical/motor action*).

The number of potential being-experiences (impressions) of each independent brain system is determined by what Beelzebub calls "Bobbin-kandelnosts" that act as "mechanical watch springs" for each brain function. When a "Bobbin-kandelnost" completely unwinds itself, the result is, that that particular brain function comes to its end and dies. Under the Itoklanoz principle of being-consciousness (which is limited) these three distinct functions of the human psyche unwind in a disharmonious and disordered fashion. So an individual disproportionately uses up their Bobbin-kandlenosts during their life. This causes an earth-human to not only die faster, but to die by "thirds."

(Now brace yourself! Because "dying by thirds" is evidenced by various forms of illness that presently affect humans.)

For instance, the premature exhaustion of the Bobbin-kandelnost located in the "spinal brain" produces such diseases as "hemiplegia" "paraplegia," "paralysis progressiva," "paralysis essentialis," "tabes dorsalis," "paralysis agitans," "sclerosis disseminata," etc. Those earth-humans who are most likely to use up the "springs" of their "spinal-brains" the quickest are those who have adopted that maleficent invention of the ancients called the "sports profession."

Those who prematurely unwind the Bobbin-kandelnost-spring of their "feeling-brain" are those who become by profession various types of terrestrial artists and poets. These terrestrial professionals usually become inflicted with some form of "psychopathy." Beelzebub tells Hassein that one of these various forms of "psychopathy" manifests as "altruism." (Certainly, many "creative" people side with those who promote the ideology of supporting the common good—the collective—but this ideal is separated from their own individual embrace of, and personal efforts at, genuine cosmic being-duty. These types of earth-humans become mere emotional misfits.

The third kind of partial death by "thirds" happens when the springs of the "thinking-brain" run themselves down through the practice of learning by rote, or, superfluously reading various articles and journals and associating only by mental thoughts. Those most inclined to exhaust their thinking brain are the scientists of *new formation*.

Under the *Itoklanoz* principle of being-existence, earth-humans are inordinately influenced by the associations of only *one* brain system. This situation makes it impossible to create a "harmonious association" or proper equilibrium between all of an individual's three distinct brain systems, by which the energy is created for living an "active" rather than "passive" (or *enslaved* life). Furthermore, the heavy dependence on only one being-function (and its spring) causes it to steal vital energy from the other functions. (Gurdjieff used the example of *vehemence* in the tone of one's voice as being a form of "sexual deviance" because the speaker's thoughts are being overly animated by the influx of a more powerful sex energy. You can observe this "stealing" of vital energy and the resulting perversion in many of Hitler's speeches, or in anyone pounding their fists during speeches.)

Swedenborg agrees with Gurdjieff that this inner disharmony of energies can be temporarily corrected especially during the hours of sleep. He discovered that during our nighttime sleep, the unconscious and involuntary (cerebellum) part of the human psyche takes over the organic reins and *restores* balance (harmony) to the bio-system that was knocked out of alignment during the day while one was exercising his/her voluntary idiosyncrasies (one's various passions and flawed thinking, which favor some limited function in the split psyche).

This predicament thwarts the completion of their astral bodies and reaching its corresponding degree of reasoning—the sacred Ischmetch (I am inclined to conjecture that the term *"Ischmetch"* is possibly taken from the biblical name "Ishmael," which symbolizes a civic level of rationality, but maybe not). The main point is that proper human rational development also helps regulate the three Bobbin-kandlenosts to function harmoniously along with each other.

Beelzebub wraps up this chapter by informing Hassein that another kind of "sport" emerged from the dysfunction of a split psyche in the countries of England, and also Russia—the drinking of alcoholic beverages to induce "good times." Booze and flat-screen TVs at "sports bars" is certainly a big part of the experience of enjoying (worshipping) athletic events. Booze is even enjoyed when there are no sports to be seen and is always used to celebrate "good times."

Only hangovers are produced by these "good times."

SUMMARY

▪ Beelzebub informs his grandson that the beginning of western civilization brought about the final end to Ashiata Shiemash's great teachings, as their growing military might allowed them to sweep across Asia and force their inferior values upon all people.

▪ The Greeks invented delusional (Hasnamuss) sciences and the Romans destroyed the being-sense of *organic shame* (through their seeking of perverse sexual pleasures). That these groups both lived in caves during "storms" symbolizes that their historic contributions were made in a state of spiritual darkness, obscurity, and inner conflict.

▪ The Greeks and Romans represented the further (and worst) degeneration of the two major human psychic functions, *the intellect* and *feelings*. This mental distinction (split psyche) between the intellect and the heart was symbolized by the Greeks' main occupation as "fishermen" and the Romans as "shepherds."

▪ Germans and the English later became the more modern versions of the Greeks and Romans, and their inventions are all equally destructive (decomposing) for other earth-humans.

▪ Because of this, today's world outlook (belief-systems) and the current ordering of human daily existence, is now based firmly on "fantasy" and the "striving-for-sexual-gratification."

▪ Beelzebub suggests that even the invention of "sports" comes from a degenerating and limited mind. (A degenerating mind may also imply an involving or decomposing quality in human sperm and ovum.)

▪ Today's earth-humans (with their split psyche) have a blood flow similar to that of reptiles and mammals (*Itoklanoz* principle). This prevents them from creating the required quality of vibrations needed by the universe (and God), or for consciously forming their higher spiritual bodies and powers of reasoning.

▪ Drinking alcoholic beverages provides evidence of both a degenerating human mind and the striving to seek pleasure and the celebrating of imagined "good times."

▪ Under the *Itoklanoz* principle, earth-humans usually "die by thirds" and never develop their proper level of reasoning. (As one develops spiritual reasoning, life is extended because it *regulates* the three "Bobbin-kandelnosts" to function harmoniously and not be used up prematurely and egotistically.)

CHAPTER 30

"Art"

Having attended art school as a young man, this chapter was able to clarify for me the reality of my own flawed egoism (self-picturings) and psychic deterioration. As a creative artist, writer and thinker, I grew up believing I represented a group of specially talented and gifted individuals who could even be classified as "cutting edge" and the "tip of the spear" of modern civilization. But reading this chapter allowed me to measure my imagined talents against real creative thinking originating from a much higher level of intelligence. This genuine higher level had been obtained by wise individuals in the ancient past, but was lost over time because of the peculiar "downward" and maleficent trajectory of human life on Earth.

This was a very long and anti-intuitive chapter (74 pages) and it convinced me that I had to get rid of my *imaginary halo*. Here, Gurdjieff continues to cut us all down to size by explaining an important aspect in the decline of human mentality, offering an unflattering view of what *really* happened to "art" throughout human history. If you grasp nothing else, be assured that art was originally invented, like everything else from the remote past, to offer assistance in one's spiritual salvation—and never for the celebration of one's individual talent or "genius."

Art was originally the objective expression of God's universal laws, not self-expression or titillation.

At this point in the narrative, Beelzebub invites his faithful old servant Ahoon to speak about his own observations, since he had also accompanied their party on all six visits to the "ill-fated" planet Earth. Ahoon states unequivocally that the human invention of "art" drove the final nail into the coffin of sane and proper reasoning.

To rub salt into the wounds (of my own egoism), Ahoon suggests that the topic of art offers the choicest material for explaining to young Hassein the negative transformation of the psyche of earth-humans and its current abnormalities. (I first read this seemingly "crazy" stuff when I was in my mid-twenties and was a budding young creative writer in a large, famous advertising agency—after having also spent four years at a very progressive art school in Manhattan.)

Beelzebub agrees with Ahoon's seemingly counter-intuitive comment about art and its degeneration along with the human psyche. He even calls contemporary terrestrial art an "evil" factor that has played a strong role in blinding earth-humans to the attainments and helpful information contained in much earlier forms of art expression. Instead of helping earth-humans to become a part of God's Divine scheme, art now simply converts people from spiritual beings into mere "living flesh." (How's that for stepping on people's corns?!!)

Beelzebub recounts that on his fifth visit to the planet Earth, in the city of Babylon, he became a member of a special brotherhood called the "Adherents-of-Legominism." (Remember that a Legominism is a means for conveying great knowledge and lessons about important historic events to others—mostly stories of humankind's inner development). This "club" was organized by two special earth-humans—one whose name was Kanil-El-Norkel, a Moor, and the other was Pythagoras, a Greek. Beelzebub describes attending one of this group's first meetings in which the issue of preserving valuable ancient information was discussed.

Because of periodic wars and bloodshed in which many of those who had special ancient knowledge were also killed, they could no longer simply depend on this valuable knowledge (Legominism) being preserved and passed down to future generations through mere word of mouth. Some more permanent and fixed (extant) forms for preserving this special, vital knowledge needed to be invented to counter this "distressing phenomenon."

At the third meeting of this new organization, Beelzebub states that this was the first time he had ever heard the word "art" uttered by anyone. It came out of the mouth of a special elderly Chaldean in the group who was named *Aksharpanziar*. This Chaldean had delivered a speech to his brethren, declaring that those who shared non-ordinary interests (different from those caught up in the various attractions, pleasures and sentiments of current society) needed to find new means for preserving and transmitting their beneficial knowledge or it would be lost forever.

Aksharpanziar suggests that they "sneak" this knowledge into daily religious and civil ceremonies. The elderly Chaldean further suggests that they make special use of the universal "Law of Sevenfoldness" to inject such knowledge into all their creations. This law pervades everything in nature when viewed holistically (as complexes or comprehensive wholes) therefore, it will always exist as long as the universe exists.

So the first usage of the word "art" came from a new need to preserve and communicate God's helpful and universal truths to future generations. In other words, art was originally a Legominism. (Swedenborg claims that God's Word or Holy Scripture is such a work of art—its full knowledge hidden from most contemporary human minds. It contains *seven gravity centers* in the unfolding of all its stories. This sacred sevenfold series, within all divine order, was more familiar to Swedenborg than his followers are currently aware of.)

Beelzebub shares examples of this ubiquitous Law of Sevenfoldness—as in the seven colors of "white" light. He states that within every single sound there are seven independent tones. In every manifest form there can only be seven dimensions, and any weight that remains at rest on Earth consists of seven "reciprocal thrusts" (*reciprocal resistances*). Even more astounding, in every full state of the human psyche there are seven independent sensations or aspects. (In his book *Worship And Love Of God*, n. 122, footnote *b*, Swedenborg also breaks down the human intellect into seven functions or gravity centers called: "sensation," "imagination," "thought," "judgment," "choice," "will," and "resulting action." The *eighth* step is a new outcome and the beginning of a new sevenfold series. He also stated that, "all concord comes from octaves." So Swedenborg was quite familiar with the law of *octaves*.)

The Chaldean, Aksharpanziar, puts forth the novel idea that they can also inject "lawful inexactitudes" within these seven orderly aspects functioning in all whole phenomena—which can serve as the new way to preserve their various Legominisms. Those who participated in transmitting knowledge in this "sneaky" and "artful" way would from then on be called "artists."

Before going further into this discussion, I am sure that you, my reader, are already getting a "taste" of how Beelzebub is using the term "art" to show how the human psyche has atrophied over the centuries. But you may be asking, "What is a lawful inexactitude?" (Swedenborg's *science of correspondences* is an example of lawful inexactitudes. It means that something can have a lawful [ontological] reality even if it does not represent an exact literal reality. The Seven Day Creation story of Genesis in God's Holy Word represents a lawful description of the process of Sevenfoldness—but the inexactitude in this orderly process is that the story doesn't portray mere outer historical events. Rather, it is injected with symbolic and spiritual expressions within its literal words, which deal with humankind's inner history and reality.)

Also, the Law of Sevenfoldness made it possible for new (and higher) principles to be injected at several mathematically precise intervals along the whole process of established rituals and ceremonies in their worship services to hopefully alert people to move beyond their normal thinking about such customs.)

Well, the members of the club were so impressed by Aksharpanziar's speech that they began to think of ways to insert special knowledge into things relating to the Law of Sevenfoldness. Some members brought in solutions based on colors, others music—even examples of architecture were used. Then, they each gave explanations to the others as to their various creative strategies of using the Law of Sevenfoldness to contain their important knowledge.

Not long after, the "Adherents-of-Legominism" even decided to organize their novel techniques into various branches according to the *seven* days of the week. Beelzebub tells Hassein that the division of a week into seven days was also based on the Law of Sevenfoldness and was formulated earlier by the beings that originally lived on the continent Atlantis (Swedenborg's Noachian Church—whose spiritual growth and quality was represented by a "rainbow" in Genesis 9:16).

It was decided by the club members that Mondays would be devoted to the exploration of using their novel techniques within common rituals—like that of their religious or civil ceremonies. (Gurdjieff once told his student P. D. Ouspensky that the Christian Church got its rituals from ancient Egypt.)

Tuesdays focused on architecture.

Wednesdays were called "days of painting." (Some of these Babylonian "artists" even worked with different combinations of black and white or using different combinations of fragrances.)

Thursdays were reserved for dancing.

Fridays involved sculpture.

Saturdays consisted of theatrical plays.

And on Sundays, the members participated in song and music.

None of these creative (artistic) activities consisted of any subjective viewpoints of any individual member, but rather, used God's universal laws to communicate deeper, objective realities and transmit *true knowledge to distant generations.* These forms of creative expression contained mathematical exactness, with "lawful deviations" and seeming "illogicalities" inserted within various everyday human products (called Afalkalna) like pottery, and also into their common rituals (Soldjinoha). These "lawful deviations" were consciously designed to challenge the customary thought processes of the worldly human *habitual* mind. In these deviations, unexpected and deeper knowledge was hidden. (Again, a lawful inexactitude or deviation could involve something that does not literally exist on the Earth's surface—like dragons, mermaids, unicorns or talking serpents—but which contain higher psycho-spiritual meanings that are still ontologically real and true on higher levels. But generally speaking, these *illogical deviations* actually represent special expressions and ways to alert an audience that something special is being communicated to them—because they are witnessing something "illogical" to their habitual way of thinking.)

Beelzebub offers simple examples of how this strategy was applied by all seven branches of this unique Babylonian club (but not enough to immediately give away the full secret to the average person reading his account). For instance, in one such example, he says that participants of some ritual or ceremony would adopt unusual postures (like bending one's leg in an unexpected position) and within these unexpected postures (lawful deviations) of a given ceremony, a special "alphabet" was created to communicate their intended knowledge. This alphabet was incorporated at precise intervals.

In another book by Gurdjieff, *Meetings With Remarkable Men* (pages 161-162), he offers a more detailed description of such a strategy and alphabet. He describes a strange construction that he observed as a younger man after coming in contact with a particular brotherhood somewhere in central Asia.

This construction consisted of a long column mounted on a tripod. It was taller than a man. On this column were placed seven appendages, each divided by seven segments decreasing proportionately in size from the central column. Each segment, which was a precise interval, was connected by a ball and socket joint. The outer socket had a space that allowed one to see the ball inside. On the inside ball were various markings or alphabet. As one moved the positions of the various appendages, different markings appeared. When these markings appeared (as a result of the changing position of the segments) they could be compared, using a special codex to decipher the message communicated by the specific posture of the construction. Dancers would learn and practice these postures. (Gurdjieff suggests that the materials on which these codices were inscribed were at least 4,500 years old.)

Ouspensky's book, *In Search of the Miraculous* (page 27), also recounts Gurdjieff's story of discovering in a desert, at the foot of the *Hindu Kush*, a strange religious statue of some ancient god or devil. The more Gurjieff's group studied this statue, the more they became aware that its features contained information of a complex system of cosmology.

This kind of communication, according to Gurdjieff, was *real art!*

(Also, during a Gurdjieffian instructional class that I attended, I was told that the position of the crossed arms used by early Egyptians on the bodies of their deceased symbolized "Emanuel" or "God is with us." I believe the "key," and alphabet, for unraveling this hieroglyphic positioning of the dead person's arms is to be found in the ancient *knowledge of correspondences*.)

On that account, it will be interesting to note that Swedenborg also claimed that more ancient races of humans had devised codices by which later generations could decipher profound heavenly knowledge. But the most unexpected news of all, alluded to earlier, is that God's Holy Word is the greatest "Legominism" of them all. Its narratives contain the sacred system and laws of God's divine cosmology (which includes human salvation)—with infinite complexity! As I mentioned above, Swedenborg, in his theological writings, offers the key for deciphering this Divine hidden material and divine Art in Holy Scripture—called *correspondences*.

Concerning the mathematical exactness of true art, Swedenborg stated "That is not art which reaches its effect by chance" (*The Swedenborg Epic*, page 13). He also describes the art and architecture of Heaven as distinctly different from the types of terrestrial art on Earth. The difference is that heavenly art promotes God's universal laws and order, rather than one's personal self-expression.

Swedenborg also observed that space in Heaven is a derivative of the quality of Love that one experiences, so the space inside spiritual buildings would represent some degree and measurement of Love.

This supports Gurdjieff's claim that ancient architects (with the knowledge of the Law of Sevenfoldness) could influence a person's state of mind with mathematical precision, through the special dimensions of the space a person occupies, because it correspondingly affects the quality of vibrations of the atmosphere that it enclosed. (God creates these special dimensions and proportions immediately, for all the angelic beings to experience while they live within Heaven's sacred, non-physical structures and "spaces.")

Symbolically speaking, that the special column in the construction mentioned above (with its seven moveable appendages), that Gurdjieff described seeing at this brotherhood was made of "ivory," inwardly represents God's universal laws ruling from Heaven all the way down into external phenomena. "Seven," according to Swedenborg, also symbolizes what is "full," "holy," and "sacred."

Next, after discussing the ancient use of colors in paintings and carpets (Persian) to transmit special knowledge (their Legominisms), Beelzebub supplies his own "deviation" to the order of his Tales (he actually adds these lawful deviations all throughout the story, which itself is cleverly written and structured according to the Law of Sevenfoldness with unexpected insertions at intervals to add "new wrinkles" to the narrative).

Beelzebub's Tales is itself a Legominism.

This next deviation of *Beelzebub's Tales* now has Beelzebub describing how the sensation of "seeing" in human beings of the planet Earth has also diminished over time. He makes the unexpected and seemingly far-fetched claim that normal humans were originally designed to be able to perceive one million, nine hundred and twenty-one thousand and six hundred tonalities of color. And, that a more spiritually evolved human could detect even twice that number of tonalities. But on the very highest spiritual level, humans could detect all (three times as much) the tonalities of color except for just one, which only God can perceive.

But according to Beelzebub, contemporary humans can now, at best, only distinguish a pitiful 49 tonalities of color. This ability to see more tonalities of color transcends optic eyesight. The message here is that contemporary humans have lost the ability to detect (rationally observe) many details from higher realms and deeper dimensions of reality (especially phenomena originating from the spiritual world and generated by the Spiritual Sun—such as receiving Divine Truths.)

Swedenborg claimed that in more remote times, the human race had the capacity to see (celestial perception) even into Heaven itself and communicate with the angels there! Their enhanced psychic perception most certainly had to increase the spectrum of colors and blendings that these earth-humans could enjoy! (Furthermore, Swedenborg learned that all angels were once citizens of some planet or another.)

Lawful inexactitudes were also incorporated into many ancient forms of sculpture. Beelzebub also relates to his grandson that ancient sculptors created forms of various allegorical or mythical beings. And, to enhance the spiritual symbolism represented by these allegorical beings, the ancient artists also distorted some of the lawful dimensions of these sculptures so that additional useful information could be introduced and hopefully noticed. This distortion included giving a sculptured form extra arms or adding wings, even inventing strange combinations of these various features in its sculpted creatures.

Unfortunately, the Law of Sevenfoldness is not even suspected by contemporary scientists as a ubiquitous law pervading and operating throughout the entire universe—nor by contemporary theologians, as operating in the steps of human salvation and the orderly unfolding of the sacred narratives and stories of God's Holy Word!

So looking for some "lawful illogicality" intentionally placed within a scheme of "seven-ness" would obviously go undetected or be seen as some silly or superstitious oddity by modern scientists and theologians (on the bright side, this deeper information would be safely preserved and protected for later, more rational generations to re-discover and decipher).

In fact, Swedenborg said that such metaphysical information would be seen as most foreign to the academic world. He also insisted that if such higher knowledge was made available prematurely, before human hearts could be properly purified, people would profane this vital information and destroy (damn) their souls.

In ancient theater, Beelzebub purports that performances were also used to communicate higher knowledge. The actors of this Babylonian club would insert some movement or statement that was seemingly "illogical" within the natural flow of the dialog. (An amusing example of this "illogical" technique was given in the introduction of this very book, when as a child, Gurdjieff hopped and skipped while reciting a silly poem at his grandmother's memorial service. This action was not expected within the general flow of his family's established customs.

While discussing similar strategies employed in the ancient theater (called "reflectors-of-reality") Beelzebub again spends some time explaining to Hassein how the abnormal lifestyles of earth-humans has a psycho-organic effect that disharmonizes their three different brain systems. So, instead of acting in unison (corresponding to each other), the *thinking brain* may wish to go on a diet, the *emotional part* of the brain may be wishing for fancy restaurant food and the *moving/instinctive* brain may wish for pizza, a football game and a soft recliner chair. (This condition is why people often end up doing something contrary to their original good intention—not all of their brain-systems were involved in the original decision or even cared about the outcome.)

These three quite different brain-wishes (inclinations) manifesting in one and the same individual can only be harmonized through proper spiritual development, which fuses these competing influences and energies into a more noble *unity of purpose*. Otherwise, a person's differing life forces and desires constantly wreak havoc within one's common presence and biofunctioning. (Even religion has atrophied, in that it no longer understands how the process of spiritual *regeneration* fuses—and thus unifies—these often competing and distinct brain systems to function harmoniously together.)

Again, I will reiterate that nighttime sleep will temporarily restore some of the balance and harmony of energies in the three-brained systems of humans. Swedenborg and Gurdjieff both agree that in pre-regenerated individuals (prior to their spiritual rebirth), these life energies flow properly only during sleep, when the cerebellum (one's involuntary) takes over the organic reins for the sleeping cerebrum (one's voluntary) and restores the damaging effects that all our conflicting inclinations have on our bio-systems throughout the day's activities. This damage is caused by all the competing (and contradictory) inclinations of a person's divided three-brained character, which upset our bio-harmony and health.

So during daytime, a person must consciously choose to partake in spiritual duty (and self-combat), or their three-brain systems will go haywire and continue to develop independently into three different personalities having nothing in common with each other, as characterized earlier. These separated "brain-functionings" have their own separate "experiencings" and associations which, through habit, produce mechanical manifestations consisting of conflicting *automatic* needs and interests.

(You may be wondering how a *three-brained* being can be described as having a *dual* personality. This is not easy to describe, because the split referred to earlier takes place in the *human natural mind* as we are growing up. That is, a mature person's natural mind contains both an *inner* and *outer* life—its external life communicates with its lowest corporeal or worldly nature but its interior [subconscious] life has the potential to communicate with, and develop, a higher rational function.)

That is why God implants *conscience* within this split of the human natural mind as a third and future mediating influence. So while this split represents a real duality in the human psyche, it refers only to our natural level of understanding and its preferences. Our interior natural mind (or astral body), through the purification of our middle blood (and its self-centered passions), can potentially connect with— and be influenced by—this new third function that is implanted in us as a gift from God's love and mercy.

This third function, called *conscience* (or remains) helps create a new rational function that can then serve as an elevated *mediating plane* between our higher spiritual and lower natural levels. (Otherwise there would be no unity, harmony or correspondence between our higher spiritual and lower natural lives.)

Again, the *potential* for developing this new rational plane is first given to us as a free gift from God's mercy, in the form of a *conscience* (also called remains). But this divine gift must then develop further (be awakened by shocks) through our sincere efforts to *resist* our natural inclinations, loves and egoism now hiding deep inside the *interior natural mind*. So, if one chooses, one can always improve on the elevation of this reconciling rational mind or mediating principle of conscience by adopting higher principles of self-less and innocent love. Such life-choices will not only further increase the development of our conscience and its bio-plane to receive more of God's influence into our lives—through an evolving *spiritual rational*—but this evolving plane is also what forms our spiritual bodies (the reconciling result between our two realities).

Gurdjieff described the three parts of the human psyche as the moving/instinctive center, the feeling center, and the thinking center. These centers correspond exactly to Swedenborg's description of the three distinct levels that constitute man—the corporeal mind (moving center), the natural mind (feeling center and its proprium) and the rational mind (thinking center). Both men teach that the psychical split that we are to be vigilant about occurs in the human natural mind.

Beelzebub then explains to Hassein why the ancient actors of this club/brotherhood always performed in unexpected ways. He claims that they understood how associations flow within the human mind—from impressions accumulated in all three being-brains according to their "kindredness" with the material previously deposited there, and proceeding according to a sevenfold series. Having knowledge of this process, these special actors would then add a sudden deviation to their expected roles, that is, respond in some *unexpected way* and jump into a more *unexpected role*.

These club actors discovered that by producing such "shocks," they could help others both notice and free themselves of their acquired automatism and the usual mechanicality of their divided psyches, which always creates a "mix-up." (I find it hard to act mechanically with just one or another brain system when you are attempting some new posture or hear and see something quite new, which forces us to create unexpected responses. It is during these strange "shocks" that the players inserted, in special ways, the new information that they wanted to share for future generations to discover. The audience was not allowed to take in these performances in the usual and habitual way.

Humans develop a mechanized functioning of their actions as their various externally and accidentally produced associations within their three disjointed brain systems become second nature over time, where their automatized behavior no longer can be noticed or ever challenged. (For instance, when people get on an elevator they will almost always make some kind of innocuous reflex-comment, with a mechanical smile, over and over again—often concerning the weather.) But true rational and conscious action requires the "comparative mentation" of all three brain-systems being vigilant and watchful over each other (a form of spiritual Djartklom which occurs in a person during *conscious labors* and *intentional suffering*).

These ancient actors eventually discovered, over time, that there were *twenty-seven* specific types of humans who could be studied and imitated on the stage merely by reproducing particular associations of a particular brain-system, which generated a certain habitual series of mental states to unfold in people's behavior. That is, they learned to produce twenty-seven combinations of flawed three-brained being experiences and actions. Then, these actors could expertly insert their new information through their shocks of making some unexpected behavior). This allowed these special actors to influence every kind of dysfunctional individual and psychic anomaly that existed.

The final group that Beelzebub describes (who met and performed on Sundays), consisted of ancient musicians and singers who found another very interesting way of verifying to an audience that earth-humans had three separately functioning brain systems. They discovered what *density of sound-vibrations,* made from their musical instruments and voices, could affect each of the three separate brain systems and the three kinds of independent associations operating in one and the same individual.

Using this knowledge, with their special melodies, they could then create *three separate reactions—simultaneously within one individual!*

For instance, with their special music, the thinking brain of a listener might be made to experience *joy*, the feeling brain, *sorrow*, and the moving-center *"religiousness."* Within these unique and unusual melodic influences, and the unusual impulses or *inner promptings* they created, these ancient musicians and singers could cleverly incorporate new knowledge (new Nirioonossian vibrations) into the listening experiences of their audience. This produced unusual experiencings and reflex movements not proper or familiar to them. Also, the audience was put into a state where they could more easily absorb new ideas under this psychic state of alertness and stress.

This is a far cry from what we call art and creativity today. And it shows the extent to which art and the human psyche have both deteriorated within a relatively short period of time. Instead, because of the sacred being-impulse of conscience having been driven back into a subconscious level of the human psyche, art is now annexed (like Love, Faith and Hope) by the egotistical and vacuous aims of a more exterior and artificial personality (mask) that gains strength from worldly influences (its vanities and allurements) and becomes habit. This situation is true slavery.

(Swedenborg refers to this same division of the human psyche into three separate functions as aspects of the *innermost, interior* and *exterior* parts of the human natural mind.)

Swedenborg, as well as Gurdjieff, both saw this division and divided functioning as leading humans into becoming "slaves" of the whims of egoism—which cannot exist under true conscience and a unified psyche. This is not the outer slavery of one person to another but an inner servitude toward one's faulty loves, that have been separated from *a spiritual affection for truth*. True freedom comes from being willing to be led by the Lord God into *true and unselfish Love*. (See *Apocalypse Revealed*, bottom of n. 208) This spiritual affection resides within a healthy functioning conscience, which Beelzebub implied contained *particles of Divinity*. (God can only flow into what is His—for instance, His Divine qualities stored within our deeper psyche.)

Another result of the atrophy of the human psyche from the covering over of the genuine being-impulse of conscience (sinking of Atlantis) is that earth-humans have lost the ability to vocalize lots of consonants. Over a period of five centuries, earth-humans went from vocally producing three hundred and fifty-one definite "letters" to only thirty-six or less. Swedenborg does make the point that the muscle fibers of the human lips now no longer act as distinctly as they once did and could communicate much more profound and subtle ideas that passed through a person's Eustachian tube (bypassing the physical eardrum) directly to the inner ear. I suspect that a deteriorating psyche would have the same corresponding result on the muscles of the vocal chords and lips and especially with a person's ability to grasp and communicate intricate concepts.

(Unless I am mistaken, contemporary archeologists have admitted that they are not quite sure about the types of vocal sounds made by early Egyptians. Well, if the modern humans failed to produce all the proper "being-articulate-sounds" from ancient inscriptions, the translation would obviously suffer.)

As a powerful philological example of this vocal decline, Beelzebub tells his grandson about the two Greek letters "theta" and "delta" which are used in words to convey *opposite* meanings. Beelzebub points out that no matter how hard they try, Russians cannot pronounce "th." However, they can actually sense the difference between "theta" and "delta" and will never use these opposite-meaning letters incorrectly in their words. On the other hand, the English can correctly pronounce these two letters but no longer sense their difference. Beelzebub further explains that when the English say "thank you" you can detect the letter "theta" but when they say "there" one can paradoxically also hear the letter "delta." (This philological oddity shows that there are different *inner* and *outer* developments between the psyches of different peoples arising on different parts of the globe.)

In this explanation we also see why Gurdjieff actually stated that "philology is a better route to Truth than philosophy (Bennett's *Talks On Beelzebub's Tales*, page 8).

Beelzebub then returns to the topic of theatrical artists who originally communicated true knowledge, but because of the maleficent properties of the organ Kundabuffer, an element of "swagger" entered into the human psyche whereby both theatrical actors and audiences alike gained the organic need to "astonish" each other through their fashions and manipulations of their external appearance. (We see this today in many celebrities' behavior to astonish the public with their wardrobes, trinkets and actions.) This organic need to decorate their exterior appearance always resulted from a loss of conscience and an instinctive desire called "the-covering-of-their-nullity." This created an illness unknown to three-brained beings living everywhere else in the universe called "dramatizing" everything. This "high drama" is most evident in the manifestations of certain contemporary beings whom we call "drama queens."

Seven symptoms of this peculiar illness among earth-humans are:

1) The vibrations of such individuals stink up the environment.

2) One's speech will be punctuated by a special cough.

3) We become frightened of every little thing (making mountains out of molehills).

4) We are no longer able to understand those around us.

5) We criticize everyone and anything not tied to our self-exaltation.

6) Fame more often than not creates "air-heads."

7) Finally, this illness gives rise to "hemorrhoids" which is the only thing such "living automatons" carry with any kind of "modesty."

(Notice that various subjects throughout this story are all arranged into groups of "sevens.")

Beelzebub does, however, mention one positive result that can be obtained from contemporary theaters. Watching movies or stage spectacles puts the thinking and feeling functions of the human psyche of the contemporary three-brained beings of the planet Earth into a passive state much like it is "during sleep." Because the body restores its life energies during sleep (mentioned a couple of times earlier) this allows for some temporary benefit and relief. However, the downside of all this is that modern theaters add an additional factor for preventing earth-humans from sensing the "need-for-real-perceptions"—especially those perceptions that would lead to "being-confrontative-associations" necessary to shock and awaken conscience. These are the same spiritual combats and temptations that Swedenborg says are necessary to allow one's spiritual transformation to begin developing.

It is not a rare phenomenon to witness various "creative types" and actors behaving in pathological ways (we see this all the time in "Hollywood"). According to Beelzebub, these contemporary artists offer some of the best examples of inappropriate behavior resulting from the disappearance in humans of the instinctive need to perform their God-given cosmic duties.

Old Ahoon begins to chime in again about how the three-brained artists he observed with Beelzebub during their sixth and final visit to the planet Earth had an inflated "being-self-appreciation," and that their completely automatized Reason produced false notions that allowed them to feel "immeasurably superior to what they really are." Ahoon then offers the young Hassein some practical advice. He warns Hassein that if he ever found himself in a position where he had to interface with such odd earth-humans, he must proceed with great caution and always remember to "tickle" some aspect of their self-delusional self-image to keep in good standing. (While one can attract more flies with sugar than with vinegar, titillation is a sweetness that only strengthens the self-delusion of those who are little more complex than flies.)

After taking all this in, Hassein turns to his grandfather and questions whether it was really possible that nothing has survived today from the great efforts of the Adherents-of-Legominism. Beelzebub replies that because of decay over time and the periodic destruction due to various wars, not only were the Legominisms that carried the keys to deciphering the lawful inexactitudes injected into the Law of Sevenfoldness, but even the notion of such universal knowledge had totally evaporated from their belief systems and scientific worldviews. (As mentioned above, scientists are totally unaware of this ubiquitous law—even though they will organize cosmic energies into sevenfold-spectrums and acknowledge that octaves are a real part of physics.)

But Beelzebub informs Hassein that there still were some exceptions to the survival of ancient wisdom reaching contemporary humans on Earth.

Apparently, while doing his own research concerning this exact topic, Beelzebub tells Hassein that he learned from a female "pythoness" or "medium" during his last (sixth) visit to the planet Earth that four individuals still existed on Earth who had inherited the keys to understanding this ancient form of art. One individual was an American "Redskin." Another lived in the Philippines, a third lived in Asia from a country called "The-Source-of-the-River-Pianje," and the fourth was an "Eskimo." Beelzebub further admits that one example of this ancient method of transmitting ancient knowledge still exists today in certain "sacred dances." Another branch, which only recently disappeared from the planet Earth, was a type of "painting" or blending of colors. This branch was alive and well as recently as three hundred years ago and was incorporated in the making of "Persian carpets."

Two other exceptions also occurred from two relatively contemporary "Western" individuals who managed to crack the ancient code, due to their own persistent being-efforts. Beelzebub identifies these two individuals as the monk Ignatius, who directed the building of the foundation for the temple called "Mont-Saint-Michel," and Leonardo da Vinci. Both individuals had noticed various "lawful illogicalities" in many ancient productions. Because these "illogicalities" seemed consciously incorporated into these ancient productions, rather than seeing them as mistakes, they began to study the matter with great intensity.

Beelzebub also explains to his grandson that because contemporary artists no longer suspected the existence of such advanced forms of communication, through cosmic universal laws, they would always be susceptible to new artistic "movements." Such movements in painting have been called "cubism," "futurism," "synthesism," "imagism," "impressionism," "colorism," "formalism," "surrealism," and other such movements with names ending in "ism." Another word for these changing movements in art is "trends."

These various trends (including fashion) are usually used by contemporary artists and performers to further *astonish* the already disharmonized brain-functionings of their fans, and those who can no longer properly sense reality.

This emphasis toward *outer* appearances only changed everyone's tempo of bloodflow to the more passive *Itoklanoz* principle, which operates just as if people were *asleep*—that is, in a lower form of consciousness. Today we see this *outer* principle in action, that is astonishing fans at all "red carpet" events.

Beelzebub then adds another distinguishing point to his discussion. He states that these ancient "artists" were originally called "Orpheists," not to be confused by the followers of the historical Greek personality Orpheus, by those in their audience who sincerely appreciated their lofty, elevated efforts. This word originally meant performers who "rightly sensed the essence of a thing." But since that noble word no longer explained what later generations of performers ("living automatons") actually did, they concocted the word "artist" to better portray their craft. Today, the word artist simply implies one who is occupied in some manner with "art."

At this point in Beelzebub's narrative, everyone's "hooves" begin to glow from the sacred substance, Omnipresent Okidanokh, being directed into their compartment from the engine room, indicating that they were near their destination. Symbolically speaking, the ends (goals) of their intentions or wills (the engines) were close to reaching their outermost realizations (symbolized by "hooves.") Hooves represent the outermost structure of the the travelers' bodies.

SUMMARY

■ According to Beelzebub, art—like everything else—was originally invented to communicate God's universal laws to future generations. But this cosmic expression of critical knowledge, or art, eventually turned into the mere personal expression of one's subjective talents and degenerated as verything else did within the human psyche.

■ Genuinely concerned individuals in Babylon created an organization to find ways to make their special knowledge more permanent—so that it could be available for future generations. At one of the club's meetings Beelzebub first heard the term "art" being used.

■ Since the Law of Sevenfoldness was a permanent part of universal law and God's sacred order, this group of concerned beings chose to preserve their knowledge within this ubiquitous series, participating in all processes.

■ Through "lawful inexactitudes and illogicalities" higher knowledge (Legominisms) was inserted (and preserved) within the Law of Sevenfoldness to shock the human habitual mind into elevated thinking.

■ These concerned individuals even invented seven distinct ways to preserve this knowledge, and this group who promoted these various approaches were actually "scientist-artists." Each one of their seven branches or specialties of their new science was devoted to a different day of the week.

SUMMARY

▪ True art has both mathematical exactness and a conscious goal—to save humanity.

▪ Human eyesight (sensing Truth and the various higher blendings of color or "complexes of results") is continually perfected during spiritual growth. This higher sensitivity takes in the blending of ideas, which can also be represented by colors of higher (heavenly) spectrums. The human organs of sight, hearing (and the voicing of many kinds of consonants) all degenerated in earth-humans.

▪ Ancient artists were called "Orpheists" by those who appreciated their works. This meant a performer who could *rightly detect the essence* of something (and were not those followers of the historical-Greek-personality called Orpheus). Today's artists and actors, who have lost this ability to detect the *essence of things,* are now swept up by all kinds of changing outer trends. These changing trends and fashion statements are used by contemporary artists and performers to *astonish* some disharmonized brain-function in their fans' psyche (and all those who can no longer sense reality).

▪ This emphasis toward promoting outer appearances also changed the tempo of earth-humans' blood circulation in a corresponding way—called the (more passive) *Itoklanoz* principle, which creates lower forms of consciousness—similar to that of mollusks and mammals.

CHAPTER 31

"The sixth and last sojourn of Beelzebub on the planet Earth"

Two months have now passed in Beelzebub's cosmic journey.

As the *intersystem* (multi-leveled travel) spaceship *Karnak* carries Beelzebub, Hassein and old Ahoon back to the planet of their birth (*Karatas*—after their visit to the planet Revozvradendr) we are again challenged to grasp that their new trajectory represents another shift in one's spiritual "gravity." This new movement in space (forward motion) represents a deeper change of *intentions of the psyche*, which— similar to a new "wish"—changes the inner direction of where one's heart and mind seeks its stability and equilibrium (Law of Falling).

I bring this up to remind the reader that this story is an immense allegory and addresses the psycho-spiritual journey (*inner* story) of human experience. Please remember also, Karatus is not in spacetime, but is meant to represent a living plane under the direct influence of the Spiritual Sun (Sun Absolute), which gives off emanations in the form of God's Word.

This change in mental gravity-centers now focuses on a unique discussion of *human sincerity*—along with the medical profession and its abnormalities, as was observed by Beelzebub on Earth.

Again, Hassein wants his grandfather to tell him more and more about the strange three-brained beings living and breeding on the planet Earth. Beelzebub tells Hassein that it was during his sixth and last visit to the planet Earth that he received information concerning his pardon and permission to return to the center of the universe and bosom of OUR COMMON UNI-BEING ENDLESSNESS, the sphere of the Sun Absolute (Swedenborg's Spiritual Sun), of which his home planet *Karatas* was a part. But he was already committed to investigating another psychic abnormality in the lives of earth-humans and needed to follow through.

The reason for his sixth trip was that he began to observe from his telescope on Mars that certain "advances" were made among different earth-humans that allowed them to kill each other from much greater distances and in much larger numbers. The inner message here is that humankind was successfully distancing itself from the true horror of their negative manifestations—making it even more difficult to awaken their conscience and perform their God-given duty.

This difficulty is why Swedenborg calls the turning around from such an unacceptable condition of the human mind and its heart an inner and personal state of "devastation" and "vastation" (*Arcana Coelestia*, n. 5360). He states that this atrophied condition of the human mind is variously described in Holy Scripture as a "pouring out," a "cutting off," a "consummation," a "desert," and a "void." Also, the "great day of Jehovah," the "day of His wrath" and "vengeance," a "day of darkness," and "thick darkness," of "cloud," and of "obscurity," a "day of visitation," also the "day when the Earth shall perish." (The "Earth" represents humankind's quality of worship at any given time.)

In fact, the split in the human psyche by which *spiritual conscience* is driven downward into the subconscious mind and stored away is depicted in the biblical story of the famine in Egypt. In this Genesis story (and divine Legominism) Joseph convinces Pharaoh to put grain in the storehouse so that it could save innocent people in the future when things took a bad turn and *food* became scarce. Similarly, the Lord God stores things of heavenly goodness and knowledge in the human subconscious (internal natural mind) to be used later to awaken, feed, and exalt spiritual conscience to our waking lives— that is, if we accept such a duty and allow ourselves to be led by the Lord God.

Swedenborg not only fully acknowledged the split in the human natural mind, he even stated that the cause of this human psychic split comes when individuals, as younger children, grow up and learn bad habits from the world (thus losing their innocence and sincerity). Through this growing up process, children learn how to *divide* their minds to manifest *pretense*, just as their adult parents and teachers do. (The slogan for this negative situation is "Do as I say, not as I do.")

Because of this real split in our psychical condition, even any true information learned in life by us will merely lodge itself in our external memory function, where it becomes "walled-off" and separated from uniting with—and being compared with—our God-given level of heavenly innocence, which has been driven deeper within our subconscious. The Lord God's protection and implanting of these remaining heavenly influences of innocence happens in the part of our consciousness that was driven deep down during our childhood. This divine action ensures that this precious sacred data will not be muddied or destroyed by the vanities and allurements of the physical world.

When "Joseph" opens the storehouses in the biblical story (Genesis 41:56) it symbolically represents a re-connection between the subconscious mind (where heavenly food is stored) and our worldly consciousness. Spiritual temptations, sincerity and self-examination (self-shocks) open up these storehouses deep within the human heart and mind. As our compulsions and negative habits are acknowledged and resisted they lose their grip, and the beneficial sacred knowledge secretly implanted by God arises upward into one's worldly consciousness where it meets with the information of our outer memory banks and puts it into correct order, so that our lives can act from sincere (innocent) acts of goodness.

Without this unifying process, goodness can easily be feigned to serve the unrestrained passions of our egoistic natural mind by the learned (and separated) worldly information of our outer habitual mind. The unregenerate internal natural mind of humans is self-centered and in the constant pursuit of financial gain, reputation, power and worldly honors. (This is why Swedenborg claimed that a *new will* is created in the human understanding or internal natural mind.)

The arising clash of values from the sincerity of connecting our inconsistent passions with our best convictions releases our God-given and protected remains, whereby spiritual growth becomes a part of our unified conscious life. This new (more vivified) life represents both an expanding plane of spiritual conscience and a new organic matrix (ground) for the birth of a genuine spiritual body to gestate inside us, and our understanding.

I will address this bio-truth of the lawful need for us to develop higher bodies in a later chapter—otherwise our spiritual growth will only be a thought-dream.

Just as the sinking of Atlantis symbolizes the submergence of spiritual conscience and God's merciful protection of one's remains, its re-appearance in our *waking* lives is symbolized (lawful inexactitudes) by the rising and re-appearance of "dry land" in the Seven Day Creation story in Genesis (epigenesis of the human spirit and its deeper ecosystem). Swedenborg stresses that the split human natural mind is what allows for hyprocrisy and deceit to manifest in the universe. (There is no deception without the ability to separate one's mental functions.)

Beelzebub tells Hassein that he was quite perplexed by the being-need of earth-humans to mutilate and destroy each other's existence with greater and greater efficiency. So he decided to travel back to the planet Earth for the final time because he senses that he still needs to discover some additional causes for this growing deadly "anomaly" in the earth-human psyche. For this reason, he decides to land this time on the continent of Asia called "Afghanistan," where the process of reciprocal destruction (wars) was most active.

On this sixth and last visit to Earth, his stay would last three hundred years!

Beelzebub decides he will make an even more detailed study of the strange Earth-human psyche with the help of certain branches of general knowledge called "medicine," "physiology" and "hypnotism" (also called "Samonoltooriko," "Gasometronoltooriko" and "Sakookinoltooriko"). He becomes convinced that the biggest obstacle among earth-humans is not their mechanically driven and artificial consciousness—which they falsely believe is their true consciousness—but that their real consciousness had been driven back into what is now called their "subconscious" and is put out of reach to them, due to their abnormal approaches to living. Instead, this subconsciousness, which was meant by God to be their real conscious mind and essence, now remains buried in earth-humans in a *primitive* and *childlike* state—an underdeveloped state—because additional knowledge gained in the world can no longer reach it and add anything real to it.

Beelzebub then reminds Hassein that it is in this subconscious level that the Very Saintly Ashiata Shiemash discovered that sacred data for the impulse of "Objective Conscience" still remained intact deep inside all earth-humans. Swedenborg states that The Lord God takes extreme care and stealth to implant remains (sacred data) safely among our various primitive inner perversions and rotten urges, by which heavenly influences can maintain some connection with outer terrestrial human life.

A lesser-known idea among today's humans is that the Lord God *only* operates through this protected plane of sacred data tucked away in our interior natural (subconscious) mind. The divine protection of this distinct and deeper sacred functioning is why we cannot easily connect with it without making serious inner efforts, such as new sincerity and spiritual combat (*conscious labors* and *intentional suffering*).

As previously mentioned, Swedenborg stated that without these divinely implanted remains, we would be incapable of any kind of rationality and become vicious beasts. The phenomenon of war and its atrocities provides evidence of human "bestiality" and a rejection of one's heavenly remains.

Because Beelzebub feels he needs a large sampling of earth-humans from as many different places as possible to verify his suspicions concerning the causes for all the abnormalities of the human psyche, he soon becomes frustrated by the fact that earth-humans have developed so many different languages and dialects. (His mastering eighteen of their languages was not enough to grapple with this *excessive absurdity*.) He informs his grandson Hassein that these diverse languages on Earth are formed every time a new split in their groupings occurs, while everywhere else in God's great universe (on other planets) three-brained beings enjoy one common "sound-manifesting-mutual intercourse." (Swedenborg calls this atrophied mutual intercourse an instinctive spiritual language, which operates on the higher level of mental ideas and concepts. Early earth-humans communicated in this rarefied manner.)

However, the current worldly mix of languages and dialects ("polyglotism") of course makes it difficult for the different groupings of earth-humans to communicate to (and understand) each other. Beelzebub even ascertains that some of these languages are so odd that they even defy nature's intended design of the vocal chords.

Beelzebub next recalls attending a special meeting on Earth in which certain "important" communities tried to solve this precise problem of differing languages. While this endeavor had a promising beginning, as always, the same "dissensions" inherent in these peculiar earth-humans created obstacles because each faction embraced its own perceived "greatness." Some wanted to use the Greek language as a universal way to communicate. Others wanted Latin. A third group thought a newly cooked-up artificial language called "Esperanto" should be used. In spite of this original noble effort, Beelzebub sadly admits that none of the earth-humans' strategies for improved communication created any positive *inner* change in the beings themselves or modified their various "heights of absurdity."

Once again, while it may appear that Beelzebub (Gurdjieff) has digressed and gotten a bit off the topic of war, he is actually making the point that none of the earth-humans' strategies to communicate with each other embraces the important need for individuals to communicate from their deeper *essence*-properties hidden within their subconscious, which is important for true peace.

Beelzebub makes the astounding and anti-intuitive discovery that the biggest difficulty is that this healing communication and intercourse first needs to take place between an individual's own split consciousness—the external (worldly) habitual mind with their true deeper essence-mind.

Unfortunately, the only successful means of communication for this dual psyche in humans is called "sincerity." Acquiring this sincerity is painful, for it requires an individual to truly self-examine—and objectively self-criticize—their own "illusory inflated" self-importance. The resulting connection and friction (from the influence of the Spiritual Sun) represents a personal and psycho-spiritual form of "Djartklom" called self-remorse).

As a result of the failure to perform this cosmic duty, earth-humans are neither sincere with themselves nor sincere with others around them. Over time, earth-humans learned to lie to themselves by stifling the function of self-criticism (inner Djartklom), preferring the more comfortable and pleasurable activity of "self-calming" to liberate their *passive nature*. This disturbed the proper coordination and harmonious ordering of their common psyche into a state of *impotency* and allowed them to overlook their various personal flaws and never to see reality. (Swedenborg observed in the Spiritual World that many of those who represented the Reformed Christian Church were petrified at uncovering any details of their own dirty laundry. Any new improvements in religion or worldly organizations will require humans embracing such introspecive sincerity.)

According to Beelzebub's long and detailed investigations, the reasons why earth-humans continue to lie to each other was caused by another worldly circumstance—the unfortunate division among them into "castes" or "classes." (Class warfare only furthers this unfortunate human condition of living in terrible lies.)

Beelzebub continues to reveal to Hassein more unflattering traits of earth-human behavior and the predicament earth-humans have gotten themselves into. It seems that over time, dividing people into classes takes on a life of its own and is no longer dependent on either one's ordinary consciousness or subconscious (involuntary mind).

Two new properties in human behavior arise from these class distinctions whereby people no longer can appreciate each other on sincere "equal terms." Instead, a person either looks down at one person or "brown-noses" another. This inconsistent activity in human relations not only corrodes the "awareness-of-one's-own-individuality" but leads to a worsening condition where people cannot even be sincere with members of their own caste. (We see this phenomenon today as cheating between friends and even between spouses.)

During Beelzebub's further investigations of earth-humans on his sixth and final visit, he discovers that earth-humans can be sincere, up to a point, with those individuals occupied in the positions called "physician" and "confessor." This gives Beelzebub an idea for furthering his human studies, which rely on people being sincere with him.

Of those two professions, Beelzebub decides to take on the role of physician as the best way to uncover new details about the strangeness of the earth-human psyche. As a result he offers Hassein—and you, the reader—another vivid example of how there is a serious lack of sincere conscience taking place in most of the daily affairs of human commerce. (Swedenborg discovered that Heaven was a place of heavenly commerce through mutual support and genuine innocence.)

Disguised, and assuming the role of a physician on Earth, Beelzebub quickly makes friends with a "pharmacist" and takes full advantage of his unique new position of *trust*. Like everything else, the medical profession has degenerated correspondingly along with the general human psyche, and is now just as influenced by people representing various classes.

Beelzebub was familiar with physicians in other parts of the universe who were all concerned with, and assisted in, both a person's *inner* (spiritual) and *outer* well-being—helping fulfill his or her being-duties—regardless of their worldly status (or the size of their wallet).

Beelzebub describes his observations of how earth-human doctors behave very differently toward patients who have lots of "English pounds," versus "cancelled-German-marks." The first type of patient gets the physician's full attention while the latter gets a hasty "prescription," so that the doctor can more quickly make his escape.

While this behavior is obviously counter to a physician's inner-being obligations and duty, Beelzebub also sees the absence of a proper *inner dictate* throughout the entire medical field. So Beelzebub next turns his attention to how these medical prescriptions are actually filled. That is the reason for his making friends with an earth-human pharmacist.

Beelzebub learns from the pharmacist how they constantly cut corners on the ingredients and "mixtures" in order to increase profits. The pharmacist also enlightens Beelzebub as to shortcuts taken by those who are supposed to regulate these medicines in order to verify the integrity of the mixtures. (Today, in the United States, even though more sophisticated technologies and tests are performed by the FDA, financial pressures will often force these professionals to withhold negative information concerning various chemical mixtures and accept the findings of the manufacturer.) After all, everyone has mouths to feed and pockets to fill.

Again, Beelzebub uses these examples to illustrate to his grandson what happens (loss of sincerity) when the three-brained beings of the ill-fated planet Earth become focused solely on *outer* worldly success and their self-centered preservation. They become more and more disconnected from the sacred being-impulse of *conscience*—to where it is driven back into a deeper or subconscious level. (While Beelzebub is picking on the medical profession in this part of his Tales, he is also giving the reader a unique opportunity to examine his/her own motives and behavior in life.)

Beelzebub next invites his faithful servant Ahoon to again share his personal experience of Earth, especially concerning a misunderstanding of the word "doctor." Beelzebub also happens to slip in the idea that Ahoon, although "clothed" with a higher being reason (inner body), was also confused by this name used for physicians. (Interestingly, Swedenborg also described "Truth" as mental *clothing* for one's "Love." This allows for one's level of understanding and reasoning to form the *higher spiritual organic structures* (bodies) necessary for enveloping the human soul as we become more bio-sensitive to the *Theomertmalogos*—influences coming from God's Word and Spiritual Sun.)

As Ahoon responds, he recounts a silly event on the planet Earth for Hassein where a friend's wife was about to give birth and was in need of a doctor. (He also suggests that human pregnancies served the noble purposes of God's universal scheme, which Swedenborg claimed, was the highest spiritual use of human marriage.) Well, the husband was away at the time and Ahoon was called upon to quickly find a doctor for her. Next, Ahoon hurriedly searched out everyone in the town who was called "doctor."

The first person he came upon was a "doctor of philosophy." The second person he ran into was a "doctor of jurisprudence." The third was recommended by a restaurant headwaiter, who directed him to a "doctor-accoucheur." After running around town for several hours looking for a "doctor of medicine," Ahoon finds out that the pregnant woman gave birth alone and quite naturally (which women are normally designed to do).

After hearing this story from Ahoon, Beelzebub shares with everyone in their spaceship compartment a wise saying from the highly esteemed earth-human Mullah Nassr Eddin concerning these contemporary physicians. His statement goes: "For our sins, God has sent us two kinds of physicians, one kind to help us die, and another to prevent us living."

Stepping back a bit to get a wider look at the medical profession and the deteriorating human psyche, we hear that the pharmacist in this Tale has also informed Beelzebub of an unexpected result—that many of these less than perfect mixtures work, regardless! This is because of the human vulnerability to *suggestibility*, which causes many people to have a strong belief in a particular remedy given to them by "professionals."

The phenomenon of suggestibility (the placebo effect) in the Earth-human psyche catches Beelzebub's attention and curiosity. He knows that this strange psychic condition of suggestibility never happens among three-brained beings from other planets of God's great universe.

But why earth-humans?

Beelzebub is next determined to understand the reason for the earth-human's susceptibility to almost any dang suggestion made by a terrestrial "expert." This investigation produces more details concerning the negative outcomes of Earth citizens having a split psyche. He discovers that earth-humans are now living on the surface of their planet in a semi-conscious and trance-like state, which has even affected the tempo and gravity center of their bloodflow.

SUMMARY

■ Beelzebub feels he needs to study the human psyche more deeply to find out why earth-humans periodically seek to destroy each other in ever-greater numbers—called war.

■ Beelzebub gives his opinion concerning the lack of human sincerity and its necessity.

■ The medical profession, as well as all other human pursuits, has degenerated along with the disappearance of inner sincerity. This is why people have learned to cut corners.

SUMMARY

■ Children lose their innocence when they pick up and imitate *pretense* from their parents, teachers and the adult world. This deceit splits a youngster's psyche and drives their conscience (sacred data) down into a subconscious level, where it is still protected by God for future use.

■ This split psychic condition and its reunification during our spiritual growth is portrayed *symbolically* in the Bible story of Joseph opening up the Egyptian grain storehouses (Genesis 45:51).

■ In the current split condition of the human psyche, new—even vital—information is kept locked up in the memory function and prevented from going any deeper, where it can help feed the subconscious mind (internal natural mind) and allow it to develop beyond its starving and primitive state.

■ Lying to oneself comes from an impotency of sincere self-criticism—while lying to others comes from placing individuals into different classes and castes.

■ Beelzelbub learns of his divine pardon from the center of the universe at this time, but decides he must continue his earth-human investigations before heading back to his own birth planet.

■ One's level of understanding *clothes* a person's bio-spiritual reality and loves.

■ Married couples having children is the highest use serving God's expanding universe.

■ Because of a strong "belief" in a doctor's prescription, and human suggestibility, even watered-down medicines can be effective cures (the placebo effect).

■ Beelzebub becomes interested in why earth-humans are so susceptible to *suggestion*—when other humans in the universe aren't.

CHAPTER 31

"Hypnotism"

Gurdjieff's onslaught of contemporary humanity's false self-image and self-importance continues. No one believes they are hypnotized!

Hypnosis (and suggestibility) is more relevant to our lives than we are ready to accept. In this chapter, Gurdjieff uses the topic of hypnotism to offer an organic basis for our split psyche.

I love this chapter. It covers a topic that few people believe could have any correlation with living a moral and spiritual life, or with living their own particular lives. We refuse to believe we are hypnotized (yet the world still seems crazy and illogical to us). As a result, we do not acknowledge and completely underestimate the reality of our true split *organic* situation and the very real obstacles facing our spiritual responsibility and salvation on earth.

I consider this chapter a deadly serious extension of the Ashiata Shiemash's unflattering Legominism titled the "Terror of the Situation." As you will remember, Beelzebub claimed that the noble being-impulses of "Faith," "Hope" and "Love" are no longer effective means by which to counter and conquer human *egoism, self-love, vanity, pride, self-deception, bragging* and *arrogance*. These negative human traits sneak into all our worldly activities and become mixed with even our best intentions. Now, they have become second nature and fixed into the bio-functions of a psyche that has "twice" become split and divided over time, to the point where earth-humans can no longer properly criticize or correct each other.

Twice?

Swedenborg fully agrees with this premise of human trance. (This is what is symbolically meant by God putting Adam "to sleep" in the Garden of Eden. He further stated that after the "fall of Man," God was forced to change the functioning of the human mind from having an instinctive and heavenly perception of Love and Faith from the cerebellum (involuntary) to that of the cerebrum (voluntary) which reasons from evidence it receives through its five outer senses. This represents one split in the human psyche. And while this divine maneuver led the human race to rely on outer sensation and memory- data (*est sensuale et scientificum*) as to what was important and true, thus preserving their free will in all matters, it also divided the new cerebral human psyche into discrete functions of thought and feelings which had to be re-unified (again, this divine action put some of the blame on the strategies of a higher intelligence to maintain cosmic harmony).

But according to Swedenborg, God also countered this loss of *angelic perception* in early humans by placing the function of *conscience* into the human psyche as a new kind of *inner* dictate (*Arcana Coelestia*, n. 607), between the thinking mind and insane will. However, over time, the abnormal lives of people who started to abuse their divided psychic functions (especially for the purpose of deceit and pretense—and the inevitable distortion of religion) caused this God-given gift of conscience to be driven deeper down into another level of consciousness where, thankfully, it could still be protected from the vanities and allurements of the external world and from evil influences bubbling up from Hell.

Unfortunately, this outcome divided the human psyche yet again, not just between the will and intellect, but in forming a whole new outer (corporeal) kind of intellect and will, called the external natural mind (*True Christianity*, Vol 2, n. 593). Thus, our earthly lives were no longer focused on or dependent upon conscience.

Because earth-humans now believe this second will and intellect represents their true personality and consciousness, God's same divine protection also serves to naturally block even helpful information, learned from the external world, from reaching deep enough inside to affect our inner world. Instead, all learning is annexed by one's outer fabricated consciousness (external natural mind and memory, which is corporeal/sensual and mechanical).

These two split mental situations allowed humans to imagine and dream they were changing in positive directions and evolving, even when they weren't. Beelzebub—and Swedenborg—tried to warn us that this imagined evolution is a form of *trance* (and hypnosis) because it leaves one's deeper conscience and reality in the dark. In most cases, the reality of this human hypnotic state is only noticed in life when such trance-manifestations are seen in people who have been put into a more concentrated and exaggerated state—where pneumonia smells like roses.

Because of this predicament, Ashiata Shiemash realized religion was now ineffectual and earth-humans had to take the splitting of their psyches into account. Swedenborg believed that when the mind was elevated to inner spiritual realities, attention was *awakened* (*Apocalypse Explained*, n. 263). So in our current un-awakened circumstances, we are simply snoozing through life.

It breaks my heart to suggest that even Swedenborgian scholars and theologians fail to grasp the significance of this notion of humans having a split natural mind, which keeps them hypnotized. As yet, no tie has been made between our implanted God-given "conscience" and our implanted "remains." But both serve as a deeper mediating plane and matrix for God's saving action and something for angels to flow into. One is a perception of truth; the other, a perception of true goodness. Both require sincerity to become active. Both represent the Lord God's presence in us.

But both operate on a distinct level—far deeper than our ordinary worldly human consciousness works. This usually places our conscience and holy remains far deeper than a minister's helpful articles and sermons can reach. I say this because so many followers of Swedenborg's potent theology now prefer to sidestep the unflattering process of self-examination (such sincerity alone brings information deeper into the rational of the human psyche). Rather, these worshippers never truly perceive their broken (fallen) situation in which egoism sneaks in. They falsely come to believe—from hearing repeatedly to "Love God and the neighbor," or "perform uses and good works"—that such holy advice is reaching their spirits and is never blocked by their disconnected minds.

As a result, they believe (with their disconnected minds), that outer acts of friendship, altruism, community building and simply becoming more loving with each other will bring about spiritual transformation and heavenly happiness. But any good deed done without imploring sincere self-examination is *simulation* and merely *passive worship*. (The innocence in one's God-given remains must expand and become an active part of one's outer charitable actions.)

Swedenborg observed that many traditional Christians (mostly of the reformed church) will easily admit to having every kind of flaw but are absolutely terrified of *self-examination* and *confession* of specific flaws. So to gain God's favor, they will assume "proper" outer activities, like attending church services, engaging in acts of kindness and joining organizations with positive worldly goals—all without inner vigilance—so most of one's bad traits are not rooted out and stay put.

The belief in helpfulness is noble, but again, this alone does not take into account that we have a divided mind (external and internal) and that our deeper, inner reality needs to be purified and re-unified with our current waking consciousness. Forming this inner unity within us is what spiritual transformation is all about. This cleansing and psychic unity qualifies our helpfulness and acts of friendship.

God's Holy Word addresses this unification (called conjunction) within its deep symbolic language (which demands an elevated mind to grasp) and urges us throughout its narratives to "awaken."

It is because of our having divided minds that our best intentions don't always prevail, and even backfire. Under these conditions our unchallenged egoism can pervert, pollute and defile every good thing we do—without our ever noticing. This blindness or inability to see our true situation is evidence that people's external natural minds are not open to, nor communicating with, the deeper passions of our essence. The Lord God has wisely set up a mediating dictate to do so—our spiritual remains and conscience.

Yet well-meaning people have learned to take the easier way out by side-stepping an important part of God's regenerative process in which *real love, faith* and *hope* can be genuinely obtained. It is only through *re-awakening conscience* (our objective observer) in one's remains through vigilance, regeneration, intentional suffering and temptation, that our Love, Faith and Hope can become spiritually sincere, genuine, cleansed and *innocent*. We have to consciously choose to uncover the hidden crap of our lives in order to lawfully make contact with our conscience (remains) so that it can grow and properly take hold of our outer actions. This process is painful because it is felt as torture in the expanding plane of conscience. But this process is our real cosmic essence-duty.

(And when we awaken and elevate our minds, our split mental functionings begin to unite, correspond and cooperate with each other.)

Unfortunately, we have falsely learned to experience ourselves as a "single" person. Instead of having a divided consciousness in which the outer mind is focused on the *artificial* and the inner one is *asleep* (lacking proper attention) we go through life, school, work, friendships, marriage and even church worship in a *hypnotic* and self-illusory state. And thus, we earth-humans botch up most things.

According to Beelzebub, this hypnotic state and trance is made possible because of our split consciousness, in which different mental functions—working alone—can never correct each other (as in Djart-klom). Furthermore, these divisions are actually strengthened by churches and academic institutions that fail to notice and grasp this problem. In fact, the second division in the human psyche (symbol-izing the submergence of Atlantis), with its delusional self-worth, is empowered by all "high-sounding" institutions that promote pleasant pursuits, cheerfulness and personal validation—such as "chumminess" and "hugging" (for self-calming). Of course, this seeking of pleasantness sidesteps the real challenge that people must endure—the unflattering procedure of identifying their personal "dirt." Instead, people want to always be comforted and look at the bright side of things, despite Swedenborg's sober claim that humans all have an *insane will* and are born into *evils of every kind*. In fact, he claimed that even the angels of the highest heaven would rush headlong into hell if it were not for the Lord God's constant attention. It takes a powerful form of self-delusion and trance to overlook such an abnormal and illogical predicament.

Swedenborg calls the orderly process to correct this situation *Repentance, Reformation* and *Regeneration*, which relies on self-exam-ination, sincerity, resisting negative traits (as sins) and imploring the Lord God for divine help. Instead, I often find the church experience of community and fellowship as simply "gushy" and "chummy" (all in the name of Christian Love and compassion). This is to be expected, because of our split psyches. Most church institutions are in the business of making people feel good and offering *hope*—but rarely focus on assisting their members to bravely cultivate inner friction and endurance for the sincere self-criticism and personal difficulty that is necessary to make contact with, and activate, a worshipper's sacred God-given remains and conscience.

Temptation and spiritual conflict connects our outer *fabricated* consciousness and all its memory-information with our inner reality. I cannot over-emphasize Swedenborg's claim that the Lord God only operates through a person's deep-seated remains and conscience, which is a divinely protected state of *innocence*. It is innocence that we must embrace and cultivate—not merely talents and friendships. So we have to go deeper with our sincerity than we are accustomed to going, in order to cooperate with the Divine plan.

If I had not studied Gurdjieff, I could have easily overlooked how Swedenborg actually addressed this same issue of human trance in our ordinary waking states. One needs simply to look at the Bible's use of the word "sleep" or the phrase "wake up," then insert the more modern term "hypnotism" to get a correct picture of the "Terror-of-the-Situation."

The problem for today's students of Swedenborg's theology is that they may have to be informed about *both* splits in the human psyche. One split took place after the "Fall," between the understanding (intellect) and will (heart), but the second took place in the human natural mind, where the insertion of conscience from above was a necessary solution. Statements by Swedenborg definitely suggest that the human psyche even goes through a second split during childhood, in which innocence is lost and our conscience and remains is covered over by deceit.

I repeat, the first split took place after the demise of the Most Ancient Church (Beelzebub's First Transapalnian Perturbation) on earth-humans embracing a false principle (from self-love), and involves the human mind being divided by God into two distinct functions capable of operating independently of each other—called the "will" and the "understanding." This split allows the human understanding to learn things that surpass the human heart and its worldly desires and then challenges the heart to apply these noble ideas to one's life (unifying the two through a third principle called action). Next, to offset the loss of having direct perception of heavenly knowledge, the human race was given "conscience" by God to mediate between the human intellect and flawed human will.

But the lesser known (or talked about), *second* split (Beelzebub's Second Transapalnian Perturbation) occurs when the natural (worldly) mind itself now divides into interior and exterior functions (*True Christian Religion*, Vol 2, n. 593). This happens when in childhood we learn from adults and through contemporary education to cleverly divide our worldly (natural) minds, in order to create pretense and phoniness through our separate outer actions (*Arcana Coelestia*, n. 8247). This second split is what causes "conscience" to become covered over by a new, more artificial and corporeal/mechanical mind, where it is buried in the subconscious and out of reach of our habitual minds and daily activities.

Over time, and through habit, we have falsely come to believe that this outer, artificial mind is who we really are.

This second split negates proper self-criticism between what we know (external and worldly nature) and what we actually are (our more internal and real nature). It is this negation of self-criticism that makes it possible for humans to become hypnotized and be vulnerable to suggestion (and worldly trends).

Well, let me get off my soapbox and back to *Beelzebub's Tales*, because there is much more on this topic of trance to explore, including its unique organic consequences (such as bloodflow).

Beelzebub informs Hassein in this chapter that he not only became a physician during his sixth and final visit to the planet Earth, but became a "physician-hypnotist" so that he could penetrate the "innerworld" of earth-humans and gain further insights into the causes of their strange psyches. He had learned that the strange capacity for earth-humans to be put into a "hypnotic state" had arisen soon after the destruction of Atlantis (dividing of the human natural mind).

After that second catastrophic event, the human psyche was divided into two kinds of natural consciousness—what is called one's worldly or "waking-consciousness" and the "subconsciousness." In this new split of the human natural mind, the outer or waking consciousness becomes aligned with the artificial and mechanical, while the subconscious, which was our original and real consciousness, is lulled to sleep. Theologically speaking, this sleep represents a form of trance and laziness, keeping us from performing any cosmic duty. In fact, the covered-over and separated internal natural mind becomes quite offended if you try to wake it up from its peaceful slumber and dream-fantasies.

As I mentioned earlier, earth-humans only ascribe the term hypnotism to describe those individuals who are affected by its process in an "accelerated" and "concentrated" manner that makes its effect obvious to all observers. What earth-humans fail to notice is that the illogicality of many of their daily manifestations and relationships with others is due to more subtle expressions of living in a trance-like state.

We humans must *snap ourselves out of this slumber* if we are to make any real changes to our lives and the rest of the world. In fact, few religions even recognize that Jesus (and all saintly individuals and legitimate prophets) sought to "de-hypnotize" the world. (As evidence, the Buddhist term "Maya" also refers to the human condition of trance, which makes it impossible to see reality. As does Jesus' remark about the "blind leading the blind.")

Beelzebub relates to his grandson that the learned-beings of the ancient city Gob, in the country of Maralpleicie, had noticed this particular abnormal property in the human psyche—or trance—and were the first to turn it into a genuine branch of their science. They called this strange mental property of trance that affected humans the "non-responsible-manifestations-personality." (One's inner essence, split from its outer mind, imagines and dreams of great things, but actually rejects any serious conscious duty.)

Unfortunately, during the course of periodic warfare on the planet Earth, this real branch of science and its knowledge was also eventually lost to the world.

According to Beelzebub, an Austrian-Hungarian doctor named Anton Mesmer revived this ancient science, when through his weird experiments, he clearly noticed the duality of consciousness in his patients. He would have gotten to the bottom of this strange phenomenon if he had not come under extreme attack from the scientific community of his day (which included Benjamin Franklin). This "pecking to death" was so effective that even today, this coura-geous individual is considered a quack by authorities (in spite of his successful cures). Beelzebub was saddened by this outcome because if Mesmer would have been able to revive this real science in the way that it was originally intended, it could have provided earth-humans with a potent means for saving themselves from many of their igno-ble tendencies.

Beelzebub also remarks that at the time he was leaving Earth for the sixth time, a learned being from the country known as France had discovered a non-traditional cure for "cancer" and was also "ganged-up on" by the so-called experts of that time, who enforced their standards and (abnormally) established conditions.

Beelzebub does not specify to Hassein whether the cure for cancer involves hypnotism or not, but it most certainly involves treat-ing the disharmony of the functioning of people's common presence (which can potentially be rectified by hypnotic strategies). There are indeed some stories of individuals curing their own cancers and other abnormalities through a form of self-hypnosis. Hypnotism is also successfully used as therapy for our habits like smoking (later in the chapter, I will touch on the bio-psycho dynamics of why hypnotism might accomplish this).

What Beelzebub does reveal is that because of the abnormal condition of life on Earth, the learned beings of new formation (post-Atlanteans) have learned to attack everything outside the status quo, so that genuine objective truth, learned over the centuries, evap-orates. In more ancient periods these cosmic truths were allowed to accumulate, and over time, became the property of all earth-humans, regardless of their status or position in life. This accumulation of cosmic truth assisted the third sacred force (Holy Spirit or "sacred reconciling") operating in their being-nature to grow conscience and create a new will in their understanding (this is the purpose of spiritual transformation and being "reborn").

Now, only erroneous knowledge has become the guarded property of the few who belong to various worldly circles.

Relating all this to the subject of hypnotism, Beelzebub explains to his grandson that earth-humans, because of their abnormal approach to life, cause the functioning of their *true consciousness* to function in a completely *passive* state (just like when it is asleep and dreaming), while the entire functioning of their corporeal planetary body (including the five senses) continues to operate normally (actively). This abnormal existence, becoming habitual and "fixed" in the human psyche, forced nature (and God) to form two independent kinds of consciousness (a two-system Zoostat) within these strange earth-humans. (Again, Swedenborg called this particular psychic split the *internal* and *external* natural minds. [*True Christian Religion*, n. 593])

Here comes the unexpected big bio-news.

We cannot look at this split without including its biological and organic ramifications within the scheme of human anatomy. Beelzebub tells Hassein that each of these distinct types of consciousness evokes a *certain blood circulation*, or tempo, and vice versa—where through a change in blood circulation, one or the other of these types of consciousness becomes activated (usually at the expense of the others, in the modern functioning of humans).

Swedenborg's research into the human brain, which included dissection at several universities in Italy and France, revealed to him that the cerebrum and its cortical cells (neurons) consisted of a multi-level architecture or scaffolding, within its various lobes, compartments and sections. Each of these distinct neural levels and substrates supported a different cognitive functioning, occupied different brain lobes and were fueled by a *different species of blood.*

In this multi-leveled brain design, Swedenborg discovered that *sensing, imagining,* and *reasoning* (and the affections associated with each) could either be unified or act independently from each other according to various kinds of blood circulations operating. Through these various types of circulations of the blood, the cerebrum could therefore either harmonize and connect its distinct mental functions or cut one off from the others. When a singular mind-function and its corresponding blood circulation gets cut off from the others, and its segregated action is *intensified* by some strong affection, passion or belief, we have a form of "trance" and limited awareness. (Meditation that does not include all our three distinct brain functions is a form of trance.)

So what Beelzebub is trying to convey to Hassein is that the earth-humans, with their split psyches, now go through their lives with their deeper, essential mind in a trance-like or dream state (this is why some people will even remark that life somehow doesn't seem real to them).

One sure-fire way for earth-humans to promote the disconnection between and limit the harmonious development between their three distinct cognitive functions is to ignore our God-given cosmic *responsibility*. That is why those of the ancient civilization in the city of Gob called hypnotism the "taking-away-of-responsibility." In other words, the moral degradation of the human psyche had a correspondingly negative physiological and real bio-functioning consequence.

One cannot act illogically—within the absurdities set up in current human life—without cutting off some self-correcting and confrontational mental function from taking part that might actually know better (like conscience). This subversive mental predicament is why many of us often sense that we are always playing some kind of game in our lives. (We are.)

Now perhaps, you the reader, can more easily appreciate the true nature of the "terrifying" outcome from this strange psychical property of the human mind, which rendered as ineffectual, the otherwise normal being-impulses of "Faith," "Hope," and "Love." As mentioned before, the split in human consciousness created an *outer* (artificial) mind, which became active while the *inner*, real consciousness was put to sleep and made passive.

It is this deeper, sleeping part of human reality that has to be affected, take responsibility, become rational, and be awakened by spiritual forces (such as conscience) during one's efforts toward personal transformation and rebirth—or the noble impulses of "Faith," "Hope" and "Love" will always be tarnished by egoism and the proprium. (Again, this is why Holy Scripture has many warnings for us to "sleep not" and to "awaken.")

You will remember it was in this deeper consciousness (our internal natural mind) that the Lord God's sacred "information," implanted during the innocence of our youth, is protected. These remains—Holy data stored up by God—are carefully immersed among our selfish passions and desires. They are hindered from developing further because the new split outer mind, now disconnected and operating independently, has control over the five senses. It intercepts all incoming data (true or false) where it is accumulated in the external memory and does not go any deeper into our psyches (where our worldly egoistic desires hide).

Information which could be helpful and better organized is instead held up in this worldly or corporeal memory as a "prisoner" and is "enslaved" (like the Israelites in Egypt under the Pharaoh). Under this enslavement our learning cannot reach the deeper subconscious and "feed" the sacred influences already in one's remains. Our remains forms the bio-matrix for spiritual conscience and the evolution of our spirit to continue and form spiritual bodies.

This abnormality in earth-humans is a two-way process.

The subconscious, being cut off from the outer world, falls asleep and fails to communicate its genuine God-given being-impulses to the artificial (habitual mind) of our daily life. Meanwhile the outer (false) mind fails to give up its own data (which can contain valuable and useful info) to one's deeper essence. So the inner mind starves and is thwarted from gaining the proper material needed for *self-evaluation, confrontation,* and criticism. Thus one's spiritual potential remains frozen in a childlike, primitive state, surrounded by a crust of worldly ideas and allows our egoistic and self-centered leanings to continue to expand unchallenged.

These two forms of consciousness must reconnect for a person to become genuinely spiritual—to wake up spiritually.

Both Beelzebub (Gurdjieff) and Swedenborg are in agreement that *Sincerity* (through self-examination) reconnects these two distinct forms of consciousness so that the process of salvation and spiritual rebirth can begin. The problem and tragedy here is that the human race, through modern education, focused on developing only one function (the intellect). Our living successfully in the physical world of senses has made us accustomed to artificial lifestyles and a limited worldly consciousness that has earth-humans now believing that their dreaming is who they really are.

So any change made to improve one's outer, worldly consciousness only amounts to a change of "masks" in the person's terrestrial personality.

According to Beelzebub, earth-humans go to great lengths to protect their false self-image, especially from any process that might challenge it by reconnecting its delusional beliefs with the sacred data stored in their subconscious. This protection keeps us calm, but profoundly asleep. And when asleep, we are prone to evils of all kinds.

Such a contact between conflicting consciousnesses leads to an uncomfortable clashing of loves and worldviews that is nothing short of a death struggle between our old selves and our new self, including our take on God's existence, character and truth. (As I have alluded to earlier, this intense drama and "battle" is played out most notably in the symbolic images and deeper language of the Revelation chapter in Holy Scripture. All genuine spiritual change requires this inner battle to take place, and is not to be understood as a physical confrontation.)

But again, I digress. I need now to return to the topic of distinct species of blood types circulating through our brains and their neural structures to make this conversation more visceral and organic to our understanding. This topic of bodily fluids (and their distinct viscosities) is essential in any serious study of the ideas of both Gurdjieff and Swedenborg.

Early in Swedenborg's scientific career, he discovered that sensation and awareness in humans depended upon where the blood was flowing in their organic bodies. Bloodflow caused bio-membranes to tighten and thus become more sensitive to vibrational influences, while the blood's departure caused these same bio-membranes to slacken and become deprived of sensation (*On Tremulations*, pgs. 6, 7, and 30).

According to both Beelzebub (Gurdjieff) and Swedenborg, humans have three distinct species of blood, in order to activate different levels of sensitivity—including the highest spiritual sensitivity to God's truths issuing from the Spiritual Sun and Holy Word. (I am not aware of any theological Seminary offering discussions on these three distinct kinds of human blood—red blood, animal spirit, and from the soul.)

In clinical hypnosis, where the human psychic property of a divided consciousness is *intensified* and *exaggerated* (and becomes an obvious phenomenon), a person can be made to think (imagine) that ammonia smells like roses, merely from the suggestion reaching one's activated primitive and undeveloped subconscious (internal natural mind).

What has happened is that through a change in blood circulation, our outer worldly consciousness, which has learned what ammonia actually smells like from its five senses, is temporarily shut down (and its particular membranes slacken) and the deeper subconscious mind with its lack of experience and uneducated functioning is brought to the surface (because its deeper membranes have become more taut and active than the slackened membranes serving our outer mind).

Because this deeper mind has been cut off from the outer world for so long (and left only to its imagination), it is gullible and open to *suggestion*. Beelzebub describes this predicament as the subconscious mind putting its hopes on anything newly perceived or communicated to it. Therefore, not having access to the things learned by the outer senses and stored in the outer or corporeal memory, to criticize a particular suggestion, it can be made to believe (again, imagine) that ammonia smells like sweet roses.

Beelzebub is suggesting here that our abnormal lifestyles have segregated our real essence to such a degree that it contains no contradictory information by which to challenge or criticize any new influence.

(A hypnotist, unknown to him/her, can modify the *tempo* and *center of gravity* of the blood flow, by which one's ordinary or habitual mind [the false and incomplete ruling master] gets shut off, whereby the deeper subconscious mind, in its undeveloped state, begins to actively take part in the entire functioning of a person's organic presence.)

Hypnotism however can be used in a beneficial manner because when the artificial consciousness and its memory are suspended, new positive ideas, also through suggestion, can be more easily *fixed* into the bio-fabric, cognitive architecture (neural substrates) and organic *states* of an individual's deeper mind. The subconscious (which was ruled by our preferences) can now blend with the harmonious operations of the whole body, much of which is under the involuntary control of the cerebellum (and ruled by Heaven's processes).

Swedenborg discovered that the human cerebellum knows all the inner states and qualities of the cerebrum. Unfortunately the cerebellum counts on the cerebrum to inform it as to what's going on in the outer world. So when the deeper, subconscious mind of the cerebrum and its passions (animus) is made to believe, though suggestion, that it no longer has an urge for smoking cigarettes or that an illness has been cured, the cerebellum jumps in and responds by directing its harmonizing action to the proper area and modifying the blood circulation for removing the disharmony there and fixing some new or alternative belief.

This is why hypnotism (with the cerebellum) can create miraculous cures associated with some strong faith and trust (again, suggestibility).

Beelzebub then goes on to educate Hassein about how the former earth-humans from the city Gob could maniuplate the human psyche through hypnotism by means of their being-Hanbledzoïn (middle blood) or Swedenborg's animal spirits.

Being-Hanbledzoïn or "animal magnetism" is the blood of the astral body. Like the red blood, which nourishes and maintains the planetary body, being-Hanbledzoïn has a finer viscosity and nourishes the more subtle astral body, which is formed according to the inner development and bio-organization of one's level of understanding.

This higher or middle blood influences the more corporeal, lower red blood and its center of gravity, determining where it will flow. If one has enough of this rarefied fluid-substance (as Beelzebub did) they can use it to affect the tempo and flow of another person's circulation of red blood and even create a hypnotic state in the individual whereby new information can be injected into their organic, neural fabric.

Swedenborg made the exact *three* distinctions of human blood that Gurdjieff/Beelzebub makes. One type is for the physical body, another for the mind, and a third or highest blood was for the soul's use.

In Swedenborg's terms, the second (subtler) species of blood (above the red blood) is called the "animal spirit" and serves as a nervous fluid. Whereas the lower red blood is made from planetary substances through the intake of normal physical food, being-Hanbledzoïn (as called by Gurdjieff) or Animal Spirit (as called by

Swedenborg) is formed from atmospheric substances given off by more subtle elements—like the spheres originating from other planets and even the Sun itself.

These rarefied elements are drawn in from the circumfluent and aerial atmosphere by our breathing and through pores of the skin. So air from the atmosphere acts as a higher-level "food" to maintain one's animal spirits. Swedenborg identified this higher food in the atmosphere as various kinds of "effluvia" and "atmospheric" or "ethereal salts." (A person, during spiritual transformation, takes in more of these atmospheric salts than others do.)

That Swedenborg and Gurdjieff had both discovered that humans could take in nutrition (aliments) from the atmosphere as a second kind of food—according to one's disposition and qualities of love— tells me they had similar special knowledge about the details of spiritual growth. Both men believed that an individual would draw in elements and substances from the air that *corresponded to their state of mind*. During spiritual growth, one's animal spirits (being-Hanbledzoïn), was also purified by one's understanding—and application of—God's cosmic truths, which would perfect (crystallize) the development of an "inner" body inside the outer, physical body.

Gurdjieff's "astral body" is similar to Swedenborg's concept of a "spiritual body" that is made from subtler substances in nature. This true bio-structure can also represent either a civic (Ishmael) level of rationality (from a self-centered principle) or a higher level of human *rational* understanding (Jacob) which represents the first step in the maturing of a new organization from out of the spiritual remains (and conscience).

(The lesser, or worldly development of one's rational mind—still ruled by egoism—is why Gurdjeff referred to some people's astral bodies as *stinking*.)

Swedenborg speaks of the purer blood or "animal spirits" (Beelzebub's being-Hanbledzoïn) in his theological work, *Divine Love & Wisdom*, n. 423. This "higher blood" species (animal spirit) is purified and purged directly by a person's mental state, rather than one's lungs. The human lungs clean up and rectify the red blood according to the inner process being made in one's understanding. So even the outermost purification of our lower corporeal red blood proceeds according to the state of purity obtained in one's animal spirits (and thought picturings).

I find it fascinating that both Swedenborg and Gurdjieff agreed that there was even a higher (or third) species of blood in humans— more primary and exalted than either the red blood or animal spirits. Swedenborg called it the "spirituous fluid" and Gurdjieff (through Beelzebub) called it the "sacred being-Hanbledzoïn." Both men claimed that this unique species of blood was a preeminent fluid-essence that served the human soul. This preeminent "blood" was formed from the direct emanations of the Most Holy Sun Absolute, or as Swedenborg would say, God's Love and Truth flowing in orderly series out from the Spiritual Sun.

An individual would take in the proper aliment (food) for this rarefied fluid-substance through appropriating and applying genuine spiritual principles to one's heart and rational mind—that is, into one's life choices and behavior. This sacred and preeminent blood would then create the ultimate formation (crystallization) of a proper angelic body to house the soul after the death of the gross planetary body. (One who had an astral or lower-level psychic body had to still undergo further education and purification in the spiritual world to obtain this purer angelic body—through the application of teachings and lessons given by angelic beings already deserving of being on this holy plane.)

But if one's reasoning and rationality, no matter how highly developed, could not be separated from egoism in spite of these angelic lessons, that individual would be expelled into a "hellish" spiritual society and realm with those *Hasnamuss* individuals of similar selfish qualities. So again, Heaven and Hell are not places you go to, but what you become. The purpose of religion is to protect this highest spiritual blood from absorbing foul elements and principles of a self-centered love (the opposite of mutual spiritual love) issuing out from the various noxious spheres of Hell.

So, the quality or center-of-gravity of person's planetary (red) blood—and one's desires in the world—is according to the quality of the two other species of blood within it, which inwardly take part in the red blood's compounded structure. But the process of purifying both the red blood and purer bloods is thwarted by the dual psyche of modern earth-humans because sincere introspection and comparison (personal Djartklom) between one's outer and inner realities has been cut off—to the point that a proper purifying operation is now even more dreaded by most earth-citizens who are unwilling to part with their silly dreams and fantasies.

That is why even the helpful and sacred data stored away by God in the subconscious or *internal natural* mind during our more innocent youth serves no use to purify our lives—unless we can force some contact (through sincerity) and create a clash between the material beliefs of the outer natural mind (the data held in one's corporeal memory) which lords over and steals practically everything learned from the outer, physical world of the five senses. Whether one reads holy books or celebrity news magazines, it doesn't matter. Because the internal human mind and its consciousness is segregated from one's five senses and corporeal memory, a person's accumulated knowledge never takes part in criticizing and perfecting anything other than showing its outer mask to the world).

Now I can better explain to you the bio-differences between a person living under the "Itoklanoz" or "Fulasnitamnian" principles, because they represent the blood circulations and tempos ruling our two main types of manifestation (internal and external) of consciousness (or split "Zoostat"). This will provide the necessary insights for describing the true mechanism of hypnosis, which even modern science and psychology has yet to fully grasp.

Beelzebub states that hypnotism is caused by a change in "bloodflow" from a corresponding change (active or passive) in the center-of-gravity of one's psyche—thanks to earth-humans now having a split psyche or two-system Zoostat.

Beelzebub explains to Hassein that through abnormal living, the human psyche eventually had to adapt its blood circulation to function by the principle called "Itoklanoz" which responds only to worldly or *external* stimuli (as animals do) and has segregated itself by forming into a new independent and more external (corporeal/mechanical) operation of the mind. Beelzebub further states that originally, the human race had functioned from the "Fulasnitamnian" principle of blood circulation, that is, from a more unified *internal* function which allowed meritorious individuals to evolve beyond their physical limitations (with increased reasoning). This increased reasoning provided additional judgment for properly evaluating and reducing to order, all kinds of otherwise heterogenous, external and worldly inputs of data. Swedenborg concurred that our understanding improved by how well we could organize our data and put it into a rational, connected series as God intended.

Furthermore, the "Itoklanoz" principle only permits earth-humans to breathe in "air" to assist in the metabolism and excretion of terrestrial food (for the red blood). Therefore, this process can only serve the planetary or physical body—which is perishable. The more noble Fulasnitamnian principle on the other hand, allows even the air itself to evolve further, thus helping serve the continued development of a higher organic body-structure within us.

Another negative consequence of the "Itoklanoz" Zoostat (blood circulation) is that important elements in the atmosphere that were providentially intended by the Creator to help the human race start to create their higher-being bodies (to house the soul) now—through abnormal human living—lost this important mechanism to properly evolve further and spiritually. Instead, these aerial elements fail to be transformed and metabolized according to God's Wise cosmic scheme by earth-humans. Being exhaled from our lungs, these elements then mix with other substances in the atmosphere and degenerate (involve) into harmful crystallizations that cause various kinds of "disease."

Beelzebub describes the names of these various diseases in earth-humans as "grippe," "influenza," "Spanish influenza," "dengue," and the like. Here, Beelzebub is showing the superiority of his "other-worldly" knowledge by giving an unexpected answer to the medical mystery behind the origin of viruses. (In fact, I have heard researchers marvel at how flu viruses are so well adapted to the conditions of the human lungs. Apparently, the answer is that viruses are constructed from elements in the atmosphere that were designed to enter the human lungs in the first place to help fill God's higher purpose—but are now being rejected! From this rejection, other crystallizations, formed in the atmosphere, come back to our lungs to roost—but in a more dangerous form.)

In Gurdjieff's earlier book, *Views from the Real World* (p. 194) he states that the secret behind our properly absorbing these special aerial elements from the atmosphere is by contemplating one's true significance and the significance of those around you. This process involves both sincerity and true compassion (a state of one's spiritual progress). This is what Beelzebub and his fellow passengers were doing in a special compartment of their spaceship.

Again, Swedenborg is in full agreement that our state of mind and its passions determine what components from the atmosphere our lungs can draw in!

Beelzebub also learned on this last visit that a particular earth-human, an Italian abbot named Pedrini and his acquaintance, Doctor Gambini, discovered that humans could fall into a peculiar mental state where they became vulnerable to suggestibility when gazing upon shiny objects while experiencing intense emotional states. The Italian abbot shared this discovery with others and soon, various individuals discovered that they could put each other in this state and change their old notions and impressions into new ones. But Beelzebub tells his grandson that they still hadn't a real clue as to why this state is possible in most humans. Nor to this day, will earth-humans become successful in solving the mystery of the bio-mechanism behind hypnosis.

Far worse, earth-humans do not recognize how this limited mental state of trance actually plays such a big part in their daily lives. In more ancient times, the knowledge of bringing others into this hypnotic state for the noble purpose of removing negative states was originally considered *sacred*. But this, too, would later begin to be used in ways by modern humans to simply "tickle" people's vanity and egoism.

Beelzebub observed this abnormal functioning and turnaround at various ceremonies, parties, and weddings on the planet Earth, where people gathered and were determined to bring one another into this hypnotic state. (My readers can easily see this abnormal activity, taking place at the Academy Awards and on the Red Carpet each year in Hollywood and its obvious effect that "astonishes" fans.)

Besides shiny objects, other methods include all sorts of "titillation" and spurious, but well-aimed compliments to flatter.

Beelzebub ends this part of the narrative by telling his grandson that he hopes the earth-humans never learn about other methods for bringing individuals into this hypnotic state.

Beelzebub obviously doesn't trust human egoism—in life, politics or in religion.

SUMMARY

■ We humans are hypnotized! We need to better understand the mechanism and relevance of hypnosis to gain our freedom.

■ The split in human consciousness (outer and inner) caused different kinds of blood circulations to emerge, disconnect, and dominate.

■ Beelzelbub calls this split a two-system Zoostat (blood-flows). One of these two systems is called "Itoklanoz" which centers on the physical body and physical life only. The "Fulasnitamnian" principle is the proper condition of humans and allows the further development of higher-body structures (like the Astral) through metabolizing air and atmospheric salts.

■ Contemporary earth-humans live under the "Itoklanoz" principle, which is similar to living like animals do.

■ Through the Itoklanoz principle in humans, air cannot properly evolve inside humans and serve to form their higher being-bodies. This air, unused for its predetermined and sacred purpose, degenerates into diseases, such as viruses.

■ Anton Mesmer was very close to finding the truth about hypnotism but was mocked by "experts" who thought they knew better.

■ The clinical hypnotist causes the blood circulation responsible for our outer mechanical habitual mind to become passive.

■ This allows a new blood circulation and its corresponding subconscious mind to come to the forefront and take an active part in one's waking bodily existence. Because of its primitive state, it is prone to suggestion.

■ Having been "imprisoned" on a subconscious level, our mind's spiritual evolution became stifled and stayed underdeveloped. Because of this lack of development and proper connection to the inputs of the outer world (which would have provided the mental data needed for confrontational logic and rational judgment), this childlike and essential mind will always *believe* in, *hope* for and *love* every darned new idea that comes its way (as from a hypnotist's, politician's, or minister's suggestion).

SUMMARY

■ The contact and clash between these two distinct kinds of human consciousness (from sincerity) can add to the growth of conscience within God's implanted matrix called the remains.

■ We use various sneaky forms of hypnotism to put other people into favorable states of mind toward us. One of these methods is "titillation," another is "astonishment."

CHAPTER 33

"Beelzebub as professional hypnotist"

At least parts of *Beelzebub's Tales* are autobiographical. I say this because Gurdjieff was himself a professional hypnotist as a young man and even treated wealthy clients in Paris of certain addictions through hypnosis in order to raise money for his Institute at Fontainebleu, France, during the 1920s. What is most interesting from my Swedenborgian viewpoint is that Gurdjieff, probably through hypnotic techniques, verified Swedenborg's revelation that God implanted special spiritual data into the human psyche, which later was pushed deeper into one's subconscious level by the formation of another, more external and corporeal mind.

These findings add a new, more modern twist to understanding Swedenborg's doctrine of "remains" and the difficulty of reaching it, by bringing hypnosis into the discussion of the human predicament of "sleep" and the actual obstacles to our spiritually "waking up."

This topic is so important to our spiritual welfare that it deserves extra explanation and repeating from things already said.

Swedenborg indeed addressed these splits in the natural human psyche as inner and outer functionings. And the split happened twice in human history! The first split of the human psyche was a split into spiritual and natural minds—the human understanding became a distinct function, separated from the will (which had become perverted). This was done so that individuals could learn ideas and concepts that were superior to their actual passions, and then apply these superior concepts to their life in order to also elevate the heart to higher spiritual levels.

In between the rotten human will and the distinct intellectual functioning of the human understanding, God placed *conscience* (as a "medium" plane) to assist in this evolutionary process. But Swedenborg also spoke of yet another split that followed, where the original will and thought becomes covered over by an even more external functioning (muscular memory or pulmonary thought) of the natural mind.

This further split in the human natural mind was what he described as the *internal natural mind* and the *external natural mind* (*The True Christian Religion*, n. 593). Swedenborg gave additional clues that this second split occurs when as young children we learn how to deceive others (and ourselves) by imitating the adult world (*Arcana Coelestia*, n. 8247). This process gradually removes innocence from our lives by destroying sincerity.

But Gurdjieff, being more contemporary than Swedenborg, was able to describe this second split of the human psyche in more modern terms—into the subconscious mind and our outer everyday (*habitual*) mind. Again Swedenborg knew the subconscious mind as the *internal natural mind* and the new outer mind as the *external natural mind*—which leans toward *corporeal* qualities.

The Lord God can only give us sacred data when we are in a state of innocence (a state removed from egoism). It is during our infancy and childhood (state of innocence) that God stores sacred data in the natural level of our mind. When as children, we begin to learn pretense and deception, both our spiritual conscience (the remains) and passions get covered over and sink into our subconscious mind. Then as God's sacred data becomes re-activated in later life, it serves as a matrix for *spiritual conscience* to re-emerge and reorganize the passions of the human heart though an involving intellect. The appearance of "Dry Land" on the third day of the Creation Story in Genesis actually symbolizes the emergence of a spiritual conscience in a person's daily life.

What those who study Swedenborg can benefit most from in Gurdjieff's cosmology, cosmogony and human psychology is grasping that the external natural mind—because of its separation—is absolutely *artificial, mechanical,* and not the seat of one's true being. However, because this external mind rules over the five senses it steals most of the sensory data and knowledge streaming into it from the outside world and keeps it imprisoned in the corporeal memory, where it cannot successfully feed our separated essential nature and deeper subconscious mind.

So the "real" person within us simply dozes off and starves. Whereas Swedenborg (and Scripture) calls this disconnected state of mind "sleep" and living in mental fantasy, Gurdjieff uses a more modern and less flattering term—hypnosis! Our not believing that we are hypnotized keeps everything in us from truly changing. And this limits our grasp of what *spiritual sleep* really encompasses—living in trance and illusion.

The issue of good and evil (salvation) is pointless to a person who is asleep at the wheel (terror of the situation) because under the divided conditions of the human psyche, only fantasy is promoted (including imagined halos). The split consciousness of the natural mind in earth-humans can often convincingly feign goodness in front of others, while allowing the same individuals to hide their deeper ego-driven intentions from the eyes of the world. Such deception is evidence of humans living in a trance-like and dual mental state. (You can't deceive anyone without a split psyche.)

So we must de-hypnotize ourselves before we can sincerely follow the two great commandments of *Loving God* and *Loving the Neighbor*. Otherwise, even noble and charitable deeds can be used to cover up and hide our real character flaws (and our inner nullity). This is what Ashiata Shiemash meant by the Terror of the Situation.

In genuine spiritual growth, these hidden (and less noble) intentions must be observed by us, resisted and removed (all while asking for the Lord God's help). This is the duty of all true religion, so that we are able to live in accordance with our God-given conscience. Without making this purifying effort, Love, Faith and Hope become impotent terms.

Swedenborg warned that this split behavior of pretense in the natural mind only succeeds in hiding our negative qualities from the outer world (but not from the eyes of Heaven's angels). Even God's truth can be used by the separated corporeal and artificial mind as a mask to hide our true intentions—thanks again to our dual psyche and its constant efforts to live in an unchallenged way. Only *sincere* introspection can *connect* the knowledge of the external mind and its memory with the deeper subconscious mind so that one's "remains" and spiritual conscience can continue to grow and become a harmonizing force in our lives.

This harmonizing action is the Holy Spirit of God proceeding through our lives. But because of this split in our consciousness, and lack of nurturing one's God-given *remains* and conscience, humans have become open and vulnerable to suggestion from being asleep within, and acting mostly on "automatic pilot" and mechanically from without.

Human suggestibility is the outcome and perversion of true sacred function of "hope."

While building loving communities through a "church" is the true goal in God's cosmic scheme, a "true church" must first create an environment that encourages worshippers to *individually* examine their behavior and flaws, before their acts of kindness can gain the quality of true *innocence*. I find most church organizations pass over this crucial step—because it makes people uncomfortable (which is a "no-no" in post-modern society). Rather, everyone is anxious to become "good" as soon as possible and to be seen as a good person by their peers. But even goodness, kindness, friendship and compassion can be spurious when one fails to make the proper preparations—to take personal inventory and then doing some appropriate house-cleaning.

The main point to all this is that achieving *noble deeds* and *charitable uses* is not what we must first seek to do, but instead, to regain our spiritual *innocence* through personal inner conflict which will then spiritually qualify the deed. That is why Swedenborg states that Spiritual innocence is never gained without inner conflict (temptations) and combat. This special combat is the true dynamic behind spiritual purification and transformation. It is our cosmic duty. Until we allow the unflattering and ego-popping process of regeneration to take place in our lives, we will all live in *the terror of the situation*. But never even suspect it!

In his book *In Search of the Miraculous*, P. D. Ouspensky reports on a conversation he had with Gurdjieff about hypnotic experiments which revealed that the dual psyche of humans was so segregated that each type of consciousness, more often than not, had different (opposing) interests. The outer-worldly mind might be interested in scientific discovery or noble philosophical ideas while the subconscious mind may have infantile and primal self-serving concerns. But it is alongside this crude, underdeveloped and deeper mind that the Lord God secretly sets up a heavenly beachhead with the yet-to-be germinated seeds of *spiritual conscience* (called "remains," which can later help us grow a new spiritual will within our individuality).

Beelzebub continues his Tales about studying the strange and troubled human psyche, which he hopes to fully solve on his sixth and final visit to the planet Earth. He tells Hassein that he continued to use hypnosis to both cure and study the abnormalities of contemporary earth-humans.

At first he used his own being-Hanbledzoïn (animal spirit) to stir up his patients' subconscious "Zoostat" into action. But since this expenditure of his own "middle blood" was ultimately dangerous to Beelzebub's health, he quickly learned other means to re-direct the tempo and flow of blood to *certain* blood vessels by which a patient's normal habitual mind was made passive, allowing the inner (deeper) natural mind to become active and begin taking part in a person's waking consciousness. (Beelzebub had also invented these new techniques and means for modifying a person's blood circulation because he soon discovered that just using a shiny object to put people into a trance-state would only work in those individuals whose thoughts and feelings could also be focused on some *intense expectation*. Advertisers discovered this when they found out that they could often control others simply by learning about and taking advantage of another's intense expectations.)

Swedenborg even described these intense expectations in people as their "Ruling Love" and concurred with the notion that when you knew what a person really loved, you could control them (he mentions this in his book *On Tremulations*). Just as important, both Swedenborg and Gurdjieff understood that blood flow could be hindered or intensified in people's bodies to change their states of mind (and vice versa). Unfortunately, Swedenborg wrote about this dynamic of blood in his earlier scientific and anatomical works, which today, are seen by many as unrelated to his more important theological writings (even though he addresses the purification of one's purer or middle blood in his theological work, *Divine Love & Wisdom*).

Having returned to the planet Earth for the final time and land-ing in Central Asia (Turkestan), Beelzebub finds himself in a perfect setting to operate as a hypnotist-physician and do his research on the deteriorating human psyche because the inhabitants who lived in an area nearby known as Chinese Turkestan were abusing "opium" and "hashish." While in an adjacent area known as Russian Turkestan, the inhabitants were destroying themselves with "vodka." These two types of Asian addicts made good guinea pigs for Dr. Beelzebub's hypnotic experiments. The pernicious actions of opium and vodka represented the various and misguided tactics earth-humans use for the self-calming of their inner nullity and keeping one's God-given conscience buried, where it will be ineffectual and unburdensome.

Apparently, Beelzebub works with so many patients with these pernicious afflictions that he becomes totally exhausted and feels he needs to leave Turkestan for a mental break. The reason he has so many patients in Turkestan is because everyone there had learned how to recognize someone of his profession—so that he could never get the required rest.

Eventually, he would come to choose some *European* towns to live in, whose cafes served a strange dark liquid (probably coffee) instead of the delightful teas served in the cafes of Turkestan. But before doing even that, he decides to immediately revisit the country of Egypt, and there, get his much needed rest (and probably some tea).

It was on this final trip to the planet Earth that he becomes aware that the wonderful constructions he witnessed earlier in Egypt on his fourth visit (for the purpose of collecting specimens of "apes") were now mostly gone. These interesting Egyptian constructions were either destroyed during various wars or covered over by desert sands. (So Beelzebub, on his fourth visit, witnessed a "pre-sand" Egypt!)

Beelzebub then acknowledges to his grandson that he was in error for saying that none of the spectacular scientific achievements of the earth-humans of past generations had ever reached later generations. He speculates that the exciting news of his divine pardon, allowing him to return to his home planet, made him temporarily forget an occurence on Earth that happened just before his final departure.

He recounts to Hassein that the inhabitants of ancient Atlantis, who belonged to the learned society named Akhaldan, knew of the existence of the sacred substance *Omnipresent Okidanokh* (substance of universal endeavor and nature's incessant disposition to promote God's three-fold design) and they subsequently learned how to sepa-rate its three sacred parts from the atmosphere and from certain materials. They could even accumulate and concentrate each of them for their various experiments, just like Gornahoor Harharkh of Saturn did. (This is nothing short of knowing how God's Holy Trinity operates as three distinct forces in the universe, then teasing out each of these singular forces from the sacred operation of threefoldness in the compound element Okidanokh.)

Apparently, the Akhaldan researchers discovered that when the separated *neutralizing-force* (third part of the sacred Omnipresent Okidanokh) was applied to different organic forms, it would arrest the process of decay. This profound scientific knowledge was eventually passed on to certain Egyptians who were the descendants of the learned members of Akhaldans in Atlantis. These early Egyptians (from pre-sand Egypt) used this unique knowledge to preserve the planetary bodies of special beings there and are today called "mummies." (On the higher spiritual level, when we create this same neutralizing principle within ourselves, through conscience, we stop the process of decay or entropy of our spiritual individuality—giving us the inner stability needed to enjoy *eternal* life.)

Beelzebub then describes to his grandson the procedure of just how the Egyptians used this special knowledge to prepare human bodies for mummification (again, this was an outer and more external representation of the effects of conscience, and the use of a sacred reconciling influence—outwardly—instead of applying it inwardly to acquire one's spiritual permanence). First, these Egyptians kept the physical body in castor oil for about half a month. Then, they would introduce the "neutralizing-force" from the sacred Omnipresent Okidanokh into the body in question.

Beelzebub later learned that on one occasion, during a time of war, those in charge of processing a particular Pharaoh's body were forced to make this procedure in haste. They did not keep the Pharaoh's body in castor oil for the appropriate length of time, and chose instead to place the body in a hermetically closed chamber. Then they filled the chamber with a specially dissolved form containing only the reconciling (neutralizing) sacred substance-force of the Holy Triamazikamno law operating in the Omnipresent Okidanokh.

Beelzebub hints that the shortcuts that were used help lead to the so-called superstition of the "Pharaoh's curse."[8] Because, when this tomb was later opened after many centuries, the sacred neutralizing substance of Okidanokh was released, and upon entering into the bodies of some of the contemporary men-beings who had broken into the tomb, it caused a dangerous imbalance of forces that ultimately resulted in many of their deaths.

This tragic consequence represented a real past achievement reaching contemporary earth-humans. Also, Egyptian mummies represented another ancient achievement still existing on Earth today. But even these examples weren't the only surviving ancient discoveries to reach modern earth-humans.

---

8. I believe this refers to King Tut's Curse where more than a dozen people met mysterious deaths after having been involved in the opening of the tomb. Furthermore, this particular tomb shows evidence of being hastily prepared and painted.

Returning to the topic of his organic need to find rest, Beelzebub says that while in Egypt, on his last visit to Earth, he would take relaxing daily walks in the direction of the "Pyramids" and "Sphinx," which were the sole surviving great constructions, erected by the descendants of the Akhaldans who came to Egypt. On one such walk he met someone who would cause him to make yet another excursion to another part of the Earth's surface.

Swedenborg claimed that early Egyptians had indeed cultivated the sacred *science of correspondences* (that spiritual forces *correspond* to and flow into material objects), which they received from even more ancient races, but later—due to their psycho-spiritual degradation—they turned this Divine knowledge into forms of magic for their personal gain and titillation.

SUMMARY

■ In a hypnotic state, people never change, but think they do. They can only create "imagined halos."

■ Beelzebub discovered that earth-humans could be brought into a trance-like state by uncovering and taking advantage of their most intense expectations (Ruling Loves).

■ For this reason, he only used hypnosis to help people remove their pernicious habits, addictions and vices, rather than to gain control over them for selfish ends.

■ Drugs and alcoholic beverages are used by weak-willed people to calm their conscience and continue to live "illogically."

■ To get much needed rest from the curing of his many patients (from both Chinese and Russian Turkestan), he heads for Cairo, Egypt.

■ Most of the great Egyptian monuments and constructions that he witnessed earlier, during the fourth trip to the planet Earth, were now gone.

■ Beelzebub recalls something and then apologizes to his grandson, Hassein, for telling him that none of the achievements had survived on Earth from the great Akhaldan society of Atlantis. He corrects himself.

■ The Akhaldans had discovered how to separate the three force-substances from the sacred Omnipresent Okidanokh in the atmosphere—like Goonahoor Harharkh did on Saturn. They then discovered that when its Third (neutralizing) force was applied to some or another organic formation, it would arrest the process of "decay" and entropy.

SUMMARY

■ (When this same "third" force is consciously applied to our inner lives, it manifests as conscience, and we gain eternal spiritual life and immunity from the destructive effects of physical time.)

■ This special knowledge was transferred later to the Egyptians, where they learned to make use of it externally, to preserve physical bodies, called mummies.

■ Also, the "Sphinx" and "Great Pyramids" represented early constructions and other past achievements that have survived to the present day.

CHAPTER 34

"Russia"

Soon, Beelzebub will get an even bigger opportunity to study the strange need for vodka among certain earth-humans.

Beelzebub now recounts to his grandson how on one of his morning strolls near the Egyptian Pyramids he was met by a complete stranger who sought to make an acquaintance and asks if he can accompany Beelzebub on his walks and converse. This elderly stranger turned out to be an important Russian figure who belonged to an organization in that large country that was formed to help rid his beloved fatherland of alcoholism. He, too, had come to Egypt to find rest and meditate on the problem with a refreshed and re- focused mind.

This sympathetic Russian (like everybody else) recognizes Beelzebub as a "doctor-type" and wishes to converse about the growing (and destructive) passion for alcohol among his people.

They discuss the weak-willed nature of human beings and how they are prone to all kinds of "vices." These vices take on the importance of providing a new and *distorted sense of aim* (misguided psychic centers of gravity) and always created a negative quality in their being-manifestations. Over time, this negative behavior (drinking liquor) not only destroys their planetary bodies but also affects the mutual relationships between citizens—which always seems to destroy the previous positive gains and beneficial attainments of the society.

He informs Beelzebub that he currently heads an organization in Russia called "The Trusteeship of People's Temperance." He confesses that he feels that the organization's future success is at best, "iffy." As a result of this tenuous situation and his instinctively recognizing Beelzbub's unique knowledge of the human psyche, he invites the "doctor" to come back to Russia with him and help in solving its pernicious alcoholic problem, which affects the lives of millions of people and all of its classes.

But there is also another problem to be solved.

This important Russian believes that the real challenge facing the Trusteeship is not just vodka, but comes from various groups and factions within the organization (the politics) itself. Instead of focusing on the problem of alcoholism, each of these groups continuously increased its demands that its own agenda be followed—which only leads to greater misunderstandings, personal considerations, gossip, intrigue, plots, etc. (This is usually the downfall of any human institution, despite its goals.)

Beelzebub agrees to help. He sees a great opportunity to carry on his experiments and learn more about the various details of the negative manifestations of the earth-human psyche by studying such a large population. The two men arrive in St. Petersburg just in time to participate in the inauguration of a large new building, built specifically for the Trusteeship.

As Beelzebub mingles with various Russian citizens in the crowd, representing all of its "classes," he observes that the *dual-nature* of their particular "Ego-Individuality" has become even more sharply obvious and illogical than ever.

He elucidates that this *strengthened* duality and segregation between functions of consciousness in Russians resulted from *non-correspondence* between the quality of their life-choices (tempo-of-the-place-of-their-arising) and the quality of their knowledge (from their being-mentation). A striking example of this non-correspondence between their life-choices (behavior) and their knowledge is the fact that most Russians have heard about the dangers of alcohol, yet they keep on drinking it. This completely illogical circumstance could only emerge from a real split in consciousness between what one knows and what one actually does. Again, Swedenborg agrees with this human predicament—that there has become a *non-correspondence* between one's external (worldly knowledge) and internal (spiritual) realities, or desires (*Arcana Coelestia*, n. 5511).

(Interestingly, Swedenborg, while he was serving as a member of Sweden's government, actively addressed the problem of drinking in his own country.)

Beelzebub now takes another apparent detour in his story—to add new details about the strange Russian psyche (and earth-humans' split personalities). He admits to Hassein that during his last (and sixth) sojourn on Earth he was given additional insights to this "Russian" predicament from several "side trips" that he made to Persia, where he had met the wise Mullah Nassr Eddin.

He had gone to Persia during the latter half of his sixth visit to Earth to further investigate the Most Saintly Activities of Ashiata Shiemash (who created the Legominism "The Terror the Situation"), with the intention of nailing down the causes of a strange new form of "politeness" arising among earth-humans. (Swedenborg would define this strange form of "politeness" as the mechanized manifestation of kindness and smiling—without innocence or the participation of conscience, and therefore, insincere. Today, this *outer* form of politeness has become a growing movement called "political correctness.")

Beelzebub and Mullah Nassr Eddin sat on the roof of a house to have their discussion. Apparently, it was a custom in Persia to sit on a roof while discussing various topics and "subtle-philosophic-questions" with others. (A "roof" also has a *spiritual meaning* of speaking from an elevated or higher point of view.)

Beelzebub describes an event he witnessed one day while he and Mullah Nassr Eddin were sitting on a roof and having one of their subtle discussions. Beelzebub suddenly noticed unusual activity on the streets below. Townspeople were carefully sweeping, cleaning and hanging up various decorations along the streets. He assumes that some festival is about to take place.

Beelzebub asks Mullah Nassr Eddin what is going on below them. Suddenly they hear the sounds of "town criers" and the clamoring of many horses. Apparently, the townspeople had prepared themselves and their town for the arrival of Russian "Cossacks" who rode in and provided security for a special coach with two special people inside. One of these special people was a dignitary from Persia itself and the other was an important Russian general.

Mullah Nassr Eddin tells Beelzebub, using metaphor—and with an obvious tone of disgust—that the Persian dignitary in this special coach was a "molting crow" and that the Russians were "well-bred-turkeys." He remarks that Persian dignitaries were always seen with these Russian "turkeys" in the hopes of restoring the luster to their own feathers. (I find this description by Mullah Nassr Eddin quite rich in psychological meaning and imagery—for "birds" symbolize the qualities of our thinking.)

Beelzebub patiently listens as his wise earth-friend gives an explanation of his *allegorical* bird remarks. He tells Beelzebub that he could make similar insightful analogies between all different countries by using various kinds of bird species to describe their character. Persians were "crows" because over the centuries they had developed a certain type of intelligence (street smarts). Nassr Eddin describes Europeans as "peacocks" because their growing influence and *refined outer forms* of culture were seen as beautiful. But Russians, who were essentially Asians, were simply crows trying to become peacocks. As a result they ended up becoming something in between—like "turkeys," which like to "puff up" and manifest "swagger." And, because of their being neither a crow nor a peacock, they have cultivated a more intensified dual consciousness within their nature.

Hearing this clever allegorical explanation, Beelzebub obtains a further insight as to why Russians manifest such a powerfully sharp duality within their individuality. Inwardly, their egoism had developed a powerful desire to look more refined and special to the outer world.

After this enlightening event in Persia, Beelzebub returns to his investigations of castes and classes to uncover the causes for the "organic need" in Russia for alcohol. He determines that this strange psychic need comes from two specific causes. One cause comes from a negative response to a cosmic law called "Solioonensius" (planetary and solar tensions which affect people's moods), and the other was a "stimulating factor" to release this tension, called "Bolshevism." (Beelzebub will give more details later in the chapter about these causes.)

Swedenborg would probably add that "Solioonensius" or astronomical tensions, originates from great clashes taking place in the deeper spiritual realm. And, as these clashes flow into the ultimates of the natural world, they would most certainly affect the tensions between stars and planets). These clashes would normally cause earth-humans to reflect (and want to transform), but instead, these astronomical tensions now only cause irritation and discomfort to their psyche).

Liquor quells this discomfort.

Beelzebub then seemingly goes off into yet another tangent concerning his story. However, as always, he is simply providing more background and details to underscore his unique findings about the deteriorating Russian psyche. He now explains to his grandson Hassein that he originally intended to establish a chemical laboratory in Russia for the secret purpose of making special experiments and learning additional facts about the more pronounced split of the Russian psyche. But when he sought a legitimate "permit" to establish such a laboratory in Russia, he gets the "bureaucratic runaround."

For almost two whole months he is sent from one "department" and "ministry" to another, without success (getting the run-around). He soon discovers that the officials in these various departments never actually learned how to accomplish their duties because they had not acquired the "automatic-habit" for doing such things. In other words, if something could not be accomplished by "automatic pilot," it was considered outside one's ability, cognitive function or expectation to perform such a duty, and especially not through any additional and genuine being-effort issuing from one's deeper inner dictate or conscience.

Beelzebub observes that the leaders of various Russian communities operated through *automatic/mechanical* behavior even more intensely than other citizens over the whole planet Earth. He then makes a pragmatic discovery that in this strange automatic behavior, the "administrative body" in Russia gives out permits based on one's proven "loyalty," called political "favors."

In other words, these permits could not be obtained unless one was willing to submit one's psyche to some abnormality or another.

Beelzebub discovers the true intensity of this "alien," but real-world, dynamic when he is invited by his important new Russian friend to meet with the "Czar" (Emperor Nicholas ll) during the inauguration of the completed building which was to house the *Trusteeship of People's Temperance* in Saint Petersburg. His Russian friend had continued to seek Beelzebub's advice all through this period, which made other members of the Trusteeship quite jealous—even beyond their usual political aim called "mutually-to-get-rid-of-each-other." The various "intrigues" from plotting and subterfuge brought on by these various jealous members (personally and from their allied groups) guaranteed the doom of the Trusteeship before it even moved into its new building.

Abnormalities pile up on top of abnormalities.

Beelzebub is next informed that in order to meet the Russian Czar he must first be fully educated on the "protocol" of how to properly act (playing the game of *outer politeness*). On reading Beelzebub's description of this tortuous learning process, one gets a vivid visceral sense of the artificiality of it all and how it opens the human psyche for an "imposter" to take over (and overlord) one's personality and consciousness—thus, lulling one's real essence-individuality into a state of slumber and slavery. (The fairy tale "Sleeping Beauty" is actually an imaginative allegory for expressing this psychic predicament of our will's inner world of snoozing!)

At the inauguration ceremony of the building, Beelzebub describes the pomp and splendor of it all as creating an "exitless magical circle" that is, a large but artificial fanfare *from which there is no escape*. However, his Russian friend eventually finds him among the captivated crowd and informs him that a personal meeting has been arranged with none other than His Majesty.

Several days later, Beelzebub notices that the streets are being frantically cleaned (like what he witnessed from a rooftop in Persia), anticipating the arrival of an important power-possessing being—a Russian general! This general is coming to see Beelzebub concerning the upcoming important personal meeting with the Czar. What happens next offers the reader (if he or she is paying serious attention) a wonderful illustration of the split psyche operating in this particular "powerful" Russian general.

In their short meeting, the Russian general informs Beelzebub that he has been sent over to teach him about the protocol *one must adhere to* when in the company of the Czar. As Beelzebub is listening to the general's words the general happens to catch a glimpse of some Chinese antiques in the room. Apparently, Beelzebub and the general share a similar deep interest in these ancient Chinese productions. Without any formal ceremony (unlike the one they are preparing for) the general makes himself more at home in one of the chairs in the room and starts up a conversation about various Chinese antiques. Later, before leaving, he decides not to prepare Beelzebub for the Czar himself, but to send someone else to actually educate Beelzebub on the official protocols. (One gets a real sensation during this meeting that the general is jumping between two forms of consciousness—his learned and artificial consciousness concerning protocol and decorum, and his deeper legitimate consciousness, which is not fabricated and is genuinely interested in Chinese antiques.

When the general's younger replacement shows up later that evening, Beelzebub describes how he has to endure learning about the ceremonial procedures for meeting the Czar. This education served only as "food" for his artificial consciousness and outward personality. Beelzebub describes the younger soldier who showed up to teach him these special protocols as a "mama's and papa's darling."

Beelzebub suddenly notices a strange change in the young man's attitude toward him (also representing the results of a pronounced split in his consciousness).

At first, the young man simply treated Beelzebub automatically—according to data fixed in his memory for interfacing with people of a *similar* or *higher* class than his. But when the young man detects that Beelzebub seems to represent a class of beings not much better than "savages," he "downshifts" his efforts to another, just as automatically learned, mannerism which made the young officer suddenly become *harsher*. The young man now sternly warns Beelzebub to practice all he is being taught, and that he will show up the very next day to make sure there are will be no screw-ups.

Beelzebub finally meets with the Russian Czar and humorously, never noticed what he looked like because he had to carefully and continuously fit into the recently learned automatic behavior and contorted psyche of the Russians and their "turkey-ness." Beelzebub admits that keeping up with these foolish manifestations, with all his spiritualized parts, caused him great *fatigue*. But he points out to his grandson, Hassein, that procedures like this greatly contributed to how the Russians appraised each other and their "individual significance" through the gradual habit of judging things only by *outer appearances*. This psychical shift caused the citizens of this very large community to lose the "taste" and "desire" for obtaining a true spiritual and unified objective consciousness.

To underscore this observation, Beelzebub (again, humorously) informs Hassein that after his royal audience with the Czar, citizens of his Russian district who learned of this special meeting began to treat him with new respect and that the permits he was seeking over the past several months for his chemical laboratory were now even personally hand-delivered to him. He hilariously describes the new manifestations of the Russian citizenry toward him as not different from those who would be expecting to be named in his last will and testament.

Beelzebub then returns to the theme of the process of reciprocal destruction in Russia of everything previously obtained, a process, which at that time was called "Bolshevism." He now begins to fulfill his promise to Hassein for providing more details about the two fundamental causes of this negative predicament. The first factor, as I mentioned earlier, was from the little-known cosmic law "Solio-onensius," and the second factor was the abnormal conditions of being-existence established by these earth-humans themselves.

Modern science does not yet know of this astronomical reality from space, which Beelzebub calls the cosmic law of "Solioonensius." But astronomical bodies in space have an influence upon three-brained beings throughout the universe from the "periodic tensions" arising from the movements (center-of-gravity-of-causes) between their Sun and activities from neighboring solar systems. Beelzebub explains to Hassein, that in the case of earth-humans, their sun is periodically influenced by, and put into tension with, a neighboring solar system supporting a particular comet. This tension acts on the general presences of three-brained beings.

As I mentioned earlier, whereas in all other solar systems three-brained beings will sense a need and thirst for evolving and self-perfecting during these periods of cosmic tension, most modern earth-humans feel "nervousness." And instead of seeking spiritual or inner growth, begin to sense a new and misguided outer need "for freedom." Such an outer need for freedom gave rise to "Bolshevism" in Russia.

(It seems to me that every new movement or revolution by earth-humans is for the cause of establishing some new freedom or another which, when sincerely pondered, is concerned mostly with external and worldly issues—not internal ones. The *redistribution of wealth* is just such an external movement [called social justice] to give everyone similar and equal *terrestrial* freedoms.)

So, instead of seeking genuine inner (spiritual) freedom during the action of "Solioonensius," earth-humans sought freedom and bliss through making changes in their *external* living conditions. Hmmm... sounds quite familiar with lots of similar movements taking place today. Beelzebub remarks to his grandson that if the sacred (from God) data hidden in their subconscious for engendering the being-impulse of conscience was operational within the artificial and habitual consciousness which has taken over their waking state, the periodic need to solve problems through mere external changes could not possibly happen.

Beelzebub puts the main blame of this need for making changes solely on external conditions (and without spiritual conscience) on the *automatic* sorting out of people into various classes or "subdivision-into-castes."

This sorting of people into various classes originally occurred through those individuals who cultivated a certain kind of "cunning" and could threaten others through an accumulation of "weapons." This special group of clever individuals came to be called the "ruling class." The main activity of this ruling class was to compel others to do their bidding, which most often meant doing the menial jobs. Since no one wanted this responsibility of menial labor placed on their backs, the being-responsibility of making certain required efforts in life was continually passed down to others, until lower and lower classes emerged, where those at the bottom of the totem pole were left with no choice in the matter but to do all the grunt work.

"Shit" runs downhill (but the "hill" is a human construction).

This sorting out into diverse classes happens naturally according to the degree of skill in artfully manifesting human artificiality. Over time, these "groupings" become fixed or crystallized (well established) into the psyche of earth-humans so that they start to view those outside their own caste with "hate." This hate is expressed in different forms, such as envy, jealousy, and even adultery, etc. (Class warfare is a real outcome of this acquired "hate.")

This smoldering hate creates more psychic degeneration in earth-humans.

Not only does the cosmic law "Solioonensius" and the need for external freedom cause earth-humans to lose their "sane-awareness-of-the-sense-and-aim-of-their-existence" but certain individuals who come under these cosmic influences and tensions more strongly than others—and believing they see reality better than other people—become "clamoring orators" and convince crowds of listeners to replace the current ruling class with members of their own class.

Beelzebub tells Hassein that while neither the older ruling class nor the upstarts who obtain new power through a revolt had cultivated the information necessary to create real and spiritual being-conscience in its citizens, the older ruling class had at least acquired a habit (from experience) of ruling that generally improved things over time.

So new rebellions (always to improve only external conditions) ensure that things will keep getting worse among the societies of Earth. (I have heard it said that if the famous revolutionary leader Che Guevara had become fully victorious, he would have gone on, simply starting up another revolution somewhere else.)

Beelzebub throws an additional barb at this degenerating process of society by observing that with each "regime change" by this process, there seemed to be an increase in the populations of *slugs, snails, lice, mole crickets* and other such *parasites* that destroy everything that is good. (Swedenborg would agree with the symbolism of this statement, since these "icky" creatures correspond to "lower" qualities of the human heart and mind, which destroy God's cosmic plan for spiritual growth and genuine goodness.)

As a negative three-pronged result from all this: 1) important information and lessons from the past were forgotten; 2) the ability to anticipate the future consequences of their actions evaporated from their psyches; and 3) important cosmic laws, which were once known, also evaporated from their minds.

Because of this widening gap and evaporation in their world-views, the earth-humans of contemporary generations falsely believed that "Bolshevism" happened for the first time in the country of Russia. Not true. These kinds of revolutions have occurred many times before. Beelzebub, having visited the planet Earth six times over thousands of years, personally witnessed this same terrifying process of the "destruction-of-everything-in-sight" (and looting) in the name of freedom at least forty times. He points out to his grandson that the different dynasties in Egypt each emerged out of similar terrifying processes, and that contemporary Bolshevism was "merely child's play" when it came to regime change. At least under Russian Bolshevism, one could recognize the bodies of those killed.

Beelzebub recounts one particularly terrifying process in ancient Egypt by which revolutionaries determined their next leaders. Individuals earned various positions of leadership in a new Egyptian regime based on the number of eyeballs they could collect from the individuals of the current ruling class (men, women and even children) and placed in special collecting jars! (I will not mention other terrifying methods used against the ruling class.) So the change of leadership in Egypt was not the peaceful passing of power from Pharaoh to son. In fact, much of the changing of the guard on the planet Earth is not done peacefully.

(Such unhinged behavior also symbolizes the accumulating sands of a desert.)

We can see this awful process of hate and "protest" in many regime changes today, throughout the globe—all demanding outer improvements. (Will this bring about the continued spreading of desert conditions on Earth? That would be real climate change!)

Returning to the topic of Bolshevism, Beelzebub describes such a being-manifestation as "vainly-to-grow-sincerely-indignant," this is, to be "agitated" and "outraged." This abnormality in the psyche of earth-humans (of new formation) proceeded as a natural consequence of everyone's diminishing "being-horizon" as well as the degenerating "instinctive-sensing-of-reality-in-its-real-light." So, the cosmic law "Solioonensius" (cosmic tension) has a particularly adverse effect on those shallow individuals whose inner impulse of conscience does not take place in their normal waking consciousness (habitual mind). Instead, such cosmic forces, which normally stimulate a need and desire for spiritual growth among three-brained beings all over the universe, now turn these earth-humans with their abnormal psyches into mere "puppets."

But they are very scary puppets!

After hearing this, Hassein asks his grandfather why helpful data doesn't accumulate over the centuries in a way that would allow earth-humans, over time, to learn and sense something approaching objective reality. Beelzebub replies that good customs and information concerning positive moral habits do appear in the lives of earth-humans, but they strangely either disappear or are transformed into their opposite. (Swedenborg observed that those spirits living in hellish and hateful conditions were in a constant effort to change the Lord God's positive loving influences and influx into their opposites.)

Beelzebub puts the main blame for good information not taking hold in the human psyche again on a special property called "suggestibility." The three-brained beings of planet Earth have developed an organic need and strong preference to influence others and be influenced by others. To offer his grandson a clearer example of this need, Beelzebub feels that the "Russians" could serve this purpose most effectively.

Russia represented a large community, which over time had indeed developed many good customs and useful moral habits. But because of their being open to *suggestibility*, these great customs manifested in "parrot-like" ways—in outer appearance only (pretense). Gradually, instead of being influenced by the useful wisdom in neighboring Asian communities and correctly participating in God's cosmic plan of inner growth, they became attracted to the more outwardly "refined" and artificial culture of European communities, particularly France.

Beelzebub next offers Hassein two examples of useful customs developed by the Asian communities close to Russia that the European influence of refined living caused them to ultimately reject and destroy. One wise custom was the chewing of a substance prepared from certain roots called "keva." This elastic substance was later called *chewing gum*. According to Beelzebub, chewing this substance strengthened and cleaned teeth, increased saliva flow to aid digestion (of the first-being food), and even helped to remove any fool odor in the mouth.

The second good custom from Asia was called the "hamman" (Turkish bath). This custom helped to clean the pores of one's skin of oily residues that the body forms from filtering out impurities from the air (our second-being food) that we all breathe in. This second custom was created because Asians discovered that wearing "clothes" prevented the ordinary process of skin pores being cleaned properly through natural evaporation into the atmosphere. Without the proper cleaning of these skin pores, humans put themselves at risk for contracting additional illnesses. These Asians also discovered that ordinary washing, even with hot water, could not reach deep enough into the skin pores to clean them properly. But Turkish baths (hammans) could remove the accumulated oily substances from skin pores.

(Gurdjieff constructed one of these "hammans" at his scientific *Institute for the Harmonious Development of Man*, outside of Paris.)

However, due to their suggestibility (and while trying to become peacocks), the Russians got rid of these two good customs because, they were considered "unintelligent" and "indecent" by the more "refined" and highly educated Europeans. Furthermore, the more educated citizens of the European community called "France" found that such types of bathing made it more challenging to maintain their "artificial" appearance—which took a long time to get "just right." (Beelzebub does give credit to the Americans for picking up the positive habit of at least, chewing gum.)

To replace these good Asian customs, the Russians picked up new moral (artificial) habits from the Europeans such as "kissing a lady's hand," "being polite only to young ladies," "looking at a wife before her husband with the left eye," etc. (Swedenborg had learned in the Spiritual World that the Europeans, who were predominately Christian, were the most likely to commit adultery.)

Beelzebub hopes that he has explained to his grandson why "suggestibility" and "imitating others" (through refined outward mannerisms) cause the deterioration in the psyche of earth-humans to find—and meditate on—real meaningful values. Instead, they have become "adopters-by-compulsion" of some trend, fad, or another. (Swedenborg would call this situation a form of real slavery to outside influences and maintained that no amount of *coercion* affects the human heart deeply—it needs to be changed inwardly and by new personal convictions.)

This desire by the Russians to throw away good customs for bad ones, based on outer conditions and considerations, is the true expression of their "turkey-ness."

Beelzebub wraps up this part of his Tale by informing Hassein that the length of the existence of any community or country, indeed, affects how many useful customs become fixed into the instinctive habits of the citizenry. Unfortunately, on the planet Earth, war always cuts short the existence of one or another of its communities.

So, "bye-bye" to the orderly accumulation of positive customs.

SUMMARY

▪ Beelzebub goes to Russia to help solve their big problem with alcoholism.

▪ Beelzebub observes that Russians manifested the most pronounced split of earth-human consciousness.

▪ The division of humans into classes comes from laziness toward personal responsibility and putting those responsibilities on the backs of others—through extra cunning—until this responsibility is placed lower and lower, on those least able to complain. This is how the ruling class now comes about.

SUMMARY

■ Cosmic and planetary tensions ("Solioonensius") felt in earth-humans who have no true conscience creates an irritation and their organic need to seek some new external *freedom* (instead of a thirst for personal *inner* change). Bolshevism, caste systems, and constant revolution are major outcomes of this new need for obtaining external freedoms for self-calming.

■ Russians, who are essentially Asians (represented by crows), but trying to embrace European "refinement" (represented by peacocks), end up as mere "Turkeys."

■ Beelzebub was originally to receive personal direction concerning the protocol of meeting with the Russian Czar by a Russian general. The Russian general has a remarkable change in personality when he notices one of the Chinese antiques in Beelzebub's room. This change represented a split in the general's psyche between two different interests, stemming from his two different forms of consciousness. One consciousness—the real one—was enthralled with Chinese artifacts, but the other was concerned only with preserving the proper *outer* decorum of his mission. Since the general spends too much time conversing about his "other love" of ancient Chinese artifacts, he has to send a young adjutant later to finish the lessons. But the young military man, perceiving Beelzebub (from outside appearances) as being a part of a lower class of people, has an automatic change in his demeanor, which becomes more harsh and bossy. Russians *strove* to judge all others in this ephemeral manner.

■ Just before meeting the Czar, Beelzebub had to learn to subjugate all his three spiritualized parts to the "tune" of Russian protocol—down to the blinking of his eyelids. This was so fatiguing that Beelzebub has no recollection of what the Czar actually looked like!

■ Even beyond the absurdities of this "torturous" procedure, when news of this special meeting with the Czar reached others in that community, they all (automatically) began treating Beelzebub with extra importance. Beelzebub believes that "suggestibility" prevents positive customs from taking hold.

CHAPTER 35

"A change in the appointed course of the falling of the transspace ship *Karnak*"

At this point in the story, while still on their return journey from having attended a conference on the planet Revozvradendr (which was mentioned in Chapter 2, but the details of the conference were never discussed), the Captain of the transspace ship *Karnak* reminds Beelzebub of his original request to visit his son Tooilan (Hassein's father) on the holy planet Purgatory. The Captain needs to know if this is still the course that Beelzebub wishes to make on his second return to the center of the universe and back to his home planet (which was possible because of his Divine pardon).

The Captain needs to make the proper adjustments soon, or their flight will be greatly delayed.

Beelzebub says "yes," but thinking things over, he adds an additional request—that he would like the Captain to make yet another stop after visiting Purgatory, to the planet *Deskaldino*, where his first teacher—the Great Saroonoorishan—resides, before returning to the sphere of his arising (the planet Karatus). The Captain agrees to make the extra adjustments necessary to allow the transspace ship to "gravitate" (fall) past all the extra obstacles of this more complex trajectory.

Having made the trip from different planets to the center of the universe before, Beelzebub grasps the difficulty of his new travel request to the Captain.

This diversion of changing trajectories is a metaphor that Beelzebub will now be changing tactics (mental direction) again before arriving at the ultimate destination (goal or aim of his talks), which he anticipates will now become more complex and difficult. Keep in mind that the *transspace* ship *Karnak* (and the intersystem ship *Omnipresent* before it) can travel between levels (dimensions) of reality—from the physical planets, even to spiritual planets (distinct ontological planes of existence in the multi-universe system).

I believe that each change made in the trajectory of the *Karnak* represents a new *state of mind* (change of gravity) and endeavor in Beelzebub's inner world. The particular maneuver and adjustment by the Captain will now require a more difficult course (explanation) in reaching Beelzebub's ultimate destination (goal of the story) and home planet.

This symbolizes the extra difficulty (new cosmic details) his story will now need to examine in order to provide enough extra evidence for the reader, to help verify the unflattering message about the peculiar degeneration of the psyche of humans on the planet Earth and their continued inability to properly sense reality.

SUMMARY

■ On the return journey from attending a conference on the planet *Revozvradendr* and back to his birth planet, *Karatus*, Beelzebub asks the flight captain to make an additional adjustment and extra stop along the way. This will complicate the route.

■ Beelzebub, after his request to visit his son, Tooilan (Hassein's father), now living on the holy planet Purgatory, also wants to include a visit to the planet *Deskaldino*, where his first great educator and teacher lives.

■ This more complex route represents Beelzebub's anticipation of a more difficult *psycho-spiritual* talk ahead, with greater challenges (psychic maneuverings) and his providing more detailed information about the actual laws ruling the great universe.

CHAPTER 36

"Just a wee bit more about the Germans"

Beelzebub returns to his narrative and admits to Hassein that he is now indeed changing tactics (a change in the center of gravity of his talks) to further make his point about the specifics concerning the abnormal psyche of the earth-humans. He returns to a short discussion on the Germans, whom he claims are now the modern substitutes for the ancient Greeks when it comes to inventing new "sciences."

To point out a particular detail of their abnormal psyche, Beelzebub focuses on an oddity in the German language and quotes a German saying that is sung during various celebrations:

> Blödsinn, Blödsinn,
> Du mein Vergnügen,
> Stumpfsinn, Stumpfsinn.
> Du meine Lust.

Beelzebub challenges Hassein to contemplate the words of this German song.

To give his grandson a little help, Beelzebub points out that there are certain words to the above song that have no corresponding words in any other terrestrial language on the entire planet Earth. Secondly, due to the deterioration of "logical-being-mentation," this grouping of earth-humans has also invented a strange "grammatical-rule."

This odd grammatical rule consists in placing the *particle of negation* after the affirmative. Thus, instead of saying "I do not want this," they say "I want this not." Beelzebub tells Hassein that by the Germans adopting this strange rule *without any challenge or resistance* hides the secret to the specific strangeness of their psyche.

Their strange grammatical rule reflected the order of their thinking and their passive acceptance of it, which was illogical to Beelzebub.

Swedenborg learned from the spiritual world that Germans were particularly prone to being submissive (passive) to those of rank and authority (*True Christian Religion*, n. 814), rarely challenging it. This submissive behavior was the "secret" to the suggestibility of the German psyche and the disintegration of their "logical-being-mentation" and which ultimately affects how they experience the world.

SUMMARY

■ Beelzebub shares a short German song with his grandson to provide a useful example and detail of the workings of their particular illogical psyche.

■ The song contains words with no corresponding expressions in any other of the world's languages and contains a strange order or "grammatical-rule" in which the *particle of negation* is placed after the *affirmative*.

■ This strange order (grammatical-rule) is the result of their warped (illogical) thinking ability and passive experiencing of reality.

CHAPTER 37

"France"

Since the Russians acquired their "turkey-ness" from trying to imitate western culture, particularly from the French, it is only natural that the story moves to this part of the planet Earth and its inhabitants. Beelzebub now continues to take aim at Western civilization through the strangeness and suggestibility of the human psyche from observations he personally made in Paris, France during the early twentieth century (1920s).

In this chapter, Gurdjieff uses Beelzebub to provide simple, everyday examples of why the knowledge accumulated by earth-humans does not correspond with reality. (This is to show that most humans indeed live in a delusional state, are susceptible to suggestibility, believe in many wrong things, and can only see reality in a topsy-turvy manner.)

For instance, during his travels to the West, Beelzebub learns through hearsay (like everyone else), of the reputation of the French as an immoral, immodest and depraved people. But rather than putting his faith automatically on the correctness of the subjective essence-opinions of earth-humans (from all parts of the planet's surface) he decides to investigate this charge of immoral behavior among the French for himself.

Beelzebub is surprised that, on observing the French people, he could not perceive any truth to these allegations. Instead, he finds them the most "patriarchal" and "modest" of all those making up the European community. (This investigation is another example of how Gurdjieff would follow up on a subject, going the "whole hog including the postage.")

I remember for myself that as a young man I heard the expression "French whore." This phrase implied that French women were the best at this particular profession to the point that the human psyche, with its "automatic opinion," eventually accepts this premise as a "cosmic truth." But when Beelzebub visits the various "bad" districts in Paris, he discovers no French citizen or Frenchwoman there. Instead, those offering the "immoral services," as well as those who were patrons of these suspicious services, *were all from foreign countries!* The French citizens themselves, stayed clear of these shady districts, which also included places where homosexuals and lesbians pursued their "nocturnal quests."

Beelzebub also noticed another abnormality of the human psyche, which further promoted ideas that do not correspond at all to reality. Because of the fact that Paris was, at that time, considered not only a "center-of-culture" on the planet but the "capital of the world," foreign visitors flocked there to tickle their vanities and partake of the many "fashionable novelties" offered. Such novelties included women's clothing styles, hair fashions, perfumes, popular dances, fancy hats and the bragging rights of saying you purchased these things in Paris itself (which has nothing to do with spiritual transformation or one's innermost qualities of character).

Beelzebub informs Hassein that he saw many Americans there and that they were now replacing the Russians for "turkey-ness" and having an intense passion to visit Paris and be more like Europeans. One humorous example of the abnormality of earth-humans to be prone to suggestibility is that many Americans came to Paris to learn the "Foxtrot," ironically, a dance style invented in America itself. It was simply much more fashionable and self-elevating to be able to boast that one had learned the Foxtrot not in America, but in Paris.

It was here in Paris, after seeing all this nonsense going on, that Beelzebub experiences—for the second time in his life—an inner revolt (being-Sarpitimnian-experiencing) of cosmic unfairness in God's providence, on account that much of this tragedy could be blamed directly on Saintly Cosmic Individuals (probably God's angels) who originally failed to foresee the collision of the comet Kondoor with the ill-fated planet Earth. If these Saintly Individuals had only done something to stop this collision from happening they would not have had to implant in earth-humans the maleficent organ Kundabuffer, which caused the three-brained beings of that planet to become self-deluded. And although these Saintly Cosmic Individuals eventually removed this organ from earth-humans, there were unintended consequences for the earth-humans of future generations.

Having attended Gurdjieff work sessions, I can verify that this topic of higher intelligences being responsible for the negative condition in earth-humans is even somewhat perplexing for Gurdjieffians. How could higher beings, working for God, have made this mistake of robbing earth-humans of the ability to sense their cosmic duty, and only mechanically fulfilling the needs of the growing universe by their own deaths? (According to Swedenborg, this apparent "unfairness" was necessary. Permitting human self-delusion was a gamble that God had to take in order to preserve human *free will*, through a false sense of self-importance. This kept the door open for our potential spiritual growth in the future.)

Beelzebub regrets that these Saintly Individuals also made a second miscalculation. This miscalculation concerned the future of spiritual transformation for earth-humans. They failed to take into account that because of the fundamental cosmic Law of Sevenfoldness (Heptaparaparshinokh) and its periodicity, plus the nature of human *habit*, the negative properties of this maleficent organ Kundabuffer would become *second nature* and transferred to future generations of earth-humans through heredity—this cosmic law would ensure that their deteriorating desires would grow and work against them, keeping them from ever developing in a positive direction.

Swedenborg offers an explanation as to why this would happen. He states in *Apocalypse Explained* (n. 211) that a principle chosen (even a false one) "draws things to its own side," since they (homogenous things of the desire) must be connected with it. This creates a coherent series of events (gravity-centers) leading to a *whole* phenomenon, with a common equilibrium, whether it is good or bad.

So, these Saintly Individuals had also failed to calculate that the Fundamental Cosmic Law Heptaparaparshinokh (Sevenfoldness) with its "Mdnel-Ins" (bearers of new directions) would simply maintain the negative trajectory of earth-humans, even after the maleficent organ's removal (instead of promoting proper human evolution and spiritual growth). So the organ Kundabuffer, once implanted, would engender false principles that would have bad lasting effects for future human generations. (Swedenborg called this *inherited* evils. He understood well that universal cosmic laws and God's Order ensured that beginnings ran to ultimates through established increments. This process allowed results to correspond to first principles.)

Beelzebub remarks that it should have been foreseen by these Saintly Individuals that the negative consequences of the organ Kundabuffer would become inherent in the human psyche from the repeating nature of this fundamental law. (Although this put God "behind the eight ball," it was indeed foreseen that He would have to personally enter into the world's spacetime fray, called the *Advent of the Lord,* and do battle with the consequences of this Law of human hereditary evil [which he got from his mother]. I will address this relatively unknown theological issue more in the next chapter.)

Unfortunately, because of lingering human perversions left by the organ Kundabuffer, the process of further spiritual evolution—the lawful means for coating or organizing a higher being-body (spiritual body for the soul)—also by means of the Fundamental Cosmic Law of Sevenfoldness, became almost impossible. Worse yet, because most earth-humans not only fail to develop their inner bodies up to certain required degrees, now they don't even know about it. So they are doomed, after the death of their physical bodies, to languish forever in all kinds of *exterior* planetary forms.

This last statement almost sounds like reincarnation, which is quite "un-Swedenborgian." However, someone who is intimately familiar with Swedenborg's ideas can find similarities with Gurdjieff's notion of various after-death realities for the human race, including in this case, those who only cling to terrestrial qualities.

Swedenborg claimed that non-angelic spirits who continue to favor worldly things have their Limbus (cutaneous covering or coating made from both spiritual substances and the finest substances of nature) above them. Whereas, true angels have their Limbus below them. So during the lives of more materialistic individuals, they will fail to develop and raise their rational mind up to a certain required spiritual degree—above their memory function. This means that these underperforming types of human spirits have their subtle bio-structure and its orientation always aimed downward, toward worldly qualities. So from necessity, their life-energies mostly flow into corresponding physical forms.

And those individuals who, through duty and being-efforts (spiritual combat) obtain the required levels of spiritual reasoning, have their deepest bio-formation and results always oriented toward higher heavenly qualities. To "languish forever in all kinds of exterior planetary forms" means that one's spiritual reality—if not spiritually regenerated and purified—will remain natural and worldy, thus tied to and continuing to flow (terminate) into all sorts of corresponding expressions of lowly terrestrial forms. In God's top-down universe, spiritual forces are always endeavoring to clothe themselves in corresponding physical (earthly) forms. God's angels need properly developed human minds (with a conscience) as a terminating plane for their heavenly forces to flow into.

So Beelzebub is actually touching on the consequences of different forms or vessels we humans inwardly become. In humans, that represents the top-down results of spiritual flow from our life-choices and actions ("influx according to afflux").

Swedenborg observed from Heaven that the Creator's Love and Wisdom flows (influx) by means of the Sun Absolute into the hearts and minds of those inhabiting Heaven and the spiritual world. But this happens only according to receptivity. This life-giving influx continues downward from angelic and spiritual beings (true top-down causation) into all the processes and structures of the physical universe and its order, including influx into the hearts and minds of various men and women on Earth who can receive it—through proper inner order—and put it into action.

Unfortunately, some of this sacred, life-vivifying influx becomes twisted along the way by wrongly developed (self-centered) human hearts and minds.

Those earth-humans who are oriented downwards toward love of the self (egoism) and the world, instead of developing a sincere and higher love toward God and the neighbor, not only twist and distort this spiritual flow (mixing their garbage and self-centeredness with Heaven's life of innocence and duty) but they also falsely believe that they think, feel and live from themselves—rather than from God. This delusion was the major maleficent property and consequence of the organ Kundabuffer's illusory effect upon the human psyche. (See Swedenborg's *Arcana Coelestia*, n. 5660 and its earlier chapter on Adam and Eve.)

So Beelzebub is describing something a bit different than the current Hindu or Buddhist notion of reincarnation. He is describing a state of languish by which spiritual beings remain trapped *forever* in mere worldly qualities and thus their distorted life-energy is eternally damned to flow only into corresponding constraints of inert terrestrial structures or lowly bio-forms.

Beelzebub comes to the conclusion that this last result of inner languish is the fault of the individual earth-humans themselves, who have not taken the proper spiritual responsibility for their lives. His inner revolt to all this causes him to reflect on all those earth-humans he observed during his six visits to the planet Earth. He is further saddened by the fact that nothing has really changed for humankind over the past *ten thousand* years because of an original cosmic screw-up and miscalculation. (Even religion and its prophets have failed to correct this screw-up, which is why the descent of the Holy City, the New Jerusalem, down from Heaven, is being stalled.)

In this funk-mood, Beelzebub continues to point out to Hassein the various weaknesses of Americans who now visit France. One very humorous observation about these American weaknesses is that they learn much about France from bus tours. Another weakness is that many Americans are duped (through their vanity) by foreign business "sharks" into buying "Paris fashions," that were actually made in Germany, where labor is cheaper. These businesses were run "legally" through "triple-bookkeeping" and "Shachermacher-accounting" (more maleficent properties of deception, thanks to the organ Kundabuffer). But besides all this, there is another deeper—and quite shocking—cause as to why earth-humans form opinions not corresponding to reality.

Beelzebub calls this "modern education."

Whoa! Isn't that an anti-intuitive notion? Certainly, education is to be desired. This is a real slap in the face for all of us!

How does Beelzebub prove this unique position?

Well, he states that modern education hinders Nature's process from forming appropriate ideas concerning reality by filling the human brain (especially children, who are sponges) with all kinds of false and fantastic ideas. As these children mature, the functioning of their psyche adapts itself to respond *only* to these false and fantastic ideas, and to judge all new information, not according to God's design, but according to these *implanted* and incorrect worldviews ("cultured European manifestations"). This causes the human psyche to split.

Such resulting incorrect worldviews diminish the two primary being-impulses upon which "objective-being-morality" or *conscience* is based, called "patriarchy" (love of family) and "organic-shame."

(Shame is noticeably absent in many modern activities and this is becoming ever more prevalent, with activities like *sexting* and *twerking*.)

Paris, therefore, being a great Center-of-Culture, became a magnet for all earth-humans of different countries that became slaves to an "Evil-God" (negative ruling love) which Beelzebub describes as: "to-attain-to-a-complete-absence-of-the-need-for-being-effort-and-for-every-essence-anxiety-of-whatever-kind-it-may-be."

Contemporary earth-humans achieve the temporary calming of this "Evil-God" (besides booze and sex) through "new fashions" or the "current rage" (their Hasnamussian susceptibility). This "calming" is accomplished because new fashions provide earth-humans with ever-creative means for changing and disguising the reality of one's appearance (another method of making life not correspond to reality). These strategies only provide temporary relief because they are always the results from one's personal insignificant aims, which are trivially egoistic and issue from their automatic (and artificial) Reasoning.

One such harmful fashion, which grew out of European culture, was the invention of "hair fashions" for those of the female sex. Since a woman's long hair was adapted by Nature to perform an important function in the exchange of certain cosmic substances for the universe, the cutting of this hair led to three additional abnormal conditions. Beelzebub informs Hassein that one of these abnormal results of cutting female hair was that it would lead to the appearance of "Amazons" and a "religion of the poetess Sappho." The second condition produces "suffragettes," "Christian Scientists," and "theosophists." And thirdly, when the custom of cutting the hair of the female sex spreads universally all over the globe, various women's diseases and venereal inflammations of the sexual organs begin to emerge, such as "vaginitis," "uteritis," "ovaritis," and "cancer."

Cosmic harmony is further altered, often leading to "divorce."

The reason for these negative outcomes is that according to cosmic law, those of the female sex serve as the "passive" principle and force in God's Great Holy Law Triamazikamno (the Trinitarian law of "three-ness"). Cutting the long flowing hair of the female sex thwarts this important universal process in Great Nature, causing women to change their God-given cosmic roles. (Feminists and post-modernists won't like this assessment, but please keep in mind that most men are not properly fulfilling their cosmic roles within the Law of Threefoldness, either.)

Beelzebub further admits that France had its own elite (ruling) class that felt it necessary to invent an even better means for calming people's inner "Evil-God." These means were called "fairs" and offered all types of gambling games, tasty treats and various whirling rides, designed to cause "stupor" in their customers. Beelzebub states that these fairs were usually set up in town squares, where just two centuries earlier, people gathered to have noble discussions on "religious-moral-subjects."

SUMMARY

■ Beelzebub now visits Paris, France, to find examples of how the knowledge possessed by earth-humans doesn't correspond with reality (the Truth).

■ Beelzebub finds the French people to be much nobler than their worldwide reputation for depravity and immodesty would suggest. In fact, only foreigners had created the shady districts of Paris, while real French citizens stayed clear of these dens of vice.

■ Going to a "French brothel," Beelzebub is surprised not to find a single Frenchwoman there.

■ At places where homosexuals gather, Beelzebub refers to these "haunts" and "evil hearths" as more examples of abnormal behavior (which is counter to current trends).

■ Americans began to replace the Russians in manifesting "turkey-ness" and came to Paris in order to boast about their specialness by acting like cultured Europeans. This "artificial specialness" is made humorously evident by Americans coming to Paris for the newest fashions, and gaining additional bragging rights by also learning the "Foxtrot" overseas, instead of at home.

■ Modern education serves to imprint false notions of reality into children's noggins—with data that does not connect with their inner being.

■ The universal cutting of women's hair (called hair fashions) results in three negative consequences—lesbianism, suffragettes and even female diseases.

■ Community leaders in Europe also devised town fairs and bazaars (to create stupor from various whirling rides plus all kinds of cheap games of chance), in order to further mollify the abnormal psyches of their citizenry.

CHAPTER 38

"Religion"

After having explained to his grandson the many, many causes for the strange functioning of the psyche of earth-humans, Beelzebub is now able to offer insights on the important topic of religion (called *Havatvernoni*) and its lamentable trajectory in human affairs—that is, its failure.

The strange and ever dwindling psyche of the earth-humans is evidenced by the "fictions" (an artificiality that is symbolized in Scripture by the *hand-hewn* stone used for the building of the Tower of Babel to reach Heaven and represents most modern human institutions) that they fabricated everything, including their "religious teachings."

This generated a large number of religions having nothing to do with each other or with creating sane cognition. Instead of using religion to free themselves of their egoistic aims, "religious doctrine" became a man-made concoction to actually further their egoistic aims and only contributed to promoting more and more confusion among them (*confusion of tongues*). We see blatant signs of this confusion in the long history of wars on Earth that were based solely on religion (including the *Crusades*).

(Swedenborg's unique interpretation of the Bible shows that it contains "interior truths"—a deeper, symbolic message touching on the universality of humanity's perversion and rejection of God's tenets, and the heavenly duty of the human race to resist all their own egoistic aims. Furthermore, these interior truths are organized into a *series of gravity centers* from the Lord in Heaven by means of the Word. Under this divine and heavenly order (Truth proceeding from Love) Swedenborg believed—like Gurdjieff—that it was extremely dangerous for humans to mess with the mysteries of faith through their own warped thinking and limited terrestrial intelligence.

But earth-humans are glad to do it anyway.

In his great theological work *The True Christian Religion*, n. 508 [3], Swedenborg observed that this situation has now been changed in that it is now divinely *permitted* ("Nunc licet") for humans to intellectually probe the mysteries of Faith (through more interior levels of meaning and true divine order within the multi-structure of God's Word). This advantageous timing is even why I believe that Gurdjieff was also permitted to discover (150 years later) deeper *truths* in his own genuine searches and to share with others all about this new mind-stretching material.

He and Swedenborg both believed that it was time to elevate the highest reaches of human understanding (to the level of God's angels) by revealing not just deeper truths, but *truths in series*. This sacred series contains the lawful steps by which earth-humans are to put their egos aside and even learn how science, psychology and true religion actually follow these same universal rules. This new information becomes perfectly and organically unified into a proper worldview about reality. Such a new worldview is symbolized by the descent of the New Jerusalem—out of Heaven, to the Earth—where human hearts and minds dwell.)

However, permission and accomplishment are two different things. If I were to ask even the followers of Swedenborg's theology, they would not be able to tell me how *truths run in a lawful series*. This will quickly change, however, when people at some future time realize that Swedenborg's *Circle of Life* is Gurdjieff's *Enneagram*. (I first wrote about this connection in my book, *Proving God*.)

According to Beelzebub (and Gurdjieff), the particular theological confusion that has most adversely affected the earth-humans' overall take on religion is their faulty and fabricated notion of "Good and Evil." Furthermore, Beelzebub hints that this faulty notion of *good* and *evil* also had a negative effect on those human souls dwelling on the Holy Planet Purgatory (the spiritual region that all human spirits first enter, after physical death, to be properly prepared and challenged for a life worthy of Heaven).

Beelzebub promises to explain this strange notion later. However, he states in this chapter that this negative effect stemmed from the "Choot-God-Litanical-period" (Fall of humanity) in which human souls could no longer blend immediately with Heaven and the realm of its Spiritual Sun (the influential rays and flow of God's Holy Word or Theomertmalogos).

It is toward this holy planet "Purgatory" that their *intersystem* spaceship is now "falling" (which again indicates that their special spacecraft can travel between spiritual and physical dimensions or levels of reality).

Beelzebub explains to Hassein how religions arise legitimately on the planet Earth and also how they degenerate over time (Swedenborg calls this the formation and final vastation of a church).

He informs Hassein, that because of the consequences of the accursed organ Kundabuffer, which caused earth-humans to see reality in a topsy-turvy way, thus making it almost impossible for spiritual evolution (crystallization of their higher-being-bodies or spiritual body of the soul) OUR ABUNDANTLY LOVING COMMON FATHER wisely decided to prepare various Saintly Individuals in order to guide the flawed functioning of the separated spiritualized parts of other earth-humans and destroy the negative traits and properties fixed into their psyches from the organ Kundabuffer.

Without these steps, even legitimate religion wouldn't have the desired effect of true salvation.

After the physical deaths of these specially prepared Saintly Individuals (I include Swedenborg and Gurdjieff in this mix) it would become the responsibility of those who still remained to gather their various instructions (from bits and pieces), before putting them back into a whole collection of religious doctrine. But after constantly pecking these original teachings to death, these earth-humans could only fail at such a heavy responsibility.

Here is where Gurdjieff shows that he has an understanding of God's new revelations similar to that of Swedenborg—especially concerning sacred symbolic writings.

Beelzebub hints that many of these extant religious teachings left behind by these true messengers *actualized from Above* were never meant to be understood only "literally!" So, over time, the distortion of the deeper meanings intended from the original Saintly messages leads to two negative factors. First, the ruling class begins to artfully juggle these distorted ideas into creative ways that can more effectively promote their egoistic aims (i.e., honor, power, status and worldly gain). Second, certain ordinary beings with a strong leaning toward "psychopathy" and "parasitism" make themselves authorities on the trifling details of these emerging concocted religious doctrines and become extremely judgmental.

These two factors are the main reason why even quite legitimate religions, soon after their foundation, begin to break up (become vastated) into various sects and factions, increasingly promoting false thinking and fantastic new religious teachings.

Swedenborg's theological writings most definitely concur with this process of degeneration in earth-religions over time. He states that these religions/churches come to an end (vastation) when all the original truths of their teachings are rejected or perverted and become profaned by those who embrace the allurements of the physical world and the vanity of self-love, which ultimately takes hold of people's reasoning powers and psyche. He also maintained that a living spiritual organization (church) kept enjoying the revelations of ever new truths!

Having made six trips to the planet Earth, Beelzebub had witnessed this same negative process occur over thousands of Earth-years. He believes that of all the Saintly Individuals actualized from Above, only the ideas of the Most Sacred Ashiata Shiemash escaped this brutal process. All the other legitimate religious teachings fell into the hands of those earth-humans manifesting the two types of psychic factors mentioned above. These teachings by genuinely Saintly

Individuals, which fell into the hands of delusional earth-humans has led to the creation of five basic religions which survive today, called:

1) The Buddhistic
2) The Hebrew
3) The Christian
4) The Mohammedan
5) The Lamaist

Beelzebub gives a short description of each of these formerly legitimate religions, and why they are no longer viable. (Swedenborg referred to such religions as "dead churches.") Beelzebub had already described to his grandson some of the particulars of the Buddhist religion, earlier in his talks (Chapter 22) in which individuals wrongly shut themselves off from others (and from worldly influences) in their specially prepared rooms—in order to increase "suffering" and gain the inner endurance needed for their successful spiritual evolution.

Next, Beelzebub states that Saint Moses was the intentionally actualized messenger from Above whose teaching founded the *Hebrew* religion. (Swedenborg makes a distinction between Hebrews, started by Abraham, and the Jewish or Israelite Church started by Moses). Beelzebub states that if the earth-humans of this once great religion had followed the directions given them from Moses, who received his instructions from Above (on Mt. Sinai), then they would have had the means to *free themselves* of the consequences and maleficent properties of the organ Kundabuffer and prevent new crystallizations from getting a foothold in the human psyche. (This is the true spiritual meaning of escaping the Egyptian Pharaoh.)

Rather, "Hasnamuss" or corrupted earth-humans, added new "spices" to these genuine teachings—to the point where Moses himself would no longer recognize anything of his original contributions. (Swedenborg goes into great detail concerning this negative outcome in his *Arcana Coelestia* translation of Exodus, where the Jewish nation kept changing religious views to suit their own egoistic purposes—like worshipping a golden calf.) Beelzebub hints that some of these "spices" were very similar to the fantastic ideas invented by King Konuzion concerning heavenly reward (in Chapter 20), all so that he could keep his earthly kingdom operating smoothly and keep his subjects from chewing poppy seeds.

The third great religion, called *Christianity*, was founded by another Sacred Individual, actualized from "Above," and named Jesus Christ. (I do not know what "actualized from Above" is intended to mean. Swedenborg claimed that Jesus was Jehovah God in the flesh, and that Jesus was to come back again, meaning that his original mission on Earth was not yet completed. So Gurdjieff is correct in saying that all these saintly messengers failed in their original missions and goals to reach the human split psyche.)

Something else has to happen from our following the normal doctrinal requirements of any religion (it has to do not with the "collective" but with individually unifying our external and internal realities, from building our conscience).

After Jesus, two other Saintly Individuals appeared on Earth—Saint Mohammed, among those called Arabs, and Saint Lama in Tibet. As all these various religions kept dividing into various sects, due to the warped thinking of their terrestrial leaders or "professional dignitaries," these sects even began to develop an "organic hatred" for each other.

Beelzebub does point out to Hassein that a small group of terrestrial beings had indeed successfully preserved the original teachings of Jesus Christ. This small group of Christ-followers was called the "Essene Brotherhood." They even succeeded, from these teachings, in ridding themselves of the negative consequences of the properties of the organ Kundabuffer—seeing reality upside down (the inverted order from God's true order). They made real efforts at putting one's own needs and interests always behind others (through inner work).

Gurdjieff claimed to make contact with this brotherhood during the turn of the 19th Century!

The fourth great religion, which arose several centuries after the Christian religion, was founded on the teachings of Saint Mohammed. (Swedenborg does state that this religious teaching was a legitimate part of God's Divine Providence and was formed to match the particular psyche of those living in Arab nations and to offset the big Christian mistake of dividing God into three Persons.)

Beelzebub says that this religion had the potential of delivering a "hearth of hope and reconciliation" if it had not been turned by the earth-humans there into a "hodgepodge." This hodgepodge, created by its followers, included adopting fantastic theories from the earlier Babylonian dualists and adding their own concocted version about the various blessings found in "paradise." This not only produced two "schools" from an original (and unified) teaching—the "Sunnites" and "Shiites"—but also led to an organic hatred (permanent property of their psyches) between the two.

Beelzebub hints that various European communities have benefitted from, and even helped to further promote this animosity between these two major schools of the Mohammedan religion, in order to insure their own security. (In his charming book *Boyhood With Gurdjieff* (pg. 160), author Fritz Peters writes about hearing from Gurdjieff that "he predicted that a day would come when the eastern world would again rise to a position of global importance and become a threat to the momentarily all-powerful, all-influential new culture of the western world... dominated by America.")

The fifth major religion, started by Saint Lama, also a true messenger from God, was more successful in helping individuals break free from the bondage of the maleficent properties of the organ Kundabuffer simply because they lived in a mountainous region in Tibet which kept them from making contact with other spoiled beings who perpetuated and established quite abnormal conditions of being-existence. Unfortunately, the real benefits and cosmic hopes from this particular Prophet's teaching were destroyed by a military expedition called the "Anglo-Tibetan" war.

Beelzebub also provides evidence of another, and more dangerous type of war—that *modernity* (Western influence) helped to further diminish the effectiveness of the teachings of both Jesus and Mohammed.

Western technology and the unending inventions of new machines (for increased convenience) insured that Christians' ability to think would not rise above the sphere of their terrestrial planet (materialism and the rising importance of making "cash").

The same Western influence for modernization caused the Mohammedan country of Turkey to start closing up the monasteries of an *esoteric* religious order known as the "Dervishes." According to Beelzebub, Turkish officials began to prohibit the wearing of the fez by males and the wearing of the yashmak by females, in order that their country could more closely imitate everything that was considered cultured and European.

This imitation also included a diminishing of religious morality and patriarchy—especially when its future leaders were always sent to Europe to get the best education money had to offer. (Swedenborg concurred that the European Christian world often manifested the worst decline of objective morality, and as I have already mentioned, participated in more adultery than other religious types.)

Next, Beelzebub's narrative returns to the mountains of Tibet and how the "Anglo-Tibetan" war had closed the doors for earth-humans to benefit from the more arcane and rarefied (deeper) teachings of Saint Lama, who showed what *individuals* must do to free themselves from the negative consequences of the properties of the organ Kundabuffer (Swedenborg's "proprium").

Apparently, a special group of seven individuals in this region had obtained a high level of spiritual growth, and one of them, their leader/teacher, had even succeeded in becoming the guardian of the deepest secret instructions of Saint Lama. Unfortunately, this esteemed leader was killed by a "stray" bullet during one of the skirmishes from the "Anglo-Tibetan" conflicts before his having a chance to share these final secret instructions with the other six.

The remaining six individuals made a desperate attempt to reconnect themselves with their departed leader and continue to communicate through their higher (astral) bodies—which are consciously formed by those who participate in acquiring and fixing spiritual Reasoning and Conscience. These six Tibetan individuals had the proper advanced knowledge to partake in such a sacred process called "Almznoshinoo" (notice that this process has the word "alms" in it). However, the success of such an attempt required their having made the proper preparation before their leader had died. But the sudden and unexpected death of their teacher caught them off guard and no such preparations were made.

(It seems curious to me that Tibet had *seven* individuals who possessed great knowledge, and that this country enjoyed the wisdom of *three* genuine messengers sent from "Above." These three genuine teachers were Saint Krishnatkarna, Saint Buddha and Saint Lama. Come to think of it, the Levant region also had *three* genuine teachers— Moses, Jesus and Mohammed!)

Beelzebub shares with Hassein some basic information concerning how this sacred knowledge of the process for after-death communication was accomplished. Those who have their astral bodies developed to a high degree can infuse their being-Hanbledzoïn (Animal Spirits, middle or "magnetic" blood) into another person. This subtle magnetic-like blood is capable of creating a highly stretchable "thread-like" connection between its originating-source (such as an evolved individual), and wherever else it has been introduced, preserved and fixed (as in another individual). In this way a physical and psychical connection (and communication) can be kept open for a limited time between terrestrial earth-humans and the mind of an individual who has passed on to the next realm. According to Beelzebub, this connection can last for a year, or during one complete orbit of their birth planet.

(You will remember that back in Chapter 32, Beelzebub had used his being-Hanbledzoïn [purer blood] to put people into a hypnotic state. This procedure allowed him to make contact with and influence the psyche of other humans. Swedenborg also agreed that subtle elements, like ethereal and magnetic substances, which go into forming the fluid of our higher "blood," were quite "elastic" and could form a basis of communication or sphere between those who shared similar affections. Humans living in the same spiritual realms share and communicate with each other through similar loves and thoughts. See *True Christian Religion*, n. 365 [4] concerning the notion that sympathies and antipathies attract others according to similitudes.)

But not having made the proper preliminary preparations, the attempts of these six individuals at infusing their being-Hanbledzoïn into their departed leader only caused this subtle magnetic blood to chaotically accumulate all over his dead physical body. Worse, Beelzebub adds that a thunderstorm was raging overhead (the reinforced *blending* of the sacred active element Okidanokh).

Swedenborg tells us that *thunders* and *lightnings* in the Holy Word represent the understanding and illustration of Divine Truth in Heaven coming from the Lord (*Apocalypse Explained*, n. 273).

This circumstance would certainly symbolize a reinforced example (blending) of God's distinct attributes and character.

Unfortunately, these two cosmic processes (improper Almznoshinoo plus thunderstorms) intermingling with each other (Sobrionolian contact) caused a terrible explosion to occur, which vaporized everything (back into the prime-source substance Etherokrilno) within one whole square kilometer of space.

Great knowledge, valuable to all future earth-humans, went up in smoke!

Also, the unfortunate war in Tibet serves as a great example of Jesus' words on the cross when He said, "Forgive them Father, for they know not what they do." The irony is, that the Creator's Divine strategies and steps for saving humankind, throughout history, have always been "checkmated" by the egoistic aims of those needing salvation the most. All the major religions of the planet Earth have been "poisoned" by faulty human prudence, mixed with various envies, jealousies and vanities (even savagery). As a result, all religious doctrines today have become a means for enabling humans (the pseudo-learned) to continue with their "mental perversity." (Swedenborg's doctrine of the New Church is equally susceptible to human perversity, except that the Lord God's *New Jerusalem* will only legitimately descend from Heaven to those individual earth-humans who meet special spiritual requirements.)

Beelzebub ends this sad chapter of his Tales with a surprising revelation concerning the famous ritual of "communion" performed by Jesus Christ. These revelations will even raise the eyebrows of well-read Swedenborgians who are acquainted with the inner meanings of this event called the "Last Supper"! The "sacrament" of the sacred Almznoshinoo (sharing the purer blood) was also carried out between Jesus and His disciples to ensure continued communication of special teachings after the crucifixion. (The sacred ritual of Almznoshinoo has led to the phrase "blood-brothers.")

According to Beelzebub, this sacred ritual was actually performed during the "Last Supper" ceremony. Jesus knew that he would soon be arrested and executed. So He did not have the time to share all His deepest and arcane instructions with the disciples. (Swedenborg confirms that Jesus was teaching His disciples about the hidden levels of meaning in the Old Testament stories and how these deeper meanings were all about the Lord's own temptations and ultimate glorification while in the world of spacetime.) Therefore, the sacrament Almznoshinoo was performed so that that the disciples could maintain contact with their teacher after His crucifixion. (These disciples did in fact see and communicate with Jesus after His bodily death.) Swedenborg also agrees that during the Last Supper event, Jesus was indeed attempting to communicate additional new ideas to His disciples, and this communication was from the principle of divine mercy and compassion (alms to the poor of spirit).

Physical substances were indeed exchanged (bread and wine). Swedenborg states that bread and wine corresponded to the Lord's body and blood, which on a deeper level corresponded to divine "goodness" and "truth." Sharing this understanding (spiritual food and drink) with His disciples necessitated the sharing of his purer blood to create a deeper connection (conjunction) between them (see Swedenborg's *Apocalypse Explained*, pages 214-215) after death. In this ritual, Beelzebub is implying the same idea—that a real, lasting connection was being made between Jesus and His disciples—through real mediary substances.

To understand the symbolic side of this sacred event one had to enter into an elevated, higher (non-ordinary) state of mind (holotropic). This higher state of mind is symbolized in Scripture by the disciples having to find a particular dining room on an "upper" level. Therefore, this *psychical* assent of the human heart and mind was the necessary preparation for the disciples to receive more of the Lord's new teachings. But to keep this special channel of communication open after the crucifixion, Beelzebub suggests that Jesus infused His being-Hanbledzoïn (purer blood) into the bread and wine, which was then shared among the disciples. This infusion of ideas into physical objects can be tricky to explain, unless it is known that ideas are real forms and substances, as well.

Even so, I admit this presents an irksome theological problem for Swedenborgians. Why? The reason is, Swedenborg does not describe the sacrament of the first Holy Communion in quite this same way—or at least, his readers don't come away with a similar take—but he does claim that only the Lord God can *instruct* men and women through a sacred (and secret) symbolic language. This instruction (revelation) requires an intermediate means—through spiritual truth—which, not being written down anywhere, must be provided by an actual exchange of *living substances* from the Lord. (Swedenborg pointed out that God's *Love* and *Truth*—like ideas—are also real substances and forms, representing a higher manifestation of physical flesh and blood.)

Swedenborg certainly suggests that the purpose of the Holy Supper was to form a deeper connection and communication between Jesus with His disciples, by revealing (sharing) new information through a deeper, symbolic language. His new information was his flesh and blood.

We can assume that Jesus needed to maintain this psychical elevation and intimate connection with His disciples—even after His execution and departure from the Earth. Swedenborg states that the Lord was resurrected in a physical manner and that His human nature had been fully united with His Divine heavenly nature. This unified dual nature of Jesus would consist of a perfectly purified quality of his purer bloods. Jesus then reappeared to His disciples to resume teaching. Only His closest disciples experienced Jesus after the crucifixion—but they indeed experienced their "undead" teacher in most perplexing and remarkable ways.

Again, this continued communication between Divine Teacher and disciples occurring between distinct planes of existence necessitates preparation through an ontologically real mediating sphere. I must candidly admit that there might seem to be an apparent disagreement between Swedenborg's and Gurdjieff's notions as to how "physical" the Lord's resurrection really was. Swedenborg claimed that the Lord's resurrection included his physical flesh and bones—thus, there was an empty tomb. Gurdjieff claimed that the Lord reappeared among His disciples through the *materialization* of His astral body (which is composed of finer, but still real, physical stuff and worldly substances). Through Beelzebub, Gurdjieff also stated that the astral body could be materialized to the density that can acquire, for a limited time, some of the functions of the actual physical body! The disciples didn't always recognize Jesus when He first reappeared before them. So their recognition of their teacher went beyond mere physical facial features and must have included their understanding. Something really profound and miraculous was made available to the Lord's closest followers that was not made available to the rest of the general population. (I would also like to mention that the Lord's resurrected body, while being touchable, could do things that ordinary human bodies cannot do—like walk through walls and suddenly appear or disappear.)

What I like about Gurdjieff is that he has successfully forced me to view his unexpected data in a way that produces real "being-pondering" and real "head-scratching." Swedenborg himself would say that we should not accept anything that we could not verify for ourselves, and in our intellect.

My personal study of Gurdjieff over the years has convinced me that he understood well that God's Word (*Theomertmalogos*) was written in a text that contained the unfolding of truth and order from a deeper symbolic language. He warns us that we are not to simply interpret religious ritual or Holy Scripture *literally*. Gurdjieff even understood this symbolic language as containing *correspondences* between the literal words and elevated spiritual interpretations of the sacred biblical text (he described this method of allegorical writing in Holy Scripture as "Similnisirnian"—obviously taken from the word "similitude").

And there is Swedenborg's announcement of a new dispensation (the New Jerusalem) being made available to the modern world. Does Gurdjieff make any similar claim? Yes, I believe he did.

Gurdjieff also knew that a new school (consisting of higher teachings) was being established on Earth. But I cannot honestly say whether he knew that Jesus was actually Jehovah in the flesh, as Swedenborg discovered. In fact, Swedenborg stated that individuals from all religious backgrounds could obtain a heavenly life through their conscience, and for those who could be further instructed by angelic teachers, they would be taught new revelations concerning the Divine Human of the Lord. It seems that Gurdjieff was most interested in reaching the conscience of all serious people, and just emphasizing Jesus (with their current associative thinking) could damage that strategy.

Again, both Swedenborg and Gurdjieff are in complete agreement that Jesus shared, and continues to share, secret knowledge with those who become His disciples, and that the problems with the religions of the world arise from the made-made "spices" that were added to these otherwise legitimate teachings over time by different people for their "titillation."

In this chapter, Gurdjieff is not commenting on which religious doctrine is the most correct, but whether these doctrines prove effective at transforming humans out of their precarious predicament. In Swedenborg's terms, does a practice help them create conscience to spiritually transform and regenerate? Gurdjieff (and Beelzebub) believed that religions have all become forms of *titillation*.

In a nutshell, instead of allowing genuine religion to offer ways for earth-humans to free themselves from the maleficent properties left over from the organ Kundabuffer, human egoism (self-love) has concocted its own new doctrines through the ages that actually strengthen the negative influences of this organ. Again, one of these negative influences is to see the world in a topsy-turvy way—from an inverted order contrary to reality.

The big negative result of this self-delusion is that earth-humans falsely believe and perceive that they themselves are the source of wisdom and goodness (instead of the Divine Creator) and claim righteousness for themselves. Beelzebub states that nothing is ever attempted by such deluded individuals unless it regards self and has self as the ultimate focus and orientation of its energies. This leads to earth-humans wanting to obtain predominance and prestige in spite of God always asking for their humility.

According to Swedenborg, this negative behavior is *spiritual theft*, because all truth and goodness comes from the Creator-God alone, and one has to develop the ability to be receptive, through *humility*, to the sacred influences issuing out from the Sun Absolute (Spiritual Sun). Otherwise, God's influence becomes passive instead of active in our lives. (Genuine humility is a sign that God's influence is active in a person's life.)

God's Word serves as a medium for communication between Heaven and Earth. It not only acts like the *purer* blood shared between Jesus and his disciples, its message can also purify one's own purer blood, and thus improve the connection with—and one's understanding of—heavenly Truth. But if only understood literally, the Bible gives up few of its deeper secrets. (Beelzebub says that an ancient culture called the deeper or allegorical language of Holy Writing "Podobnisirnian.")

I will add here that I believe that Swedenborg's theological writings, which cover the inner truths (and their sacred *series*) contained in Scripture, serve as offering a more approachable medium and intermediary between God and earth-humans on how to approach religion and salvation properly, lawfully and rationally. We can all sup with the Lord God and have a seat at His table. This includes our suffering to learn about the symbolic language of correspondences (inner truths) that Jesus was trying to convey to His closest disciples concerning the Scriptures and the detailed descriptions of human life in the spiritual world.

If one pays attention, they will also see that both Swedenborg and Gurdjieff were communicating the amazing idea that any *whole* series of events issuing from the Creator (and out from the Spiritual Sun) are organic forms (living Truths).

I also know that Swedenborg's theological writings came as a big shock to traditional European religious sensitivities when they were first published. Without new information providing a real *shock* in us, nothing will penetrate deeply enough to break through our worldly masks and reach our inner reality and awaken our God-given remains. This is where the spiritual warfare needed to transform us must take place.

In other words, a genuine religion should not simply offer comfort (self-calming) to a group of people, but must constantly provide "wake-up" shocks to our individual systems and inspire each of us to engage in self-examination and resisting (struggling against) anything negative we find harbored inside us. Swedenborg calls this form of personal suffering "true temptation" or *spiritual combat.* Gurdjieff called it the need to *work on oneself.* Such *intentional* and *conscious suffering* in the individual is what Gurdjieff was always promoting and stressing. This is also why God permits misfortune and sorrow in our lives. No pain, no gain.

As Beelzebub ends this segment of his story, everyone on the inter-solar-system ship *Karnak* begins to sense a special sour-bitterish taste on their tongues from a *magnetic* current released by the Captain, indicating that they were close to their next destination—the holy planet *Purgatory.* Beelzebub promises that when they later arrive at their home planet *Karatas,* he will discuss the mysterious time period of Jesus' life between the ages of twelve and twenty-eight.

If Gurdjieff had this information about Jesus' missing years, it is truly a very special accomplishment. And, if he revealed this "lost" information about Jesus anywhere in the pages of these Tales, it is, at this time, going way over my head. (Swedenborg does suggest that Jesus, while in the world, had to learn like every child and young person does growing up on Earth. That means that Jesus also had to spend time learning this special knowledge from those who still possessed and protected it on the planet Earth. Jesus also had to be inwardly regenerated like we all do—but more completely!)

The only other clue that Gurdjieff has given concerning the Lord's missing years is that he said that Jesus was in a place that had *sacred dancing*. Another clue comes from the fact that the baby Jesus received a visit from three Kings of the *East*. This tells me that Jesus, and His teachings, would have a connection to ancient knowledge and conscience (such as the Church of Noah had), which included an understanding of *inner truths in series*, and was symbolized by a "rainbow."

SUMMARY

■ All legitimate religious doctrine is based on the removal of improper human behavior and egoism in the *individual*.

■ Human egoism has muddied-up all the Creator's religious tenets, actually turning God's original laws toward promoting various selfish and worldly goals.

■ Beelzebub gives examples of how human artificiality has crept into all the world's major religions.

■ Earth-humans have a terribly flawed concept of "Good" and "Evil."

■ Today's religions are "dead." That is, they have muddied-up all of God's genuine teachings and no longer receive the heavenly influences of the Spiritual Sun (Sun Absolute). Everyone wants to obtain predominance and prestige—even if it means fighting, killing or starting wars to obtain it.

■ Because of all the above, most earth-humans can no longer directly go to Heaven after their physical death, but to a spiritual realm of further preparation. Beelzebub calls this ontological plane for further preparation the *Holy Planet Purgatory*, while Swedenborg refers to this preparatory realm simply as the Spiritual World, which exists directly "below" Heaven.

■ The "New Jerusalem" is a state of the human heart and mind that embraces the Lord God's true plan for the universe, which Gurdjieff and Swedenborg were tirelessly promoting.

■ According to Beelzebub, the relatively small country of Tibet was influenced by three genuine messengers sent from "Above"— Saint Krishnatkharna, Saint Buddha and Saint Lama! It is no wonder why Tibet's government became a theocracy and is still considered

SUMMARY

a highly spiritual place on Earth. But more important, certain special Tibetans had received the secret instructions for continuing communication (through the middle blood of the Astral body) with a teacher who had passed into the other world.

▪ Beelzebub claims that a similar ritual took place during Jesus' Last Supper among His disciples. (This ritual also led to the phrase "blood brothers.")

▪ A materialized *Astral Body* can reach a density where it can perform some of the functions of the physical body (like eating or even feeling solid). The resurrected Jesus could eat fish and be touched, yet He walked through walls!

▪ Beelzebub calls the allegorical style of Holy Scripture "Podobnisirnian" and also "Similnisirnian" (Swedenborg's *correspondences*).

CHAPTER 39

"The Holy Planet 'Purgatory'"

Chapter 39 is an intellectual whopper! It addresses how God created the manifest universe and physical spacetime through "truths in series." (Even the best Swedenborgian scholars can learn new things here.)

According to John Bennett (author of *Talks On Beelzebub's Tales*), Gurdjieff himself regarded this chapter as the central topic of his epic Tales. Here, he unifies universal scientific laws with God's ultimate purpose for creation, evolution and humankind's salvation, by illustrating *truths in series* (the power of truth advancing) coming directly from God's providential actions in a pre-spatial and pre-temporal realm. However, these laws represent an objective (or theistic) science, which is not yet known or recognized by the authorized terrestrial scientific community—especially by those who embrace a purely materialistic paradigm of reality (scientism). The knowledge contained in this chapter represents *supra*terrestrial (angelic) wisdom—straight from the Creator.

(In his own work, *Principia, Part III*, Chapter I, Swedenborg states that, "all dissimilarity implies imperfection." Thus, everything in the universe follows the same rules. Again, modern science does not know this—even though they will admit that the entire universe is somehow *unified*.)

Although the Roman Catholic Church invented the word "Purgatory," I believe that Gurdjieff is using the concept of the Holy Planet Purgatory to represent an ontological, lower plane of the non-material Spiritual World, where according to Swedenborg, the spiritual bodies of all humans (after their physical death) first go in order to learn God's universal and spiritual truths and be inwardly prepared (purified) for their final eternal abodes.

This chapter communicates sacred universal laws—most of them unheard of—to challenge and prepare us in a similar fashion for a heavenly life, while we are still on the planet Earth (as Swedenborg's books do). These special laws, or *truths in series*, follow the organic, living patterning principles and structures of the human anatomy (which Swedenborg called the "Grand Human"). All things in the created universe strive toward the human form—which is God's likeness.

Why do these laws follow organic (living) principles? Swedenborg states that "life comes from life." Gurdjieff made a similar statement that "Consciousness came from consciousness." In other words, both men believed that living intelligence came from a Divine Creator, and not from various combinations of dead matter.

So only by understanding these great unifying laws can an individual gain the true sense of how to properly strive (spiritual duty) to exist in a manner that corresponds with the Lord God's purposeful plan.

When Beelzebub returns to his Tales in this final chapter of Part 2, we find out that he and his ship and crew have already visited and left the Holy Planet Purgatory—which as I already indicated, represents a spiritual plane for learning and for further purification. (Nothing is mentioned about his visit to the planet *Deskaldino* to meet his first teacher.)

His grandson, Hassein, was struck by how often God Himself makes personal visits to this "planet." Hassein asks his grandfather why this is so. (Swedenborg states in his spiritual writings that angelic support is given to those suffering to be regenerated in the world of spirits and that the Lord even makes Himself visible at times, as an angel, to those still suffering and still going through the process of inner cleansing—which causes temporary, but great suffering. This appearance is actually God's mercy, and why God is often referred to as an angel, in a visible and evolved human form, in the narratives of Holy Scripture.)

Beelzebub replies to Hassein that the Holy Planet Purgatory serves as the heart and focus of concentration for all the results and functions created in the pulsating universe. In other words, this ontological plane of existence is a major *center of gravity* for a universe in process and its "directionality of complexity" (reverse entropy or evolution).

It is almost as if Beelzebub tried to sneak this last statement in while no one was looking. I myself missed this idea in many of my earlier readings. Now this topic of complexity (and its directionality) is dear to my heart, for it embraces the increased bio-organization of evolving spiritual bodies. Stated theologically, the *directionality of complexities* represents the focus of God's evolutionary plan, and particularly of the souls (inner bio-complexities) of men and women who have left their gross terrestrial bodies and have moved on to a higher realm of existence.

Swedenborg expressed a similar idea of the *directionality of complexity* by stating that all nature was a striving toward the human form, which is in the spiritual image and likeness of God. Using other terms, this high-level complexity represents the ecosystem of the spiritual world, where souls (higher-being-bodies) and their worldviews are further prepared for a heavenly life (or for Hell).

Many human souls being prepared for Heaven on this lower, spiritual eco-plane can experience harsh sufferings (vastation) during the purifying process of obtaining an angelic bio-structure. This suffering depends on how "off" their beliefs are and how much they are willing to adjust. So, from Divine mercy, God visits these still-suffering souls to alleviate their anguish and anxiety while they are enduring this often internally painful purging process.

(Swedenborg assures us that this purifying pain is not simply physical—it is the *agony of conscience*.)

As the directionality of people's inner complexity crystalizes and fixes its form (from the results or ends of their deepest thoughts and feelings) they gravitate to a similar (corresponding) spiritual environment—either an environment that promotes self-centeredness or one consisting of mutual support and profound genuine friendship.

Beelzebub informs his grandson that originally, human souls did not have to go through this "purging" process. Rather, earth-humans originally possessed the inner complexity to go straight to the blessed sphere of the Most Most Holy Sun Absolute (heavenly plane of the Spiritual Sun). Swedenborg describes these early humans as beings of a *celestial genus* whose inner complexity was such that they could communicate directly with angels and gain great insights and first-hand knowledge concerning reality. But after the "Choot-God-litanical period" (Gurdjieff's Fall of Man) the unimpeded reunion with the living source of the universe became impossible because humans picked up too many disharmonious ideas and passions.

The "Choot-God-litanical period" describes a terrible period in creation where God's cosmic plan to create a *Heaven from the human race* was almost completely foiled.

Beelzebub goes on to describe the unique beauty of this spiritual planet Purgatory, but also describes the human souls there as living in various *caves* structured from all kinds of "interior forms." *Interior forms* is code for these caves as consisting of psycho-spiritual realities. (Swedenborg also put forth the concept that the outer environment of the spiritual world perfectly reflects the inner qualities of a person's heart and mind!) Similarly, Beelzebub also maintains that these cave-forms are representative of the *inner qualities* of the various souls there. Swedenborg also claimed that "caves" symbolically represent *mental obscurity* in the human understanding toward some universal or spiritual truth and needs to be educated.

A further, and very imaginative clue that the Holy Planet Purgatory can reflect the inner *psychical* qualities of the souls living there is that its atmosphere contains what Beelzebub calls "Egolionopties" or "omnipresent-platforms" which can quickly move in all directions (a motion apparently not hindered by physical constraints). These rarefied atmospheres represent the combined spheres generated by the activities of the hearts and minds of those there (which, I imagine, is why the strange word *Egolionopties* has the word "ego" in it).

At this point in his Tales, Beelzebub feels that he can offer the best answer to his grandson's question about the frequent visits God makes to this plane of existence by first describing the process of the creation of the world and the sacred laws that now maintain and sustain the entire universe. Such knowledge is indispensable for anyone who sincerely strives "to exist in that direction which corresponds just to the aim and sense of existence," that is, in the *coating* and organizing of one's higher-being body, or organic vessel for the soul—a body capable of resonating with the emanations of the Spiritual Sun (harmonizing and conjoining one's inner life with the Lord God's Divine Love and Wisdom).

As a Swedenborgian, I like Gurdjieff's approach to God's universal scheme because he offers new details and a more visceral way to discuss and experience similar knowledge. (For instance, Swedenborgians—because they focus on group worship—have too few discussions about the orderly formation of the spiritual body in individuals through regeneration and the functions that the three discrete human "bloods" play during the process of our spiritual re-birth.)

Nor do Swedenborgians adequately grasp the dynamical difference between God's triune law (three-ness) and His sacred Law of Sevenfoldness, acknowledging only that both laws somehow symbolize a state of fullness. The Law of Sevenfoldness, as we will soon see, more accurately (even mathematically) depicts the genuine and sacred steps of the unfolding of a completed physical, mental or spiritual process (truth in series producing cyclic orbs).

Now hold on to your hats, folks!

Beelzebub shares with his grandson not only why God decided to create the physical world in the first place (to become more relevant) but *how*. I find this lawful explanation quite amazing!

Originally, God and the Most Great and Most Most Holy Sun Absolute (Spiritual Sun) existed alone—except for the presence of the prime-source cosmic substance "Etherokrilno." A Swedenborgian can easily understand the idea of the Holy Sun Absolute as being the Spiritual Sun and serving as God's sacred abode. The prime-source cosmic substance "Etherokrilno" is more difficult, but I believe that it is also quite translatable into Swedenborg's terms. Rationally, my current understanding of this prime cosmic substance is that it represents "possibility space" like the Buddhist term sunyata meaning "pregnant void" or "swollen with possibility" (*Buddha of the North*, pg. 104).

Theologically speaking, this prime substance is the *internal state* of Divine Love in a state of perpetual effort and pure endeavor—that is, in an untargeted or potential state! (Swedenborg also describes this pure effort as a "motion in the Infinite" or first "Ens" that existed before the physical universe and its spacetime arena.)

Well, God became aware of the fact that under these original circumstances His sacred abode or Spiritual Sun, which encompassed His holy activity (along with His *cherubim* and *seraphim*—symbolizing guards or protectors of Divine Providence), would ever-so-gradually, diminish in "size." (That Beelzebub mentions *cherubim* and *seraphim* tells me that Gurdjieff is in possession of deep theological secrets.)

Since there is as yet no formal time, space or matter, this notion of any shrinkage of size becomes a real head-scratcher and seemingly makes no logical sense! But psycho-spiritually speaking (which we need to do to elevate our thoughts to higher and abstracted ideas), it makes a whole lot of sense. I believe that God, while infinitely good and wise, was faced with *irrelevancy*—God's Divine Love and Wisdom (providence proceeding) through His orderly laws went *nowhere*. And just as important, this loving action was not being reciprocated by any outside subjects or objects (reciprocation perfects love). This situation would certainly diminish God's sacred importance and influence that was flowing out of this special Sun and its Divine sphere.

So it didn't matter whether God was full of resplendent Love and Wisdom or not! God had no kingdom to rule. So Beelzebub suggests to Hassein that the reason for the creation of the universe was that a *higher intention* and relevancy could be realized through the emergence of a created physical reality that God could Love and which could serve God's intentions by *reacting* to (being recipients of) His Divine influences.

This "higher intention" is symbolically represented by the Creator's *cherubim* and *seraphim*—theological terms which Swedenborg states are symbolic code for representing the guards and protectors of the proper unfolding and sacred order of God's Divine Providence or ultimate plan (which is, creating a heavenly kingdom from the human race). These guards also ensure that all spacetime processes (series) correspond to heavenly processes (*Apocalypse Explained*, n. 277a [3]) and that all the laws of salvation are preserved. So again, I believe that Gurdjieff is using these two terms of *cherubim* and *seraphim* with Swedenborgian precision, since they would represent qualities that could indeed exist before the act of creation!

Swedenborg also suggests a similar problem of Divine irrelevancy before the actual creation of the finite universe. Simply put, God's Infinite Love needed a subject and object (outside of Himself) to love and focus on. Swedenborg pointed out in his book *Divine Love and Wisdom* (n. 47) that self-love is contrary to Divine Love, so it was necessary for God to create an external (outside) focus for His Love, including the eventual appearance of an intelligent creature (like humans) with the cognitive powers to recognize God's heavenly Love and choose to *reciprocate* that Love. Swedenborg claimed that such reciprocation between creation and God was needed for Love to find its perfection in the fullness of time, become relevant and create unity.

This important need produces a divine anxiety, which Genesis (Chapter 1, verse 2), portrays as God "brooding."

So God next takes action to ensure that His Spiritual abode will not become ultimately irrelevant (and diminish in importance). God had to create something to Love that was outside of Himself. This meant that God had to change the way He was doing things. (One of the big questions that often arises in a theistic viewpoint is "what did God do before the creation event?" Surely God was not inactive. We get a great answer to that question in this wonderful chapter of *Beelzebub's Tales.*)

Both Gurdjieff and Swedenborg state that the creation of the physical universe proceeded from a sacred and Spiritual Sun. Swedenborg even claimed that no proper view of creation could be entertained by either scientists or theologians without seeing all process in the universe as emerging from this sacred source of spiritual *light* and *heat*. But since this "sun" encompassed God's activity throughout eternity, what did God change in order to create the finite universe, which had a finite beginning in time and space? What kept God and the Spiritual Sun, which was equally eternal, from creating a physical world?

Something had to change in God's activity to create physical spacetime.

Swedenborg doesn't seem to offer a direct answer to this important creation question of God's needing to make a change in the principles of how divine laws function, in order to create a limited and *external* universe in his angelic book, *Divine Love and Wisdom*, which touches on the topic of creation.

But Gurdjieff does—in this chapter of *Beelzebub's Tales*!

Beelzebub explains that before the creation event, God's sacred activity indeed proceeded through His two fundamental laws—the *Law of Threefoldness* (triads) and the *Law of Sevenfoldness* (octaves)—but under an original system called "Autoegocrat." This meant that these laws were perfectly maintained by God's direct influx from *within*. As we will see shortly, this inner system of perfect activity cannot create an *external* world of processes or a spacetime arena for God to be able to both Love something outside of Himself, and remain relevant. The Creator God needed forces to come from both within (immediately) and from without (intermediately) for such a purpose.

(Swedenborg actually understood the external change involved or he wouldn't have been able to write the chapter, "Organic Forms Generally," in his great anatomical work, *The Animal Kingdom*. I therefore believe that this extra dynamic will represent a future revelation and insight for those of us on Earth—which Gurdjieff, through *Beelzebub's Tales*, was fully prepared to disclose.)

Those who study Swedenborg will recognize the Law of Threefoldness as end, cause and effect, which are derivatives of God's *threefold* character (Holy Trinity) and sacred functionings. As mentioned in an earlier chapter, Beelzebub describes this Divine Law of Threefoldness as the sacred *Triamazikamno*. The Law of Sevenfoldness is called the sacred *Heptaparaparshinokh* and is much harder to grasp.

The Law of Sevenfoldness is more obscure to Swedenborg's students but Swedenborg indeed addresses it as "Truths in series," that is, the *Holy* (*sacred*) trajectory of all coherent process organized into periodic or cyclic series of successive order (intermediary steps of stability or gravity centers) by which all phenomena, on all scales, find common equilibrium (simultaneity) and harmony (wholeness). For now, I will only say that this cosmic law of repeating cycles can be applied to Swedenborg's *Doctrine of Series* and his *Circle of Life* (which I explored in my earlier book, *Proving God*).

Gurdjieff describes the Law of Sevenfoldness as "the-line-of-the-flow-of-forces-constantly-deflecting-according–to-law-and-uniting-again-at-its-ends." (This is similar to Swedenborg's karmic notion that all process returns to its first principles—in the form of circles, gyres and orbs, which he called "the gyre of nature.") Each deflection (step) along this sacred and universal trajectory represents a distinct "center-of-gravity" and the intervals or "distance" between these gravity-centered steps of stability (and constancy) are called by Beelzebub, "Stopinders." (In his book *The Fibre*, n. 65, Swedenborg called each of these centers of gravity their *punctum immobile* and I believe he also mentions "centers of gravity" in his great theological work *Divine Providence*.)

Gurdjieff states that according to objective (cosmic) science, all coherent and holistic process (natural or spiritual) always passes through seven Stopinders (and gravity centers) in order to reach its harmonic (corresponding) completion or *common equilibrium*. This means that the universe, its laws, and inner consistencies are even more mathematically precise than contemporary scientists would ever dare to imagine. (Swedenborg was in full agreement that all of nature obeys the same rules—otherwise there would be no correspondence, harmony or unity in the universe.)

The second sacred and fundamental cosmic law of Triamazikamno is formulated as: "the higher blends with the lower in order to actualize the middle and thus becomes either higher for the proceeding lower, or lower for the proceeding higher." Gurdjieff calls this *threefold* process of end (active force), cause (passive force) and the effect (reconciling or equilibrating force) of their conjunction (producing either an evolutionary or involutionary direction), the "Harnel-miatznel." Swedenborg describes this same universal threefold process in his work *Divine Love and Wisdom* (n. 172), stating:

> *"That these three, end, cause, and effect, are in each and everything created, can also be seen from this, that all effects, which are called last ends, become anew first ends in uninterrupted succession from the*

First, who is the Lord the Creator, even to the last end, which is the conjunction of man with Him."

This divinely planned intimate conjunction with the human race is why the Lord God mercifully appears to those still-suffering being-spirits dwelling on the Holy Planet Purgatory—to help them overcome the painful challenges of purification and assisting the further evolution of their inner bio-complexity to create a more perfected human/angelic form.

So not only did God create a physical universe by modifying the functioning of His two universal laws, these two sacred laws of "World-creation" and "World-maintenance" were providentially changed to allow for the increase of spiritual complexity—in a way that creation could also serve to bring God and evolving humans closer together by forming the ultimate inner (non-physical) conjunction between Creator and the created. This conjunction preserved the relevancy of the Spiritual Sun and would create a heavenly realm.

This indeed, is theistic science. Gurdjieff (as well as Swedenborg) more than hints that the Sacred-Triamazikamno consists of three independent (and holy) forces, because they mirror God's threefold character. That is, these three forces are holy because they correspond to the Trinitarian doctrine of *God the Father, God the Son,* and *God the Holy Spirit* (which are three unifying functions of One God, not three Gods or Persons).

This triune dynamic is what causes all future created elements to potentially divide and re-blend by the process of *Djartklom* (separation of being-forces).

According to Beelzebub, before the negative properties of the dreaded organ Kundabuffer had been fully crystallized and fixed within the psyche of earth-humans (Swedenborg's Celestial race) they had a proper theological (and scientific) understanding of these three independent and holy functions. (According to Swedenborg, these holy terms became totally confused by the theological wiseacrings and even political decisions concerning Trinitarian doctrine made during the Council of Nicea in 325 A.D.)

Now we can return to God's ongoing activities and the holy mechanism (and change) behind the act of creation as described by Beelzebub.

Before the creation of the manifest universe (Megalocosmos) God's Spiritual Sun (Divine emanations) was maintained solely by God's internal activity through these two sacred laws of *Heptaparaparshinokh* and *Triamazikamno.* This internal system was called "Autoegocrat." But in order for the Spiritual Sun—the sacred place of God's holy residence—to not diminish in importance and relevancy (spiritual size), our ALMIGHTY ENDLESSNESS devised a plan to modify these two sacred laws so that they would also become dependent on *forces coming from the outside.*

Wow!

This shift made in the functioning of these two sacred laws for the guaranteed maintenance of the Sun Absolute then began to be called "Trogoautoegocratic" (which John Bennett translates as, "I hold myself together by feeding"). In other words, the universe came into being when creation and existence became tied to building relationships and mutual support through a "common-cosmic-exchange-of-substances." With this new dynamic of sharing (eating), the entire universe would have to take part in its own creation and maintenance through cooperation and the sharing of everything with everything else, including ultimate reciprocation with the Creator God (this exchange between outside influences is an analog of the dynamics of Love, which unifies through mutual sharing).

The original condition in which the Spiritual Sun existed before spacetime was created was a one-way ticket, where God's influx was not outwardly targeted and therefore represented only potential qualities. But the creation of the physical universe was based on a new *two-way* system of cooperation. This two-way system, with every created thing providing *external* help to everything else, was how God now planned to ensure the eternal relevancy and importance of the sole place of His most glorious existence.

Again, I find Swedenborg's apparent omission to be curiously amusing—that there was a modification in Divine Law, making it necessary for forces "from the outside" to take part in sustaining all process—because, as I have already addressed, he certainly mentions this dynamic in his wonderful scientific work, *The Animal Kingdom* (Vol. II, chap. "Organic Forms Generally"). While commenting on *the progressive series of causes* he even states, "*Every* object, *or* all the material out of which and by means of which [the effect is produced], comes from without ..."* (n. 547). Furthermore, in his *Worship and Love of God* (n. 96), Swedenborg acknowledged that ordered (circular) process has to be fed to maintain the connection [of Stopinders] between successive operations to maintain its series (this creates the simultaneous order found in all systems). In the same book he also expressed that "subsistence is perpetual existence and conservation is perpetual creation." Subsistence is another word for eating, which holds everything together.

So, exactly how did God modify His two sacred laws to obtain this result of universal subsistence and cosmic sharing in the act of creation?

According to Beelzebub, the biggest modification to allow for this mutual sharing of all whole processes to proceed to their ends was made to the sacred *Heptaparaparshinokh*, or Law of Sevenfoldness. God, from Divine Will, lengthened the Stopinder (interval) between its third and fourth deflection (centers of gravity). This "lengthened" interval in the periodic cycle of the Law of Sevenfoldness was called the "mechano-coinciding Mdnel-In." This interval represented a discontinuity of process, in the form of an aperture (a "way in") where outside influences could enter into the process as a kind of supporting "food."

God also "shortened" the Stopinder or interval between the last deflection in the process and the beginning of a new cycle of the Law of Sevenfoldness. The Creator predetermined that through shortening this particular deflection, external influences would be determined by the actions occurring in some particular big cosmic concentration (like the Earth's astronomical sun or God's Spiritual Sun) during the process of completing its trajectory.

The reason for this second modification to the Law of Sevenfoldness is that any larger active external influence—issuing out from some great cosmic concentration—can lawfully intervene and become a directing force to the manifestations and qualities of the processes of some coherent series and keep it going. In the case of the Spiritual Sun, it can act as an *intelligent* guiding force for bringing on the required principles for new possibilities (evolution) and higher complexity to occur (like in humans).

This interval, allowing for an outer active influence to come in and take part in the completing process of the Law of Sevenfoldness (operating in some whole phenomena), was called the "intentionally-actualized Mdnel-In." This modification, at this interval, made it possible for a *directing influence* (active principle) and even consciousness (from the Spiritual Sun) to enter into a process, great or small.

And finally, a third modification to the Law of Sevenfoldness occurred at its fifth deflection or middle Stopinder. This middle interval (the Holy Ghost of the new system) was then called the "Harnel-Aoot." This deflection (Stopinder) is very important because it normally displayed a *disharmony* (chaotic nature), according to the flow of the entire completing process and cycle of the law of Heptaparaparshinokh. This disharmony arises from the natural asymmetry of the two other (active and passive) influences now coming into the system from the outside. This special chaotic condition allowed for change to take place in the "heart" of the organic process. (God planned for conscience to act as this third [reconciling] principle in the human species.)

These three new features in the Law of Sevenfoldness, divinely modified by the Creator, now brought both potential *hazard*, or *good fortune*, into any whole process by allowing this fifth deflection and middle interval to act like a cosmic "loose cannon" (which could not happen with the *ideal causality* of the original one-sided *Autoegocratic* system that was originally maintaining God's Spiritual Sun—whereby everything was automatically predictable, perfect and indistinct—but going nowhere).

This final modification of the middle interval is why "s – – t happens" in the universe and things can go wrong. But this "chaotic" function is also necessary for human free will to develop, and allow earth-humans to make their own conscious choices in spiritual matters and values—whether right or wrong.

Beelzebub explains that three possible results can occur because of this new open and free-swinging condition in all organized and complete cosmic processes. (That is, three results can happen at the chaotic "Harnel-Aoot.") If the process of Sevenfoldness is completed in a cosmic unit or organization where it is affected by many "extraneously-caused-vibrations," then only external results will be generated (for instance, if you saw an axe coming toward your head, you would duck).

If there are no extraneous influences during this completing process, only *internal* results will occur (like when we are alone, thinking or dreaming at night).

But, if neither of these two conditions were present during the completing process (that is, through all the deflections of the Law of Sevenfoldness), then the results of the action of its process will *split* between the *external* and the *internal*.

The change made to the sacred and fundamental Law of Tria-mazikamno was that at various points along the way, in order to manifest according to its third (harmonizing) force, it also had to rely on outside influences coming in at precise mathematical points to sustain its three-ness.

These modifications to God's sacred laws then began to take place in the process of actualization of all things in the created world. As mentioned earlier, the physical world could only emerge from a new external need by everything for mutual support. Existence was now relationship. And the greatest relationship would be that of the future human race with the Lord God.

Gurdjieff's Beelzebub is adamant that not only is knowing about these two fundamental laws necessary for humans, but only with a proper understanding of these new Divine changes within those cosmic laws of world creation and maintenance can three-brained beings (humans) ever become capable of pondering the true sense of their existence—because earth-humans had to apply these same changes in a responsible manner to their own lives. Only in this way can individuals acquire the necessary data (scientificum) for becoming aware of their genuine and objective place (and duty) in the universal scheme of God's providential plan.

Beelzebub calls this awareness "Semooniranoos," which he states can be roughly translated as "impartiality." (This holistic and objective view of reality reverses the flawed and topsy-turvy judgment engendered by the organ Kundabuffer, or as Swedenborg would call it, the human *proprium* of selfhood, which is delusional. See *Divine Providence*, n. 321 [8] (e).

Beelzebub again asserts that it was from these cosmic changes in the functioning of the two fundamental and primordial sacred laws that our "COMMON FATHER CREATOR ALMIGHTY" began to direct the action of His forces (Divine Love and Truth) from within the Spiritual Sun in an outward manner that was called the "Emanation-of-the-Sun-Absolute" also called the "Theomertmalogos" or "Word-God." Swedenborg describes the Word of God emanating from the Spiritual Sun as the *Divine Proceeding* (Love and Truth advancing).

So both Swedenborg and Gurdjieff are in complete agreement that the creation of the universe had a theological beginning (as opposed to the current irrational theory in scientism that the world was somehow created from absolutely nothing (*ex nihilo*).

Love is a substance!

Beelzebub now begins to explain to his grandson more details about the successive steps by which the creation of physical universe proceeded from the modifications made by God of the two primordial sacred laws—changing from the "Autoegocratic" to the "Trogoautoegorcratic" system (which allowed for the *reciprocal creation and maintenance* of the universe). To again remind the reader, Swedenborg called this same system of mutual support and sharing in the universe "perpetual existence and subsistence" and noted that "creation is perpetual subsistence." And he did so in both his scientific (*Worship and Love of God*, n. 57 [5]) and theological publishings (*Divine Love and Wisdom*, n. 152 and *The True Christian Religion*, n. 46).

Next, Beelzebub explains to his grandson that due to the change in the sacred law of Heptaparaparshinokh at its *fifth* (middle) interval, the harmonizing emanations of the Spiritual Sun (Divine Proceeding) began to act at specific points in possibility space (Etherokrilno—or prime source cosmic substance—now gained pure points of action from the Infinite). The total (pure) action of the Spiritual Sun now became focused in a way that created real targeted points of pure activity in possibility space (Love's creative soil).

So the new changes in both sacred laws allowed God's profound sacred action to be constrained and concentrated by acquiring its first limit and *boundary*. The Infinite became "finitized" at these "points," meaning that the physical universe and geometry had the exact same origin and beginnings. (In theological jargon, this dynamic is referred to as kenosis or the *self-limiting of Divine action*.)

These points of activity in the *Etherokrilno* represented pure motion or infinite endeavor and were directed by God to begin to occupy space and determine moments (which I also describe in greater detail in my book *Proving God*). Later, these points, from their outer motions, began forming new aggregations and concentrations (Beelzebub calls this the "aggregations of the homogeneous"). These aggregations eventually grew and grew and evolved into a whole new order of suns and stars, which were physical analogs (likenesses and images) of their parent—God's Spiritual Sun—and began to radiate (outward) their own (now physical) energy.

As these new cosmic formations were created and built up, the Laws of Sevenfoldness and Threefoldness could begin to operate together on different new levels and distinct scales. For instance, any one of these second order suns (physical stars) now represented the *active* holy force in the sacred law of Triamazikamno, while all the neighboring suns of its cluster (galaxy) served to act as the constraining or *passive* force of this law. And the emanations of the Spiritual Sun (the Divine Proceeding) served as the third (*neutralizing*) and unifying holy force in this process. (This triune dynamic kept the process of creation in sync and always corresponding with God's character and conscious design.)

From these new scales of activity in both cosmic laws, new crystallizations were again generated from each of the star's own prime-source Etherokrilno, and these crystallizations grouped together around each physical sun, forming the planets (third order suns). According to Beelzebub, the creation of planets represented the first "full cycle" of the fundamental and cosmic Law of Sevenfoldness (Heptaparaparshinokh).

Now even smaller scales of this whole completing process were needed to create increased complexity and receptivity for God's *living* and *conscious* influences (influx) to ensure that His Spiritual Sun is forever relevant. The human race evolved for serving this Divine trajectory and anticipation.

At the formation of planets, the original momentum of this first completed outer cycle had lost half the force of its vivification, and because of the change in its fifth deflection (called the Harnel-Aoot), the process now continued with half of its action manifesting *outside of itself* and the other half *within itself* for its own functioning. This splitting action resulted in the creation of "similarities-to-the-already-arisen" to form over the surface of these planets—new corresponding units representing smaller scales of previous creations. This process led to the emergence of life forms.

Swedenborg concurred that new creations (novitiate orbs) imitated and were effigies of previous creations—corresponding to their "parents" or form of their prior *genetrix* (*Worship And Love Of God*, p. 32, footnote 1). Beelzebub then states that afterward, everything created and existing in the universe became established according to the second particularity of fifth deflection in the Law of Sevenfoldness at the Harnel-Aoot. As mentioned earlier, this second particularity of the Harnel-Aoot always creates internal results (increased inner complexity) beginning an *evolutionary* trajectory back to God from its completed outer cycle by creating more intricate complexities. This is why the universe is occupied in a ceaseless drive toward greater organization and complexity. Therefore, *inner* trajectories began to become more predominant in the way all created things—on all scales—went through their various stages of transformation and change—in a universe ruled by a new kind of dynamic process and sharing. These transformations produced both "involutionary" and "evolutionary" trajectories (away from, or toward God—through increased vivification or increased entropy).

Next, these "similarities-to-the-already-arisen" or new independent formations on the surface of the planet, grouped themselves together—again and again—according to the "aggregation of the homogeneous." (Swedenborg claimed that this aptitude in nature originated from the dynamics of God's Love to unify through relationship according to spiritual correspondence.) From the evolution and involution of these new formations on the Earth's surface, which underwent crystallization and de-crystallization, all kinds of additional active elements were eventually created.

All these concrete (formal) results stemming from "evolution" and "involution" through the new *Trogoautoegocratic* principle of existence—which held everything together as a whole by reciprocal feeding (cosmic sharing) and the maintaining of each other's existence—produced the common-cosmic process "Iraniranumange," that is, the ongoing necessity for the "common-cosmic-exchange-of-substances" (cosmic food) everywhere among all existing things in the universe.

(Again, this mutual sharing and feeding is a physical analog of God's Divine Love and Wisdom—to unify and conjoin everything through mutual support). This dynamic support of sharing allows God to enter into a profound relationship with the created world through *similitude* (correspondence) with His character and bolster His relevancy and the relevancy of His Love and Wisdom—emanating from the Spiritual Sun (the Word) into a growing and increasingly receptive universe.)

Beelzebub underscores this idea by telling Hassein that thanks to this new system of reciprocal feeding (mutual cooperation and sharing) of everything existing in the created universe in which the Spiritual Sun Itself participated, an *equilibrium* was established by which the ALMIGHTY UNI-BEING ENDLESSNESS no longer had to be anxious over the future relevance of His eternal place of dwelling—the Most Most Holy Sun Absolute.

The eventual emergence of human beings onto the scene would play a key role and duty in perfecting this Divine cosmic scheme of equilibrium and keeping the Spiritual Sun (God's Love and Wisdom proceeding in series) eternally relevant, because humans, throughout the universe, had the psychic potential (inner complexity) to receive its sacred influence and be affected by it. Thanks to Swedenborg, we've learned that Verse 2 of Genesis concerning the Seven Day Creation Story (Heptaparaparshinokh), that the phrase *"and the Spirit of God was brooding upon the faces of the waters"* alludes to God's original anxiety over His grand scheme and the important part that humankind would ultimately play in it—creatures with free will (and who determined their own "Harnel-Aoot" in proper ways).

Beelzebub states that after this Divine actualization of modifying the two sacred laws was accomplished, the triumphant *cherubim* and *seraphim* (the guards of God's providence which protect His sacred and Divine Truths of Love from any human nonsense) named the various orders (cosmoses of different scales), distinguishing and designating the different qualities of these distinct and independent worlds, relative to Divine order. (Swedenborg stated that "names" symbolize qualities).

The Spiritual Sun was named the "Protocosmos." The emanation (not radiation) and divine influence from this first (primary) cosmos was called the "Theomertmalogos" or "Word-of-God." Heaven is part of this Protocosmos system.

Each astronomical star or "Second-order-sun" was named the "Defterocosmos." The radiation (no longer called "emanation") of each separate star was called "Mentekithzoïn."

The planets or third-order-suns were called "Tritocosmos." Each planet of this world radiated "Dynamoumzoïn."

The radiation given off from the microcosmoses (living microrganisms) was called "Photoinzoïn." (Although some ancient and esoteric traditions call a human a microcosmos, in reality, the human race was also designed to become micro-heavens, absorbing the *emanations* of the Protocosmos and its Spiritual Sun.)

The radiations issuing from the "Tetartocosmoses" (higher order or complex living organisms in the animal kingdom, which includes warm-blooded mammals and the human race) was called "Hanbledzoïn." This radiation comes from a subtle blood called the "Animal Spirits" and has a magnetic component. (Interestingly, Swedenborg had called animals "living magnets" in his scientific works.)

The radiations from all the planets taken together from any one solar system, was called "Astroluolucizoïn."

The general radiations of all the stars in the universe, was called "Polorotheoparl."

And all these cosmic influences taken together were called the "common-cosmic Ansanbaluiazar." (These distinctions, made by the guardians of God's Divine order, offer us a whole new way to appreciate the entire multi-dimensional universe.)

Beelzebub also gives an objective scientific definition of what he called the "common-cosmic Ansanbaluiazar" participating in all things of the new universe as: "Everything issuing from everything and again entering into everything." (Swedenborg understood this karmic principle as *everything returning to, and finding equilibrium in, their first principles.* This universal cosmic law of consistency turned all process into coherent and mutually supporting cycles or orbs, which he called the *Circle of Life*. Swedenborg's Circle of Life is mentioned in both his scientific and theological writings and it refers to the universal steps and Divine order in all things of dynamical and periodic process.)

Furthermore, Beelzebub tells his grandson that names were also given to the various "centers-of-gravity" (steps), which all substances within these independent cosmoses were transformed into during the processes of involution and evolution preceeding in them. (FYI: these centers-of-gravity and nodes of stability correspond to the biblical rungs of "Jacob's Ladder," from which God's angels and Divine process make an orderly descent [involve] and ascent [evolve] in all coherent and completed processes.)

Beelzebub shares with his grandson the names given to the particular substances that are transformed through the seven gravity-centers of *Tetartocosmoses* or higher order animals and mammals (including humans). They are classified as:

1) Protoëhary (chyme)
2) Defteroëhary (chyle)
3) Tritoëhary (oxygenated or arterial blood)
4) Tetartoëhary (ideas)
5) Piandjoëhary (perpetual will or endeavor)
6) Exioëhary (male sperm or female ovum)
7) Resulzarion (results or "births")

After sharing this cosmic *sevenfold* knowledge with Hassein, Beelzebub feels he has now offered enough background information to fully address the topic of why and how "higher being-bodies" arise in the universe and why God placed particular importance on, and His Divine attention to, these *higher organic vessels for the soul* or what Swedenborg called "spiritual bodies."

This is what all religion should be focused on.

These higher (spiritual) bodies are obtained through individual humans becoming increasingly sensitive to the influences of the Sun Absolute (the non-material Spiritual Sun) from their conscious life-choices and actions. Here, Gurdjieff's Beelzebub is giving us a bio-structured (increased complexity of organic forms) understanding of spiritual transformation and rebirth, in order to render this normally hidden process as more visceral to our cognition—and not just a bunch of words.

Gaining more of God's influx requires *personally* gaining new inner forms of complexity and bio-structure. (Most traditional church-goers normally give no attention to these personal and increased structural demands of spiritual transformation, and thus have an incomplete picture of how they can actively become proper apparatuses and bio-mechanisms for serving God's great *Trogoautoegocratic* plan—the acquiring of noble substances for themselves and for the needs of Heaven's higher ecosystem and equilibrium.) Both Gurdjieff and Swedenborg were adamant that such process happens on an individual level and not the group level.

Three-brained beings throughout the universe, including the human race on planet Earth, have the potential to change the functioning of their own being-ness (through the same modifications made by God in all sevenfold completing processes). This divine opportunity would give all humans the possibility of distinct, new purer bodies to develop within their gross physical bodies.

As I hinted earlier, through the *Harnel-Aoot* or chaotic Stopinder/ step of this modified sevenfold law, an individual has been given the freedom of choice and opportunity to overcome the physical body's inertia (and challenge the more passive and negative worldly influences created by the organ Kundabuffer upon the spinal column).

This spiritual challenge goes hand-in-hand with a bio-change in the functioning of certain Tetartocosmos-beings (like us humans) to acquire "individual Reason"—and *rational* mind.

So, inherent in the changes of God's two fundamental laws, certain lifeforms gradually began to consciously absorb cosmic substances of a higher order through the atmospheres of their planets (particularly substances from the astronomical Sun and radiations from other planets—called *Mentekithzoïn*), which contained vibrations of "greater vivifyingness," and leading to increased intelligence and consciousness. This is evolution.

Becoming rational is evidence of humans having the additional ability to consciously change the functioning of their behavior and become influenced by ever-higher principles.) So earth-humans are designed to evolve even further and become *spiritually* or *angelically* rational (absorbing influences from God's Spiritual Sun—and making its influence relevant to their lives.

In the course and directionality of bio-evolution, this process of gaining greater vivifyingness (more liveliness) first led to certain Tetartocosmoses (warm-blooded mammals) being called "beings" after their having acquired a dual-nature through a second or astral body (body-Kesdjan). This dual nature incorporated a new emotional level and nerve structure added to the motor/sensory nerve system.

With a certain additional kind of *change of functioning*, these two-natured beings could further absorb and assimilate into themselves even the sacred cosmic substances emanating from the Most Most Holy *Theomertmalogos* Itself (God's Word). This now added a rational level to the two other levels of creatures, creating a *three-brained* system of beings capable of further angelic evolution.

The human race became such a three-brained hope for the Creator.

This special and *third* extra assimilation (now of spiritual food) represents a conscious acceptance and personal metabolism of God's sacred teachings and commandments. Swedenborg described the emanating rays of the Spiritual Sun as God's Divine *Love* and *Truth* proceeding harmoniously together in series (and that "Love" was the primary substance and mover of this entire dynamic).

This new assimilation of sacred spiritual substances (Divine teachings) within the human species would in turn begin the organizational building of an even higher and truer eternal spiritual body—to house the soul within the individual. The "change of functioning" alluded to above by Beelzebub is a conscious choice by an individual to live a higher, more spiritual life under God's tenets, instead of a merely physical life, like other two-natured beings. (Again, this higher assimilation of spiritual food in the human species would further help to ensure that the non-physical Spiritual Sun would remain relevant forever by making God's plan the "intentionally-actualized-Mdnel-In," or active principle in the completion of one's own personal *sevenfold* circle of life.")

When an individual succeeded in coating (fixing) one's "highest being-body" within his or her presence, through the proper assimilation (appropriation by living a more noble life) of spiritual data necessary for "objective Reason" (spiritual rationality), then that individual had the possibility of uniting (forming an all-important conjunction) with the Cause-of-Causes—the Divine Creator and His Spiritual Sun (and its heavenly cosmos). Without this rarefied *inner* body one cannot maintain the proper matrix and bio-form to hold God's heavenly influence in place and live under God's laws with sincerity. Instead these values would be feigned and thus not part of a person's true essence.

The Holy Planet Purgatory served to test one's "Harnel-Aoot" and help this process along—that is, if individuals sincerely accepted their ultimate cosmic duty.

This special conjunction and partnership between Creator and the created, through the human race, was the ultimate plan in which God placed His hope and focused the directionality of His Divine Providence when modifying the universal Laws of Threefoldness and Sevenfoldness to sustain His Spiritual Sun (and eternal abode).

Swedenborg claimed that God's purpose and goal in creation was to *"create a Heaven from the human race"* (*Divine Providence*, n. 27). Heaven (and the hearts and minds of humans) gives God's Spiritual Sun an inner kingdom (plane) to shine upon and flow into. (This is why Jesus said to Pontius Pilate that His Kingdom was within us—and thus beyond any external Roman rule).

Heaven (the kingdom of God's Spiritual Sun) is not a place you go to, it is something you inwardly become—from personal being-efforts and cosmic duty. Most religions still treat the heavenly kingdom as a wonderful place you go to, like an eternal vacation destination, and usually as a reward of great pleasure. (But this is not true Justice for beings with an inner and outer reality.

True religion is ultimately rational, logical, and *lawful*. Swedenborg underscores this idea of lawfulness by stating that all process—including life—needs a corresponding organic (bio) structure in order to properly react to stimuli. This includes heavenly stimuli, where life is much more intense, and therefore requires higher organic complexity for us to fully appreciate its values.

But little information—even from religion—is given today about the necessity of higher being-bodies. Beelzebub supplies the details nicely.

He states that the astral body (also body-Kesdjan) along with the highest being-body of the soul both survive the death of the terrestrial, physical body. After this death, they rise together and gravitate toward a *sphere of vibrations* corresponding to the substances of the astral body obtained from their solar system.

After the astral body also later disintegrates (dies), the third (higher) being-body, with its spiritual individuality and reasoning, can lawfully unite with the heavenly sphere of the Spiritual Sun.

Apparently this process took place relatively smoothly up until the time of the "Choot-God-litanical" period (Fall of Man). After this terrible period, human life acquired extra "baggage" (false principles, conflicting desires and extra psychic weight) during its spiritual journey to reunite with the Source of all things. This extra baggage also included the spiritual realities of other human beings who now began attaching themselves (after death) to our terrestrial lives and loves. These human spirits either promoted or resisted God's duty-journey.

Before the "Choot-God-litanical" period, higher being-bodies could be perfected on their own, without the spiritual baggage. But after this period, those spiritual individuals needing extra time for purification, after the disintegration of their own astral bodies, now had to rely on the astral bodies of others to continue the process of spiritual evolution. (This gives human spirits access to our memories and passions.)

Since even the astral body eventually decomposes, these souls have to constantly search for, and depend on, a similar and corresponding astral body from somewhere else, in order to continue their inner development (or oppose it).

This information about the dependence of unperfected souls on others' astral bodies was gradually distorted over time by the later doctrine of *reincarnation*, which mistakenly assumes that spiritual growth is automatically occurring through continual births.

This predicament of soul migration ("Techgekdnel"), while seemingly alien to Swedenborg's ideas, actually supports his notion that spiritual forces must always terminate in corresponding forms of the natural world—including human forms—so that terrestrial humans and human spirits keep needing each other to co-exist. (Most people are indignant to the organic idea that there is a vital connection between spiritual and physical realms—creating mental dependence between spirits and earth-humans).

But this top-down reality was actually observed by Swedenborg, where it was revealed that individuals in the spiritual world must have continued access to the hearts and minds of terrestrial humans on Earth, (or on some other corresponding earthly form.) Swedenborg further observed that all spirits had access to the memory-functions of those still living on Earth, where they could easily find similar views they can relate to, by being able to walk through anyone's inner ecosystem. In other words, spirits have real access to the organic states and qualities of our middle blood and the states of its nervous fibers. In fact, Swedenborg observed that our ideas and thought processes actually originate on the spiritual plane, so that terrestrial humans and human spirits need each other to continue functioning and support each other's different realities. God now uses this situation so that both terrestrial humans and human spirits can more easily find their ultimate destinies and harmonies from their shared worlds.

It just so happens that one's astral body and its middle blood is his or her "Harnel-Aoot," which represents the nature and quality of one's life-choices and *neutralizing* principles (uses).

So, the strange concept of spirits and terrestrial humans needing each other supports Beelzebub's discussion with Hassein that human spirits need to migrate to the different *psychical environments* (mental outlooks) created by people still on Earth who have a more fixed presence in spacetime and who from their preferences support a similar behavior, disposition and belief system. Therefore, as a human individual living on Earth changes the functioning and orientation of his or her life, spiritual beings in the other realm (with similar or dissimilar inclinations) become either attached to, or flee, from that person's astral body and the medium of their purer (middle) blood or animal spirits, which affect the living states of people's hearts and minds.

I cannot stress this point enough that all spirits represent the extra baggage we now assume, since the "fall." Human spirits (higher being-bodies) have real bio-access to an earth-human's middle (purer) blood or magnetic "animal spirits," (formed from both spiritual and earthly substances according to one's life choices). This rarefied species of blood (nervous fluid) causes the various changes of state in the human brain and its neurons to produce feelings, memories and thoughts! Spirits can dwell within the activity of this middle blood and affect human behavior as long as there is a similitude of desires.

It is a mistake to believe that these ideas belong to an antiquated or fairytale belief system. Swedenborg, a true genius, incorporated these same ideas into God's new theological revelations and divine settlement or disposition.

In *Divine Love And Wisdom* (n. 423) Swedenborg more than hints that an individual's purer blood or animal spirit (and not simply the corporeal red blood) is purified during the process of spiritual growth through genuine enlightenment and spiritual temptations. What is overlooked by current churchgoers is that this purer blood creates and maintains the bio-quality of the astral body—just as the red blood builds and maintains the quality of one's corporeal physical body.

The astral body's quality (and the quality of its purer blood) is always aligned with the qualities of a person's behavior, conscience and inner value system. So what Beelzebub is telling his grandson is that a human spirit, without properly developing its highest metaphysical body (body of the soul), cannot go directly to the realm of the Sun Absolute but instead becomes associated with and dependent upon the various psychical qualities of those beings still living on Earth, and perhaps even including the lower structures of organic and non-organic forms on Earth (like rocks and trees).

The reason for this migrational pressure on astral bodies is that even with their incomplete development, spirits still contain some amount of substances from the Spiritual Sun, which never decompose, so they have an eternal problem before them. As mentioned before, it is these spiritual beings, not yet fully purified, that have become both the extraneous "baggage" for us Earth-citizens and a living necessity for us to genuinely acquire a spiritual life by resisting their unpurified states—long after the "fall of man" (Choot-God-litanical period).

Swedenborg remarks that through temptations, we on Earth are given the opportunity to ignore the bad influences from these spirits or give better spirits the opportunity to transform and evolve further (right along with us)! He also concurred that as we make real changes in our lives, our spiritual cohorts in the other realm change.

It is important to understand that the three distinct bodies of human beings are fixed bio-qualities corresponding to, and housing, the three types of distinct kinds of being-reasonings that can be developed during one's lifetime. These levels of reasoning become a "fixed" quality, and bio-structure, according to one's personal efforts (conscious choices) at becoming more spiritual. The lowest (corporeal) and worldly level of cognition consists of mere memory data taken in by the bodily senses, and over time and through abnormal usage (as a kind of undigested food), leads to merely automatic (habitual) responses.

Higher up is an independent understanding and reasoning ("Okiartaaitokhsa") acquired through the increased and developed cognitive function of imagination and intelligence—which creates new ideas and new combinations of ideas from the homogenous things already deposited in one's memory banks from our life's experiences and preferences. But the precise mental process necessary for forming a proper second body inside the physical body—in a way that will allow for further lawful development to occur—requires the intentional effort of sensing (change in functioning) one's true significance in the world and the significance of other human beings. The resulting humility creates a change from a mere worldly rationality and civic morality to a genuine or spiritual rationality.

This higher rationality and understanding (symbolized by Isaac in the Bible) also allows us to take in extra substances (ethereal salts) from the circumfluent air and atmosphere that we breathe in every day (our second being-food for the astral body).

Above this second level of individual reasoning and its corresponding inner organic structure, one can go on to obtain true spiritual wisdom—which lives off the spiritual sustenance provided by the Spiritual Sun (God's Truths). Those who study Swedenborg's writings are quite familiar with the notion that God's influence emanating from the Spiritual Sun (or Sun Absolute) serves as a higher form of food, feeding angels and providing nourishment for a human's deeper needs and development. This inner development forms the higher bio-spiritual bodies of angelic spirits and angels. It is this third level of human cognition and metabolism (with its special spiritual food) which takes part in the coating and maintaining of the highest being-body for the human soul.

This higher being-body is not simply an imagined construct, but a real bio-structure, containing real human organs, but in a spiritual form. That is why this rarified structure and body cannot be properly united with the sacred emanations of the Spiritual Sun until human *egoism* is replaced by genuine *spiritual* love within one's life and reasoning mind (this highest "spiritual rationality" (or wisdom) is acquired by functional changes of both the human heart or will—not just the head-knowledge of the intellectual mind). This new spiritual quality in the reasoning mind becomes fixed into a new psycho-organization and an appropriate organic structure (higher body) to allow an individual to assimilate further divine influences from the MOST MOST HOLY SUN ABSOLUTE—only when selflessness, from a spiritual principle, becomes (as Beelzebub says) the "center-of-gravity-initiator-of-the-individual-functioning" of one's entire being-presence.

This principle in our evolving loves must become creatively equal to the intensity of our physical sex energy, because it gives birth to our spiritual possibilities. More on this topic, coming later.

(Gurdjieff is brilliant in using the organ Kundabuffer to give us a bio-grasp of what effects must be removed from our lives before God's goodness can take hold and create a purified state of innocence within us. Even though Swedenborg states that detesting and removing ignoble traits (in the first several chapters in the second volume of *True Christianity*) is the first step toward obtaining genuine goodness and producing good uses, this unflattering self-criticism is currently being overlooked as distasteful, self-degrading and therefore unnecessary. People want to jump from where they are directly into goodness (as if enhancing an already positive state).

But Swedenborg even states that unless we label our behavioral flaws "as sins," nothing real or deep will ever happen or be changed. Since genuine goodness only comes from God, our negative traits (that normally fly under the radar and instill vanities into all our activities) must be removed *first*—by both our permission and by the Creator's mercy, in order to make room for the genuine innocence of Divine influences to enter our lives. (Heaven wouldn't be heaven without the goodness of innocence.)

The first level of being-Reasoning is acquiring noble data. Swedenborg describes these divisions or discrete levels of human reasoning as different marital conjunctions (nuptuals) between heart and mind.

The second level of being-Reasoning obtained by human evolution (now the love of understanding what one knows), represents the successful coating and organization of the astral body, within the gross physical body. (Swedenborg concurs that one's understanding produces a real body or bio-organization from one's affections and inclinations.) This level of rationality still represents worldly reasoning and values, but can potentially lead to true compassion, introspection and humility (Isaac), which begins to connect us to our God-given remains and allows for our conscience to appear and grow further.

Above this, the highest body (third body) is coated and organized from the emanations of the Spiritual Sun (which leads to wisdom).

All three organized body-levels represent one's "Ruling Love" or "center-of-gravity-initiator-of-the-individual's-functioning."

The lowest level of consciousness and human cognition is simply from data and influences of the external world, which enters into the five senses and creates habitual associations and mechanical reactions. This automatic behavior is purely corporeal and is fixed in the human memory (by the outer natural mind), according to both accidentally and previously perceived sensory inputs. This data (accumulated knowledge) is disconnected from our more vital inner reality because of our need for deceit. (The organ Kundabuffer was designed to keep us in this life of delusion and inner slavery to lies so that we would continue to function without rebelling or sensing our true predicament and cosmic duty.)

Beelzebub admits to Hassein that they, as well as their earth-human cousins, are (from a cosmic perspective) actually only *half-beings*. To this, Swedenborg informs us that *male* and *female* angels are really only "half-angels"—until they enter into a heavenly marriage and re-unify. (And yes, he even suggests that the female sex was created from the male sex and that they now possess a property that was taken from the man, so they must re-conjoin.)

Beelzebub now throws in a peculiar and unfamiliar cosmic situation into the narrative. He states that since the formation of moons around planets, the Law of Sevenfoldness, concerning the completion of its process, now had the placement of its last gravity-center shifting to a more extraneous form. This same shift in the law also affected the dynamics of the process in the continuation of the species, by allowing a division of genders to emerge, because the Law's last gravity center now also had to shift its placement in some new extraneous living form (like the female ovum).

In other words, the female sex was now needed to provide the last Stopinder in the changed Law of Sevenfoldness occurring on the human scale—just as the Earth's separated Moon had become a last center of gravity on the larger planetary scale. This is why two sexes are now required (active and passive) to assure the continuation of the species and why marriage was originally designed to re-unify male and female sexes in order to complete the process of Heptparaparshinokh in a way that would create new beings. Beelzebub hints to his grandson the strange notion that originally, Tetartocosmoses could reproduce singularly but that later, the seventh or last deflection (called *Ashagiprotoëhary*) of the sacred Heptaparaparshinokh was focused to terminate on a planet's moons, instead of the planet itself.

This is a most challenging metaphor of spiritual reality. Apparently, the formation of planetary moons has something to do with the dividing of the sexes. As crazy as this sounds, it is a scientific fact that reproduction cycles in women on Earth often follow the cycles of the moon.

Continuing on this same topic, Swedenborg admits observing an angel coming toward him in Heaven and that this apparently singular angel appeared as a male and female *married* couple, as they got closer to him. This couple was perfectly unified in heavenly marriage, as if this profound unity expressed their real inner life— even more than their separated genders ever could.

As I mentioned earlier, Swedenborg mysteriously stated that women have something that was taken from the man (*Conjugial Love*, n. 88), and are born from male wisdom (*Conjugial Love*, n. 91) after which there is an inclination in the female to reunite and become one (*Conjugial Love*, n. 89) with the male. This outcome of two sexes may also represent, on a higher psychical level, that human cognition and its functioning became more separated, external, and finally terminated outside of one's real being or spiritual essence—causing the female principle (and matrix) to split off and move to a more external representation of a passive principle in gender.

The moon could represent this same split on a larger cosmic scale.

Women's fertility has over history been tied to the cycles of the Moon. The human memory and its worldly imagination (the Moon's representation within our inner universe) actually lies outside of a person's inner living essence—just like the moon lies outside the planet Earth. This situation represents information separated from the reality of our true lives and actions.

Swedenborg describes our beliefs and actions as a person's "spiritual" children (or psychical births).

Without spiritual growth, we unavoidably feed and sustain only this lower, split-off functioning of our mentality by seeking and collecting mere memory data, thinking that in this *passive* state, our accumulated data and education is enough for generating genuine wisdom and measuring our stature. This kind of dead memory knowledge in the intellect (as a mere reflection of true living knowledge or wisdom) by itself represents a "moon" or external satellite within the human psyche.

According to Swedenborg, this situation is what happens when knowledge is allowed to accumulate beyond one's living capacity for *goodness*. Here, knowledge becomes split off from the actual qualities and choices of our lives and is only used to put up an outer face.

This means spiritual growth (and wisdom) requires that information seek a deeper plane of one's being than is customary by modern standards. This deeper plane, when developed, acts to promote "conjugial partners" (psychic nuptials) and a unifying principle for the memory-data and knowledge of our corporeal psyche to become intimately united to and fully "engaged to" our interior psyche and will (loves).

Similarly (but on another scale), a man who loves wisdom will seek the woman who best represents that love.

To further complicate the matter (and bury the dog deeper) Gurdjieff's character, Beelzebub, states that on another unique planet in the Megalocosmos called *Modiktheo*, three distinct individuals came together to produce offspring through their completion of the Sevenfold process. This unique planet exists in the system of the Protocosmos or Spiritual Sun, so this is a strong clue that allegory and symbolism is also being used here to describe a highly sacred and advanced form of *tri-unity* (active, passive and neutralizing modes), which all heavenly angels enjoy in the Protocosmos of Heaven.

This clue is further evidenced by the fact that this special plane or "planet" is where Beelzebub even claims angels arise in the universe! So it must represent an innermost plane of reality and unity that is potentially within all of us. Therefore, I understand the third "individual" taking part in this "triunal copulation" as a proper harmonizing principle (Holy Spirit) or living goal, the results of which—on this special plane of existence—conceive *spiritual offspring* (more inner development) through what Beelzebub calls "psycho/spiritual-organic-attraction" and "Aklonoatistitchian longing." (This striving for unity is the creative re-blending of triunal forces within human hearts and minds.)

As I have already mentioned, Swedenborg describes a similar spiritual conception and progeny in Heaven among married angels. These rarefied progeny (spiritual births) are born from a prolific inner principle to promote, unify and perfect Divine qualities within us. These spiritual progeny represent a *multiplication of God's Loves and Truths* though created beings.

I suspect that this rarefied plane of existence, which did not require special external efforts (conscious labors and intentional suffering) among its citizens, also represented an original genus of *internally* directed earth-humans that Swedenborg called the *Most Ancient Church* (before the "Fall"). These spiritually superior human beings received direct influences from God's Spiritual Sun—they could perceive cosmic truths (without reading books). So, as to their hearts and minds, these ancient earth-humans were already *inwardly* inhabiting this special planet/plane of the Protocosmos, ruled by the Spiritual Sun.

Furthermore, this sacred top-down influence from the Sun Absolute of the Protocosmos (Heaven) could be directed and terminated within the deepest organic fabric of those special ancient beings *immediately,* grasped instinctively and *synthetically,* without weighing anything *analytically* (unlike more modern human species who must gather information from their lower five senses). Now, learning no longer comes from interior planes, but from more external influences and *extant* writings that could be picked up by one's outer natural mind and its reliance on *corporeal/sensual* receptors.

Beelzebub names this new outer termination and last step of God's influence toward finding stability through reproduction (within the Law of Sevenfoldness of all human species), the sacred *Ashagiprotoëhary* (as opposed to personal *Resulzarion*). But this last step is now fulfilled on a more external level through another gender (cosmically represented by the Moon). So human sperm is excused from its need to evolve further or create an inner, spiritual birth (higher body) through the more external activity and pleasure of sexual intercourse.

(But in the Revelation chapter of the Holy Word, we are given a depiction of a pregnant female standing "above the Moon," representing a spiritual affection *elevated* from worldly memory and worldly concerns, who is about to give birth to a *new paradigm.* The *Great Red Dragon* represents our resistance to this new paradigm and our efforts to stop this "spiritual child" from maturing!)

The extra step now needed for the downward trajectory of the Spiritual Sun's Divine influence to reach us at a more external and lower level (which is an outer "satellite" of human cognitive functioning), allows its proper qualities to be twisted and perverted along the way. This unfortunate twisted situation is explained by Beelzebub through the current earth-human misunderstanding of the phrase "We are images of God."

Most earth-humans now perceive God (as in everything else) in a most distorted way—like having a beard or five fingers and toes. But Beelzebub suggests that we are *images of God* for other reasons—because we each represent a smaller-scale unit of the whole created world and share in all its God-given hopes and possibilities. (Swedenborg also agrees that the "image and likeness of God" notion represents a potential capacity in humans toward gaining spiritual understanding and love, thus becoming the smallest unit of Heaven— or in Beelzebub's terminology, the Protocosmos.) In this way, humans play a special role in maintaining creation's continued harmony and unity through their continued success at spiritual transformation. The entire human race was inwardly designed to become God's special helpers (actual angels) on ever-higher and higher levels of the multi-universe.

However, this noble divine role and duty, especially for modern humanity, is now threatened by the increasingly diminished and "passive" activity of human cognition— which has a proclivity to invent falsities, maleficent fictions and poppycock. Beelzebub states that in more recent times, the atrophied "being-Aimnophnian-mentation," that is, "perceptible logic" of humans, now almost pictures God with a "comb sticking out of his left vest pocket."

(As mentioned above, Swedenborg promoted the concept that for humans to be made in the *image and likeness* of God, they were to manifest elements of His spiritual love and wisdom. God can only flow into and develop those qualities that are His own. In that way, if individuals receive that celestial influence, they can each represent smaller scales of heavenly life.)

Angels are *spiritual microcosms*—the smallest units of Heaven.

In this vein, Beelzebub now teaches Hassein how to view the proper functioning of human experience and existence—as representing a smaller scale model of the functioning of the entire universe—incorporating its sacred *triune* design.

What now follows is truly elevating and carries us above our common, daily worldviews. Here, Beelzebub displays a profound and uncommon understanding of *correspondences*, especially as God's triune law works in humans.

He explains to his grandson that the cells of the human head-brain (neurons) *correspond* to the active functioning of higher being-bodies (angels), living in the sphere of the Spiritual Sun or Protocosmos. It was in the development of angels from the human race that the Creator had put His hopes—in order to make His place of abode (the Spiritual Sun) eternally relevant, and where the human species could serve as an aid for the administration of the expanding universe (beyond their terrestrial planets).

Swedenborg stated that the innermost reality of human beings was ultimately designed to *serve the Lord*, both in the physical and spiritual worlds (*Arcana Coelestia*, n. 5947). Swedenborg also put forth the non-traditional idea in his theological writings that all angels evolve from some planetary existence, and from some terrestrial human species. This is God's plan for creation, so that the innermost reality of all human species can evolve, and further serve God, on higher planets (planes of existence).

Angels are not independent creations in the world!

Beelzebub now moves beyond the active principles of the human head-brain and continues his description of how this micro-design and image of the laws of the greater universe are represented perfectly within the human bio-architecture and psyche. He picks up with his explanation of the Law of Triamazikamno (Three-foldness). This is important in order to explain—and clarify—just how humans are images of God.

As mentioned above, the neurons of the head brain represented the *active* part of the *law of triads* in humans. Beelzebub goes on to explain that within the spinal column of three-brained beings there was localized the denying, *passive* or reactive force, relative to the more active neural cells (neurons) of the head-brain (you will remember that the spinal column is where the organ Kundabuffer had its original placement, and therefore, promoted passivity and laziness in human mental activity—which led to fantasy and dreaming).

On the larger scale of the Megalocosmos, this same relationship between active and passive forces is played out between the physical stars (second order suns) as a group, whose combined action is relatively passive to—and puts limits on—the activity of each individual star (representing active principles). The Spiritual Sun (and angels of Heaven), provide the neutralizing (orchestrated) influence and patterns of God's conscious design into the formula of the universe.

While Swedenborg states in his book *Worship And Love Of God* that the physical world of matter is *reactive* to spiritual forces, he qualifies this dynamic. Spiritual forces can only act as a *neutralizing* agent between various active and passive causal principles, and combine them in a way that *creates* a coherent series (successions) of productions on higher levels of organization—much as the human will and its level of love determines one's actions and organizes its data into a worldview. (The physical sun acted as a neutralizing principle for plant life, but the Spiritual Sun was the neutralizing agent for animal life.)

In human transformation, the active, passive and reconciling principles all correspond and promote unified results. So the reconciling principle manifests itself in the image and likeness of its active principle.

Concerning special knowledge of the human spinal column, Beelzebub relates the fact that during more ancient times, earth-humans knew what specific parts (nodes) of the spinal column *corresponded* to, and which particular active parts of the head-brain they reacted to. From this profound knowledge, these individuals of former epochs had developed mechanical means to address and correct various disharmonies that arose in people's "psychic state." But as human cognition deteriorated and became more "superpeculiar," this great knowledge gradually evaporated among them like everything else and they lost access to it.

The third (reconciling) principle emerges from the results obtained between the triunal activity (combination) of the Spiritual Sun and all the shades of action and reaction from the second order suns and their individual stars within the great universe—which also had a corresponding representation in earth-human anatomical design. Beelzebub describes the reconciling principle in this tri-fold design as being basically located within the human "breast"— more specifically, in the solar plexus (nodes of the *sympathetic nervous system*).

It is because of this three-pronged design, corresponding to the universal Law of Threefoldness (and Holy Trinity) that earth-beings can be said to be images of God. But they become *likenesses*, from spiritual effort—when they acknowledge they have a special responsibility—not only to serve the universe as an apparatus for transforming substances required for maintaining the Great Trogoautoegocrat system, but also have the possibility of assimilating and metabolizing additional substances needed for the coating, organizing and perfecting of their own higher, spiritual bodies.

All true religion originally provided the directions for guiding earth-humans through this process of gaining inner (psycho-spiritual) bio-complexity. But not any more! Today we seek titillation.

To understand this special process and higher potential in the human species more viscerally, Beelzebub tells his grandson that each of these *three* basic localizations in earth-humans relies on its own distinct kind of food, and their ability to properly metabolize these threefold kinds of sustenance. (While Swedenborg touches on these distinct foods, the bio-subject of building spiritual bodies during one's spiritual growth, and the metabolism required, is little discussed among his theological followers.)

Turning now to the other major sacred Law (of Sevenfoldness) operating in the universe and in humans, Beelzebub next describes to Hassein that the first type of food is created by Nature through the *evolutionary* ascent of substances from the last Stopinder ("Ashagiprotoëhary") of the fundamental Sacred Heptaparaparshinokh—as an evolutionary substance or result heading back toward the Spiritual Sun.

(*Ashagiprotoëhary* seems to represent a form of *Resulzarion* (final step) that is capable of entering into a new upward series and octave of process, including reproduction.) Its continued evolutionary ascent (gaining greater vivifyingness) represents the various substances and lifeforms arising on the planet, that provide *sustenance* for earth-beings, i.e., rising to the level of physical food. So in digestion, humans play an important role in continuing this upward, evolutionary trajectory back to God. (Also keep in mind that the sacred Heptaparaparshinokh unfolds its successive sevenfold series, in both a downward (involutionary) and upward (evolutionary) gyre or cycle. Swedenborg calls this sacred cycle the universal orb or *Circle of Life*.)

The second distinct type of being-food is produced from the combined radiations of the astronomical sun and physical planets of its system, which then enter into the Earth's circumfluent atmosphere. These substances nourish earth-beings as a second type of food through the air (Swedenborg referred to this food as *atmospheric* and *ethereal* salts (which go into the maintaining of one's middle blood). We breathe in this aerial (second) food according to the quality and values of our inner reality.

Finally, a third distinct type of food, consisting of what Beelzebub defines as our *first-sourced substances* (sensory data), which all earth-humans have been given the ability to absorb from all the sensual impressions of the physical world, is crucial for the final coating and perfecting of their higher-being body—the spiritual body of the soul. This highest food is absorbed and properly metabolized during genuine spiritual transformation and rebirth. But, this higher metabolism only happens when we can discriminate between higher (spiritual) and lower (terrestrial) ideas flowing into our sensory organs, and choose from them correctly.

Unfortunately, while these three types of food continue to automatically enter into earth-humans, because of their adopted abnormal lifestyles they no longer consciously [know how to] absorb all these substances, and therefore only enough to guarantee the automatic continuation of their species, demanded by Nature. In fact, only physical foodstuffs are recognized by today's earth-humans as actual food, and even this they have managed, thanks to their abnormal lifestyles, to turn into a vice.

Again, this abnormal being-existence (against God's design) can be blamed on the maleficent properties of the long-gone organ Kundabuffer, which unfortunately have now become "fixed" by habit into the human psyche. As a result, earth-humans have forgotten that they were originally designed for a sacred cosmic duty to also absorb the second and third cosmic foods—*consciously.*

While earth-humans do acknowledge the importance of the first being-food, these terrestrial substances only maintain the lower, perishable, physical body and offer nothing for building the higher and more important potential bio-structures (higher bodies) within an individual's presence and life. Furthermore, since the physical body only serves as the denying (opposing) source for spiritual growth, the terrestrial individual lives life completely within a denying (passive) and corporeal framework of existence. Without embracing a higher (God-given) duty, nature allows terrestrial earth-humans to absorb just enough of these higher cosmic substances, mechanically, for the continuation of their species, and this is done without their conscious participation. (This means that the *Ashagiprotoëhary*—the final step of their personal octave—represents a most limited goal.)

Additional efforts (that have been forgotten in our religions traditions and education) are necessary for the proper absorption and further metabolization of the these two more rarefied "foods."

Beelzebub explains to Hassein that certain individuals of the ancient continent Atlantis (after the destruction of the functioning of the organ Kundabuffer) actually considered the absorption of these two higher being-foods, the *chief aim* of their existence. These Atlantians called the conscious absorption of the second being-food (air) as "Amarloos" or "help-for-the-Moon." The conscious assimilation of the third being-food (divine information from the Sun Absolute) was called the sacred "Amarhoodan" or "help-for-God."

Over time, the failure of earth-humans to consciously absorb these two higher cosmic substances necessary for building up their potential higher being-parts, resulted in the disappearance of both a striving for inner perfection and the possibility of "intentional contemplation." (Because of this lack of sane thinking, traditional religions fail to make the rational connection between faith, friendship, compassion, charity and higher *organic* processes. The universe not only follows the laws of organic process, it always strives toward the human form, because this form has a correspondence with the highest unifying principles of God's operation. Swedenborg even observed that the different heavenly societies of angels were designed just like all the organic structures, systems, organs and cells that would be operating in one Great Human Being. Which again, is a wonderful bio-model of mutual support and analog of the Lord God's Living Love and unifying rational operation.)

Swedenborg stated that humans were born for the benefit of other humans, which now requires a change in our functioning.

Beelzebub stresses that the active process of *intentional contemplation* (genuine pondering) in humans (rather than reacting passively and automatically to everything) is the principle factor for the proper assimilation of these two higher and rarefied cosmic substances for food. (That is why the process of eating and digesting food corresponds spiritually to mental *ruminating* and one's "chewing on something."

Since humanity walked away from its original God-given duty (and triple digestion), Nature was then forced to adapt herself to the resulting abnormal life conditions made by more shallow thinking earth-humans—in order to ensure that the bare minimum of these rarefied cosmic substances would be, at least, automatically assimilated in them. Still, even this mechanical assimilation of all three foods would be further dependent on various "unexpected" and "intense experiences" taking place over the course of people's lifetimes.

While Beelzebub does not identify these *intense experiences* to us, my "Swedenborgian hunch" is that a certain amount of tragedy and misfortune is built into everyone's worldly fate—to allow for some serious contemplation and questioning about life to take place. This forced contemplation would create the minimum vibrations needed from humans to maintain the universe and their species.

During such times of misfortune one's perspective on what is important in life certainly changes. This allows us to cut through all the crap, even if only temporarily!

Beelzebub next summarizes for Hassein just how cosmic energies and substances evolve and involve through the Sacred law of Heptaparaparshinokh and differentiate themselves into new independent *Sevenfold* groupings, according to which Stopinder (direction of stability) they emerged from, and also through their "affinity of vibrations" (harmony) with other similar substances.

To be more precise, all these various classes of substances manifest particular subjective properties, that is, "proportions of vivifyingness" according to what form of functioning of the *fifth Stopinder* of Law of Sevenfoldness (the Harnel-Aoot or reconciling action) was flowing during their arising. And secondly, whether these substances had arisen from the conscious intention of independent beings or merely arose automatically from the cosmic law of "Attraction-and-Fusion-of-Similarities." (These two outcomes from the fifth Stopinder is determined by influences from either the Spiritual Sun, or from some physical source entering into the Sevenfold series of events as first principle.)

The various substances and elements making up the entire universe always arrange themselves into seven "Okhtapanatsakhnian-classes," for which all process either *involves* or *evolves* (going up or down Jacob's Ladder). This Sevenfold order has supreme (and sacred) significance in that it comprises the grand cosmic scheme of the fundamental and cyclic process of the common-cosmic Ansanbaluiazar (transformation and mutual support), by which God's Trogoautoegocrat system now keeps the Spiritual Sun relevant—thus outwitting the tyranny of physical entropy and thermodynamic time.

The great *common-cosmic Ansanbaluiazar* is the reciprocal movement by which all process returns in an orderly and lawful fashion to its beginnings (first principles), like the Most Most Holy Sun Absolute or Theomertmalogos does when creating any whole process, through Truth advancing in series. Again, Swedenborg called this sacred, repeating operation and reciprocation *the Circle of Life*—in both his scientific and theological publications.

Beelzebub now describes to his grandson some additional details as to how every concentration in the universe emerging from the

Etherokrilno (Love's possibility space) and formed from the cosmic law of "Attraction-and-Fusion-of-Similarities" gained formal existence (Since everything comes out of Love, everything created finds its partners and true form.)

Beelzebub states, in a most mentally challenging way, that if the (virtual) particles of Etherokrilno already occupying the different spheres of all seven Stopinders of the fundamental Ansanbaluiazar (God's sacred law of holistic succession) make contact (and assume similar harmonic or corresponding motions) they begin to collaborate and form new crystallizations or substances. Furthermore, if this harmonic collaboration is taking place in conditions where the "Harnel-miatsnel" (*end, cause and effect*) is occurring, they will fuse into more compound (and complex) unities.

Each time these compound unities enter into other processes and conditions of "Harnel-miatsnel," new active elements and compounds are created in another "Okhtapanatsakhnian class" (a new octave or spectrum).

Moving the discussion onto a new scale, the process just mentioned is extremely relevant to an individual's spiritual growth. Beelzebub tells Hassein that if he can grasp the order and successive process of the transformation of cosmic substances (especially back toward the Spiritual Sun) through the organic apparatuses of earth-humans, such as the substances which enter into them as physical foodstuffs (first being-food), then he will be able to gain an approximate understanding of a spiritually important particularity of the sacred law of Heptaparaparshinokh—the involution and evolution of higher being-foods, within the human organism, to assist in God's plan of perfecting mutual support and also our gaining greater bio-complexity (spiritual bodies).

Here, we are now given a totally unique look at human digestion.

Beelzebub explains that when the first physical foodstuffs enter into the presences of earth-humans on their ascent and evolution from their own last interval (as "Ashagiprotoëhary") of the Law of Sevenfoldness, they come under new conditions of the *Harnel-miatznel* from the enzymes in the human digestive system. These foodstuffs react with active elements (such as enzymes) in the human digestive system according to the "affinity of vibrations" already present in the individual. (Swedenborg, in his scientific works, is adamant that this organic affinity is according to an individual's *affections, animus, passions* or *Ruling Love*, creating an orb. The differences in human affections and passions is why our individual digestive systems will automatically absorb different elements from the foods we eat and create *chemically different* types of red blood in each of us.)

Beelzebub now describes the full process of digestion through which substances evolve though higher gravity centers (steps of stability or Stopinders) according to the *combined* Laws of Sevenfoldness and

Threefoldness operating in the human anatomy. The process starts (*see figure 1*), *Trogoautoegocratically*, from foodstuffs entering the human bio-system from the *outside*.

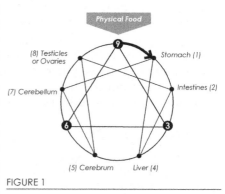

FIGURE 1

In the human stomach, physical food is first transmuted into "being-Protoëhary" or *chyme*. (Since new readers, unfamiliar with Gurdjieff's expressions of the two fundamental laws operating together in a universal and organic model, called the *enneagram* or nine-diagram, I have illustrated this dynamical model here, so that the novice reader can better follow the order of succession in the processes of this discussion.) Beelzebub states that this first step in the transmutation of physical food into chyme within the stomach *corresponds* (*figure 2*) (vibrationally) to the ascending *fourth* Stopinder of the sacred Sevenfold process (*arterial* blood

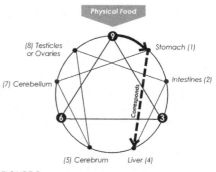

FIGURE 2

leaving the Liver). Gurdjieff is here touching on an inner movement by which seemingly diverse external operations can be inwardly united by profound relationship and moved toward a common goal (equilibrium). Swedenborg described a similar bio-process to Gurdjieff's "Harnel-miatznel" operating through the organs of the human body, by which *help from the outside* always intervenes, in his great anatomical work, *The Animal Kingdom* (chapter titled: "The Glands Generally.").

The chyme, which has gained a new trajectory (*figure 3*) and "gravity-center vibration" from that of its previous form as physical food, next goes through the same process of Harnel-miatsnel (change through the Law of Threefoldness) all along the human duodenum or small intestines. Here, the chyme is now transmuted into "being-Defteroëhary" or *chyle*.

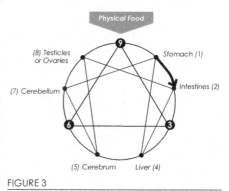

FIGURE 3

Next, the chyle, with a modification made to its center-of-gravity, from the Law of Threefoldness (Harnel-miatsnel), evolves "upward" to the *liver* where it is then transformed into "being-Tritoëhary," which now has the same vibrational equivalent as *fire* (See Ouspensky's *In Search of the Miraculous*, page 321).

Because of the change in the system of creation and maintenance from the *Autoegocrat* to the *Trogoautoegocrat*, it is just at the place of the liver in humans, where the process of Harnel-miatznel needs a new level of outside help and *support* to continue to its next evolutionary step. (This detail in the process of human digestion strongly convinced me that Gurdjieff and Swedenborg were talking about a similar concept.)

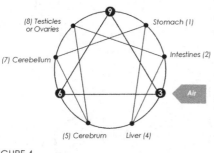

FIGURE 4

Both men claimed that the liver could not perform its functions without the external help of the second being-food or "air" (*figure 4*) entering into the process. This external help takes part in the process of Sevenfoldness in humans by the oxygenated (arterial) blood entering the liver from the lungs through the hepatic artery, as a further emollient or diluting menstruum (*The Animal Kingdom*, Vol. 1, n. 208 [r]). Beelzebub calls this critical interval or Stopinder in the sevenfold process, the "lower" or "mechano-co-inciding-Mdnel-In," because it takes place naturally. In this part of the process, God's Great Nature has designed an automatic "way-in," (through our breathing) for air to come in and help in the feeding of the astral body's purer blood, as well as supporting the continued evolution of the first being-food for the physical body.

However, the air entering the lungs from the circumfluent atmosphere is now also transmuted in a similar (corresponding) fashion as physical food was in the stomach, but instead, into a higher level and distinct substance called "Astralnomonian-Protoëhary."

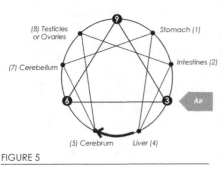

FIGURE 5

The substances from these two distinct being-foods (physical food and "Astralnomonian-Deftoëhary from the air) (*figure 5*) now help each other pass through the liver and evolve together, creating "being-Tetartoëhary" (which, if consciously metabolized, can pass through the blood barrier, and communicate its passions, leanings and inclinations to the cerebrum and lead to increased rationality).

But in an unconscious state, "Being-Tetartoëhary" has the center of its gravity concentrated at the surface of both hemispheres in the cerebrum (and travels there through the external carotid arteries). Here, these cosmic substances undergo further transmutation through the continued process of Harnel-miatznel and evolve their vibrational state to that of being-Piandjoëhary—with the external help of sensory impressions coming from the outside environment that we are most attracted to. This new substance has its center-of-gravity and trajectory now concentrated toward the *cerebellum*, where all the inputs from the various qualities of an individual's choices and passions accumulate, take form, and are prepared for some future action.

This special interval, between the cerebrum and cerebellum, is chaotic and represents *free will* or the Harnel-Aoot in humans. This is a place for either rational actions or potential screw-ups to occur along the whole bio-process. Because of the change in the functioning of the *fifth* Stopinder, enacted by God, this chaotic step in the Sacred Heptaparaparshinokh can bring proper or dissimilar results within the lives of three-brained beings (if they adopt bad principles and make misguided choices). This interval is where religion and God's commandments were designed to help keep earth-humans vigilant and on guard, in order to avoid undesirable consequences.

Why? Because the cerebellum, knowing what's going on in the cerebrum, can turn our ideas and feelings into sperm and ovum (*figure 6*), whereby human progeny (or any created result of our chosen actions and deeds) will inherit similar qualities and principles, becoming effigies of their parents (genetics)! This is why our inner ideas and feelings represent spiritual children and births.

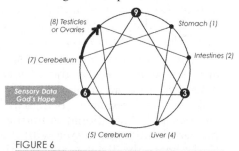

FIGURE 6

In *The Five Senses* (n. 63), Swedenborg states that the cerebellum, because of the connection of its nerves, knows everything the cerebrum is doing. And because the cerebellum also shares and communicates its perception with the higher human soul, it gets the power to induce changes in the organic states of the cerebrum, according to its affections and give these affections prolific form. Also, in his book *Organs Of Generation* (n. 44), Swedenborg had anatomically observed that the cerebellum affects our prolific principle because it was from the nerves of the cerebellum that vital seminal fluids (containing spiritual influences) are transferred to the human testicles. (In n. 36 of the same work, he even mentions *involution* and *evolution*.)

This is exactly where Beelzebub is going with his discussion. He states that from the human cerebellum, being-Tetartoëhary is transformed into new cosmic substances in the male testicles and female

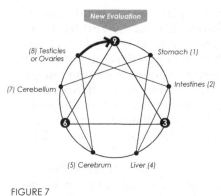

New Evaluation

(8) Testicles or Ovaries

(7) Cerebellum

Stomach (1)

Intestines (2)

(5) Cerebrum   Liver (4)

FIGURE 7

ovaries, called "being-Exioëhary."

For both genders, being-Exioëhary is their most sacred possession. According to Beelzebub, this final substance can either contribute to the "automatic justification" of earth-beings through the natural continuation of the species (from terrestrial sex) or it can *evolve further* (*figure 7*) (though consciously receiving influences of the Spiritual Sun and God's Word) whereby our Exioëhary can create new degrees of vivifyingness and intensity in our relations with others, as it enters the last Stopinder and interval of its otherwise natural cycle, called the "higher-intentionally-actualizing-Mdnel-In."

In other words, nothing additional, beyond physical sex, happens to this special substance at this stage—unless it comes under the conscious influence of a more noble active principle (like the Spiritual Sun) and is accepted by a new functioning (affection and evaluation) of an individual's heart and mind, This change of functioning not only allows our Exioëhary to evolve further, but by correspondences, represents the change of choices being made at one's chaotic fifth Stopinder (the human free will).

The proper assimilation of spiritual influences as *outside help* at this rarefied stage (at the *intentional* Mdnel-in of one's sevenfold bio-series) is not automatic like air helping our liver metabolize physical food, and requires "being-Partkdolg-duty," that is, "conscious labors" and "intentional suffering." In Swedenborg's terms, this proper assimilation means willfully subjecting oneself to the Lord God's heavenly dictates and entering into the process of spiritual regeneration and re-birth through sincere humility and innocence, which re-activates *conscience*. (And creates a new will in the intellect.)

This re-birth is the chief aim of our existence and puts our Exioëhary (sexual energy) under the guiding influences of the Spiritual Sun! (But few earth-humans today grasp the necessity to intentionally absorb higher "foods" to change the focus of their prolific principle.) Terrestrial humans of the Earth no longer know that their genuine spiritual re-birth goes hand in hand with multi-level feeding and the forming of spiritual bodies from within.

According to both Swedenborg and Gurdjieff spiritual transformation and evolution is an extension of organic processes into higher, non-physical realms.

Ironically, Swedenborg observed that as we faithfully follow these transforming steps, *we* also become appetizing food for the larger and superior organic system of Heaven, whose societies function as a grand analogy of all the organic forms found operating in humans. So, after our physical deaths, when we enter into the grand bio-stomach of angelic enzymes and teaching, which opens up the constitution of our inner realities, we can either become a part of the angelic commerce in the spiritual world or be eliminated out of its butt-hole as crap.

We each serve as food and as *help coming from the outside* to nourish this grand bio-system. Swedenborg described the heavenly process of digestion as separating all the knowledge we learned but which took no part in our actual lives—so we are left with only the knowledge that conforms to the actual quality of our spiritual reality (Ruling Love).

We can be food and nourish God's heaven!

The challenge and duty we each have been given is to get this process started—even before we die. Because we need our physical bodies to act as a lawful denying principle to spiritual influences—in order to help determine our inner qualities and Exioëhary. Otherwise our ultimate essential fluid and prolific principle (sperm), especially in males, remains worldly, terrestrial, and only capable of producing physical offspring.

The cosmic and dutiful *labors* necessary for spiritual transformation here consists in one consciously deciding to fight against one's self-love (egoism) and love of worldly possessions and status, through a special form of inner *sincerity* (obtained through self-observation and introspection) and *humility* (spiritual self-remembering of one's real situation and cosmic duty). This purging activity and increased vigilance changes the vibrational quality of male sperm in a way that allows it to help create (coat) higher spiritual bodies, and intensity of life within the individual.

(Swedenborg personally witnessed that angelic wives, through the love of their husband's growing wisdom, form an accepting matrix (spiritual ovum) in which to receive these evolving prolific principles developing in their husbands. This intensifies their marital conjunction and closeness and brings forth spiritual births and progeny—in the form of the inner perfection of their unity.

This may all sound misogynistic, but both Swedenborg and Gurdjieff expressed the anti-intuitive notion that each gender was only a half-human. In God's universe, everywhere, there are expressed real, lawful, *active* and passive principles, which must come together through a third force to form a unified whole. These active and passive principles are also represented by the different human genders for expressing the fundamental law of Triamazikamno on a particular scale. On this scale it takes both a male and female to make one angel.

The "suffering" in the process of purification is the *intentional* submitting of oneself to the scrutiny of higher heavenly principles, which the Lord teaches from His two great commandments—*loving God* and *loving the neighbor*. This new application of love nukes our self-centered love and first necessitates a "housecleaning," which allows heavenly life from the Spiritual Sun the room it needs in our psyche to lawfully flow into people's hearts and minds.

Most people want to jump the gun on becoming good before any serious purging (and suffering) can take place. But such purging also allows our being-Exioëhary to evolve further and participate in forming spiritual births (intensifying our life energies and heavenly goals). This rarefied "offspring" is also represented by the formation of a spiritual body for the soul, through a rebirth of the human will and heart in one's understanding and rational mind.

(When Swedenborg describes coming into a state where he no longer has an interest in sex, nor lusts for the female form, in his *Journal of Dreams*, I believe that his sperm, or being-Exioëhary, had evolved further to become influenced by a higher spiritual and evolutionary desire to help and love all humankind. I never forgot that statement or admission when I first read it!)

Beelzebub next informs his grandson that there is a poisonous downside to one's being-Exioëhary (especially male sperm) when, from abnormal living and bad life-choices, is not being allowed to evolve further or help in the formation of one's higher spiritual bio-complexity. Nothing in a universe of process stays where it is. Everything must go either up or down in God's creation. So, even the special substance being-Exioëhary, when humans are failing to engage in being-Partkdolg-duty (God's plan), begins to *involve* back to those lower substances from which its evolution began.

This backward process of involution in one's being-Exioëhary (that is no longer evolving), begins on its descent to manifest as various illnesses and poisonous viewpoints, which "de-perfect" one's essence-individuality and continues to shorten the general duration of earth-people's physical and planetary existence.

Beelzebub tells Hassein that the physical satisfaction and pleasure derived by the abnormal blending (from lust) of being-Exioëhary between male and females, all of us terrestrial humans can thank our inheritance from the ancient Romans as the chief vice of contemporary living, and the quelling of any self-perfecting and spiritual impulses called "thirst-for-being" (which is also a thirst for Truth—an undertaking that affects the creation and formation of our Exioëhary).

The number of abortions performed every year is evidence of a serious failure in human society of grasping the true cosmic significance of this most sacred sacrament between men and women. Rather, then, as a sacred being-fulfillment, earth-humans are more and more viewing pregnancy as a great misfortune, hindering their lifestyles, and which has even generated a whole new industry of specialists for earth-humans and described by Beelzebub as "makers of angels." Swedenborg stated in his book *Conjugial Love* (the angelic expression of marital love) that God sees the creation of children as the greatest use for His universal scheme because it adds to the potential of creating an ever-larger Heaven from the entire human race.

In a lamentable way, Beelzebub points out to Hassein that even two-brained and one-brained creatures, which do not enjoy the mental function of *comparative logic*, such as "hyenas," "cats," "wolves," "lions," "tigers," "wild dogs," "bagooshis(?)" or "frogs" act out this sacred function in no other way than is lawfully foredesigned by God's cosmic purposes. Earth-humans are the only creatures that perform the sex act in ways that do not always promote God's great plan for the universe.

In fact, many people today fool themselves into believing that unnatural sexual acts and preferences of all kinds are all simply extended expressions of God's heavenly love—equating deep love with personal physical pleasure.

Beelzebub now feels he can return to the main topic of the chapter—of perfected-higher-being-bodies of souls that continue to suffer upon reaching the Holy Planet Purgatory.

These higher being-bodies, having originally been perfected to a required level of wisdom and reasoning (through the proper assimilation of the second and third types of being-foods), were first deemed worthy of uniting directly with the sacred sphere of the Most Most Holy Sun Absolute. That is, after the disintegration of their physical bodies, they could directly enter a heavenly sphere and begin to take part in their Divine foreordained purposes (uses).

The process of spiritual evolution, even among earth-humans, originally proceeded without any major obstacles—until that terrifying cosmic incident took place, which Beelzebub calls the "Choot-God-litanical" period. As I have said previously, I believe this unfortunate period corresponds with Swedenborg's notion of the "Fall of Man."

Why? Because after this event, Beelzebub claims that higher being-bodies were no longer immediately sent to the Most Most Holy Protocosmos (Heaven), because individuals were no longer able to obtain the required corresponding results needed to immediately blend (harmonize) with the Holy influences of the Spiritual Sun.

Before the "Choot-God-litanical" period, the sacred emanations of the Theomertmalogos (God's Word), which issued from the Spiritual Sun was still in a pure state. But later, because higher being-bodies were no longer properly perfected in a corresponding manner, when they rose to a higher plane, the influences (influx) from the Spiritual Sun became mixed with their heterogenous qualities and manifestations (like human vanities getting mixed into spiritual processes from all those who entered this higher plane unprepared and unpurified).

Swedenborg supports this theological claim by stating that individual souls in the spiritual realm who continue to manifest negative traits can intercept and even twist the emanations of the Spiritual Sun (which Beelzebub calls a "Geneotriamazikamnian contact"). Then, from the resulting universal directionality of top-down causation (involution), God's beneficial influences are turned into hurtful and ignoble compulsions within those human-receptacles of similar bent who still exist on terrestrial planets. Thanks to this new mixture of influences bubbling up in terrestrial human beings, their involving preferences eventually began to internally assimilate these negative influences as "sins-of-the-body-of-the-soul." These bad influences began to fix themselves into the deepest fabric of human experience.

According to Gurdjieff's Beelzebub, the resulting disharmony caused a particular planet to become separated from its usual system in the cosmos. He calls this planet "Remorse-of-Conscience." The symbolic language being expressed here is that the functioning of *conscience* in the human psyche was displaced from its normal relationship and importance. So even when higher being-bodies perfected their Reasoning to a high level (like Ishmael), without spiritual conscience, they still failed to live in a way that corresponded to the conditions of *innocence* necessary for living harmoniously in the sphere of the Most Most Holy Protocosmos (Heaven).

Swedenborg also agreed that God implanted the function of conscience between the human intellect (thinking function) and the spoiled human heart (insane desires). The split in the human natural mind into internal and external functions was represented by the Land of Goshen being separated from the rest of the consequences happening in the rest of Egypt. Also, a careful reading of his *Arcana Coelestia* offers strong clues that conscience was lost among earth-humans mainly between the Genesis and Exodus chapters of Scripture, upon Joseph's death and where a new Pharoah had taken control of Egypt.

God, from His Infinite justice and mercy, would counter this loss. So providentially, He came up with a solution for this grievous phenomenon by creating a whole new planet (plane) called Purgatory, where flawed higher being-bodies in the other realm could continue to receive all the possibilities (and further teachings) for self-perfection from the undesirable elements they had picked up during their previous physical existence.

In Swedenborg's terms, the Holy Planet Purgatory represents the outer spiritual plane of existence and conscience now separating Heaven and Hell, where souls are carefully prepared for one eternal reality or another.

The confusion of minds in most earth-humans concerning the two opposite spiritual realities of "Heaven" and "Hell" is the flawed and false belief that these realities both represent *places* instead of the inner qualities of one's character and inner spirit.)

But this new mediate plane allowing for continued self-perfection and self-correction guarantees nothing. It still requires each of us to choose to submit ourselves to the personal suffering from the purification of our self-centered loves. So, if we sincerely wish for God and his angels to properly remove harmful properties that we have picked up from the vanities and allurements of terrestrial life, it will happen.

Laws of universal order must always be followed. Heaven is not a vacation destination.

Beelzebub explains to Hassein how this order is to be understood. He states that throughout the universe, all those three-brained beings from different planets who have developed a strong wish of going to this holy plane of existence, can eventually gain the happiness of becoming a particle (angelic unit) of God's Greatness. They clearly understand that their physical bodies (operating on the scale of their own law of Triamazikamno), must always oppose, *as passive principles*, all the aspirations of their higher and spiritual being-parts. (Spiritual forces always act, and physical forces react). These passive (bodily) principles usual take the form of hedonism and laziness. From the voluntary conflict between active (spiritual) and passive (worldly) influences, these noble humans throughout the universe understood, and eagerly participated in this struggle, which Beelzebub calls "Disputekrialnian-friction."

This required "friction" for spiritual growth is the result of an individual always challenging the "wishes" of the lower planetary body. Swedenborg calls this struggle (battle) between our higher and lower desires vastation, temptation and spiritual warfare (See *Arcana Coelestia*, n. 8403).

During this constant inner struggle and personal regeneration, the neutralizing (harmonizing) principle also operating within an individual's own Law of Threefoldness is his or her astral body and the quality of its being-Hanbledzoin (middle blood or animal spirit) that is, one's level of reasoning. As I mentioned earlier, Swedenborg supports a similar idea in that the struggle between higher spiritual and lower worldly ideals is what purifies the middle blood called animal spirits (*Divine Love And Wisdom*, n. 423). The astral body (one's personal quality of reasoning) and its higher blood, always has a viscosity according to the dominant or Ruling Love of an individual. So it can favor a corporeal and worldly constitution or a spiritual and heavenly one.

Unfortunately, the special knowledge of this *neutralizing* astral body and the passive role the human physical body (with its sensory and motor nerves) plays in this spiritual warfare, began to "wither" in earth-humans, from the time of the disappearance of Atlantis to the Babylonian epic—and still continues to wither with those individuals of "new formation" who make up the modern and post-modern world.

Swedenborg's purpose in both his scientific and theological writings was to serve the Lord God by fulfilling the holy duty of reviving this and other hidden and forgotten knowledge back for the human race—so that they could again properly enter into this grand conflict. (He stated that proper spiritual conflict required a physical body, to set the parameters and constraints for one's higher aspirations, inner development, and the qualifying of one's efforts and struggles.)

In reading the text, Gurdjieff's *Beelzebub* seems to contradict Swedenborg's idea that Heaven ("Paradise") and Hell actually exist. It doesn't. This contradiction comes from faulty human understanding based on physical assumptions, because as I said earlier, neither Heaven nor Hell is an actual *place* that you go to—a misguided idea that confuses human understanding even today (and fouls their middle blood). Rather, Heaven and Hell are *states* and *qualities* (preferences) of the human heart and mind (which represent one's true inner spirit). That's why Jesus said to Pontius Pilate, "My kingdom lies within."

So Heaven is not a reward, or retirement destination. It is something you become and keep improving on! Gurdjieff confirms this notion by also describing Hell in *psychical* terms, where higher being-bodies (which are not physical constructs) dwell and suffer. These unfortunate higher being-bodies live in constant anguish, grief and oppression, which is mental torment, rather than physical pain.

Beelzebub indicates that during the general psychosis (confusion of minds) of the Babylonian epic these two terms, *Heaven* and *Hell* became misunderstood as being actual physical places. He further informs his grandson that from this current discussion the young man now has the proper information and material to form a judgment concerning the general misunderstanding that earth-humans have concerning the "questions of the beyond." Beelzebub then jokes with Hassein that if the peculiar notions and human understandings about these questions were shared with their hens, the chickens would laugh so hard that the same thing would happen to them as happens among earth-humans when they ingest castor oil.

Beelzebub shares yet another spicy "tidbit" concerning the consequences of the fairylike thinking of earth-humans—especially concerning their being-Exioëhary. He wants to provide additional data for his grandson in understanding certain concrete results issuing from the processes of sacred law of Heptaparaparshinokh.

Apparently, after the loss of the continent Atlantis, some partial knowledge was preserved concerning the original significance of being-Exioëhary, particularly male "sperm" in the process of spiritual evolution. Unfortunately, this real knowledge was only preserved and handed down in a limited (fragmentary) form. As a result, later earth-humans who sensed the emptiness of their existence, vaguely knew that somehow their being-Exioëhary was an important substance in their efforts to perfect themselves. But they no longer had a full or correct idea of just how this sacred substance played a lawful part in their spiritual struggles.

(Those who have studied Swedenborg's writings have yet to make this connection—even though he states that human seed, or sperm, has as its primary form and nucleus, the soul. See *Organs of Generation*, n. 170. In *Divine Providence*, Swedenborg even states that human sperm comes from one's Love.)

Pondering this problem of how sperm might play a part in spiritual transformation, some of these later and misinformed earth-humans, with their small bits of information, then became convinced that if they simply abstained from ejecting this substance from themselves this practice would eventually give them the anticipated and favorable transformative results that they were expecting.

After this method of abstinence produced many failures, the next generation of earth-humans discovered, through constant trial and error, that such expected results could only be obtained by the ceaseless fulfillment of being-Partkdolg-duty (sincere spiritual vigilance and combat—which changes one's Love).

Unfortunately, this discovery was only temporary. Because, according to Beelzebub, by the fourth generation, terrestrial three-brained beings simply began to "imitate" those before them (and only from their outer observations). So they continued their ritual of abstinence without making the proper inner efforts, which are invisible to ocular vision.

Even at this day, Beelzebub reports that earth-individuals gather together into special "monastaries," and as "monks," they continue to practice this outer form of abstinence. Of course, no sensible result is ever obtained from this silly practice, especially when it is removed from the cosmic responsibility of fulfilling "conscious labors" and "intentional suffering."

(Equally absurd, Aleister Crowley promoted a spiritually degenerate method of *magic*, by which one made a "wish" during the sex act and ejaculation. No responsibility or introspection was required.)

While no reasonable results of spiritual growth were obtained from the monks' misguided sexual practices, two concrete (empirical) results indeed were.

Beelzebub explains, that without one's participating in being-Partkdolg-duty, one cannot assure that the proper food (help from the outside) will enter the two higher "Mdnel-Ins" of the sacred Heptaparaparshinokh. This oversight leads to the normally helpful substances in one's physical body beginning to involve back to their original states from which they began their evolution, which creates lots of organic troubles.

This same involution happens even to male "sperm" when abstaining monks (or anyone else) also abstain from their legitimate and cosmic being-Partkdolg-duty in order (from their own faulty reasoning) to intentionally aid the continued spiritual evolution of this sacred substance from the first being-food.

Instead, the resulting *involutionary* trajectory of their sperm leads to two kinds of negative organic actions in these monks. In one kind of action, these involving substances will promote the depositing of superfluous "fat." (So, could the mysterious obesity crisis in America, be partially caused by individuals not properly participating in their divine evolutionary duty?)

The second type of negative organic action produces *skinny* monks—plus, the dispersing over the whole of their physical bodies with "Poisonioonoskirian-vibrations" (pimples).

So, some monks will become fat during periods of sexual abstinence while others will become skinny, with blemishes. Beelzebub adds that the skinny monks also develop sharply dual psyches— where, no matter how they *outwardly* try to manifest kindness, *inwardly* they still remain hateful to a high degree.

Beelzebub ends this long chapter by offering an additional theory for why he thinks some of these monks become skinny and get pimples, rather than fat. He suggests that those who become skinny probably cheat a little in their abstinence, and engage in sexual practices (like masturbation) on the sneak, which is what brings forth skin eruptions of the face called "pimples"—a sign that their astral bodies (inner reconciling principle) are still leaning toward worldly wants and pleasures.

Even worse, this involving or degenerating process of being-Exioëhary occurring in both these unfortunate types of monks only hastens the fixing of various negative properties of the organ Kundabuffer into their psyches. (Hmmm… I wonder if this degenerative process has anything to do with the epidemic of ordained priests and ministers acting in sexually deviant ways?)

Beelzebub's talk is then interrupted. A ship's servant brings him a special audio message (called a "Leitoochanbros") to listen to, being sent from another part of the universe.

SUMMARY

- The holy planet "Purgatory" represents the universal focus of all evolution and increasing complexity in the universe. This complexity is psycho-spiritual and its trajectory is toward the human form, which is in the image and likeness of God.

- The Lord God often comforts those human souls who have to still suffer and purify their inner complexity to make it correspond more closely to heavenly qualities.

SUMMARY

▪ God created the physical universe by changing His two sacred Laws (Threefoldness and Sevenfoldness) to rely on outside influences for help. Thus, everything that came into existence had to enter into supporting relationships. This unifying and mutual sharing is an analog of God's Divine Love, which unifies.

▪ The highest manifestation of this unifying partnership (conjunction) is between God and the human race. In this way, God's Spiritual Sun can inoculate itself from irrelevance by having created subject/objects (such as humans) to focus its influence on and be properly acknowledged.

▪ The modification in God's two Laws allowed the directionality of complexity and evolution to help humans create more rarefied (spiritual) bodies, through increased powers of reasoning, so that the human race could become *angelic*. Genuine religions used to promote this knowledge, but now it is perverted and forgotten.

▪ Each of the three distinct bodies that earth-humans can acquire and develop during life (physical, rational and spiritual), represent distinct "Ruling Loves" or "centers-of-gravity-initiators-of-one's-individual functioning."

▪ A planet's moons cause the completion of the Law of Sevenfoldness to require male and female sexes. Male and female humans represent only half-beings or half-angels.

▪ Spiritual process relies on the further evolution of male human sperm, which Swedenborg states is created in the human understanding (intellect) as a higher seed and given form in the ground of the human will (love). This is why in Heaven, women come to represent this spiritual ground of Love in order to re-unify eternally with men as their wives (the two no longer half-beings, but one complete angel).

▪ The human, triune-design (three-brained system) is represented by the head-brain (as active part), the spinal column (as passive part) and the various nerve plexuses of the breast (as reconciling or harmonizing part).

▪ Beelzebub also describes how the Law of Sevenfoldness operating in humans gives them the bio-potential of using the Spiritual Sun's influence as "food" to create angelic bio-structure (spiritual bodies) for a heavenly life. In Heaven, angel-humans take on the corresponding active duties of neurons relative to terrestrial citizens.

PART THREE

"Beelzebub tells how people learned and forgot again about the fundamental cosmic law of Heptaparaparshinokh"

After Beelzebub finishes listening to his audio message in the "Leitoochanbros," his grandson, Hassein, is bothered by a seeming contradiction concerning the two sacred cosmic laws.

He tells his Grandfather that he can more easily grasp the details of the sacred law of Triamazikamno (Law of Threefoldness) than that of the sacred Heptaparaparshinokh (Law of Sevenfoldness). Even so, he admits that both these laws are difficult to comprehend. This gets Hassein wondering how it was that earth-humans, particularly after the *second Transapalnian perturbation* (disappearance of Atlantis and spiritual conscience) when their abnormal psyche and education (Oskiano) produced only "automatic-Reason" could ever have contained such potent and complex laws.

It seemed impossible to Hassein for such abnormal earth-humans to ever grasp these two cosmic laws with their deteriorating powers of cognition.

At this point in my interpretation of these Tales, I would like to point out that even most of those who intensely study Swedenborg's writings have—like Hassein—a better sense for the Law of Three-foldness (God's triune order) operating in all things than they do of Sevenfoldness. (I have come to believe that the Law of Sevenfoldness represents the arrangement and order of the knowledges of Truth and their application, by which the Lord God brings forth all process, including His ultimate Church on Earth—*the New Jerusalem*.)

Swedenborg did offer some interesting clues relating to the sevenfold successiveness and orderly series of events unfolding in all things, especially within the sacred stories of Holy Scripture. One of these clues is His statement that "three" and "seven" have a similar symbolic meaning of *wholeness*. The difference being that the number "seven" is used particularly in communicating the holiness and sacredness of a process (*Apocalypse Explained*, n. 20), while "three-ness" is used for all process in general.

He alludes to the sacred sevenfold series of the Seven-Day Creation Story of Genesis, also, as the order of functions in the "octave" of the human intellect (*Worship And Love Of God*, n. 122. footnote b.), plus the *cyclic* stages of tree growth from *seed, root, stem, branches, leaves, flowers, fruit* to *seeds* again (*Divine Love and Wisdom*, n. 314). All God's processes follow this cyclic course, which is why all universal progressions are sacred (from first principles to outmosts and back to first principles). Every coherent (and whole) process represents an image of creation.

Other than that, Swedenborg does not shine additional light on this important second fundamental law or take this Arcanum further to make it more obvious to the reader, stating that first, more must be known concerning Divine action (that is, from first principles to ultimates) before such a profound understanding can be acquired (*Apocalypse Explained*, n. 41).

God's Law of Sevenfoldness is no ordinary knowledge.

The law represents how successive progressions mutually cooperate to form simultaneous operations, as in the organization of *systems*. In *Conjugial Love*, n. 314, Swedenborg states, "It is extremely difficult, however, to present to the perception the mode in which things successive carry themselves into things simultaneous, and the nature of the order they form there; for among the learned there is as yet no idea that can serve for the elucidation of the matter."

Without this sevenfold cyclic law, the other fundamental Law of Threefoldness could never both descend outward (involving) nor ascend inward (evolving).

The special understanding of Divine order, process and concord, through the combination of both laws (Threefoldness and Sevenfoldness) leads to a *Mathematical Philosophy of Universals*, which Swedenborg claims would represent the one science of all the sciences, because it is the complex of them all. Just as profound, this combination of laws produces an organic pattern and would also be called the *Circle of Life* (and by Gurdjieff, the *Enneagram*). Therefore, the full understanding of such all-embracing, and living-laws lies well beyond the current comprehension of material science (or scientism).

This means that Gurdjieff acquired the rare and additional understanding to take this spiritual Arcanum about the progressive series of mediating causes (truth advancing) further than most of those who are even aware, that the Holy City, *The New Jerusalem*, is now descending to Earth (and into the hearts and minds of people)! I believe that Gurdjieff as well as Swedenborg both tapped into their purer minds. So, sacred knowledge is still streaming in from Heaven, awaiting higher human minds to receive it! (Swedenborg claimed that continuous revelation is the criteria for determining whether an established organization can be called a true *living* church or school.)

Another difficulty in elucidating the second fundamental *Law of Sevenfoldness* is that everything can still be broken down into triads and understood as an operation of triads. Triads (end, cause and effect) indeed operate within all the distinct steps in the sequential

Law of Sevenfoldness, creating its seven points of stability or common equilibrium through its reconciling outcomes (which relates them harmoniously to all the other triunal outcomes). I illustrate this point in my book *Swedenborg's Circle of Life.*

All larger and smaller scales of progressive series operate in this holistic process—when viewed in their complex.

So, it is only when a *series of triads* proceed to form a coherent and common equilibrium (harmonious goal) from all their mediating causal effects that the sevenfold nature of all process can be illustrated and become evident. In other words, the sacred Law of Threefoldness creates, from the blending of its three forces, a single step or gravity center (reconciling principle) as it progresses through the steps of the Law of Sevenfoldness. By the time a series of triads reaches its eighth progressive step or reconciling result, the process has been harmoniously completed.

The Law of Threefoldness then re-emerges to act as three opening points (Mdnel-Ins) for outside influences, such as "food," to enter into the newly created greater whole (octave), producing on a larger scale, a new comprehensive system and organic pattern that will allow for *outside support* to help the new process continue and be connected to everything else. So both laws are needed to act together to unify the universe in a way that resembles God's love!

As I describe this dynamic I am painfully aware of how greater explanation can often obscure a topic. But I must continue.

Due to the change from God's original *Autoegocratic* system to the *Trogoautoegocratic* system (mentioned in the previous chapter), passive elements in some of the (mathematically precise) mediating triads now have to be brought in from outside sources (like food) to maintain the integrity of the process and allow for every function to stay connected through mutual support, forming a web of universal unity.

This divine organic (living) order and sharing necessitates looking at the connections and completion of a series of triads in a harmonic sevenfold series as needing to be "fed." (Sorry folks, but I would rather write a complete new book about further details concerning the two laws in this sacred process of unity than agonize here to make sure that you understand all this more clearly. So I did. Furthermore, this unique knowledge, and its understanding, is a gift from God—not from me.)

Still, I personally believe that at some future time the sacred Heptaparaparshinokh will eventually become the property of most earth-human scientists and theologians. This will also offer a new organic wrinkle in understanding Swedenborg's *science of correspondences* (from the sacred framework and patterning principles of living, dynamic and holistic world processes—and not just in terms of static symbolism).

This unified model and design of connected steps and whole series of process is both multi-leveled and alive!

Theologically speaking, this living, cyclic design represents the *Divine Power of Truth Advancing* (through various orbs and wheel-like circuits), which is also called the *Divine Proceeding*, whereby Love emanating from the Sun Absolute (Spiritual Sun) providentially comes forth into existence and gains a *corresponding* form called *Truth*. This is why Swedenborg states that all Truth represents various ontological forms and expressions of God's Love.

Nothing can proceed (emanate) from God but what is consistently Himself, and therefore also Divine (*The True Christian Religion*, n. 6). This is why all true process in the created universe is sacred!

Returning to Hassein's perplexity as to how flawed humans could have ever discerned such a complex law as the Law of Sevenfoldness, Beelzebub tells his grandson that from time to time various individuals on Earth escape many of the abnormal influences of human automatic Reason occurring around them and develop a genuine objective "being-reason" that is more in line with that of other three-brained beings throughout the great universe.

Beelzebub assures Hassein that even among earth-humans, the germs and possibilities of higher reasoning proper for responsible existence within God's grand scheme are always present. These germs are the Divine being-data secretly implanted deeply within an individual's *subconscious* mind to form a "representative-of-the-Very-Essence-of-Divinity" or "conscience." (As a reminder, Swedenborg also called this secret and protected holy data that is divinely implanted within each of us the *remains*—a plane for God's heavenly influence to operate in the lives of people on Earth.)

Swedenborg maintained that without this Divine implantation, we could never be rational or be saved. Only God is Love and life and any belief of one's personal goodness without God is a delusion. Furthermore, God's Love and Truth can only flow into what is God's, and God's work of transformation can only proceed from such a holy plane.

As to Hassein's question, Beelzebub replies that in some cases, an earth-human, during his or her preparatory age, gains the right evaluation of being-Partkdolg-duty (cosmic responsibility) which stirs up this divine being-data implanted in us (this "stirring" is symbolized by God's moving across the face of the waters in Genesis, ver. 2) so that one's "essence-center-of-gravity" and education is anchored to the Divine impulse of Conscience, whereby an individual gains the "potency-not-to-be-identified-with-and-not-to-be-affected-by-externals-through-one's-inevitably-inherent-passions."

In a way that is similar to Swedenborg's claim of the importance of this special plane for salvation, Beelzebub assures Hassein that only this Divine being-impulse (of conscience) engenders the proper mental development required for correctly perceiving all true phenomena and cosmic laws. (Again, Swedenborg made the point that God only works through the remains and conscience implanted within people's lives.)

In other words, for the human mind to recognize and develop the Divine data stored in one's deeper consciousness, one has to remove their natural and habitual notions of self-importance and worldly status. Only then can God's influence flow in. This state is obtained by submitting oneself to the tenets of God's Love—from a sense of personal duty and humility. (Beelzebub also states that it is extremely important that such a fortunate individual, who embraces such a duty on Earth, finds a teacher or guide who has had some level of success and experience with persevering through the labors and real requirements for inner growth.)

I would like to add here that Gurdjieff and Swedenborg are the only two teachers I have come across who emphasize that love and *intention* operate the cockpit of human intelligence. So the real challenge of raising one's intellect to both grasp and appropriate higher cosmic and spiritual truth into one's life must also focus on raising the quality of one's heart and desires. Otherwise one's knowledge remains just *head-knowledge* and adds nothing to our being. In fact, it splits our psyche.

When one embraces spiritual love, it arranges (organizes) the ideas in the human mind to operate from proper Divine order and therefore creates an inner ecosystem (or psycho-kingdom) for itself within the human intellect through greater rationality. This psycho-spiritual organization represents one's "other-world" reality and is accomplished through connecting with God's sacred data implanted in one's interior natural mind, and forming an expanding plane for Conscience to grow and bio-develop into a spiritual body.

(So, making higher bodies depends on spiritual labors and inner combat—not comfort. According to Swedenborg, an individual's higher [spiritual] body is organically tailored [from one's efforts] for a particular eternal reality and spiritual environment.)

After explaining to Hassein that such fortunate individuals can still arise on Earth, even at the present day, Beelzebub now offers to explain to his grandson how earth-humans first became aware of the more complex fundamental cosmic law of *Heptaparaparshinokh*. Beelzebub feels that his explanations will also help Hassein visualize how earth-humans gradually forgot about this fundamental law.

It was, at first, out of the question for earth-humans to discover this law when they had the organ Kundabuffer still operating at full force within their planetary bodies, because this organ caused individuals to perceive only false illusions rather than reality (God's Truth). Later, when this maleficent organ was destroyed, the human psyche was temporarily freed up to enjoy relatively sane being-mentation.

As previously mentioned, on the continent of ancient Atlantis, certain alert individuals (Akhaldans) began to notice in themselves that something "not-quite-right" proceeded in them. That is, something in their behavior and actions (heart) did not correspond to the more noble ideas and values they held (in their intellects and memory banks). They also became aware that they had the real possibilities of destroying these "not-quite-right" manifestations from their lives by making certain kinds of efforts. These concerned individuals began to search out the causes of these surprising and "abnormal functionings."

(This concern actually was turned into a branch of their science, and an individual named *Theophany* was the first to lay down a rational foundation for this science. It centered around the "most-necessary-functioning-of-Reason.")

Swedenborg stated that the ultimate goal of human reasoning and rationality is to become spiritual—through the application of the noble values learned in one's intellect. This special type of reasoning is above merely being civil or looking naturally (outwardly) moral to the eyes of others. It relies on receiving God's heavenly truths into one's heart and actions—that is, sincerely living for others.

As Beelzebub had chanced to learn during his visits to Earth, this Theophany fellow was once pouring a particular liquid mixture onto a marble slab so that it could dry. (Beelzebub describes the liquid as containing an extract from a plant on Earth called "Patetook," some pine-resin, and also cream of the milk of "Khenionian goats." This mixture would then harden into a mastic—that was used as a chewing gum after eating.) During one occasion, Theophany noticed that after pouring this mixture onto the marble slab, it cooled in a way that revealed seven *definite plane surfaces*. (Remember that as a young boy, Gurdjieff noticed seven tints in his blood's color on the roots of his wisdom tooth that was knocked out of his mouth by another boy's punch.)

Theophany and a growing number of his interested friends began additional experiments (from a *conscious aim*) to discover the cause of this unexpected law-comformableness in the liquid. What they eventually discovered was that all cosmic results issuing from transitory states (process and causation) always consist of seven different aspects. The branch of science that emerged from their discoveries was called "Tazaloorinono" or "the-seven-aspectness-of-every-whole-phenomenon."

Swedenborg maintained that the highest angels of Heaven view reality from *comprehensive wholes*—they see all things in unifying patterns and connection through series (*Heaven & Hell*, n. 270 [5]). In my earlier book Proving God, I showed how even the Lord's Prayer consists of a connected (sevenfold) series of mediate causes (including two food Mdnel-Ins—making it the *Law of Ninefoldness*) and also forming a comprehensive whole.

Unfortunately, this knowledge was lost after the continent of Atlantis (proper Conscience) perished (and instead, people began building the Tower of Babel). Beelzebub explains that because this science was so widely known on the continent Atlantis, nobody anticipated the need to preserve its knowledge in an extant Legominism to be saved for future generations. However, the knowledge of the law of Heptaparaparshinokh was still, centuries later, rediscovered by twin Chinese brothers, named "Choon-Kil-Tez" and "Choon-Tro-Pel." ("Choon" means "prince.")

It is worth our reflecting on the idea that these twin brothers were also "princes" because it provides an additional clue that Gurdjieff, like Swedenborg, understood the abstract language of correspondences, because the term "princes" symbolizes primary truths—and that is exactly what the twin Chinese brothers' research would reveal!

To add further support to my view, Beelzebub states that these twin princes were descendants of King Konuzion, who himself was a direct descendent of those belonging to that great society of learned beings from Atlantis, called *Akhaldan* (a society that possessed unusual knowledge). This positive genealogical situation allowed the twin princes to inherit, and be brought up in, a more positive environment where proper being-data was made available to them. This gave them the power to actualize "being-Partkdolg-duty" during their terrestrial lives.

This situation also spared the twin brothers from the cognitive atrophy happening to other earth-humans around them. Rather than seek knowledge for the satisfaction of "vainglorious," "proud," and "self-loving" weaknesses, these exceptional twins had as their ultimate "aim," the attainment of a higher gradation of Being. Put in Swedenborg's theological terms, this means they were willing to submit themselves to the challenges of spiritual and angelic evolution.

These twins first grew up in the city of Gob, in the Asian country Maralpleicie, but after the great windstorms of the third Transapalnian perturbation (which created deserts), they moved further east into China. It is interesting to note that concerning the ancient wisdom, called by Swedenborg the "Ancient Word" (a Bible before the Bible), he states that it is still protected in the "Great Tartary" (is this Gurdjieff's Maralpleicie?), and if one cares to find this ancient sacred knowledge, to "Seek for it in China" (*Apocalypse Revealed*, n. 11 [2]). This statement by Swedenborg tells me that the Law of *Sevenfoldness* might also have been easier to discern from the earlier unfolding narratives of symbolic language used in the extant writings of God's first sacred stories (the Ancient Word) than in the later Judeo-Christian version, where true scientific principles were also abandoned.

Beelzebub tells Hassein a curious fact—that these twin princes had ironically chosen to study the cosmic substances of the *poppy plant*—substances that their great grandfather, King Konuzion, had tried to stop the chewing of among the citizens of his kingdom by inventing a "religious teaching." Beelzebub then informs his grandson that there are three classes of flora (plants) that have evolved on the Earth's surface to help in the transformation of cosmic substances during the process of "Iraniranumange" (universal interdependence).

The bio-formations of the first class of flora are called "Oonastralnian-arisings." This class of vegetation contributes to the evolution and involution of active elements simply found on the surface of a planet.

The second class of plantlife, called "Okhtatralnian-arisings," are apparatuses for the transformation of similar terrestrial substances, but in addition, they can also transform influences issuing from the Sun and other planets of a given solar system.

Through the arising of the third class of plants, called "Polormedekhtian" even substances issuing out from other suns and star systems in outer space are transformed. The poppy plant represents this third class. So, extraterrestrial influences from far-off star systems are absorbed and metabolized by the poppy plant, from the "ubiquitous-diffusion-of-the-radiations-of-all-kinds-of-cosmic-concentrations" occurring in a planet's atmosphere. (Modern science doesn't classify plants this way nor is it aware that certain plants can absorb cosmic influences from deep space.)

Swedenborg informs us that the plant world represents various functions of the human intellect, so similar forms of receptivity are built into the human brain—terrestrial, astral, and cosmic.

The Twins, while living in China, began to investigate the totality of cosmic substances obtained from this Polormedekhtian plant. The main substance of this totality was named *opium*, which at that time meant "dream-maker." They were intrigued by the fact that when this substance, opium, is ingested by humans, every sort of painful sensation temporarily vanished. They began to wonder if there was a possibility, by means of the extraordinary properties of this plant, that they could reverse a special form of "psychic illness" which was spreading through the population of refugees (from Gob) around them.

However, they later abandoned this particular medical aim when they discovered that opium itself consisted of seven independent crystallizations defining its "wholeness," and that each of these seven independent subjective properties consisted of seven others—and so on and so on. They discovered that the splitting of seven properties from smaller and smaller whole units continued almost to infinity, and this unexpected discovery greatly sparked the intellectual curiosity of the twins. They believed that this astonishing discovery had to represent some (as yet unknown), universal law.

Beelzebub's own private research showed him that these two *Saintly* Chinese twin scientists had become convinced beyond all doubt that opium consisted of a whole range of compounds, each containing seven "diversely-subjectively-propertied-active-elements."

So the Twins decided to begin investigating whether "cosmic results" and "phenomena," other than opium, manifested this same law-conformableness.

Beelzebub also found out that the twins had concentrated their further experiments on the "white-ray" of visible light, plus the vibrations of "sound." It was from these additional studies by the twins that **the Law of Heptaparaparshinokh was rediscovered on the planet Earth.**

The twin Chinese princes then went on to give specific names to the seven independent aspects discovered in all whole results (distinct things representing one complex or comprehensive whole), including their secondary and tertiary derivatives or offspring. (Again, Swedenborg indicated that Heaven's highest angels perceive and understand all phenomena happening around them as *comprehensive wholes*—coordinated series of things in their complex or composite form—that is, as complete units.)

The first seven fundamental aspects of each whole, the twins called:

(1) Erti-Pikan-On
(2) Ori-Pikan-On
(3) Sami-Pikan-On
(4) Okhti-Pikan-On
(5) Khooti-Pikan-On
(6) Epsi-Pikan-On
(7) Shvidi-Pikan-On

And the second class:

(1) Erti-Noora-Chaka
(2) Ori-Noora-Chaka
(3) Sami-Noora-Chakoo
(4) Okhti-Noora-Chaka
(5) Khooti-Noora-Chaka
(6) Epsi-Noora-Chaka
(7) Shvidi-Noora-Chakoo

In addition to this, the Twins distinguished the sevenfold results of *sound* and their number of vibrations by adding the word "Alil." For the sevenfold results of color obtained from the composite of the "white-ray" they added the words "Nar-Khra-Noora." And to the active elements of the "Polormedekhtian" product called *opium* they simply added the appropriate numerical value of their "specific gravity."

The twin reseachers were able to define these specific vibrations and specific gravities of distinct phenomena by taking, as the standard unit of the vibrations of sound, what they called the "Nirioonossian-world-sound."

Beelzebub promises to explain the "Nirioonossian-world-sound" at some future date to Hassein, but that it is more advantageous for him to know that genuine scientists all over the universe take as their standard unit for calculations of specific gravities and specific-vibrations from that part of the sacred *Theomertmalogos* or Word-God, that which contains all the fullness of "lifeness" in each of its three holy forces of the sacred Triamazikamno, and what current earth-humans call an "atom of Hydrogen."

While hydrogen is a good standard unit for confrontative calculations, Beelzebub suggests that hydrogen (which indeed is an elemental unit containing all three triune forces in equal amounts) can still be broken down further into smaller whole units for measurement. (Both Gurdjieff and Swedenborg had cosmologies that contained smaller whole units of substance and were quite different from today's particle theories and quarks. Any smallest whole unit could be called an atom in their world models. So atoms could represent ethereal particles, magnetic corpuscles, including smaller elements of the primordial universe, and even units of non-material [psychical] substances emanating from the Spiritual Sun.)

Beelzebub further informs his grandson that Hydrogen is one of the seven cosmic substances that contribute to the "inner Ansa-palnian-octave" of a given solar system, which in turn, represents a *one-seventh* independent part (unit) of the larger fundamental "common-cosmic Ansapalnian-octave." Beelzebub gives the names of the heterogeneous substances contained in the "inner Ansapalnian-octave" as they are called from their home planet of *Karatas*. They are:

(1) Planekurab (Hydrogen)

(2) Alillonofarab (Fluorine)

(3) Krilnomolnifarab (Chlorine)

(4) Talkoprafarab (Bromine)

(5) Khritofalmonofarab (Iodine)

(6) Sirioonorifarab (?)

(7) Klananoizufarab (?)

Beelzebub does not give the corresponding scientific names of the last two cosmic substances (in Earth-terms) because earth-humans of the early twentieth Century did not yet know of them. Apparently these last two substances are essential to human existence. However two centuries earlier, alchemists called these last two substances "Hydro-oomiak" and "Petrkarmak." (Looking at the current chart of the *Periodic Table of the Elements*, I can only surmise that the *sixth* cosmic substance is *Astatine* and the *seventh* substance has the atomic number "117." But this is only a guess, so don't hold me to it.)

(Even though these scales of different octaves are not recognized by contemporary science, I trust that the reader can still instinctively sense the cosmic correctness of this order in the universe. In fact, even earth-scientists use octaves to classify different higher energies and wavelengths—but not yet with the organization of different solid materials and substances. Both Gurdjieff and Swedenborg even incorporated this spectrum into the functioning of the human mind!)

So, after their discovery, the two Chinese brothers began to formulate the special information of this knowledge into a scientific model—to make it more discernable to their intellects.

According to Beelzebub, their model included the discovery of two of the three main law-conformable *particularities* in the great cosmic law of octaves. That is, the twins had successfully identified two "Mdnel-Ins" (missing halftones) of the octave (which tells me they probably failed to discern the significance of the chaotic fifth interval in this process, called the *Harnel-Aoot*, which corresponded to the holy reconciling force of the sacred Triamazikamno.

However, by including these two Mdnel-Ins (portals or appertures) within their scientific model, the "seven-aspected-ness-of-every-whole-phenomenon" then came to be called the Law of "Ninefoldness" (Swedenborg acknowledged that the number "9" represents all things in their *complex* (or *wholeness*) and that certain connections in such a periodic process or gyre needed to be "fed" to keep going. *Worship And Love Of God*, n. 96).

Exactly what these twin Chinese scientists had discovered was that there were *always* two "obligatory-gap-aspects-of-the-un-broken-flowing-of the-whole." (Remember, these two "gaps" were originally caused by the Creator *lengthening* and *shortening* two intervals in this fundamental law to change everything over to the Trogoautoegocratic system of mutual sharing and external support.) A correct universal theory of process and causality must include missing *causal links* (today, this idea is even portrayed as missing "black keys" on the common piano keyboard!). These two causal links always enter at precise mathematical points along the dynamical completing process of this law—no matter what the scale or dimension of the "transitory result." These two gaps are what allows for cosmic "sharing" and all full processes to be connected to everything else, and thus be representative of an organic blueprint of relationship and an analog of God's Love.

This means that the "fine-tuning" of the laws of the universe is even more mathematically exact (and organic) than current earth-scientists now believe.

To further verify their results of this fine-tuning, these two Chinese researchers had at their disposal an experimental apparatus called the "Alla-attapan," which they also invented. With this unique apparatus, the twin princes could obtain valuable objective results from "chemical," "physical," and "mechanical" experiments.

So they began to use this apparatus to experiment with *opium,* *white-light* and *sound,* to see not only if these three distinct "transitory results" or "actualizing constructions" proceeded from the same laws of orderly process, but whether each of these distinct manifestations (Dooczako) can affect each other in correspondingly precise ways! For instance, does a certain color in a series have some affinity with a certain sound or chemical in a series? (Again, such an ordered universe and design would be unfathomable to current scientists and would blow their minds away.)

Beelzebub states that he saw this unique apparatus (Alla-attapan) with his very own eyes and was therefore, in a perfect position to describe its various parts to his grandson. He had gotten a request from his good friend Gornahoor Harharkh (the same individual who invented a means to artificially separate Okidanokh into its *three* essential parts and who wanted to study earth-apes) to bring him one of these experimental apparatuses back from Earth to his home planet Saturn.

Beelzebub procured an Alla-attapan and brought it back to Mars before sending it off to his extraterrestrial essence-friend. During the time that the Alla-attapan was on Mars, Beelzebub made himself familiar with all the features of its design. He next describes these features in detail. (I found that mentally following Beelzebub's explanation of the peculiar design of this unique apparatus was itself a real exercise for my mind and consciousness. But here goes. Please try to follow Beelzebub's description as best as you can.)

The Alla-attapan consisted of three major parts.

The first (and front) part was called "Loosochepana," a cone-shaped pipe whose wide end was hermetically fitted into the frame of a sole window in the room where the experiments were made. At the other end (opposite the window) was a smaller aperture and "collecting disk" where light gathered from the window could be focused to form a more concentrated ray or light beam.

This light beam was then sent through a second part of the apparatus that was a crystal or what earth-humans would call a "prism." This second part of the Alla-attapan broke up the white light ray into seven different colors, which were projected onto an ivory slab (called "Pirinjiel"). The surface of this ivory slab was constructed in a special way that allowed the colored rays landing on it to again be concentrated (but in a different way which Beelzebub does not describe) and sent off toward another crystal which projected the results onto a second and larger ivory slab (called "Polorishboorda").

Opposite this Polorishboorda (the larger ivory slab), was a small specially designed apparatus (another prism?) that, by shifting its angle, one could choose a particular color and even direct this color to the third major part of the Alla-attapan.

Beelzebub stops here and tells Hassein that although the contemporary earth-humans know about prisms, through a prism, they only obtain the seven "negative colored rays" of light, but to actually gain a true understanding of other phenomena connected with the transitory changes of the white-ray they must extract its "positive colored rays." Apparently, the negative colored rays or spectrum obtained by modern prisms does not portray the true order in which these rays actually arise from their sources. Poor Newton.

Thanks to the arrangement of the *two* crystals (yes, another prism!) of the Alla-attapan, positive colored rays were indeed obtained and able to be directed to the third part of this astonishing apparatus, called the "Riank-Pokhortarz."

This third part consisted of a three-legged stand, on top of which were two ivory balls. The larger ball was specially fitted on top of the smaller ball. On the lower (smaller) ball, facing opposite the movable second ivory slab, a special cavity was made where opium was placed. The upper (larger) ivory ball was bored straight through, horizontally, to the first cone-shaped pipe of the Alla-attapan, which focused light from the window. Radially perpendicular to this first bore, another was drilled—this time only to its center.

This second bore of the larger ball could be aimed in a way that the colored rays could be directed from the Loosochepana or reflected from the special cavity bored in the lower (and smaller) ivory ball. Through the bore of the larger ball, a specially prepared piece of "bamboo" could be moved freely inside. These specially prepared bamboos were soaked in absolute darkness in a liquid consisting of four ingredients. They were:

(1) The egg whites from a bird then called "Amersamarskanapa"

(2) The juice squeezed from a plant called "Chiltoonakh"

(3) The *excretion* from a quadruped animal called "Kezmaral"

(4) "Mercury-amalgam"

The soaked bamboo, again in absolute darkness, was fitted inside other non-soaked and thicker shoots of bamboo, which were then hermetically sealed at their ends. When an experiment was about to take place, the thicker bamboo was specially inserted into the bore drilled all the way through the larger ivory ball of the Riank-Pokhortarz. A small hook attached to the inner and specially soaked smaller bamboo allowed it to be moved inside the larger bamboo at any speed desired.

Now, we get a most amazing display of the *correspondences* that can take place between all orderly, lawful series and their transitory results.

During an experiment with this apparatus, the part of the soaked bamboo that a positive colored ray fell upon, either directly from the

Loosochepana or reflected from the cavity of the smaller ivory ball, became instantly dyed the same color as the ray that was directed upon it! Even more amazing, exposed parts of the smaller bamboo would also become dyed according to colors corresponding to particular *sound vibrations* made from a stringed instrument, or middle part of the experimental apparatus, called Dzendvokh.

Beelzebub describes the Dzendvokh as having a strong frame made of mammoth tusks, upon which were stretched strings of various lengths and thicknesses. The strings were made partly from twisted goat's intestines and partly from the tail-hairs of various other animals.

Hassein becomes curious to know what the heck a mammoth is.

Beelzebub tells his grandson that mammoths were large two-brained animals that became *suddenly* extinct due to extreme climate changes. These climate changes were the result of the Moon's atmosphere trying to harmonize itself within the equilibrium of the rest of the solar system, which caused great winds to be stirred up on the Earth's surface, where certain parts became covered by sand, and its two polar regions became subjected to constant snowstorms. (It is still a big mystery to modern earth-scientists why mammoths and other large mammals quickly disappeared. According to Beelzebub, this intensified snowfall was the reason for the mammoth's sudden extinction on Earth.)

Beelzebub reminds us that the Moon is a "planetary upstart" and chief enemy to the planet Earth (and us humans). He also points out that mammoths can still be found fully preserved in the hermetically closed and protected conditions below the snow and frozen Earth strata. What I find most relevant is that Beelzebub is offering the reader clues that the experimental apparatus he was describing may have been created more than 10,000 years ago (the time in human history that Swedenborg would probably have said that the Ancient or Church of Noah had already passed on from the Earth—and whose members possessed the profound universal knowledge called *the science of correspondences*).

So, the entire three-part experimental apparatus "Alla-attapan" allowed ancient investigators to verify that *light, sound* and *opium* equally expressed (corresponded to each other) "mutual-actions-ensuing-one-from-the-other-and-forming-one-common-functioning" in their "transitory results" in the evolutionary (upwards) and involutionary (downwards) particularities of the law of Heptapara-parshinokh. (Swedenborg called each of these completed transitory results a "common equilibrium." So here, Beelzebub is describing an experimental apparatus capable of providing physical evidence for Swedenborg's *science of correspondences*—a multi-leveled affinity!

For instance, a colored ray directed on any active element of opium transformed it into another active element that *corresponded* in its newly acquired vibrations to the vibrations of the colored ray, which acted upon it! The same result could be obtained when sounds made from the various strings of the Dzendvokh were directed upon elements of opium! In other experiments, if a colored ray were made to pass straight through an active element of opium or through wave-sounds of particular vibrational rates, that ray would be transformed into a corresponding color as well.

That is potent stuff!

Beelzebub further adds that experimental success also came when phenomena, with a higher rate of vibrations, were directed on "transitory-cosmic-results" containing lower vibrational rates. (Swedenborg concurred that higher influences flowed into and directed lower ones. Scientifically speaking, this influx would be referred to as *top-down causality.*) This relationship allows so-called miracles to occur.

Thanks to the twin brothers and their amazing apparatus, this knowledge eventually became an independent and genuine branch of science in ancient China. Unfortunately, within two to three centuries after the death of these two brothers, and the failure of later generations of humans to use this potent knowledge (and its two Mdnel-Ins) to help them with their "inner struggle" of spiritual evolution and free themselves of the negative influences of the organ Kundabuffer, this science evaporated.

Beelzebub gives two causes for the loss of this great knowledge.

First, because of the accursed organ Kundabuffer itself, earth-humans developed an "organic-psychic-need" to be considered *important* and began the practice of "cunning-wiseacring" (making shit up). It is these types of individuals, possessing such a specific inherency to bullshit (wiseacre) that Beelzebub describes as "learned beings of new formation," after the loss of Atlantis. (Remember, Beelzebub is talking about us!)

The second cause operated from a larger cosmic scale.

During times when these self-centered earth-humans came under the influence of the action of the law *Solioonensius* (this is where phenomena in different solar systems affect each other and create tensions) their intuitive ability to sense and properly forsee things began to weaken. As a result, this genuine branch of scientific knowledge also began to be distorted by them as it was passed down to future generations—until it became almost forgotten.

However, according to Beelzebub, some actual bits and fragments of this important knowledge automatically reached later generations of earth-beings. One of these fragments concerned methods of separating from the Polormedekhtian product called *opium*, certain of its independent active elements (as "dope"). Another fragment concerned "the law of combination of colors." And a third fragment reaching later generations of humans involved the "seven-toned scale of sound."

The first fragment was preserved mainly because the substances derived from opium produced pleasant and agreeable actions upon the abnormal general-psyche of the earth-humans. In other words, these substances obtained from opium were used to satisfy the peaceful functioning of the properties left in them from the maleficent organ Kundabuffer. So, these mind-altering substances allowed earth-humans to continue to view reality in a delusional way.

Beelzebub then relates to Hassein that a contemporary "comical" scientist named *Mendelejeff* even collected the names of these particular active elements, separated out from opium, and classified them according to their "atomic weights." Although this classification does not correspond to reality or to objective science, Beelzebub states that these atomic weights can still offer an approximation of the earlier classification made by the great terrestrial twin scientists of early China.

These twin brothers from ancient China had succeeded in identifying nearly *four hundred* active elements of opium, but knowledge of how to obtain only forty-two active elements have reached contemporary "chemists of the Earth." These forty-two active elements have currently the following names:

(1) Morphine
(2) Protopine
(3) Lanthopine
(4) Porphiroksine
(5) Opium or nicotine
(6) Paramorphine or thebaine
(7) Phormine or psuedophormine
(8) Metamorphine
(9) Gnoskopine
(10) Oilopine
(11) Atropine
(12) Pirotine
(13) Dephteropine
(14) Tiktoutine
(15) Kolotine
(16) Khaivatine
(17) Zoutine
(18) Trotopine
(19) Laudanine
(20) Laudanosine
(21) Podotorine
(22) Arkhatozine
(23) Tokitozine
(24) Liktonozine

(25) Makanidine

(26) Popoverine

(27) Krintonine

(28) Kodomine

(29) Kolomonine

(30) Koilononine

(31) Katarnine

(32) Hydrokatarnine

(33) Opianine (mekonine)

(34) Mekonoiozine

(35) Pistotorine

(36) Phykhtonozine

(37) Codeine

(38) Nartzeine

(39) Psuedocodeine

(40) Microparaine

(41) Microtebaine

(42) Messaine

Beelzebub confesses to Hassein that during his last trip on Earth he had heard that their scientists had discovered several other independent active elements from opium. However, since nothing truly positive ever comes from these contemporary discoveries he did not interest himself in learning the names of these additional substances. (I wonder how many more substances were obtained from opium after Gurdjieff's death in late 1947?)

Moving along to the second fragment of ancient knowledge discovered by the twin brothers from ancient China that had reached contemporary earth-humans was the "law of the combination of colors." Beelzebub informs his grandson that until two centuries ago, most of this knowledge was handed down to the "Persians" but because of the growing "European" influences, and their paintings, this knowledge was also quickly forgotten. (Gurdjieff indicated that Persian rugs over three hundred years old still contained this special knowledge of color.)

The third fragment of objective knowledge that reached contemporary earth-people from remote times was the "seven-toned scale of sound," which the twin brothers called the "seven-gravity-center-vibrations-of-sound." To add context to the discussion, Beelzebub says that he brought back to Mars, from Earth, a stringed instrument whose vibration-engendering "strings" could be arranged like that of the second and middle major part or *Dzendvokh* of the experimental apparatus Alla-attapan used by the twin princes. But it was much simpler.

Today, it would be called a "piano."

Beelzebub informs Hassein, that about a century and a half after the death of the Chinese twin brothers, a genuine learned being named King-Too-Toz worked out new details of the Law of Sevenfoldness, based on the second part of the Alla-attapan, or Dzendvokh. This new theory was called the "evolution and involution of vibrations."

He was able to confirm this theory from his own specially invented apparatus called the "Lav-Merz-Nokh" (a kind of piano instrument on steroids). This special elucidatory apparatus, like the Dzendvokh (and piano), also had a strong frame supporting many stretched strings made from the intestines and tail-hairs of various animals. At one end of the frame were pegs, which could be turned to tighten or loosen the strings to create the required number of vibrations. The apparatus contained forty-nine white strings, each of which represented a whole "center-of-gravity-of-the-octave" or "whole note."

Each grouping of seven strings or seven gravity-center-sounds" was called an octave and the totality of vibrations from each octave corresponded to the totality of vibrations issuing from all the cosmic substances that compose one of the units or one of the seven-centers-of-gravity of the "fundamental common-cosmic Ansapalnian-octave" of the universe.

King-Too-Toz categorized these octaves so that each had its own name, including names for each whole note in its scale. The highest octave obtained from the Lav-Merz-Nokh was called "Arachiaplnish." This octave was followed by six others named "Erkrordiapan," "Eror-diapan," "Chorortdiapan," "Piandjiapan," "Vetserordiapan," and "Okhterordiapan."

Each of the seven gravity-center-strings, or whole notes within the larger octave was also given its own name. In descending order these names were "Adashtanas," "Evotanas," "Govorktanis," "Maiki-tanis," "Midotanis," "Lookotanis," and "Sonitanis." Contemporary earth-people call these same seven descending subdivisions: "do," "si," "la," "sol," "fa," "mi," and "re."

Beelzebub reiterates that the mathematical preciseness of the "vivifyingness-of-the-vibrations" of these whole notes correspon-dended quite accurately to the vivifyingness of sources of substances issuing from the cosmos at large—that is, one of the seven-centers-of-gravity of the "fundamental common-cosmic Ansapalnian-octave." Together, the seven octaves of this apparatus coincided with what was called the "Nirioonossian-World-Sound." (My conjecture is that this "World-Sound" or grand octave was illustrated by the Buddhist chant "Aum," and which could also be obtained from the Judeo-Christian word "Amen.")

In addition to the seven white strings of each octave on the Lav-Merz-Nokh apparatus, King-Too-Toz placed five black strings in certain locations. These black strings represented "half-notes." But he did not place these black strings where the twin brothers had determined that the independent process of the evolution and involution would become mathematically retarded and interrupted. Instead, at certain precise "gaps" in the Law of Sevenfoldness—where the process was actually haphazard—King-Too-Toz placed hair strings from animals called the "horse."

Why?

Because these placements of (black) horse-hair strings in his Lav-Merz-Nokh apparatus came to represent the *Harnel-Aoot*, within each octave of the universal process of sevenfoldness. These horse-hair strings were perfect for this particular placement because they did not produce consistent vibrations, but always "chaotic" ones. In other words, the number of vibrations from these horse-hair strings did not depend on their being stretched by pegs, but on three causes issuing from surrounding (extraneous) cosmic results in the environment. (So, these black horse-hair strings signified where the chaotic reconciling actions of the sevenfold process [Harnel-Aoot] could be found.)

These chaotic results included the influences from other strings on the Lav-Merz-Nokh, the temperature of the atmosphere in the room, and the radiations (qualities issuing from living spheres) of individuals who were present in the same room (including other animal species).

Then King-Too-Toz provided extra complexity into this scheme by adding *fourteen* additional "red" strings of "twisted intestines" as "quarter notes" to each octave.

The "red" quarter notes that were stretched *on either side* of the (five) black horse-hair strings served a special purpose. It seems that they could be stretched in a way that they could blend with the chaotic vibrations given off by the black hair strings from horses. These *red* and *black* strings represented the new details King-Too-Toz added to the Law of Sevenfoldness.

Beelzebub warned that if these particular "red strings" did not properly blend with the chaotic vibrations of the black horse-hair-strings, the sound issuing from them would be very harmful to the human psyche. (I understand this to mean that these special red strings (quarter notes) kept all the varying and possible outcomes of process, good or bad, in consonance. Swedenborg stated that the human anatomy would be torn apart without such an adaptable consonance and consistency for the changing states taking place in a whole organic system.

Whether one makes good or bad decisions, is angry or considerate, everything in a coherent series has to maintain its harmony. (See *A Philosopher's Notebook*, p. 473).

These quarter notes (placed on either side of the horsetail strings), represent the level or scales on which this harmony can be maintained on every whole process.

Unfortunately, the Lav-Merz-Nokh invented by King-Too-Toz met the same fate as the Alla-attapan apparatus invented by the earlier Chinese scientist twins. So the sense and signification of the discoveries from these two remarkable inventions was gradually forgotten by earth-humans. Worse yet, after a certain "confused period" had passed on Earth (probably representing the "Tower of Babel"), Beelzebub states that another Chinese scientist came along, named Chai-Yoo, and became informed about the details of the Lav-Merz-Nokh apparatus and the seven-toned scale of sound.

However, being a scientist of *new formation* (with the organic need to feel important) this Chinese scientist began to concoct his own theory, also constructing a simpler sound-producing version of the great original apparatus. As a result of his limited thinking (and not taking into consideration the red or black horse-hair string arrangement of the Lav-Merz-Nokh) his incomplete invention only included strings representing the white (full) notes, and black strings, indicating half-tones.

A further imperfection resulted from the fact that his new instrument contained only *two* octaves—one whole octave in the middle and two half octaves on each end.

While the theory of sound developed by Chai-Yoo didn't survive either, versions of his simpler sound-producing instrument did. These various sound-producing instruments (which Beelzebub compared to child's toys) were called "clavicymbals," "clavichord," "organ," "grand piano," "upright piano," "harmonium," etc. But thankfully, at least the basic principle called the "alternation of gravity-centered sounds" was preserved in much the same way as was originally discovered by the twin Chinese princes, Choon-Kil-Tez and Choon-Tro-Pel on their Dzendvokh—the middle independent part of their Alla-attapan.

This is how a "simplified" version of the original "Chinese seven-toned subdivision of the octave of sound" has reached contemporary human beings of the planet Earth.

In spite of this incomplete knowledge reaching contemporary earth-humans—which could be used to contemplate how, in the Most Great Trogoautoegocrat system, the "flowing-of-some-vibrations-from-others," creates cosmic substances with different "densities" and "vivifyingness"—and how they can unite and disunite into larger and smaller independent units, actualizing the common cosmic Iraniranumange, this vibrational dynamic is, instead, used in all their sound-producing instruments to merely tickle their fancy.

Here, Beelzebub is giving the reader an astonishing way to grasp the extent to which the human psyche has deteriorated when it comes to sensing reality from what would be called "quickness of instinct" (in his book *Rational Psychology,* n. 147, Swedenborg called this mental speed *presence of mind,* which can become perfected when the human intellect forms a closer partnership with the involuntary mind or pure intellect, n. 154). I believe both Swedenborg and Gurdjieff tapped into this higher intelligence.

This cognitive deterioration, from the alienation between our normal intellects (the external) and the pure intellectory (the internal) is what has led to new "types" of earth-beings (with split psyches), which Beelzebub described both here and earlier in his Tales as learned beings of new formation.

Contemporary earth-beings (including those of the post-modern era) who widely make use of the "Chinese seven-toned subdivision of the octave" in their lives, have no clue that such a subdivision was originally constructed on the universal principles and laws from which the Great Megalocosmos was created and is constantly maintained! This higher and nobler understanding is a far cry from using the octave to create such Rock 'n' Roll classics as Little Richard's "Good Golly Miss Molly" (which certainly does tickle one's fancy). So instead of providing direction for obtaining wisdom, music now simply titillates (thanks to the residual but powerful properties of the organ Kundabuffer).

Gurdjieff is cleverly using Beelzebub, an extra-terrestrial (or perhaps, even a *supra*-terrestrial), to both humble the reader and initiate *remorse of conscience* in each of us. Swedenborg, in his theological writings, would say that this strategy was a good thing because genuine humility is absolutely essential for acquiring true wisdom and sincere spiritual growth.

Beelzebub goes on to explain to Hassein, that among all the branches of contemporary scientific knowledge, little focus is given to the "law of vibrations," which should represent the most important branch of knowledge—especially when it comes to recognizing ontological reality and the unifying laws ruling the universe.

However, various misunderstandings further arose even about the "theory of sound" among the later earth physicists and musicians, which further confused them and prevented them from gaining any genuine information concerning the universal law of vibrations or sacred *Heptaparaparshinokh*. (So, the Tower of Babel is still being constructed today by all those learned individuals of "new formation," and plays a central role in the blueprints of most contemporary human-built edifices.)

This further unfortunate situation and confusion with a fundamental cosmic law occurred because a theory of vibrations reached contemporary humans from two different sources—the ancient Greeks and ancient Chinese.

Beelzebub explains.

The Chinese theory, as we have just discussed, consisted of seven "restorials" or seven "gravity center sounds." But in the Greek theory, a whole octave consisted of just five "restorials," or five whole notes.

This contradiction led to the "troubled perplexity" over which theory was to be included among the rest of their "official sciences." Both theories seemed plausible.

Eventually, in a process which embraced a form of *political correctness* by which no one would be offended, an individual named *Gaidoropoolo* took on the task of uniting these two theories so that it could indeed be included as a branch of their science. He sought out a mathematical explanation for this misunderstanding of how there could be two different ways to subdivide the octave. And Gaidoropoolo succeeded with a mathematical explanation for this discrepancy which, to this day, has pacified and quieted the conscience of all concerned researchers.

Gaidoropoolo's mathematical explanation went as follows: he calculated the vibrations of all the seven whole notes of the Chinese scale and determined that the notes called "mi" and "si" were not whole notes at all, but really only half notes. He assumed this because the number of vibrations these notes contained "almost" coincided with the number of vibrations of those Greek half notes in the Greek subdivision of the octave occurring just between the whole notes "re" and "fa" and between "si" and "do" of the Chinese octave.

Gaidoropoolo made the further supposition that the Chinese, simply from convenience, placed emphasis of the voice on these half notes, whereby they eventually became used as additional whole notes. Beelzebub claims that what Gaidoropoolo failed to recognize, by his thinking only in terms of the "restorials of voice," was that the Greeks, for genetic and cultural reasons, could create from the range of their voices, only five whole notes. (I personally find this to be an extraordinary and even hilarious genetic explanation of the difference between the these two theories of sound!)

It never occurred to Gaidoropoolo, that earth-humans from different parts of the planetary globe reproduce a different number of gravity-center sounds from their voices. Beelzebub then relates to his grandson how he personally witnessed groups of earth-humans who could reproduce thirteen or even seventeen whole notes within the restorials of their voice. One special group described by Beelzebub could even reproduce up to forty separate definite sounds from just three restorials of voice, through special chanting. Their effect on the listener was quite powerful. (Beelzebub admits that he later conducted experiments using three tuning forks and measuring devices called "vibrometers" to find out why their unique chanting could have such a powerful reverberation or "organic echo" within the physical bodies of the listeners.)

But the main point of Beelzebub's discussion was that the Chinese octave was not created from the mere restorials of voice. Rather, it was mapped out and incorporated into the science of comprehensive wholes or Law of Ninefoldness, from the *conscious labors* and *intentional sufferings* of the Chinese twin brothers.

Beelzebub laments that the sound-producing instrument called piano, which he brought back from Earth, could not demonstrate for Hassein the laws of vibrations from all sources, which partake of the common-cosmic Ansanbaluiazar, (but was indeed possible to demonstrate on the remarkable Lav-Merz-Nokh apparatus). However, Beelzebub tells his grandson that the piano is still capable of demonstrating the laws of vibrations issuing from any single fundamental common-cosmic octave of substances. And, since all the sevenfold sources of vibrations have the same reciprocal actions on all scales, studying just one of them can help an individual obtain knowledge of the laws of vibrations for all centers-of-gravity—assuming that one takes into account their differences of scale. (Each whole note, or center of gravity, can be further subdivided into additional octaves of another scale.)

Beelzebub assures Hassein that if the earth-invention called the piano is correctly tuned, then the resulting blending of vibrations obtained from this sound-producing instrument will coincide (even mathematically) with the law-conformable totality of vibrations of substances issuing out from corresponding cosmic sources according to the sacred Heptaparaparshinokh (Law of Sevenfoldness).

Such a demonstration would show how each whole note and half note pass from one to another exactly, according to the law of the sacred *Heptaparaparshinokh*, by which vibrations can mutually help each other to either evolve or involve. As I have said previously, this mutual process and connection is a physical analog of God's Divine Love *advancing through the power of Truth!* (The *science of correspondences*, which Swedenborg heavily discussed, cannot be fully grasped in terms of dynamic process or life, without an understanding of God's *sacred* sevenfold process.)

Gurdjieff himself must know of this universal similitude and correspondence, because his Beelzebub character goes on to state to Hassein that the success of the ancient Chinese scientists was owed to the fact that the standard unit, which they took for their calculations, was a unit from the Theomertmalogos (God's Word). Therefore, this standard unit contained all the fullness and power of vivifyingness (life-givingness) found in its theological origins. That is why Beelzebub describes this holy unit as the "Nirioonossian-World-Sound" or absolute vibrations of the note "do" (and I am almost positive that this sacred *world-sound* is also similar to the eastern religious concept of "Om" or "Aum," and the western Judeo-Christian concept of "Amen," which according to Gurdjieff, if properly voiced, can produce the sound of a full octave!)

Symbolically speaking, Swedenborg understood the word "Amen" to represent a confirmation of the orderly and successive sacred process of divine communication and flow (truth in series), which preceded and entered into its fullness.

According to Beelzebub, this sacred *world-sound* was first discovered by that same learned individual who had belonged to the ancient

Akhaldan society, on the continent of Atlantis, and who later moved to the country called Maralpleicie, where he was elected as its chief leader (and who was the great grandfather of King Konuzion's grandfather). Apparently, this former member of the Akhaldan society found that while making observations of different cosmic phenomena occurring on the planet Earth and beyond, had perceived that in a definite locality where the town Gob arose, twice a year, during certain meteorological perturbations in the Earth's atmosphere, this world-sound could be heard, and for quite a long time. This led to his constructing an elevated observatory in which to study this "cosmic result" more closely.

So afterward, when the Chinese twin brothers began to study the cosmic law of *Heptaparaparshinohk*, and having also gained knowledge of this cosmic result heard by this Akhaldan, set up their own operations in this very same place, where they succeeded in elucidating the true character and nature of this strange sound and decided to make it the standard unit of measurement in all their calculations.

Next, Beelzebub goes on to make a most important connection (correspondence) between the sacred *Heptaparaparshinokh* and human physiology. He describes to Hassein that the chaotic nature of the fifth Stopinder in an octave manifests the same way on a piano as in human digestion (metabolisim of food). In other words, in the same manner that physical food is unable to acquire its proper vivifying power until after it is transformed into being-piandjoëhari (in the cerebellum from the cerebrum) the vibrations of a musical chord will also not acquire a corresponding vivifying power until they have been fused with the preceding vibrations from the note "sol."

This concept is full of insights and meaning relevant to an individual's spiritual evolution and salvation because "sol" is the Russian word for *salt*, which spiritually represents the human striving to conjoin goodness with truth within one's life—or its opposite.

Similarly, the *fifth* interval in the Seven Day Creation story between "day four" and "day five" is the most critical and chaotic step in one's spiritual transformation. This interval symbolically represents the *Harnel-Aoot* within one's personal spiritual journey of evolution, because here is where the human will (and its salt or what an individual really savors) either becomes more animated by God or it goes horribly off course from one's self-centeredness and stubbornness—or rebelling against the notion that the Lord God must get all the credit.

To provide some further scientific evidence concerning the verity of some specific details contained in the Law of Sevenfoldness, Beelzebub tells his grandson just how this law can be put to an empirical test.

He states that if the notes "mi" and "si" are produced on a piano (which is placed in a hermetically sealed room), their vibrations will either immediately cease (ka-poof!), or from the momentum obtained from the first shock given for their arising, they will involve either back to the lower note "do" or to the lower note "fa" and then cease trembling. This is because of the "gaps" of discontinuity in the octave (since the fundamental change of this law's functioning was made to create the *Trogautoegocratic* system, and a needy universe).

So, unless the process of changing sounds gets extraneous support from other vibrations and influences originating in the (outer) atmospheric space, to support (and feed) its continuation, this dynamical process will stop dead in its tracks.

Again, Beelzebub blames the loss of this great knowledge from earth-humans becoming lazy and giving up the practice of being-Partkdolg-duty (conscious labors and intention suffering). Swedenborg describes this same activity of conscious labors and intentional suffering as an individual suffering oneself to give up egocentricism and voluntarily following the teachings of the Lord's Commandments.

It next occurs to Beelzebub that he must now explain to Hassein an important experiment on vibrations that he also witnessed on planet Earth, made by another special individual who had a unique understanding of the particularities of the law of *Heptaparaparshinokh* and octaves. (This special terrestrial being of the planet Earth also came to discover, because of his unique experiments, Beelzebub's true identity (as belonging to another planetary system), and who possessed extraordinary knowledge that allowed him to enjoy certain immunities from some of the effects of his experiments).

Concerning Swedenborg's early study of vibrations, he states that, "all concords emerge from the octave" (*A Philosopher's Notebook*, pg. 470), also, that the human body was constructed "like a musical instrument" (*On Tremulations*, pg. 33). The inference here is that our physical body and its organic fibres are designed according to all the laws and strings of the Lav-Merz-Nokh!

SUMMARY

■ Hassein asks Beelzebub how it was possible for earth-humans, with only automatic reason, to have ever constated the complex *Laws of Threefoldness* and *Sevenfoldness*.

■ The answer given is that it just so happens that now and then, an individual escapes the abnormal influences of those around him and develops the "potency-not-to-be-identified-with-and-not-to-be-affected-by-externals-through-one's-inevitably-inherent-passions" (self-loves). Also, such a fortunate being may come in contact with a genuine teacher, who through personal being-Partkdolg-duty, has made use of the data that remained in his subconscious to grow the Divine impulse of "Conscience."

■ (I believe that Swedenborg and Gurdjieff represent such fortunate beings.)

■ Swedenborg also knew of the law of *Heptaparaparshinokh* (sevenness) and knew it was sacred but felt that his readers did not have the appropriate knowledge to grasp its workings. This guarantees that a new dispensation by the Creator-God (the descent of the New Jerusalem from Heaven) will continue even further into the future.

■ The Law of Sevenfoldness is actually a mediating series of triads reaching a mathematically precise common and harmonious equilibrium. This sacred arrangement represents Swedenborg's *Mathematical Philosophy of Universals—the science of all sciences,* by which successive order carries into simultaneous order, making comprehensive (connected) wholes.

■ A mentally curious individual from Atlantis named *Theophany* first constated that by pouring a certain mixture onto a marble slab it would always dry into a form composed of *seven* definite plane surfaces. Later, he and his friends discovered that all transitory trajectories of *whole* phenomena were composed of seven aspects.

■ This idea became so well known that no one thought it was necessary to preserve its knowledge for future generations (specially in a written or extant Legominism).

■ Later, two Chinese twins (who were "princes") rediscovered this law while studying the poppy plant, which absorbed cosmic influences from far-off star systems.

■ The real "theory of sound" degenerated as it was passed down from generation to generation (along with the parallel degeneration of the human psyche). Later, the *science of octaves* became further distorted by incorporating the "restorials of voice," which is different among people of different countries (i.e., the Greeks only could voice *five* sounds instead of seven). Beelzebub also provides a way to scientifically test the sacred law of *Heptaparaparshinokh*.

■ Beelzebub tells Hassein that another extraordinary earth-human conducted special experiments on the law of *Heptaparaparshinokh* that would ultimately expose his extra-terrestrial nature.

CHAPTER 41

"The Bokharian dervish Hadji-Asvatz-Troov"

Beelzebub informs Hassein that about three years prior to his final departure from the planet Earth and its solar system, he met a remarkable *contemporary* terrestrial being, whose efforts will eventually cause, in the future, the fundamental sacred cosmic law of *Heptaparaparshinokh* to be re-established among all those earth-humans who possess a true thirst for knowledge.

(This certainly gained my attention and interest!)

On a journey through Asia, in a place called "Bokhara," Beelzebub first chances to meet a dervish named "Hadji-Zephir-Bogga-Eddin," who always loved to discuss "higher matters." On one particular day the dervish brought up the topic of the "ancient-Chinese-science," or Sevenfoldness, which he called "Shat-Chai-Mernis." Beelzebub discerned that through this incomplete science, the dervish was only aware of "fragments" of the discoveries of the twin Chinese brothers, the totality of which was actually called the "Law of Ninefoldness."

(Beelzebub adds that if even these bits and fragments of genuine knowledge were to fall into the hands of contemporary scientists, they would soon "cook up" a sloppy mess of new theories concerning reality, and thus destroy even this amount of valuable information.)

The dervish next tells Beelzebub that he would like to introduce him to another dervish, whose experiments had made him a great authority concerning this ancient Chinese science. This second dervish lived in an elevated region in what was called "Upper Bokhara."

Beelzebub tells Hassein that "Upper Bokhara" was located in a mountainous region, which was a *three-day* walk from where they were. (I have suspicions that this journey may be an allegory for an inward journey of the human heart and mind, because Gurdjieff's focus was always directed on the development of man's inner spiritual potentials). In fact, as I mentioned earlier, Swedenborg stated that "three" symbolizes a holy state of *fullness*. He also says that "three" represents one's completed spiritual journey of *repentance*. "Mountains" symbolize a higher (elevated) state of thought and spiritual level obtained in humans.

On the subject of symbolism, I recall P.D. Ouspensky (one of the most reknowned followers of Gurdjieff's ideas) once asking Gurdjieff where his unique knowledge came from. Gurdieff's reply was "Upper Bokhara." You won't find Upper Bokhara on a map of central Asia, which further confirms to me that he was talking about an elevated state of the human mind—not just a physical mountainous region, that is, one's *journeying to inaccessible places.*

Also, when Ouspensky began to pull away from Gurdjieff, every meeting the two had after this separation seemed to take place further and further from Gurdjieff's Institute. So Gurdjieff was using physical distance to display the closeness and *inner reality* of how far Ouspensky's understanding was getting away from the true nature of Gurdjieff's ideas. One of Ouspensky's biggest blunders was his belief that he could connect with the same people and esoteric schools where Gurdjieff had acquired his unique cosmology. He did not grasp that "Upper Bokhara" might be a place that was inaccessible to physical legs and physical climbing.

Now, back to Beelzebub's ultra-fantastic Tales and journey.

At a gorge in the mountains of "Upper" Bokhara, Beelzelbub's dervish friend comes upon a small stone slab. Together they move it aside. As the stone slab was set aside it revealed a small aperture from which two iron rods were projected at the edges. The dervish put the two metal bars together and appeared to be listening to something. Then a strange sound was emitted from these iron bars. To Beelzebub's surprise the dervish began speaking into this aperture in a mysterious language or code. After placing the stone slab back over the aperture, the two travelers walked a considerable distance before coming to an enormous boulder. The dervish stopped in front of the boulder and acted as though he expected something to happen. Suddenly, the huge boulder moved, revealing an opening to a cave. (Spiritually and symbolically interpreted, the moving of this large stone symbolized an opening from external and worldly knowledge to more interior [spiritual] secrets.)

So "caves" not only symbolize mental obscurity, but the depths of reality that hide great revelations. (This also suggests to me that tales of the "Arabian Nights" were written in a similar, symbolic language.)

Once inside, Beelzebub was further astonished to find that the tunnels of the cave were alternately lighted both by gas and electrical devices—despite being far from any center of civilization (also, this was during the early part of twentieth century, where such devices were still quite rare). As the two made a turn at the end of a long tunnel they were greeted by the dervish experimenter, who was tall and elderly, named *Hadji-Asvatz-Troov.*

The two travelers were then invited into a small section of the cave and given something to eat as they sat on a felt-covered floor. The first dervish mentioned to the knowledgeable host that Beelzebub also had a strong interest in the ancient Chinese science Shat-Chai-Mernis (Sevenfoldness). The dervish Hadji-Asvatz-Troov then tells

Beelzebub that he not only made a long study of this great science, but that for the last ten years he had focused his efforts on creating practical applications from its laws. As a result he had attained results far beyond that of what contemporary terrestrial humans can discover. (That includes Einstein and Schrödinger.)

Knowing that this ancient knowledge had long ago ceased to exist on the planet Earth, Beelzebub wanted to know how this respectable Hadji could have come upon this lost branch of true science.

After establishing that Beelzebub was not wearing a "mask" of friendship or feigning some external calculated manifestation based on empty words, the Hadji, convinced of this visitor's benevolent intent, was able to confide in him as a sincere friend (even though they had just met).

On the question of true friendship, Beelzebub takes a short detour here in his Tales and describes to his grandson the downside of the human psyche falling victim to associative thoughts, whereby people can easily (automatically) take the statements of others in wrong ways. (Political correctness is an outcome of this predicament of how to verbally address others in all circumstances—externally, and not with inner sincerity.) This abnormal and cowardly existence of "verbal amenity" among earth-humans has not only spoiled their psyches, but the psyches of other lifeforms as well!

Apparently, animals of all kinds sense the negative radiations and inner fears (laying below the surface) of humans as enmity toward them. The result is that each lifeform—humans and animals— perceives the other as a "menace." Beelzebub adds that those humans who manage to attain a high degree of inner growth and *love for all things,* from actualizing being-Partkdolg-duty, can live in complete harmony with all other creatures on Earth. (In one case Gurdjieff even stated that if one had accumulated a certain amount of rarefied substances in their being, during inner evolution, "bugs would not bite them.")

Earth-humans that do not obtain such a high degree of livingness, act just like those one- or two-brained creatures (lower lifeforms) when it comes to various word/sounds that reach their ears—that is why every society or locality relies on certain verbal formulations of "outer amenity" for maintaining proper mutual relationships. (Likewise, animals have adopted special non-threatening, *external* postures to communicate similar states toward each other.)

The friendship between Beelzebub and the two dervishes went beyond such concocted formalities (remember all the artificial crap Beelzebub had to learn before being allowed to meet with the Russian Czar). The conversation now turns to the significance of vibrations— especially with regard to the octave of sound.

Hadji-Asvatz-Troov informs Beelzebub that the octave not only consisted of seven relatively independent whole manifestations or units but that each of these units also obey in their arising and manifestation, the same conformity to this law. (According to Swedenborg's scientific research and his work called *Principia*, "all nature obeys the same rules." Also remember that Swedenborg's first major work, which directed the rest of his scientific studies, was titled *On Tremulations* [vibrations]. So he would certainly applaud the study of vibrations because "Love" is the universal first principle of emanation in the world, which conjoins all things, and manifests itself in the physical world through the principles of *harmony* [*A Heiroglyphic Key*, n. 30-38].)

Hadji-Asvatz-Troov now shares some background information with Beelzebub.

Before entering into a dervish brotherhood, Hadji admits that he had a fondness for making various kinds of stringed musical instruments. (As stated before, Swedenborg claimed that humans were designed by God to be just like a stringed musical instrument. Later, he stated that the human voice and vocal chords acted like both wind and string instruments.) Hadji's fondness for making stringed musical instruments continued even after entering the brotherhood. Then on one fateful day, the Sheikh (leader) of his monastery presented Hadji with a curious mystery.

The Sheikh had noticed at a former monastery that during sessions where the dervish musicians were playing the melodies of their sacred canticles, the listeners experienced sensations *corresponding* to the text of the given sacred canticle. Here Gurdjieff uses the term "sacred" as a non-terrestrial influence. (Swedenborg, had also made the amazing statement that when earth-humans read the sacred text of God's Holy Word, it would *reverberate* with a specific angelic society in Heaven. This reverberation would also *correspond* with the function of a particular organ in the human anatomy! So maybe this sheik noticed that these sacred melodies were somehow causing the listener's sensitivities to feel these sacred vibrations in various parts of their anatomies!)

But when the Sheikh came to the present monastery he noticed that these exact same melodies failed to produce those particular effects in the bodies of the listeners. Since Hadji was a specialist in making musical instruments, the Sheikh asked him to help in clearing up why this was so.

After studying the matter, both men came to the conclusion that the special effect sensed at the other monastery came from performing the sacred melodies with *stringed* musical instruments—rather than the wind instruments that were being used at their current monastery. They then decided to replace all the wind instruments with stringed instruments and seek out dervishes who were expert at playing these stringed musical instruments. But the Sheik found it difficult to find enough musicians to play the stringed instruments.

So after having thought the matter over a little longer, the Sheikh wondered if Hadji could also design a *mechanical* stringed instrument, capable of automatically playing their sacred melodies, through various turning motions, pressing motions and striking hammers. (This would then only require one operator to perform their sacred melodies.)

Hadji accepts the challenge and seeks the help of another friend, the dervish *Kerbalai-Azis-Nuaran,* who had once been a watchmaker with quite unusual ideas. At the time, Kerbalai had come up with a "Freakish Idea" and was working on a clock that would keep time without springs, by means of the Earth's motion and its gravity.

Since gravity occupies only half the space of a planet's volume (the other half is outside the planet, directing its trajectory toward its place of stability), he sought to obtain the perfect equilibrium of special levers that would move according to the movement of the planet's tempo—and in a way that also could be made to correspond with the hands of a clock. (Free mechanical energy!)

Both dervishes started on the project of making a mechanical stringed instrument. It was during the construction of this apparatus that Hadji became greatly interested in making further experiments concerning the laws of vibrations.

Hadji admits that he was already familiar with the idea that half the length of any string would produce twice the number of vibrations of a whole string with the same volume and density. He had once arranged on a zimbal "bridges" for the strings, based on this very principle, and tuned each string for an ancient sacred melody according to "one-eighth-toned" sounds, and checking them with a tuning fork. It was during this tuning that Hadji experimentally verified for himself that the number of vibrations of a string is inversely proportional to its length.

Then something quite mysterious happened.

To his complete surprise, this effect did not always coincide with what he described as obtaining the "common blending harmonic consonance." (I understand this to mean that the repeatability of results in these experiments, which is required by modern scientific methodology, was not always guaranteed. This was due to the inherent and chaotic nature of the *fifth* Stopinder in the octave, called *Harnel-Aoot.*)

Seeking an answer to explain this chaotic result in his experiments soon consumed all of Hadji's time. In spite of this extra challenge, Hadji and his friend somehow managed to finish their "zimbal" by which sacred music could be mechanically produced. It was described as looking like a "new Greek hand organ," only a little bigger, and could play *quarter-tone* sounds. After presenting this musical invention to the Sheikh of the monastery they were given both permission and the money to continue their own personal studies on vibrations.

Hadji and his friend settled in an area near the Amu Darya of Central Asia. Hadji tells Beelzebub that on a trip into a town to pick up additional supplies for their experiments, his friend was killed by a "stray" bullet. (Gee, this has happened before in the story—a "stray" bullet" killing the *seventh* member of a special group of Tibetans.)

Not only was this an area where the Russians and Anglo-Afghans were exchanging shots between each other, it seems that the insanities brought on by earth-humans to destroy each other are always having their negative consequences upon genuine truth seekers. This brutal outcome is why the "common blending harmonic consonance" [like world peace] is never reached in most human affairs.)

Finishing this sad story, Hadji-Asvatz-Troov next stands up in the cave and motions for Beelzebub and the other dervish to follow him. They come to the main passage of the cave where Hadji stops in front of a stone projection and presses something. The stone block "magically" moves aside and another passage of the cave is revealed. Beelzebub feels it is necessary to give a detailed description of this special section of the cave. (Stones or rocks, in front of some chamber, represent and spiritually symbolize the protective power of hard or solid truths, formed from goodness, which can be moved aside to bring a genuine seeker—with the proper heart—into a higher or deeper level of discovery.)

Beelzebub describes the walls, floors and ceiling of this section of the cave as being covered by several layers of very thick felt. Due to its special natural and artificial design, this area of the cave did not allow any sounds or vibrations penetrating from outside its walls. In this unique room Beelzebub also observed several experimental apparatuses, including a sound-producing instrument called the *grand piano*. The cover of the piano was open and Beelzebub could see "vibrometers" attached to its various series of strings—to measure the "degree of vivifyingness" when they were each struck.

Seeing all these vibrometers astonished Beelzebub, as did seeing the gas and electric lighting throughout the cave, and in a place so remote from centers of civilization. Beelzebub wondered how an old dervish could obtain all this equipment, living in such a wild mountainous region. Then he spots and describes another unusual apparatus in that part of the cave in which pipes made from the throats of cows were attached to "masks" coming from the ceiling. Since this special room could be hermetically closed, these special masks (like a skin diver's mask connected to air tanks) served as breathing apparatuses to bring in air for those inside who were conducting the experiments on vibrations.

All three men then seated themselves on the floor and Hadji-Asvatz-Troov began to speak. He states that he and his now deceased friend Kerbalai-Azis-Nuaran had begun studying all the existing theories on Earth about vibrations. These theories included the "Assyrian theory of the great Malmanash, and the Arabian theory of the famous Selneh-eh-Avaz, and the Greek theory of the philosopher Pythagoras—and of course, all the Chinese theories."

The two dervishes also reproduced the same instruments that these original sages used in conducting their own experiments. They also modified one of these apparatuses that were similar to the one Pythagoras used, called a "monochord." They named their own modification to this instrument the "vibrosho." Hadji then points to a "vibrosho" in the room they are sitting in. Beelzebub describes it as consisting of a two-meter board on which the front half was divided into segments called "frets," similar to the neck of a sound-producing instrument called "guitar." It had only one string stretched across it.

(In Swedenborg's book, *On Tremulations* [pg. 33], he illustrates how the study of vibrations also leads to the study of humans, since humans are anatomically designed exactly like stringed musical instruments—the porous human cranium working as an acoustic and resonating sounding board, the nerves as the strings, and the foramen of the skull acting as a bridge to attune the sound.)

On the other half of the board on Hadji's special instrument (the modified monochord), were a great number of vibrometers, which were attached to measure the vibrations of the different frets. Also on this back half of the board were fastened a whole network of sound-producing metal and glass pipes. These particular objects produced sounds from artificially compressed and rarified air—like wind instruments.

So the vibrometers could measure the vibrations made from the sounds of both *blowing air* and *string plucking*. (This would allow the two dervishes to observe differences made between wind and stringed instruments—in the hopes of solving the problem that their Sheikh had observed.)

At this point in the story a small Uzbekistani boy came from another part of the cave to bring some green tea for the three men. (Gurdjieff may be offering some extra clues here to help us verify that they where indeed somewhere in Bokhara, but I still believe "Upper Bokhara" represents a parallel place and state of the mind and spirit with physical mountains and dwells in an elevated reality above the physical landscape.)

While they are drinking the refreshing cups of tea, Beelzebub takes the opportunity to ask Hadji about several questions that were troublesome to him. Beelzebub asks Hadji how he came into the possession of instruments that could make exact measurements of vibrations. Beelzebub, from all his visits, believed that such unique apparatuses existed nowhere else on Earth!

Hadji replies that these inventions were made by his now deceased friend Kerbalai-Azis-Nuaran but also added that during the time that the great Tikliamish (Sumerian?) civilization existed, many such apparatuses were already invented and built. He admits that indeed no such apparatuses exist at the present time on the planet Earth to measure vibrations—with the exception of a "childish bauble" in Europe called a "siren." Hadji describes this childish toy as consisting of a revolving disk with various sized holes drilled into it. As the disk was rapidly turned, air flowed though it from a pipe and made an even-pitched sound. One could then measure the revolutions recorded on a clock mechanism and multiply this with the number of holes on the disc to give a measurement of vibrations that a particular sound made at a given interval of time.

Unfortunately, this European apparatus (siren) could not be used to fully serve Hadji's experiments, since it only measured vibrations of sounds made from the *flow of air*, rather than from the action of genuine (natural) vibrations such as those made by *strings*. The fact that sound could be produced from two distinct causes had interesting repercussions. Hadji proceeded to give a demonstration of these two outcomes on his modified monochord, first invented by Pythagoras.

(There must also be interesting repercussions from the fact that human voices are a combination of "wind" and "string" design. Interestingly, it was revealed to Swedenborg that an ancient genus of humans existing before the "Fall" (called the celestial race of the Golden Age) did not communicate with air passing through vocal chords, but made much finer reverberations through intricate tremulations of an extraordinary series of muscle fibers in their lips. So their communications were still string-related, but far more subtle than today's languages and speech. The resulting finer vibration produced by this genus of humans traveled not to the ears of another, but through the *Eustachian tubes*—to one's inner ear. Thus this early race of humans could communicate more ideas, more perfectly, than those who later used vocal chords! Verbal speech, and the position of the hyoid bone in the human throat, is no indicator of evolving human intelligence.)

Hadji next begins to produce five different tones of sound from the air pipes and asks that his two visitors observe a pot of flowers in the room, their watches, and the various vibrometers on his apparatus. He continues creating the monotonous melody of five tones by sending air into corresponding pipes with a pair of bellows. He does this for ten minutes.

Beelzebub observes that no change occurred to the flowers in the pot.

Next, Hadji moves over to his grand piano and produces the same five monotonous tones, but this time from strings. Beelzebub observes that the vibrometers register the very same numbers, but strangely, the flowers in the pot have now faded and withered in the period of just ten minutes. (In another book, Gurdjieff claimed to have personally watched individuals from a surviving Essene Brotherhood reverse this process and make flowers *grow* faster from the simple melodies they were producing on their instruments!)

After this experiment Hadji sits back down with his guests and offers an explanation for what just occurred. He explains that after long years of investigations he became convinced that the claim made by the ancient Chinese science Shat-Chai-Mernis was true and that two distinct kinds of vibrations existed in the world. He called these two types "creative vibrations" and "momentum vibrations."

Vibrations created from the *flow of air* produced only momentum vibrations. But strings produced creative vibrations. Furthermore, only strings made from a certain metal, or from goat guts, could produce creative vibrations. (This was the full answer to the Sheik's question as to why some sounds reverberated in people's bodies and some didn't.)

The piano, in the possession of Hadji, was made from strings of this precise metal. Hadji states that his now deceased friend Kerbalai-Azis-Nuaran had purchased this particular grand piano at an auction from a Russian general in an undisclosed town in Bokhara.

Hadji describes the hardship of moving the grand piano up the mountains. Once delivered, the piano was properly prepared for the experiments on vibrations. Hadji and his friend tuned the piano according to the absolute sound of the ancient Chinese "do" and took into consideration, as this ancient science suggested, the local geographical conditions, pressure of the atmosphere, the form and dimensions of their interior room, and the mean temperature of the surrounding space as well as the interior itself—even considering the amount of radiations issuing from the humans in the room during the experiments! After all these preparations, the grand piano was finally ready to illustrate the cosmic properties of the mentioned great Chinese science.

Hadji now tells his two guests that he is ready to show them what is possible to do on this specially prepared grand piano, when one has the proper and precise knowledge of the laws of vibrations. He gets up and writes something on a piece of paper, then goes over to the piano and starts playing a certain monotonous melody. This melody consisted of only two tones made from the lowest octave of the grand piano.

After a short while, Beelzebub begins to notice that his dervish friend Hadji-Bogga-Eddin began to fidget a little with his left leg. Something on his leg was giving him increasing pain. Hadji-Asvatz-Troov then asks Beelzebub to read what he had written on the piece of paper. On the piece of paper it stated that the two guests would have a "boil" an inch below the knee and half an inch to the left of the middle of the leg. The two guests where then asked to roll up their left pant leg.

Hadji-Bogga-Eddin indeed had a painful boil on the precise part of the leg indicated on the paper. However, Beelzebub had no boil on his left leg! This produced extreme amazement in Hadji-Asvatz-

Troov—which would later convince him that Beelzebub was not of this Earth, and was a very special being of another order!

But under the stress of the present moment, Hadji began to have doubts about his long and hard-fought-for knowledge of vibrations. Devastated, he explains to Beelzebub that he gave up his many caravans (containing 10,000 camels) and great wealth to acquire this very knowledge—knowledge that saved him from the wearisome "burden" and emptiness of ordinary life. This great knowledge cannot be obtained from ordinary, habitual life, no matter how superabundant it is. Personal *sacrifice* was the key.

In fact, only the thoughts of his aging mother had given him strength and kept him from ending his life by suicide before he re-discovered this important ancient Chinese science.

We have to sacrifice our egoism and love of this natural world to gain this special knowledge, and a proper evaluation of its significance. Before making this sacrifice, and when Hadji's mother had finally died, nothing of importance was left for him in this natural realm and his feeling of inner emptiness returned.

His only way out of this misery and emptiness was the study of vibrations. But now even this knowledge was being threatened by his inability to create a boil on Beelzebub's leg. Again, Hadji felt inner emptiness.

After sharing his depressed soul-state with Beelzebub he goes over to the piano and by playing two "good-carrying" notes, one from among the highest octaves and the other from a lower octave, he successfully shrinks the boil on the other dervish's leg. After this he sits down again with his two guests and shares his rekindled feelings of despair.

He recounts that *four* days ("Four" spiritually symbolizing the restoration of genuine goodness) after the death of his mother, a benevolent wandering dervish passing through the area was chanting some sacred canticles. Hadji sent a servant out to invite this dervish into his home. They talked for awhile and the wandering dervish, listening to his new friend's agony about his deceased mother, suggests that the only way out of this desperate situation is for him to devote himself to religion.

This turned out to be the reason that Hadji-Asvatz-Troov decided to join a far-off "brotherhood of dervishes" in the Bokhara region. Over time he transferred to several brotherhoods until he settled in the one run by the Sheikh who gave him the original task of creating a mechanical stringed musical instrument. This undertaking eventually led to his decision to study the laws of vibrations, which occupied his mind (and heart) up to the present time.

Hadji confesses that this science took the place of his loving mother, (Swedenborg, in his *Diary of Dreams*, discovered that women symbolized the love of various sciences, and that women were replaced by ever more beautiful women in his dreams when a new science caught his attention and *desire*). But the Hadji's failure to form a boil on Beelzebub's leg was the first time his knowledge of vibrations had ever failed him. Now he was faced with the fact that the science, which had taken the place of his loving mother, was itself on its deathbed. He was now feeling intense and indescribable grief.

To spare himself from this new death agony, he pleads with Beelzebub to explain to him what supernatural powers stopped the otherwise infallible process of forming the anticipated boil on Beelzebub's leg.

Beelzebub's unique answer will offer truth seekers an important dynamic to clear up misunderstandings concerning sincere inner growth and the nature of our knowledge.

Beelzebub assures the Hadji that his failure to produce a boil on his leg from the "evil-carrying" vibrations of the grand piano was actually further proof of the truth and precision of the great laws of world vibrations. (However, Beelzebub also feels he is in a tight spot because he could only share the truth about himself in private and to beings of a similar *elevated* stature.) Beelzebub indeed knows how he differs from most earth-humans because his race (from the planet *Karatas*) had cultivated the "knowledge of being," as opposed to a knowledge of "things." (Swedenborg calls this second kind of learning mere "memory-knowledge" or the memory stuff in one's external [corporeal/sensual] mind, which can delude people into thinking they are smart and special.)

The "knowledge of being," (obtained from *sincere* self-examination) which is the sole means of connecting a person to his or her sacred "remains" and "conscience" also seems to have offered Beelzebub special protection from various "poisonous" vibrations and influences of external life. (In spiritual transformation, this connection to deeper sacred data, through temptation, offers healing help and immunity from confronting our character flaws and negative intentions, which otherwise, leaves us vulnerable to poisonous vibrations and various self-delusions.)

Having shared this secret of immunity (with the reader), Beelzebub then promises the dervish Hadji-Asvatz-Troov that he will give a more satisfying answer later, in private, about why a boil did not appear on his leg—information he feels cannot be shared quite yet with the other dervish sitting in the room. (But we readers have been given the heads-up as to how to lawfully offset negative "creative vibrations," from affecting our minds, which have correlations to precise parts of our physical bodies!)

At this place in the story, Beelzebub now makes it clear to his grandson that the only means left for humankind to escape the negative consequences of the organ Kundabuffer (and its poisonous vibrations) and gain true *spiritual liberation* is through the "knowledge of being." Otherwise, even true knowledge cannot save humankind if it simply remains as mere mental knowledge (head-knowledge) in the human memory, which is one-dimensional and putrefying.

(Again, Swedenborg calls this type of mental learning mere *memory-knowledge* [*scientiarum et cognitionum*], which offers no real help in the process of spiritual re-birth and transformation, because such info doesn't reach deep enough into a person's heart and will [*inner natural mind*, where one's insane perversions live] to create a personal confrontation and the proper inner friction to evolve.)

But there is more to Hadji's discoveries from his study of vibrations.

Beelzebub next notices a nook in the Bokharan cave where colored strips of silk material are hanging and asks Hadji their significance. Hadji informs him that these colored strips also were used for his experiments on vibrations and how they could be manipulated to influence the behavior of both people and animals. Hadji then brings three types of animals into their enclosure—a dog, a *sheep* and a *goat*. Next he places a special bracelet on his arm and on that of the other dervish while also fitting special "collars" on the three terrestrial quadrupeds (mammals). These special bracelets and collars all had vibrometers attached to them. Hadji asks his guests to jot down the various readings of the vibrometers on writing pads, once the experiments began.

He then sits down and begins to explain the scientific basis of his next experiment. He tells his guests that all lifeforms have their own signature or their own "totality" of vibrations. This totality is created from the various operations of the organs functioning in a particular lifeform. So this living totality varies according to the intensity of the vibrations being produced by the various organs. (Swedenborg refers to this totality as "spheres" and "auras.")

Through the various vibrometers, Hadji demonstrates that the dog has three times the vibrations of a sheep and half again as much as the goat—but less than he and his dervish friend manifested. Hadji then explains to Beelzebub that humans, particularly modern humans, now produce fewer vibrations than a dog! This unique explanation gives us a more unexpected, yet more visceral, perception of the important theme running through this entire Tale—that the human species has atrophied over time and now manifests less vivifyingness because of this downward trend.

Something has definitely gone wrong with the psyche and *life* of earth-humans, especially modern humans! Some important function of the human presence has lost its intensity, and this makes us vulnerable to negative (poisonous) influences.

Here, Hadji gives an important clue for the reader to what is the critical difference between having mere "mental knowledge" and "knowledge of being." The knowledge of being *includes* the proper functioning of *emotion*, which gives humans their proper "life-intensity."

In Swedenborg's language, this means we underestimate the importance of the human heart (will) in human consciousness and learning. What is not taken into account in our current educational systems is that the human heart (will) and its affections operate the cockpit of the intellect—the thinking brain. Love and its affection is the being or living principle, which resides in, and *adapts information to its own disposition* and order. In fact, Swedenborg was adamant that spiritual love and goodness enlightens human understanding (*Arcana Coelestia*, n. 6405). This theistic dynamic runs counter to modern academic and scholarly approaches which stress and focus on instructing the human intellectual mind only (this is why science stays clear of "values").

The function of *feeling*, which actualizes the main quantity of a person's subjective vibrations, has been ignored and thus has atrophied in modern human life and education. Also *higher-being bodies* (spiritual bodies) are developed from the quality of one's love and heart (*Arcana Coelestia*, n. 1900). That is the reason why true religion has always focused on elevating the human heart, not just the intellect.

Again, it is worth reminding you, the reader, that Gurdjieff is merciless at conveying *Beezebub's Tales* in ways that will frustrate anyone's accustomed and mechanical approach to acquiring mere "mental knowledge." His Tales ingeniously create an environment of "shocks" to promote our self-examination and personal pondering—all to bring about greater "knowledge-of-being" in the reader.

The ancient phrase "know thyself" refers to the "knowledge-of-being" (and having it will protect you from many, many poisonous influences). Swedenborg would also add that the "knowledge of being" is spiritually represented by the *Tree of Life*, while mental (head) knowledge, is represented by the *Tree of the Knowledge of Good and Evil*.

After describing the differences in the totality of vibrations of various living beings, the venerable Hadji-Asvatz-Troov goes to the room containing the colored silk strips. He is able to unroll the various colored silk materials in ways that *completely* cover the walls, ceiling and floor of this special section of the cave. His experiments showed that each color change made in the room also changed the vibrational number of all the living beings exposed to it.

Hadji then took his guests, followed by the dog, sheep and goat, to yet another nook—which was the most important section of his underground laboratory. He then points to a pile of some material, shaped like a tent with a strange color. This material was woven from the fibers of a plant called "Chaltandr." This plant had the rare quality of being able to change the vibrations of other nearby sources, yet is itself unchanged by other influences. In Hadji's experiments he could change the shape and direction of this tent. He therefore also displayed that he had learned the means to test vibrations on beings by making "architectural" changes to the special tent.

By moving the flaps of the tent's special material, Hadji experimentally proved that all his geometric modifications would produce real changes in the vibrations of the air space inside its walls. These changes would further contribute changes for the better (or for the worse) on the subjective vibrations of the people and animals also put inside its walls.

Hadji adds that the vibrations created inside this special large tent acted more strongly on modern earth-humans than on all other lifeforms. Hadji chalked this up to the abnormal inner and outer conditions brought on by modern life (which continue to weaken the human psyche).

Other experimental rooms were also revealed to Hadji's two guests, which further showed how variously caused vibrations acted upon the subjective chords of people's vibrations. These experiments included the effects of vibrations coming from other people, including one- and two-brained beings, and the vocal sounds made by each.

Surprisingly, Hadji informs his guests that his experiments showed that modern works of art, like pictures, statues and music, also had harmful vibrational effects on terrestrial contemporary beings. (Not only has human art degenerated over history, as we learned in Chapter 30, it has now actually become harmful to the human psyche.)

But even more surprising, he eventually discovered that the most harmful of all influences to contemporary people was their "medical remedies." (Oh-oh, this does not bode well for today's pharmaceutical companies, whose products all admittedly have "side-effects"—just read their labels or listen to all the "legal" disclaimers in their advertising and the increasing numbers of lawyers now going after them.)

Beelzebub again states that he stayed at this special remote place in the mountains for *four* days. This underscores my strong belief that Gurdjieff understood the symbolic significance of numbers—because, according to Swedenborg, "four" represents a mental state where one is being spiritually *challenged*—in order to unify the heart (emotions) with new information coming into the intellect from the outside world. In other words, the number "four" represents the inner challenge to increase one's "knowledge of being."

Gurdjieff knew that the knowledge of vibrations and knowledge of being would greatly challenge most of today's worldviews and strongly held misconceptions. But these new revelations are the whole point of these Tales!

During that "four-day" visit, the dervish Hadji also explained how gas and electric lighting came to be installed in such a remote spot on the planet. Beelzebub promises his grandson that Hadji's story about the gas and electric lighting will be beneficial concerning the *idiosyncrasies* of personal destiny, which may seem (at least outwardly) unjust at times, especially what happened to Hadji's friends.

Hadji explains the origins of both kinds of lighting (gas and electric) separately. The inflammable gas had its source not far from their cave from the action of a river over a particular mineral medium. Hadji and his other dervish friend, Kerbalai-Azis-Nuaran (who was shot dead) simply re-routed the inflammable gas through pipes of clay and bamboo to different sections of the cave.

The electric lighting came from another one of his friends, a young European traveler, who shared the same interest in the laws of vibrations, particularly those that caused various diseases in people. This European friend eventually succeeded in discovering the cause and cure for cancer (whoa!!!) but also suffered a cruel personal destiny. Apparently this unique cure involved that a healer adopt a certain mode of life and a certain preparation, by which positive vibrations could be accumulated and directed upon the sufferer over a period of time. (I suspect this is an accumulation of the purified and magnetic *being-hanbledzoïn*—Swedenborg's animal spirits—which happens through the process of genuine spiritual transformation.)

This second friend of Hadji's (a magnetizer) returned to Europe and married. Over time, Hadji had received reports that his friend indeed succeeded in the complete destruction of this terrifying disease cancer in his patients with his "unorthodox" approach. After receiving these initial favorable reports, Hadji heard no more news of his friend—for another ten years.

One day, immersed in his own experiments, Hadji heard the "secret signal" made from the communications system in his cave and recognized the voice of his European friend. He was coming for a visit. Hadji's friend had packed some new experimental equipment and brought it to the underground cave on camels. This new equipment from Europe included a "Roentgen apparatus," close to fifty "elements of Bunsen," several accumulators and bales of material that could be used for "electric wiring."

As they unpacked the camels, Hadji's friend told him a disheartening story. Several years earlier, because of higher World-laws, surrounding conditions became such that hardly any place on Earth offered *security for the morrow* or any place to *comfortably settle*. He then suddenly noticed that his wife had come down with cancer. (Hmmm, is this deep insecurity the cause of cancer?) To his greater horror, the surrounding and deteriorating conditions he found himself in also made it impossible to actualize his unique cure on his wife. So he waited for conditions to change, but in the meantime, did everything he could to at least slow down the progression of his wife's cancer.

Two years later, conditions became favorable to employ his cure to his wife. Unfortunately, after preparing himself to employ this cure he was hit by a car and became incapacitated for several months. During that unfortunate period, his wife's cancer spread at an accelerated rate. By the time he returned to full consciousness he discovered that his wife was suffering the last stages of this dreaded disease. Not having the proper time to prepare himself for acquiring in himself the vibrations of the quality he needed to affect the cure, he was forced to use the standard European methods of medicine of that time. This method involved the use of X-rays.

(One could discern from this tragic story and automobile accident that Hadji's young European friend, from all *outside* appearances, indeed had a most unfair and unjustified destiny.)

Hadji's European friend observed that while this X-ray treatment caused the original area of cancer (its "gravitational center") to indeed shrink, the cancer began to appear in other places after several months of this procedure. (Physical X-rays cannot cure an illness or disharmony originating in the state of one's psyche.) Horrified by this metastasis, he abandoned all contemporary European medicine and was able to keep his wife alive for two more years using his own methods. Hadji reiterates that this process involved acquiring the necessary positive vibrations within his being and saturating the body of his wife with these same helpful vibrations.

(This part of the story seems blatantly autobiographical to me, since Gurdjieff had himself implored "special" treatments to personally cure his own wife of cancer—but an automobile accident, mentioned at the introduction of this book, made this impossible. One of Gurdjieff's followers—I don't remember who or where—describes seeing Gurdjieff hold up a glass of water to a sunny window and focused his attention on it. When he gave that glass of water to his wife to drink, her appetite for solid food returned! His wife's ultimate death and his seemingly "unfair" destiny changed very little in his own approach to life—he refused to identify with the outwardly negative aspects of this most intimate event.)

Similarly, after the death of Hadji's friend's wife, this remarkable individual returned to his studies, which now included the desire to find out why X-rays caused cancer to metastasize in other parts of the body. It was for this very reason, that he returned to Hadji with his new equipment to begin his new experiments. Hadji offers his friend a room in the underground cave to perform these experiments with the Bunsen elements and Roentgen apparatus. One of the results of these experiments led to the implementation of electric lighting throughout the cave.

As Hadji and his European friend conducted their experiments, which included using vibrometers to measure the electric current needed to create X-rays, they noticed from their readings that the current obtained from their Bunsen elements either gradually increased or diminished. They then realized that they needed to create an electric current that was more consistent. (Human energies in the distinct functionings of people's psyche also require a "regulator.")

Three days later ("three" symbolizes fullness) while the two friends were crossing over a small bridge in the cave that was built over an underground stream, the answer for producing a more consistent electric current came to the European researcher in a flash. On the next day they had local helpers gather three types of ore from the caves, which were placed at certain intervals at the bottom of the stream's bed. From this ore placed in the stream, Hadji's friend was then able to connect two terminals to some slightly charged accumulators. This created a consistent electric current but they next discovered that the "amperage" (strength of current) still needed to be increased for their experiments to be successful. Hadji's European friend then built some "condensers" from goatskins, a certain kind of clay, crushed "zinc ore" and pine resin. These condensers created the required amperage and voltage for the Roentgen apparatus to be useful in their experiments. (As I hinted earlier, I suspect that these efforts to create a more consistent, strong current *corresponds* to the inner efforts one needs to sustain and intensify spiritual action and usefulness—otherwise this would be superfluous information.)

The two men did elucidate from their experiments that although X-rays caused the gravitational center of a cancer to atrophy, the process also increased the sowing and flourishing of this disease in other glands and parts of the body. After these results were satisfactorily verified, the European friend finally became bored with this question and returned home to Europe (abandoning his cancer research was another seemingly unfair and negative outcome of destiny). As a result, Hadji was left with all the technological equipment necessary to install electric lamps throughout his entire underground laboratory.

Beelzebub ended this part of his Tales to his grandson when everyone on the transsystem spaceship Karnak began to experience a "sweet-sour" taste on the inside of their mouths. This meant that they were entering the atmospheric sphere of some planet. They had now reached a new planet called Deskaldino, where they would make a short stop so that Beelzebub could visit his personal teacher.

SUMMARY

■ Beelzebub meets with a special dervish in "Upper Bokhara" whose efforts will someday help to re-establish the sacred law of *Heptaparaparshinokh* back to all earth-humans who have a sincere thirst for greater knowledge.

■ "Upper Bokhara," although seemingly describing a mountainous region of Turkestan, may be code for a higher, spiritual level of thinking and representing a journey to an otherwise *inaccessible* (non-physical) place.

■ There are two kinds of vibrations—*vibrations of momentum* (mostly from air) and creative vibrations (from strings made of special substances).

■ There are also two kinds of knowledge—mental knowledge (memory data) and *knowledge-of-being* (from the intentional and conscious suffering emerging from one's personal circumspection and spiritual combat).

■ *Knowledge-of-being* protects one from poisonous influences.

■ We all give off a sphere of subjective vibrations that represent both the true quantities and qualities of our lives (our chord of vibrations). The main generator of these vibrations should come from the proper functioning of *emotion*—or heart, which is obtained from a sincere *knowledge-of-being*.

■ Modern humans, with only mental knowledge in their noggins (this includes scholars and academics), give off fewer vibrations than a dog!

■ Hadji conducts vibrational experiments not just on a grand piano, but with colored silk strips (that can cover the whole room) and a special tent whose flaps (walls) could be changed to create different geometrical enclosures.

■ These experiments also showed that modern works of art have a negative effect on the totality of vibrations in humans. But the most surprising revelation was that modern medicines have the most poisonous effect on our vibrational health (called "side-effects").

■ Cancer may be caused by deep-rooted mental uncertainties (insecurities and anxieties that plague us, and find their *centers-of-gravity* in corresponding parts of the body), yet can be cured by those who have elaborated within themselves a special quantity and quality of beneficial vibrations (*living forces*) that can be transferred to others or to a suffering individual.

CHAPTER 42

"Beelzebub in America"

If Swedenborg were reading all this today he would agree with Gurdjieff that the powers of human reasoning were diminishing over time because of spiritual causes, and that a better term for describing humankind's becoming "asleep at the switch" is the more unflattering but modern term *hypnotism* (a term that was coined years after Swedenborg's death). On other important levels, this downward psychic trajectory into cosmic human snoozing also led to the diminishing quality of people's belief systems (one's Faith and worldview) and inability to see reality, which included trading in a God-given reality for a counterfeit and artificial (man-made) externally dead reality—like scientism.

The human race, seeing everything in a "topsy-turvy" way, is mostly oblivious to the hole they have dug themselves into by descending into a pitiful state whereby they would easily forsake God if they could not obtain what they personally desired during their short existence on the planet Earth. And, what they desired and sought was increasingly becoming more external, worldly and self-centered—like personal status, reputation, power and cash in the wallet. (In other words, if God exists and truly loves us, He would treat us extra special and cater to all our desires, whims, and demands.)

Unfortunately for us, the Lord God cannot set up a genuine church on Earth (Heaven's representation, or *Protocosmos*, effecting the earth-human's psyche) from such perverted and warped belief systems, as we now have. So as a consequence, all our cherished notions and institutions are being challenged, everywhere—now!

To this heavenly challenge, Swedenborg states, "divine providence is never acting in the same direction as our deliberate love. It is always acting *against* it. This is because from our own inherited evil we are constantly hungering for the deepest Hell, while the Lord, through His divine providence, is constantly leading us away from it and drawing us out of it—first to some milder Hell, then out of Hell, and eventually to Himself in Heaven. This effort in divine providence is going on all the time; so if we were able to see or feel vividly this carrying off and pulling away, we would be outraged. God would become our enemy, and in the evil of our self-centeredness we would deny Him. So to prevent us from knowing about this, we are kept in

379

a free state where all we can know is that we are leading ourselves" (*Divine Providence*, n. 183).

So we are allowed to live in a deceptive trance and see things "topsy-turvy." But not knowing this situation is what I have discovered as being the most important obstacle to our genuine spiritual growth. Earth-humans were "put to sleep" because it was more *comforting*, and according to Gurdjieff, we were given the maleficent organ Kundabuffer to calm down any potential outrage with God's going against our terrestrial loves. In Swedenborg's statement above, he fully agrees with this scenario.

However, dealing directly with this outrage (from our delusions) is all part of the biblical "Apocalypse," The "Great Red Dragon," and the descent of the Holy City, the New Jerusalem from Heaven to Earth. This descent happens as we receive new heavenly (but challenging) knowledge about reality into our hearts and minds. Unfortunately, we must give up something very dear and important to us as well—to make room for this new heavenly dispensation. At the top of the list for this personal sacrifice is our egoism, which comes from a sincere *knowledge-of-being* that something is not quite right in our lives—no matter how much outer success, respect, or wealth we gain (or how clever we become at fooling others).

Now in this chapter, Beelzebub takes aim at Americans, who have become the new world leaders of "turkey-ness."

As an American citizen, I personally found Beelzebub's visit to my birth-country the most humorous chapter of the whole book (which was greatly appreciated, since reading these Tales three different ways, was a very long haul). Thankfully, Gurdjieff always uses humor at the right time, but always to convey the same seriousness and unflattering message concerning the disintegration of the human psyche, and humankind's decreasing ability to perceive reality correctly and act responsibly—our God-given duty.

(At least we know Americans chew gum!)

I would like to interject here that while Americans have continued on the same trajectory of earth-humans to manifest diminished cognitive abilities, Gurdjieff still places greater hope on the contemporary beings living and breeding on this part of the planet Earth, because when compared to other societies which are older and more settled, Americans are comparatively like "little children." Gurdjieff claims that children are still capable of learning!

Chapter 42 begins with Hassein asking his grandfather to tell him more about those peculiar three-brained beings, the Americans, who are great champions of the "fox trot." I told you this would be humorous. (You can insert any modern form of prancing—even twerking—to get beyond this dated 1920s viewpoint.) Beelzebub replies by telling Hassein that from the city of Paris he took a steamship to the North American city of New York. Beelzebub admits that he is anxious to observe this so-called "melting pot of the races of the Earth."

Beelzebub even carries a letter of introduction to meet with a certain American businessman there, who was always up to his eyeballs in various projects for making "dollars." Beelzebub concludes that practically everyone in this country is obsessed with "earning money."

To offer a creative mental picture for describing the "manufactured" and "false" conditions of these odd ducks of North America, Beelzebub quotes a wise saying from the venerable Mullah Nassr Eddin, "a soap bubble that lasts a long time only in a quiet medium." This statement is rather insightful in that America has gone through several economic crises where "bursts" periodically occur to their financial bubbles! In other words, Americans have created an artificial world and artificial rules for themselves by which they can play their moneymaking games, but which eventually explode in their faces.

Beelzebub says that such breakdowns in their financial systems and the resulting slowdown of foreigners who come into their country to make these same dollars are particularly disastrous to Americans, because being concerned only with making money, they now no longer know how, or care to do something as simple as baking real bread.

In America, dollar-making has replaced many essential crafts for living. (We can see this especially today by how making money has become so abstracted from anything real, and instead, consists of increasingly convoluted and esoteric financial schemes (like "derivatives"). Those who become good at these schemes become less and less able to fix leaks, do plumbing, attach new wires or bake a loaf of bread—the real and necessary chores of everyday life. This trend for pushing the importance of making dollars (at the expense of becoming handy and truly useful) is seen in today's school systems by their removal of "shop" and "home economics" classes from their curriculums. (Today, everyone coming out of school or college wants a "corner office" handed to them—immediately.)

Beelzebub blames the causes of this psychical abnormality, particularly in Americans, on two factors. The first factor is due to their concocting peculiar laws that set up a condition whereby parental wisdom becomes less influential. (Evidence for this first unnatural direction, can be seen by laws that permit younger and younger girls to obtain birth control pills without any parental permission.)

The second factor lies in their institutionalized strategy of teaching children to both save and love dollars. This love of making dollars is strongly implanted in children before they reach adult age. (It certainly was in my own younger life.)

An additional factor providing further evidence of the psychological decline in this country was discovered by Beelzebub as he presented his letter of introduction to the American businessman he was seeking out. While the businessman was reading this letter, Beelzebub notices a quick change in the businessman's behavior (much like the soldier who prepared him for meeting the Czar, but this was more positive), which he calls "unconscious preening." This unconscious preening was due to the fact that Beelzebub's letter of introduction was written by an individual with a reputation for being "damn clever and an expert when it came to making dollars." This is what got the businessman's attention!

In spite of the fact that this American businessman now felt willing to offer his services to Beelzebub, he still had to put this effort off for another day, because he was so swamped in his own various business affairs, making dollars.

Beelzebub makes a passing joke to Hassein that such dollar makers are only free on Sundays, and unfortunately, he did not visit this man on a Sunday. (Even this has changed because in many cases in America, the act of dollar-making has now been extended, even into Sundays.)

The two men then agree to meet at a later time on a street called "Broadway."

On the appointed day of their agreed meeting Beelzebub takes a taxi to the designated place on Broadway, but arriving early, he decides to stroll about and take in the local color. Beelzebub tells Hassein that this famous street is the foremost and principal street of the city of New York. Also, that it is the longest street in any of the major contemporary cities of that planet. It so happens that Beelzebub turns his attention next to the many restaurants and eating establishments on this unique and bustling American street.

Beelzebub amusingly describes the proprietors of these various restaurants on the main section of Broadway as chiefly "Armenians," "Greeks," and "Russian Jews" (at least this is what he observed during the 1920s). Beelzebub then informs his grandson about a curious custom that emerged among these American proprietors. During that particular time of Beelzebub's visit, "alcoholic beverages" were prohibited in America by the powerful political leaders there. Therefore, one would expect that obtaining such liquids, under such strict conditions by the average American citizen was quite impossible.

Nope!

Rather, Beelzebub observed that alcoholic beverages of every type, distilled on "off-shore" barges, could easily be obtained at any of these New York restaurants.

A restaurant customer need only make some suggestive signal and such a liquid would be quickly served at the table. The bottle would always be labeled as "lemonade" or some other benign beverage. (Feigning proper decorum is a sure sign of psychical decline, like pretense and hypocrisy.)

Beelzebub next shares with his grandson the curious and suspicious means by which these various alcoholic liquids were stealthily prepared. These liquids all seemed to be made from some acid, like sulfuric, nitric, or muriatic acids (modern money-making ingenuity). Then, for the purposes of economy of effort, a fraudulent but precise ritual was introduced into the process of booze-making.

For every thousand bottles (or batch) to be prepared, one genuine bottle of the particular alcoholic beverage was to be placed among them. Next, and by some "wishful" process of osmosis (and the proper prayer), the other thousand bottles would be instantaneously transformed into that same liquid from the single genuine bottle. As a final touch, labels similar to the one on the genuine bottle were placed on the other thousand bottles.

(In Swedenborg's terms, this "magical" ritual represents an *inner* principle operating among those individuals who trust only their own prudence and value craftiness and cunning over wisdom and truth. Such self-deluded individuals, and their always-perverted "hope," are psychically prone to such concocted magical rituals of self-delusion and contrived various arts—*Arcana Colestia*, n. 6692.)

Beelzebub recounts that this same solemn, yet hypocritical contrivance of production, also went into the making of "German chicken soup" during the First World War—as a solution to their growing food crisis. This feat of illusion involved putting water in a big pot, adding some finely chopped leaves of parsley, opening the doors (or window), then chasing a poor chicken through the kitchen at full speed. Presto—one now had created a most delicious chicken soup—that could feed many, many people.

And, when the chased chicken became utterly tired they would roast it and invite their family members over for a special dinner. But the real chicken never went into the soup—only its imagined influence.

That this final procedure (family chicken dinner) was also given deep spiritual credibility, was hinted by Beelzebub, in his tongue-in-cheek description of the family hostess, as looking up to Heaven and pointing to the chicken as having a human soul, and attributing their good fortune (and good meal) to some nephew in a far away place who sent them this bird and who was always looking after their well-being. (Fat chance! I am often amused at how Americans believe that their dead relatives and friends are always looking down on them with angelic concern.)

This delusional ritual apparently made it okay to shortchange others.

Beelzebub observed that these self-deluding incantations and congeries were used for every kind of purpose on the planet Earth. This "make-believe" practice also increased, as more and more people entered into careers called "occultists," "spiritualists," "theosophists," "violet magicians," and "chiromants (palm readers)," etc. Such people even envisioned themselves to have supernatural powers.

Hassein is then told that further insights into the atrophying psyche of earth-humans could be distilled from the American Prohibition going on—since they were still able to continue their consumption of alcoholic beverages.

Hassein is further informed by his furry grandfather that the same phenomenon was now occurring to these American consumers of alcohol that occurred with the chewing of poppy seeds in the ancient country of Maralpleicie. Then, to turn the screws deeper into the sensitivities of the post-modern American psyche, Beelzebub states that the individuals in Maralpleicie at least became addicted to genuine poppy seeds, whereas modern earth-humans in America were becoming addicted to any darn liquid labeled as "alcohol." (One only has to think about those who ingest cough medicine to get a "buzz" in order to verify Beelzebub's seemingly harsh accusation.)

Beelzebub next describes to Hassein how contemporary Americans have become far more clever at hiding their addiction than those ancient citizens of Maralpleicie (cleverness trumping wisdom). American ingenuity has taken "pretense" to a new level of absurdity. For instance, when sitting in a restaurant or dance hall, many Americans were drinking alcohol from containers designed to look like a cigarette or cigar case. Beelzebub had even observed one female patron stealthily pouring some suspicious "liquid" into her glass from a hollow umbrella.

So Beelzebub gives credit to the Americans for being much more "civilized" than modern Russians in concealing their consumption of such beverages so damaging to their planetary bodies. (Swedenborg says that hiding one's bad behavior and compulsions from the eyes of the world, only ensures that one will take these unrepentant negative traits into the next world. That is why he also maintained that one's personal evils had to be seen and acknowledged—in order to be removed.)

Beelzebub also has some negative things to say concerning another famous American drink called "orange juice." He tells Hassein that while such a drink has a real cooling effect on hot days, its acidic content damages the "mucous membranes" of the stomach and intestines, causing further destruction in the Americans' *digestive* function. (Some recent research seems to point to alkaline and lower ph levels as being more beneficial to the human body.)

Beelzebub makes yet another unique observation concerning American *ingenuity*. On the table in the restaurant where Beelzebub was sitting while waiting for his American contact to show up, he notices a printed "menu." He is astounded to read that this menu offered *seventy-eight* different dishes that a patron could order. Having watched earth-humans prepare food down through the centuries he wondered what kind of stove was capable of preparing so many choices in a day. He also calculated that the restaurant's kitchen had to contain about three hundred pots and pans to create so many dishes. So he gives a "good tip" to one of the waiters in order to go into their kitchen to observe their massive operation.

Instead of the expected massive operation, Beelzebub sees only a "midget gas stove" and a "fat-necked" cook reading a newspaper. As he was looking around this kitchen in astonishment, a waiter came in with a food order for a very elaborate dish. From the waiter's accent, Beelzebub concluded that he came to America, like all other Europeans, to fill their pockets with "dollars."

After giving the order, the fat-necked cook took out a small frying pan, lit the "dwarf stove," pulled out a tin can from one of their many cupboards, opened it, and poured its contents into the pan. Then the large (meaning clumsy) cook went to another cupboard, got out another can, and poured a small amount of its contents into the pan, stirred it up and presto—the resulting mixture was served to a customer, but was first put on a fancy copper tray with fashionable cutlery.

After this contemporary ritual in food preparation had run its course, the cook sat back down to continue reading his newspaper. Beelzebub takes his seat back at his table and observes a customer "smacking his lips" as he is being served the strange food prepared from that kitchen.

What Beelzebub was discovering about Americans, was that they were *masters of illusion* (this is a theme throughout the chapter and represents a further negative outcome and expression of the consequences of organ Kundabuffer in human life).

But wait—there is more to "American strangeness." Much more.

On his arrival to America, Beelzebub discovered, that while having mastered the English tongue, he found some difficulty picking up and communicating the particular "conversational English" used by the Americans. To correct this difficulty he decided to find a teacher, and thanks to an outdoor "American advertisement" he was led to such a school. The instructor there had created a unique system by which "American English language" could be learned in anywhere from five minutes to twenty-four hours. This made no sense to Beelzebub, who had mastered many other languages, but he took the course anyway.

When Beelzebub showed up for the lesson, the inventor of this unique language system, Mr. Chatterlitz, informed him that the lessons came in three forms—each corresponded to some particular and special requirement. The first form was described to Beelzebub as having been created for those interested mainly in making lots of "American dollars." The second form was created for those who wanted to come off as already successful and as a gentleman with a good English upbringing. The third form was devised for those who wanted to procure Scotch whisky—anywhere—and at any time of the day.

Beelzebub decides that the second form of the English language would suit him best and immediately pays the appropriate amount of dollars to learn the secret of Mr. Chatterlitz's system.

Once Mr. Chatterlitz had received the money and tucked it safely into his inside pocket (closest to his heart), he reveals to Beelzebub that in order to learn this second form, one had to memorize just these five words. They were:

1) Maybe
2) Perhaps
3) Tomorrow
4) Oh, I see
5) All right

Lesson over! Cha-ching!

Mr. Chatterlitz assures Beelzebub that these five words were the only words he would ever, ever have to use to effectively converse with other influential Americans—and that he only needed to utter them every now and then.

These five words offer a wonderful picture of how easily contemporary humans can operate as mere automatons and without any deep self-pondering. On top of that, Mr. Chatterlitz also assures Beelzebub that using just these five English words will convince everyone that he is an old pro in making American dollars.

On the very next day, Beelzebub meets a European acquaintance on another New York street. He was a professional "editor" of a newspaper there. He told Beelzebub that he could even offer him an additional secret concerning this local language. This further secret to becoming a master of the American version of the English language involves imagining that you have a hot potato in your mouth—that is even sprinkled with some ground "red pepper." Instantly, the result would be the blurting out loudly of some appropriate and genuinely sounding American word. Even if one spouted loudly an unfamiliar term, using the hot potato method will quickly convince others that the word, now obviously given importance, must be quite legitimate.

GEE-WILLIKERS!

From New York City, Beelzebub next travels to the city of Chicago and takes another letter of introduction with him from his first American acquaintance, to meet someone there—a person named "Mr. Bellybutton." Upon their meeting, Mr. Bellybutton suggests going to the house of some of his friends, so that Beelzebub would not become bored in this strange new city. When they arrived at the house, Beelzebub observed a happy group of young people sharing jokes and other funny stories. Beelzebub, literally being from another planet and culture, found that the laughter from their stories seemed to linger in the room like *"smoke blowing in from American sausage factories that made 'hot dogs'."* (That description certainly landed on all three of my psychic functions!)

While Beelzebub was mildly amused by these various funny stories he was still quite astonished by their "ambiguity" and "obscenity." Nothing with real depth or real importance was ever mentioned by these contemporary American partiers.

The next day Mr. Bellybutton took him to another American party. At this party a "young lady" came over to sit next to Beelzebub where they began to converse (chat) about any darned thing (so nothing of importance). Suddenly the young lady, for no apparent reason, began to stroke the back of his neck. Beelzebub, in complete innocence, thought that this must be some act of American kindness, and that she probably noticed a "flea" on his neck and simply wanted to offer some soothing relief. But he then notices that everyone at the party was stroking each other in the same way and that it was too much of a coincidence that they could all have fleas on their necks.

After leaving that house Beelzebub asks Mr. Bellybutton to explain this strange coincidence. This causes Mr. Bellybutton to break out into laughter and call Beelzebub a "simpleton" and a "hick." He informs Beelzebub that they had just attended a "petting party." Tommorrow, he was planning to take his guest to a "swimming party." But he added, that if one sought something less tame, he could provide it because he was also a member of several groups that offered such parties.

Before Beelzebub leaves for New York to take a boat back to Europe, he spends an additional day studying an American invention that was now a chief cause in the further dwindling of the human psyche. This invention gradually took the place of the being-function in humans called "sane instinct to believe in reality."

Beelzebub tells Hassein that before coming to America he had read in a magazine that Chicago had famous slaughterhouses. These slaughterhouses were promoted as having specially designed machines that allowed their operations to be both "humane" and impeccably clean, and that no human hands were ever involved. The article he read made it seem to Beelzebub that a live cow could go in one end, and ten minutes later, hot sausage, ready to eat, would come out the other. The article convinced him of the unprecedented results of these modern meat factories. Now that Beelzebub was in Chicago, he decided to personally inspect these miraculous factories for himself.

In the same way that Beelzebub was shocked by the fat-necked and lumbering cook, with the small gas stove in the fancy New York restaurant, he was now just as shocked by the "true" conditions of these Chicago slaughterhouses. The magazine article he read distorted reality—just as the restaurant's wonderful menu had. While indeed being larger than the slaughterhouses he had seen on other continents, the Chicago operations were in reality much dirtier, more brutal, and pools of blood could be seen everywhere. He observed no special machines there other than ordinary "rollers and rails."

Beelzebub had now been exposed to the American idea of "selling the sizzle instead of the steak." In other words, American advertising and marketing was adding to the diminishing state of the human psyche by successfully replacing the instinctive function to perceive reality with mere illusion.

Such deception, and human gullibility are the result of modern humans being highly susceptible to suggestion, hypnotic spell and exaggerated claims. Apparently, American advertisers and market-ers (with their now atrophied sacred functioning of conscience) could create these illusions better than anyone else on Earth and turn this "expertise" into making plenty of dollars. In fact, this expertise and practice has become so effective that the human beings breeding on the planet Earth have to summon all their psychical powers to remind themselves, for short moments, that they are being deluded.

(I have to admit that I thought I was "hot shit" when I was working as a young copywriter for some of the biggest ad agencies in America—but I was actually involved in a form of hypnosis/ suggestion, and helping to speed up the further psychic "dwindling" of large numbers of people!) There is even a comic strip joke about advertising that compares it to *cleaning out the stables.*

(I believe Beelzebub is actually making a more cosmic compar-ison between the affect "Advertising" has on the human mind with the comet *Kondoor* striking the planet Earth and creating fragments!)

When Beelzebub returns to New York from Chicago, he again continues his research on contemporary illnesses and the subjec-tive vices affecting this comparatively new group of earth-humans. After gathering his statistics he concludes that almost half of the three-brained beings living in America have disharmonized *digestive* systems, and as a result, a quarter of them also suffer from *sexual impotency.* (The wide usage of antacids for indigestion and pills to cure *erectile* difficulties seems to support these particular claims— now, more than ever!)

Beelzebub predicts that if this trend continues, the same kind of destruction will befall America as happened to "monarchic Russia." The only difference in the fate of these two cultures is that this destruction in Russia was from faulty minds, whereas in America, it will result from organic abnormalities—faulty digestion and the diminished functioning of their sexual organs. (I have even heard reports that "sperm counts" are going down in men and it is getting more and more obvious that a malicious cultural divide is brewing in America similar to what happened during "monarchic Russia" and its so-called "great revolution.")

Beelzebub points out to Hassein that because digestion and sex represent the two *motors* of existence, which are atrophying in these earth-humans and causing FRUSTRATION, they must become, from reasoning, evermore carefully vigilant (and suspicious) of any *initiating* factor, inclination or intent, arising in their hearts and minds (appetites and lusts).

Everything we do has an eternal consequence. All such initiating actions, which drive the human psyche (like eating and sex), come under cosmic laws and acquire a universal momentum and trajectory that heads back to Prime Being itself. But do we eat and have sex to celebrate the works of the Creator? Heck, no.

Swedenborg would say that such a *circular* "Karmic" law or cosmic "orb" involves the first causal principles (initiating factors) of our actions eventually returning back to the original ground from which they came. "What goes around comes around." For coordinated unity everything must return to its source—good or bad. What we eat and how we expend our sexual energy goes into determining our ultimate karma.

So, from sane reasoning, we must always be vigilant.

Any reader of *Beelzebub's Tales* can easily confirm that a sincere, objective view of humanity points to a general strangeness in the psyche and manifestations of three-brained earth-beings. Beelzebub informs Hassein that the causes for the disharmony in the functioning of digestion and sex in Americans, which leads to their negativity, personal agitation and frustration, will offer new and useful details to the underlying problem facing humankind.

Beelzebub starts with the reasons for why American earth-humans are wreaking havoc on their digestive systems and ruining their health.

In a nutshell, the quality of people's food has come to reflect the quality of their being and lives (you are what you eat). In all areas of human living, the current emphasis has been placed on "external" beauty. (In the restaurant business, this "beauty" or creating a "striking appearance" with food is called *presentation*.) In other words, the nutritional value of food has been replaced by cosmetic (external) concerns. Furthermore, because of the need in modern society for extended "shelf-life" and long distance distribution, food products are not only becoming less fresh and more processed, but that everyone has become accustomed their digestive systems to food products that are already in a "decomposed condition." By the time earth-humans chow down, most of the vital active elements required for normal health have been volatized out of their food products.

The three-brained beings of the planet Earth have not only disconnected themselves psychically from reality, but their *first-being food* has been similarly severed from its connection with common Nature. Beelzebub tells Hassein that none of the preservation techniques like freezing or canning halts the cosmic *Trogoautoegocratic* process, by which active elements lawfully *involve* and separate themselves in the reverse order from which they were first fused. So even in "hermetically sealed cans" the vital active elements in food, necessary for health, infallibly separate from the general mass—and disintegration results. As soon as these cans are opened, the import-ant active elements inside simply volatize into space, returning to their corresponding origins, according to cosmic law.

Beelzebub has nothing good to say about earth-humans eating fresh fruit either, because human tinkering (engineering) has turned these fruits into "freaks." Contemporary scientific manipulation of these fruits have merely turned them into "feasts for the eye" and not a proper form of being-nourishment for the physical body. It turns out that this manipulated, nutrient-deficient fruit now only provides cosmic substances serviceable for maintaining one's "automatically self-reproducing subjective presence," or the mentality to view all true value in external terms only—that is, whether something is "fashionable" and does it have "a striking appearance."

Again, Beelzebub believes that Americans have become the masters at this game of illusion. They have created many colorful labels and artful jars that convince the buyer of the "rapture" one will experience by tasting the equally colorful and artful contents within.

(Again, I played a role in this deceptive practice, having been an advertising writer for many clients, including food clients. However, I did rebel from time to time when this deception (and a client's claims) made no sense to me. For instance, I once worked on a hair shampoo that emphasized "natural purity," yet it was produced in a lab from complex chemical mixtures—so the product claim differed significantly from its actual design. This trend toward hiding scien-tific manipulation continues today with GMOs (genetically modified organisms), which have been ruled "natural." However, once some-thing is severed from its actual connection to nature it begins to change its form and decompose in the reverse order of its forma-tion—no matter what is done to improve or preserve it.)

Another cosmically important food item that Americans have botched up (to make more dollars) is the making of "good" bread, which Beelzebub calls one of the most important first-being foods for the physical body. This botched effort, based also on maximizing profits, includes extracting the wheat germ from the flour and robbing the resulting bread of its otherwise natural and nutritional essentials. (Conversationally, the term "white bread" has come to be used to describe something lacking anything meaningful, special, or essen-tial.) Even though food manufacturers "scientifically" try to put these nutritional elements back into the bread, it is never the same again.

Beelzebub is saddened by this "deformity" in American bread-making because the continent itself has a great and very rich soil. Not only does this American bread offer nothing useful to those who consume it (except gas and worms) but that this product of "Amer-ican ingenuity" has caused this young nation to gain a warped "sense of superiority," having created a marvel of contemporary civilization.

This sense of pride and superiority in succeeding to obtain the greatest possible sensation of self-satisfaction from their money-making feats more than makes up for the health problems they might experience arising in their stomachs. (A full wallet makes up for a bad stomach.)

As a cruel irony, Beelzebub points out to his grandson that the more nutritionally important parts of American grain, after being removed, are simply fed to pigs and livestock. (This is before antibiotics were given to such livestock.)

Even the natural process of "taking a dump" has been negatively affected by the inventiveness of the diminishing human psyche.

Beelzebub also blames modern "water closets" and "fashionable" toilets for the further disharmonizing of the American digestive function. He points out to Hassein that in more ancient times, earth-humans could instinctively adopt the *correct posture* of squatting for removing solid wastes from their bodies. But now, the invention of "comfortable seats" (with magazines, phones and radios nearby, so that they can continue making dollars without skipping a beat or a flush) have caused important muscles to atrophy. The result is that obstructions form in what normally would be a smooth process.

(Remember John Wayne's issue with digestive blockages?)

These obstructions further cause new diseases to occur—diseases unknown to three-brained beings living in other parts of the universe. Beelzebub adds that problems occurring in the human "appendix" are one such "modern" result of using these seats of extreme comfort. Beelzebub tells Hassein that the appendix was designed by Great Nature to gather the various gases forming in the intestines and use these gases to assist in the discharge and elimination of human waste (much like the gases of a repeating rifle are used to exit a bullet cartridge and allow another bullet to enter into the chamber).

Beelzebub explains to Hassein that the proper action of the human appendix is naturally established according to biological timing mechanisms established from an individual's daily habit. But once this habit is broken, as for instance, when one travels to another country, this timing mechanism becomes seriously disharmonized in a way that the accumulated gases in the intestines could then be released at any time of the day, *unproductively*, apart from the elimination function (like farting). One can easily imagine how these continued disharmonies could add up over time through non-natural living and cause such obstruction and damage to this little understood organ's proper functioning and utility that it would often need to be surgically removed.

Today's increased speed for traveling far distances has even created a whole new term for the physical disharmony of our biological timing, called "jet lag."

Beelzebub recounts that during the ancient Tikliamishian civilization, the beings there, had succeeded in creating inventions similar to that of the American comfort seats. In fact, the American invention would be considered a mere "child's toy" compared to those created by this former civilization.

This ancient civilization created not simply "seats of ease," but according to Beelzebub, even developed a certain kind of "comfortable couch bed." One could simply lie on this wonderful contrivance and without making any *being effort*, perform the function of bodily elimination. One simply moved a lever at the side of the couch and everything was taken care of. These wonder couches were cozy and "chic." Unfortunately, these seats eventually caused momentous events to occur in the process of their daily existence. (I suspect that Beelzebub is alluding to the increased frictions that irritated people have with each other, and were partially caused by the these *effortless* comfort seats.)

Beelzebub next makes another amazing claim about organic gratification, which had profound significance for blocking the self-correcting activities needed for restoring the human psyche to normal. From my Swedenborgian vantage point, the "comfort seats" symbolize a psychical change in what earth-beings were striving for—more physical pleasure and comfort. (This comfort seeking and increased hedonism, represents a *downward* change in the center of gravity of one's conscious aim in life.)

This deteriorating psycho-condition is augmented (and finds its new analog) by the fact that Beelzebub's story now moves to another scale—a much larger planetary scale. He describes to Hassein that at the time these comfort seats were being put into great use throughout the former country of Tikliamish, the planet Earth was also experiencing a cosmic process called "Chirnooanovo" (which is different from Solioonensius). The Chirnooanovo represents the specific action of the *solar system* in maintaining its common-cosmic harmony and causing the Earth's center of gravity to be modified and displaced a bit. This represents a cosmic correction within the solar system itself, which unfortunately, is felt in people's lives *as a need to correct their outer social situation*. So Beelzebub is using a large-scale planetary event as a metaphor and cosmic connection for what is also happening deeper within the human psyche—a psyche that also finds itself needing to re-orient itself to a more harmonic situation.

As above, so below.

In three-brained humans throughout the universe, this mentioned cosmic corrective process in the solar system routinely brings about the being-experience of "Remorse-of-Conscience," where one becomes inwardly motivated to purposefully compare *one's past deeds* with *one's stated convictions* and make the proper corrections. (This creates the important *knowledge of being*.) Only in this way can humanity regain its proper harmony and a nobler center of gravity within the universal motion and sacred endeavor of God's eternally unfolding plan, that is, divine providence. But without this conscious effort, one merely seeks *external* improvements to solve all problems.

Swedenborg makes it clear that *spiritual truths from good* are implanted in humans by temptations (*Apocalypse Explained*, n. 283b, [4])—by which one's deeds and passions are compared with one's stated convictions and knowledge. (Understanding and enjoying "spiritual truths from good" is another way of saying one has "knowledge of being.")

But in earth-humans seeking mere organic gratification and comfort, the cosmic process of sincere self-reflection and correction is ignored, and its necessity never penetrates people's inner reality or changes their center of gravity to a more noble and eternal pursuit. Being oblivious to self-correction also causes a corresponding disharmonious result to occur on much, much smaller scales—such as increasing diseases in humans. Harmful microorganisms, pathogens and epidemics begin to spread throughout human communities when self-correction is not practiced. Swedenborg concurs that disease and harmful things correspond to spiritual illnesses and that all illnesses have spiritual causes in how one approaches his or her life.

According to Beelzebub, as a result of these illnesses, "revolutionaries" popped up in Tikliamish. So they got rid of these harmful pleasure seats (toilets), blaming the "parasitic bourgeois," who made great use of them, and thus bringing about these terrible diseases and spreading these diseases among the masses.

These "revolutionaries" had no problem convincing populations to follow their lead, because the negative placement in the centers of gravity of everyone's true being—to seek mere pleasure and personal comfort—created a "loss of sensation of self" (separating oneself from oneself). This opened them up to propaganda and further "suggestibility." The "loss of sensation of self" is a problem that is difficult to prove because most people do not want to learn about, or be shaken out of, their comfy dream-states.

(Concerning disease and comfort, I would like to share something I heard said to my Gurdjieffian work group by our teacher at a meeting in the early 1980s. She said, "If one only seeks comfort and pleasure, the first thing to go is one's health.")

This pleasure principle, when it represents our true *center of gravity* (or *Ruling Love*) wreaks havoc on our physical wellness—particularly when we dismiss the more uncomfortable responsibility of engaging in spiritual vigilance (of our various-sourced personal *initiating* factors) and transformation, which is our inherent God-given duty.

As a student of Swedenborg's ideas, it seems to me that the "Dark Ages" and the various plagues that raged through Europe at an earlier time were brought about by Christian bishops (fathers of the Orthodox Christian religion), who misinterpreted true religious doctrine at the Council of Nicea, which was full of politics and intrigues to consolidate power. They misinterpreted the Holy Trinity as consisting of three Divine Personalities, instead of One God with three functions, and successfully sold this idea to the masses.

As I addressed above, it seems to me that "Solioonensius" and "Chirnooanova" represent a similar cosmic law (the first, from a tension outside the solar system and the second, within the solar system) since they both produce similar pressures on the human psyche to make some change in their lives. However, earth-humans no longer respond correctly to these cosmic tensions.

Normally, when the human psyche is feeling some kind of "displacement" happening in the universe, a tension arises between what a person knows (in the intellect, or his stated convictions) and what a person actually does (from the heart). But in those individuals who overlook this cosmic duty of inner comparison (psychic Djartklom and remorse), they instead sense this tension as an irritation and aggravation concerning the quality of their *physical* or *outer* lives only. And they tend to demand external changes to fix this irritation by some "social change" or revolution.

Beelzebub is not yet finished with the problems of the American digestive system. He now moves to the topic of modern food preservation and adds that it is odd that modern Americans consider themselves to be the prime originators of time-saving, economically convenient, preserved food products (and comfort seats). This is further evidence that humankind is becoming more disconnected from its true history. He tells Hassein that ancient cultures also sought to minimize the time spent on feeding themselves with food products, but that in each case, they became convinced that these strategies all led to the degeneration of food quality.

Beelzebub informs his grandson of the various methods of preserving food that he witnessed during prior visits to the planet Earth. In one case, during a time when the country of Maralpleicie was in a fierce competition with the inhabitants of Tikliamish to determine which society deserved to be called the "center of culture," methods of food preservation were at the top of the list. Those from Maralpleicie invented something similar to the hermetically sealed cans of the Americans but they used something much less toxic than metal tins. Their sealed containers were made from finely ground "mother of pearl," yolks of hen's eggs, and a glue obtained from a fish called the Choozna sturgeon. These food-preserving vessels had the appearance of unpolished glass jars.

In spite of the advantages over tin cans, certain wise beings from the country of Maralpleicie began to notice that individuals who habitually used products preserved in this manner began to lose their sense of "organic shame." (Swedenborg would say that such "gross" food would affect the *animus* [passions] of the cerebral cortex in negative ways because it reinforced depraved appetites in one's red blood.) These Asian wise leaders then convinced their community to abandon this method of food preservation, whereupon even the knowledge of this method was forgotten within just five generations.

Beelzebub points out that various methods of food preservation were devised throughout the ages, but none of these methods were as harmful as the poison-exuding tin cans invented on the continent of America. (What is hinted at here is that promiscuity and vulgarity, which is increasing in America, is an outcome of our eating more and more artificially preserved and poisonous foods—which negatively affect our blood and its passions.)

As the saying goes, "you are what you eat."

Furthermore, Swedenborg also put forth the same notion that human illnesses and disease were caused by the improper regulation of *food*—and this on three distinct levels of blood qualities, the red blood (physical body), the purer blood (in the mind) and the purest blood (from one's soul), *The Fiber*, n. 371–374. (The notion of food preservation itself can represent the ingestion and appropriation of a false, or *involving*, belief in the human mind and spirit.)

Beelzebub does admit to Hassein that one method of food preservation in ancient Asia was somewhat satisfactory. This method relied on the fat of a sheep's tail, which did not give off active elements that could turn "poisonous" for the human gut.

The problem with hermetically sealed tin cans is that the metal used gives off elements that cannot properly volatilize into the atmosphere and therefore must lawfully fuse together with the by-products given off by the deteriorating food itself. The result of this unfortunate toxic fusion is that it now enters into the organisms of these contemporary beings that consume such preserved food items. Beelzebub also states, that besides using sheep's-tail fat, this particular Asian culture had the wisdom to roast or broil their food first—rather than preserve food in raw states (because it is thought to be fresher). This Asian culture learned that the cooking process retards the speed of food decomposition.

Beelzebub changes scales again. He now feels it is advantageous for his grandson to put this part of his narrative, about the importance of boiling and roasting in food preparation, into a larger, cosmic perspective concerning universal laws (including spiritual growth). As I was hoping to communicate to you, the reader, the same laws operating in the cooking process also work in the larger processes occurring over the entire universe and human mind.

Beelzebub uses the process of making bread to illustrate the universal principles of how new products are formed from *fusion*. This knowledge reveals the *sacred* significance of "bread" (which was used by the Lord at the sacred ritual of the "Last Supper"). Bread is made from *three* distinct cosmic substances (according to the Sacred Triamazikamno or Law of Threefoldness). "Water" represents the *active* ingredient (holy affirming) in this threefold law. "Flour" represents the *passive* (denying) aspect in this law. Finally, the third or *neutralzing* and reconciling influence, which brings the whole process of fusion to completion, is "fire," or some source of heat.

The combination of these three universal principles creates a new and more permanent fusion between each one of them, resulting in a new totality of substances now called "bread." This procedure allows the bread to more easily resist the tyranny of time (entrophy due to the merciless Heropass). Even as bread dries and begins to crumble, the integrity of the bread, as a new product, is still preserved by this universal process of fusion. (Similarly, Swedenborg communicated that in humans who are going through spiritual regeneration and transformation, psychical "heat" from the friction of inner challenges is created to fuse together a spiritual body, which can resist the influence of physical time.)

Beelzebub gives other examples of ancient methods of food preservation, but just like Swedenborg, the main point of this part of the narrative is to set the reader up for understanding how this same law of Triamazikamno, which takes part in bread-making, can also create an inner fusion within a person's being—to produce a spiritual body that is capable of ultimately overcoming the tyranny (entropy) of physical time—in order that one can enjoy eternal life and spiritual happiness.

So the challenge to earth-humans is that they must create a similar process of fusion within themselves—between their best knowledge (passive principle) and their actual intentions (active principles). The conflict arising from this psychical mixture creates the "heat" necessary for the fusion (reconciling principle) of one's inner unity and spiritual integrity.

In fact, Beelzebub informs his grandson that he had personally met an Asian who was part of a Brotherhood, and whose name was *Asiman*, who conducted special investigations to verify whether this universal triune law could be used to free humankind from their *inner slavery*.

This individual had previously lived in the country formally called "Pearl-land" and now called "Hindustan." When westerners from the continent of Europe began to move in, disturbing their valuable work, Asiman and his Brotherhood moved to the "Himalayan Mountains" in Tibet and also into the "valleys of the Hindu Kush." Brother Asiman himself had settled into one of the valleys in Hindu Kush. (Hindu Kush seems to be a special area that still contains ancient wisdom.)

This Asiman fellow believed that if he could reduce the time spent eating and preserving food, they could all spend that much more time on self-perfection.

So Asiman, an alchemist, had concocted a unique kind of powder that, with an amount of just a thimbleful, kept his brethren alive while also diminishing their appetites due to "wandering nerves of the stomach." (Americans trying to lose weight would today jump at such a product—even without sensing a need for spiritual growth.)

But after five months, the harmful effects of this powder began to be noticed. The Brothers' functions of seeing, hearing and speaking became weaker. Negative manifestations in their general psyches began to appear as well. These negative manifestations caused otherwise good-natured people to become quite *irritable, pessimistic,* and *troublesome.* Thus, these individuals discovered the unflattering truth that their qualities of goodness had more to do with whether they had full bellies rather than full hearts. True spiritual development goes much deeper and is more consistent, but one must also be fair to the physical body and its needs, for it supports (like a foundation) the mind and spirit.

At this point in the story Beelzebub humorously predicts that the author of these Tales (Gurdjieff), who is not afraid to speak the truth to earth-humans, will become a hated man by "full-bodied materialists," "ninety-six carat deists" and by those contemporary earth-humans who are irritated because of empty bellies and whose mistresses are causing scenes.

(As I stated earlier, during his anatomical investigations, Swedenborg discovered that the quality of the red blood coming from the digestive system, had a real effect on the *passions* of the cerebrum. These influences could penetrate the brain's blood barrier by a process of dissolution, whereby the red blood is broken down to its more essential elements, consisting of chemical substances in the foods that correspond to one's leanings and moods. When these chemical influences (leanings) enter the cortical brain they act as *initiating factors* for mental picturings in one's imagination and which become powerful human compulsions.)

Moving from his discussion concerning the disharmony in the Americans' digestive function, Beelzebub now takes aim at the disharmony occurring in their second important function and motor in life—the function of sex.

As mentioned in an earlier chapter, this problem arose from European customs which brought about bad hygiene and an uncleanliness concerning their sexual organs. This tradition of uncleanliness migrated to the continent of America.

Americans now spend more time and care of their faces and hair (with cosmetics and conditioners) than with the cleanliness of their sexual organs. As a result, "venereal diseases" occur in Europe and in America more than anywhere else on the entire planet (certainly much more than in Asia). In fact, the problem has almost reached epidemic proportions in these *modern* western nations. Beelzebub also found that the disease called "gonorrhea" was mostly only found in parts of Asia, which either shared a border with European communities, or its inhabitants had increased contact with westerners or Russian people. (Even epidemics of sexual disease in Africa, which is a modern phenomenon, are associated with their picking up contemporary western behaviors and a loosening of values.)

Again, because of wise traditions developed over time in Asia, among those who lived more or less normally (for earth-humans), these Asian societies were relatively protected from such sexual diseases. Beelzebub points out two traditions, which spare earth-humans from many sexual diseases and "sexual abnormalities." Circumcision is one of them. This keeps the male penis cleaner, reducing the causes of irritation and thus reducing the acquired habit in children for self-gratification called *onanism* (masturbation).

(Swedenborg, in his scientific book on the human generative organs, *The Animal Kingdom, Generation,* n. 153, suggested that a spurious form of erection in the male penis was caused by *irritation or impure thoughts,* rather than a noble principle of spiritual [marital] love, forcing the red blood to expand the male organ by a different order and entering into different expanding tissues.)

The second wise custom mentioned by Beelzebub requires cleaning the sex organs, with *just cold water* after every visit to the toilet. This very simple custom spares many, many Asians from contracting most venereal diseases.

Expanding this theme on sexual disharmony in America (and the western world), Beelzebub shares with Hassein a conversation he once had with a young Persian male acquaintance who acted as his guide in the city of Paris. Beelzebub had arranged to meet this Persian guide at a particular café and when the Persian showed up, he seemed "more drunk than usual." Besides the heavy drinking, this Persian male was also a "petticoat chaser." Beelzebub observed that every time this Persian saw a pretty face of the female sex, his whole body, including his breathing would suddenly change. (Swedenborg also discovered that a person's breathing would change along with his or her various mental and emotional changes of state.)

Beelzebub asks his Persian friend, point blank, why he ingested this "poison."

The young Persian man responds by honestly saying that he has become fully addicted to alcoholic beverages and that only through its consumption could he *calmly* look at all the obscenities and depravity occurring all around him in this western center of culture. He began his drinking only after life conditions forced him to move to Paris (to make money). Everyone in this maleficent European community drank, and if they noticed you were not drinking, they would question your manhood (the late actor, Humphrey Bogart, is reported saying that he "trusted no one who didn't drink"). The Persian man did not want his business acquaintances to call him offensive names so he began to drink along with them. Drinking also helped him to alleviate the shame and inner pain he felt from being exposed to the strange morality and patriarchy of European life, which contrasted to the values he was brought up with.

Lending a sympathetic ear, Beelzebub next asks his Persian guide how he picked up the inexcusable vice of "petticoat drooling."

The Persian man places part of the blame on his drinking but also explained that this particular weakness developed out of another interesting psychological cause. He then explains to Beelzebub about the different attitudes Persian men have toward their women.

Persian men, over the last two and a half centuries, were brought up to place women into two distinct classes. Either as a "woman-mother," or a "woman-female." (There is a growing trend in America for girls to become "woman-females.") Furthermore, Swedenborg discovered in the spiritual world that "mothers" receive the special heavenly sphere of conjugial love (marital love) and the protection of infants more than others (*Conjugial Love*, n. 393, VI).

The Persian man said that these two "organic attitudes" toward women emerged out of a period of declining piety because wars were intensifying all over Asia. Certain wise Elders in these warring societies concluded from their impartial observations that a certain psychic disease began to appear which was contracted by those men whose subconscious minds never seemed to contain any *impulse of faith* in anything. (Since human seed comes from the "soul," according to Swedenborg's *Conjugial Love*, n. 220 [2 & 3], such individuals have no desire or determination to propagate God's plan for cosmic usefulness and wisdom.) This psychic disease would often lead to insanity and suicide. However, the wise Elders also noticed that men (even if they had no faith in anything) who continued to have normal sexual intercourse with women were not subject to this very same illness and mental breakdown.

(Swedenborg also suggested, in his spiritual work *Conjugial Love*, n. 450, [V] that normal sex can help maintain health in the physical bodies of men and also protect them from sicknesses of the mind. This situation seems logical, since sex helps men eliminate hundreds of millions of sperm cells that would otherwise *involve* backwards and create toxins in their bodies—especially if they were not participating in intense spiritual activities or usefulness.)

When this second discovery of mental breakdown was passed along to various chiefs and leaders throughout Asia, they became concerned about the *fighting ability* of their young male soldiers, who would often spend long periods of time away from their wives. These leaders and their consultants concluded that the problem could be easily remedied if they allowed *prostitution* to be established everywhere throughout Asia (as is now the case throughout the European continent and America).

These leaders, without experiencing any "remorse of conscience" began encouraging many women (except their own daughters) to embrace this new "abhorrently repulsive" occupation in order to keep their soldiers in the best fighting condition (and to protect their own behinds).

The Persian guide tells Beelzebub that during a celebration of Ramadan he once had a discussion about this "scourge" with his Mullah uncle. This uncle advised the young man to never blame or despise these kinds of women. It is the parents, husbands and guardians who are to be blamed for this, because they failed to provide the proper principles of life for the proper cosmic organization of the female psyche (engendering innate modesty). Therefore, instead of acquiring their own good sense, young maturing women have allowed an element of laziness to take hold. Catchwords like "equal rights" and "equal opportunities" and "sexual revolution" further served to convince the inherent female psyche and its "passive consciousness" to reject innate prudence and organic shame. (Swedenborg stressed the importance of innate prudence governing all angelic women in Heaven.)

Interestingly, these unguided women tend to leave their native countries in order to more easily adopt this profession and live their lives as "woman-females." Men guided by the same essential organic need to do nothing except enjoy oneself, assist in enticing women to leave their native land for some foreign country to enter this profession—with the least amount of embarrassing consequences.

The young Persian said that similar kinds of *woman-females* had eventually reached Persia. Because these "new" women were unable to merge with the traditional women of Persia (and adopt their values), the Persian men began to easily distinguish among them two distinct kinds of women (even when both were wearing veils).

The native women were viewed as *woman-mothers* and the free-living foreigners were simply referred to as females. This dual perception of women became so ingrained in the psyche of Persian men that if somehow a most beautiful woman of the first category were to find herself in a Persian man's bed he would be unable to treat her sexually as a mere female (unless he was under the influence of opium or alcohol). And even if such a potential "woman-mother" made advances toward him he would simply treat her as his sister and offer help to treat her from this "unclean power." This was the moral and cultural tradition that the young Persian who was speaking with Beelzebub grew up in.

But later, this young Persian, at the age of twenty, became a partner and chief European distributor of a dried fruit business. He confesses to Beelzebub that he observed that European men made no real distinction between a *woman-mother* and *woman-prostitute*. (This phenomenon is underscored in modern "rap music" where all women are seen, depicted, and referred to, as "hos.")

He tells Beelzebub that he believes that European men's attitude toward women is purely mental (stemming from their artificial thoughts), and no longer *instinctively* organic. Persian men and women, on the other hand, instinctively know when their husbands and wives are cheating.

This instinctive or "psycho-organic" ability even holds for Muslims who have more than one wife. Such wives will instinctively pick up on infidelity if their husband has strayed beyond his lawful wives. Because of all the cheating going on between husbands and wives in Europe, the young Persian was able to gain a new appreciation for his native country's custom of polygamy. He observed that Persian husbands manifested more honesty and conscientiousness toward their several wives than European Christians who, through their religion, were allowed only one wife, but still cheated anyway and often. (As I mentioned before, Swedenborg learned from his observations in the spiritual world that Christians engaged in more adultery than anyone else. He also stated that polygamy was not a sin with those with whom it exists from religion (*Conjugial Love*, n. 348).

The young Persian points out to Beelzebub that lots of couples sitting at the various tables of the café they were in, were most probably involved in some kind of "hanky-panky." In fact, he suggests that a man is respected more in Europe if he can support several mistresses. (When President Clinton got into sexual trouble, the Europeans found this situation to be quite trivial.)

Those European men who do not have the financial means to support "illegal wives" are sentenced merely to "drool" at women. These droolers nevertheless betray their one legal wife in their thoughts and hearts—in their *inner* lives or *interior* spirits. As to the European women, he believes that few of them are now properly educated to form in their being, that ideal called "organic shame." (Again, Swedenborg called this ideal, and instinctive spiritual value in women "innate prudence.")

Under such abnormal conditions, European men have no incentives to divide women into two categories. Unfortunately for this young Persian man, he came to Europe at a time when his hormones were exploding and his animal passions were particularly powerful. Being handsome and a foreigner, European women saw him as a unique (exotic) type of male and hunted him down. These women could also sense a special gentleness and courtesy in his character (which was instilled in him from his Persian childhood). But conversing with these European women admirers transformed into something much more vile, once he came under the poisonous influence of alcohol.

At this point in my interpretation, I would like to again point out the three-dimensional nature of Gurdjieff's unique writing style. He always designs his narratives to communicate in a *triadic* way—with the human *intellect*, the *emotions*, and viscerally; that is, to our bodily or *organic sensory* and *motor* functions. So when he describes the moral fall of this young Persian man, he will not only give the intellectual rationale for this bad behavior or describe the man's remorse of feelings, but also add a physical and visceral element (like lust and boozing it up) of how everything ("three" symbolizes fullness) in this man's life, is heading down an "inclined plane."

After the young Persian states that he is hopelessly addicted to women and booze, Beelzebub asks him if he is not afraid of being infected with the terrible diseases that these women-prostitutes usually suffer from. The young Persian man answers that he believes that he was spared of these diseases because he had never stopped the Mohammedan (Shiite) tradition of unfailingly washing his sex organs with simple cold water, after every trip to the toilet. The Persian asks Beelzebub, who he believes to be a doctor, why it is that the Christian countries offer no such beneficial customs, while the Mohammedan religion offered many.

Beelzebub responds by saying that there were actually more good customs originally in Christianity than in any of the other religions. But during the "Middle Ages," the "elders of the church" mixed many new spurious ideas into their religion (As mentioned earlier, Swedenborg suggests that the Council of Nicea was such a turning point, where harmful doctrines were added to the Christian faith system—particularly of turning the three essences of the One God into three Persons. The Dark Ages and plagues providentially followed closely after that grievous event.)

Beelzebub instructs the young Persian that all religions are based on the same *universal truths*. As new religions appear, these truths are adapted to the particular psyche and spiritual development of the people of that given time. (Swedenborg would concur with this.) If it were not for the unfortunate changes made in Christianity from its original beginnings, it too would have kept many wise customs for the welfare of people—both body and soul.

For instance, *circumcision* was one of the beneficial customs that was no longer deemed necessary by Christianity (Pauline doctrine mocked it as being too Jewish). Symbolically speaking, circumcision represented the cleaning or purification from worldly and filthy loves. Swedenborg claimed that this ancient custom of purification, called circumcision, was later replaced by the ceremony of *Baptism* in Christianity. This new ritual also symbolized the "spiritual cleansing" of a person's heart and mind, but circumcision offered the extra benefit of simplifying *bodily* hygiene. It is easy to see from this how Gurdjieff is using the bad hygienic practices of the Europeans (and Americans) to depict a deeper abnormality in their psyche and inner spirit.

Again, I call to your attention the ancient saying, "As above, so below."

Beelzebub tells his grandson an interesting tidbit—that he learned that Moses had first introduced the health-promoting custom of circumcision from his coming upon an ancient Chaldean manuscript! This manuscript stated that when Moses was leading the Judaic people out of Egypt to the land of Canaan he noticed that their youths and children were habitually rubbing their sexual organs.

Substances for the proper function of these sexual organs eventually collect in the foreskin of the penis in males and the covering of skin over the clitoris in females. This substance is generally called "Smegma" and is secreted by various glands. These substances were normally removed by nature through the activity of the planet's atmosphere. However, with the invention of clothing, the separation and volatilization of these substances into the atmosphere was hindered, causing perspiration and bacteria to grow and accumulate in the areas of the sexual organs.

This caused "itching" in these sensitive areas. From the unconscious scratching of these areas—where there just happened to be a concentration of nerve endings that produced pleasure—the children eventually learned to rub these areas even when there was no itching. (Many ancient cultures saw this practice as quite harmful and considered stopping it their chief duty in raising and educating their children. Beelzebub underscores this by claiming that reaching orgasm before adulthood affected the nervous system in a way that made acquiring full normal mentation impossible.)

Moses, having learned methods of ancient medicine from the Egyptian high priests, (who acquired their vast medical knowledge from the *Akhaldan* society of the continent Atlantis—Swedenborg's Church of Noah), created procedures to eliminate the itching in youngster's sexual organs, in both male and females due to clothing. (Beelzebub suggests that most of what contemporary children now learn through their abnormal education is created by older "masturbating psychopaths.")

Beelzebub states that after the death of the great King Solomon, the custom of helping young boys out of this condition (through circumcision) continued, but it ceased for the female sex. And, after the divine teachings of Jesus Christ were introduced to the world, for some reason or other, the fathers of Christianity (like Paul) removed this rite from boys as well.

At this point Beelzebub declares that Christianity would have become the greatest of all existing religions on Earth if it had properly followed Jesus Christ's actual teachings. (Swedenborg claims that Christianity has been vastated and a deeper, more proper understanding of Jesus Christ's teaching is now at hand, which embraces our cosmic duty and spiritual regeneration!)

Beelzebub also informs Hassein (and the reader), that besides the custom of polygamy, there is nothing in the Mohammedan religion that was not also in the Judaic and Christian teachings.

Beelzebub next tells the young Persian man that the Mohammedan religion was created after the founding of Christianity—because people were losing the power of *contemplation* (replacing it with blind [false] faith). Serious contemplation alone allows individuals to understand the deeper truths of all genuine religious teachings, to offset the downward mental trajectory taking place in Christianity, and to adapt religion, specifically to the psyche of Asian people. The creators of the Mohammedan religion focused their attention on certain customs and simplified religious teaching so that its followers could still receive its benefits—regardless of any lost capacity for contemplation on universal truths. Due to these simplified customs, the Mohammedan religion has built up a *stable family foundation* rarely found among Christians.

Swedenborg stated that the Mohammedan religion was heavenly inspired to change the Asian psyche to abandon idolatry and embrace the theological concept of One God. No further contemplation was required. As hinted above, this was also a providential counterbalance to the Christian downward movement of going away from the idea of One God and toward polytheism, by dividing their God into three Persons, called the Trinitarian Doctrine. As I mentioned above, the Dark Ages (as a result of a degenerating psyche and lack of proper contemplation) followed from this false Christian doctrinal trajectory. But the early Mohammedan scientists continued to advance knowledge and scholarship during this same dark time of Christian cognitive atrophy.

Swedenborg claimed that a new Christian dispensation was now coming from Heaven with potent ideas that would return serious contemplation to the human psyche and offset the old ideas being promoted by the current Christian church! (He also stated later in his theological works that those [of all religions] who showed a desire for increased contemplation would be specially educated toward the universal principles of a new theology.)

The young (and contemplating) Persian man, knowing that half of the human population now calls itself Christian, had to ask Beelzebub why it was that this very large religion contains no good customs, like the Mohammedan religion does.

It was news to me that, according to Beelzebub, the Christian religion had originally contained the greatest amount of good customs for its followers—more than any other religion. And these original Christian teachings, if carried out in conformity with the original plan, would have become the best of all religions (which Swedenborgians would be glad to hear).

I knew that the elders of the Christian Church changed doctrine in a negative way. But I did not know that the "elders of the church" had also put an end to some holistic, health-producing customs. According to Beelzebub, the only surviving positive Christian custom designed for the preservation of health and morality is their periodic *fasting*. But even this wise custom is changing to the point that it no longer produces a proper "shock" or "wakeup call" to the Christian psyche.

Beelzebub is adamant that producing such a shock in worshippers was the reason fasting was originally established. This shock, through real bodily sacrifice, was a remedy for those individuals who were particularly suffering from the "loss of sense of self." Affirmation and positive feedback by friends and others does not actually remedy one's *lost sense of self.* Only the conscious labors and intentional suffering of an individual, through the realization and activation of one's cosmic duty, properly returns one's real sense of self. Many times this requires a "shock" to a person's system and habitual living (however, people prefer comfort to "shocks").

As a further illustration of how the human psyche is still atrophying, Beelzebub provides a look into how the Russian "Orthodox" Christians observe this one surviving custom, and with a little history on how *fasting* was passed down to them. The Russian Orthodox Christians took their religion completely from the "Orthodox Greeks." While the Russian Orthodox Christians strictly follow the literal code of fasting (through their lack of genuine contemplation) they totally missed the spiritual essence and significance of this beneficial practice. Now, these Orthodox Russian Christians have become confused as to what to eat and what not to eat during their sacred periods of fasting that they call "Lent."

To explain this confusion about fasting, Beelzebub describes to the young Persian man a conversation he had once with a Russian friend who was an "Old Believer" of the Russian Orthodox tradition. This Russian could not fathom why it had ever been decided that it was permitted to eat the flesh of fish during Lent, since the Greeks, from whom they took this custom, never eat fish during their fasts. Eating fish reduced the intended "shock" that would be beneficial to the fasters because it was still a form of "flesh" and contained the substance Eknokh like all other meats.

Beelzebub next shares with the Persian man some information that he read from an ancient Judaic-Essenian manuscript that he came upon. (As I mentioned earlier, Gurdjieff made the claim that he personally came in contact with the Essene Brotherhood sometime in the late 19th Century or early 20th Century! So he probably had a knack for gaining access to their documents as well.) This particular manuscript stated that the custom of fasting, designed for the followers of Jesus Christ, was established two hundred and fourteen years after his birth on the shores of the Dead Sea by the *Kelnuanian Council.* This special council laid down the rules of what foods should be abstained from during particular periods of the year. The special shocks intended by these fasts were designed to challenge one's habitual pleasure principle and rekindle an instinctive sense of reality (this would challenge the self-calming inclinations inherited from the organ Kundabuffer).

The initial cause for instating this custom at the Kelnuanian Council was over a dispute that had arisen between two of their important learned members—the great *Hertoonano* and the great Greek philosopher *Veggendiadi.* Hertoonano represented the Christian followers who settled on the shores of the Red Sea, while Veggendiadi represented the Christians of Greece. Hertoonano was by far the more famous of the two men and was considered an authority on the laws of the inner organization of man, as well as alchemic science.

From this unique Judaic-Essenian manuscript, Beelzebub learned that Veggendiadi was the first to address the council on the importance of the teaching of Jesus—that killing animals for food was not only a great sin but was actually harmful to one's health. (Swedenborg mentions that our earliest human ancestors, representing a Celestial race of humans on Earth, detested eating meat and the cruelty of slaughtering animals for such a purpose. Swedenborg also added that while the God of Heaven, is not pleased by humankind's eating the flesh of animals, the practice is *permitted* by divine providence. God permits various transgressions to occur, so that they can be observed, in order to be challenged and even resisted.)

Hertoonano comes to fully agree with his Brother in Christ, the philosopher Veggendiadi. But because of his own detailed investigations into this same matter, he discovered that there are some real downsides to abstaining completely from meat. First of all, because it is not practical to believe that all followers of all religions in the world would adopt such a custom of abstaining from consuming meat, those who do abstain, and continue to live among the other meat-eaters, will suffer a worsening of their psychic state.

Hertoonano discovered that such fasters inevitably lose their "will power" when living around those whose morality is deteriorating from the consuming of the harmful substance "Eknokh" found in all meat products (in other words, there will be a dwindling desire to go through life as an "A-Personality" in a highly competitive world of human predators and "sharks.") Therefore, the true health benefits from abstaining from eating meat can only be obtained by living in complete isolation (which is not the best condition for developing genuine spiritual growth).

Hertoonano became convinced that if humans continued to eat meat, great harm would come to them. Yet, because of life's competitive requirements, nothing good would come to those who abstained, either (unless everyone on the planet abstained). So he looks for a solution to help humans get out of this unhappy cosmic situation. As a result of his lengthy researches he discovers that while people's psyche indeed deteriorates from the constant ingesting of the substance *Eknokh* found in meat, this substance has its most harmful effect only at certain times of the year. (The hint here is that the pre-Easter Lenten season, during the early Springtime, is one of those periods where eating meat is most harmful to human health).

Therefore, Hertaoonano recommends to the esteemed council that if the eating of meat is abstained from during just those certain harmful times of the year, the followers of the teachings of Jesus Christ could derive some real benefit to both body and mind from the practice of the timing of one's fasting. Unfortunately, as I mentioned earlier, it was originally discovered that the harmful substance *Eknokh* was also produced in fish (even milk and eggs).

This is pure conjecture on my part, but if Swedenborg's ancient Celestial race of humans detested eating "flesh," and they had an instinctive grasp of the symbolic language of *correspondences*, I wonder if the harmful substance *Eknokh* also represents some deeper negative spiritual quality? In his *Apocalypse Explained*, Vol. 1, n. 295 [d], Swedenborg informs us that the term "flesh" in reference to humans, represents a preference (appetite) for trusting one's own self-judgment (*proprium voluntarium*). Therefore, abstaining from such a self-centered appropriation (psychical eating) and orientation would be spiritually healthy.

Beelzebub goes on to say that this Judaic-Essenian manuscript further reported that Hertoonano's suggestions for establishing a new custom of fasting during certain fixed times of the year were then officially adopted. Beelzebub laments however, that the Russian Orthodox Christians now mistakenly believe that eating "tasty fish diners" during these fasts will guard them from any harmful effects that the custom was originally designed to protect them from. But it was also discovered that the harmful substance *Eknokh* was also produced in milk, eggs, and fish! So instead of producing shocks, fasting humans have made Lent "too yummy." (How can a tasty fish dinner evoke real sacrifice?)

Plus, the observance of this custom is also fading throughout modern culture, and further eliminating any helpful shock (against self-love and its pleasures) that was designed into it.

That ended Beelzebub's discussion of his conversation with the Persian man.

He now tells his grandson Hassein, that contemporary people-beings of the planet Earth are only able to create customs that continue to derange (and titillate) their psyche. One example of such a modern custom is the dance called the "Fox Trot." The real harm such seemingly innocent customs do is that they take the focus away from individuals to become aware of the sense and true aim of their arising and existence. (This higher aim is certainly not the focus of those who watched and participated in the TV shows *American Bandstand* and *Soul Train*, or who now embrace "twerking.")

In fact, Beelzebub asserts that the experiential process of one participating in the "Fox Trot" is exactly similar to that which proceeds from what Moses addressed as children's tendency toward "Moordoorten" or *onanism*—that is, masturbation. (I even remember a dance in my youth once called "the jerk" in which the participants made hand motions suggestive of masturbation. And now, today's rappers and entertainers, dancing to their music, perform highly suggestive and titillating movements that seem to be lacking in any organic shame or innate prudence.)

However, Beelzebub tells Hassein that most of the truly beneficial customs that have reached contemporary humans from the past still survive in Asia. To the modern Westerner, many of these Asian customs seem quite absurd, barbaric, and backward. Beelzebub supplies his grandson with an example of just such a seemingly senseless and primitive custom, adding that hygienic and even moral benefits have been skillfully incorporated into these rituals. A certain tribe of Asiatic beings called "Kolenian Loors" or "Kolenian gypsies" dwelling between Persia and Afghanistan take part in a very odd ritual of "self-fumigation."

This gypsy tribe lives in such filthy conditions that their clothes are infested with lice. In spite of these filthy conditions this gypsy tribe neither knows of venereal diseases nor that such things can even possibly be contracted. Beelzebub believes their ancient custom of self-fumigation is responsible for this hygienic bliss.

The ritual involves a sacred chair or stool called "Ateshkain." This stool is placed over a pit in the earth called a "Tandoor." Usually this earthen pit is used as a hearth to bake bread and prepare food. Animal dung is used as the fuel for these hearths. The animal dung burns slowly so that the heat lasts for long periods of time. Each evening these gypsies take off their clothes and shake them over this heat source. The lice, in their attempt to escape the heat fall off their clothes but are destroyed in the fiery pit. (The lice even make melodic popping sounds as they are cremated.)

Next, they solemnly and respectfully bring their sacred stool to the pit and place it over the pit. Every family member of this tribe steps up onto the stool, then, reciting special prayers, lowers his or her body, exposing their sexual organs to the heat. While this ritual is being done, sacred canticles are sung by the other members of the tribe.

Apparently, Gurdjieff doesn't just want to share doctrinal revelations that were originally incorporated into all genuine religions, but to bring back practical applications for obtaining cleanliness and health to the outer physical body, which houses the human spirit. This allows religion and its purifying dynamics to lawfully and properly be designed into terrestrial customs.

Beelzebub also describes another custom of self-fumigation from a small tribe called the "Toosooly Kurds," who lived in Transcaucasia near Mt. Ararat. Besides bathing daily in the river Aras and living in the open air, these Asian people created special guest huts, in which a front section includes what is called a "sacred Mungull"—a hearth, which was filled with smoldering charcoal. Every member of the family and every guest had to enter this section of the hut for self-fumigation before moving on to the main area where the festivities were held. Every person participating in this rite of purification grabs some special plant roots from a nearby hanging box and throws them into the hearth to create a special kind of smoke. Women would lift their skirts as they stood over this smoking Mungull, while men would drop their trousers. A special screen created privacy.

Beelzebub describes having observed hundreds of similar and seemingly silly customs among the Asian people. And, on further investigation he discovered that these rituals were always created to rid people of the noxious carriers of various diseases or to strengthen their sense of moral shame and humility. Beelzebub adds that Western civilization, on the other hand, now has customs which tend to only disguise and hide undesirable aspects of a person's exterior form. This modern focus on *outer* manipulation and deceit progressively increases the duality or split between the two personalities that have occurred to the human psyche. Again, Swedenborg would call this a split in the human natural mind into interior (or true animus) and exterior (mechanical) aspects of the human psyche.

The cosmic peril of this negative human trajectory is that earth-humans have adapted their education only to advancing the outer and artificial consciousness of the split human psyche condition. Thus "Western" education destroys the important data, once ingrained in us, that we are all an "image of God." Beelzebub states that such an artificial education now merely fills a person "with everything except himself" (head-knowledge rather than a knowledge of being.)

Lacking a tradition of positive patriarchal customs, and substituting this with their pseudo-education, has slowly transformed the beings of Western society into "automatons" and "living mechanical puppets." Such individuals only become animated when certain buttons, created by impressions mechanically absorbed during their terrestrial life, are pressed. When these buttons are not being pressed, these earth-humans are no more than "pieces of pressed meat."

What does this all have to do with sex?

Beelzebub next makes the shocking assertion that this problem can be somewhat alleviated if parents simply spoke sincerely to their children about sex, and did not consider such a conversation as being "improper." He concludes that parents putting such an important topic into a category or question of simple "decency" and "indecency" when talking to children, is not enough, and is the chief cause of promoting "psychic mechanicality" to future generations.

The question of what is deemed decent or indecent to tell children, under the modern western view of education (and the negative consequences of their terrestrial misunderstanding and hang-ups), is elucidated by Beelzebub, from an occurrence he experienced firsthand in the country of Russia. He says that this is a very characteristic occurrence and offers a good general picture of the kind of silly education children receive from modern civilization. (It is viewed by many, that schools are failing in America.)

As the story goes, Beelzebub once became acquainted with an elderly Russian couple in St. Petersburg. The husband was a "political leader," and the wife was a "society lady" and patron of several "welfare institutions." They had several daughters, the oldest of which was settled and married. The youngest daughter, who was twelve years old, was still living at home. The elderly Russian couple decided to do something special for their younger daughter and give her the very best education available at the time. They sent her to an "institution" called a "boarding school."

Beelzebub got to meet and know this youngest daughter when she was home for holidays, as he was often a guest of the Russian couple. The young girl, named Sonia, was charming and unspoiled. Beelzebub found her to be "alert and thoughtful" and the two became trusted friends. But because of a government assignment and "liver trouble," her father, the Russian senator, was sent on a trip to faraway Siberia. The wife, of course, wanted to stay by her husband's side. So they asked Beelzebub if he could visit their daughter at school while they were away.

Beelzebub agrees. On his first visit to this "genteel institution" he notices that although all the young girls wore similar outfits and had their hair braided in similar ways with ribbons, some of the girls had the ends of their ribbons tied together in special ways. Later, during a holiday, when Beelzebub was able to take the young girl home he asked her to explain the significance of some girls tying their hair ribbons in this different and special manner.

The young girl immediately blushed.

She admits to Beelzebub that this was a code kept secret from the adults of the institute. The practice of tying their ribbons in special ways was purposely devised so that the girls could know which category a pupil belonged to—the "men's club" or the "women's club." Those belonging to the "men's club" and tied their hair ribbons in special ways were the rebels and acted this out in several ways. This club of *rebellious* girls met in the dormitory bathrooms. Their special privileges included pulling rank over the other girls, so that those of the other club would be ordered to fix their beds, copy the day's lessons, and share presents from their parents. In a nutshell, the girls of the "women's club" were subordinate to those of the "men's club" and had to make the latter group's stay at the school as pleasant as possible, gratifying every wish.

Because these girls were never given a proper discussion about sex from the adults, one of the chief activities of those girls in the "men's group" was to read books on "forbidden" topics. It seems that the most widely read book concerned the teachings of the famous Greek poetess *Sappho*. These teachings involved special details concerning the "way to real happiness" for women. Sappho lived on the island of "Lesbos." The name of this island eventually was used to describe the followers of this unique teaching and who came to be called "Lesbians." The girls of the "men's club" could have as many partners as they wished to fulfill this pastime and in full accordance with the teachings of the poetess Sappho.

Beelzebub tells his grandson, point blank, that such a phenomenal ugliness could not exist among the rising generation if there were not the prevalent and false notion among parents that it is quite "indecent" to talk to children about sex. As a result, children grow up without proper guidance in this important matter. He tells Hassein that this faulty notion of "decency" was handed down to contemporary civilization from the nonsense concocted by *Hasnamuss* beings living in the "Middle Ages." These were the same faulty individuals (many of whom were bishops) who were the chief agents in the destruction of the real meaning behind the teachings of Jesus Christ. (Swedenborg said these falsified teachings led to the vastation of the original Christian Church.)

So, the original teachings of Jesus were then replaced by a new standard of regulations called "Bon Ton." This new outer standard has become so ingrained in the weakened human psyche that it is almost impossible for people to overcome the abnormal mental fixation of the indelicacy of parents discussing sex with their children—even if these parents see their children "rotting" before their eyes.

When the parents of this Russian young girl returned and relieved Beelzebub of his obligation, an unfortunate outcome occurred at another, similar, boarding school as a result of their modern "decency" regulations. Two girls had hung themselves after being harshly and unfairly reprimanded. Beelzebub was so horrified by this event that he personally investigated the case. Apparently, the two girls, on a school excursion through the countryside, happened to notice a farm bull grazing in the pasture. One of the girls shouted to her friend, "Look, there goes a bull!"

Soon, the young girl was surrounded by adult supervisors who accosted her about using the word "bull." After the young girl defended her use of the word "bull," the headmistress further persecuted her by saying that in their special institute one was responsible for finding ways to describe things that do not sound indecent to the *educated* ear—like using the word "beefsteak" instead.

Having been ridiculed in front of her friends the young girl let loose with a name-calling tirade. This prompted the adults of the establishment to hold a "teachers' council" there, on the spot, where they ruled that the young girl was to be immediately expelled from the institute and from all other similar institutes throughout the entire Russian Empire.

This incident caused the two girl companions to hang themselves rather than live among such "nonentities" and in an "improvised box."

The psychoanalytical message in this story is that great harm comes to young minds from the tyranny of established *artificial* standards in society. This artificial education is one of the chief causes of the split psyche in modern earth-humans. (Political correctness now represents such an artificial or "Bon Ton" standard.) Beelzebub adds that the young girl who uttered the word "bull" was raised in a rural area, where she was spared from the many abnormal conditions of city vanities.

Beelzebub apologizes to Hassein for getting off-topic and describing earth-humans of other continents besides America. But in terms of the "degree of degeneration" of those found on the young American continent, Beelzebub asserts that Americans represent the largest group on Earth where the "acquisition of being" is not yet entirely lost. (Hooray!) He attributes this to the fact that most immigrants moving from Europe to America were not from the more educated "upper class" or "ruling caste," but simple folk looking to better their lives. This spared America from importing many of the abnormal (and psychically harmful) customs of cultured European civilization. Americans are relative upstarts and free spirits. (However there is a movement growing in America to become more like the so-called progressive and cultured European societies.)

On Beelzebub's last day in New York City, while sitting in a Childs Restaurant in the Columbus Circle area and awaiting friends to take him to the dock of an outgoing steam ship, he amusingly observes all the pedestrians passing by. He concludes from this that the main problem of the American psyche was its slavery to "fashion." Although this phenomenon of fashion allowed individuals to make different personal statements, Beelzebub found that the "inner content" of their lives was profoundly shallow. Beelzebub's final deduction was that this slavery to fads was the "periodic fundamental source of the issuing of *new causes* of abnormality," and it was being embraced most strongly by the beings living on the American continent.

Strangely, Beelzebub observes that Americans continue to imitate outer gestures and manifestations—long after "freed beings" of other groupings coming there had found these same external values and the process of ordinary existence, to be quite disappointing (and unfulfilling) to their real *inner* needs.

This observation of American stubbornness with fashion astonishes Beelzebub—because it involves a seeming contradiction. Especially since this abnormal behavior of following trends, preceding out from such a young country as America, is now being imported and fixed right back into the psyche of other older groupings of human beings living elsewhere on the planet Earth (these imported trends include American blue jeans and rock 'n roll).

Through his observations at the Childs Restaurant, to his taxi ride to the docks, and finally to the steamship back East, Beelzebub ponders this question of "terrestrial incongruity." How could this happen to people who should know better?

Eventually he identifies the originating cause of this abnormality in earth-humans. The chief cause is a new twist to their abnormal education. Earth-humans are all wrongly educated into believing that contemporary civilization is superior to that of previous epochs! (I even have Swedenborgian friends who believe this notion!) Humanity tends to think and believe that it is getting smarter and thus, growing wiser all the time. (This belief puts the kabosh on the need or concern for spiritual growth.) Beelzebub, who had observed thousands of years of human history, is flabbergasted by this modern (and false) assertion. He personally witnessed that this false assertion had been gathering steam among earth-humans, over the last 3,000 years!

This modern psycho-need of earth-people to constantly be trendy and desirable (usually through imitation), even interferes with the occasional discovery of some authentic ancient wisdom or another from the past. The discovered remnant of ancient wisdom is then quickly turned into a "new discovery" by these modern imitators who put pressure on everyone else to immediately adopt (that is, imitate) in order to appear sophisticated and, of course, up-to-date. Yoga is a good example of how Americans turn an ancient form of practice into a means of becoming desirable and looking "cutting edge." (Americans even talk about older scientific theories as being "out of fashion" and are all too quick to embrace the newest scientific fads such as the "many-worlds theory.")

This lack of self-critical thought (contemplation) comes from the false teachings of contemporary education that early man was stupid (like the current "lumbering and savage image" of Neanderthals) but that today's earth-humans have developed superior powers of reasoning. Not so! Not even close!

Beelzebub asserts again that most contemporary earth-humans, due to their abnormal education, have lost the ability "to ponder" or "contemplate." (When I was attending theological school, I ran into peers who seriously believed, from their educated view, that contemporary humans were more advanced than previous humans on Earth. (But Swedenborg disputes this. As I mentioned earlier, he even discovered that an ancient race of humans lived on Earth, called *Celestial*, who had developed the inner technology of the human heart and spirit. As a result, they could converse with angelic beings living in a non-material plane of the universe.)

Because of this abnormal condition of feeling superior, now reigning in the belief systems and worldviews of modern humans (which also prevents these earth-citizens from properly coating their body Kesdjan or first spiritual body), nature was forced to change their functioning and *living tempo* from the *Fulasnitamnian* principle to the *Itoklanoz* principle (their blood flow was redirected as discussed in Chapter 32, called "Hypnotism").

Putting this organic redirection into Swedenborg's terms, I believe the Itoklanoz principle represents blood entering into the lungs though the *pulmonary* artery and veins, while the Fulasni-tamnian principle represents blood entering the lungs through the *bronchial* artery and veins (see *Divine Love And Wisdom*, n. 407, 413). The latter blood path connects our feelings to our intellectual convictions, whereupon spiritual conflict can begin, and subsequently, our purification from *envy, greed,* and *jealousy.* This purging process is our rebirth—and the creation of a spiritual body within us.

While everyone knows that there are problems in the world, few know that the negative progression to a more *artificial* lifestyle has a real effect on people's bloodflow (their tempo-of-life) and their "second-being food"—that is, on the quality of the substances people are able to absorb from the air and circumfluent atmosphere. The proper absorption of this higher food (through a change in our attitudes) is what perfects and purifies our middle blood (Hanbledzoïn or animal spirits) necessary for creating higher bodies—which can survive the death of the physical body.

An artificial lifestyle throws off the proper fusion of substances, which would normally take part in the Sacred Triamazikamno (Law of Three) of those individuals who choose to participate in their own conscientious being-existence and honorable service to the ALL-COMMON FATHER MAINTAINER, OUR ENDLESSNESS.

Swedenborg concurred that proper living consists of our consciously choosing unselfish *usefulness* according to the Lord God's plan for our personal rebirth and the spreading of genuine mutual love. But genuine spiritual transformation first relies on our realization that something has been lost and must be regained. (After all, how can one act with genuine humility if they believe that because of technology, they live in superior times?) This oversight throws off proper (conscious) absorption of atmospheric substances necessary for individuals to successfully crystallize their spiritual bodies, through a process of inner *fusion* from logical confrontation and inner combat of the heart and mind. (The proper, re-directed blood circulation in earth-humans, results from the re-embracing of our cosmic duty and the inner confrontation between our split personalities.)

On a funnier note, one of the unexpected maleficent downsides of this artificial lifestyle and worldview (of modern superiority) in humans is a "disease" called "writer's itch."

Beelzebub observed that practically everyone on the American continent seemed to embrace the idea of authorship. (I can vouch for this—I was one of them!) Those author/individuals, who simply were more "cunning" and clever than others, were least able to refrain from leading their fellow-beings into error. (My first efforts to write "great" books, from a need for self-importance, certainly were chock full of erroneous thinking!)

All these contemporary authors, while being inwardly only *nullities,* became experts at creating books with "loud" titles that seduced many readers. As these books, the result of "wiseacreing" (the love of the principle of self-intelligence) became more popular, it led to the further dilution of everyone's cognitive powers. (In other words, individuals whose personal lives have become a complete mess will offer consultation and false expertise to others.) This is a hilarious insight, but again, I too, first started writing books with high-sounding themes, which I had no right to write about. But from painful self-sincerity, I now know I was a complete jerk, merely seeking attention and importance!

Next, Beelzebub strikes a more serious tone. He tells Hassein that he isn't kidding about the possibility that these contemporary earth-humans might not continue to produce descendants. He observed a phenomenon among the female sex on the American continent that he had also witnessed much earlier on a small island situated west of ancient Atlantis. (Symbolically speaking, "west" is not a positive thing. It represents the furthest distance from God's influence, which rises in the "East," like the Sun.)

This small grouping of earth-humans eventually ceased to exist because the pelvises of their women were progressively narrowing! The quality of this group's inner manifestations produced a corresponding morphism to occur in their females' bodies. (I have even heard some American women wishing that they had narrower hips, like teenage boys—to better wear even more *fashionable* clothes.) Beelzebub adds that these ancient females that he had once observed, as well as those contemporary women now living on the American continent, resorted more and more to "Caesarian operations." The implication here is that women are trying to live a more masculine lifestyle, distancing themselves from the natural order of things and the cosmic responsibilities of their passive consciousness—due to the abnormal and artificial conditions created by the earth-humans themselves.

(I suspect that seeking abortions is another negative outcome of women trying to become "freer" and to be more like males. Swedenborg stated that producing offspring ultimately represents the marriage between the Lord God and the church, or quality of worship, and is therefore, the highest spiritual *use* between two truly *conjugial* married partners on Earth—because it provides the potential to increase the population of the Heavens. Otherwise, men and women will only get together for the terrestrial, selfish love of venery and lust.)

This part of the narrative ends as Beelzebub detects a crosscurrent in the *ether* of the spaceship, which was a signal that it was time to go to the "Djamdjampal" for dinner. This dining room was the special place where the passengers consciously fed on *both* the second (air) and first (terrestrial) being-foods.

The second being-food, from air, is properly absorbed when three-brained beings sincerely contemplate their true significance and the true significance of others (*Views from the Real World*, pg. 194).

This contemplation allows substances in the air to be rendered "passive" and thus become more easily acted upon and absorbed by new active forces.

SUMMARY

■ Beelzelbub now takes aim at Americans. They have become the new world leaders for "Turkey-ness."

■ Americans are obsessed with "making dollars." This obsession has led these earth-humans to become less *handy* and *useful*.

■ Americans, seeking dollars, have become *masters of illusion*, especially at promoting things that are not in correspondence with reality—like "selling the sizzle instead of the steak." Or believing that food comes from stores instead of slaughterhouses. This imagined and fabricated reality requires a sharp split in the functioning of the human psyche.

■ America's specialty for masking motives through *pretense* extends into all areas of business and human relationships.

■ How American ingenuity and inventiveness got around the prohibition of alcohol provides an additional demonstration of how the human psyche has deteriorated.

■ American "advertising" further helps to diminish the human psyche.

■ *Digestive* and *sexual* problems (the two motors of existence) particularly plague Americans. The quality of their food has quickly diminished along with their psyches—due to their demands for "external" and cosmetic beauty.

■ "Comfort Toilets" have allowed various important muscles to degenerate, causing earth-humans to adopt bad postures for the elimination of solid waste.

■ No process of food preservation stops the decomposition of food and loss of its vital nutriments, which causes human digestive problems—not to mention promiscuity and vulgarity, by changing for the worse, the chemical make-up of one's red blood.

■ Earth-humans, particularly Americans, spend more time caring for their faces and hair than on the cleanliness of their sexual organs. Venereal diseases result, which are more rare among Asians who have healthy customs.

SUMMARY

■ Food can be *terrestrial, mental* and *spiritual,* which affects the quality of an earth-human's three distinct bloods and one's ultimate health.

■ Modern humans neglect contemplation and true depth of thought. The next great religion will offer deeper ideas that will require true contemplation.

■ Eating fish is just as bad as eating meat during "Lent." But, we would rather minimize all discomforting "shocks" from customs wisely designed to wake us up and give us a true sense of self and our cosmic duty.

■ Parents who consider a discussion about *sex* with one's children to be *improper,* is a leading cause for creating within them, the strange phenomenon of "psychic mechanicality."

■ Having a frank and important talk with children about sex has been replaced by *artificial standards of decency,* that were concocted by flawed beings during the "Middle Ages" in Europe, and who undermined the original teachings of Jesus.

■ On the bright side, Beelzebub asserts that Americans represent the largest percentage of individuals on Earth that have not yet entirely lost the "acquisition of Being." This is because most immigrants to this new country were simple beings, and not of the "ruling class." Therefore, they had not developed the maleficent property of "inner swagger" nor had they the predisposition toward *Hasnamuss* (bullshitting), which has a harmful effect on the "subjectively-natural-inner-forces" of earth-humans.

■ One of the worst ideas for the human psyche, spread by modern education, is the worldview that contemporary society is more evolved than previous earlier human epochs. This flawed belief has curtailed the development of spiritual bodies and put the kabosh on one making the proper efforts for spiritual growth, causing the bloodflow in earth-humans to be re-directed into different arteries and veins. This modification allows the human *intellect* to be separated from—and non-responsible toward—the human *will,* allowing for the promotion of hypocrisy and pretense (from the outer *imitation* of proper protocols). This organic modification also affects the quality of substances that we can breathe in from the atmosphere.

■ Modern education is the chief cause of spreading abnormalities in earth-humans, by strengthening their dual natures.

SUMMARY

■ Americans, particularly, are slaves to *fashion* (a sure symptom of hypnosis).

■ (This cracks me up.) Cunning individuals, whose personal lives are a complete mess, will become authors and *specialists*, who then offer consultation (for dollars) and (false) expertise to others.

■ Because of abnormal living (and a corresponding morphism), American women are developing narrower pelvises and needing more Caesarian surgeries. Beelzebub claims he witnessed this same phenonemenon in females on an island west of "Atlantis," who were no longer able to continue the human species.

CHAPTER 43

"Beelzebub's survey of the process of the periodic reciprocal destruction of men, or Beelzebub's opinion of war"

After Beelzebub, Hassein and Ahoon, had finished their *dual meal* (of physical food and air) in the "Djamdjampal," which they had approached *consciously* as a sacred sacrament, Hassein had another urgent question for his grandfather. While convinced of the strangeness of the earth-human psyche, Hassein felt that something was still illogical about their living manifestations.

Hassein was interested in learning why, ever since the *third Transapalnian perturbation* (formation of the great deserts from powerful wind storms), when earth-humans were able, despite their "automatic reason" to grasp all kinds of cosmic laws, that they developed the parallel need to periodically destroy each other's existence. He wanted to know why these three-brained beings, after thousands of years, were still unable to see the horror of this strange psychic property.

(The famous poster which reads, "War is hell," certainly didn't put a stop to this awful psychic property in humans.)

Beelzebub, after a remorseful smile, begins to share with his grandson the "muddled logic" of earth-humans and the causes of this most terrible of all horrors that could possibly ever exist in the whole universe. Again, he wisely chooses to inform his grandson in a special way that will provide the necessary mental material for *logical confrontation*, so that Hassein could form his own opinion about the matter in the most helpful and genuine way possible.

Hassein is told that while some earth-humans do ponder this great horror at times, and even start "peace movements," nothing positive ever comes of it. The reason is that this pondering usually happens in isolated individuals, and because there is no common-planetary organization, they have no means of spreading their ponderings to the minds of other earth-humans in other countries. (Hmmm... I wonder if the internet will help here?) And unfortunately, even these isolated thinkers are only capable of this sincere contemplation *when their bellies are full* and *other organic needs are satisfied*. (Swedenborg agrees that the human understanding can ponder and rise above the quality of a person's heart and inner character, but if the heart isn't elevated as well, nothing actually changes.)

Beelzebub reminds his grandson that this sincere thinking has, over time, become a luxury, because too few earth-humans are fortunate enough to be able to be so completely satiated. Only important and "power-possessing" individuals have the means to become so satiated, yet for other reasons, they still fail to offer solutions.

As always, few earth-people are willing to take a deep and sincere look at *themselves*, and discover that peace requires *personal* inner cleansing and transformation. The world changes *one person at a time*. And an individual can only change if it is a change made in one's deepest spiritual fabric—which is separated from one's daily consciousness due to people's split psyche.

Beelzebub blames this inadequacy of powerful people (our politicians and leaders who can more easily fill their bellies and other organic needs) to make real and lasting improvements in the world, all on their abnormal education. This education only increases one's negative properties, which were begun by the organ Kundabuffer. Such harmful properties included "egoism," "partiality," "vanity," "self-love," etc. In fact, earth-human education serves to further deepen and fix (crystallize) these harmful attributes *organically* into the psyche of earth-humans—even without the Kundabuffer.

(Modern education does not recognize the *dual nature* of the human psyche, and therefore, does not adapt its data to address that condition.) Individuals who are educated by this limited system and then rise to power, instead of remedying the nasty situation of war, only indulge themselves in "self-calming" activities to pacify their "wandering nerves." This leads to a kind of mentation that operates in such individuals as purely *automatic* and without any intentional exertion.

Instead of their associative thoughts proceeding in a proper and orderly manner, these powerful people only receive *shocks* from the reflexes of their *stomachs* and *sexual organs*. These pleasure-demanding organic influences, flowing freely and without being *inwardly challenged*, produce kindred (corresponding) negative associative thoughts. These resulting negative thoughts and impulses, which bubble up unchallenged, include *revenge, discontent* and *contempt* for others. (Without sincere self-examination we don't even notice these negative thoughts and impulses inside us, because from habit, they have become so natural to us. And have become a part of what we love.)

(In the first several chapters of Swedenborg's *The True Christian Religion* (Vol ll), he stresses how *Repentance, Reformation*, and *Regeneration* require that we sincerely examine our tendencies and challenge those which seem opposed to God's tenets—even our calling them *sins*.)

Beelzebub assures Hassein, that in some rare cases, power possessing earth-humans will indeed have a sincere thought or two about the horrors of war in their noggins—apart from the ongoing influences of their stomachs and sex organs. But even these sincere moments are usually caused by yet other *external* causes, such as the unexpected and violent end of someone that was near and dear to them (like a loved family member or friend), or when a great favor is given to them that was totally unexpected, or seeing the approach of their own inevitable death.

But here lies the problem—no sooner do many such sincere thinking individuals vow to solve the terrifying reality of war (at any expense), than their stomachs become empty again or they finally recover (over time) from some powerful *external news*. They then forget their vows and even begin to participate in the same kinds of things that cause communities to fight against each other in the first place. (Because of this human tendency, Gurdjieff called men "great swine.") This same principle is why it is so difficult for most people even to keep their "childish" New Year's resolutions.

Because of our dual nature, everyone is screwed up—not just our leaders. But we all expect better things from our leaders!

In a nutshell, there cannot be any other outcome than periodic wars among leaders and other power-possessing individuals—who have not used the time given to them by God and Great Nature to become worthy, responsible (spiritual) beings. This lack of cosmic responsibility is why their mentation consists mostly of *automatic* associations, and they act like living automatons.

Also, in their current degenerated reasoning, many of these *power-possessing* earth-beings have even come to expect "egoistic profits" from increasing the size and scale of these deadly conflicts. (Great profits and dollars are certainly made by the American military industrial complex—as President Eisenhower had warned. Dealing in arms has become a highly profitable business.)

Beelzebub informs Hassein, that just as he was leaving the planet Earth for the last time, certain important and power-possessing beings of that ill-fated planet decided to unite and form a special organization to come up with solutions for this "archcriminal" property of war. This organization was to be called the "League of Nations." Beelzebub had witnessed the formation of many similar organizations throughout human history, and observed that they all ended in a similar death.

He recalls such an organization in the town of Samoniks in the Asian country Tikliamish, when it was considered a chief center of culture for all the three-brained beings on Earth. The motto of this ancient organization was: "God is where men's blood is not shed." (Swedenborg stated that bloodshed symbolized violence done to God's laws of mutual love, and that war was a larger-scale outcome of personal hate because it was an outgrowth of many individuals embracing delusional self-love.)

As usual, the people in power, because of various egoistic and vainglorious inner aims, quarreled among themselves and finally left this Asian organization—without ever accomplishing anything.

Several centuries later, there again arose a similar organization on the continent of Asia, but in a country called "Mongolplanzura." Their motto was: "Love one another and God will love you." This organization was also terminated because of similar manifestations among its leaders. (Apparently, no one in power ever notices these disruptive negative manifestations in themselves.)

Later, in a country today called Egypt, Beelzebub describes seeing, firsthand, that there had also been formed a similar "noble" organization. Their motto was: "If you learn how to create a flea, only then dare you kill a man." (In other words, if you cannot create the simplest of life forms, you will not have authorization to kill the "crown of God's creation.")

After this, another such noble organization also arose, in the country of "Persia." Their motto consisted of the words "All men are divine, but if only one is violently killed by another, then all will be as nothing."

More recently (about four or five centuries ago), another similar organization of concerned individuals in Asia, who lived in a city Beelzebub calls "Mosulopolis," was formed with the motto: "The-Earth-Is-Equally-Free-for-All." After a dispute among their members their motto was changed to: "The-Earth-Must-Be-Only-for-Men."

Before this change was made in their motto, Beelzebub felt that this group of Asian leaders from Mosulopolis actually developed a workable (actualizable) program. The reason for his thinking this, is that its leaders were *elderly* and had the time to fully experience that their ordinary planetary existence (regardless of the pleasures received in life) only brought disillusionment. On account of this *experienced frustration* with everyday life, they had fewer egoistic and vain properties for obtaining personal gain, which had ultimately caused all such noble organizations to finally melt down. Beelzebub promises to inform his grandson later in his Tales about the specific reasons why this particular organization, with the potential to put the kibosh on the terrifying property of reciprocal destruction among earth-humans, ultimately failed as well.

Beelzebub feels confident that he has now given Hassein the appropriate context upon which to address the problems that would inevitably face the newly formed League of Nations. He gives two main reasons for this inevitable failure. (As we know today, it did fail.) The first reason will be made clear by the end of these Tales, while the second reason has to do with a lack of "self-remembering" by which individuals keep proper vigilance on their deeper, inner compulsions.

The result of this failed self-responsibility among its members is that this "official" organization would simply be used for pulling the wool over everyone's eyes. Instead, these leaders will partake in and arrange many "cocktail parties," all in the name of some "high-sounding" cause. (The United Nations, created more recently to do the same thing as the League of Nations, is not immune from such rompings and promenades by its members and leaders. I personally witnessed a representative of the U.N. at a New York bar, acting like a highly developed, self-important *hedonist.*)

To further help Hassein assimilate (metabolize) this information properly, Beelzebub describes the downward process by which these organizations first come into being and then finally fail. Usually, they are started up after the end of some nasty war or another, in which such heavy losses are sustained that temporarily, the being-impulse of true "conscience" begins to be activated even within their normal habitual or "automatic consciousness."

This temporary "resurrected conscience" among some of the leader-beings allows them to truly see—for the first time—and even perceive reality, almost in its true light. These concerned earth-humans then unite in order to actualize a sincere wish to stop all wars. But as more and more individuals later join such operations, those who are motivated by *self-importance* and *status* rather than *conscience* begin to outnumber the original concerned beings. Eventually, this causes the original aim of the organization to go up in smoke—ka-poof!

On the other hand, over many centuries of observing these strange earth-humans, Beelzebub noticed that in general, highly evolved individuals who consciously worked at spiritual self-perfection, never seemed to belong to these "noble" organizations. Nor do these highly evolved beings ever seek to become ostensibly "famous." Having developed true "conscience," such individuals never seek to become known as important, nor do they promote their reputations. (Swedenborg stated that any good deed done for the mere purpose of reputation, worldly gain, money, or for some improved status, is spurious, and not an act of sincere spiritual love.)

Furthermore, other less-noble individuals will always see to it that those who manifest wiser, more humble traits will never take part in their societies (clubs). So, this same fate will (did) come to the League of Nations, because various regulations and contrivances devised by those *devoid of spiritual conscience* will make sure that everything truly positive will come to no effect. Unfortunately, and completely unsuspected by these "Hasnamuss" individuals (who are oblivious to their dual personalities and the *Terror Of The Situation* in their own lives), this hideous property of self-centeredness and hedonism has become fixed so deeply into their psyche (internal natural mind or subconscious) that it cannot be easily observed by their separated and now degenerated habitual consciousness (symbolized in the New Testament as a "log" or "beam" in one's eye).

In spite of this, Beelzebub assures Hassein that contemporary earth-humans could still achieve positive results—if they only restrained themselves to solving those questions which remained within their sphere of competence and understanding (as opposed to the "Peter Principle"—of rising to one's own level of incompetence). And, it is also still within the reach of their understanding to be able to verify that horrible and ignoble properties are deeply ingrained in their psyche and that these traits cannot be *decrystalized* immediately and forever. (Swedenborg states that a person can indeed observe his or her ignoble leanings, but that one's evils are never fully removed, even by spiritual growth—only shoved to the outskirts of our psychic environment and reality).

Also, if these same leader/individuals of the planet Earth simply stopped the custom of promoting "heroes" of warfare and making war statues (which sustain the false feeling of *goodness* that a particular society seeks) and abandoned one of their main false but equally silly worldviews—that without war, conditions of over-population would result (in their Godless, material world), producing economic woes, and forcing earth-humans to cannibalize and eat each other—things could change for the better.

Beelzebub asserts that if earth-humans got rid of just these two types of behavior they would begin to free themselves of their "automatic responses" (slavery) to life and abandon their now powerful tendency to "doubt in the existence of Divinity," a tendency which interferes with the development of their "instinctive sensing" of cosmic truths. (The current trend in modernity is toward *atheism, secularism* and *doubting the infallibility of God's Word.*) Because of their doubting the existence of Divinity, earth-humans become *incompetent in all things.* (Swedenborg lamented that although people see everything, they understand nothing.) In contemporary society, important persons manifest themselves only according to the dictates of the residual properties left in them from the organ Kundabuffer.

Under this trance-like state and self-delusion, such egoistic individuals always make decisions about topics that are quite beyond their reasoning capacity, and they fail to address the actual problems at hand, most of which would indeed fall within their mental powers to solve (minus their ego).

Beelzebub again warns his grandson to never offend such earth-humans— especially those who now consider themselves to be "representatives of art" (who have wrongly developed and psychopathic feelings). Instead, one must always be prepared to "tickle" their numerous weaknesses (brown-nosing), that include *self-love, pride, vanity* and many, many others. If one "tickles" these properties in contemporary humans, particularly those called artist-beings, not only will they *never* harm you, they will even worship you!

Beelzebub then retracts this advice because he realizes that Hassein would also have to learn about all the other properties that needed to be tickled among the other, "non-artist" types of earth-humans as well. So he shares a strategy that would assure Hassein of a tranquil and happy existence while living among *all* types of these strange earth-people. This great strategy includes the "big secret" to earth-human's abnormal and disharmonious psyche—which is one's conviction of self-importance.

This broader, surefire strategy involves "tickling" an earth-person's need to offer *advice* (always to gain self-importance and self-affirmation from others). Swedenborg called this secret psychic need in people, the principle of "self-love."

If one simply approached these odd earth-people and *pretended* to want to learn something from them, their self-conceit will be immediately and successfully pacified.

Beelzebub suggests that this negative property of *self-conceit* springs from a person who is only able to see the defects of others, but never the defects in themself. (Again, Jesus made this an important issue in his teachings when He spoke about the "log" or "beam" we all have in our own eyes; also "not to throw the first stone.")

Besides their constant complaining, blaming others and feeling self-pity, Beelzebub adds that the resulting *indignance* of earth-humans, from observing only the defects of others, always leads to long-term anxiety, depression, and the inevitablility of coming under the influence of someone else—who can, just as naturally and easily, see through them and their own masks as well.

But things get worse—especially concerning human incompetence.

When someone's inner nullity becomes exposed to another being, whereby an individual loses his or her worldly *mask*, this creates even more inner frustration, indignation and dissatisfaction (instead of humility and proper spiritual growth). These overly dissatisfied individuals usually find psychic relief in becoming overnight "experts" in areas where they have little understanding—including everything from giving health tips, to how governments ought to be run, and even becoming spiritual counselors for others. (I have personally noticed this trend to become an "expert" *in myself*, and have also noticed it in many divorced people, including people whose personal lives actually suck.)

People resort to this maneuver to regain their feeling of self-importance, and not to suffer any more, or in any way. (However, Swedenborg, as well as Gurdjieff, viewed this kind of suffering and personal discomfort as the raw material necessary for sincere spiritual combat and inner fusion, which is often mechanically activated by misfortune, but is better activated consciously through worldly temptations— from one's sincere introspection.) Here, Beelzebub is pinpointing the biggest obstacle of (flawed) humans trying to make the world a better place, and why the road to Hell is paved with seemingly good intentions. (These roads are actually paved with the powerful psycho-need for personal self-importance, which most people see as "good" and the means of self-improvement.)

Beelzebub tells Hassein that on Earth, he met such "needy" experts at every step. These individuals negate their inner suffering (true duty) and instead, find pleasure by lording it over others. He warns Hassein that if he were to ever live among these odd beings he would experience a mixture of emotions—both pity and inner laughter—called "an-essence-palnassoorian-grief." (Swedenborg called such laughter "an affection of truth," whereby one senses the discord.)

This abnormal particularity of the earth-human psyche to reject conscious inner suffering is especially strongly developed in those regarded as the "intelligentsia" (This is why Swedenborg had lamented that intellectuals and scholars, including scientists, "see everything, but understand nothing," and are thus further from seeing reality and God's Truth than the more simple-minded—who have smaller egos.)

This dynamic is precisely why *the meek shall inherit the Earth*. Merely acquiring brain-knowledge (memory data) is spiritually analogous to *justification by faith alone*—the notion that knowledge, abstracted from one's actual life choices and actions, is what counts most. Humble humans (the seemingly meek) know better.

Rather than manifesting a real "force-in-oneself" (which the Greek term "intelligentsia" actually means) for introspection, or of having perfected the ability to direct their functions as they wished (instead of being slaves to all their inner whims), the intelligentsia now do the complete opposite. They are not much more superior to other inanimate cosmic formations, like rocks, which react only to *external* stimuli.

Beelzebub adds that those on Earth who have developed *real force of being* are usually considered as "unintelligent" and simple. Beelzebub suggests to Hassein that it would be more correct to call the modern intelligentsia of the world, with their automated reasoning, the "mechanogentsia."

Contemporary earth-humans, through their abnormal existence (and education), have squashed in themselves any valuable information that would lead to creating the impulses toward "essence-initiation" that Great Nature (and God) had placed in their psyches during their infancy. (Again, Swedenborg would explain this "essence-initiation" as the activation of the "remains" that God embeds in the *internal natural mind* or *subconscious* of humans to form a plane, and matrix, from which angels can focus their influence in our lives and allow conscience to grow, and inner bodies to form.)

Instead, contemporary earth-humans are animated only by external stimuli (shocks) from the world, or influences coming from their blood and bodily organs. As a result, the manifestations of most earth-people do not proceed from the directives of their legitimate beingness (inner dictates) or from the whole of their entire presence—called their true "I" which has become buried (like Atlantis) by modern life.

Today most people have learned how to hide their true inner and outer flaws from the eyes of others by wearing a "mask" (and keeping up appearances). This causes *inner slavery* in humans because it means that in order to find acceptance in the outer world, one must always put themself under somebody's thumb. This "thumb" extends to negative influences coming from the spiritual world and which makes such people-slaves always indignant of the manifestations of others, because of their refusal to suffer any real humility.

(I have found this manifestation of being *indignant* toward others quite pervasive in my own life.)

Beelzebub informs his grandson that contemporary intelligentsia have been given other names that have their origins in the roots of other, more ancient Greek names. Such as:

"Bureaucrats"

"Plutocrats"

"Theocrats"

"Democrats"

"Zevrocrats"

"Aristocrats"

and on, and on it goes.

Beelzebub gives his grandson a short description of each of these types of intelligentsia now arising from earth-human populations. The types of intelligentsia called "Bureaucrats" display the following abnormal behavior. Their experiencings have become quite limited. No matter how varied the external inputs of data are that reach the organs of perception in this category of beings, from repetition, the same limited experiencings always result. This acquired and limited result manifests into a specific character and behavior quite independently, and apart from any participation of their legitimate spiritual and God-given psycho-functions. Nothing they do comes from the soul or reaches the soul.

In the Foreword to JG Benett's book *Talks On Beelzelbub's Tales* (page 8), Louise March is quoted as saying that Gurdjieff clearly stated that, "philology was a better route to Truth than philosophy." (I find this interesting since Swedenborg's theological works often included the philology or roots of words for further explanation.) In that spirit of philology, Beelzebub next gives Hassein some of the roots behind the names given to these distinct groups of intelligentrics living among the earth-citizens (of new formation).

The word "Bureaucrat" comes from two Greek roots—"buro," which means "chancellery" and "crat" which means "to keep" or "to hold." In other words, the chief duty of such esteemed beings is *to hold on to their positions.*

"Plutocrats" represent those *phonies* who through cunning and cleverness manage to convince other naïve fellow countrymen to labor for them, so that they can procure wealth and "slaves." These types of intelligentsia represent the major category from which most Hasnamuss-individuals (bullshitters) now arise on Earth.

Beelzebub declares that the use of such high-sounding Greek names to dignify (and create forceful names) for earth-people's suspicious manifestations had occurred over the past twenty-five centuries. However, the name "Plutocrat" is a more recent invention from about seven or eight hundred years ago. The first half of this word was taken not from any Greek word but from the Russian word "plut" which means, "rogue." The joke here is that "Plutocrats" are satisfied with being distinguished by such a title, not knowing that they are actually being called the genuine "freaks" that they really are, and thus, from their self-delusion, strut around like "turkey-cocks" instead of being insulted and getting angry.

(This reminds me of an ironic occurence that happened to Swedenborg. A group of individuals banded together to deny his assertion that the Bible had higher levels of meaning. This group picked a "bear" to represent their organization. Swedenborg mentioned that a "bear" symbolizes the literal sense of the word—as separated from its interior meanings!)

Beelzebub further informs his grandson that the difference between the Plutocrats and Theocrats is that the former satisfy their abnormal needs through the function which they call "trust," while the latter rely on the function called "faith."

Concerning the group called Democrats, Beelzebub states that they do not become such from inheritance, but from originally being ordinary terrestrial beings (simple folk) who chance to become influenced by the ideas of the intelligentsia, whereby their proper being-function of "Conscience" also becomes atrophied, and they develop a warped psyche similar to that of Plutocrats and Theocrats, and then finally become Democrats. When these Democrats happen to gain a position of power, nothing useful happens either. The reason is that these individuals have *no inherited aptitudes* for instinctively being able to govern or properly offer direction to the existence of those under their power. Thus, these particular individuals have a hard time implementing their ideas. (Hmmm… sounds like what is currently happening by America's increasing lack of leadership, in spite of "Ivory Tower" ideas.)

Beelzebub admits to his grandson that it is difficult to explain the differences between the last two types of intelligentsia on his list—the Zevrocrats and Aristocrats, through ordinary terrestrial speech, other than that they both represent "jokes of nature." In spite of their

different names they both share the exact same inner psychical properties, which go by the name "vanity." However, where a country's
state organization is "Monarchic" they are called "Aristocrats," but
where a government's state organization is "republican" these individuals are called Zevrocrats. (As a student of Swedenborg, the term
"vanity" suits such educated individuals quite well. He stated that
many members of the modern and educated intelligentsia falsely
favor their own prudence, possessing a misguided and warped sense
of themselves and reality. This condition resulted from the spiritual
and original "Fall of Man" or "Choot-God-Litanical-period.")

Since these ignoble manifestations usually diminish one's lifespan, Beelzebub is surprised that these types of intelligentsia can live
almost as long as other earth-humans. Especially since the experiencing of reality by these so-called "special" beings is so very limited.
Beelzebub reduces their limited experience to three series of mental
process: 1) the question of food, 2) the memory of the former perfor-
mance of their sexual organs, and 3) the memories of their first nurse.

The question of how beings with such limited experiencings can
have a relatively lengthy existence seems to be an insoluble puzzle for
Beelzebub. But he makes an educated (and highly inventive) guess.
Using a hilarious metaphor, he comes to believe that it is one's *inner
reality* that actually diminishes, because it has become prone to fantasy
and is entirely made up. He describes this made-up fantasy in contemporary earth-humans as their fondness for arranging "puppet shows."

These puppet plays (made-up realities) gain additional credibility if Zevrocrats and Aristocrats take part in these performances
(symbolizing, they are the actual puppets, and that puppets always
need to be supported by others doing the *string pulling*). Since many of
these intelligentsia are vacuous beings, and inwardly quite weak, they
must constantly get "support" from other beings of their community
(an audience of similarly deluded individuals who believe in their
own self-importance). This kind of spurious support can keep these
intelligentsia outwardly alive and ticking for quite awhile.

The method of support (strings) during these puppet plays
differs between Zevrocrats and Aristocrats. In countries where there
is a "monarchial state organization" it is the custom to support the
Aristocrats with one's right arm (emotionally). Zevrocrats of "republican state organizations" are supported with the left arm (thinking
function). Despite these different outer rituals to dignify the lives
of these scoundrels, Beelzebub emphatically states that men's inner
emptiness and guilt is the same everywhere.

Moving from his seemingly creative digression of puppet shows,
Beelzebub returns to his talk concerning the society of terrestrial
beings who go by the motto of "The-Earth-Is-Equally-Free-For-All" in
Mosulopolis. He then explains how this society first arose then died
out, and the chief causes as to why the process of periodic destruction, or war, must almost inevitably occur among these unfortunate
earth-humans.

War seems to be a lawful outcome, because when something hinders Nature's proper functioning, within the common-cosmic *Trogoautoegocratic* system, it is forced to adapt itself so that a *correspondence* is continually maintained with the harmony and equilibrium of the greater cosmic process. This adaptation includes tension among the motion of planets (called *Solioonensius*), which also produces a feeling of tension (nervousness) among various people on Earth. (Swedenborg called this multi-leveled causality the *science of correspondences,* by which all things and distinct levels in the universe, like mental and physical, are kept in harmonious [common] equilibrium with each other.) Because of the split in the human mind, this tension is felt as a need for changing one's *outer circumstances*—even if it means the destruction of others.

The particular society that Beelzebub is now addressing arose six or seven centuries ago because frequent "civil wars" were occurring on the Asian continent. The chief cause of these "civil wars" was from a new religion—the Mohammedan religion, which was quickly spreading across the land.

A fraternity of brothers in Central Asia named "The Assembly of the Enlightened," concerned about this *warring* situation, then began to create a new charter. This society of brothers was originally formed from earth-humans who had noticed in themselves the consequences of the organ Kundabuffer and banded together in order to help each other in obtaining their deliverance and freedom from these negative properties. Their new mission was to attempt to put a stop to the terrible process of war on their planet, though an individual's desires and efforts to transform.

The members traveled throughout Asia, preaching about the colossal criminality and sin of these deplorable actions among fellow men. (Swedenborg maintained that the proper place for war and conflict was within one's own *inner* world, where God's tenets do battle with one's false principles of self-importance and self-centeredness.)

In terms of addressing the true and cosmic equality of everyone's system of justice, Beelzebub recounts a remarkable saying he personally heard from the wise earth-sage Mullah Nassr Eddin, who said, "Is there such a thing anywhere on Earth as a wise legal examination of men's guilt?" I understand this statement to mean that true inner realities cannot be determined by any outer form of human judgment. Beelzebub says he always remembered this quote every time he had to make impartial comparisons. (Swedenborg stated that justice goes *inward* and deals with the spiritual qualities a person has adopted—not on some outer measurement of equality or accomplishment.)

One of the results of the philanthropic labors of this Asian assembly was the formation within the city of Mosulopolis, of a new and large society of men-beings called "The-Earth-Is-Equally-Free-for-All." Beelzebub states that they had reasonable success because their plan was well drawn up with regard to actually being "doable" within the current conditions found in Asia.

They aimed at creating *one common religion* based on the teachings of a sect called "Parsis" and one common language called "Turkoman," which was the oldest language on the continent and whose roots had already become a part of many other Asian languages. And finally, in another city called Margelan, the capital of what was then the "Ferghanian Khanate," a new kind of government was formed under the name of "The-Council-of-the-Elders." This government was different from others because only those mature earth-humans who were the most impartial and just, *irrespective of what religion and/or nationality they belonged to*, were chosen as its leaders. (This goes beyond simple diversity because it depends on one's spiritual merits—not genetic factors.)

Other leaders of this new diverse society (who lived outside of Margelan), in the city of Mosulopolis, were similarly chosen—from wise individuals representing many nationalities, called "Mongols," "Arabs," "Kirghiz," "Georgians," "Little Russians," "Tamils," and even the personal representative of the then-famous conqueror, Tamerlane. Because of the efforts of this great society, wars and civil wars began to actually diminish. But then something happened which caused the eventual breakup of this incomparable earth-organization.

Beelzebub explains that this unfortunate end came about from a special theory given in a treatise by a very famous Kurd philosopher named *Atarnakh*. His address to the society was titled "Why Do Wars Occur on the Earth?" This speech confounded all the nations of the assembly. This highly learned Kurd had made a life study of every possible angle concerning the question of "what in general is the sense of man's existence?" During this study by Atarnakh, an ancient "Sumerian manuscript" also happened to fall into his hands.

Beelzebub was also familiar with the contents of this manuscript and seemed confident that he knew exactly what part of this ancient text had caught the philosopher Atarnakh's attention. It was a statement about how the laws of reciprocal maintenance most probably always existed somewhere in the world and that the cosmic purpose of people's lives were to serve this *Trogoautoegocratic* system on some small or great scale. (In Swedenborg's theological language, reciprocal maintenance of the universe was to be understood as God's Doctrine of Mutual Love and cooperation. Heaven represents the highest degree of humans serving this universal reciprocal dynamic.)

In fact, there is no way around this ubiquitous cosmic law.

Even if a person refused to live up to his or her cosmic duty, Nature would still end up using that person to serve its grand purpose in at least some *automatic* way or another. (Swedenborg says that there are even evil uses. This is why the Lord God of Heaven and Earth will permit evil under the laws of Divine Providence—as long as that evil can serve and help maintain the ultimate harmony and equilibrium of His grand eternal end.) This will not necessarily bode well for the reluctant individual who removes him or herself from the sacred demands, uses and duties of life—because such an individual will then be unwittingly forced by the demands of Nature into lowly servitude and menial labor (a slavery, producing only low quality vibrations).

The Philosopher Atarnakh was so captivated by this unique Sumerian concept concerning the *inescapable laws of utility* that he then devoted himself entirely into studying its full significance. As a result of this study, the Kurdish philosopher produced his theory called "Why Do Wars Occur on the Earth?"

Beelzebub informs Hassein that he himself became totally familiar with this theory of war *and that it came very close to describing reality.* The theory established that there was indeed a great fundamental cosmic law *Trogoautoegocrat* maintaining the harmony of the entire universe. This law of reciprocal creation and maintainenance required that energies, chemicals and substances, for assisting this holistic process be created by all life forms.

However, many of these important substances and their vibrations are made available to maintain all that exists *only after a life form dies*—where everything returns to its place of origin. Furthermore, Great Nature required these chemicals and substances at certain precise periods. So, a certain number of increased human deaths must lawfully proceed during these same periods. (Swedenborg agrees that people providentially die when they are needed to maintain equilibrium in the Spiritual World. He also mentions that at death, every degree of substance in one's body returns to the place of its arising. But it is through proper spiritual growth and rebirth that an individual can *die consciously* and create the high quality vibrations necessary for the needs of the Spiritual Sun and the rest of the physical universe.)

This unique finding in the Sumerian manuscript of meeting Nature's maintenance quotas through death is what Atarnakh delivered in his address to the society called, "The-Earth-Is-Equally-Free-for-All." Hearing this address, the members of the society at first became confused and discombobulated; then they rallied behind the speaker. By the end of the day this learned society of earth-humans picked special individuals among them to fully familiarize themselves with this fantastic theory of cosmic balance and give a final report to their general assembly.

Unfortunately, there were several members of this society who had not yet become convinced of the inability to actualize their terrestrial dreams and greedy fantasies. They were not sufficiently disillusioned enough by ordinary terrestrial life to be impartial and just. This disagreement caused the society to split into two groups—one that took this hypothesis completely on faith, and the other, who completely rejected these ideas. But the worst part of it all was that those challenging Atarnakh's astonishing theory worked themselves up to into a *frenzied state of enmity*—not only against the theory but also toward the philosopher. So instead of offering unifying insights to the other members of the society, these elected individuals only added to the agitation existing among them. As a result, ideas began to arise automatically among them for *always* sustaining two opposite convictions. (Sound familiar?)

One conviction held that wars and civil wars were necessary on the Earth despite the level of consciousness obtained by men, while their original belief was that by gaining the consciousness of the programs the society had set for itself, this evil would be destroyed—root and all.

But before this situation of inflamed psyches got totally out of hand in the city of Mosulopolis, another learned society, "The Assembly of the Enlightened" arrived to calm everyone down and give new direction as to what to do next. They even choose Atarnakh to oversee this new trajectory. Finally, a conclusion was unanimously reached.

Astonishingly, they all agreed that wars and civil wars must periodically proceed on the Earth, in spite of the will of men, to provide Great Nature with its vibrational needs. In other words, by no mental decision of man could such bloodshed be abolished and interfere with Nature's needs. So with grief and inner resignation, the whole group felt compelled to disband their organization and head back home to simply drag out their inescapable "burdens of life." This decision causes Atarnakh to again address this society and apologize for unintentionally being the cause for the group's dissolution. Hoping to turn things around, he decides to share some final and recent conclusions concerning his astonishing theory.

Atarnakh informs his assembly members that while Nature indeed requires, at certain periods, a certain number of deaths, Nature is indifferent to which kinds of deaths these are. Therefore, the number of deaths of humans needed by Nature could be reduced, simply by increasing the deaths of other living creatures. So the Kurdish philosopher suggests that they continue the work of the original program of their society, but to reinstate on Earth, that former ancient custom of animal sacrifices to their various gods—but now on a much greater scale than ever before.

This speech caused even more commotion among the members than when Atarnakh first introduced his unique theory. After four days of intense deliberations, the society then decided to change how they conducted themselves. Several days after that, the society revised its motto to now be "The-Earth-Only-for-Men." The members spread out across the continent Asia with the purpose of re-establishng the custom of sacrificing animals for "making themselves agreeable" to their gods.

According to Beelzebub, this practice was mostly put into the hands of the Mohammedan "clergy" but also became a part of certain Christian feasts. But then, so many creatures were destroyed during these procedures that Great Nature was again forced to make adjustments due to the deterioration of the *quality* of vibrations being released into the cosmos. As a result of Great Nature having to again re-establish its cosmic equilibrium and harmony, the birth rate of humans now also had to greatly increase, so that the equally rising human deaths could affect the quality of vibrations being produced. (By "Great Nature" Gurdjieff is always referring to God's universal order and entire creation.)

This horrible balancing scenario continued until the arrival of the famous Persian dervish, *Assadulla Ibrahim Ogly*. Beelzebub hints that this individual had begun to view the sacrifice of animals as an anti-religious custom around the end of the 19th century. He wandered among various dervish communities in order to persuade and teach them of the "truth" behind his idea. He convinced many people that such a practice was not only not pleasing to God, but that they were "sins" and that they would be damned to "another world" called *Hell*.

But Beelzebub surprisingly informs Hassein that the Persian dervish's success at reducing animal sacrifices actually led to a most tragic and unintended consequence—World War I! (One is therefore left to surmise that with the decrease in animal sacrifices, Great Nature was forced to again take it out of many men's hides to maintain its equilibrium and cosmic needs through war.)

So, the reason for this horrible miscalculation, and Great War, was that the hypothesis put forward by the earlier Kurd philosopher Atarnakh *only approximated reality*, and that he had failed to grasp what was truly most important. There was more to fulfilling Nature's needs. It was found out that the vibrations required by Great Nature, which are formed by living creatures during their lives and deaths, have no significance quantitatively, but only *qualitatively*.

Beelzebub asserts that Atarnakh would not have made this mistake if he had become familiar with the teachings of the Most Saintly "essence-loving" Ashiata Shiemash. You see, during the time of Asiata Shiemash's important teachings, both the rate of human mortality and birth rate had indeed declined because many people were helping to create the required *quality of vibrations* (through their spiritual transformation). Those closely following his unique teachings had created vibrations more akin to the needs of the cosmos—the Most Great common-cosmic *Trogoautoegocrat* in general—and for the maintenance of the Moon and Anulios *in particular*. And since the requirement of vibrations for the Moon from the deaths of earth-beings was then lowered, Nature adapted herself by diminishing the human birth rate as well.

Beelzebub stresses to his grandson the importance of understanding the significance of the sense and aim of human existence.

434

(Humans were specifically created to produce a higher quality of vibrations for the needs of God's expanding universe on the highest scales—for the Spiritual Sun and its Protocosmos.) Only this knowledge offers real insights into the processes that occur on the Earth, including the causes of war, when these higher quality vibrations are not sufficiently being produced—as when people become indignant and hateful to the point of killing each other.

Beelzebub reminds Hassein that long ago, he learned from the Archangel Looisos, that the destiny of living creatures was to pull from the process of their existence and death the proper vibrations for the upkeep of those former fragments of their planet, called *Moon* and *Anulios*. Sacred Individuals made sure that a "corresponding" substance, called *Askokin*, would continuously issue from the planet Earth (mechanically through the death of creatures) to ensure the harmony of these satellites' movement. But this mechanical solution had a downside for earth-humans. Another challenge to universal maintenance still had to be taken into account—the potential of conscious human spiritual growth to provide quality vibrations for higher realms.

Archangel Looisos had also explained to Beelzebub that the substance Askokin was generally found blended with two other sacred substances, *Abrustdonis* and *Helkdonis*, and had to be separated from these other two substances in order to become "vivifying" enough for such planetary maintenance. Later, Beezebub learned that these other two substances (Abrustdonis and Helkdonis) were not to be ignored. They are necessary for the perfecting of a person's higher being-bodies—the body Kesdjan (Astral body) and the higher body of the Soul.

So, here is what the implanting of the organ Kundabuffer in earth-humans failed to take into account—that during proper spiritual development (and *death* of the old will), Askokin could be released consciously (during life) and the other two substances could be used for the formation of higher bodies.

In other words, during the creation and organization of these two sacred substances into higher being-bodies, within three-brained beings throughout all the planets of the universe (from their *conscious labors* and *intentional suffering*), the substance Askokin is naturally liberated—without one's physical death. (Swedenborg would say that this process occurs through another kind of death—our spiritual death and rebirth—when we choose to give up our worldly and selfish loves. This is why Holy Scripture speaks of humans having two deaths.) But knowing the human psyche and its worldly preferences, the ability to produce higher-grade vibrations would be a great gamble and threat to the harmony of the universe.

From Swedenborg's teachings, I understand that *Askokin* represents terrestrial and corporeal/sensual life force, including memory-data. *Abrustdonis* represents the more rarified substances formed from the ideas developed from increasing rational thought and *Helkdonis* represents the form and substance of spiritual truths! (Swedenborg even states that the quality and structure of one's understanding represents both a real bio-organization of the quality of one's love, and a higher type of body.)

Beelzebub, after studying earth-humans over thousands and thousands of years, is convinced that if they sincerely pondered over their existence and served Great Nature honestly, with this endeavor in mind, their otherwise ill-fated planet would not have to "puff and blow" in order to constantly adapt Herself to remain within the common cosmic Trogoautoegocratic harmony (God's order and eternal plan) and mess with human duration and its shrinking experience.

Unfortunately, earth-humans do not act in honesty with respect to their cosmic duty. Beelzebub quotes a saying from the wise Teacher Mullah Nassr Eddin which sums up this exact conclusion: "Plague and Cholera are, at any rate, less ignoble than human honesty, since people with a conscience can at least live at peace with them."

Ever since an instinctive need for *conscious labor* and *intentional suffering* disappeared from the psyche of earth-humans—in order that they might absorb and metabolize the sacred substances Abrustdonis and Helkdonis (and therefore naturally release the sacred substance Askokin for the maintenance of the Moon and Anulios)— Great Nature was compelled to extract this substance from humans by other (and more drastic) means.

One of those means is war and the taking of many human lives as they are.

Beelzebub points out to Hassein that after the destruction of the organ Kundabuffer in earth-humans, the first generations after that quickly learned that a certain cosmic substance had to be transformed through them—and their assistance in this process was one of their chief being-duties during physical life. On the continent Atlantis, this life-effort was called "Help-to-the-Moon."

To accomplish these being-duties, Beelzebub had learned that in every populated locality of Atlantis, three special buildings were always set up. One was designed specifically for the male sex and was called "Agoorokhrostiny." The second building was designed for the female sex and was called "Gynekokhrostiny." A third sacred building was designed for the "middle sex" and called "Anoroparionikima." The first two sacred Atlantean buildings were considered their "churches," "temples" and "chapels." (I understand the "middle sex" as representing all those living confused and improper lives— which indeed affects their sexual energies.)

Beelzebub informs Hassein that he became well acquainted with the purposes of these sacred buildings. In the building in which the males of the district congregated, they would participate in certain "mysteries" while getting into a special mental state called "self-remembering" (remembering why one was put on Earth and one's ultimate aim).

The Atlanteans considered those of the male sex to be the sources of active manifestation. The men therefore participated in active and conscious contemplation as they participated in performing corresponding sacred mysteries, so that there could be transubstantiated within their being-ness the sacred substances Abrustdonis and Helkdonis for the coating of their higher being-bodies. This procedure allowed these males to free up that other sacred substance, *Askokin* (one's physical/sexual life force), which is not needed for this spiritual process. In this way, Askokin would gain its own vivifyingness and act as the *active part* in the sacred law they called the "Holy Trinity"—to be used by the Moon for its very own maintenance.

In the building for females (the sacred Gynekokhrostiny), the women portrayed the *passive* principle, allowing their vibrations to serve as the passive part of this great sacred triune law and help promote further vivifyingness of Askokin. Unlike the men, the women tried consciously not to think of anything. They spent time in this building during periods called "menstruation." Everything was arranged so that these women's thoughts could be directed, the whole time spent there, toward wishing well to their present and future children.

The third building, designed for the so-called "middle sex" included earth-beings of both sexes who were out of sorts (incorrect or chaotic manifestations). Atlantean society recognized these "misconceptions" if their citizens manifested these peculiar symptoms:

1) If a being believed in any kind of "balderdash."
2) If a being began to prove to others anything about which he himself knew nothing whatsoever, or was not sure of.
3) If a being failed to keep his word of honor, or took his oath in vain.
4) And finally, if there appeared in any being tendencies to "spy" upon the others and to be occupied with "Took-soo-kef."

But the most conclusive symptom of all was when a property would appear among any of them called "hemorrhoids."

These third type of humans could do anything they liked within the period that they were given to stay in their sacred building—except they could neither meet with, or speak, with normal beings. In this way their "tainted" radiations would not interfere with the peaceful and regular existence of the surrounding normal beings.

Unfortunately for the being-humans of this ill-fated planet Earth, the continent of Atlantis entered into the planet and along with it vanished their beneficial customs that were aligned to sacred cosmic laws (God's Truth). However, Beelzebub admits that the need for such special buildings was re-established under the great king Solomon. This Hebrew king had noticed that during times of menstruation women became psycho-organically harmful to those around them. So special buildings were provided to keep these females separate from the rest of society, during these periods where the property of "hysteria" was most likely to happen.

In contemporary times, where females go about freely in the world during menstruation (and behave as though they represented the active function of the sacred Triamazikamno), has now caused human life to become nonsensical and men to be unable to have healthy relations with each other. When the Hebrew nation had fallen from its greatness and dispersed, this beneficial custom for isolating menstruating women was also rejected.

(Beelzebub adds that this unique custom still exists among a very small community in the mountains of the Caucasus called the "Khevsoory," who give modern researchers no sleep because their origin still remains a mystery.)

Returning to the theme as to what extent Great Nature must constantly adapt herself to remain within the cosmic-common harmony due to the chaotic actions of earth-humans, Beelzebub states that World War I serves as a good example. This war resulted from the successful efforts of the Persian Dervish Assdulla Ibrahim Ogly to convince authorities throughout Asia to desist from sacrificing animals. This put increased pressure of harmonizing Great Nature back on human deaths and wars. But this time, due to the German invention of "poison gas" and the English invention of "rapid-fire machine guns" there resulted many more deaths than Nature actually required. This was over-kill.

Once again Great Nature had to "puff and blow" and "jump out of her skin" in order to correct this situation and adapt in a corresponding way. The "corresponding" reaction by Nature was to increase the birth rate of other beings called "wolves," "mice" and "rats." Since most of the men-beings killed during this World War were from Russia, these vermin increased particularly fast in that country. (Swedenborg said that things are multiplied according to their first principle—and men, during war, act inwardly like wolves, rats, and other vermin.)

Hassein becomes silent and thoughtful after listening to all this. Then he sadly says to his grandfather, "How will it all end?" Hassein then wonders if earth-humans are eternally doomed to remain unperfected and be endlessly coated into various lower planetary forms, endlessly toiling on account of that accursed organ Kundabuffer placed within their planetary bodies for reasons extraneous to themselves.

He wonders about the "justice" of all this.

Hassein believes something must be wrong here, especially since he has never doubted of the existence of *justice* in the Megalocosmos. He is now more determined than ever to make it clear to himself why the souls of these terrestrial three-centered beings are in such an unprecedented and terrifying situation. He lowers his head in all these melancholic thoughts.

Beelzebub looks upon his grandson with love and with a special gladness that Hassein was experiencing such grief and depression for others (an empathy that helps in the absorption and digestion of the second being-food, or air). The silence between the two lasts a long time.

Then Beelzebub answers, conceding that something is indeed not quite right here.

He tells Hassein that if the deliberations of the Very Saintly Ashiata Shiemash, entitled "The Terror of the Situation" could do nothing, then *Time alone* can do it. Only Time alone will erase the property of earth-humans to periodically destroy each other—*"either through a certain Being with very high Reason or to certain exceptional cosmic events."* (Hmmm… Swedenborg possessed very high reason. I wonder if this means that his writings will bring news of a certain great cosmic event before the populations on Earth—like a new dispensation and teaching from the Lord God of Heaven, and that will take effect over time? In fact, both men have brought a new understanding to the planet Earth. Gurdjieff claimed that a new "school" was now being prepared on Earth while Swedenborg called this new learning influence a "church." Also according to Swedenborg, this great cosmic event and new disposition for humans on Earth, is symbolized by the descent of the Holy City, *The New Jerusalem*, down from Heaven.)

"Thy will be done."

But first, and because of a seemingly faulty interpretation of fairness in our ancestors' lives—that ended up deluding all of us, Hassein still needs an answer to his question, "is there such a thing as justice in the universe?"

SUMMARY

■ Modern education only serves to strengthen negative properties in individuals, because without personal self-examination and vigilance, our negative desires and influences (hideous emotional properties) organically bubble up—regardless of any kind of thinking or intellectual convictions that might exist passively in one's corporeal (worldly) memory function or psycho-database (this situation has given rise to the spiritual idea of justification by faith alone).

■ Politicians will only ponder the horrors of war when their bellies are full and their sexual organs are satiated—which is an ongoing process.

■ Individual self-importance between members cause all the organizations ever created to end the horrors of war to ultimately fail. And, the resulting bickering between people is just a smaller scale version of hate and war!

■ Organizations for world peace can start from individuals with "resurrected consciences" (due to experiencing the real shocks of war), but later, other individuals join who merely want to establish their personal status and self-importance. Thus, the original aim of such organizations goes up in smoke.

■ Individuals who have developed their conscience, but not their worldly popularity, or who haven't increased their wealth, never belong to such organizations.

■ Beelzebub states that if people just stayed within their sphere of competence, many problems could be solved. And even these problems cannot be solved overnight. Plus, stopping the custom of creating and honoring "war heroes" and abandoning the peculiar belief that war keeps populations to manageable levels will also lead to big improvements. These efforts will help future generations, and even stop that property in them that "doubts the existence of a Divine Being," and also that of no longer *instinctively sensing cosmic truths*. Instead, modern society is moving in the opposite direction and teaching their Hasnamuss views to other generations.

■ *Inner slavery* results from hiding one's true inner and outer significance from others. This pretending always puts one "under somebody's thumb" and creates the need to always seek outer approval (brown-nosing).

SUMMARY

▪ The big secret to the strangeness of the earth-human's psyche is that if you honor their individual Hasnamuss ideas, and pretend to want to learn from them, they will embrace and even consider you an honored friend. This shortsightedness and blindness comes from *self-love*—that is, being able to see abnormalities in others (and become indignant) but never in one's self.

▪ We mostly don't notice or acknowledge that our indignant nature toward others is a real obstacle to genuine happiness.

▪ The simple-minded can sense reality better than intellectuals and academics.

▪ Great Nature takes advantage of wars to gain the required quality of vibrations needed to maintain its cosmic equilibrium. Only through human spiritual growth are the proper vibrations provided for the universe, not through physical death, but the death of the old human ego.

▪ Real change will happen on Earth, only over time—either through an individual with highly developed reason or from some great cosmic event— like the *Apocalpyse* in Revelation!

▪ Thy will be done!

CHAPTER 44

"In the opinion of Beelzebub, man's understanding of justice is for him in the objective sense an accursed mirage"

There is a movement on Earth at this time for (external) social justice, which makes this chapter particularly timely and enlightening.

After hearing Hassein's concerns about *justice* in the universe, Beelzebub stares affectionately at his grandson (and future replacement) for a long time. He then decides it is now the proper moment in his conversations to explain to Hassein that terrestrial question he had promised to divulge earlier concerning the main idea behind the "kink" in the psyche of earth-humans. This maleficent idea concerns not only human self-centeredness, but also the concocted concepts of "Good and Evil" taught by traditional earth-human religions. (Our understanding of these concepts of what is *good* or *bad* certainly affects how we view justice in the world.)

Beelzebub states here that we don't really have a correct picture of what is good or evil, and he is about to give us all a fresh look at understanding these two opposing but important essence-concepts—in a much different way than our religions have previously described them! As you will soon see, he will help us understand these concepts from the more rational point of view of universal laws, which govern all things.

Hassein learns that certain of his ancestors, now living on the Holy Planet Purgatory (which exists on a non-material spiritual plane) were brought into a mental state of turmoil chiefly because of the earth-humans having acquired a warped understanding of these two concepts. (Swedenborg would agree that the concepts held by earth-humans concerning these two notions would indeed, because of their causal connections, affect the mental states of those living in the spiritual world.) Beelzebub feels that it would be beneficial to describe some long-past events in order to provide a good background for this important discussion and anti-intuitive lesson.

Beelzebub goes back in time to his fifth and very short visit to the planet Earth. During this visit, he was notified from the "Center" by some friends, that a special cherubim, very close to our ALL-EMBRACING ENDLESSNESS, was coming to Mars with some important message for him. (Cherubim are guards to the secret knowledge of God's providence of salvation—only allowing access to these secrets when individuals are genuinely following the heavenly protocols of *celestial* love. Therefore, this secret knowledge is unavailable to many of today's scholars.)

Because of Beelzebub's tireless efforts to rid the planet Earth of its horrible practice of "sacrificial offerings," plus a personal petition made by Angel Looisos before our COMMON FATHER ENDLESSNESS, the message was that his punishment of cosmic banishment and exile had been reduced (that is, Beelzebub was pardoned) so that he and his family could return to the "Center" (Heaven's Protocosmos) and take part in the appropriate obligations to God's divine scheme and governance. (In Swedenborg's terms, a visit by a cherubim would represent such grace and mercy.)

After this divine pardon, Hassein's father and his uncle Tooilan soon left Mars for the Center, where they were each given their divine assignments.

Hassein's father was given an important leadership role (called "Zirlikner") on their birth planet Karatas, while his uncle Tooilan took a post on the Holy Planet Purgatory as an assistant to the director of communications for the "etherogram connection" between most of the planets of the Great Universe. (Swedenborg observed that all realms of the spiritual world, including Hell, are governed by God's angels. And that all these inner realms and planes of life are kept in communication with each other.)

Among those members of Beelzebub's tribe who had also been originally exiled, a one-time leader on the planet Karatus, named *Pooloodjistius,* was promoted after this all-gracious pardon to become the assistant to the Great Observer of the movements of all cosmic concentrations in the Megalocosmos, the Archseraph *Ksheltarna.* Pooloodjistius had offered Beelzebub wise council and direction on establishing his observatory on the planet Mars, as well as tutoring his two sons, and setting up the proper inner and outer conditions for their acquiring the proper data necessary for crystallizing in themselves the principles necessary for becoming responsible three-brained beings (future angels).

Pooloodjistius taught Beelzebub's children why and for what purpose a particular cosmic concentration occupied a certain designated place in the universe and informed them about the particular *mutual* influences these concentrations had on each other within the grand scheme of the common-cosmic Trogoautoegocratic process of reciprocal creation and maintenance.

Only God's most advanced angels could have this degree of knowledge of the order of the universe. (Swedenborg, who had his spiritual eyes and understanding opened by the Lord God to reach into angelic levels of reality, stated in his theological works that the planets and stars took up positions in the universe that corresponded to the *organic* design, structures, functions and scheme of the human anatomy—just like the societies of Heaven are organically arranged in a Grand Human form! Swedenborg also observed that all things in the created universe are in perpetual endeavor toward the human form, which is in the image and likeness of God's Divine Human nature and His Word. See *Divine Love and Wisdom*, n. 56–68.)

Beelzebub tells Hassein that his father favored studying the mutual influences between those cosmic concentrations that were nearest to the Prime Source, the Most Most Holy Sun Absolute (Spiritual Sun),but that his uncle Tooilan became interested in the planet Earth and the three-brained beings that existed on it. Tooilan made his father, Beelzebub, promise to always keep him informed of the events on Earth after he left for the Center nearer to Our Lord. (Swedenborg had received a similar request from angelic spirits when he was asked by them, "What news from Earth?")

Beelzebub did not know what became of his quarterly etherogram reports that he sent to his son Tooilan (who was existing as a higher being-body) until receiving information about the turbulent events taking place on the planet Purgatory. Apparently, the great governor of the holy planet Purgatory, His All-Quarters-Maintainer the Arch-cherub *Helkgematios*, asked Tooilan to reproduce these reports, so that if they wished, various other "higher being bodies" dwelling on this holy planet could keep tabs on the psyche and mental states of those breeding down on that most peculiar planet Earth, located on one of the very remote corners of the Megalocosmos. (Again, the symbolism here is that the planet Earth is quite remote and distant from God's direct influence, and therefore, its human inhabitants cause disturbances in the grand scheme of universal harmony from their faulty beliefs. And, these disturbances would also have a negative affect on the hearts and minds of those living in the spiritual realm—like the Holy Planet Purgatory.)

These reports from Earth had attracted a large following from interested souls existing on the planet Purgatory and their contents created a great turmoil among them. As these higher being-bodies and souls delved into the abnormal psyche of the earth-humans, and pondered its causes, they began to suspect that the problem seemed to originate from what they first felt was *an injustice coming "from Above."* (This kind of thinking about justice and fairness in God's universe was the reason for Beelzebub being exiled in the first place.) Many unperfected souls are quick to blame God when things don't go their way! The topic of theodicy or evil in the world—when things don't go someone's way—is considered a *cosmic injustice*, and that it is all God's fault (operating from "Above"). They also believe this injustice should be immediately changed to remedy this obviously unfair situation.

These "righteous" souls of the Holy Planet Purgatory became so *indignant* over this "suspicion" that they chose fifty of their members, who were all bonafide candidates for promotion to the Most Most Holy Source of Everything Existing, to make a deeper investigation into the true causes of the seeming injustice as to why it had become almost impossible for earth-humans to perfect themselves. (Symbolically, fifty represents a stage of transformation whereby ideas become arranged into either spiritual or natural categories).

After rigorous investigations they determined that the fundamental cause of the psychic abnormality of earth-humans came from a faulty notion that these three-brained beings entertained concerning the concepts of "Good" and "Evil." Earth-humans had come to falsely believe that these two diametrically opposing forces acted *outside of them,* and were the two instigators of all their good and bad manifestations in life. (No earth-human seemed to want to blame these forces and instigators as coming from *within* themselves.)

This maleficent and absurd notion in earth-humans became crystallized (fixed) into their worldview where it ultimately served as both a tranquillizer to justify all their stupid actions, and also to prevent any real possibility of self-perfecting their higher being-parts (soul parts)—which is a process of *inner,* not *outer* change.

The "righteous" souls of Purgatory began to gather together and deliberate how they might fix this cosmic mess from their end. They came to a unanimous decision and even sent a petition to God that HE in HIS Providence send a special Messenger to Earth with the wisdom and ability to uproot this maleficent dogma. (Could Swedenborg or Gurdjieff have been used for this purpose?)

They also petitioned God to prevent the individual who first invented the terms of "Good and Evil" from ever entering their holy planet. Instead, they wanted to doom this person to exist and suffer eternally on the planet *Remorse of Conscience* (Hell). Turmoil soon broke out among the inhabitants of this holy planet when they succeeded in identifying the actual individual who first spread this faulty idea of "Good" and "Evil" to the earth-humans below.

This individual's name was *Makary Kronbernkzion.*

The turmoil and frustration was increased by the fact that this individual's higher being-part was already perfected (from personal spiritual efforts) to the required gradation of Reason that made him worthy to go not only to the Holy Planet Purgatory but also to be a main candidate to eventually be taken on to the Most Most Holy Sun Absolute (the sphere of Heaven).

God then graciously decided not to punish this individual, but to allow this deserving soul to exist on that holy planet until the future results of his apparently "bad" deed could be revealed and objectively assessed.

In spite of the fact that this highly developed individual was indeed the fundamental cause of the failure of earth-humans to perfect their lives *inwardly,* God had made this gracious command because He hoped that earth-humans would still eventually recognize *their own personal errors* and begin to exist in a more proper way. After all, why should this individual, Makary Kronbernkzion, be punished for having successfully overcome adverse conditions and mercilessly struggling with his own passive denying principle (the physical body and its worldly desires) and perfect himself to a level necessary for reaching the *threshold of the basis of everything existing in the Universe?*

Even to this day, anyone on this holy planet who gives thought to this question "shudders."

However, the future for the higher-being part (soul part) of poor Makary Kronbernkzion, despite his positive inner achievements, rests completely with the outcome of those now inhabiting the planet Earth—how much eternal damage will the earth-humans' misunderstanding of the terms "Good" and "Evil" (because of Kronbernkzion) result in?

The news of this distressing situation had reached Beelzebub during his sixth visit to the surface of the planet Earth. He then began to investigate the details of this problem firsthand concerning the severity of this maleficent idea among earth-humans concerning the concepts of "Good" and "Evil." He admits to his grandson that although Kronbernkzion's maleficent ideas did, indeed, fundamentally cause the "dilution" of the psyche of earth-humans, he personally fell short of confirming this categorically.

So Beelzebub looked into this distressing situation more deeply.

One of the things Beelzebub did was to research the life story of Makary Kronbernkzion (going the whole hog, postage included). He discovered that although this individual was indeed the first to use the words "Good" and "Evil," he was not to blame for the way earth-humans reinterpreted these same terms in such a destructive manner.

Beelzebub tells Hassein that he received a lot of good help in studying Kronbernkzion's history from an elderly member of his own tribe that had existed on the continent Atlantis. This elderly individual happened to be the uncle of the young being from Beelzebub's tribe on whose account he first came to the planet Earth to diffuse a great problem. This elderly being had existed on Atlantis at the same time Makary Kronbernkzion existed there. (So Makary had conscience!)

Kronbernkzion indeed grew up under favorable conditions, from receiving a positive heredity from his parents, to obtaining a good education in order to be prepared for a "scientific career." His scientific accomplishments allowed him to later become a member of the great society *Akhaldan*. During his life he had clearly determined the real value of his own significance and sincerely realized his "nullity" (something most earth-humans are unwilling to do—especially famous earth-humans and those with celebrity status).

As Makary Kronbernkzion pondered his true inner situation, he became convinced that he could, through *conscious labors and intentional sufferings*, transform himself from a "nothing" into a "something." He then began to labor consciously and mercilessly toward setting up *intentionally disturbing conditions* for the denying-aspect of his being—challenging the unconscious need for pleasure in his physical body and corporeal/sensual mind.

(This inner bravery speeds up spiritual growth and is certainly a different approach from those who normally seek affirmation and comfort from others—mistakenly calling it love. *Affirmation is a cover-up, not neighborly love.* And Makary labored intensely in this unusual manner—always within the sphere of his daily responsibilities and scientific investigations. I can't overstress that most modern earth-humans desperately try to remove themselves from any disturbing conditions, particularly from those that point to flaws within themselves.)

Since most beings on the continent Atlantis at that time had data still crystallized in them for engendering the genuine being-impulse of "love-of-kind" (love of the neighbor), Kronbernkzion wished to share with others the cosmic truths he had learned from his own challenges and individual efforts. For this purpose he created, on a piece of marble, a kind of "book" (a *Boolmarshano*), titled "The Affirming and Denying Influences on Man." (Swedenborg concurred that the human physical body was passive and reactive, usually negatively, to God's evolutionary and *active* spiritual influences.)

Beelzebub informs his grandson that a later copy of this Boolmarshano, carved on tusks of a creature called "Chirniano," had survived to the present day and came into his possession during his sixth visit to the planet Earth. Beelzebub claims he succeeded in deciphering it, whereby he became quite familiar with all its details.

The original marble copy was so admired and approved by other members of the society Akhaldan that it was placed in the middle of their "cathedral." (In other words, severe self-examination became a central component of their religious approach. This self-examination is on a whole other level than self-deprecation.)

And because interest grew in this Boolmarshano among the Akaldans, *seven* copies were made of it and distributed to various other branches of their "Church" in other cities on the continent Atlantis—even to other continents. One of these copies reached a church on a landmass not far from the continent of Africa called "Sinndraga." Before this landmass sank along with the continent Atlantis, the copy was taken to Africa where it lay beneath some *ruins* (destruction by falsities) and was later covered over by desert *sands* (disconnected knowledge and data in the human memory).

About thirty centuries later, when earth-humans had again multiplied and the process of reciprocal destruction (war) was proceeding between two African communities, called the "Filnooanzi" and "Plitazoorali," those of the community "Filnooanzi" happened to uncover this important text while digging for water. But like all things pillaged during times of war and divvied up, this great ancient work was also divided among these two warring communities, during a so-called declared "peace." (Reminds me of Roman soldiers dividing up the Lord's clothes among them.)

One of the halves of this text, after seven centuries, fell into the hands of "Egyptian high priests." This half of the copy changed hands again when a certain Persian King made a "clean sweep" of Egypt. Finally, moving to the continent of Asia, this half-copy ended up in the hands of an *Aisorian* priest, where Beelzebub was personally able to examine it on his sixth visit to the planet Earth.

The second half of this important marble text also passed from hand to hand to one of the central communities in Asia, until it was finally swallowed up by an earthquake. (Earthquakes symbolize a paradigm shift.)

Beelzebub reminds Hassein that it was during his sixth visit to the planet Earth that he became a "physician-hypnotist." He used hypnotism to study the strange psyche of earth-humans. Through the use of hypnosis, Beelzebub was able to prepare various earth-humans—through the manipulation of their blood circulation—to enter into a mental state whereby they could act as "mediums." During this special mental state, Beelzebub was able to tap into the subconscious minds of these specially prepared earth-humans where special holistic data existed and consisted of the "seeing-and-sensing-of-what-has-occurred-in-the-remote-past."

Swedenborg insisted in his book *Rational Psychology* (n. 563) that humans have a connate knowledge of all things, kept deep in their psyches (in the higher involuntary part). Humans are also connected to spiritual beings in higher realms, who possess even greater heavenly knowledge. So Beelzebub used hypnosis to turn his subjects into versions of "Edgar Cayce."

Beelzebub also used this method of mediumship to learn about more details concerning the life of Makary Kronbernkzion, who supposedly destroyed the chances of earth-humans to perfect themselves because of his having introduced the terms of "Good" and "Evil" into their abnormal noggins. Beelzebub strongly suspected that there might still exist on the surface of the planet Earth something tangible and extant that was intimately connected to this individual's life and used hypnotism to explore this suspicion. It was in this way that Beelzebub learned that half of the ancient text created by Makary Kronbernkzion had landed in the hands of an Aisorian priest living in the locality called "Urmia."

Beelzebub located the Aisorian priest and persuaded him to allow an alabaster copy to be made of this ancient text. Then he used the same method of mediumship to locate the other half of the text. Getting to this other copy required obtaining excavation equipment and concocting a plan that would not create any suspicions about his true purpose. He was able to dig for the second part of this rare ancient document under the pretext of preparing a shaft for a copper mine.

So Beelzebub succeeded in acquiring and deciphering both halves of this important text by Makary Kronbernkzion, titled "The Affirming and Denying Influences on Man." It was in this ancient text that Makary Kronbernkzion indeed first coined the terms "Good" and "Evil," but to represent *two* of the *three* universal forces of the sacred Triamazikamno (the active and passive forces), which participate in all created things. All three-brained beings (including earth-humans) consist of the same three independent forces, which participate in all the processes of the reciprocal maintenance of the universe.

Now pay close attention.

The first of these independent fundamental forces constantly issues forth from the Prime Source itself (God's Spiritual Sun), where it descends by momentum through the pressure exerted on it by other created units of the World. When this first force spends the energy of its outward momentum it begins to strive to re-blend (and turn the corner) back with the source of its arising, and becomes a new "second World force" or endeavor. Beelzebub describes the dynamics of this second direction in the fundamental cosmic law, as "The effects of a cause must always re-enter the cause." (As mentioned earlier, Swedenborg addresses this same universal law as "First principles returning to their first principles—though mediate causes.")

The first independent force, which moves outward from the Prime Source of Eveything that Exists, always creates the process of *involution* (top-down causality). The second force, which strives to re-blend (and return) with the cause of its arising (and first principle) always creates the process of *evolution* (or reverse entropy).

Since the first force that issued out of God and the very foundation of the cause of everything is involutionary and *outward* (away from God), Makary Kronbernkzion labeled this directionality as "Evil." But since the second independent force resisted this outward direction and instead, began moving against this downward stream (and back toward God) Kronbernkzion labeled it as "Good."

From this point of view, in the grand cosmic scheme of things, the first force is to be considered as *passive* (and moving by momentum). The second force, which must overcome top-down causality and entropy and regain vivifyingness, could therefore be considered as the *active* force. (The third force in this fundamental cosmic scheme consists of the results of the clash between the first two forces happening everywhere in the universe.)

Beelzebub, from his reading of Kronbernkzion's original document, was simply describing "Good and Evil" objectively in terms of forces—*moving either toward or away from God.* (You may have been taught that the concepts of "Good" and "Evil" are contained in the Ten Commandments, but these laws are a means of measure to let us see, in principle, if we are moving closer or away from God. If we look at our own actions and choices as either getting us closer to God or further away from God, our notions of "Good" and "Evil" will be more cosmically correct. Self-love and love of the world are *involutionary,* and therefore, move us further from the Creator.

(Again, Swedenborg describes similar active and passive principles in the universe as *action* and *reaction,* and in terms of a person's spiritual evolution we must consciously play *active* roles in working with God's special descending influences, thus turning the created world and cosmic truth *passive*—where it can serve us as proper spiritual food and be digested, psycho-metabolized and finally appropriated—absorbed into our innermost bio-fabric or spirit. More is discussed on this topic in Chapter 46. Swedenborg also makes comments on God's influx into Ultimate Nature or *involution* in his *Arcana Coelestia,* n. 7270.)

Both Gurdjieff and Swedenborg offer an interesting wrinkle to the idea that we humans cannot allow God's influx (influence) to simply pass through us like a sieve, where it dissipates and continues to move downward, terminating beyond us into dead matter and mechanical energy. Rather, we must consciously suffer to create new organic substrates (matrices) and bio-vessels (through the clashing and fusion of active and passive forces in our own lives) that can hold God's influx on an increasingly higher (and evolutionary) plane. This new trajectory takes the individual back up the evolutionary rungs (gravity centers) of "Jacob's Ladder."

The resulting inner development (and fusion of active and passive principles) results in a new bio-structure within us. This is what forms a higher plane and organic vessel for God's increased influx into our lives.

This higher bio-structure (spiritual body) is the spiritualizing result (third force) of the chosen conflict between the two fundamental forces or influences in our lives that are constantly flowing from opposite directions. (Swedenborg stated that even Jesus, who had a physical body and human hereditary frailties—but a divine soul—had to also take part in this cosmic clash, until He cleansed and unified His human nature perfectly to His divine heavenly nature. This was the essence of *Glorification.* In humans, this same ordeal leads to increased *conscience.*)

Beelzebub explains to his grandson that it was this precise description of cosmic forces where the words "Good" and "Evil" were first used in the scientific thesis of Makary Kronbernkzion. As such, Kronbernkzion cannot be personally blamed for the flawed and *external* understanding of "Good and Evil" that eventually took hold of earth-humans' minds, then took on such a destructive and fantastic imagining in their abnormal psyches.

Instead of cultivating a proper worldview, Makary Kronbernkzion's actual definition was replaced by warped and weird notions of "Good" and "Evil" among the earth-humans, who judged everything in *external and physical terms*. (Swedenborg described this external viewing as looking at spiritual things, naturally.)

Beelzebub goes on to explain that such weird external notions and judgments permitted humans to never have to take responsibility for their own bad actions, but to always blame it on some "foreign" external cause—and not as issuing from anything related to themselves or their essential egoism. *Today, all revolutionary and freedom movements also deal with blaming some outside cause.*

True justice can never be obtained from such a warped and limited belief system. (This is why Swedenborg maintained that true justice operates deeper and deeper within—on an eternal and spiritual level. True justice has to do with where we all end up spiritually—*not* whether we are treated fairly during our 70–80 years of life on the terrestrial planet Earth.)

Beelzebub then relates a tragic/comic story relating to members of his own tribe when they first began to live on the planet Earth among those weird humans. This story began as a consequence of Beelzebub's tribe being allowed to emigrate to other planets of the same solar system during their exile from the center. This emigration took place during the emergence of the *Tikliamishian* (Sumerian?) civilization, and at a time when a new religious teaching was just being established by an individual named *Armanatoora*.

He came up with a unique description of "external Good and Evil" as being spread by either good spirits called "Angels" or bad spirits called "Devils." Both kinds of spirits cleverly hid themselves while living among the humans on Earth.

The notion then began to spread among these silly earth-humans that all the members of Beelzebub's tribe (who suddenly appeared and then disappeared from their sight—after the pardon), were in fact, these same sneaky "Devils" who, fearing that their activities would be "found out" (thanks to this new external religion), instead went into hiding, where they could cleverly infect innocent humans and bring about various misfortunes without ever being detected.

(While Swedenborg does talk about angels and devils as being real, they are not terrestrial, and instead live in the higher psychical realms of our shared inner (spiritual) reality, where they can conjoin themselves to the qualities of our will and its loves—to those that are similar to their own bent and preferences. Because of this deep and profound relationship, their influences are never foreign or external, but always perfectly personal and intimate.)

Beelzebub states that because of this concocted new faith-system and religion now affecting the hearts and minds of these earlier terrestrial humans, the names of various individuals from his own tribe were eventually used to identify and name *all kinds of Devils* and their evil roles. (The name "Beelzebub" certainly has a negative connotation, and he also states that "Lucifer" was the name of one of his honorable tribesmen!) These "named villains" were blamed for all the bad things that happened during earth-people's lives. Earth-citizens now considered themselves as always being mere innocent victims to all these villians' shenanigans. (Most traditional religions indeed now depict "Beelzebub" and "Lucifer" to be external causes of misfortune to humans in the world.)

However, earth-humans failed to grasp (and admit) that they are in fact personally responsible for permitting these "villainies" to be formed within their own hearts and minds. It is much easier to blame outside forces for all these criminal transgressions. This "finger-point-ing" permits people to personally remain comfy and calm, rather than getting consciously upset about their character flaws, nullities, blunders or anything depending on them personally. (Swedenborg underscores this notion by insisting that evil has no real *ontological source* in the universe—but is only a contingency.)

The theme of this chapter is that *Justice is an illusion* if it is based on external thinking and worldviews—which leads only to external solutions (like political correctness, worldly self-esteem, and the forced redistribution of physical wealth in order to equalize every-body). But true, genuine eternal justice is actually built into the cosmic system of laws and duty, because it is based on the results of our individual efforts and the conscious clashing between our own involutionary (passive) and evolutionary (active) forces. In layman's terms, this means we are personally responsible for our life choices and ultimate eternal fate. (For this reason Swedenborg insists that true justice goes deeper within to uncover our true inner quality, and its fairness is built into a system that allows us to change the spiritual coordinates of our hearts and minds—according to our choices and acquired loves.)

At this point in his Tales, Beelzebub receives a message ("Leitoo-chanbros") from a servant elsewhere on the cosmic ship *Karnak*, who joyfully communicated that visible reflections from their home planet Karatas were now coming into view.

SUMMARY

■ Our current view of *Good and Evil* needs to be looked at more personally and deeply, as does our understanding of true justice and cosmic fairness.

■ Beelzebub, his family, and members of his tribe were all pardoned for his tireless work on the abolition of animal sacrifice on the planet Earth. After the divine pardon, Beelzebub sent updates to his son Tooilan (Hassein's uncle), who had been given an important position on the Holy Planet Purgatory, and always wanted to know the status of earth-humans.

■ But the *self-righteous* inhabitants of the Holy Planet Purgatory (the spiritual plane where one gets the chance to be further purged and perfected) were put into turmoil and became indignant through their false notion of a cosmic injustice being committed from "Above." They wanted the individual responsible for first spreading the ideas of *Good and Evil* to earth-humans, and making it impossible for them to perfect themselves, to be punished by God.

■ Those who blame God for any cosmic injustice have a flawed understanding of "Good and Evil." They tend to believe that Good and Evil come from *outside* causes and these *external forces* are the instigators of all the good and bad consequences of their lives—and not from anything within themselves. (This faulty idea of *good* and *evil* is evidenced today by people's growing belief that there is no *inner* individual evil in the world—but only bad external systems that are unjust.)

■ Makary Kronbernkzion, who first used the terms "Good and Evil" on Earth, was likewise misunderstood. He wrote a treatise on a marble tablet called "The Affirming and Denying Influences of Man," which clarified his position.

■ "Evil" can be objectively understood in *involutionary* terms—as that which takes us further from God, while "good" can be understood in *evolutionary* terms—of doing things that bring us closer to God. And, the direction of evolutionary or spiritual growth must come from an inner dictate or active conscious choice.

■ True justice cannot be obtained by anyone who always blames everything on *external* causes, or who quickly embraces the title of *victim*.

CHAPTER 45

"In the opinion of Beelzebub, man's extraction of electricity from Nature and its destruction during its use, is one of the chief causes of the shortening of the life of man"

Eating meat is bad for us, western comfort toilets are bad for us, and now we are about to learn that generating and using electricity is also bad for our psyches (and even those of our planetary neighbors). This negative notion of using electricity first came as a real shock to me, especially when I considered the profound dependency of modern civilization to run on electric power and our reliance on electric devices.

So, looking for a free source of electrical energy won't help us either—all of which makes this part of the Tales particularly disturbing for the reader. Remember, Gurdjieff feels it is most important to create intentionally disturbing conditions (shocks) in order to make us engage in logical confrontations.

I suspect that most readers will simply ignore this chapter and flip the light switch at home to a *brighter* setting.

I have to admit to knowing ahead of time (from earlier readings) where this chapter was heading, I found myself somewhat impatient and uncomfortable with Beelzebub's message. While the information has become less shocking to me over time, because I am now becoming more willing to accept such a premise, still, much of my own life has depended heavily on the use of electric power, and without my giving its usage much serious thought.

(Was my mindless use of electricity the problem or was using electricity causing me to become more mindless?)

But I also became aware, after some reflection, that the author's (Gurdjieff's) motive is not simply to share important information in shocking ways, but that the intended clash between passive and active (exterior and interior) components of our being-ness would eventually transform our own thinking (from a new inner fusion) toward a more correct view of reality—particularly toward the bio-mechanism behind real and genuine spiritual transformation.

Increased convenience (from electricity) tends to obstruct inner growth, contemplation and promotes inner laziness.

In the early 1980s, I did build a solar house on some rural property hoping to become less dependent on "the grid." But energy conservation is not the point Gurdjieff is making here. Convenience, through electric power, tends to diminish our psyche. And, in terms of our generating electric power, a claim is made that we humans destroy important substances that were originally meant for supporting our mental activity and the building of higher being-bodies.

As mentioned throughout these Tales, Gurdjieff knew how to create unique mental challenges concerning the universal laws of cosmic order and process to keep the reader's mind "on its toes." From this strategy there would hopefully result a powerful inner conflict between this new information and the reader's accepted worldview, and not simply become some data that drains into the basin of one's memory-function—where it gets stale and putrefies. I will discuss this unique strategy by Gurdjieff more in the next chapter. But I am sure you are now becoming familiar with the strategy of *Beelzebub's Tales* to force your brain to make uncommon efforts and judgments (including your heart making uncommon observations and perhaps, even some self-confessions).

Such mental efforts and unflattering admissions are demanded by the fantastical cosmic setting of Beelzebub traveling through the great multi-leveled universe, which is populated by many other intelligent (three-brained) beings—who live more normally than we do. (This kind of stuff drives academics crazy!)

Beelzebub returns to his Tales by informing Hassein that the abnormalities of the existence of earth-humans would be only half a calamity if they became concerned with the lost capacities of their perfecting, within themselves, their own higher being-bodies (needed for proper living and happiness in the eternal realm). But even more terrifying, the repercussions of the abnormal existence of earth-humans, and their use of electric power is now having harmful effects that also make it more difficult for the three-brained beings inhabiting other planets (of that same solar system) to obtain proper spiritual growth.

Our responsibilities are connected even to those beyond our birth-planet.

Beelzebub became aware of this worsening situation after receiving his Divine Pardon, as he was making his final preparations to leave that solar system and return to his home planet Karatas.

This distressing new fact became "imperishable" being-data (a fixed conviction) with the help of the son of Beelzebub's essence-friend Gornahoor Harharkh, who lived on Saturn. If you will recall, in Chapter 18, (called "The Arch-Preposterous") Gornahoor conducted "electrical" experiments to discover in detail the special properties of the cosmic omnipresent substance *Okidanokh*. Harharkh's son (Beelzebub's godson), whose name was Gornahoor Rakhoorkh, put the "fly in the ointment" of his father's research on this important substance.

In order to explain more fully to his grandson how it became a conviction, crystallized in Beelzebub's mind, that earth-beings were also having a negative effect on the self-perfecting efforts of other three-brained beings in that particular solar system, more background information had to be provided. So he informs Hassein that he had to return to the planet Mars to get all his personal affairs in order for them to travel to Saturn, including changing spaceships for his long journey back home.

During this last stay on Mars, Beelzebub learns that the Martian king (named "Toof-Nef-Tef") wanted to speak with him. Beelzebub knew this king in his youth when he was a Martian "physician." (Again, this background context challenges our habitual mind to fathom reality through the conflicts of mixing real data and allegory together, that is, higher levels of meanings with lower, terrestrial-level concepts.) Swedenborg used a similar hybrid writing style (of science and metaphor) to elevate human minds in his work *The Worship and Love of God*.)

Beelzebub, in describing this Martian king, underscores the fact that individuals everywhere else in the Megalocosmos rise to become leaders based solely on their being-merits (not on slogans, promises or campaign war chests). This Martian king or "Toof-Nef-Tef" was now close to *twelve thousand years old* and was nearing the state of self-perfection called the sacred "Ischmetch." A three-brained being acquiring this level of self-development, as regards to the Most Great Cosmic Iraniranumange, has mastered an individuality which becomes dependent on the substances emanating directly from the Sun Absolute (such as spiritual truth), and not as the reciprocal exchange of substances taking place in other creatures (according to the common-cosmic fundamental Ansanbaluiazar.)

Since the "Iraniranumange" and "Ansanbaluiazar" both represent processes by which substances are exchanged throughout the universe, I am led to believe that the process of "Iraniranumange" represents the higher, *conscious* and *willful* exchange of psycho-spiritual substances (God's objective Truths) within a three-brained being, rather than the automatic exchanges of natural substances occurring in lower life forms and unregenerate earth-humans to simply maintain the status quo of life. (Swedenborg calls the reciprocal exchange of higher psycho-substances or energies from the Spiritual Sun, angelic *mutual love*.)

Beelzebub states further that when an individual, through being-efforts, perfects his or her reason to the level of "Ischmetch," that individual becomes capable of even choosing their time of death, where their highest being-body is then taken directly to the holy planet Purgatory (the Spiritual World).

Beelzebub finally meets with the Martian King, who with his fellow Martian subjects, all understood why he and his tribe were first compelled to live in this solar system (after his having some youthful, misguided notions). And these Martians also understood the nature of his divine pardon.

The King then shares with Beelzebub the disturbing observation that his subjects were losing their "willfulness" and as a result, their "potency" for active mentation and the drive toward self-perfection was also diminishing. The King tells Beelzebub that he has failed to find out where the trouble lies and what corresponding measures needed to be carried out to uproot and destroy this "evil" taking place among his subjects.

Beelzebub promises to look into the matter.

Several Martian days later, Beelzebub heads for the planet Saturn. Upon arriving there, he is informed that the larger intersystem ship *Omnipresent*, that would finally take Beelzebub and his family back to their home planet Karatas, would not arrive until the next "Hre-Hree-Hra" (a period determined by the position of the planet Saturn in relation to the Sun and the planet Neptune). There are apparently "seven" of these Hre-Hree-Hra periods on Saturn in each yearly cycle. This news leaves Beelzebub with about a month and a half to burn before the larger spaceship, the *Omnipresent*, arrives to pick him up.

Beelzebub decides to use this time to visit his old friend Gornahoor Harharkh on Saturn. Since Beelzebub was the godfather of Harharkh's son Gornahoor Rakhoorkh, he asks about how the young Saturnian man was doing in life. Gornahoor Harharkh said that his son was doing well and that he continued in his own footsteps to study the details of the cosmic substance Okidanokh. However, owing to the results of his son's further investigations he was sadly forced to destroy all his scientific equipment. Apparently, it was discovered that during the operation of this equipment in doing the experiments on the cosmic substance Okidanokh (which produced electricity), an "unredeemable sin" was being committed.

Since Beelzebub had always kept his Saturnian friend up to date on the strange psyche of earth-humans, Harharkh wanted to know if the existence of these unfortunate beings was still diminishing.

Just then his son, Gornahoor Rakhoorkh, entered the room and took his place on his "perch" and welcomed Beelzlbub with an "angelically musical voice." (I believe that the *height* of these perches represented the mental level on which one's whole being rested.)

After this welcome, the young Saturnian took part in the conversation. It was during the conversation of Beelzebub's godson about his own experiments with the element Okidanokh, that Beelzebub began to put two and two together and realized how the abnormal manifestations of earth-beings was also having a harmful effect on those living on other planets in the solar system.

457

They were making and using up too much electricity!

Rakhoorkh explained to Beelzebub that at a very young age he was preparing himself to be a responsible being and devoted much of his effort to increasing a mental potency defined as "to-deliberate-actively-and-long." Later, when he started to use his father's scientific equipment he would notice that the force and degree of his active mentation definitely became worse.

After long observations of his mental state and his surroundings, he became convinced beyond all doubt that this undesirable mental state had proceeded in him every time the large "Lifechakan" (dynamo, generator or turbine) in the experiment room was switched on.

In Swedenborg's scientific writings he described the action, and active state, of the human brain-fibres as being *turbinated* (a curved motion). So it is conceivable to me that when one was around a turning mechanical generator, extracting electricity from the atmosphere, one would have less personal energy for his or her own psyche to operate and properly *turbinate*.

The young Saturnian investigator further discovered that the Omnipresent Cosmic Substance called Okidanokh, was to be found not only in his planet's atmosphere but in the atmosphere of all planets in the solar system and was essential in the formation of all planetary and surplanetary formations. This substance is also important to the health and maintenance of every being that exists, including human three-brained beings.

This cosmic substance and element, owing to the universal common equilibrium, is distributed in a precise proportion among the various planets of a given solar system and must, without fail, be replenished to maintain the equilibrium of this common proportionality. So, if for some reason, more than the established norm of a planet's portion of this substance is being used up, it must be replaced. The re-balancing of the Okidanokh due to any portion of it being exhausted must inevitably flow in from the atmosphere of the other planets (which means less for those living on those other planets).

He also proved for himself that Okidanokh was crucial for the external coating of the organic bodies of beings of all brain systems (including higher being-bodies in humans). Therefore, the possibilities of three-brained beings to be able to perfect themselves and re-blend with the Prime Cause of everything strongly depended on this substance being in abundance as well.

(JG Bennett, a leader of Gurdjieffian studies, described "Okidanokh" as *the substance of will* in his own book, *Talks on Beelzebub's Tales*, pages 113 & 135.) That is a pretty good description! However, Okidanokh may support the human "will," but the will is actually a non-material and living substance. As stated in an earlier chapter, Swedenborg would understand this subtle elemental substance similarly as an "endeavor" or "striving" in Nature [outside the

Spiritual Sun] to unify its three distinct forces and perfect itself—which takes part in all material creation and self-organization. This cosmic elemental substance must be a derivative of spiritual love proceeding through truth [finding form], but once outside the Spiritual Sun, this endeavor or striving becomes classified as *conatus* in the physical spacetime arena.)

Rakhoorkh then strongly suggests that the destruction of the cosmic substance Okidanokh from a planet's atmosphere is very similar to (corresponds to) the conscious destruction in the human psyche of the labors and results of the First-Sacred-Cause of everything that exists (God's Love and Divine plan for humans).

Whoa! The strong hint here is that a similar process of creating electricity takes place within the hearts and minds of humans on Earth when they reject God and proper contemplation through creating artificial values—resulting in wars, hatred and other assorted conflicts. (Ancient societies did discover electric power and even invented batteries, but they all strangely abandoned this technology and did not care to advance it.)

Beelzebub, remembering the earlier experiments of Rakhoorkh's father, Gornahoor Harharkh (whereby the blending, clashing and destruction of the *active* and *passive* parts of Okidanokh [incomplete Djartklom] created "electricity"), made him suddenly realize the cause of why the Martian king observed a deterioration in the mental potencies of his subjects. The now widespread use of electricity on the planet Earth was sucking off the Okidanokh from other planets in the solar system and causing their inhabitants to become more and more lethargic (will-lessness).

Whether one believes that the use of electricity destroys a cosmic substance that supports proper mental activity in humans or not, certainly electrical appliances on Earth are designed to make our lives easier and require less thought. (Kids today don't need to learn how to add, subtract, multiply or divide—they now have a calculator in their hand. Mobile phones and computer screens don't make us wiser—just more efficient. People are having more artificial [and impersonal] relationships with others, communicating through advanced technology.)

Destroying the substance Okidanokh to extract electricity for naïvely egoistic aims indeed throws out God's wise cosmic plan (and third reconciling force).

The point that electricity creates "artifical light" is also a metaphor, used by Gurdjieff to communicate the concept that contemporary humans have created an artificial and destructive intellect based on *opposites*. This artificial mentality (and limited mechanical attention) is represented by both the wrongly ordered corporeal memory of earth-humans and the Kundabuffer, which is the Moon's representative within the microcosmos (smaller world) of earth-humans.

(Swedenborg would agree that the satellite Moon, by itself, corresponds to man's illusory self-importance and self-intelligence, which happens when natural knowledge is separated from spiritual knowledge [and knowledge of being] based on genuine mutual love. The reason for this is that, like the Moon, which is not a true source of light but only reflects it, humankind fails to see that they are not the source of wisdom, but at best, only reflect it. In the "Revelations" chapter of the Holy Bible, a pregnant woman is depicted as standing above the Moon. This symbolizes a higher orientation of the heart toward spiritual influences.)

Beelzebub also comes to realize that individuals, who through practical *self-confrontation* and *being-Partkdolg-duty*, and who come to experience and understand the same hardships in others, are far more competent and helpful to the rest of the world than the angels or cherubim—who were initially and more easily prepared before the "Fall" (pre-Kundabuffer age) and who carried no "baggage."

In other words, early three-brained beings on Earth, who were instinctively aligned to Heaven, can not be as helpful to us as those later flawed humans, who endured and challenged their personal flaws. (Perhaps this is why Swedenborg observed that the Heaven of our early celestial ancestors is separated from the Heaven of later generations.)

At this point in the story, a vibration is sent throughout the ship *Karnak*, which tells the passengers that they are now to assemble in that special room to collectively absorb, *in a sacred way*, the second being-food. (Again, this is the *contemplating* of one's true significance and the significance of others.)

SUMMARY

■ The King of Mars notices that his subjects are losing their potency for self-perfection and asks Beelzebub to look into the matter.

■ Beelzebub, after his divine pardon, goes to Saturn to exchange spaceships for his long journey back to his birth planet, Karatas. While staying on Saturn he learns some surprising details about the extraction of electricity.

■ Beelzebub learns that earth-humans' extraction of electricity from the atmosphere is hurting the entire solar system, especially decreasing the *active contemplation* in three brained-beings and making everyone lazier.

■ The destruction of Okindanokh to create electricity (for naïvely egoistic aims) is very similar and analogous (almost equivalent) to humans rejecting God's plan for salvation and adopting a more artificial lifestyle.

CHAPTER 46

"Beelzebub explains to his grandson the significance of the form and sequence which he chose for expounding the information concerning man"

In his book *Views from the Real World*, Gurdjieff states, "The secret of being able to assimilate the involving part of air is to try to realize your true significance, and the true significance of those around you . . ." (page 195). Involving? Yes, all true "nutrition" must be in a passive state to be assimilated properly by the active processes of a living organism as any kind of food, including the air we breathe and also the information coming into our organs of sensation.

This is even a cosmic principle for how God's eternal *Truth* (which is information) becomes rendered as "food." It is made passive so it can be digested, absorbed and acted upon, and thereby appropriated—becoming a real part of our deeper spiritual (inner) fabric. (When individuals take part in genuine spiritual growth they acquire important substances from both the surrounding air and from the Spiritual Sun—that will change the center of gravity of their blood, directing its path to more dynamic blood vessels—according to the Fulasnitamnian-Zoostat (tempo-of-life) principle.

So this "eating" is what Beelzebub and members of his tribe were again doing in that special room of their spaceship in which they collectively and consciously absorbed the passive elements out of their second being-food (air). This practice, when properly understood, seems to point us to a forgotten but very noble ritual of our past, and tells us humans that we are all disregarding something very special in our daily approach to life.

This disregard of cosmic responsibility, even in the way we breathe, is a symptom of our being psycho-spiritually *asleep* at the wheel, which adversely affects our tempo-of-life and our blood circulation. (Swedenborg observed that our breathing corresponds to the way we think.)

After taking in this second being-food in a sacred and conscious way, Beelzebub goes to his cabin to stick his old decrepit "tail" into a certain liquid to cool it off. (Tails symbolize the outermost manifestation and projection of one's *inner* qualities, which can heat up during prolonged intense activity.) As Beelzebub resumes his epic Tales and returns to the area of the spaceship where everyone had gathered for most of the trip, he notices something that concerns him.

Hassein is now weeping.

Beelzebub addresses Hassein with his concern. His grandson first responds in a most technical way. He had been pondering his grandfather's description of the ill-fated humans on the planet Earth. This pondering caused a new and unaccustomed "tempo" to proceed within the normal and whole tempo (blood flow) of his general presence. Hassein also realizes that when this new tempo finally harmonizes with the other tempos of his common organic functioning, the weeping would come to an end.

This heightened impulse of sadness for earth-humans struck Hassein's full being, while he was taking part in the sacred ritual of feeding on the second being-food (in which one considers their own significance and the significance of others). Associative thoughts then arose in Hassein's mind during this sacred process in which he was saddened by the fact that earth-beings, through no fault of their own, but because of their ancestors having an organ implanted in them by sacred individuals. (God did allow Adam to be put to sleep and no longer see reality, but only dreams.) Now their "higher being-bodies" were deprived of being properly coated and of experiencing the same kind of "bliss" that he himself felt during the sacred absorption of the second being-food (air). This bliss is what Swedenborg described as peace from the Lord. (*Apocalypse Explained*, n. 365b.)

Beelzebub looks at his grandson with a loving smile, and is grateful that during his Tales, Hassein did not "inwardly sleep" but kept his proper mental focus. Beelzebub tells Hassein that he is happy that this "crisis" is taking place in his grandson, because it will help him mature as he reaches closer to the age of responsible existence. Such a disquieting mental state is essential for the cultivating of a harmonious and positive tempo during one's life.

Beelzebub then continues his theme of God's ultimate plan.

He tells Hassein that his sobbing ensured that the proper data for forming a foundation of Reasoning based on the direct formulation of our COMMON FATHER in words that now are placed over the chief "entrance" of the holy planet Purgatory would occur in his grandson. These words are:

"ONLY – HE – MAY – ENTER – HERE – WHO – PUTS – HIM – SELF – IN – THE – POSITION – OF – THE – OTHER – RESULTS – OF – MY – LABORS." This thought is similar to the concept of "walking in another person's shoes." Gurdjieff called this effort "external considering" which removes us from our habitual self-centeredness.

Beelzebub comforts and ensures Hassein that this exact kind of empathy and sincere sobbing was activated during his personal feelings of bliss, while remembering, at the same time, that others were deprived of it. To repeat, Beelzebub is quite happy and grateful that this crisis was taking place at a time during young Hassein's development, because ideas and worldviews were being formed in him from outside exchanges of energy, that is, from all kinds of external data and influences.

Beelzebub now explains to Hassein that he delivered his Tales in a special sequence (order), which would be most beneficial for the youth's education (and ours). The purpose of this conscious form and sequence of storytelling was to assure that his grandson's various functions would learn and harmonize in a way that produced "sane-mentation." It was in this manner and order that he chose to reveal to Hassein the various things concerning the lives of earth-humans.

To accomplish this, he applied two principles. The first principle was to tell the story as an objective third party so that Hassein would not form convictions mechanically based on the opinions of another. (Swedenborg described this flawed approach as having the faith of another, who was deemed worthy of credit, within oneself—and not from one's own seeing or understanding, *Apocalypse Explained*, n. 232.)

The second principle was to convey his Tales in a premeditated and selected sequence (Swedenborg's Doctrine of Series), the history of the inner and outer lives of the earth-humans, which has lawfully led to the abnormalities of their psyche. This sequence provided the data from which Hassein could form his own conclusions through his own being-efforts and legitimate active mentation, creating the required "Egoplastikoori" (new sensing or perceiving organs) for removing any doubts.

This calculated unfolding of information (truth advancing) would promote the proper elaboration of the *reconciling* substances of *Abrustdonis* and *Helkdonis* for the coating and perfecting of both of Hassein's higher being-bodies. This elaboration comes from the development of a proper level of *understanding* (which adds new spiritual qualities and the "sublimation" of one's "seed" and prolific principle). Swedenborg also mentioned that the human understanding is the medium whereby the Lord God now reforms a person's heart and will. *Apocalypse Explained*, n. 295 [b].

Beelzebub brings up an earlier discussion about how earth-humans tend to confuse the two mental values of "knowledge" and "understanding." Basically, the mental function of conscious "Reason-of-understanding" requires that through being-contemplation, data and information becomes an inseparable part of an individual's fabric, creating a "knowledge of being." In other words, "to know thyself." (Remember, that Beelzebub was protected from *poisonous vibrations* that would produce a boil on his leg by the Bokharian dervish, Hadji-Asvatz-Troov, because he and his tribe had developed their "knowledge of being," which is above the mental operation of acquiring data.)

Furthermore, the more common *Reason-of-knowing* (memory knowledge), which habitually operates in most contemporary earth-humans, causes new inputs or impressions to be only tempo-rary, whereby such information must be *freshened*, and repeated often, or it will "evaporate" out of the presence of a three-brained being. Modern education works mostly under this second principle, called "learning by rote." Under such conditions even *truth* can't protect people! (In fact, Swedenborg observed that this kind of important knowledge, which doesn't really belong to us inwardly, is gradually removed in the Spiritual world, so that all we really end up knowing is kept in perfect consonance with what we love and actually intend.)

But Beelzebub (through Gurdjieff) is now going to offer a more detailed illustration of the differences between these two kinds of knowing—based on the cosmic triad and universal law.

The two distinct mental functions of "Reason-of-knowing" and "Reason-of-understanding" operate under different actualizations within the three separate holy forces of the Sacred Triamazikamno (Law of Threefoldness). During the formation in an individual of the "Reason-of-knowing," all kinds of contradictory data stored in the corporeal memory function serves as both affirming (positive) and denying (negative) principles, and the new impressions coming into our senses from the circumfluent world serve as the third (or recon-ciling) principle between the two. In this case all outside data merely serves to sustain one's limited, subjective views and cause *acciden-tal* and automatic behavior from the neutralizing influence of such external inputs (even "dead" rocks respond to external influences).

In the spiritual realm, Swedenborg observed that his first tutor and brother-in-law, Erik Benzelius, had to change his notion that all true reasoning was a manifestation of data in the memory function. That is, Erik had wrongly embraced the principle of the *Reason-of-knowing*. But this would change.

Explaining the two types of human mental functioning from the strict cosmic *law of triads* makes our thinking less fuzzy, vague or flat, whereby the two kinds of operations can stand out so clearly that the differences between them become unchallengeable—even by all the world's different faith systems and their various teachings about the doctrines of salvation!

Beelzebub further illustrates this difference in that the human psyche uses the Sacred Triamazikamno (Law of Threefoldness) in a completely *different order* when it has obtained the "Reason-of-un-derstanding" (of one's true being). During the process of the "Reason-of-understanding" newly perceived impressions become the *active* force. The *passive* force is represented by *corresponding* data already present and stored in one's memory. The *neutralizing* force (third holy force, or "Holy Spirit") is represented by the personal striving, inner combat and conscious efforts of the individual perfect-ing one's true God-given individuality and potentials.

The distinct and spiritual being-strivings (called being-Autoko-lizikners) are formed in all three brain localizations of three-brained beings, exclusively from the results of a person actualizing his or her cosmic "being-Partkdolg-duty." In other words, this inner effort and duty causes similar (or corresponding) notions to become equally fixed and *harmonically fused together* in all three earth-human mental divisions (whereby they can all act together as an individual's third force in life and become one's eternal and immovable property). This fusion creates in three-brained beings a continuing desire to seek out only certain spiritually relevant information.

So then, the more beneficial "Reason-of-understanding" is created through the active contemplation from what Beelzebub calls "Zern-ofookalnian-friction" which alone produces the sacred substances Abrustdonis and *Helkdonis* of higher triads (to assist in the evolution of a person's sex energy) for the coating and perfecting of both of a person's higher being-bodies. (Swedenborg would describe "Zern-ofookalnian-friction" as *temptation* and *spiritual combat*, creating the heat to fuse together an inner body of the spirit.)

It is only through this challenging process of conscious mentation that newly perceived ideas are properly arranged into an organized bio-series of order with the other data already in the memory. (This is why *Beelzebub's Tales* was written in a style that forces us to confront strange new ideas that can cause us some doubt, creating a more vivified *inner* organization.)

The resulting psychic organization in the human understanding from this conflict also brings about a new bio-reality (spiritual body) and utility within us. (Swedenborg maintained that this spiritual organization creates new organs and functions within us.)

That is why seeking affirmation from others, whether from friends or even supportive church communities, only shuts this sacred process of *inner clashing* down! This is one of the most diffi-cult notions for even well-meaning people to accept—because they believe (prefer) that love (gentleness and friendly deeds) works well enough, without having to experience the discomfort of inner conflict. But Swedenborg is adamant that love only comes from God. So our acts of friendship can only become genuine from spiritual *reformation, regeneration,* and *repentance.* Innocence must be obtained through sacrificing mere outer actions of caring and the hope of receiving peer approval.

(Swedenborg discovered that spiritual bodies [higher being-bod-ies] are organized and structured around new levels of usefulness, that is, one's particular manifestation of third force through a genu-ine sacrifice of one's self-love.)

Interestingly, Swedenborg also stated that the mental conflict (Zernofookalnian-friction) needed to promote human spiritual ratio-nality is created by *"mixing truth with ideas that cause doubt"* (*Arcana Coelestia,* n. 7298 [2]). This mixture of ideas forces one to actively use his or her noggin in new ways (called *pondering* and *contemplation*).

Again, Gurdjieff, throughout his Tales, is a master at mixing the two to ensure this conflict and friction takes place among his readers.

This process of inner conflict perfects the quality of one's true identity and lawfully leads to a psycho-spiritual re-organization, as ideas are organically arranged into a new value system and coherent series, whereby they can become *classified*. Swedenborg even claimed that this new organic order represented actual *genera* and *species* in the evolution of the *inner ecosystem* of three-brained beings. (That is why animals and plants in Holy Scripture can lawfully symbolize, [correspond to] various human *feelings* and *thoughts* arranged in their proper order.)

We must seriously come to realize that not only is one's *understanding of being* dependent on a person's ability to arrange and organize data into their proper series (through contemplation and sincere self-examination) but that this new inner arrangement is to be looked at as the development of a *real psycho-organic structure* that forms the spiritual body (higher being-body) of a person's spirit. No genuine development ever takes place (even spiritual) abstracted from real forms and organized structures. Swedenborg stated that ideas— even non-material ideas—are real finite forms and that the human understanding acts like a body to house one's loves and affections.

(Those who are oblivious to this organic self-challenging procedure, even if they are well-meaning, will suffer the proper purifying process, which is painful, in the Spiritual World—Gurdjieff's *Holy Planet Purgatory*. Swedenborg even observed many human spirits suffering greatly in the Spiritual World before being introduced into Heaven.)

Both Swedenborg and Gurdjieff also refer to this cosmic organizing process (in accordance with sacred guidance), as a formation of "armies"—*to do battle with false ideas*. This new inner organization of human ideas into a more sacred order is also alluded to in Exodus (6:26), by God's command to lead the Israelites out of Egypt, symbolizing memory data and ideas arranged "according to their armies." Gurdjieff and Swedenborg both understand that this special arrangement and order of the things in our heart and mind is God's design for our salvation.

Truth always fights falsities.

But this cosmic battle rarely happens among most earth-humans who live merely terrestrial lives or worship as automatons. Rather than obtaining the proper classification of data (inner organizing) in one's value system, the more common "Reason-of-knowing" in most earth-humans, only allows newly sensed impressions to settle in three-brained beings at *random* or willy-nilly. This leads to artificial worldviews that are disconnected from reality and not based on the whole picture. Swedenborg stated that angels view all things in terms of *comprehensive wholes*. (Gurdjieff's Enneagram arranges all series of coherent process into such comprehensive wholes and orbs. Swedenborg calls this arrangement the Circle of Life.)

But under the artificial and limited system of habitual mentation called "Reason-of-knowing," even valuable knowledge is reduced to mere random information and disjointed data (like desert sands), providing no significant usefulness for the eternal welfare of an individual who comes by it (other than for pretense). Because of this, earth-humans only acquire subjective memory-knowledge in their lives, which has nothing to do with "Objective Knowledge" (universal truths that God intends for us to have and to be used for our self-perfecting).

Beelzebub admits to Hassein that he learned about the details of how to make sure a story would create *Zernofookalnian-friction* (real contemplation) in humans so that new impressions could be properly used for the formation of their "Reason-of-understanding" (*truly knowing oneself*) during his investigations as a "professional hypnotist."

As a hypnotist, he discovered the "laws-of-the-fixing-and-unfixing-of-ideas-in-localizations." So he constructed his Tales in a way that would create legitimate being-logical confrontation within his grandson (and us) so that the "totality of information" of his Tales would not settle in Hassein's mind randomly as mere "data and stuff," and therefore, without generating any genuine understanding of it all.

(It may be pure conjecture on my part, but I believe that Gurdjieff wrote this work not just from the order of the laws of the sacred Triamazikamno but also according to the Laws of Sevenfoldness—based on how these two fundamental laws work together within the context of the *Enneagram*, discussed in Chapter 39. But since my making such an additional effort to provide extra details about the Enneagram would only confuse the matter and make it more obscure, I will refrain and perhaps put these views in another book to be written later on. However, in one of my previous books, *Proving God*, I suggested and offered some evidence that Gurdjieff's Enneagram is Swedenborg's "Circle of Life.")

It was by his cosmic story-telling strategy of *form and sequence* that Beelzebub shared with Hassein details of the psyche of earth-humans, as well as the laws governing the universe on all its scales, so that *Zernofookalnian-friction* could proceed in his grandson's youthful thinking. The resulting manifestation of this contemplation had caused his grandson's sincere weeping for the earth-humans. This weeping also assured Beelzebub that the time spent conversing with his grandson was not done in vain.

As they were getting closer to their home planet Karatas, Beelzebub tells his grandson that it is time to take a rest from his active mentation and simply go with the flow of the "harmony of the common-cosmic tempo."

Beelzebub tells his grandson that the higher, spiritualized parts of his being should always treat his lower (and unconscious) physical body with fairness and never demand more of it than it is able to give. In order that one's planetary body can properly serve the essence of one's spirit, it should not be pushed beyond its inherent possibilities. (Otherwise one's tail would overheat—or even worse!)

Also, in addressing the topic of *Justice* further, Beelzebub tells Hassein that one must de-activate certain mental functions from time to time in order that the unconscious part (cerebellum and the physical body) of a human being can gradually blend any newly acquired (recently learned) subjective "tempos" with the objective tempo of our common Megalocosmos. (Swedenborg agrees and says in his anatomical writings, that during rest and sleep, the involuntary part of the brain in humans, or *Cerebellum*, restores order and harmony to the whole organic system from the various passions and personal attitudes of the faulty voluntary mind and its cerebrum. He also mentioned that heavenly forces flow into the human cerebellum first, which is why it is usually in harmony with the objective "tempos" of God's universal creation. But when conscious changes are made in one's life and thinking, this needs to gradually align and harmonize itself to all the current tempos of one's living processes before creating a new, more harmonious general tempo.)

Beelzebub warns Hassein that if one does not get proper rest and allow this process to proceed gradually, within the cosmic scheme of things, undesirable results will come from such extended or overactive mentation, which inevitably leads to a harmful tempo and *lopsided* development. He then stresses that earth-humans frequently become such lopsided beings at their maturity.

Furthermore, the gradual process of procuring a proper change of tempo requires that such a change, from the results spiritualized in a person's life, must proceed equally in all three brain-localizations— the *"thinking-center," "feeling center,"* and *"moving-motor-center."* Swedenborg identified the harmony of similar distinct psychic functions in humans as the "will," the "understanding," and their unifying marriage, through *use*, in the reconciling "action" of the motor neurons and their nerves. These *three* distinct brain-functions must operate in corresponding (unified) ways, and therefore have corresponding aims.

(Gurdjieff had developed his three brain localizations to such a harmonic order that he was able to fully heal himself from his automobile crash.)

SUMMARY

■ Beelzebub notices that Hassein is crying over the crises in his mind concerning his own feelings of bliss and the horrible situation earth-humans are now in.

■ Beelzebub is pleased to see this crisis happening to his grandson, because it will help perfect him toward obtaining a responsible existence, based on the *Reason-of-understanding* instead of the *Reason-of-knowing.*

■ These two distinct forms of the human intellect use the Law of Threefoldness (Triamazikamno) in different ways. In those individuals whose intellect functions from mere memory-data, the active and passive principles both operate from one's memory and the reconciling principle comes from all-new external sensory impressions coming from the circumfluent world—which is willy-nilly. This causes *automatic* and *mechanical* behavior based on external stimuli—thus, living like a rock.

■ A person, who has developed the more noble *Reason-of-understanding,* has his *active* principle (from the Law of Triads) in the new impressions entering any part of his psyche. The *passive* part is represented by corresponding data already present in the psyche (memory). But the third or *reconciling* principle comes from the conscious efforts one makes between any conflicts created from the active and passive principles making contact with each other. As an example, this conflict results when our behavior (passions) favors something that is at odds with our stated intellectual convictions and forces us to reconcile both of these opposite *tuggings.* This voluntary contact allows the emergence of real *conscience* to act as a reconciling force.

■ This voluntary contact and conflict also fuses together a spiritual body (from one's third force or conscience) by weaving together a new bio-form arranged according to new levels of *usefulness.*

■ The true purpose of religion is to activate this conflict in us.

CHAPTER 47

"The inevitable result of impartial mentation"

Suddenly a pale blue light flashes throughout the spaceship *Karnak*, indicating that they were slowing down and that one of the great Cosmic *Egolionopties* in the universe had arrived and pulled up beside their spaceship!

With Beelzebub's symbolic clue that there are only *four* Egolionopties in the whole created universe, my best guess is that an Egolionopty is a special *supra*-natural (spiritual) vehicle, representing *the means of conjoining with God through the highest love,* and therefore, this cosmic event is on the order of what Ezekiel observed in his famous biblical vision concerning four living creatures and their "divine" mode of transportation (wheels within wheels).

(The color "Blue" also signifies the *truth of celestial love.*)

All the passengers and crew of the Karnak gathered in the main hall to greet this most sacred visitation. In one of their hands they were each holding a branch of *myrtle*—which Swedenborg tells us symbolizes *those who are willing to learn.*

The scene that follows is chock full of such spiritual symbolism.

A procession of archangels, angels, cherubim and seraphim enters into the ship's main hall from this Cosmic Egolionopty—and, they are holding palm branches! The "palm branches" are similar to the welcoming of Jesus into Jerusalem. (Swedenborg states that palm branches symbolize the *wisdom from God's goodness* and its *pleasantness.*)

At the head of the procession was a venerable archangel being closely followed by two cherubim carrying a special container radiating an orange glow. (This special container reminds me of the *Ark of the Covenant,* which glowed as it was carried by the Israelites! Furthermore, "orange" represents a quality of Spiritual Love from which Divine Truth is derived.)

The procession stops right near Beelzebub and the members of his tribe. Then everyone joins in to sing the "Hymn to our ENDLESS-NESS." After the singing of the sacred Hymn, the venerable archangel tells Beelzebub that because of his merits and divine pardon, he has personally come here to officially restore what had been taken away— Beelzebub's horns! (Horns have an interesting spiritual meaning—*the power of Truth in ultimates.*)

The venerable archangel takes a sacred *rod* from the container carried by the two cherubim. (Swedenborg described a sacred rod as symbolizing the "power of Divine Truth from the Word of God.") When such a sacred rod is waved or directed toward something, it further symbolizes divine power "which is shown" (*Arcana Coelestia*, n. 7292, 7295). It becomes visible and obvious to observers. Everyone present then gets down on one knee as the angels and cherubim sing more sacred canticles. With the sacred rod, the venerable archangel goes through a special ritual to restore the horns to Beelzebub, who is also kneeling (in a passive posture).

Many of those in the room are asked to *sacrifice* and transfer some of the material from their own horns to this process. In a gesture of support, they touch the sacred rod and share their good wishes and good vibes to promote the anticipated new horn growth atop Beelzebub's head. Since the members of Beelzebub's tribe display the virility and degree of their Reason by the size of their own horns (symbolizing the power of truth in one's faith) on their head, all in the room become anxious to see to what length Beelzebub's horns would now develop and grow.

Little by little, horns began to appear atop Beelzebub's head. Excitement grows as these horns split into their first fork, then again, and again and again and again! (With each new fork or branching of the horns, there was signified a new measurement and complexity of Beelzebub's powers of Reasoning.) Everyone soon falls prostrate, including the old archangel, before Beelzebub—as his horns eventually forked for an amazing and unprecedented fifth time! This meant that Beelzebub had reached the gradation of reasoning called the sacred *Podkoolad* and was only one gradation below the sacred Anklad (the highest level a finite and created being could obtain in God's universe) and was just three degrees below the Absolute Reason of the Creator.

Beelzebub had succeeded in reaching a level even higher than that of the venerable archangel who was performing the ritual! As Beelzebub stood up, he looked "transfigured" with his new majestic horns. (Transfiguration symbolizes that the onlookers were getting a deeper and more holy view—from their more interior spiritual eyes—of Beelzebub's new significance. He now represented a certain level of glory of God's Word and laws—that is, a special degree of conjoining his three-brained being-ness with God's divinity.)

The archangel then tells the audience of the transspace ship, that Beelzebub's new worthiness as one of the sons of their COMMON FATHER should serve as inspiration for all of them to continue their struggles against their personal denying source (passivity) through *conscious labors* and *intentional sufferings*. After this proclamation, the venerable archangel led the entire assembly in singing a final sacred canticle titled "I Rejoice." Then they returned to their Egolionopty and disappeared into space.

Hassein and the faithful servant Ahoon were deeply moved by the solemnity of the ceremony and the transfigured appearance of Beelzebub, resulting from his life's accomplishments. Ahoon suddenly feels remorse, that until now, because of life circumstances, he had failed to grasp the full significance of intensifying his own efforts of *being-Partkdolg-duty* (God's cosmic duty).

Hassein, witnessing all this, now senses even greater love and compassion toward Ahoon (and even for the three-brained beings of the planet Earth). He also feels gratitude that he was a part of a journey and story that allowed him to personally experience such a great and rare event as his grandfather's newly formed horns—and their unprecedented degree of forking.

Beelzebub wishes for both of them to sit again and talk some more before their final landing on their birth planet Karatas. He asks Hassein if he has any remaining questions that could be stated briefly. He hopes that such a question will help him to find out to what extent his Tales about the strange psyche of earth-humans have promoted Hassein's own powers of logical mentation.

Hassein replies, except now addressing his grandfather as "Sacred Podkoolad" and the "cause of the cause of his arising." He asks Beelzebub what he would personally say to God if God summoned him about the question of whether it was still possible, by some means, to put earth-humans back on the proper path.

This question convinced Beelzebub that his stories had brought his grandson the desired psychic results of both contemplation and compassion. Then, with a serious countenance, Beelzebub stands up and (stretching his right hand outward and his left hand backward) looks off into the very depths of space and begins to give Hassein his answer. As he is doing this, a "something" *pale yellow* begins to envelop him, representing some holy quality (like a halo).

Beelzebub answers Hassein that he would personally tell God that the only means remaining to save the humans of the planet Earth would be to implant again a new organ in them, much like the organ Kundabuffer. However, this new organ would manifest, during the earth-human's entire existence, the unique property of always reminding them of their *inevitable death* and the deaths of everyone else upon whom their eyes gaze, or attention rests. Only such an organ, producing that kind of constant pressure of awareness, could de-crystallize the *egoism* that has swallowed up the whole of their essence, and has produced only abnormalities in their lives and to God's plans.

Since we do not have such an organ, we earth-humans must consciously create (or awaken) such a "reminding-organ" from our own spiritual efforts and conscious duty. This organ is called spiritual *conscience*. (Mark Twain seemed to have acknowledged the importance of this awakening function—of contemplating the inevitability of one's death. And perhaps he even made some efforts in this direction.)

SUMMARY

■ This chapter is loaded with spiritual symbolism, similar to what Swedenborg understood such heavenly and abstracted terms to mean.

■ As Beelzebub and his crew got closer to their birth-planet Karatas, their transspace ship was boarded by a great divine commission—consisting of archangels, angels, cherubim, and seraphim.

■ The commission had arrived to restore Beelzebub's horns through a sacred ceremony, because of his merits and divine pardon.

■ (The number of "forks" in one's horns determines the level of reason that one has obtained in life.)

■ In that sacred ceremony, the venerable archangel has everyone grab hold of a special rod, and asks all of them to sacrifice, and to share, in the good wishes toward Beelzebub in order to help with the growth of his horns.

■ To everyone's surprise, Beelzebub's horns produce *five* forks! This means he has reached a level of reasoning just three degrees lower than the Creator and one degree lower than is obtainable for finite three-brained beings.

■ Beelzebub then becomes *transfigured* before everyone's eyes.

■ When asked, Beelzebub says he would tell God that what earth-humans now need to turn things around (and destroy their egoism) is a new organ to be implanted in them, that would constantly remind them of their inevitable death and the inevitable deaths of all those around them.

CHAPTER 48

"From the Author — an 'Afterword'"

In his closing epilogue, Gurdjieff reveals that he has worked on the manuscript for *Beelzebub's Tales* under intense mental pressure for six years. He describes this particular writing project as the first book in a series of three, in which he will share his discoveries, made over an entire lifetime of great personal challenges.

Gurdjieff states that *Beelzebub's Tales* was written "to corrode without mercy all the rubbish accumulated during the ages in human mentation." The second book in the series (titled *Meetings With Remarkable Men*) would be written to offer "new constructional material" to replace that rubbish. And finally, the third book (*Life Is Real Only Then, When "I Am"*) would provide the means "to build a new world" out of that rubbish.

Gurdjieff indicates that he went back over his "Preface" (to this book), written six years earlier, titled "The Arousing of Thought," and decided that he needed to write an *Afterword*. This new effort would ensure that a "logical fusion," was formed between the beginning and end of the book—by taking ideas from the Preface and making sure they *corresponded* to the conclusion of his book ("ends" returning to their first principles).

He admits that this mentally intense writing project seemed to take more than six terrestrial years because, according to the ancient science called "the law of association of human mentation" known to only a handful of contemporary earth-humans, "the sensing of the flow of time is proportional to the quality and quantity of the flow of thoughts." And Gurdjieff's writing labors certainly contained both an unmatched quality and quantity of ideas. So this represents a period in which he was able to stretch out his lifespan (life experiences) by a more intricate and deeper sensing of processes and phenomena occurring during that period of the flow of time!

Furthermore, Gurdjieff's extreme mental activity during these six years of writing was motivated by the *self-willed* acknowledgement of his own inevitable death (and that his time on Earth to get all his valuable ideas across to humans was being threatened). In fact, he was in the challenging situation of starting his epic writing project while still recovering from a most serious automobile accident, which the medical experts believed should have ended his life.

The automobile accident was a strange event. He is said to have hit a tree at 80 miles an hour, yet somehow he got out of the car and laid himself off to the side of the road. (He had asked a car repairman to check the brakes a day before the accident.) One thing is for certain. Gurdjieff consciously used this tragic event to make the point that humans—even specialists—understand little about the workings of the real world and what a person could accomplish.

(It may even be that Gurdjieff actually planned the car accident to make his point. I have my suspicions.)

Gurdjieff also admits that one of his personal weaknesses was getting satisfaction from watching the facial expressions of those who represented contemporary science, and who were baffled by how such a mangled body (from the car accident) could heal itself. Gurdjieff chalks up this feat of unprecedented healing to the fact that his correctly disciplined "spirit" had never once entertained the normally expected state of depression.

Gurdjieff confesses that he even became more energized from both his repeated disappointment in modern human academia to grasp reality, and an inner dictate and commandment formed in his childhood psyche—that "the highest aim and sense of human life is the striving to attain the welfare of one's neighbor."

(Swedenborg would have nodded and applauded this spiritual aim of self-sacrifice for the benefit of others. He, too, was disappointed in human academia and his book *The Worship and Love of God* represented his alternative view to their low-level and flawed worldly thinking—which was so full of false pride.)

Such a noble aim to sincerely seek the welfare of others (which is one of the two great commandments that Jesus spoke about, and from which all the other sacred laws hang) was possible only through the conscious renunciation (and inner death) of one's own self-importance and self-centeredness. (This "spiritual death" lies at the core of human salvation for all religions, and qualifies our ability to perform genuine good in the world, from the principle of *innocence*.)

At this point the reader is made acutely aware of the self-sacrifice and personal hardships Gurdjieff himself endured, in order to share his rarified and vast information with humankind. He did not make a penny on this manuscript, in spite of all the long years he put into it. This is an act of real heavenly love (both to God and humankind). With each reading, I became more aware of Gurdjieff's unselfish love for humanity—even when he was sharing seemingly unflattering and harsh information about us all.

The world isn't getting any better, simply because we ourselves are not getting any better!

Reflecting upon the data in the various chapters of his book, Gurdjieff is finally quite satisfied that it will produce unusual impressions (shocks) in the minds of his readers, and these shocks will lead to "substantial results" (it has in me). He states that due to his acquired ability to penetrate the psyche of humans with complete impartiality, and the sincere impulse called "love of kind," he decides to add nothing more to this first book—except some previously delivered lectures read by an advanced pupil at his "Institute-for-the-Harmonious-Development-of-Man," outside Paris (which he was now, regretfully, closing).

These original lectures contained further information fully corresponding to the aim and the Preface of this first series of his writing. Therefore, this additional information would help to finalize the "concluding chord" of his first book and create the perfect fusion (correspondence) between his Foreword and Afterword (thus making it, I believe, a complete octave—a comprehensive whole.)

Gurdjieff had decided to close down his Institute because it became painfully clear to him that as he got older, other people would not be able to step up and make the same *superhuman* efforts to keep the institution viable. He also observed that many of his top pupils were threatening the very gist of his work—because of their predisposition toward becoming *self-important* (Hasnamuss individuals), a predisposition which his Institute tried to uproot. So he dismantled it.

But to keep his ideas alive and pristine, he next chose to become an author, so that they would survive his inevitable death. (One of the main criticisms of Gurdjieff's system is that he failed to create individuals who obtained a similar level of self-perfection as its founder and teacher. That is like criticizing Swedenborg's theology for not creating, immediately from the human race, angels of the highest heavens. The principle of one's self-importance is extremely difficult to curb—even with the Lord God's help.)

The following lecture by Gurdjieff is provided here (in an appended form) for the benefit of those readers who seriously seek to become true "images of God."

THE VARIETY, ACCORDING TO LAW, OF
THE MANIFESTATIONS OF HUMAN INDIVIDUALITY
(Last read in New York in the Neighborhood Playhouse, January 1924)

I will address (paraphrase) the main points made in this early lecture, which concern the investigations and researches made at the Institute-for-the-Harmonious-Development-of-Man according to the methods developed by George Gurdjieff.

These researches lead to the elucidation and conviction that *all* humans, regardless of their heredity and surrounding environments, consist of four definite and distinct personalities. (Swedenborg also promoted the concept that humans possessed several distinct [or discrete] cognitive functions, which could operate independently as a limited and disjointed manifestation of individuality, or they could develop these functions to work harmoniously together through one's spiritual efforts.)

The first of these four independent personalities consists of the *automatic functioning* proper to man and all other animals, which includes the sensory and motor nerve system of the brain. (Swedenborg, who first developed a neuron theory of the brain, also identified this same lower level of brain functioning as the corporeal/sensual mind or *external natural mind*, which includes memory-data and the life of the physical body.) This "lower" mind is totally *mechanical* and reflexive. It is our habitual mind. (Swedenborg calls the artificial quality of thought of such an external mind as "pulmonary" [*True Christian Religion*, n. 593]. Both Gurdjieff and Swedenborg are in agreement that without sincere spiritual development, this level of thinking, or habitual mind, becomes both second nature and accepted as one's true state of consciousness, operating in our daily and worldly affairs and providing cover for our real egoistic passions.)

According to Gurdjieff, the second independent (discrete) functioning of the human psyche is one's *intellect*—that is, one's thinking capacity or "understanding" and "discernment," including the level of one's personal judgment.

The third discrete personality of human beings, *which represents the prime functioning of one's organism*, deals with the *emotional* or *feeling* operations in the human psyche (one's real loves). This central functioning subjectively favors certain new impressions over others according to one's heredity and the circumstances at play during one's preparatory upbringing. (In Swedenborg's various anatomical and psychological writings he describes this distinct brain function as the *animus* or *affection* of the cerebrum.)

Natural living or merely terrestrial living (with all its worldly concerns and pressures) only allows for these three separate personalities to develop in a way that leads to "automized functioning." (Living a Godless life only produces human robots.)

The fourth personality in humans is a *potential*.

It only comes from conscious spiritual growth, which *unifies* the disharmonious operations of the first three functions mentioned above. As a result, this higher (psychic) inclusiveness allows one's true individuality or legitimate "I" to surface. (Swedenborg describes this higher functioning in the mind as the *spiritual rational*—and its unfolding process is the emergence and development of one's God-given "remains" which serves as a plane on which genuine spiritual "conscience" develops and grows into an actual, but rarefied, new bodily organization.)

Furthermore, Gurdjieff suggests that each of these first three distinct mental functionings have their own "gravity-center-localizations" and their own organic bio-structures (neural substrates) to operate in, thus they usually develop apart from each other. So for these distinct functions to become holistically unified within a person's entire being-ness, they each require a special education to address their particular peculiarities and predispositions.

Unfortunately, modern education does not acknowledge nor does it provide the correct methods for the proper inner development and harmonizing of these three independent personalities to fuse together as a fourth type. (The Latin root of the word "religion" means to *bring together* or *bind*.) Without such inner harmony, humans exist as a pseudo "I" or a "Man-in-quotation-marks," not an image of God.

What I like most about Gurdjieff's explanations is that he strives to make them more and more viscerally clear to us. So he next offers a helpful analogy for our further grasping these distinct personalities and mental functions—as representing a *carriage*, a *horse*, and a *coachman*, having to carry competing passengers to different destinations.

Only those passengers who obtain genuine spiritual growth and a proper harmony between their distinct personalities become the rightful owner of this "hackney carriage" and enjoy perfect control over where it should go. But those who lack such unifying development simply pay a fare with great loss of control. The reason for this loss of control is that other passengers can also get in and pay their fares—but again, all these passengers have different destinations. (Swedenborg associates this constant change of passengers with various influences, good and bad, coming to us from beings in the Spiritual World—whom we must carry around.)

Gurdjieff points out that problems also exist concerning the design of the carriage, which represents our *physical/corporeal body* and its spinal brain system. It was originally designed to go over bumpy roads, so that its various lubricants could be spread by the various parts constantly being shaken. But in more modern times of increased convenience, this carriage (our bodily function) has preferred a more pleasurable path, traveling over "smoother roads," causing many breakdowns to occur—especially when it does have to occasionally endure a bumpy ride or two—because its parts got rusty quicker and it began to wear out prematurely. (Today our bodies similarly get rusty, living as "couch potatoes.")

In this creative analogy of a hackney carriage, the emotional (feeling) function of the human psyche is represented by the *horse*. This horse is harnessed to the carriage and must pull it. (It is our emotions and loves that pull our physical bodies in the desired direction.) Unfortunately, this horse has been treated so badly during its life (through the insensitive actions or negligence of others) that now, because of its solitude and lack of education (suffering from constant thrashing and vile abuse), never wants to go where the coachmen (our intellect) wants, and doesn't even want to pull the carriage anymore. Instead, its "inner life" is driven *deep inside* (becoming the subconscious mind) where it only cares about food and sex, and is always focused on running toward places where it can gratify these needs.

479

Never having been treated with any kindness, it will surrender to anyone who gives it the slightest caress and attention. (So it is prone to deceit and suggestibility.) In Swedenborg's terms, the human feeling function never develops *rationally* or with *conscience*.

The thinking function of the human psyche and personality is represented by the driver or "coachman." Gurdjieff describes the coachman as often being drunk, but he wears a top hat and flower in his lapel to feign cultivation and education. His desire for tips has taught him through the art of pretense to become a "flatterer." This function suffers from self-intoxication and unrestrained self-importance, from its independent and disjointed development. This humorous portrayal by Gurdjieff of the thinking function in contemporary humans reminds me of the *know-it-all* "Cliff Claven" character on the TV sitcom *Cheers*.

Because of modern education, no conditions are in place for a person to gain "ownership" of this hackney carriage—the three functionings of his psyche never work together or in spiritual correspondence. Therefore, these three parts develop *arbitrarily* during a person's lifetime and he or she is forever robbed of obtaining a real "I."

This is the picture of the contemporary human predicament. (The problem is that few of us see the arbitrariness in the development of functions in our lives.)

To complete this analogy between a "hackney carriage" and the separate parts of the human psyche, Gurdjieff adds that there are even similar (corresponding) connections between them—representing our three different types of blood!

The shafts connecting the horse to the carriage, symbolize the *red blood*, which connects a person's feeling-organization to their physical body. The "reins" between the coachmen and horse, which determines how well they will communicate, representing the higher blood called *Hanbledzoïn*. (Again, Swedenborg calls this purer blood the "Animal Spirit," and that it, too [the reins] must be purified by God's truth, *Apocalypse Explained*, n. 167). This rarified "magnetic" or middle blood is a substance produced and purified only by a person's intentionally made being-efforts (genuine spiritual transformation toward *rationality*).

> *I, Jehovah, search the heart, I prove the reins, even to give every man according to his ways, and according to the fruits of his works.*
> (Jeremiah, 17:10)

Unfortunately, modern education has led to the coachman, (thinking function in humans) to cease having any real effect on the horse (our feeling center), other than by means of the poorly constructed reins (poor or unpurified Hanbledzoïn). And now the human thinking function, though this imperfect connection, can only communicate three simple ideas to the emotional function: "right," "left," and "stop." (This, instead of going in a more spiritually rational direction and aim.)

The unique purpose of Gurdjieff's "Institute-for-the-Harmonious-Development-of-Man" was to educate each of these independent brain-functionings and personalities so that they could form the proper reciprocal relationship and join together, correspondingly, so that they would engender in a person his or her own legitimate "I." Without such development within the inner organization of man, humans cannot act under their own initiative (this creates inner slavery—especially among all the other passengers).

The researches of Gurdjieff's Institute categorically confirmed that everything without exception happens *through* contemporary man and there is absolutely nothing that he does *from himself*. This includes all things and activities involving personal, family, communal life, politics, science, art, philosophy or even religion. (So this slavery also includes those who clamor for social justice and equality in the world!)

Contemporary men and women are mere machines!

Humankind is only a more complex machine than other animals when it comes to reacting to *external stimuli*. Gurdjieff is insistent on this point—that humans are simply more complicated transforming apparatuses (transmitting stations) for cosmic forces. People are simply wind-up toys, set in motion by external forces, acting on springs that govern the lifespan of their three independently developing mind-functionings.

In other words, Gurdjieff denies the existence of real "will" within the presence of the average person now being born on Earth. Instead, what most humans call will, is simply the result of many contradictory desires passing though him or her at that moment. (Swedenborg stressed that only God has true *will* and *proprium* but God also shares that heavenly will with properly aligned individuals.)

That is why Gurdjieff claimed that real will is actually a sign of a very high degree of spiritual development. (While, according to Swedenborg, God has given humankind "free will," but humankind has distorted this gift into becoming mere *licence*, making us slaves to a slew of competing passions/passengers.) And while Gurdjieff's Institute admits to great inner possibilities for all humans, it denies them any real value or status—as a unit of God's creation, with proper individual conscious aims— especially as long as he or she remains as they are.

-◆- -◆- -◆-

To prove his point that humans lack a real, coherent will and inner dictate, another of Gurdjieff's early lectures is referred to next, in his *Afterword*.

In this second lecture, Gurdjieff sets up the scenario of an individual who, by all modern civilized standards, represents an *external* human success story. This person has plenty of money, luxury living conditions, and universal esteem and respect from those around him. In fact, many people rely on and are devoted to such a successful individual. One would assume that a person of this merit, who disposes his time as he pleases, is a patron of the arts, solves world problems over a cup of coffee, and even has interests in the development of latent spiritual forces, therefore possesses real "will" in life

Not so! Not by a long shot!

Even this so-called model of contemporary culture, whose very life and existence is deserving of imitation, and a person to be envied, has no real will at all, and is a slave to external stimuli.

Gurdjieff's lecture goes on to describe a typical day in the life of such a seemingly "successful" individual. I will refer to him simply as "Mr. X." But he can represent any one of us on a given day, responding to *external stimuli.*

"Mr. X first wakes up in the morning after having an upsetting dream. Although he is now awake, the depressing dream colors the mood of the day. When he goes to the bathroom to comb his hair he drops his brush. While fumbling to catch the brush, he breaks the expensive antique mirror.

Mr. X uses some choice words.

(I have personally argued with people who chalk up these "bummers" in life as something similar to having mere "bad hair days" and that there is nothing about these mishaps that reveal anything disturbing about the inner quality of their lives.)

Next, when Mr. X doesn't find his newspaper beside his morning coffee he takes it out on his servant. Mr. X leaves his house for a walk in the sunshine but then comes across someone lying in the street from drunkenness. Suddenly, by association, this drunkard reminds him of a drunkard he bumped into on the street after leaving a party somewhat tipsy himself. That association creates another new association within Mr. X concerning some food he had also eaten at the party.

Mr. X later stops at a café where he can find a pleasant moment for himself. He notices two attractive women sitting at a nearby table. He happens to hear one of the women say to the other "that is my kind of man" as she looks in his direction. Mr. X "inwardly rejoices" from hearing these flattering words. His mood is so transformed especially after personally introducing himself to this woman and spending some time with her that he forgets to take care of the business of the day. No bother, Mr. X can simply take care of his business with a phone call.

Later he makes his phone call but gets the wrong number. He calls again but reaches the same wrong man as before, who is now indignant and tells him off.

When Mr. X returns home, he slips on a small rug. He gets up and uses some foul language as his servant hands him a letter. The letter is flattering and comes from a person whose opinion he values. Mr. X's irritation is gradually transformed into a state of "pleasant embarrassment."

The point Gurdjieff is making here is that people rarely notice these drastic inconsistencies and wild swings of their character, which are driven solely by *external influences*. All day Mr. X was bounced around by one external influence and another (good and bad), like a cork bobbing up and down in the waves and currents of the open sea. Mr. X has no "inner fusion" between his various mental qualities or responses, and therefore, his sense of possessing true individuality and *true will* is all merely an illusion.

(This illusion is what Beelzebub was referring to early in the Tales when he stated that the organ Kundabuffer caused earth-people to see things topsy-turvy. This is why even a highly esteemed and talented person can lose it when he or she can't find the slippers under the bed in the morning.)

So, how can religion even be beneficial to earth-humans living under such self-delusion? Religion has become just another *external influence*. Unless, of course, one's religion is able to mercilessly penetrate and utterly destroy such a false self- illusion. But most religions have degenerated in ways that simply offer comfort and a calming effect toward our disjointed character. (I find that even the Swedenborgian Church is guilty of producing this calming effect on worshippers when it promotes bogus affirmation and outer acts of friendship as "community love and denomination building.")

We approach life (and religion) with an assumption about ourselves that just isn't true. We go through life in a *hypnotic state* and *trance*. Even God's Truth has no value to people unless it is allowed to reveal the stark (and unflattering) reality about our profoundly trance-like lives.

You can't offer something to someone who thinks he or she already possesses it. True individuality and a proper assessment of one's actual self-worth is something we all believe we currently possess. That is our self-delusion.

In most cases, we will never believe that we are hypnotized at all, and therefore, we wrongly cling to the notion that we already possess real consciousness and real will. Under this illusion, religion is seen simply as an "add-on" and as an enhancement of a positive state. Gurdjieff is trying to prove otherwise, by showing that we have distinct and disjointed personalities that are neither properly educated nor properly harmonized.

Hypnotism and trance is only possible because these psychic functions in earth-humans operate independently. The varieties of our personal aims (different passengers) are why the Bible states

"Man is legion." Without a unifying harmony between an individual's various psychic functions, one cannot claim to be a person "without quotation marks" or an "image of God."

-◆- -◆- -◆-

(A third Gurdjieff lecture is now discussed to further capture the negative human predicament.)

In this next lecture, humans are described as coming into the world with a "clean slate." This clean slate is filled up over time with all kinds of data-stuff and knowledge dealing with morality, duty, honor, conscience, etc. However, these noble teachings become quite ephemeral and trivial when one wakes up in the morning on the wrong side of the bed, or has a "bad hair day."

Rather than being a cause of real concern, these manifestations are chalked up as simply being "human nature." We are slaves to the idiosyncrasies of terrestrial life. We fail to see our own mechanicality and slavery to the world. But genuine spiritual growth represents freedom from this autonomized situation. God's eternal plan is to provide the means by which the human race can acquire real freedom (escaping Egypt, in the book of Exodus in the Old Testament, actually represents this new direction to obtain spiritual freedom and real will).

To escape Egypt properly (inwardly), one must seek freedom though the unity of all his or her independent parts—through harmonizing one's *feelings, intellect,* and *organic instinct.* This requires sincere (impartial) self-examination to recognize and verify that this inner unity is not there yet. One must truly "Know Thyself" (the *knowledge of being*) and struggle against the established subjectivity and mechanicality within each wrongly developed independent personality formed during "regular" life on Earth (which has become quite abnormal). Instead of simply going to church or studying religious doctrine, a person must come to understand and verify sensibly, the reality of one's mechanicality. Not just mentally or emotionally or physically, but with one's whole presence!

But we fail to notice our distinct and abnormal three-fold mechanical functioning!

This is a real "shocker" to our illusory worldview. Freeing oneself of this flawed belief system (false self-unity) requires making many unflattering and painful self-discoveries. This kind of self-observation requires unconditional sincerity and follow-through. (Swedenborg describes this introspection as necessary for regaining *innocence,* without which there can be no genuine humility. Also, self-examination is God's lawful method of promoting the need for greater conjunction between distinct mental aspects within our psyche. This sincerity is the only legitimate way to connect the *external* natural man (and its outer life) properly to the *internal* natural man. Thus allowing contact and conflict to occur between these distinct person-alities, which alone, permits one's God-given *remains* to develop further into a new spiritual reality in our conscious life.

This contact and unity between higher and lower realities in humans is the symbolism behind God creating both "a new Heaven and a new Earth."

Finding such sincerity to explore one's flaws and dirty laundry and measure this against our stated convictions is not as easy as one might hope (after all, we are going up against ourselves and what we currently feel is our most important self-image—regardless of what we say or do). It requires great courage and persistence (spiritual endurance) not to lose heart during this purging process.

We must shut our eyes to nothing. The resulting discoveries will inevitably shake up many of our deep-rooted (but false) convictions and lead to the death of one's old and former self. (This is the "death before the death" that God's Word refers to.)

I would like to add my own observation here, that although Swedenborg and Gurdjieff share similar ideas about the process of spiritual transformation, those who particularly study Swedenborg these days, seem to be overlooking the notion and possibility of one's corporeal mechanicality and hypnosis. In fact, one's mechanicalty is not noticed or even considered to be an important issue in their spir-itual growth. Why is this?

It may seem like I am unfairly picking on the Swedenborgian church, but they should know better (just read the first few chap-ters of Volume II of Swedenborg's *True Christian Religion*). There has been a growing misunderstanding of God's Doctrine of Love (due to personal laziness, dropped responsibility and the external demands of being liked)! These worshippers have become way too busy seek-ing the more pleasurable activity of being *loving* (and being loved), preferring appreciation and affirmation from other members of their church organization. So they jump immediately into outer acts of friendliness—while sidestepping personal spiritual regeneration. In other words, painful self-observations and personal spiritual combat is quickly (automatically) sidestepped in favor of trying to be seen as a considerate and caring person by other people.

Therefore in their worldview, all that spiritual growth seems to demand of us is simply (and mechanically) to prefer outer acts of goodness over external (and obvious) acts of hatred. However, one must take into consideration that subtle evil intentions lurk and hide deep within us all (to elude detection). Swedenborg also stated that if some compulsion or negative manifestation is repeated often enough, it becomes second nature to us—that is, mechanical—where it becomes even harder to observe and detect because we have become so used to doing it.

But according to Gurdjieff, self-examination goes well beyond uncovering one's sins, it includes observing our own mechanicality. After all, how can one seriously look for behavioral flaws without first observing one's own *mechanicality*?

When I have a chance to warn such worshippers that they are acting as mere automatons and live in a trance (from using limited and disconnected mental functions, which do not care to observe each other) my advice is seen as incredulous. All because they overlook their split natures and how their mechanicality affects their religiosity.

Gurdjieff's "Institute-for-the-Harmonious-Development-in-Man" made the study of one's *mechanicality* the groundwork of its approach to *self-examination*. However, if one mistakenly studies his or her mechanicality with only one personality or mental function, rather than through the combined efforts of all one's separate, independent parts—from the simultaneous desires of one's *thought, feeling,* and *organic instinct*—it will only lead to psychopathy.

Living a serene and calm life is out of the question when one is in the process of spiritually removing false values (and a false self-image) that have become dear to one's heart during terrestrial living. Transformation is simply too upsetting for most people.

The next blow to one's egoism, through impartial self-observation, occurs when one makes it quite clear to him- or herself, that we are, of our own power, quite powerless and helpless toward everything around us, which always governs and directs our lives. We live as slaves. These influences of slavery are the mere attractions and repulsions (likes and dislikes) of our independently formed personalities and brain functions, which—acting as loose cannons—mold all our illusory values, conflicting tastes and incorrect worldviews (including our approach to religion).

Another downside of our abnormal psychic development and the flawed influences derived especially from contemporary education is that we no longer properly communicate, nor do we understand each other. Words in one's common language are used and interpreted by earth-citizens with great "elasticity." As an example of this "elasticity of meaning" between different individuals, Gurdjieff uses the word "world" to make his point about the human "automatized" cognition and why great misunderstandings arise even when seemingly familiar words and terms are being used.

For instance, when different people hear the simple word "world," it conveys quite different meanings to lots of different people, even to highly educated people.

Gurdjieff states that a physicist understands the word "world" to mean the creation of matter, from atomic particles to the largest aggregates, such as planets and suns.

On the other hand, a person interested in, and well educated in philosophy, would say that the "world" is only a *subjective* mental picturing, and that all the things observed by us are simply illusory—a world of appearances.

A person acquainted with the latest theories on polydimensional space (like today's string theory) would view the three-dimensional world as merely a cross section of a fourth or some higher dimensional reality.

Someone whose worldview embraces religious dogma will understand the term "world" to mean all things created by God that exist visibly and invisibly. The invisible world is where one goes after one dies, where he or she will receive either eternal punishment or reward.

A person deeply involved with spiritualism would say that there is a world of the "Beyond," and that communication has been set up with beings populating this world of the Beyond.

Someone fanatical about theosophy would say that reality consists of seven worlds interpenetrating each other, consisting of more and more rarefied matter.

So, these examples are why no individual can offer a single and precise definition of the word "world" that would be similarly understood by all people. To further complicate this communication, Gurdjieff indicates that individuals learn, over time, to become accustomed to the consonance (harmony of sound) of words as opposed to recognizing (contemplating) the real "pith" put into their meanings.

This is because the whole psychic inner life of the average person is nothing more than an "automatized contact" between two or three series of experiences already perceived by him or her, and fixed, under the action of an impulse (likes or dislikes) arising in all three (heterogeneous) brain systems.

This process leads to mental associations based purely on the consonance of words. So, when some corresponding shock re-awakens one of these previous associations (like hearing a certain sounding word) it evokes homogenous impressions and ideas that were already established among the three independent human brain-systems.

Gurdjieff's personal research showed him that ordinary humans form their personality and subjective understanding based on the order that new impressions are experienced and the mechanically established process by which previous impressions were repeated. (Instead of having their impressions put into an order that reflects God's Wisdom and providential plan, people's automatized psyche gives things seen and heard their own subjective meaning.)

This haphazard order rules out any precise exchange of opinions among earth-humans, because they can no longer ponder what they are saying or what is being said to them. This also explains why, when people are at rest (in a passive state), they can often observe that many thoughts and feelings automatically still arise in them, without any effort, and having nothing whatsoever to do with each other. We can all witness this automatic and incongruous "chatter," taking place inside our noggins. (This chatter is something happening *through us* and *not* by us.) Some of these ideas can be so strange and foreign to us that we will think aloud—saying, "Where did that idea come from?"

Now Gurdjieff offers an explanation of the divided human psyche, and its associations, that cannot be gleaned from any contemporary cognitive theory.

A person's three independent brain systems each act as a mechanical apparatus—like reels, or tapes on a recording device. Because of this, all of a person's experiencings throughout life are recorded in several apparatuses at once, and are preserved there unchanged (See *Arcana Coelestia*, n. 7398). The arousing of these various impressions by some repeated corresponding trigger or new perception creates the activity of both one's memory function and one's thought-associations.

It is interesting to note that the average person remembers only a fraction of the memory-data that a more spiritually evolved individual can. (Swedenborg states that higher cognitive abilities [from our involuntary mind] have superior memory functions that contain not only more details, but record everything ever experienced.)

Gurdjieff also discovered this similar phenomenon through *hypnosis*. Under hypnosis, and reaching the human subconscious mind, he discovered that people could recount even the most miniscule details of their lives—including those things experienced on the first days after birth! Besides using hypnotism, Gurdjieff stated that some overt or hidden shock (evoked by a particularly strong experiencing) can also cause many long-forgotten memories to resurface.

At this point in the original reading of this particular lecture, Gurdjieff states that he interrupted the presenter in order to make a timely *addition* for the audience:

HERE IS THE ESSENCE OF *THE ADDITION*

Gurdjieff states that under these unfortunate worldly conditions, the average person cannot help being a mere slave to larger universal purposes, which are quite alien to his or her own personal well-being (individual daily priorities). Unbeknownst to us, we must all serve the needs of the greater universe—*whether we want to or not*. As such, a person who is oblivious to the real demands and cosmic responsibilities of God's greater reality, and who never consciously chooses to change, is in danger of having his or her spiritual potential doomed and destroyed forever. (Swedenborg concurs that individuals not participating in spiritual regeneration—in order to become more useful to others—will end up eternally *lifeless*, like skeletons without flesh, or having hard faces like metal or steel.)

But at the same time, God's great creation offers a contingency plan by which humans can serve not only as blind tools for the benefit of universal purposes, but acquire what has been divinely preordained for them. Gurdjieff adds that such personal liberation through spiritual evolution and transformation is actually lawfully required for maintaining the ultimate equilibrium of God's higher realms. Only humans can fulfill this higher purpose. (Remember God's pre-creation need for keeping His abode, the Spiritual Sun, relevant?)

Gurdjieff warns that although such inner liberation is possible, an individual's heredity and conditions under which one is prepared throughout terrestrial life now constitute uncontrollable conditions, which usually put the kibosh on God's ultimate plan for such liberation. As a stark example of this seemingly uncontrollable condition, not everyone on Earth will come across Swedenborg's or Gurdjieff's challenging ideas. (Even if they did, many would immediately reject them outright.)

The chief difficulty in escaping one's slavery is not making the conscious decision and having the initiative and personal persistence to eradicate from one's presence the fixed negative properties inherited from that ancient organ Kundabuffer of our forefathers—and any predisposition toward those negative consequences, which might arise in the future. (Swedenborg describes the difficulty of this undertaking as the decision to go up against our self-centered preferences and destroy our previous false notions—all stemming from egoism. We can never do this completely. This effort represents a kind of psychic or inner *suicide*. Our egoism, which arose from "The Fall," causes humans to see reality "upside down," which is a perversion and corruption of God's Divine Order.)

Gurdjieff now reminds the reader why the organ Kundabuffer was purposely caused to grow inside the presences of our remote ancestors in the first place. It was foreseen by Great Nature that the human race had become such that it favored its own self-judgment and that it would *rebel* against any opposing views (including God's views). Unfortunately, God's universal plan and equilibrium would be threatened if humans were abruptly proven wrong and decided not to take part in life at all. Therefore, to preserve the human race (and people's sense of human free will) they had to be protected from seeing and feeling anything as it truly proceeds in reality and would cause them to become indignant and rebellious. (As said earlier, the Genesis story of God putting Adam to "sleep" and then forming Eve out of his *rib*, is another representation of the functioning of the organ Kundabuffer, which produced a psychic modification and a lowering of consciousness in our ancestors, permitting them to embrace self-deception and wrongly placed pride.)

Swedenborg stated that this was God's only alternative to preserving human *free will*, which is critical for any future attempt at *genuine* spiritual growth—because it requires us to make choices.

Although, according to Gurdjieff, this organ was later removed from humans, the "oft-repeated" negative manifestations of our ancestors, who were under its influence, caused similar predispositions to become second nature (fixed by habit) and passed on to future generations through heredity.

One of the proofs Gurdjieff offers for helping us verify that these consequences of the organ Kundabuffer still cause us to see reality in a perverted way is the difficulty people have in picturing their own inevitable death. We can easily picture other people dying, but not ourselves. There is much evidence all around us, that we will all die someday.

Gurdjieff adds that besides contemplating our own death, many other facts dealing with reality would cause a similar terror in us. Humans do everything possible to keep these genuine terrors about reality from interfering with their desire to carry out, in peace, their existence of the unconscious fulfillment of Nature's nearest immediate needs for preserving equilibrium, that is, going through life as mere slaves. Meanwhile, living under such abnormal conditions, the human race fails in the possibility to serve God's higher purposes (which Swedenborg maintained was the creation of Heaven from the human race—and to keep God's Spiritual Sun relevant. In fact, Swedenborg even observed an increase in the Spiritual Sun's light when the Lord was enacting His Second Coming—which was a new dispensation in the spiritual world—and is coming our way!)

The organ Kundabuffer, although our enemy, acts as a "buffer" to protect humans from the cognition of any threatening terrors (like one's inevitable death) and instead promotes dream-thoughts (fantasy-thoughts) for the purpose of self-quieting people's hearts and minds (but this is "mind-fornication"). So, rather than being terrified by our true and genuine situation, we are instead fearful of little mice and molehills. Obviously, if everyone knew that they would die in a day or even in a week, the world would be seen differently by them and people's priorities would change in a hurry.

But in case one would question life itself, and ever wonder why people should live and toil and suffer to fulfill some grand scheme (that they never agreed to), the organ Kundabuffer was implanted so that this question would never arise. Otherwise, earth-humans would become *indignant*, throw down their shovels and walk off the scene. (Swedenborg made the point that humans are never fully free from labors, that is, from performing "uses" in the world—we either do so willingly or as mechanical slaves. To shake us out of our snoozing, God is often forced [through divine providence] to throw various misfortunes—as *shocks*—our way in order for us to experience, from time to time, real deep feelings, and get us to ponder the reality of our terrestrial situation.)

So, cosmic equilibrium would be totally threatened if humans saw an injustice in all this and refused to move a finger in God's universe. So, Great Nature was forced to take measures that would keep the human race from sensing that *there is no escape from this universal law* of mutual cooperation and sharing.

What were these measures?

Well, from that time on (after The Fall), human birth and death rates increased because Nature could only meet her cosmic require- ments of radiations through increased *quantities* of earth-humans living out their lives as mere "things." Therefore, it was in Nature's best interest to make sure human life was tolerable and took great care that human society does not prematurely perish.

Then, when the time is right, she slaughters us!

Gurdjieff anticipates that some people may find this cosmic condition quite cruel and unjust—that all our lives simply serve the purposes and needs of the Great Cosmos. So he reminds the reader how we humans watch over and take care of our own sheep and pigs—not for the sake of those animals having happy lives, but so that they can later be slaughtered to obtain their meat (and with as much fat on it as possible—the fatter, the better).

(Addressing the needs of the cosmos and our consciously serv- ing its Great Common Purpose, Swedenborg describes the Spiritual World as consisting of communities that correspond to all the organs, tissues and cells of a human body—which is analogous to the true *bio-form* of the Lord God's living mutual love. When we die, we enter the "digestive system" of this immense spiritual organism, where we are then specially prepared to take our eternal places in maintaining the equilibrium of this holistic and grand organic scheme of mutual sharing. Or, if we remain obstinate to this purposeful design, for what- ever reason, we are jettisoned out the cosmic "butt-hole" and then serve as slaves in more hellish conditions—where one's God-given and spiritually "hoped-for" identity indeed perishes forever.)

Those who acquire true "imperishable Being" choose to serve ulti- mate reality out of the principle of conscious, spiritual love (mutual support). Such individuals willingly sacrifice their hearts and minds for the sake of *serving others* and to *serve the Lord God's plan*. (When you give up your specialness, you find your specialness!)

To make his point clearer for the reader, concerning the differ- ences between being a conscious player in this system or a mere slave to it, Gurdjieff uses the analogy of human life being compared to a great river. A single human life is represented by a single drop of water in that moving river. At some point during the flow of this river it becomes divided into two streams. To me, Gurdjieff is hinting here that this separation coincides with the "dividing of the waters" mentioned on *day two* in the Genesis story of Creation. (According to Swedenborg's spiritual exegesis, this is where we, as individuals, come to separate what is from Heaven and what is from Earth—and just as important, our separating what is really important to us from that which is not.)

The first of the two streams eventually reaches the ocean (which symbolizes God's heavenly expanse and our spiritual possibilities). The other stream falls through crevices where it flows down through the depths of the Earth and its "nether regions." (But reaching the ocean is the duty of every drop of water.)

According to Gurdjieff, an earth-human manifests this same dividing of the waters when he or she reaches *the age of responsibility* or adulthood. According to one's inner convictions, at the time of adulthood, a person acquires that character which determines which of the two streams he or she will likely enter.

Gurdjieff says that one should not be disheartened by the discovery that one's life is coursing through the *wrong* river. It is not too late to change course—because through certain atmospheric phenomena such as storms (cyclones and hurricanes), it is allowable for drops of water to be sucked up and to pass from one stream to another.

Gurdjieff's unique investigations and experiments which formed the basis for his "Institute-for-the-Harmonious-Development-of-Man" proved to him that God's universe provided this contingency plan and conditions for those wanting to escape the underground river and begin the formation of the kernal of their spiritual essence or real "I." (This real "I" represents what Swedenborg called our God-given *remains* and *conscience*.)

So earth-humans, if they make the proper inner and outer efforts, can still cross from one river into the other! This crossing is referred to as "the first liberation of man."

The crossing-over requires a deeper *spiritual storm*, whereby an individual consciously renounces his or her cupidities and *dies* to one's former, ordinary terrestrial life (the struggles with one's own self-denial of cosmic laws). Gurdjieff insists that this death is not the death of the physical body but the death of the "Tyrant" inside us that keeps us in slavery. (As hinted earlier, the Bible describes this state as the "death before death." And, according to Swedenborg, this death from our inner slavery, self-centeredness and self-importance, is also represented in the highest degree by the crucifixion and resurrection of Jesus Christ, who had to reform and align his earthly heredity with his higher heavenly nature—by challenging and denying the His lower earthly wishes.)

Gurdjieff himself refers to our salvation as a "resurrection."

Unfortunately, Gurdjieff again emphasizes by this *Addition* that contemporary earth-humans, due to their abnormal lives and education, are only intensifying the negative properties left over by the organ Kundabuffer, which he calls "the-reflecting-of-reality-in-one's-attention-upside-down."

Everyone can confirm this topsy-turvy worldview if they think seriously and "without being identified" with all one's fickle passions. Humans have become such, that even frightening circumstances will become trite or laughable when we look back at them (after having jumped to some other mood or state of mind).

These disconnected changes of state, always occurring in the human mind, are why molehills can become mountains and mountains, molehills. With humans always believing that in the moment, each state is true (like our daily reactions to the changing stock market) only a little afterwards, these same states seem trivial and unimportant. In other words, we humans have no real or consistent value system governing us.

Seeing reality "upside-down" is particularly intensified during times of great scourges, like wars, revolutions, civil unrest, etc. During these terrifying events earth-humans, through their suggestibility, become helpless victims of all kinds of maleficent stories and propaganda. Instead, "conscience" and the data implanted in them from God's Grace (also Swedenborg's "remains") for their self-perfection, is replaced by "mass psychosis."

Gurdjieff states (maybe even in a facetious way) that informed and wise individuals, from all epochs, especially regret this outcome of victimization in contemporary earth-beings—especially since they have discovered that wars and mass psychosis are no longer needed by Great Nature to maintain her equilibrium. Instead, Nature and the cosmos have successfully adapted human birth rates and the "tempo of the general psyche" in contemporary earth-humans for accomplishing those same purposes. (And that ain't good.)

Gurdjieff's study of human history revealed to him that people of former epochs did not divide into two streams of life, but flowed along in a single river. He places the time of this "split" during the "Tikliamishian" civilization (Sumerians?), which preceeded the Babylonian civilization.

From then on, when this split occurred, the life of humankind and their organizations could flow, more or less tolerably, only when people were divided into *masters* and *slaves*. While it is against Divine Order as children of God to be either a master or a slave, current conditions now demanded a special compromise whereby one's personal welfare never becomes contrary to these commandments issuing from the "Prime-Source-of-Everything-Existing"—even while living in a world full of social injustices.

This special compromise consists in a person acquiring all the data for becoming a *master of oneself*, rather than having many slaves and much money. In this case, devout acts to sincerely help all others around them allow for a special "something" to grow within a person that other people can sense and who will then gladly carry out his orders with reverence—instead of feeling like a slave or "working for the man." (Possessing this special "something" is how leaders were chosen in former times.)

-◆- -◆- -◆-

With that said, Gurdjieff considers this first series of his writings to be completed. Before starting to write his second series, *Meetings with Remarkable Men* (which was adapted into a full-length movie in 1979) he vows to take a month off for a much needed and deserved rest and to slowly drink 15 bottles of "old Calvados" (Armagnac) to re-stimulate his extremely fatigued organism.

Gurdjieff, as a final gesture, before drinking his splendid and divine fluid, says that he had made a decision a year or two earlier to make this first series of writings (*Beelzebub's Tales*) available to the general public. The second and third series would be less generally accessible and would be distributed in an order that would help him accomplish one of his fundamental tasks—to absolutely prove, theoretically as well as practically, to all his contemporaries, that all their notions of Heaven and Hell are absurd.

Hell and Paradise do indeed exist, but not only "in that world" (as if being in another physical place), but here—intimately beside us on Earth. (Swedenborg is in complete agreement that Heaven and Hell are essential parts of our terrestrial life and psyche, right now! For we are either a living representative of Heaven or of Hell (*Arcana Coelestia*, n. 7366) through the inner qualities of our hearts and minds. Swedenborg discovered that neither Heaven nor Hell, are places that you go to, but they are something you become!)

Gurdjieff closes by saying that he intends to have, in the future, public readings of his second series of writings (*Meetings With Remarkable Men*). With regard to the third series (*Life Is real only then, when "I am"*), which he promises will bring genuine objective truths to light, it will be accessible only to a hand-picked group of people specially selected from those who took part in the readings of his second series.

Gurdjieff died in late October 1949. Around 1976, those of his followers who owned the rights to these writings decided to make even the publication of the third series available to the public. I, for one, am thankful for that.

SUMMARY

▪ Six years later, after finishing his first full draft of *Beelzebub's Tales*, Gurdjieff re-reads his opening Preface and decides the story now needs an *Afterword*, so that there can be a more perfect fusion and correspondence between the story's beginning and its end. (This uniformity tells me that the entire work is indeed intended to represent a complete octave or whole.)

▪ Gurdjieff gives a breakdown of the three distinct functions operating in the human psyche and how they are now discombobulated, whereby real pondering becomes less and less possible for earth-humans.

▪ These three brain-functionings have their analogy in the *driver, horse,* and *coach* of a hackney carriage. The connections in this analogy, such as the shaft and reins, correspond to the red blood and "Animal Spirits."

▪ A fourth function is created by the process of genuine spiritual growth, whereby the passenger gains full control over all the elements of the hackney carriage—through a unified and transformed *will.*

▪ The modern educated human shows no inner consistency of will throughout a normal day and rather, is ruled exclusively by external events and stimuli.

▪ The study of one's mechanicality is the groundwork of self-observation in Gurdjieff's system. Without this effort, one cannot "wake up" and gain the ability to think deeply, ponder reality or realistically change one's flaws.

▪ Our mechanicality arises from the fact that our three distinct mental functions of *thought, feelings,* and *organic instinct* develop on their own (heterogeneously) and not together. This disjointed development allows an *incongruity* of reactions (which have nothing to do with each other), to develop out from, and manifest, within a single person's life.

▪ This situation also makes people slaves to the stimuli of the external world. Under this psychic condition, even religion and its doctrines become merely another form of external stimuli.

▪ We must all serve the needs of God's Great universe—either as a slave, or consciously, like an angel.

SUMMARY

■ To fulfill these important cosmic needs (and to prevent any rebellion), early earth-humans were put into a trance-like sleep, where everyone could safely see the world from their own fantasies. However, true spiritual growth involves destroying these fantasies.

■ Earth-humans now go through life in one of two streams—one leading to a positive condition, the other, to a bad one. Individuals, like drops of water, can cross over to the better stream through the action of "storms" (psycho-spiritual combat) whereby one's self-importance is challenged and must die.

■ In a world that now produces *masters* and *slaves*, we can each make a lawful compromise to this ungodly situation by becoming *masters of ourselves*. This is the true *freedom* and *liberation* that all religion was designed to offer.

■ Our usual notions of Heaven and Hell are absurd. They are not places you go to—they are what you become.

The End

INDEX

A

active force, 93, 99, 124, 292, 416, 449-452, 465-466

actors, 204, 206-210, 213

Archangel Hariton, 31-35, 39

archangels, 30-35, 39, 46-47, 435, 471-474

Adam, 19, 55-56, 123, 136, 147, 223, 463, 489

Adherents-of-Legominism, 199-201, 210

Afterlife, 29, 94, 155

Ahoon – faithful servant, 17, 130-131, 198, 210, 220-221, 473,

Aieioiuoa, 91-92

alcohol, 196-197, 249-259, 382-384, 398-401

allegory, 17, 32, 46, 50, 97, 132, 138, 214, 253, 310, 361, 456

Almznoshinoo, 278-279

amber, 33, 144

America, 134, 266-269, 379-399, 412-418, 421, 428

angels, 30-38, 46-47, 104-104, 106-109, 158, 204, 225-226, 266-268, 273, 307-313, 316, 324-331, 343, 426, 443, 451, 467, 471

animal sacrifice, 85, 109-119, 433-435, 443

animal spirits (middle blood), 234-235, 300, 305, 327, 375, 414, 495

Ansanbaluiazar, common-cosmic, 300, 317-318, 357, 456

Anulios, 52, 72, 85, 434-436

apes, 134-139, 145, 245, 346

"Arabian Nights," 362

art, 198-213
 – artists, 195, 204, 209, 211-212, 213, 424
 – dance, 211, 266, 407
 – music, 201-207, 355, 365, 374, 400, 407, 457
 – scientist-artists, 213
 – sculpture, 201, 204
 – theater, 204-205, 210
 – true art, 203, 213

Ashiata Shiemash (divine messenger)
 also: Very Saintly Ashiata Shiemash, 20-21, 158-197, 223-224, 243, 250, 434, 439

Asia, 108-134, 168-183, 245-260, 361-366, 394-399, 404-409, 416, 430-448

associations, 18, 141, 164, 195, 205-210, 308, 487-488

Assyrian, 153-157

Ashhark (Asia), 108

askokin (life force), 48-56, 70, 94, 109 435-437

astral body, 185, 234-235, 281, 285, 304-308, 327

astrologers, 139, 143, 146

astronomers, 139-140, 146

Atarnakh (Kurdish philosopher), 431-434

atheist, 152-157

Atlantis, 69-79, 86-87, 103-108, 112-115, 119-121, 134-149, 159, 174, 201, 216, 226-228, 245-247, 327-328, 340-341, 436-437, 446-447

Autoegocrat, 76, 291, 293, 295, 297, 320, 337,

automaton, 7, 9, 16, 209, 212, 386, 409, 421, 467, 486

B

Babylon, 150-159, 165, 179, 183, 201-204

Banishment, 19, 443

Beelzebub

being-duty, 40-42, 193-195

being-Partkdolg-duty, 41, 322-324, 329, 338-341, 359-363, 460, 466, 473

being-Reasoning, 306-308

Bennett, John G., 17, 90, 294, 458
 – *Talks On Beelzebub's Tales*, 90, 95, 209, 286

Bible
 – interpretation, 33, 492
 – stories, 29, 50, 108, 111, 222
 – symbolism, 49, 78, 97-104, 227, 460
 – writing style, 63, 104, 272, 282, 428

birds (symbolism of), 53, 97, 251, 347, 383

Blake, Anthony
 – Foreword, *Talks On Beelzebub's Tales*, 19

E

F

G

inner nullity, 127, 243, 245, 425

inner slavery, 3, 94, 187, 308, 396, 427, 440, 481, 492

inner travel, 32

innocence, 7-8, 19, 61, 69, 74-75, 83, 104-107,
123-124, 169, 174-178, 215, 219, 222, 225-227,
231, 242-243, 250, 268, 307-308, 322, 326,
387, 476, 484

Institute-for-the-Harmonious-
Development-of-Man, 477, 481, 486, 492

intentional suffering (spiritual combat),
1, 123-124, 157, 177, 186, 207, 217, 226, 311,
322, 329, 356, 359, 405, 435-436, 447, 472

intentions, 29-30, 76, 89, 147, 175, 212, 214, 223,
225, 242-243, 290, 371, 396, 425, 485

internal natural mind, 8, 13, 16, 82-83,
106-107, 165, 172, 215-216, 222, 228, 231,
233, 236, 241-243, 246

Ischmetch, 196, 456

Itoklanoz principle, 193-197, 211, 213, 237, 239, 413

J

Jacob's Ladder, 301, 317, 450

Jesus, 31, 44, 75, 110, 168-169, 228-229, 275-285,
303, 328, 403-417, 425, 450, 471, 476, 492

Joseph & Pharaoh, story of, 215, 222, 326

Jung, Carl J., 87

justice, 3, 18, 58, 77, 180, 255, 326, 430,
439-445, 451-453, 481, 490, 493

justification by faith alone, 426, 440

K

Karatas, 17-21, 113, 214, 283, 344, 371, 443,
452, 455-457, 461, 468, 473-474

kenosis, 297

keva, 258

killing, 53, 70, 108, 115, 117, 156, 284, 366, 406, 435

King Tut's Curse, 246

"knowledge of being", 371-374, 378-380,
392-393, 409, 460, 464, 480

Korkaptilnian thought tapes (similar to
Swedenborg's Limbus), 140, 146

Kronbernkzion, Makary, 445-453

Kundabuffer (Swedenborg's proprium), 52,
55-60, 67-68, 74-79, 86-87, 104-106, 121-130,
155-169, 209, 266-269, 274-277, 282, 293,
296, 302-308, 313-316, 349-350, 420,
435-438, 459-460, 489-492

Kundalina, 126-127

L

Lamaist, 275

Languages, 9, 217-218, 264, 368, 385, 431

Last Supper (see also: Holy Communion),
279, 285, 395

Law-of-Catching-Up, 47

Law of Falling (see also: gravitational
order), 28-31, 47, 56, 103, 214

Law of Sevenfoldness, 89, 91, 184, 187,
199-204, 210, 212, 267, 289, 291-292

Law of Threefoldness, 89, 93, 270, 291-292,
314, 319, 327, 335-337, 395, 465, 470

Law of Ninefoldness, 340, 356, 361

lawful deviations, 201-203

lawful inexactitude, 130, 200-201, 204, 210,
212, 216

Legominism, 159-203, 210, 212, 223, 250, 341, 360

Lentrohamsanin, 155, 181-187

license (vs. free will), 60, 136

life choices, 452

Lord God, 6-7, 11-14, 19, 32, 38, 44-54, 81,
86-87, 91-95, 100, 107, 110, 129-130, 145,
148-164, 171-178, 208, 215-217, 225-227, 231,
242-244, 258, 279-289, 293, 296, 316, 327,
330, 335, 379, 414-415, 431, 439, 443, 464,
477, 491

looting, 257

Love, 37, 75, 82, 84, 89, 96, 132, 140, 150, 156,
160-166, 168-170, 173-175, 182, 184, 203,
206, 208, 220, 222-223, 226, 231, 239, 260,
272, 278, 280, 290-291, 294, 297, 303, 310,
313, 316, 318, 363-364, 420, 433, 447, 467

– angelic, 36, 37, 51, 175

– congugial, 323, 324, 329, 336, 399, 401

– devilish, 63-64

– divine (God's), 21-22, 55, 89-90, 107, 125,
146, 153, 162, 172, 206, 235, 268, 280,
290, 297, 298, 300, 303, 311, 313, 327, 331,
345, 422, 459

– egoistic, 164, 192, 206

– familial, 20, 43-44, 269, 420-421

– (of) God, 43, 81-82, 84, 118, 168, 177-178,
200, 225, 268, 294, 297-298, 313, 335, 345,
456, 476

– habitual, 65

– heavenly, 7, 61, 172, 290, 325, 476

– human, 50

– infinite, 18, 53, 290

– neighborly, 7, 15, 124, 447, 473, 483

– (as) primal substance, 89

– quality of, 30

S

sacred dances, 211

Saint Buddha, 122-129, 133, 278, 285

Saint Krishnatkarna, 278

Saint Lama, 276-278, 285

Saint Mohammed, 276

Saint Venoma, 25-26, 28-31, 35

salvation, 4, 8, 25, 30, 36, 44, 50, 107, 118, 136, 168-171, 198-204, 223, 232, 242, 274, 279, 283, 286, 290, 338, 358, 443, 461-467, 476, 492

scientism, 286, 297, 336, 379

sculpture, 201, 204

Second Coming, 129, 168, 490

second-being food, 258, 414

self-calming, 67-68, 218, 226, 245, 260, 283, 405, 420

self-centeredness, 50-52, 55, 63, 75, 144, 159, 167, 186-187, 268, 288, 358, 379, 423, 430, 442, 463, 476, 492

self-examination, 7, 34, 67, 97, 123, 125, 160, 164, 168, 171, 175-178, 215, 225-226, 232, 283, 371-373, 420, 440, 447, 467, 484-486

self-guidance, 18, 21, 55, 104, 123

self-importance, 1-4, 50, 61-64, 108-109, 124-126, 160, 186-187, 218, 223, 266, 339, 414, 423-425, 429-430, 440, 460, 476-477, 480, 492, 496

self-love, 37, 55, 60-63, 71, 93, 111, 124, 141, 164, 169, 174, 177, 182, 185, 223, 227, 274, 282, 290, 323, 359, 407, 420-421, 424-425, 450, 466

serpent (symbolism of), 59, 123, 147, 201

sevenfoldness, 31, 47, 56, 103, 214

Law of Sevenfoldness, 89, 91, 184, 187, 199-204, 210, 212, 267, 289, 291-292

sevenfold series, 81, 199-200, 206, 315-317, 335-337, 340

sex (sexual), 139, 182, 270, 322, 324, 330, 397

 – abnormalities, 398

 – depravity (deviance), 192, 196, 325, 329-330

 – discussions about, 139, 389, 409-411, 416-417, 420

 – disease, 270-271, 397-398

 – energy, 1, 196, 307, 322, 389, 436-437, 466

 – gender, 270, 308-309, 403, 415, 436-437

 – homosexuals/lesbians, 266, 271, 436-437

 – hygiene, 397-408, 416

 – impotence, 388, 416

 – intercourse, 181, 311, 322, 324, 399

 – pleasure (gratification), 136, 164, 192, 197, 270, 329-330, 440

 – revolution, 270, 400

Shiites, 276

similitudes, 48, 278

sleep, 12, 93, 100, 136, 147, 469

 – deep, 55, 71,

 – disconnected state, 242-243, 379-380, 463, 489

 – nighttime, 196, 205, 210-211, 230, 232

 – passivity, 55, 68, 71, 93, 180, 223, 231, 232

 – spiritual, 63, 176, 228, 241-242, 462

 – trance, 55, 93, 226, 228, 230-231, 463 496

slugs, 43-45, 60, 256

social justice, 11, 177, 180, 255, 442, 481

soldiers, 14, 399, 448

sound-vibrations (density of), 207, 348

space travel, 22-23, 30

spacetime, 22, 32, 80, 87, 89-90, 94, 104, 154, 214, 267, 279, 286, 289-291, 294, 305, 459,

Sphinx, 144, 146, 247-248

spiritual body, 24, 29, 57, 168, 216, 235, 267, 273, 289, 303, 315, 324, 339, 396, 413-414, 450, 466-467, 470

spiritual combat (see also: intentional suffering), 67, 123-124, 141, 168, 179, 210, 217, 268, 283, 378, 425, 466, 485, 496

spiritual heat and light (see also: enlightenment), 92

spiritual "gravity". 31

spiritual sleep/mental laziness, 63, 176, 242

Spiritual Sun (from Swedenborg), 18-21, 32, 47, 81, 88-101, 143-146, 204, 214, 218, 220, 233, 236, 273, 282-306-326, 331, 338, 344, 432, 435, 444, 449, 456, 459, 462, 489-490

spiritual theft, 282

spiritual travels (goals), 34

Spiritual World (Gurdjieff's Holy Planet Purgatory), 36, 53, 62, 75, 86, 106, 109, 121, 132, 179, 185, 194, 204, 218, 236, 259, 263, 268, 283-288, 305, 312, 323, 399-401, 427, 432, 442-443, 456, 465-467, 479, 490-491

split psyche (see also: divided human psyche), 4-6, 82, 150, 162-163, 180-182, 196-197, 221-242, 253, 275, 355, 411, 420

states of consciousness, higher (non-ordinary), 17, 280

state of mind, 82, 122, 181, 203, 235, 238, 242, 261, 280, 493

striving (see also: endeavor), 90-94, 98-105, 108, 110, 118, 142-148, 173, 178-179, 197, 287, 310, 316, 358, 392, 458-459, 465

stones (rocks), 95, 306, 366, 426, 465

suggestibility, 10, 63-64, 68, 71, 117, 169, 221-223, 234, 238, 243, 258

–◆– –◆– –◆–

Notes On Beelzebub's Tales:

Cosmic Duty was written while referencing Gurdjieff's text from the paperback edition first published by E.P. Dutton in 1973. ISBN:0-525-47348-3

Notes On Images:

Cover art: © 2016 Staircase Press Design
Moon: © 2012 David Moug

pg *x*: Portrait of Emanuel Swedenborg by Carl Fredrik von Breda in 1817.

Portrait of George Gurdjieff from http://www.gurdjieff.am/photos/photogallery-2.htm

pg 319-322: diagrams adapted from *Proving God* © 2009, Staircase Press.

George Ivanovitch Gurdjieff

The Gurdjieff Foundation
The largest organization directly linked to Mr. Gurdjieff.
http://www.gurdjieff.org/foundation.htm

The Gurdjieff Society
The activities of the Society are mainly in London. However, there are some groups elsewhere in the UK, as well as in some other countries, for which the Society is responsible.
http://www.gurdjieff.com/

Gurdjieff International Review
A source of informed essays and commentary on the life, writings, and teachings of George Ivanovitch Gurdjieff.
http://www.gurdjieff.org/index.en.htm

Gurdjieff Legacy– The Teaching for our Time
An independent exploration whose aim is to creatively apply Gurdjieff's seminal, esoteric teaching of self-transformation to contemporary life.
http://www.gurdjieff-legacy.org

Gurdjieff Internet Guide
Gurdjieff Internet Guide contains interviews, articles, videos, book reviews, event listings and other material related to the teaching of G.I. Gurdjieff. You can add your own events and contribute reviews.
http://www.gurdjieff-internet.com/index.php

Bennett Books
An online independent bookstore selling "books for serious seekers." A good source for hard-to-find Fourth Way books.
http://www.bennettbooks.org

The Study of "All and Everything"
This is an online version of *Beelzebub's Tales to his Grandson,* which includes the entire text of the book (making it very searchable, with a Chapter Index and a Term Index). This is a great tool to keep handy as you read.
http://ae.gurdjieff.org.gr/index.htm

Emanuel Swedenborg

The Swedenborg Foundation
The publisher of Swedenborg's writings in the U.S. Additionally, they publish and distribute some books applying these principles to contemporary life; also scholarly monographs.
http://www.swedenborg.com

Swedenborg Scientific Association
Preserves, translates, publishes and distributes the Swedenborg's scientific works. They publish an annual journal of scholarly articles on related topics online.
http://www.thenewphilosophyonline.org

The Swedenborg Society, London
A publisher, library and bookshop in London. They also organize lectures, conferences and exhibitions on relevant topics.
http://www.swedenborg.org.uk

The Online Swedenborgian Library
Swedenborg's theological, scientific and philosophical works online and in a searchable form.
http://www.swedenborg.org/Library.aspx

Staircase Press
Elevate your mind with these independently published books that explore how all true knowledge is connected.
http://www.staircasepress.com

TheGodGuy Blog
This lively blog is a discussion on new ideas concerning Science and Theology and their ultimate unification.
http://thegodguy.wordpress.com

Books, Articles, Sermons and Blogs
Curated by Ian Thompson, this collection of links is based on the Writings of Emanuel Swedenborg.
http://www.swedenborgstudy.com

Edward F. Sylvia, M.T.S.

Philosopher/Theologian Edward F. Sylvia attended the School of Visual Arts in New York and had a long, successful career writing for some of the world's largest advertising agencies in New York City, St. Louis and Chicago. He now advertises for God.

He has been a student of the ideas of both George I. Gurdjieff and Emanuel Swedenborg for over forty years and feels that writing this book changed his deepest views about both men. He is particularly concerned that the reader understands the chapter titled "The Terror of the Situation" and why the best ideas of religion are ineffective.

He received his M.T.S. (Master of Theological Studies) at the Pacific School of Religion in Berkeley, CA and a Certificate of Sweden-borgian Studies from the Swedenborgian House of Studies at PSR. He is a past president of the St. Louis Publishers Association, and a member of the International Book Publishers Association (IBPA), the Center for Theology and the Natural Sciences (CTNS), the Swedenborg Scientific Association (SSA), the Missouri Botanical Garden and Forest Park Forever.

Edward and his wife Susan have been married—and contributing to each other's spiritual growth—for 40 years. In 1980, they purchased 11 acres of empty farmland in southern Illinois, upon which he planted and nurtured over 300 different species of trees, an organic vegetable garden and orchard, plus an array of beautiful flowers. They lived there sustainably for over 35 years in a passive solar house. Several years ago, they left this piece of the earth far better off than they found it and relocated to an apartment in a nearby city, where Edward can focus on writing and working on his own spiritual growth and regeneration.

He is the award-winning author of several books, including *Sermon From the Compost Pile: Seven Steps Toward Creating An Inner Garden;* the children's fable *Cupid and the King of Muck;* an essay book titled *Swedenborg & Gurdjieff: The Missing Links;* and his masterwork *Proving God*, which fulfills a continuing vision that God's fingerprints of Love can be found everywhere in the manifest universe.

Edward has many other writing projects currently in the works.